Social Work Research and Evaluation

Social Work Research and Evaluation

Quantitative and Qualitative Approaches   SEVENTH EDITION

EDITED BY

Richard M. Grinnell, Jr.

Yvonne A. Unrau

OXFORD

UNIVERSITY PRESS

2005

OXFORD
UNIVERSITY PRESS

Oxford   New York
Auckland   Bangkok   Buenos Aires   Cape Town   Chennai
Dar es Salaam   Delhi   Hong Kong   Istanbul   Karachi   Kolkata
Kuala Lumpur   Madrid   Melbourne   Mexico City   Mumbai   Nairobi
São Paulo   Shanghai   Taipei   Tokyo   Toronto

Published by Oxford University Press, Inc.
198 Madison Avenue, New York, New York 10016

www.oup.com

Oxford is a registered trademark of Oxford University Press

Library of Congress Cataloging-in-Publication Data
Grinnell, Richard M.
Social work research and evaluation : quantitative and qualitative
approaches / edited by Richard M. Grinnell, Jr., Yvonne A. Unrau.—7th ed.
p.   cm.
Includes bibliographical references and index.
ISBN 0-19-517949-8
1. Social service—Research.   I. Unrau, Yvonne A.   II. Title.
HV11.G753   2005
361.3'072—dc22   2004011799

1 2 3 4 5 6 7 8 9

Printed in the United States of America
on acid-free paper

Preface

This book is now being published by Oxford University Press. With a new publishing house and coeditor (in addition to the thousands of students and their instructors who have used the previous six editions of this book), we have refined this edition of *Social Work Research and Evaluation* with their comments in mind. Nevertheless, the audience of this edition remains the same as the previous ones—advanced undergraduate and beginning graduate social work students who are taking a one-semester (or quarter) research methods course.

THE GOAL OF THE BOOK

As before, our emphasis continues to be on how the goals of social work are furthered by the research process. Our belief is that research endeavors underlie and support our profession. Thus, research in social work is presented as more than just a way to solve human problems, or to add to our knowledge base, or to guide practice—though it is all of these. For more than two decades, this book has symbolized tradition and change; it has applied timeless issues of research design and measurement to changing methodologies and social concerns. It has broken some traditions and has taught readers to try new research methods without losing sight of the old.

Many research instructors first cover basic research methodology and then apply this course content to more advanced research courses that specialize in single-system designs (case-level evaluation) or program evaluations. Accordingly, we have designed this book to give students the basic methodological foundation they need in order to obtain the advanced knowledge and skills presented in these two specialized research courses. This book provides social work students with a rock-solid foundation for future statistics courses, program evaluation courses, and case-level evaluation courses.

We have made an extraordinary effort to make this edition less expensive, more esthetically pleasing, and much more useful for students than ever before. We have strived to produce a "user-friendly," straightforward introduction to social work research methods couched within the positivist and interpretive traditions—the two approaches most commonly used to generate relevant social work knowledge. To accomplish our goal:

- We have written this book to emphasize generalist social work practice. It fully complies with the Council on Social Work Education's (Council) research requirements in this respect.
- We use numerous practice examples throughout the text in an effort to emphasize the link between practice and research in generalist social work settings.
- We discuss the application of research methods in real-life social service programs, rather than in artificial settings.
- We stress numerous ethical issues that crop up when doing research throughout this book and have also devoted a complete stand-alone chapter to research ethics.
- We have heavily included human diversity content throughout the chapters. Many of our examples center around women and minorities, in recognition of the need for social workers to be knowledgeable about their special needs and problems. We have given special consideration to the application of research methods to the study of questions concerning these groups.
- We included only the core material that is realistically needed in order for social work students to appreciate and understand the role of research in social work. Our guiding philosophy has been to include only research material that they realistically need to know to function adequately as

social work practitioners; information overload was avoided at all costs.

- This book prepares students to become beginning critical consumers of the professional research literature. Thus, it does not prepare them with the necessary knowledge and skills to actually conceptualize, operationalize, and carry out a research study—no introductory research methods text can accomplish this formidable task.
- We explain terms with social work examples that students will appreciate. We have written this book in a crisp style using direct language.
- This book is easy to teach *with* and *from*.
- Numerous boxes are inserted throughout the book to complement and expand on the chapters; these boxes present interesting research examples, provide additional aids to learning, and offer historical, social, and political contexts of social work research.
- Numerous tables and figures have been used to provide visual representations of the concepts presented in the book.
- A comprehensive glossary can be found at the end of the book.

EXPERTISE OF CONTRIBUTORS

Without a doubt, the success of this book can be attributed to its unparalleled collaborative nature. No single person can be an expert in all the areas (chapters within the book) of the research enterprise. Thus, each chapter is written by a person who can be considered to be an authority on the chapter's topic. The 31 contributors know firsthand, from their own extensive teaching and practice experiences, what social work students need to know in relation to research. They have subjected themselves to a discipline totally uncommon in compendia—that is, writing in terms of what is most needed for an integrated basic research methods book, rather than writing in line with their own predilections. To further our efforts to produce a book that is consistent across chapters, the content has been extensively revised and edited to maintain a common editorial approach and writing style.

NEW CONTENT

The publication of the seventh edition of this book indicates that we have attracted loyal followers over the past two decades. It also means, conversely, that making major changes from one edition to the next can be hazardous to the book's success. Beyond the customary routine of updating examples and material, the modifications in this edition are more organizational in nature than substantive. Like the previous editions, this one:

- Provides students with an extensive background in why social work research does not take place in a vacuum and how to be on guard regarding ways their own ethnocentric perspectives influence how they will do research studies, participate in research studies, or consume the findings of published research studies.
- Provides students with a rationale for why the quantitative and qualitative approaches to knowledge development have value, in addition to showing them that the greatest benefit that research can bring to our profession is to combine both approaches in a single research study.

New content has been added to this edition in an effort to keep current, while retaining material that has stood the test of time. As can be expected, a few research instructors have expressed disappointment that several of the chapters in the earlier editions have been deleted. In general, chapters were dropped because they were not being assigned as required reading in a majority of research courses and it was necessary to make room for new ideas and development while retaining a manageable and accessible size for this revision. The work of former contributors is still readily available in many copies of the preceding editions, however.

What's New in This Edition?

Compared to the sixth edition, this one contains eleven new chapters:

Chapter 4:   Using Existing Knowledge
Chapter 5:   The Quantitative Research Approach

Chapter 6:   The Qualitative Research Approach
Chapter 7:   Gender, Ethnicity, and Race Matters
Chapter 14:   Observation
Chapter 16:   Interviewing
Chapter 21:   Historical Research
Chapter 23:   Analyzing Quantitative Data
Chapter 26:   Analyzing Qualitative Data
Chapter 27:   Writing Qualitative Proposals and Reports
Chapter 28:   Reliability and Validity in Qualitative Research

Eight of the chapters contained in the previous edition have been rewritten by new authors:

Chapter 1:   Scientific Inquiry and Social Work
Chapter 3:   Research Ethics
Chapter 11:   Sampling
Chapter 12:   Case-Level Designs
Chapter 13:   Group-Level Designs
Chapter 19:   Content Analysis
Chapter 24:   Writing Quantitative Proposals and Reports
Chapter 29:   Program Evaluation

CONTENT MEETS ACCREDITATION STANDARDS

As with the previous editions, we have written this one to comply with the Council on Social Work Education's (Council's) research requirements for accredited schools and departments of social work at the undergraduate and graduate levels (see Box 1.1). In addition, the book is written with the 16 research principles contained in the National Association of Social Workers' *Code of Ethics* in mind (see Box 1.2).

NEW ORGANIZATION

Over the years, we have received hundreds of comments from users of the previous six editions. With these comments, and with the Council's new 2003 research curriculum requirements in mind, we determined the specific topics to cover, the depth of the topics covered, and the sequencing of chapters within the book.

As in the preceding six editions, this one is neither a brief primer in social work research nor a book intended for use as a desk reference. With a tremendous amount of instructor and student input, this edition has been reorganized into nine parts and 29 chapters. The new organization is an attempt to make the book more functional, realistic, and manageable for students and instructors alike.

Part I: An Introduction to Inquiry

Part I consists of four chapters that lay the necessary background for the remaining parts within this book. More specifically, it examines the basic tenants that make the research method different from the other ways of knowing (Chapter 1). It then explores the research context that must be considered when doing social work research studies (Chapter 2), taking into account social work ethics (Chapter 3). The remaining chapter explores how to use the existing literature within the research enterprise (Chapter 4).

Part II: Approaches to Knowledge Development

Part II consists of three chapters that present how the research method of knowing discussed in Part I comprises of two research approaches—the quantitative research approach (Chapter 5) and the qualitative research approach (Chapter 6). The following chapter (Chapter 7) then describes the relevance of gender, ethnicity, and race issues in the design and conduct of the research studies that were described in the previous two chapters.

Part III: Measurement

Part III consists of three chapters that discuss why we need to measure variables in social work research. More specifically, Chapter 8 discusses how validity and reliability are relevant to the research process. Chapter 9 presents how to select an existing measuring instrument to measure a variable, and the final chapter discusses how to design a measuring instrument if an existing one cannot be found in the literature.

Part IV: The Logic of Research Design

Part IV consists of three chapters that presents the logic of research designs. More specifically, Chapter 11 discusses how sampling is used the research process. The following chapter (Chapter 12) discusses the various research designs that can be utilized when doing a research study with a single case, while the last chapter in this part (Chapter 13) presents the various designs that can be utilized when doing a research study with groups of people.

Part V: Collecting Original Data

Part V discusses the four main obtrusive data collection methods that collect original data for social work research studies—observation, use of interviews, and survey questionnaires. Chapter 14 focuses on how observational methods can be used as a data collection method, and the following chapter (Chapter 15) expands on this content by presenting how observations can be used in participant observation. Chapter 16 then goes on to discuss how to conduct research interviews, while the last chapter presents how to construct and execute surveys.

All four chapters in Part V present obtrusive data collection methods; that is, they all require an interaction of some kind between the researcher and the research participant. In contract to Part V, Part VI presents unobtrusive data collection methods that require no involvement of the research participant and collect data that already exist.

Part VI: Collecting Existing Data

The first four chapters in Part VI discuss the four main data collection methods for collecting existing and unobtrusive data for social work research studies. Unlike the data collection methods discussed in Part V, these methods require no involvement of the research participant and collect data that already exist. The final chapter, Chapter 22, presents a model for selecting the best data collection method to answer a research question.

Part VII: Quantitative Data Analysis, Proposals, and Reports

The three chapters contained in Part VII are specifically geared to the quantitative research approach. More specifically, Chapter 23 discusses how to analyze quantitative data, and the following chapter (Chapter 24) presents how to write quantitative proposals and reports. The remaining chapter (Chapter 25) discusses how to evaluate published quantitative reports.

Part VIII: Qualitative Data Analysis, Proposals, and Reports

Part VIII follows the same format as Part VII with reference to the qualitative research approach. More specifically, Chapter 26 discusses how to analyze qualitative data, and the following chapter (Chapter 27) presents how to write qualitative proposals and reports. The remaining chapter (Chapter 28) discusses how to evaluate published qualitative studies.

Part IX: From Research to Evaluation

Part IX contains one chapter on program evaluation. Program evaluation overlaps heavily with social work research. Since most of the research techniques contained in this book are used in program evaluations in some form or another, Chapter 29 deals less with the methods of program evaluation—methods contained in the previous 28 chapters within this book—and focuses on five simple ways a social service program can be evaluated.

LOGICAL AND FLEXIBLE TEACHING PLAN

The book is organized in a way that makes good sense in teaching fundamental research methods. Many other sequences that could be followed would make just as much sense, however. The chapters (and parts) in this book were consciously planned to be independent of one another. They can be read out of the order in which they are presented, or they can be selectively omitted. However, they will probably make the most sense to students if they are read in the sequence as presented, because each builds upon the preceding one.

In general, this edition is organized to help students master nine basic research-related skills:

Skill 1: Understand the Place of Research in Social Work (Chapter 1)

Skill 2: Understand Social Work Research Contexts and Ethics (Chapters 2 through 4)

Skill 3: Understand How to Formulate Research Questions and Hypotheses (Chapters 5 through 7)

Skill 4: Understand How Measurement Is Used in Social Work Research (Chapters 8 through 10)

Skill 5: Understand Sampling and the Logic of Research Design (Chapters 11 through 13)

Skill 6: Understand How to Collect Data and Select a Data Collection Method (Chapters 14 through 22)

Skill 7: Understand How to Analyze and Interpret Data (Chapters 23 and 26)

Skill 8: Understand How to Write and Evaluate Research Reports and Proposals (Chapters 24, 25, 27, and 28)

Skill 9: Understand How Social Work Programs Can Be Evaluated (Chapter 29)

NEW WEBSITE

This book has its own state-of-the-art website (see back cover). The site can be accessed free of charge by both students and instructors alike.

Students and instructors can obtain hundreds of review questions broken down by chapter, in addition to 11 on-line published social work research studies, also broken down by chapter.

Each one of the on-line research studies contains five discussion questions. Unlike the chapter review questions, where students do not have to read additional material to answer them, the on-line discussion questions require students to read at least one additional research study to answer them. In other words, students will need to read the chapter plus at least one additional

on-line research study to answer the five questions. Unlike the chapter review questions, the on-line review questions require students to apply what they have learned in the chapter to an actual social work research study.

Thus, BSW students could complete the chapter review questions where MSW students could be assigned the on-line research studies with their corresponding application questions. Or, both types of questions can be combined if appropriate to the course's objectives. We encourage instructors to be as creative as possible and utilize the website to fulfill individual teaching goals.

Instructors can access the student section along with their own password-protected section that contains: (1) hundreds of multiple-choice exam and quiz questions broken down by chapter, (2) comprehensive PowerPoint presentations broken down by chapter, and (3) PDF files of all tables and figures contained within the text by chapter. Each file can be transposed to a transparency where it then can be used on an overhead projector.

REPETITION OF CONCEPTS

Instructors who have taught research courses for several years are acutely aware of the need to keep reemphasizing basic research concepts throughout the semester, such as validity, reliability, constants, independent and dependent variables, randomization, internal and external validity, conceptualization, and operationalization. Thus, we have carefully tied together major concepts not only within chapters but across chapters as well.

There is deliberate repetition, as we strongly feel that the only way students can really understand fundamental research concepts is for them to come across the concepts throughout the entire semester—via the chapters contained in this book. Readers will, therefore, observe our propensity to explain research concepts in several different ways throughout the entire text.

ACKNOWLEDGMENTS

Many individuals, in addition to the more than 125 contributors since the book's conception, have seriously augmented the continual development and preparation of this text. For individual chapters, a number of people aided in the production by critiquing and reacting to chapter drafts, suggesting text and/or chapter content, and encouraging others to contribute.

These include Susan Anderson-Ray, David Austin, Mike Austin, Don Beless, Martin Bloom, Floyd Bolitho, Ed Borgatta, Scott Briar, Ed Brown, Harry Butler, Harris Chaiklin, Heather Coleman, Don Collins, Kayla Conrad, Jill Crowell, Rick Dangel, Inger Davis, Liane Davis, Wayne Duehn, Eugene Durman, Paul Ephross, Irwin Epstein, Roland Etcheverry, Michale Fabricant, Phil Fellin, Joel Fischer, Chuck Garvin, Neil Gilbert, Lewayne Gilchrist, Tom Givler, Harvey Gochros, Richard Gorsuch, Don Granvold, Tony Grasso, Ernest Greenwood, Jim Gripton, Charles Grosser, Lynda Hacker, Bud Hansen, Diane Harrison, Joseph Heffernan, George Hoshino, Walt Hudson, Jackie Ismael, Ittleson Foundation, Inc., Siri Jayaratne, Anne Kincaid, Mike Kolevzon, Mike Lauderdale, Alice Lieberman, E.E. LeMasters, Charles Levy, Rona Levy, Duncan Lindsey, Mary Ann Lynch, Mary Martin Lynch, Tony Maluccio, Rachel Marks, Bob Mayer, John McAdoo, Clyde McDaniel, Grant McDonald, Lynn McDonald, Tom McDonald, Robert Morris, Ed Mullen, Judy Nelson, and Kim Ng.

Others include Dan O'Brien, Don Pilcher, Norman Polansky, Alan Press, Paul Raffoul, Reyes Ramos, Frank Raymond, Rick Reamer, Bill Reid, Joan Robertson, Peggy Rodway, Sheldon Rose, Marti Royer, Mary Russell, Beatrice Saunders, Steve Schinke, Dick Schoeck, John Schuerman, Jim Seaberg, Judith Sears, Fred Seidl, Larry Shulman, Deb Siegel, Max Siporin, Norm Smith, Harry Specht, Dick Stuart, Paul Stuart, Jim Taylor, Eli Teram, Ed Thomas, Ron Toseland, Tony Tripodi, John Tropman, Barbara Turman, Lynn Vogal, Tom Watts, Margaret Whelan, Stan Witkin, Sidney Zimbalist, and Lou Zurcher.

Within the limits of time frames and resources, we have tried to follow the suggestions offered by these colleagues. However, they should not be held responsible for our sins of omission or commission. Special thanks go to the contributors for their hard work and individual participation. This book is a product of their experiences and their desire to introduce others to social work research, which they have found so challenging and stimulating.

Finally the staff at Oxford University press, especially Joan Bossert, Jessica Sonnenschein, Keith Faivre, and Tracy Baldwin, have been most helpful in the task of seeing this huge project through to completion. They have done an astronomical job in publishing this book while at the same time keeping its cost below other similar books on the market today. Both cost and utility were our main concerns throughout the publishing process. We simply desired to produce a book that students could afford and one that they really felt was useful for their future careers.

A FINAL WORD

The field of research in our profession is continuing to grow and develop. We believe this edition will contribute to that growth. An eighth edition is anticipated, and suggestions for it are more than welcome. Please send your comments directly to:

Richard M. Grinnell, Jr. and Yvonne A. Unrau
School of Social Work
Western Michigan University
Kalamazoo, Michigan 49008

Richard M. Grinnell, Jr.
rick.grinnell@wmich.edu
http://homepages.wmich.edu/~rgrinnell

Yvonne A. Unrau
yvonne.unrau@wmich.edu
http://homepages.wmich.edu/~yunrau

Contents in Brief

Contents in Detail

17
Surveys   271
Steven L. McMurtry

Part VI
Collecting Existing Data

18
Secondary Analysis   291
Judy L. Krysik

19
Content Analysis   303
Rodney Stark, Lynne Roberts

Contributors

Jeane W. Anastas, Ph.D., is a professor within the School of Social Work at New York University, New York, New York.

Michelle Sondra Ballan, Ph.D., is an assistant professor within the School of Social Work at Columbia University, New York, New York.

Gerald J. Bostwick, Jr., Ph.D., is a professor within the School of Social Work at the University of Cincinnati, Cincinnati, Ohio.

Elaine Bouey, M.ED., is a Human Resource Consultant at the University of Calgary, Calgary, Alberta, Canada.

Heather Coleman, Ph.D., is a professor within the Faculty of Social Work at the University of Calgary, Calgary, Alberta, Canada.

Kevin Corcoran, Ph.D., is a professor within the Graduate School of Social Work at Portland State University, Portland, Oregon.

Joel Fischer, DSW, is a professor within the School of Social Work at the University of Hawaii at Manoa, Honolulu, Hawaii.

Cynthia Franklin, Ph.D., is a professor within the School of Social Work at The University of Texas at Austin, Austin, Texas.

Peter A. Gabor, Ph.D., is a professor within the Faculty of Social Work at The University of Calgary, Calgary, Alberta, Canada.

Harvey Gochros, Ph.D., is an emeritus professor within the School of Social Work at the University of Hawaii at Manoa, Honolulu, Hawaii.

Richard M. Grinnell, Jr., Ph.D., is a professor and holds the Clair and Clarice Platt Jones/Helen Frays Endowed Chair of Social Work Research within the School of Social Work at Western Michigan University, Kalamazoo, Michigan.

Catheleen Jordan, Ph.D., is a professor within the School of Social Work at the University of Texas at Arlington, Arlington, Texas.

Judy L. Krysik, Ph.D., is a program evaluation consultant in Avondale, Arizona.

Nancy S. Kyte, M.S.W., is an office manager at Vista Hospice Care, Inc., Cincinnati, Ohio.

Robert W. McClelland, Ph.D., is a professor within the Faculty of Social Work at the University of Calgary, Calgary, Alberta, Canada.

Steven L. McMurtry, Ph.D., is a professor within the School of Social Welfare at the University of Wisconsin at Milwaukee, Milwaukee, Wisconsin.

Charles H. Mindel, Ph.D., is a professor within the School of Social Work at the University of Texas at Arlington, Arlington, Texas.

Miriam Potocky-Tripodi, Ph.D., is an associate professor within the School of Social Work at Florida International University, Miami, Florida.

Frederic G. Reamer, Ph.D., is a professor within the School of Social Work at Rhode Island College, Providence, Rhode Island.

Lynne Roberts, Ph.D., is the founder of the MicroCase Corporation, Seattle, Washington.

Antoinette Y. Rodgers-Farmer, Ph.D., is an associate professor within the School of Social Work at Rutgers—The State University in New Brunswick, New Jersey.

Gayla Rogers, Ph.D., is a professor within the Faculty of Social Work at the University of Calgary, Calgary, Alberta, Canada.

Russel K. Schutt, Ph.D., is a professor within the Department of Sociology at the University of Massachusetts, Boston, Massachusetts.

Jackie D. Sieppert, Ph.D., is a professor within the Faculty of Social Work at the University of Calgary, Calgary, Alberta, Canada.

Rodney Stark, Ph.D., is a professor within the Department of Sociology at the University of Washington, Seattle, Washington.

Paul H. Stuart, Ph.D., is a professor within the School of Social Work at The University of Alabama, Tuscaloosa, Alabama.

Leslie Tutty, Ph.D., is a professor within the Faculty of Social Work at the University of Calgary, Calgary, Alberta, Canada.

Yvonne A. Unrau, Ph.D., is an associate professor within the School of Social Work at Western Michigan University, Kalamazoo, Michigan.

Robert W. Weinbach, Ph.D., is a distinguished emeritus professor within the College of Social Work at the University of South Carolina, Columbia, South Carolina.

Margaret Williams, Ph.D., is an associate professor within the Faculty of Social Work at the University of Calgary, Calgary, Alberta, Canada.

Bonnie L. Yegidis, Ph.D., is a professor within the School of Social Work at the University of Georgia, Athens, Georgia.

PART I

An Introduction to Inquiry

· ·

Part I consists of four chapters that lay the

necessary background for the remaining parts

within this book. More specifically, it examines the

basic tenets that make the research method

different from the other ways of knowing

(Chapter 1). It then explores the research context

that must be considered when doing social work

research studies (Chapter 2), taking into account

social work ethics (Chapter 3). The remaining

chapter explores how to use the existing literature

within the research enterprise (Chapter 4).

Richard M. Grinnell, Jr.

Yvonne A. Unrau

Margaret Williams

Scientific Inquiry and Social Work

1

CONTEXTS

Madame Cleo is an astrological consultant. She advertises widely on television, promising that her astounding insights into love, business, health, and relationships will help her viewers to achieve more fulfilling and gratifying lives. Hah! you think. I bet she can't do this for me! I bet she's just out for the money! But if she could, but if she could only tell me . . . ! How do I know if she's for real or if I'm just getting taken for a ride? Perhaps the Enron Corporation could have used her services.

There is a parallel here between the people who receive social services—sometimes called clients—and you, the future social worker. Most people who we help—in common with all those people who are never seen by social workers—would like more fulfilling and rewarding lives. Like Madame Cleo's naive clientele who get suckered into calling her, many of our clients also have personal issues, money issues, relationships issues, or health issues. Unlike Madame Cleo, however, who has to be accountable only to her checkbook, we, as a profession, are required to be accountable to society and must be able to provide answers to three basic accountability questions:

1. How do our *clients* know that we can help them?
2. How does our *profession* know that we have helped our clients?
3. How do the *funding bodies* that fund the programs (that employ us) know how effectively their dollars are being spent?

RESEARCH AND ACCOUNTABILITY

What is the role that research plays in answering these three accountability questions? In one word, *significant!* That is the position of both the Council on Social Work Education (CSWE) and the National Association of Social Workers (NASW). These two prestigious national accountability organizations have a tremendous amount of jurisdiction over what curriculum content is required to be taught to all social work students (CSWE) and how the students, after they graduate, practice their trade (NASW).

The Council on Social Work Education

The CSWE is the official "educational organization" that sets minimum curriculum standards for BSW and MSW programs throughout the United States. This accreditation organization firmly believes that all social work students should know the basic principles of

---

BOX 1.1

Council on Social Work Education's BSW and MSW Curriculum Research Content

B6.0—BSW Curriculum Content

- The research curriculum must provide an understanding and appreciation of a scientific, analytic approach to building knowledge for practice and to evaluating service delivery in all areas of practice. Ethical standards of scientific inquiry must be included in the research content.
- The research content must include quantitative and qualitative research methodologies; analysis of data, including statistical procedures; systematic evaluation of practice; analysis and evaluation of theoretical bases, research questions, methodologies, statistical procedures, and conclusions of research reports; and relevant technological advances.
- Each program must identify how the research curriculum contributes to the student's use of scientific knowledge for practice.

M6.0—MSW Curriculum Content

- The foundation research curriculum must provide an understanding and appreciation of a scientific, analytic approach to building knowledge for practice and for evaluating service delivery in all areas of practice. Ethical standards of scientific inquiry must be included in the research content.
- The research content must include qualitative and quantitative research methodologies; analysis of data, including statistical procedures; systematic evaluation of practice; analysis and evaluation of theoretical bases, research questions, methodologies, statistical procedures, and conclusions of research reports; and relevant technological advances.
- Each program must identify how the research curriculum contributes to the student's use of scientific knowledge for practice.

research. The Council mandates that all social work programs have a research curriculum of some sort that addresses the research areas contained in Box 1.1.

The National Association of Social Workers

Just like CSWE, NASW is a parallel "practice organization" that works to enhance the professional growth and development of practicing social workers. Like CSWE's view of social work students, NASW believes that social work practitioners should also know the basics of research that are contained in Box 1.2.

This book provides the beginning research content to comply with the research standards set out by CSWE and NASW. Unlike Madame Cleo, however, social work students and practitioners are expected to have a substantial research knowledge base to guide and support their interventions. This knowledge base is generally derived from your social work education.

Of course, we, as a profession, tend to have more credibility than astrological consultants like Madame Cleo. We have graduated from accredited social work programs (CSWE) and have recognized practice qualifications (NASW). You are expected to have not only good intentions but the skills and knowledge to convert your good intentions into desired practical results that will help your clients. It all boils down to the fact that we have to be accountable to society, and to do so we need to acquire the knowledge and skills to help our clients in an effective and efficient manner.

HOW DO WE ACQUIRE KNOWLEDGE?

Our discussion so far automatically leads us to the question of "where do we acquire the necessary knowledge base to help our clients?" As can be seen in Figure 1.1, you will acquire your knowledge base to help others through five highly interrelated sources: (1) authority, (2) tradition, (3) experience, (4) intuition, and (5) the research method. All of these "ways of knowing" overlap to some degree, but it greatly simplifies things to discuss them separately.

Authority

Some things you "know" because someone in authority told you they were true. Had you lived in Galileo's time, for example, you would have "known" that there were seven heavenly bodies: the sun, the moon, and five planets. Since "seven" was a sacred number in the seventeenth century, the correctness of this belief was "self-evident" and was proclaimed by professors of philosophy. But Galileo peeked through his telescope in 1610 and saw four satellites circling Jupiter. Nevertheless, it was clear to those in authority that Galileo was wrong. Not only was he wrong, he had blasphemed against the accepted order. They denounced Galileo and his telescope and continued to comfortably believe in the sacredness of the number "seven."

But the "authorities" could have looked through Galileo's telescope! They could have seen for themselves that the number of heavenly bodies had risen to eleven! In fact, they refused to look because it wasn't worth their while to look because they "knew" that they were right. They had to be right because, in Galileo's time, the primary source of "how you knew something" was by authority—not by reason, and certainly not by observation. Today, this may seem a bit strange, and we may feel a trifle smug about the fact that, in *our* time, we also rely on our own observations in addition to authority. Even today, entrenched opinions are very difficult to change, and facts are more often than not disregarded if they conflict with cherished beliefs.

Questioning the Accuracy of Authority Figures

Fortunately and unfortunately, you have little choice but to believe authority figures. You wouldn't progress very fast in your social work program if you felt it necessary to personally verify everything your professors said. Similarly, practicing social workers lack the time to evaluate the practice recommendations that were derived from research studies; they have no choice but to trust statements made by researchers—the authority figures—who conducted the research studies.

Experts can be wrong, however, and the consequences can sometimes be disastrous. A few decades

BOX 1.2

Ethical Standards for Evaluation Research; Excerpts from the National Association of Social Workers' *Code of Ethics*

(a) Social workers should monitor and evaluate policies, the implementation of programs, and practice interventions.

(b) Social workers should promote and facilitate evaluation and research to contribute to the development of knowledge.

(c) Social workers should critically examine and keep current with emerging knowledge relevant to social work and fully use evaluation and research evidence in their professional practice.

(d) Social workers engaged in evaluation or research should carefully consider possible consequences and should follow guidelines developed for the protection of evaluation and research participants. Appropriate institutional review boards should be consulted.

(e) Social workers engaged in evaluation or research should obtain voluntary and written informed consent from participants, when appropriate, without any implied or actual deprivation or penalty for refusal to participate; without undue inducement to participate; and with due regard for participants' well-being, privacy, and dignity. Informed consent should include information about the nature, extent, and duration of the participation requested and disclosure of the risks and benefits of participation in the research.

(f) When evaluation or research participants are incapable of giving informed consent, social workers should provide an appropriate explanation to the participants, obtain the participants' assent to the extent they are able, and obtain written consent from an appropriate proxy.

(g) Social workers should never design or conduct evaluation or research that does not use consent procedures, such as certain forms of naturalistic observation and archival research, unless rigorous and responsible review of the research has found it to be justified because of its prospective scientific, educational, or applied value and unless equally effective alternative procedures that do not involve waiver of consent are not feasible.

(h) Social workers should inform participants of their right to withdraw from evaluation and research at any time without penalty.

(i) Social workers should take appropriate steps to ensure that participants in evaluation and research have access to appropriate supportive services.

(j) Social workers engaged in evaluation or research should protect participants from unwarranted physical or mental distress, harm, danger, or deprivation.

(k) Social workers engaged in the evaluation of services should discuss collected information only for professional purposes and only with people professionally concerned with this information.

(l) Social workers engaged in evaluation or research should ensure the anonymity or confidentiality of participants and of the data obtained from them. Social workers should inform participants of any limits of confidentiality, the measures that will be taken to ensure confidentiality, and when any records containing research data will be destroyed.

(m) Social workers who report evaluation and research results should protect participants' confidentiality by omitting identifying information unless proper consent has been obtained authorizing disclosure.

(n) Social workers should report evaluation and research findings accurately. They should not fabricate or falsify results and should take steps to correct any errors later found in published data using standard publication methods.

(o) Social workers engaged in evaluation or research should be alert to and avoid conflicts of interest and dual relationships with participants, should inform participants when a real or potential conflict of interest arises, and should take steps to resolve the issue in a manner that makes participants' interests primary.

(p) Social workers should educate themselves, their students, and their colleagues about responsible research practices.

Figure 1.1   How Do You Know Something?

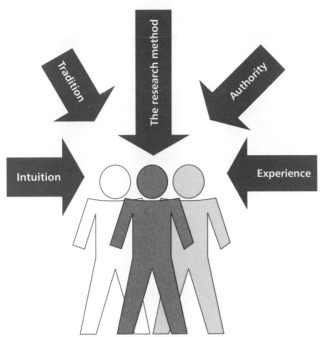

ago, for example, authority figures in family therapy believed that children who were schizophrenic came from parents who had poor parenting skills. Researchers emphasized such causative factors as parental discord, excessive familial interdependency, and mothers whose overprotective and domineering behaviors did not allow their children to develop individual identities. In accordance with these research findings, many social workers assumed that all families that had a child with schizophrenia were dysfunctional. Because the social workers focused their interventions on changing the family system, they often inadvertently instilled guilt in the parents and increased tensions, rather than helping the parents to cope with their child's situation.

However, recent research studies show that schizophrenia is caused largely by genetic and other biological factors, not by bad parenting. According to *these* findings, the most effective social work intervention is to support the family system by providing a nonstressful environment. This is what social workers *currently* do, again relying on *current* authority figures. More than likely, the authorities are correct this time—however, not as quite as exact as they will be when our knowledge of schizophrenia has progressed a little bit more over time.

So what are we to do when we need to trust the experts but the experts might be wrong? Put simply, we need to take into account the "kind of evidence" the experts utilized to make their pronouncements. This means that we must be able to distinguish good research studies from bad and from, well, quite frankly, the awful ones. One of the purposes of this book is to enable you, the future social worker, to evaluate research articles, which were written from research studies, with a more discerning eye. You need to decide for yourself which research findings you will clutch to your heart and use to help your clients and which research findings you will disregard until more information is forthcoming.

Sources of "Evidence"

The "kind of evidence" on which a practice statement is based includes the source(s) of the evidence. And the media as a source of evidence should be questioned. For example, we obtain knowledge by watching television shows and movies, in addition to reading newspapers, journals, and magazine articles. These forms of communication provide rich information (right and wrong) about the social life of individuals and society in general.

Most people, for example, who have had absolutely no contact with criminals learn about crime by these forms of communications. However, as we all know too well, the media can easily perpetuate the myths of any given culture (Neuman, 2003):

> The media show that most people who receive welfare are African American (most are actually non-African American), that most people who are mentally ill are violent and dangerous (only a small percentage actually are), and that most people who are elderly are senile and in nursing homes (a tiny minority are).

> Also, a selected emphasis on an issue by the media can change public thinking about it. For example, television repeatedly shows low-income, inner-city African American youth using illegal drugs. Eventually, most people "know" that urban African Americans use illegal drugs at a much higher rate than other groups in the United States, even though this notion is false. (4)

Tradition

The second way of adding to your social work knowledge base is through tradition. Authority and tradition are highly related. For example, some things you "know" because your mother "knew" them and her mother before her, and they are a part of your cultural tradition. Your mother was also an authority figure who learned her bits and pieces through tradition and authority.

More often than not, people tend to accept cultural beliefs without much question. They may doubt some of them and test others for themselves, but, for the most part, they behave and believe as tradition dictates. To be sure, such conformity is useful, as our society could not function if each custom and belief were reexamined by each individual in every generation. On the other hand, unquestioning acceptance of "traditional dictates" easily leads to stagnation and to the perpetuation of wrongs. It would be unfortunate, for example, if women were never allowed to vote because women had never traditionally voted, or if racial segregation were perpetuated because traditionally that's just the way it was.

Some traditional beliefs are based on the dictates of authority, carried on through time. The origins of other beliefs are lost in history. Even in social service programs, where history is relatively brief, things tend to be done in certain ways because they have always been done in these ways. When you first enter a social service program as a practicum student, your colleagues will show you how the program runs. You may be given a manual detailing program policies and procedures that contains everything from staff holidays to rules about locking up client files at night, to standard interviewing techniques with children who have been physically and emotionally abused. Informally, you will be told other things such as how much it costs to join the coffee club, whom to ask when you want a favor, whom to phone for certain kinds of information, and what form to complete to be put on the waiting list for a parking space.

In addition to this practical information, you may also receive advice about how to help your future clients. Colleagues may offer you a few of their opinions about the most effective treatment intervention strategies that are used within your practicum setting. If your practicum is a child sexual abuse treatment program, for example, it may be suggested to you that the nonoffending mother of a child who has been sexually abused does not need to address her own sexual abuse history in therapy in order to empathize with and protect her daughter.

Such a view would support the belief that the best interventive approach is a behavioral/learning one, perhaps helping the mother learn better communication skills in her relationship with her daughter. Conversely, the suggestion may be that the mother's personal exploration into her psyche (whatever that is) is essential and, therefore, the intervention should be of a psychodynamic nature.

Whatever the suggestion, it is likely that you, as a beginning social work student, will accept it, along with the information about the coffee club and the parking space. To be sure, you will want to fit in and be a valued member of the team. If the nonoffending mother is the first client for whom you have really been responsible, you may also be privately relieved that the intervention decision has been made for you. You may believe that your colleagues, after all, have more professional experience than you and they should surely know best.

In all likelihood, they probably do know best. At the same time, they also were once beginning social work students like yourself, and they probably formed their opinions in the same way as you are presently forming yours. They too once trusted their supervisors' knowledge bases and experiences. In other words, much of what you will initially be told is based upon the way that your practicum site has traditionally worked.

This might be a good moment to use your new-found skills to evaluate the research literature on the best way to intervene with children who have been sexually abused. But if you do happen to find a different and more effective way, you may discover that your colleagues are unreceptive or even hostile. They "know" what they do already works with clients—they "know it works" because it has worked for years.

Thus, on one hand, tradition is useful. It allows you to learn from the achievements and mistakes of those who have tried to do your job before you. You don't have to reinvent the wheel as you've been given a head start. On the other hand, tradition can become way too comfortable. It can blind you to better ways of doing things, and it dies extremely hard.

Knowledge versus Beliefs

At this point, it is useful to differentiate between knowledge and beliefs (or faith). Knowledge is an accepted body of facts or ideas acquired through the use of the senses or reason. Beliefs are similarly a body of facts or ideas that are acquired through reliance on tradition and/or authority. We now have *knowledge* that the earth is round because we have been into space and observed the earth from above. A few centuries ago, we would have *believed* that it was flat, because someone "in authority" said it was or because tradition had always held it to be flat.

Knowledge is never final or certain. It is always changing as new facts come to our attention and new theories to explain the facts are developed, tested, and accepted or rejected. Belief systems, on the other hand, have remarkable staying power. Various beliefs about life after death, for example, have been held since the beginning of time by large numbers of people and will doubtless continue to be held, without much change, because there is nothing to change them. For example, there is no "evidence" that we survive death and none that we do not, nor is there likely to be—for the moment, that is. A position on the matter must therefore be based on authority and tradition—and authority and tradition change very slowly, more through political maneuverings than through the consideration of emerging facts.

Beliefs are often institutionalized through religion and involve not just articles of faith but a set of values that determines how people live their lives. The Manichaean sect, for example, founded in Persia in the third century, believed that sex was wicked, even for the purpose of procreation. They relied on the natural wickedness of men to keep them supplied with disciples. More recently, the belief that one acquires worth through work is strongly held in North American society. The harder you work, the more virtue you acquire by doing the work. At the same time, it is believed that people will avoid work if at all possible—presumably they value ease over virtue—so the social service programs we have in place are designed to punish our clients' "idleness" and reward their "productivity."

Beliefs in one area tend to cluster with beliefs in other areas. There are relationships, for example, between a nation's cultural and religious traditions, its economic profile, the social welfare model it adopts, and its attitudes toward socially divisive forces such as race, poverty, age, and gender. These attitudes are rarely based on knowledge. They spring from tradition and authority and have an inertia and a complexity that resist the forces of change brought to bear by evidence and experience. This is not to say that attitudes and values never change. Of course they do.

Experience

The third way of acquiring knowledge is through experience. You "know" that buttered bread falls when you drop it—buttered side down, of course. You "know" that knives cut and fire burns. You "know," as you gain experience in social work, that certain interventive approaches tend to work better than others with certain types of clients in particular situations. Such experience is of enormous benefit to clients, and it's unfortunate that the knowledge gained by individual social workers over the years is rarely documented and evaluated in a way that would make it available to others.

However, as with anything else, experience has its advantages and disadvantages. Experience in one area, for example, can blind you to the issues in another. Health planners from mental health backgrounds, for example, may see mental illness as the most compelling community health problem because of their experiences with the mentally ill. Mental health issues may therefore command more dollars and attention than other public health issues that are equally deserving. Awareness of your own biases will allow you to make the most of your own experience while taking due account of the experiences of others.

Intuition

Intuition is fourth on our countdown of the ways of knowing. It can be described in a number of ways: revelation through insight, conviction without reason, and immediate apprehension without rational thought. In short, you "know" something without having a clue of how you "know" it. It has been suggested that intuition springs from a rational process at the subconscious level. For example, you may see something out of the corner of your eye that maybe is too small, or happens too quickly, to register at the conscious level, but your subconscious takes it in, combines it with a sound you didn't know you heard, facts that you've forgotten, a familiar scent, and/or an unfelt touch. And now you have it! Knowledge sprung from intuition!

Intuition and Professional Judgment

Perhaps intuition works that way. Perhaps it doesn't. Some of us trust it. Some of us don't. Whatever it is, intuition should not be confused with an experienced social worker's professional judgment. Professional judgment is a *conscious* process whereby facts, as far as they are known, are supplemented with the knowledge derived from experience to form the basis for rational decisions. In this eminently reasonable process, you

know what facts you have and how reliable they are, you know what facts are missing, and you know what experiences you're using to fill in the gaps. You are thus in a position to gauge whether your judgment is almost certainly right (you have all the facts), probably right (you have most of the facts) or possibly out to lunch (you know you are almost entirely guessing).

A reasoned professional judgment on your part, no matter how uncertain you may be, is far more beneficial to your client than your intuitive hunch.

The Research Method

We have now come to the fifth and last way of knowing. This way of acquiring knowledge is through the use of the research method—the main focus of this book. It is sometimes called the problem-solving method, the scientific method, or the research process.

The research method is a relatively new invention. For example, Aristotle was of the opinion that women had fewer teeth than men. Although he was twice married and the number of teeth possessed by women and men was a contentious issue in his day, it never occurred to him to ask both of his wives to open their mouths so that he could observe and count the number of teeth each had. This is a solution that would occur to anyone born in the twentieth century because we are accustomed to evaluate our assumptions in the light of our observations.

The social work profession—and modern society—is enamored of knowledge development through the use of the research method. Acquiring knowledge through the use of research findings that were derived from the research method is the most objective way of "knowing something." For example, as can be seen in Figure 1.2, when researchers do research studies they must: (1) be value aware (2) be skeptics, (3) share their findings with others, and (4) be honest.

Value Awareness

You must be aware of and be able to set aside your values when you do a research study—you must be unbiased and impartial to the degree it is possible—like a judge. This means that you, as a social work researcher, should be able

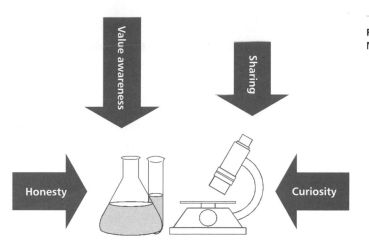

Figure 1.2   Characteristics of the Research Method

to put aside your personal values both when you are conducting research studies and when you are evaluating research results obtained by other researchers.

If your personal value system dictates, for example, that health care should be publicly funded and equally available to everyone, you should still be able to use the research method to acquire knowledge about the advantages and disadvantages of a privatized system. If the evidence from your own or someone else's study shows that privatized health care is superior in some respects to your own beliefs, you should be able to weigh this evidence objectively, even though it may conflict with your personal value system.

Skeptical Curiosity

Now that you are valueless, you must become insatiably curious. We now know that knowledge acquired using the research method is never certain. Scientific "truth" remains true only until new evidence comes along to show that it is not true, or only partly true. Skeptical curiosity means that all findings derived from the research method should be—and, most important, must be—questioned. Wherever possible, new studies should be conducted by different researchers to see if the same results are obtained again. In other words, research studies, whenever possible, should be replicated.

Replication of the same study, with the same results, by another researcher makes it less likely that the results

of the first study were affected by bias, dishonesty, or just plain old error. Thus, the findings are more likely to be "true" in the sense that they are more likely to reflect a reality external to the researchers. We will come back to this business of "external reality" later on.

For now, it is enough to say that the continual replication of research studies is a routine practice in the physical sciences but is far more rare in the social sciences, especially in the social work profession, for two main reasons. First, it is much more difficult to replicate a study of people than a study of physical objects. Second, researchers in the social sciences have a harder time finding money to do research studies than do researchers in the physical sciences.

Sharing

Like your mother said, "you must share your stuff with others." The results of a research study and the methods used to conduct it should be available to everyone so that the study's findings can be critiqued and the study replicated. It is worth noting that sharing findings from a research study is a modern value. It is not so long ago that illiteracy among peasants and women were valued by those who were neither. Knowledge has always been a weapon as well as a tool. Those who know little may be less likely to question the wisdom and authority of those who are above them in the social hierarchy. Public education is thus an enormously powerful social force that allows people to access and question the evidence upon which their leaders make decisions on their behalf.

Honesty

Not only must you share your research findings with others; you must be honest in what you share. Honesty means, of course, that you are not supposed to fiddle with the results obtained from your study. This may sound fairly straightforward, but, in fact, the results of research studies are rarely as clearcut as we would like them to be. Quite often, and in the most respectable of scientific laboratories, theories are formulated on the basis of whether one wiggle on a graph is slightly longer than the corresponding woggle.

If "dishonesty" means a deliberate intention to deceive, then probably very few researchers are dishonest. If it means that researchers allow their value systems and their preconceived ideas to influence their methods of data collection, analysis, and interpretation, then there are probably a few guilty ones in the bunch.

In this sense, the term "honesty" includes an obligation on the part of researchers to be explicit about what their values and ideas are. They need to be sufficiently self-aware to both identify their value systems and perceive the effects of these upon their work; then, they need to be sufficiently honest to make an explicit statement about where they stand so that others can evaluate the conclusions drawn from the research studies.

PHASES OF THE RESEARCH METHOD

On a very general level, and in the simplest of terms, the research method has four generic interrelated phases as illustrated in Figure 1.3. As can be seen, the research method begins with Phase 1—some kind of an observation and/or measurement. Suppose, for example, we find in the garage an unidentified bag of seeds and we don't know what kind of seeds they are. We plant a random seed from the bag into the ground, and it grows into a petunia. This might be a coincidence, but, if we plant 37 more seeds from the same bag and all of them grow into petunias, we might assume that all the seeds in our bag have something to do with the petunias. We have now reached the second phase in the research method; we have made an assumption based on our observations.

The third phase is to test our assumption. This is done by planting yet another seed (the thirty-eighth) in

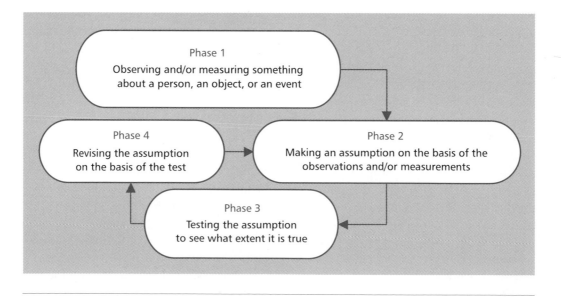

Figure 1.3   Phases of the Research Method

the same way as before. If the thirty-eighth seed, too, becomes a petunia, we will be more certain that all the seeds in our bag will grow into petunias.

On the other hand, if the thirty-eighth seed grows into a cabbage, we will begin to wonder if our original assumption—the bag contains all petunia seeds—was wrong, the fourth phase of the research method. In a nut shell, the four phases of the research method are not just something we are taught at school; they permeate the entire structure of our modern-day thinking.

Nothing Is Forever, According to the Research Method

It is possible, of course, that we are quite mad and we only imagined those petunias in the first place. We would be more certain of the real existence of those petunias if someone else had seen them, as well. The more people who had observed them, the surer we would become. The research method of knowing holds that, in most cases, something exists if we can observe *and* measure it.

To guard against objects that are seen without existing, such as cool pools of water observed by people dying of thirst in deserts, the research method has taken the premise one step further. A thing exists if, and only if, we can measure it. The cool pools of water that we observed, for example, probably could not be measured by a thermometer and a depth gauge. Things that have always occurred in sequence, such as summer and fall, probably will continue to occur in sequence. In all likelihood, rivers will flow downhill, water will freeze at zero degrees centigrade, and crops will grow if planted in the spring.

But nothing is certain, nothing is absolute. It is a matter of slowly acquiring knowledge by making observations and measurements, deriving assumptions from those observations, and testing the assumptions by making more observations and measurements. Even the best-tested assumption is held to be true only until another observation comes along to disprove it. Nothing is forever. It is all a matter of probabilities.

Let's say you have lived your whole life all alone in a log cabin in the middle of a large forest. You have never ventured as much as a hundred yards from your cabin

and have had no access to the outside world. You have observed for your entire life that all of the ducks that flew over your land were white. You have never seen a different-colored duck. Thus, you assume, and rightfully so, that all ducks are white. You would have only to see one nonwhite duck fly over your land to disprove your white-duck assumption. Nothing is certain, no matter how long you "objectively observed" it.

Another Example of the Research Method

Suppose, for a moment, you are interested in determining whether the strength of a child's attachment to his or her mother affects the social skills of the child. In order to test your assumption (hypothesis, if you will), you must now decide on what you mean by "child" (say, under age 6), and you need to find some young children and their respective mothers.

Next, you need to decide what you mean by "attachment" and you need to observe how attached the children are to their mothers. Because you need to measure your observations, you will also need to come up with some system whereby certain observed behaviors mean "strong attachment," other behaviors mean "medium attachment," and still other behaviors mean "weak attachment." Then you need to decide what you mean by "social skills," and you need to observe and measure the children's social skills. All of these definitions, observations, and measurements constitute Phase 1 of the research study.

On the basis of your Phase 1 data, you might formulate an assumption, hunch, or hypothesis, to the effect (say) that the stronger a child's attachment to his or her mother, the higher the child's social skills. Or, to put it another way, children who have stronger attachments to their mothers will have better social skills than children who have weaker attachments to their mothers. This is Phase 2 of the research method and involves *inductive* logic. In short, you begin with detailed observations and/or measurements of the world obtained in Phase 1 and move toward more abstract generalizations and ideas.

If your assumption is correct, you can use it to predict that a particular child with a strong attachment to his or her mother will also demonstrate strong social skills. This is an example of *deductive* logic, where you are deducing from the general to the particular. In Phase 3, you set about testing your assumption, observing and measuring the attachment levels and social skills of as many other children as you can manage.

Data from this phase may confirm or cast doubt upon your assumption. The data might also cause you to realize that "attachment" is not so simple of a concept as you had imagined. It is not just a matter of the *strength* of the attachment; the *type* of the attachment is also a factor (e.g., secure, insecure, disorganized). If you have tested enough children from diverse cultural backgrounds, you might also wonder if your assumption holds up better in some cultures than it does in others. Is it more relevant, say, for children raised in nuclear families than for children raised in a more communal environment such as a First Nations reserve or an Israeli kibbutz?

These considerations will lead you to Phase 4, where you revise your conjecture in the light of your observations (inductive logic) and begin to test your revised hunch all over again (deductive logic). Probably, this will not be a lonely effort on your part. Other researchers interested in attachment will also examine your assumption and the evidence you formulated it from and will conduct their own studies to see how right

you really were. This combined work, conducted with honesty, skepticism, sharing, and freedom from entrenched beliefs, allows our knowledge base in the area of attachment to increase.

PURE AND APPLIED RESEARCH STUDIES

Social work research studies can be described as pure or applied. The goal of pure research studies is to develop theory and expand the social work knowledge base. The goal of applied studies is to develop solutions for problems and applications in practice. The distinction between theoretical results and practical results marks the principal difference between pure and applied research studies.

APPROACHES TO THE RESEARCH METHOD

The research method of knowing contains two complementary research approaches—the quantitative approach and the qualitative approach. Simply put, the quantitative portion of a research study relies on the quantification in collecting and analyzing data and uses descriptive and inferential statistical analyses. If data obtained within a research study are represented in the

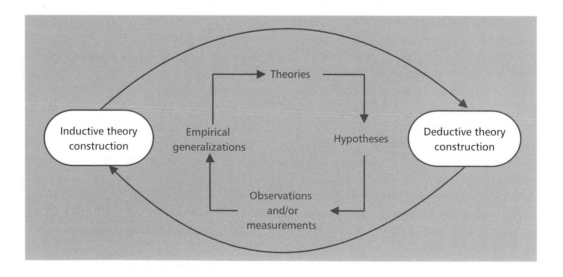

Figure 1.4   Inductive/Deductive Cycle of Theory Construction

form of numbers, then this portion of the study is considered "quantitative." On the other hand, a qualitative portion of a research study relies on qualitative and descriptive methods of data collection. If data are presented in the form of words, diagrams, or drawings—not as numbers, as in the quantitative approach—then this portion of the study is considered "qualitative."

It should be pointed out, however, that a research study can be solely quantitative in nature. It can also be exclusively qualitative. As we will see throughout this book, a good research study uses both approaches in an effort to generate useful knowledge for our profession.

The unique characteristics and contributions of the quantitative approach and qualitative approach to knowledge building are examined in Chapters 5 and 6, respectively. The quantitative and qualitative research approaches complement each other and are equally important in the generation and testing of social work knowledge.

Skills Needed to Do Research Studies

As we know from Figure 1.3, there are four highly interrelated phases of the research method. With these generic phases in mind, we now turn our attention to the skills (and the chapters within this book that discuss these skills) you will need in order to obtain knowledge that is as "error free" and "objective" as possible. Thus, when you do any research study, you will need to have the following skills:

Skill 1: Understand the Place of Research in Social Work (this chapter)

Skill 2: Understand Social Work Research Contexts and Ethics (Chapters 2 through 4)

Skill 3: Understand How to Formulate Research Questions and Hypotheses (Chapters 5 through 7)

Skill 4: Understand How Measurement Is Used in Social Work Research (Chapters 8 through 10)

Skill 5: Understand Sampling and the Logic of Research Design (Chapters 11 through 13)

Skill 6: Understand How to Collect Data and Select a Data Collection Method (Chapters 14 through 22)

Skill 7: Understand How to Analyze and Interpret Data (Chapters 23 and 26)

Skill 8: Understand How to Write and Evaluate Research Reports and Proposals (Chapters 24, 25, 27, and 28)

Skill 9: Understand How Social Work Programs Can Be Evaluated (Chapter 29)

The Research Attitude

The research method, or "scientific method," if you will, refers to the many ideas, rules, techniques, and approaches that we—the research community—use. The research attitude, on the other hand, is simply a way that we view the world. It is an attitude that highly values craftsmanship, with pride in creativity, high-quality standards, and hard work. These traits must be incorporated into both approaches to knowledge building (i.e., quantitative approach, qualitative approach) in order for the findings generated from research studies to be appropriately utilized within our profession's knowledge base. As Grinnell (1987) states:

> Most people learn about the "scientific method" rather than about the scientific attitude. While the "scientific method" is an ideal construct, the scientific attitude is the way people have of looking at the world. Doing science includes many methods: what makes them scientific is their acceptance by the scientific collective. (125)

THE KNOWLEDGE-LEVEL CONTINUUM

We now turn our attention to how the quantitative and qualitative research approaches answer various types of research questions. Any research study falls somewhere along the knowledge-level continuum, depending on how much is already known about the topic (see Figure 1.5). How much is known about the research topic determines the purpose of the study. If you don't know anything, for example, you will merely want to explore the topic area, gathering basic data. Studies like this, conducted for the purpose of exploration are known, logically enough, as *exploratory* studies and fall at the bottom of the knowledge-level continuum, as can be seen in Figure 1.5. Usually exploratory studies adopt a qualitative research approach.

When you have gained some knowledge of the research topic area through exploratory studies, the next task is to describe a specific aspect of the topic area in greater detail, using words and/or numbers. These studies, whose purpose is description, are known as *descriptive* studies and fall in the middle of the knowledge-level continuum, as presented in Figure 1.5. As can be seen, they can adopt a quantitative and/or qualitative research approach.

After descriptive studies have provided a substantial knowledge base in the research topic area, you will be in a position to ask very specific and more complex research questions—causality questions. These kinds of studies are known as *explanatory* studies.

The division of the knowledge continuum into three parts—exploratory, descriptive, and explana-

tory—is a useful way of categorizing research studies in terms of their purpose, the kinds of questions they can answer, and the research approach(es) they can take in answering the questions. However, as in all categorization systems, the three divisions are totally arbitrary, and some social work research studies defy categorization, falling nastily somewhere between exploratory and descriptive, or between descriptive and explanatory. This defiance is only to be expected, since the knowledge-level continuum is essentially that—a *continuum*, not a neat collection of categories. Let's take a moment here to look at exploratory, descriptive, and explanatory studies in more detail and the kinds of questions each type of study can answer.

Exploratory Research Studies

Exploratory studies are most useful when the research topic area is relatively new. In the United States, during

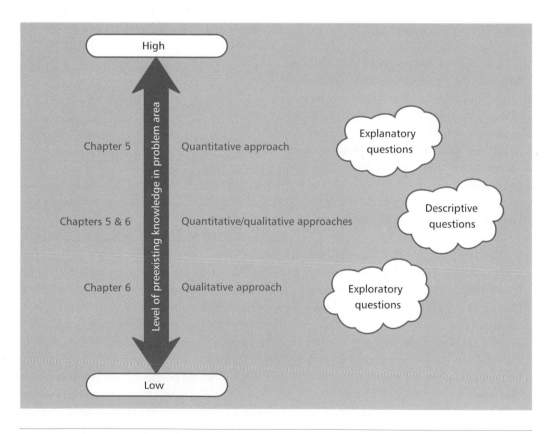

Figure 1.5   The Knowledge-Level Continuum and Approaches to the Research Method

the 1970s, for example, the development of new drugs to control the symptoms of mental illness, together with new federal funding for small, community-based mental health centers, resulted in a massive discharge of people from large, state-based mental health institutions.

Some folks applauded this move as restoring the civil liberties of the mentally ill. Others were concerned that current community facilities would prove inadequate to meet the needs of the people being discharged and their families. Social workers active in the 1970s were anxious to explore the situation, both with an eye on influencing social policy and in order to develop programs to meet the perceived needs of this group of people.

The topic area here is very broad. What are the consequences of a massive discharge of people who are psychiatrically challenged and were recently instit-utionalized? Many different questions pertaining to the topic can be asked. Where are these people living now? Alone? In halfway houses? With their families? On the street? Are they receiving proper medication and nutrition? What income do they have? How do they spend their time? What stresses do they suffer? What impact have they had on their family members and the communities in which they now reside? What services are available to them? How do they feel about being discharged?

No single study can answer all these questions. It is a matter of devising a sieve-like procedure where the first sieve, with the biggest holes, identifies general themes. Each general theme is then put through successively finer sieves until more specific research questions can be asked (Figure 1.6).

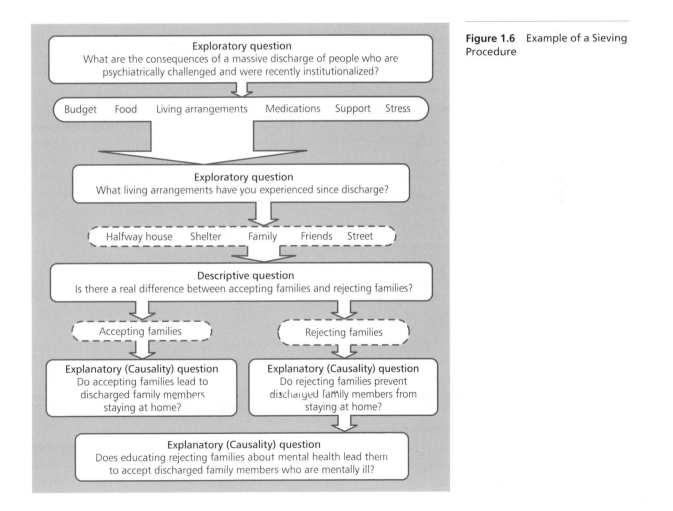

Figure 1.6 Example of a Sieving Procedure

For example, you might begin to explore the consequences of the massive discharge by gathering together a group of these discharged people and asking them a basic exploratory question: What have been your experiences since you were discharged?—what are the components that make up the discharge experience? These questions will be answered using qualitative data. Individual answers will generate common themes. You may find, for example, that the patients have had a number of different living arrangements since they were discharged, vary greatly in their ability to manage their budget, leisure, food, and medication, feel rejected or supported, suffer less or more stress, and so forth.

You might then take one of these major themes and try to refine it, leaving the other major themes to be explored by someone else at a later date. Suppose you choose living arrangements (Figure 1.6) and mount a second exploratory study to ask respondents what living arrangements they have experienced since discharge. You may find now that those who were institutionalized for a long time have tended to move among halfway houses, shelters, and the street, while those who were institutionalized for a shorter time moved in with family first and stayed regardless on how accepting the family was.

At this point, you might feel a need for numbers. How many of them are living where? How many times have they moved on average? What percentage of those who moved in with their families stayed there? These are *descriptive* questions, aimed at describing or providing an accurate profile of this group of people. You are now moving up the knowledge continuum from the exploratory to the descriptive category, but, before we go there, let's summarize the general goals of exploratory research studies. These are to (Neuman, 2003):

- Become familiar with the basic facts, people, and concerns involved
- Develop a well-grounded mental picture of what is occurring
- Generate many ideas and develop tentative theories and conjectures
- Determine the feasibility of doing additional research studies

- Formulate questions and refine issues for more systematic inquiry
- Develop techniques and a sense of direction for future research

Descriptive Research Studies

At the descriptive level, suppose you have decided to focus on those people who moved in with their families. You have a tentative idea, based on your previous exploratory study, that there might be a relationship between the length of time spent in the institution and whether this group of people moved in with their families after discharge. You would like to confirm or refute this relationship, using a much larger group of respondents than you used in your exploratory study.

Another tentative relationship that emerged at the exploratory level was the relationship between staying in the family home and the level of acceptance shown by the family. You would like to know if this relationship holds with a larger group. You would also like to know if there is a real difference between accepting and rejecting families: Is Group *A* different from Group *B*? What factors contribute to acceptance or rejection of the discharged family member? Eventually, you would like to know if there is anything social workers can do to facilitate acceptance, but you don't have enough data yet to be able to usefully ask that question. In general, the goals of descriptive research studies are to (Neuman, 2003):

- Provide an accurate profile of a group
- Describe a process, mechanism, or relationship
- Give a verbal or numerical picture (e.g., percentages)
- Find information to stimulate new explanations
- Create a set of categories or classify types
- Clarify a sequence, set of stages, or steps
- Document information that confirms or contradicts prior beliefs about a subject

Explanatory Research Studies

Suppose you have learned from your descriptive studies that there are real differences between accepting and rejecting families and that these differences seem to have a major impact on whether the discharged person stays at home. Now you would like to ask two related causality questions: Does an accepting family lead to the discharged person's staying at home, and does a rejecting family prevent the discharged person from staying at home? In both cases, the answers will probably be yes, to some extent. Perhaps 30 percent of the decision to stay at home is explained by an accepting family and the other 70 percent remains to be explained by other factors: the severity of the discharged person's symptoms, for example, or the degree of acceptance shown by community members outside the family.

Now, you might want to know whether acceptance on the part of the family carries more weight in the staying-at-home decision than acceptance on the part of the community. The answer to this question will provide a direction for possible intervention strategies; you will know whether to focus your attention on individual families or on entire communities.

Suppose you decide, for example, on the basis of your own and other explanatory studies, to focus on families and the intervention you choose to increase their acceptance is education around mental illness. In order to evaluate the effectiveness of your intervention, you will eventually need to ask another explanatory (or causality) question: Does education around mental illness lead to increased acceptance by families of their discharged family members? With the answer to this question, you have concluded your sieving procedures as outlined in Figure 1.6, moving from a broad exploratory question about discharge experiences to a tested intervention designed to serve the discharged people and their families. In general, the goals of explanatory research studies are to (Neuman, 2003):

- Determine the accuracy of a principle or theory
- Find out which competing explanation is better
- Link different issues or topics under a common general statement
- Build and elaborate a theory so that it becomes more complete
- Extend a theory or principle into new areas or issues
- Provide evidence to support or refute an explanation

DEFINITION OF SOCIAL WORK RESEARCH

So far, we have discussed the various ways of obtaining knowledge and briefly looked at the characteristics and phases of the research method. Armed with this knowledge, we now need a definition of research, which is composed of two syllables, *re* and *search*. Dictionaries define the former syllable as a prefix meaning "again," "anew," or "over again," and the latter as a verb meaning "to examine closely and carefully," "to test and try," or "to probe" (Duehn, 1985).

Together, these syllables form a noun that describes a careful and systematic study in some field of knowledge, undertaken to establish facts or principles. Social work research therefore can be defined as:

> a systematic and objective inquiry that utilizes the research method to solve human problems and creates new knowledge that is generally applicable.

We obtain much of our knowledge base from the findings derived from research studies that utilize the research method. However, all research studies have built-in biases and limitations that create errors and keep us from being absolutely certain about the studies' outcomes.

This book helps you to understand these limitations and to take them into account in the interpretation of research findings and also helps you to avoid making errors or obtaining wrong answers. One of the principal products of a research study is "objective and systematic" data—via the research method—about reality as it is, "unbiased" and "error-free."

RESEARCH ROLES

We have looked at the reasons why social workers need to engage in research. Since there are many different ways of actually engaging within the research method, it is useful to look at the three research-related roles that social workers might play. These are (1) the research consumer, (2) the creator and disseminator of knowledge, and (3) the contributing partner.

The Research Consumer

If you go to your doctor to discuss your arthritis, you expect the doc to be aware of the most recent advances in the management and treatment of arthritis. All professionals, in all disciplines, are expected by their clients to keep up with the latest developments in their fields. They do this by attending conferences, reading books and journals, and paying attention to the results derived from research studies. In other words, these professionals—which include you as a social worker—are *research consumers*, and, as previously noted, they need to know enough about the research method to consume it wisely, separating the nutritious wheat from the dubious chaff.

The Creator and Disseminator of Knowledge

You may be quite determined that you will never yourself conduct a research study. Never ever! you say, and then you find that you are the only staff person in a small voluntary social service program that desperately requires a needs assessment if the program is to serve its clients and keep its funding base. You look up "needs assessment" in forgotten research texts, and sweat, and stumble through them because someone has to do the study and there is no one there but you.

This may seem like an unlikely scenario, but in fact many social service programs are very small and are run on a wing and a prayer by a few paid staff and a large volunteer contingent. They rise and flourish for a time and die; and death is often hastened along by their inability to demonstrate, in research terms, how much good they are doing on their clients' behalf, how little it is costing, and what the dreadful social consequences would be if they weren't there to do it.

You may escape being the sole social worker in a program that needs research know-how. But even if you are a mere cog in a immense machine of interlocking social workers, the time may come when you want to try something new. Most social workers do. Most of them, however, don't try the something in any structured way. They don't write down exactly what the something was (perhaps a new intervention for raising Jody's self-esteem), they don't say why they needed it

(nothing else was working), how they tested it (they measured Jody's self-esteem before and after doing it), or how effective it was (Jody's self-esteem score rose triumphantly, from X to Y and was still at its higher level three months later).

Worse, they don't tell anyone else they did it, except for a few murmurs, rapidly forgotten, to a colleague over coffee. One consequence of this is that other Jody-types, who might benefit from the same intervention, never have the opportunity to do so because their social workers don't know that it exists. Another consequence is that the program cannot use this newly founded innovation as evidence of its effectiveness to place before its funders.

The Contributing Partner

In reality, many social service programs conduct some kind of research studies from time to time, particularly evaluative studies. Many more agree to host studies conducted by researchers external to the program, such as university professors and graduate students. Unlike studies conducted by psychologists, social work research rarely takes place in a laboratory but, instead, is usually conducted in field settings. Data may be drawn from program clients or their records and may be collected in the program or in the clients' homes.

Since social workers are usually employed by social service programs, they are often drawn into the program's research activities by default. Such activities are normally conducted by a team, consisting of researchers and program staff members. Today, the solitary social work researcher, like the solitary mad scientist, is very much a thing of the past. Staff members who contribute to research inquiry may have specific skills to offer that they never imagined were research-related.

One may be particularly acute and accurate when it comes to observing client behaviors. A second worker, on the other hand, may work well as a liaison between clients and researcher or between one program and another. Some social workers are cooperative in research endeavors, and others are less so, depending on their attitudes toward knowledge development through the use of the research method. Those of us who know most about research methods tend to be the most cooperative and also the most useful. Hence, the greater the number of social workers who understand research principles, the more likely it is that relevant studies will be successfully completed and that social work knowledge will be increased.

Integrating the Three Research Roles

Just about everything in life is interdependent on everything else. Chaos theory comes readily to mind concerning the idea of interdependence. The same holds true with the three research roles noted earlier—they are not independent of one another. They must be integrated if research is to accomplish its goals of increasing our profession's knowledge base and improving the effectiveness of our interventions with clients.

The issue is not whether we should consume research findings, produce and disseminate research results, or become contributing partners in research studies. Rather, it is whether we can engage the full spectrum of available knowledge and skills in the continual improvement of our practices. Social workers who adopt only one or two research roles are shortchanging themselves and their clients (Reid & Smith, 1989):

> If research is to be used to full advantage to advance the goals of social work, the profession needs to develop a climate in which both doing and consuming research are normal professional activities. By this we do not mean that all social workers should necessarily do research or that all practice should be based on the results of research, but rather that an ability to carry out

studies at some level and the facility in using scientifically based knowledge should be an integral part of the skills that social workers have and use. (p. xi)

A research base within our profession will not guarantee its public acceptance, but there is no doubt that the absence of such a base and the lack of vigorous research efforts to expand it will, in the long run, erode our credibility and be harmful to our clients.

SUMMARY

Knowledge is essential to human survival. Over the course of history, there have been many ways of knowing, from divine revelation to tradition and the authority of elders. By the beginning of the seventeenth century, people began to rely on a different way of knowing—the research method.

Social workers derive their knowledge from authority, tradition, professional experience, and personal intuition, as well as from findings derived from research studies.

Social workers engage in three research roles. They can consume research findings by using the findings of others in their day-to-day practices, they can produce and disseminate research results for others to use, and they can participate in research studies in a variety of ways.

Now that we have briefly explored the place of research in social work, the following chapter discusses the various contexts where the research process actually unfolds.

Research Contexts

Robert W. Weinbach

· · · · · · · · · · · · · · · · · · · ·

2

CONTEXTS

In order to conduct any research study, we need to understand the research method of obtaining knowledge as presented in the previous chapter. In addition to understanding and knowing how to use the paradigm, we need to face the fact that it is impossible to conduct any research study in a social work setting without an appreciation for the *contexts* in which the study will take place.

If we desire to do a research study in a social service program and ignore the special characteristics of conducting our study within it, then we are destined for a catastrophe. Social work research is unique because social work practice settings are unique. There are unparalleled opportunities to execute research studies in applied settings, but there are also constraints inherent within these same settings. Thus, only understanding and knowing how to use to use the research method to answer research questions are not enough. We must also be aware of, and appreciate, the "special factors" that we must take into account when we want to do a social work research study—the focus of this chapter.

FACTORS THAT AFFECT SOCIAL WORK RESEARCH

There are three major factors that shape social work research, and it is senseless to view them separately. They always interact, as do components in any system, to create a research environment whose potential for support of research endeavors ranges all the way from complete enthusiasm and sanction to virtual sabotage. This interaction is compounded by the individual personalities, values, and needs of the people who work within the programs.

The three contextual factors that serve as major shaping forces for all social work research studies are: (1) the social service program, (2) the social work profession, and (3) the social workers themselves.

The Social Service Program

The first factor that affects social work research is the social service program where the research study actually takes place. The majority of social workers are employed by social service programs. Some programs, particularly in the private sector, have demonstrated over the years a strong commitment to research. As voluntary financial support has decreased in a time of economic problems for many citizens, traditional research roles and responsibilities of social workers employed within the programs are being examined.

We cannot yet ascertain whether research in private social service programs will move in the direction of the "luxury" status that it currently enjoys in many public programs. The future of program-generated (and program-supported) research remains at best tenuous for the foreseeable future. But what happens to those of us who may merely be seeking to conduct a simple research study within a social service program without requesting extensive program or financial support? What climate exists within programs that will affect the potential for at least a minimal support of our research interests?

Generalizations regarding programs (which range from public social service settings that employ thousands to two- or three-person counseling offices) are always dangerous and rarely apply perfectly to any one setting. However, there are six general characteristics that are appropriate to the majority of programs: (1) programs have accountability concerns, (2) all research has evaluative potential, (3) accountability pressures create a market for research, (4) programs exist in hostile environments, (5) programs have scarce financial resources, and (6) programs have client files.

Accountability Concerns

As discussed in the previous chapter, accountability is the need for us to demonstrate our effectiveness and efficiency to those who pay the bills. However, accountability has resulted in a mixed blessing for social work research. As we will see in Chapter 29, evaluative research, or program evaluation, is a logical response to demands that a program demonstrate that it is doing what it claims to be doing—and doing it relatively inexpensively. At the same time, program administrators are acutely aware of the threat of unfavorable program evaluations and are fearful that such evaluations may provide justification for funding cutbacks or termination of inefficient, but needed, social service programs. These programs may seem inefficient, and a real fear may be that program evaluations will overemphasize inefficiency without paying adequate attention to the necessity for the services upon which our clients depend.

Evaluative Potential

Like all people, social workers tend to be suspicious of any research study that is evaluative in nature. We rightfully fear that the results of the study will have negative consequences for us and our clients, for many of the same reasons that program administrators fear it. These fears within programs are not limited to program evaluations, however. Despite widespread agreements regarding the need for meaningful research studies, particularly in the evaluation of social service programs, our attitude toward research remains typically one of anxiety, distrust, and apathy. A generalized fear of research is not totally unfounded.

Even simple research designs, which seek only to describe or to identify a relationship between two variables, have the potential to embarrass individual social workers, their supervisors, and management. If data are incorrectly (or correctly but tactlessly) interpreted or made available to an audience hostile to the program or one or more of its staff members, research studies of *any type* can be a legitimate threat.

A program's administrator "once burned" can be expected to be extremely wary of a proposed research study, no matter what assurances are made and what controls are included in the study's design. Only after past negative experiences are explored and the appropriate assurances made can any reasonable level of approval and support be anticipated from a program.

It must be emphasized that social work "researchers" may have perspectives and needs very different from those of the program's practitioners and administrators. The questions that interest researchers and make up the most important issues for them may not interest the staff of the programs where they wish to conduct their studies. Program administrators may prefer (and need) to see requests for research studies in terms of cost/benefit ratios.

They are especially concerned with what and how program resources will be diverted from normal client service to support the proposed study. They may have difficulty in justifying such a reallocation of funds and staff, especially if previous research studies within their programs resulted in a promised research report that was never delivered. Or, worse, they may have received a report that was written in such an esoteric form that it had little potential for utilization by anyone but the researchers themselves.

Many social service program administrators have had at least one negative experience with a research study that has embarrassed either the program or the very administrators who risked their reputations to support the research study. Sometimes all of these negative experiences have occurred to the point that the next well-meaning potential social work researcher has an especially difficult sales task. Occasionally, it is not the past negative experiences but a genuine fear that threatens support for a research study to take place within a social service program.

While accountability pressures have successfully eliminated some programs that were ineffective and/or inefficient, a few such programs still remain because they have been able to cover up their shortcomings. If we seek to do a research study in such a program, we must recognize that any meaningful support from the program will potentially be nil and that special diplomacy and determination will be required. Good program evaluations will always pose a serious threat to poorly administered programs and their administrators.

Market for Research

On the positive side, pressures for accountability and resultant fears regarding it in social service programs have created an environment of interest in program evaluation. Since we are trying to demonstrate our accountability, we are now searching for evaluative methods that will be fair to the programs, while at the same time providing useful feedback for the improvement of their services to clients.

At first there was a tendency to try to apply systems-oriented evaluation methods developed for use in business (i.e., profit-making organizations) to programs.

This seemed logical, placed a renewed emphasis on efficiency, and was supported and even imposed by people in funding organizations. Advocates of these methods had little understanding of the unique nature of social service programs committed to public service rather than to private profit.

Use of such evaluative techniques as planning, programming, budget systems (PPBS); program evaluation review techniques (PERT); and other systems analysis-oriented methods provided proof to us that "evaluation" was legitimately to be feared. The specter of cost efficiency used as a criterion for evaluation of social services was threatening and was resisted unless mandated. Workers in programs that knowingly offered services (e.g., counseling for people who have addictions) that were "inefficient" on a unit basis and had a relatively low success rate (effectiveness) were especially fearful.

Obviously, the use of only profit-oriented measurements of success within social service programs is totally inappropriate. A renewed interest in different types of program evaluation methods that take into account such factors as the need for services (*despite* inefficiency) is becoming more apparent. There now are many books and articles written by social workers that propose program evaluation methods that we feel are infinitely more fair and reasonable than those utilized in business (e.g., Gabor, Unrau, & Grinnell, 1998; Unrau, Gabor, & Grinnell, 2001).

A positive changing attitude toward program evaluation within social service programs is now being observed. Program administrators, faced with the need for evaluation, have turned to people in our own profession to provide it. Social workers, who are more familiar with both the strengths and the limitations of day-to-day social work practice, provide evaluations that are not excessively rigid or critical. We also generate more meaningful recommendations that have greater utility for improving services to clients than do researchers outside our field who may be utilizing criteria inappropriate for a social service program.

Unlike researchers in other fields, social work researchers understand the limits of knowledge that exist within our profession. We will not mistakenly assume that cause-effect knowledge exists and that this type of knowledge can be applied in a given situation in which our own professional judgment is really the only measurement instrument currently available.

The development of program evaluation methods and the increased interest among us in doing program evaluations have contributed to the fact that program administrators seem less fearful of evaluation now than in the late 1970s. Some even welcome it as an important skill by which to upgrade the delivery of services to the clients they serve. There is now an increasing acceptance of the importance of evaluation and research activities for the future development of our profession.

As we will see in Chapters 12 and 13, we have also begun to look critically at the effectiveness and efficiency of our individual practices. With encouragement from the professional literature, we have shown an increased interest in both group- and single-subject research as vehicles to evaluate our daily work and to generate suggestions for improving it.

Hostile Environments

Although most programs are readily valued and accepted within their communities, unfortunately, some are not. Public tax-supported programs, such as public assistance and criminal justice facilities, are nearly always misunderstood and frequently resented. They may be perceived by the general public as giving away the public's tax dollars to undeserving and undesirable clients. Letters-to-the-editor columns in local newspapers illustrate the low regard and even outright hostility reserved for these programs and the clients they serve.

Research, which has the potential to dispel commonly believed negative mythology about social service programs, may be especially useful, particularly in programs' ongoing public relations struggle. Any data that can improve the credibility and the overall image of a program are useful.

Scarce Financial Resources

Some social service programs that suffer from a public image problem as noted in the previous section could benefit from research studies that would result in a more accurate portrayal of themselves to the general public. However, the financial resources that are needed for such projects are often simply not available. Research related to advancing practice theory must often compete with other activities that appear more politically desirable (e.g., policing of clients, fraud investigations) within the critical spotlight of the community.

Resources that are available for a research study may be committed almost entirely to the tasks of data compilation, storage, and retrieval—a tremendous undertaking in a large public social service program. Overall experience seems to demonstrate that the programs in which we work are rarely able to provide the continuity of financing and the staff required for research studies designed to advance practice theory.

Social service programs usually cannot afford to do "pure" research. For obvious reasons, they are much more receptive to doing "applied" research. We may find them even more receptive to research suggestions, provided we are willing to conduct our study with minimal resource support. Program administrators would often like to improve their program's image by showing a commitment to greater accountability but cannot because they lack the personnel to conduct the needed research studies.

If we are interested in an area that may potentially improve the program's image, we may be permitted access to data otherwise inaccessible for pure research purposes. Research activities that suggest an interest in improving quality of services and a commitment to more efficient use of funds are a valuable tool for an administrator seeking to improve community relations, to deal with suspicious board members, or to negotiate next year's budget.

Client Files

The bureaucratic nature of social service programs provides a desirable resource for social work research. As presented in Part V in this book, there is often a tendency for us to think in terms of collecting original data. However, as we will see in Part VI in this book, a wealth of existing data in the form of case records (client files) and regularly gathered statistics often goes untapped. Data may be gathered within programs because of federal or state mandates or because administrators feel they need to have sufficient records in case of legal actions. Social workers themselves are accustomed to making voluminous notes, whether out of habit or because the notes may actually serve some need, such as jogging the memory about a client seen only occasionally.

For legal and other reasons, client files are not and should not be readily available. However, since research has many advantages for programs in the present environment, client files can usually be obtained. A program administrator is charged with both safeguarding the confidentiality of client information and creating a good public image for the program. Research that threatens either of these will result in the denial of access to the data residing in client files. Thus, it is essential that tact be used and all necessary assurances be given when proposing a research study to a program's administrator.

Program administrators are aware that research involving program data will usually require the time of program staff. To safeguard confidentiality, a staff member will probably need to be present when client files and other databases are utilized in a research study. If data are computerized, program personnel may be required simply to obtain the desired data in a form usable to the researcher. Program records are a relatively economical data source, but various limitations in the use of such databases need to be noted:

- First, generalizations of the study's findings to the clientele of other programs may not be possible. Every social service program is unique. While some phenomena (e.g., certain human problems and behavioral characteristics) transcend the boundaries of a given program, factors such as catchment areas (i.e., geographical areas served) and eligibility criteria (e. g., unemployed youths) of individual programs may result in a research sample unlike any other. As we will see in Chapter 11, we must be attuned to any biasing effects that arise from the samples we eventually use.
- Second, client files often lack standardization. Data in some programs are abundant but are not in a sufficiently standardized format to be readily accessible or analyzed. Data within client files

tend to change as federal and state requirements are modified. Sometimes it is more economical to collect original data in the usual standardized format than it is to use already existing data from somewhere within the program.

- Third, client files may be biased. The sources for most program records and client files are the individual social workers, whose effectiveness is sometimes evaluated in part by what is reflected in their clients' files. As with most human beings, few of us are sufficiently honest (or masochistic) as to record our failures and errors of judgment in program records. Certain data that result in the evaluation of our own effectiveness are especially suspect.

  Even if every effort has been made to record data in client files as accurately as possible, it must be remembered that the social work researcher who uses client files still has no first-hand knowledge of the client. The data ultimately used for a research study may easily become distorted in the necessary chain of translations from the actual behaviors of the client to the practitioner's perceptions of these behaviors (case files) to the researcher's measurement instruments (categorizations) to the data analyses.

- Fourth, client files may contain deliberate omissions. Sensitive client data that may be subject to court subpoena may never appear in clients' files. Sometimes, data (variables) that would be most valuable (e.g., assignment of clients to diagnostic categories) are deleted as a matter of program policy or worker discretion. In short, client files—for reasons of political and client interest—must be assumed to be inconsistently incomplete data sources.

Increase in computerization of client files and legal concerns regarding the safeguarding of client data may not portend well for social work researchers' using program records. Every time a program must defend itself in court either for refusing to release data (client and/or program) or for releasing data with questionable authorization, the climate for the storage of accessible client information worsens. Issues of confidentiality have led to questions of whether written client files have become a dangerous anachronism now that these necessary data can be stored in coded form accessible by only a few selected staff members. Although this is not yet a common practice, if it were to become widespread it would have a limiting effect on social work research in program settings.

The Social Work Profession

The second factor that affects social work research is our profession. What is possible and desirable in social work research is shaped by professional values, standards, and definitions that differ from those in any other discipline. There are three characteristics inherent in our profession which shape social work research: (1) the profession's values and ethics, (2) the profession's beliefs and practices, and (3) the rewards for doing research. Membership in our profession carries certain responsibilities, and these responsibilities, combined with professional objectives, constitute both supports and obstacles for those of us who seek to advance knowledge relevant to social work practice through research.

Values and Ethics

Physical scientists need not concern themselves with the rights of their research subjects. Nonorganic matter may be manipulated in a way that will minimize the researcher's three enemies, which are investigator bias, intervening variables, and chance (Weinbach & Grinnell, 2004). The following chapter presents many of the ethical issues that must be addressed in the use of human subjects as research participants. Our profession reflects special concerns relating to the protection of clients whom we are committed to help—not to harm. Some of these concerns are quite legitimate; others are somewhat less so. Nevertheless, our profession, with its protectiveness toward our clients, tends to set limits on research studies that exceed a generalized concern for protecting the rights of human research participants.

Specifically, there are research situations that our profession generally will not (and should not) tolerate, despite the apparent potential for building knowledge for practice theory. As we will see in Chapters 11 and 13, research studies that involve the random assignment of clients to different practice methods in order to compare the relative effectiveness of the methods are usually opposed.

Probably the most dramatic example of a conflict between professional values and responsibilities and research requirements relates to the issue of the denial of services. In evaluating the effectiveness of a social work treatment intervention, for example, it would be highly desirable, from a research perspective, to randomly form a group of people who are seeking help but are denied it (control group) so that a direct comparison can later be made with outcomes among those who received help (experimental group). As we will see in the next chapter, such a decision would be a violation of professional social work ethics.

Beliefs and Practices

Some characteristics of our profession are not written down so easily or so easily identified as its values and ethics. Certain beliefs, traditions, and professional definitions, while elusive, nevertheless have their effect on the shaping of research investigations in our profession. Whether they are based on a verifiable *fact* or have their basis in mythology is really unimportant.

Social work practice, particularly at the direct practice level, is believed to be highly dependent on the social worker-client relationship. Not surprisingly, any action (even in the interest of knowledge building) that might be perceived as threatening or in any way changing this relationship will be opposed.

While it may be easy for us to build a logical case for the evaluation of practice methods, or for describing the nature of social work practice through direct observation of social worker-client interactions, requests for permission for us to do this are usually not well received. Students in their field practicum courses may observe a similar resistance when they make what appears to be a perfectly reasonable request to learn treatment techniques (e.g., active listening) of a particular intervention (e.g., nondirective therapy) by observing their field instructors in an interview.

The rationale most frequently given for not permitting onsite observation of direct treatment, even in the interest of research, is that it would jeopardize the treatment relationship. While the cynic might see this as an effort to avoid exposing the errors that even a very experienced social worker inevitably makes, it is more likely a sincere belief, based in part on professional tradition and folklore. Despite the fact that skilled observers are rarely an impediment to any treatment relationship (they are soon ignored), the belief persists. This belief presents an obstacle to research studies where firsthand observation of an intervention would be the best means to collect data for the study.

While accountability pressures have recently tended to prod our profession to examine and evaluate our treatment interventions, the nature of our practice is such that effective practice remains difficult to conceptualize and operationalize. Such vague outcome measures as progress and growth—when applied to client problem areas equally as vague, such as communication, self-esteem, and social functioning—become especially elusive. As presented in Chapters 8 through 10, a tremendous amount of progress has been made in the measurement of these and many other concepts. However, our profession has a certain folklore that remains somewhat distrustful of measurement packages that do not take into consideration the professional judgment of the social worker.

Some social workers may prefer to perceive improvement in client functioning subjectively rather than objectively. Research methods that rely heavily on objective measures are likely to be suspect; thus, the utilization potential of quantitative research findings may be readily dismissed because the findings are solely based on quantitative data sources.

Research Rewards

Research has not always been synonymous with status in our profession, as it has in many other fields. Rewards in the form of promotions and recognition have more often gone to skilled practitioners, especially to those of us who have evolved a new intervention (e.g., primal scream, trust fall, trust walk) or pioneered practice methods with a newly discovered client group (e.g., people with AIDS).

Professional social work journals publish more reports of quantitatively based research studies than qualitatively based studies. Whether this phenomenon occurs because of editorial preference or the unavailability of high-standard qualitative research reports for publication is not precisely the issue. What is important is that there has been a message within the profession that tends to say that published reports of research findings are of secondary importance to other forms of communication. A constant pressure for more and better research endeavors has come from ongoing efforts to further professionalize social work. No matter which of several available lists of professional attributes are applied, social work appears especially vulnerable to accusations of nonprofessional status because of its heavy reliance on knowledge derived from other fields, such as psychology and sociology.

The lack of a clear-cut body of knowledge unique to social work practice, and hence the concern about this shortcoming, will continue to foster practice-relevant research. Current emphasis on case-level research methodologies (see Chapter 12) for use by the individual social worker is but one example of this trend. The popularity of program evaluation (see Chapter 29) is another example. As more of us become involved in doing research, we will see its value to professionalization and, thus, to practice.

Our profession can be expected to become even more supportive of research efforts as professionalization takes hold, because professionals need to do research and use research findings in their practices for reasons previously discussed. Those of us who seek to conduct research studies might well make use of this point to gain acceptance and support for our research aspirations.

The Social Work Practitioners

The final factor that affects social work research is the social workers themselves. As in the case of the social work profession, and the social service programs within it, generalizations about the characteristics of social work practitioners are dangerous. Of course, there are always exceptions, but social workers, as a group, seem to have three characteristics that are useful in understanding their role as it affects social work research: (1) social workers are people oriented, (2) social workers have a vested interest in practice, and (3) social workers need research.

People Orientation

A certain selection process takes place when people must choose a career. People who commit themselves to our profession have done more than choose an academic field or a knowledge area in which to work. They have made statements about themselves in regard to the personal needs and values they possess. In general, we choose our profession because we feel a need and a responsibility to help other people help themselves.

We believe that we are capable of interacting meaningfully with others, either on a one-to-one basis (e.g., direct practice) or on a more indirect level of helping (e.g., research, administration). Furthermore, we desire this type of interaction and probably believe that the helping process and the interaction will provide gratification for us. The selection of our profession is, in part, an acknowledgment of our desire to work with the real and the human, rather than with the abstract or the inanimate. As we saw from Chapter 1, social work research usually involves working with social workers—either as research participants, as research collaborators, or as researchers themselves.

Social workers have a certain amount of uninterest in, or even terror of, research. They have not generally exhibited either the reliance on, or the interest in, research that would be reasonable to expect among those who seek professionalization by attempting to move toward a more knowledge-based practice. Rather than using research-based practice knowledge, we often prefer to rely on what we describe as a combination of humanitarian impulse, occupational folklore, and common sense.

These phenomena should not be viewed as "anti-research" so much as "pro-people." To many of us, research is abstract, dry, theoretical, and totally unrelated to practice. This impression is not without its basis in reality. Until recently, much of social work research has lacked relevance to practice and has had little potential for utilization. The combination of researchers who were not always in tune with social work practitioners' practice needs and practitioners who were uninterested in, and uninformed about, research has resulted in attitudes of apathy and even antagonism toward research. However, this attitude has begun to change in recent years as social work graduates have come to a better understanding of research and a knowledge of more practice-relevant methodologies; the people orientation of social workers can be expected to continue.

More often than not, we have a tendency to be advocates for our clients and coworkers alike; we usually reflect optimism and hope that our clients' situations are improving and will continue to improve. Although this positive characteristic is necessary and desirable for social work *practitioners,* it can often drive social work *researchers* to frustration because of its potential biasing effects. Social work practitioners are not very good at estimating the amount of their clients' success. We sometimes tend to subjectively view clients in a positive light, which interferes with our ability to objectively evaluate our clients' success.

In evaluating the functioning level of clients, objectivity seems to be compromised even further by our need to somehow reward past client growth or even client effort by unrealistically favorable current measurements. Research measurements involving the "subjective" perceptions of our clients' functioning must always be viewed as suspect and in need of "objective" corroboration. The characteristics of emphasizing strengths and the good in people, while absolutely essential to good social work *practice,* may be almost diametrically opposed to what is necessary for valid and reliable client success measures in social work research.

Vested Interest in Practice

We not only believe in people; we also believe in the treatment interventions that we use to help people help themselves. This results in a confidence that is as desirable for practice as are optimistic evaluations of clients. Unfortunately, the confidence that we have in our interventions may give rise to a resistance both to certain types of research and to our acceptance of research findings that are not supportive of the interventions. It can result in an unwillingness or even an inability on our part to question and, hence, to revise our interventions and treatment techniques on the basis of emerging research findings.

Some social workers employ favorite treatment interventions and have done so for many years. They have become skilled at them through repetition and experience. Some of us have gone even further by writing papers and books about the interventions and their corresponding techniques.

Some of us have also been acknowledged by peers as experts in our specializations. Some social workers have sought to become more proficient at what they do and have made personal and financial sacrifices to receive advanced training in specialized interventions. If we wish to evaluate whether an intervention is truly effective, we will likely meet a wall of resistance based upon one or a combination of these investments.

Research studies that evaluate an intervention and/or its corresponding techniques must be totally objective. Its findings can challenge accepted practices and, in some cases, threaten the reputation and status of those people most associated with its theory (if a theory exists). While this type of research may be what is most needed in our profession, we must anticipate that some of us will be reluctant to participate in research studies and will be reluctant to utilize the findings if they are not an endorsement of our favorite intervention.

Need for Research

It would be erroneous to suggest that the characteristics of social workers present the only barrier to research in our profession. There is another side, based in part on the same attributes, that can provide support for those of us who wish to build a social work knowledge base for practice theory. Generally, we welcome research that is clearly aimed toward improving client services. Having been convinced that a proposed research study has this goal, we will more than likely support the study and participate in it. Until quite recently, there were few research studies that represented methodologically sound evaluations of treatment interventions.

The paucity of these evaluations and the need for them represent an excellent opportunity for research activity. Positions taken by our professional organizations such as the National Association of Social Workers on the need to evaluate social work interventions may be having an effect on the attitudes of practitioners. The entire theme of this book is that our profession needs to incorporate into program operations, and into the daily routine of practice, the developing means for continuously monitoring and assessing the results of our efforts. Research will help us in our difficult task of explaining to others what we are doing, with what success, and its importance.

As a group, we are more humble than arrogant, more open to learning from others than smug about our own knowledge. We are generally realistic about the effectiveness of our helping skills, particularly in working with client groups and problems where experience in the problem area is limited. The nature of our profession is such that a large percentage of those who practice in it are forced to make decisions and to intervene without the assistance of a vast body of sound knowledge. We will welcome research findings that assist us in functioning less on our instinct and good intention and more on a sound knowledge base that was generated through quantitative and qualitative research studies.

SUMMARY

In order to conduct a research study, we need to take into account not only the design of the study itself but the environment in which it will be conducted. The three contextual forces that shape all social work research studies are the program, the profession, and the individual social workers involved in the research studies.

This chapter presented the three contexts in which research studies are conducted. The next chapter builds upon this one by discussing the major ethical issues that must be addressed before any type of research study can take place in any social service program.

Fredrick G. Reamer

Research Ethics

3

The chapters in this book demonstrate clearly the remarkable maturation of social work research and evaluation. Especially since the 1970s, social workers have cultivated an impressive array of quantitative and qualitative methods to help them monitor and evaluate practice, conduct needs assessments, and develop practice guidelines (this book; Reamer, 1998, 1999; Rubin & Babbie, 2005).

Paralleling these developments, social workers also have enhanced their understanding of the ethical issues related to research and evaluation. Interestingly, social workers' enriched understanding of ethical issues also began in earnest during the 1970s. During recent years, for example, social workers have begun to appreciate that their mastery of technical issues pertaining to research design (Chapters 12–13), sampling (Chapter 11), validity and reliability (Chapter 8), measurement (Chapter 8), instrument development (Chapters 9–10), and data analysis (Chapters 23 and 26) must be supplemented by a firm grasp of ethical issues.

After all, even the most sophisticated and rigorous research and evaluation methodology would be suspect, and possibly destructive, if it did not conform to prevailing ethical standards. This chapter traces the development of social workers' understanding of ethical issues in research and evaluation, focusing especially on guidelines for research-based practice.

A BRIEF HISTORICAL OVERVIEW

During recent years, but especially since the 1970s, members of all professions—including professions as diverse as social work, psychology, psychiatry, nursing, medicine, accounting, business, law enforcement, and engineering—have paid closer attention to ethical issues in general. This has occurred for several reasons (Reamer, 1999). New technology, especially in the health care and the computer fields, has brought with it a number of complex and compelling ethical issues. Examples include ethical issues concerning the termination of life support, genetic engineering, organ transplantation, and the privacy of computer-based records.

In addition, widespread medial coverage of ethical misconduct and scandals has enhanced professionals' knowledge of and interest in ethical issues. For example, international, national, and local stories of ethical misbehavior involving politicians, lawyers, doctors, nurses, athletes, and social workers have helped to put the subject of ethics on the professions' front burners.

Also, our current preoccupation with ethical issues is a legacy of the intense focus during the 1960s on various social justice issues, including patient' rights, consumers' rights, prisoners' rights, civil rights, and welfare rights. That decade's visible protests and advocacy made a lasting impression. One consequence is that the language of "rights" now is firmly entrenched in our culture, and we see evidence of this in the proliferation of mechanisms to protect the rights of research and evaluation participants.

Furthermore, there is no question that increases in litigation (lawsuits) and ethics complaints filed against professionals have generated increased interest in ethics. Formal allegations of ethical misconduct and professional negligence involving ethical issues have motivated many professionals to pay closer attention to ethical standards.

Along with these factors that explain the expansion of professionals' interest in ethics in general, we must consider a number of unique developments related to research and evaluation ethics. Perhaps the most significant historical event was the trial of the Nazi doctors at Nuremberg, in 1945 (Levine, 1991). These legal proceedings broadcast the fact that profound harm can result from unethical research (Ashcroft, 1998). The hauntingly inhumane experiments conducted by the Nazi doctors for the benefit of the Third Reich military demonstrated the unspeakable pain and suffering that unprincipled research can cause.

Fortunately, from this horror came the Nuremberg Code and other international codes of ethics designed to protect research participants. These pioneering documents have shaped contemporary guidelines that require that individuals' participation in research be both voluntary and informed and that participants be protected from risk to the greatest extent possible (Levine, 1988).

Two other key historical events involving unethical research must be noted. First, the famous Tuskegee syphilis study involved a 40-year project, begun in 1932, by the U.S. Public Health Service to investigate the natural history of untreated syphilis. The study's participants included poor African American men from Alabama who were told that they had "bad blood" and that they would receive procedures such as spinal taps as free treatment. These men were not provided with what then was the standard and widely accepted treatment for syphilis, nor were they provided with penicillin when it became available later during the study. The men in the sample were not told about the research design or the risks they faced. Many of the men died, but the study's unethical design and procedures did not come to the public's attention until 1972.

In the second important study, known as the Willowbrook study, researchers investigated the natural history of another untreated disease, in this instance infectious hepatitis. A group of children who had been diagnosed with mental retardation and who lived at the Willowbrook State Hospital in Staten Island, New York, were deliberately infected with hepatitis. The researchers' goal was to study the history of the disease when left untreated and later to evaluate the effects of gamma globulin as a treatment option. Public debate about this project focused especially on the ethical issues involving the deliberate infection of the children with hepatitis and the attempts to convince their parents to enroll the children in the study in exchange for admission to the hospital (which had limited space).

The first prominent regulations designed to prevent these types of abuses were introduced in the United States in 1966 when Surgeon General William Stewart issued a U.S. Public Health Service directive on human experimentation. This directive announced that the Public Health Service would not fund research studies unless the institution receiving the federal funds documented the procedures in place to ensure research participants' informed consent, the use of appropriate and ethical research procedures, an adequate review of the risks and medical benefits of the research project, and the procedures designed to protect research participants' rights. Also during the 1960s, the World Medical Association promulgated the Declaration of Helsinki, which elaborated on the informed consent standards set forth in the Nuremberg Code in 1946 (Whitbeck, 1998).

The most prominent current guidelines for protecting research participants appear in two key documents: the Belmont Report (National Commission for the Protection of Human Subjects of Biomedical and Behavioral Research, 1978) and the International Guidelines for Biomedical Research Involving Human Subjects (Council for International Organizations of Medical Sciences, 1993). The landmark Belmont Report sets forth guidelines to protect human participants in accord with three core ethical concepts: (1) respect for persons, (2) beneficence, and (3) justice (Weijer, 1998). The International Guidelines for Biomedical Research Involving Human Subjects includes 15 specific standards for the conduct of research, addressing issues such as informed consent, the extent to which a research project is responsive to community needs, and the need for scrutiny of a project's research methods by an ethical review committee.

A key historical development that is especially important to social workers concerns the ratification of the 1996 *Code of Ethics* of the National Association of Social Workers (NASW, 1996). This code, only the third in NASW's history, greatly expands the number of ethical standards pertaining to research and evaluation. The 1979 code, which preceded the 1996 code, contained seven ethical guidelines governing research and evaluation. By contrast, the 1996 code contains 16 specific ethical standards that are explored later in this chapter (see Box 1.2).

Ethical issues related to research and evaluation can arise at every stage of the evolution of a project or research activity. Some ethical issues emerge at the beginning stages, when social workers formulate their research questions and basic methodology. Other issues arise while the research and evaluation studies are actually being conducted. Still others emerge at the conclusion of the study, particularly in relation to data analysis (see Chapters 23 and 26) and the reporting of the results (see Chapters 24 and 27).

ETHICAL ISSUES DURING THE EARLY STAGES OF RESEARCH AND EVALUATION

Social workers should be especially knowledgeable about several ethical issues when they begin research and evaluation projects. These include (1) the initial formulation of research questions, (2) sample selection, (3) informed consent, and (4) institutional review.

Initial Formulation of Research Questions

Before social workers dwell on ethical issues pertaining to the technical aspects of research design and methodology, they must explore overarching questions concerning the research project's broad goals. How compelling is the research question in the first place? In light of social work's mission and ethical norms, are the project's results likely to generate important information that will enhance social work's ethical duty to assist people in need? Research projects that are directly related to the profession's moral mission—"to enhance the basic human needs of all people, *with particular attention to the needs and empowerment of people who are vulnerable, oppressed, and living in poverty*" (NASW, 1996, p. 1, italics added)—are more compelling than projects that explore abstruse subjects that might be only remotely related to the core aims of social work.

Sample Selection

As we will see in Chapter 11, social workers also should be mindful of the research participants (or samples) they include in their work. Given the profession's enduring commitment to issues of cultural, ethnic, and social diversity, social workers must ensure that their samples sufficiently represent, when methodologically appropriate and sound, diverse groups and clientele. Studies based on narrowly drawn and culturally homogeneous samples are less likely to yield information consistent with social work's ethical obligations to address issues of diversity and social justice (see Standards 1.05 [a,b,c] and 6.04 [b,c,d] in NASW's [1996] *Code of Ethics*).

Informed Consent

Perhaps the most important by-product of the unconscionable Nazi medical experiments and of experiments such as the Tuskegee and Willowbrook studies has been the development of strict informed consent guidelines. According to this concept, research partici-

pants must be *informed* about the purposes, methods, and risks associated with the research study, and they must voluntarily *consent* to participate in it.

The landmark legal ruling in the United States on informed consent came in the 1914 case *Schloendorff v. Society of New York Hospital* (1914), in which Justice Benjamin Cardozo stated his widely cited opinion that "every human being of adult years and sound mind has a right to determine what shall be done with his own body" (President's Commission for the Study of Ethical Problems in Medicine and Biomedical and Behavioral Research, 1982, pp. 28–29). A second well-known court case pertaining to informed consent, one in which the term "informed consent" actually was introduced, was decided in 1957 (*Salgo v. Leland Stanford Jr. University Board of Trustees*, 1957). In this case, the plaintiff became a paraplegic following a diagnostic procedure for a circulatory problem and alleged that the doctor had failed to properly disclose ahead of time important information concerning the risks associated with the procedure (President's Commission for the Study of Ethical Problems in Medicine and Biomedical and Behavioral Research, 1982).

During recent years, various court decisions, regulations developed by government and private sector organizations (e.g., NASW), and scholarly writings have generated a list of core elements that should be included in informed consent procedures pertaining to research and evaluation. These are reflected in NASW's (1996) *Code of Ethics*:

> Social workers engaged in evaluation or research should obtain voluntary and written informed consent from participants, when appropriate, without any implied or actual deprivation or penalty for refusal to participate; without undue inducement to participate; and with due regard for participants' well-being, privacy, and dignity. Informed consent should include information about the nature, extent, and duration of the participation requested and disclosure of the risks and benefits of participation in the research. (Standard 5.01 [e])

More specifically, social workers must be mindful of several key elements of informed consent (for a sample informed consent form, see Box 3.1).

Not Using Coercion

Social workers should not use coercion to convince people to participate in their research and evaluation activities. People should agree to participate willingly and voluntarily. This is especially important in circumstances where clients might believe that they are being pressured to participate in studies as a condition for receiving social services or other benefits.

Ascertaining Competence

Consent is valid only when participants truly understand the nature of the research and evaluation activity, possible benefits, and associated risks. Social workers must ensure that participants' understanding of these issues is not compromised by their mental status, literacy, or language difficulties. Persons who are not competent or whose competence is questionable should not be asked for their consent. Either they should be excluded from the research study or their consent should be obtained from their legal representatives.

Unfortunately, there is no clear and widely accepted definition of competence. Some believe that professionals should consider individuals' ability to make choices, comprehend factual issues, manipulate information rationally, and appreciate their current circumstances, whereas others believe that there ought to be a single standard for determining competency based simply on people's ability to retain information or "test reality." The President's Commission for the Study of Ethical Problems in Medicine and Biomedical and Behavioral Research (1982) concludes that competency should be determined by a person's possession of a set of values and goals, ability to communicate and understand information, and ability to reason and deliberate.

Although there is some disagreement about the conceptual criteria that should be used to assess and determine competence, there is a general agreement that incompetence should not be presumed across the board for any particular client group (e.g., the elderly, children, people with mental illness) except for people who are unconscious. Instead, some groups of individuals, such as people with active psychotic symptoms and individuals who are under the influence of alcohol or other drugs, should be considered to have a greater *probability* of incompetence.

Even in instances where clients or other potential research participants do not appear to be competent, social workers still should consider explaining the purposes and methods of the research project or activity and, if appropriate, should obtain the potential participants' *assent* to participate (along with formal consent from appropriate proxies as permitted or required by law). As NASW's (1996) *Code of Ethics* states:

> When evaluation or research participants are incapable of giving informed consent, social workers should provide an appropriate explanation to the participants, obtain the participants' assent to the extent they are able, and obtain written consent from an appropriate proxy. (Standard 5.02[f])

Waiving Informed Consent

Some research and evaluation projects and activities do not require formal informed consent. Using clinical assessment tools during work with clients primarily for clinical rather than for research purposes might warrant *implied consent,* where the social workers provide clear explanations of their approach and rationale. Implied consent also might be appropriate when social workers interview social service program colleagues for their suggestions about topics such as potential in-service training curricula, needed resources, and personnel policies. According to NASW's (1996) *Code of Ethics*:

> Social workers should never design or conduct evaluation or research that does not use consent procedures, such as certain forms of naturalistic observation and archival research, unless rigorous and responsible review of the research has found it to be justified because of its prospective scientific, educational, or applied value and unless equally effective alternative procedures that do not involve waiver of consent are not feasible. (Standard 5.02[g])

BOX 3.1

Sample Informed Consent Form

[Letterhead]

You are invited to participate in a research/evaluation project being conducted by [insert name of agency]. This project involves [briefly describe the nature of the project]. I am a [social worker, student, etc.] at the [insert name of agency]. [If you are a student, explain how the project relates to your academic program.] The purpose of this project is to [describe the purpose and possible value of the project]. You are being invited to participate in this project because [state reason].

This project will involve [describe the specific procedures that will be followed; the reasons; the timetable or schedule for the various procedures; the possible risks, inconveniences, and benefits; alternative procedures or options that the participants might want to consider; and any standard treatment that would be withheld].

Any information obtained from you or about you in connection with this project will remain confidential and will be disclosed only with your permission, as permitted or required by law. [Describe plans, if any, to release information to third parties, the purpose for the disclosure, the nature of the information to be released, and the circumstances under which it would be released.]

You are not under any obligation to participate in this project, and your decision will not affect your future relationship with [insert name of agency]. Furthermore, if you decide to participate, you may stop at any time without penalty or prejudice. [For projects using mailed surveys or questionnaires, you might want to include the following or a similar statement: "Your completion and return of the enclosed survey/questionnaire will indicate your willingness to participate in this project and your consent to have the information used as described above."]

Please contact [insert names and telephone numbers of all appropriate contact persons] if you have any questions about this project or your participation in it.

Your signature below indicates that you have read the information provided on this form, it has been explained to you, you have been offered a copy of this form to keep, you have been given an opportunity to ask questions about this form, your questions have been answered, and you agree to participate in this project.

Signature:

_____Date_____

Signature of Parent or Legal Guardian (if necessary):

_____Date_____

Signature of Child (when appropriate):

_____Date_____

Signature of Witness:

_____Date_____

Signature of Project Director/Investigator:

_____Date_____

Obtaining Participants' Consent to Specific Procedures or Actions

When formal informed consent is warranted, social workers must explain clearly to potential participants the purpose of the research activity, its possible benefits and costs, and alternatives or other options that the participants might want to consider. Broadly worded and vague explanations will not suffice. Furthermore, the language and terminology on consent forms must be clear and understandable, jargon and technical terms should be avoided, and potential participants must be given reasonable opportunity to ask for clarification.

Having the Right to Refuse or Withdraw Consent

Social workers should ensure that potential participants understand their right to refuse or withdraw consent. This is a standard element of the informed consent process. According to NASW's (1996) *Code of Ethics*:

> Social workers should inform participants of their right to withdraw from evaluation and research at any time without penalty. (Standard 5.02[h])

Social workers should understand that merely having participants sign a consent form generally is not sufficient. Informed consent is a process that should include the systematic and deliberate disclosure of information and an opportunity for individuals to discuss and ask questions about the research study (Reamer, 1987). In conjunction with this process, social workers should be aware of and sensitive to clients' cultural and ethnic differences regarding the meaning of concepts such as self-determination, autonomy, and consent. In some cultural groups, the concepts of individualism and consent are contrary to prominent values; in other cultural groups, there is a greater expectation that individuals will be asked for their permission before engaging in a research project (President's Commission for the Study of Ethical Problems in Medicine and Biomedical and Behavioral Research, 1982).

Institutional Review

One of the most important developments concerning research ethics was the creation of Institutional Review Boards (IRBs). IRBs, often known as human subjects protection committees, became popular during the 1970s as a result of the national attention to ethical issues in research in general. Currently, all organizations and programs that receive federal funds for research are required to have an IRB review the ethical aspects of proposals for research involving human participants.

(There are some exceptions for research that constitutes a routine requirement of an educational or academic program, involves analysis of secondary or existing data in a way that preserves confidentiality, depends on interviews or surveys, or entails observation of public behavior.) An IRB may request additional information and details or may request certain changes in a study's research design before approving a proposal. As NASW's (1996) *Code of Ethics* states:

> Social workers engaged in evaluation of research should carefully consider possible consequences and should follow guidelines developed for the protection of evaluation and research participants. Appropriate institutional review boards should be consulted. (Standard 5.02[d])

ETHICAL ISSUES IN RESEARCH DESIGN AND METHODOLOGY

There are seven main issues that social workers must be concerned about during the actual research project or activity: (1) ethical aspects of research designs, (2) the use of deception, (3) confidentiality and privacy, (4) conflicts of interest, (5) reporting of results, (6) disclosure of results to research participants, and (7) acknowledgment of credit.

Ethical Aspects of Research Designs

Ethical issues often arise when social workers design projects that explore cause-effect relationships between variables. In an effort to control for extraneous factors in group designs (e.g., contemporaneous events, demographic factors, measurement effects), social workers may want to randomly assign participants to experimental and control groups or to contrast groups. Similarly, in case-level designs (see Chapter 12), social workers may attempt to control for extraneous factors by withdrawing and reintroducing an intervention (e.g., *ABAB* and related designs as presented in Chapter 12).

Potential ethical problems in such instances are well known. On one hand, social workers understand that it might be difficult, if not impossible, to control for extraneous factors without using control groups, random assignment, reversal designs, and so on. On the other hand, social workers sometimes find it difficult to withhold interventions from clients with demonstrated and serious needs or to withdraw interventions that might be efficacious from clients who are demonstrating progress.

Whether social workers are willing to use a control group, random assignment, or a reversal design always is a matter of judgment. Consultation with an IRB can provide useful insight into the ethical tradeoffs involved in these decisions. In some instances, compromises are reached, for example, when a program uses clients on a waiting list as a "natural" control group and as a way in which to avoid completely withholding services from a control group or when a practitioner uses a multiple-baseline design in an effort to avoid withdrawing services from clients in need.

The Use of Deception

As a group, social workers generally find anathema any form of deception in professional practice (see Standard 4.04 in NASW's [1996] *Code of Ethics*). Fortunately, the vast majority of research and evaluation activities, whether needs assessments, program evaluations, or clinical evaluations, do not call for any significant deception.

There are instances, however, when social workers may feel that some degree of deception might be necessary in order to generate meaningful research information. An example includes withholding information from clients about concerns staff have that constitute the "real" reasons for the program's client satisfaction survey; staff might feel that a completely honest disclosure about their reasons for the research project would be inappropriate and might bias clients' responses. Another example involves giving clients only vague information about changes in clinical interventions that clinicians are evaluating using a case-level design; a completely candid disclosure might interfere with the social workers' ability to evaluate the intervention.

Certainly, thoughtful and reasonable people can disagree about the extent to which any type of deception in research and evaluation is reasonable or acceptable.

Diligent consultation and IRB reviews can help social workers to make sound decisions about these issues.

Confidentiality and Privacy

Social workers have a keen understanding of the importance of confidentiality and privacy. Complex ethical issues concerning confidentiality and privacy arise in every professional capacity, whether related to direct practice, community organizing, administration, supervision, consultation, or research and evaluation.

Several confidentiality issues pertain directly to research and evaluation. Perhaps the most prominent concerns social workers' obligation to protect the confidentiality of data. Data collected by social workers often concern very sensitive issues such as clients' troubling feelings, illegal behaviors, and controversial attitudes or program employees' concerns about personnel issues or administrative problems. Social workers need to be scrupulous in their efforts to protect such data. As NASW's *Code of Ethics* asserts:

> Social workers engaged in evaluation or research should ensure the anonymity or confidentiality of participants and of the data obtained from them. Social workers should inform participants of any limits of confidentiality, the measures that will be taken to ensure confidentiality, and when any records containing research data will be destroyed. (Standard 5.02[l])

Furthermore,

> Social workers should protect the confidentiality of clients' written and electronic records and other sensitive information. Social workers should take reasonable steps to ensure that clients' records are stored in a secure location and that clients' records are not available to others who are not authorized to have access. (Standard 1.07[l])

In addition to safeguarding the confidentiality of research data, social workers should be concerned about individuals' privacy. Social workers should recognize that clients and other data sources might be uncomfortable disclosing information about very private and sensitive issues. Accordingly, social workers should take steps to prevent unnecessary intrusions into people's lives. However, once individuals disclose private information in the context of research or evaluation activities, social workers must take steps to ensure confidentiality. According to NASW's (1996) *Code of Ethics*:

> Social workers should respect clients' right to privacy. Social workers should not solicit private information from clients unless it is essential to providing services or conducting social work evaluation or research. Once private information is shared, standards of confidentiality apply. (Standard 1.07[a])

Social workers also must be prepared to assist individuals who become upset during data collection or at any other point in their involvement in research activities. Because social workers often address sensitive and sometimes traumatic issues, they need to anticipate the possibility that research and evaluation participants might become upset during the process. According to NASW's (1996) *Code of Ethics*:

> Social workers should take appropriate steps to ensure that participants in evaluation and research have access to appropriate supportive services. (Standard 5.02[i])

Conflicts of Interest

Social workers involved in evaluation and research need to be careful to avoid conflicts of interest, especially when the research participants are current or former clients. Relating to clients as clinicians *and* for research purposes (e.g., collecting data from clients for social workers' master's degree projects or doctoral dissertations) has the potential to constitute a problematic "dual relationship" (see Standards 1.06[a,b,c] of NASW's [1996] *Code of Ethics*). Social workers must avoid exploiting clients or placing them at risk for research purposes. Thus, social workers should not knowingly subject individuals to undue stress and discomfort to meet their own professional or personal aims. As NASW's (1996) *Code of Ethics* states:

Social workers engaged in evaluation or research should be alert to and avoid conflicts of interest and dual relationships with participants, should inform participants when a real or potential conflict of interest arises, and should take steps to resolve the issue in a manner that makes participants' interests primary. (Standard 5.02[o])

Several ethical issues can arise once evaluation and research data have been collected. These concerns reporting results, disclosing results to participants, and acknowledging colleagues' contributions.

Reporting Results

Social workers must be careful to protect the confidentiality of final results and to report results accurately. Practitioners need to be sure that sensitive information does not fall into the wrong hands, for example, ensuring that clients' comments about past illegal activities are not shared with law enforcement officials. According to NASW's (1996) *Code of Ethics*:

> Social workers who report evaluation and research results should protect participants' confidentiality by omitting identifying information unless proper consent has been obtained authorizing disclosure. (Standard 5.02[m])

Reporting results accurately also is essential. In some instances, social workers might be reluctant to disclose certain "negative" or unflattering results because of possible ramifications for their programs. For example, a program director might be uncomfortable reporting evaluation data showing that a major program has not had good results; this could affect future funding or the program's reputation. In spite of these understandable concerns, however, social workers are obligated to be honest and accurate in their reporting of results. To do otherwise would undermine the integrity of evaluation and research in general and, ultimately, could damage social workers' and programs' reputations and harm the people they serve. NASW's (1996) *Code of Ethics* states:

> Social workers should report evaluation and research findings accurately. They should not fabricate or falsify results and should take steps to

correct any errors later found in published data using standard publication methods. (Standard 5.02[n])

Disclosing Results to Research Participants

As a matter of principle, social workers ordinarily share evaluation and research results with their data sources, whether clients, colleagues, or the general public. In some instances, however, social workers might be inclined to withhold results in an effort to protect potential recipients from psychological harm or trauma. In clinical circumstances, for example, social workers might be tempted to withhold results obtained from rapid assessment instruments or other measures that suggest serious psychological or emotional symptoms or trauma. Ethically, of course, social workers must consider the extent to which clients have the "right to know" information about themselves, even when the information might be painful or emotionally threatening.

Unfortunately, there are no easy answers to these dilemmas. In general, social workers support clients' right to know information about themselves; at the same time, social workers have an understandable instinct to protect people from harmful information— what ethicists refer to as *professional paternalism* (Reamer, 1983). When social workers encounter these issues, they should take assertive steps to address them using available ethical decision-making frameworks, protocols, and standards (Lowenberg & Dolgoff, 1996; Reamer, 1999). When possible, social workers should obtain consultation from thoughtful and knowledgeable colleagues (e.g., supervisors, program-based ethics committees, IRBs, ethics consultants).

Acknowledging Credit

Many research and evaluation activities in social work entail some type of collegial collaboration. Common arrangements involve collaboration among program-based colleagues and between principal investigators and research associates or assistants. Social workers responsible for the dissemination of results must be careful to acknowledge the contributions of those who provided meaningful assistance. According to NASW's (1996) *Code of Ethics*:

> Social workers should take responsibility and credit, including authorship credit, only for work they have actually performed and to which they have contributed. (Standard 4.08[a])

Furthermore,

> Social workers should honestly acknowledge the work of and the contributions of others. (Standard 4.08[b])

Although there is no precise formula to determine how credit should be given in every circumstance, there are widely accepted guidelines. These include ensuring that all individuals who made meaningful contributions receive acknowledgment as co-authors, usually in descending order of their respective contributions. Individuals who contributed equally may be listed alphabetically, although occasionally the parties decide to list names in random order. Individuals who made useful contributions but who were not central to the project's conceptualization, data collection, or data analysis may be acknowledged appropriately in a footnote (e.g., a graduate student or clerical employee who conducted a number of interviews over several weeks or who helped with data entry).

A related issue concerns social workers' honest acknowledgment of literature and data sources they rely on during the course of evaluation and research. Ideas reflected in a research report or a project's instruments that are based on, or directly draw from, other professionals' work, whether published or not, should be acknowledged accordingly.

SUMMARY

Clearly, social workers must be cognizant of a wide range of ethical issues germane to evaluation and research studies. These include ethical issues involving the formulation of research questions in the first place, research design, sampling, measurement, data collection, confidentiality and privacy, and the handling of results.

Our current preoccupation with these issues reflects the maturing grasp of ethical matters in social work and other professions. In part because of past unethical practices and in part because of professionals' increased understanding of the inherent importance of ethics. During recent years, social workers have developed increasingly substantial and rigorous ethical guidelines and standards related to research and evaluation. Certainly, this is reflected in the current *Code of Ethics* (NASW, 1996).

Underlying social workers' concern about the protection of research and evaluation participants and ethical methodology, however, is a fundamental question facing the profession: To what extent do social workers have an ethical duty or obligation to incorporate research and evaluation into their practice? The short answer is that contemporary social workers strongly believe that there is such an ethical obligation (Curtis, 1996; Myers & Thyer, 1997). In fact, NASW's (1996) *Code of Ethics* asserts this definitively when it states:

> Social workers should critically examine and keep current with emerging knowledge relevant to social work and fully use evaluation and research evidence in their professional practice. (Standard 5.02[c])

We must ask ourselves, however, what social workers can do to meet this ethical obligation. The answer is twofold. First, social workers have an obligation to keep current with research-based knowledge and to draw on it routinely and systematically during their careers. Our profession's funding of research-based knowledge has grown dramatically, especially since the 1970s. The profession's journals and texts now regularly include the results of both quantitative and qualitative studies evaluating social work intervention. Social work's literature also contains many secondary reviews and meta-analyses of multiple studies on a subject. Social workers should consult this literature as a matter of course when they design and implement interventions (see Standards 4.01[b,c] and 5.02[c] of NASW's [1996] *Code of Ethics*).

Second, social workers should use the ever-growing number of research and evaluation tools available to practitioners to conduct needs assessments and to monitor and evaluate their practice (see Standard 5.02[a] of NASW's [1996] *Code of Ethics*). As various chapters in this book demonstrate, social workers in clinical and nonclinical settings now have access to an impressive assortment of research and evaluation tools that can strengthen the quality of their work.

Without question, social workers' understanding of the relevance and value of research and evaluation has progressed during recent years, especially with respect to the ways in which user-friendly tools and techniques can be used for very pragmatic purposes by social workers in all practice settings, supplementing contributions based on studies conducted by professional researchers. This phenomenon demonstrates noteworthy progress in the evolution of social work. Along with this developmental progress, social workers have enhanced their understanding of a diverse range of compelling ethical issues related to research and evaluation. This understanding, along with social workers' enduring commitment to upholding high ethical standards, will serve the profession and its clients well.

Bonnie L. Yegidis

Robert W. Weinbach

Using Existing Knowledge

4

Reference to existing knowledge can and frequently does occur at any point in the research process. For example, when you select and specify a research problem or choose from among possible research questions, you will generally seek out and use available knowledge that already exists. Answering questions about how widespread a social problem is or whether some phenomenon is easily measurable may require a quick trip to the library or an Internet search. Similarly, after data have been collected, they can best be interpreted and the research findings put into perspective with reference to what others have learned and published on the topic.

WHAT IS A LITERATURE REVIEW?

A review of literature is both a process (an activity) and a product. It is an activity that will occupy a great deal of your time and attention after you have selected a research question(s) to study. It is the phase of the research process when you will immerse yourself in any existing knowledge that may relate to your research question.

Later, when you write your research report, you will generally include a separate section that may be titled "Review of the Literature," "Relevant Literature," "Literature Review," or something similar. This is a written summary of what you have learned in your examination of the existing work of others, and it contains those findings and ideas that influenced your thinking and the research methods you have selected for conducting your research study.

Even new social problems or ones that for one reason or another have received little or no attention in the past always bear some similarity to those that already have been studied. Knowledge drawn from research studies on related topics can be productively brought to bear. For example, during the late 1980s and early 1990s, the problem of date rape and our lack of understanding of its causes, incidence, or impact belatedly received widespread attention. Research studies on date rape began. Although there initially was little or no empirically based knowledge available on the specific problem, a review of the literature on many related topic areas provided knowledge that was extremely useful for acquiring insight into both date rape and how best to design research studies to examine the problem. Research studies on this newly identified problem were greatly facilitated by an examination of reports of previous studies on literally hundreds of diverse topics. Each made a valuable contribution that saved many researchers countless hours of inquiry. Among the knowledge areas examined were:

- Cultural dating practices
- Male patterns of aggression
- Spousal rape
- Domestic violence
- Law enforcement and judicial handling of rape accusations
- Substance abuse and interpersonal violence
- Historical definitions of rape
- Intergender violence
- Gender validation rituals of males
- Media portrayal of males and females
- Spouse battery
- Incest and sexual abuse

A new social problem, our lack of understanding of the unwillingness of sexually active teenagers at risk for pregnancy to use free contraceptive injections, was identified in the late 1990s. Because such injections (and contraceptive implants) were not even available until the mid-1990s, it would seem on the surface that a person who wished to study the problem would be in the dark. But there is plenty of literature on related topics that address the problem and questions that relate to it. Related topics might include:

- History of contraception
- Success rates among various methods of contraception
- Current attitudes about use of contraception among young women
- Current attitudes about use of contraception among young men
- Fear of injections among young women
- Responsibility of males and females for contraception
- Cultural differences in attitudes about teen pregnancy

- Gender validation rituals of males
- Obstacles to use of public health services
- Societal rewards and penalties for teen pregnancy
- Relationship between injections and future fertility

For every research problem—and for its related research questions—there is a body of knowledge that is helpful for those who study them. Whenever researchers report that little is known about the problem or that no relevant literature exists on the topic, it may be an indication that (1) they probably do not understand the nature and purpose of the literature review, or (2) they probably did not invest sufficient energy and time in this important step in the research process. There is no research problem for which there is no existing relevant knowledge. Although it is conceivable that no one may have previously studied the exact research question finally selected, there is *always* knowledge available that could help to enlighten and inform the researcher.

PURPOSE OF A LITERATURE REVIEW

A literature review draws its focus from the broad research questions that have been selected. It has several complementary objectives. They are summarized in Box 4.1.

In a general sense, a literature review serves to put the researchers' current efforts into perspective. It creates a foundation for them based on existing related knowledge. It also suggests the most appropriate way to further expand what is already known. A literature review is a recognition that knowledge building is a cumulative process that goes on over long periods of time, a principle to which we will return to in future chapters.

POTENTIAL SOURCES OF "LITERATURE"

For social work researchers, the term "literature" denotes much more than just printed words. A more descriptive term might actually be "relevant knowl-

---

BOX 4.1

How a Literature Review Is Used

Before data collection, to

- Learn more about the history, origin, and scope of the research problem
- Learn what methodologies have been applied successfully and unsuccessfully to study related research questions
- Learn what answers already exist for general research questions
- Identify variables that will need to be measured and learn what methods already are available to measure them
- Decide what is the best way to acquire needed data, who or what might best provide them, and how best to analyze them
- Refine and better specify research questions and, when indicated, propose answers to them in the form of hypotheses
- Select the appropriate statistical analyses to be used

After data collection, to

- Attempt to explain differences between current findings and existing knowledge
- Identify ways in which current findings are consistent with and support existing knowledge
- Specify how current findings advance knowledge
- Develop theories and formulate hypotheses (in qualitative studies)

---

edge." As we shall see, it can be found in many different places and forms.

What qualifies a source of information for inclusion in what we have called "the review of literature"? It should enlighten and inform the researcher—and the reader of a research report—about the research problem and/or question. It must also be credible. The issue of credibility is often debatable. Even the best of sources are sometimes vulnerable to political or economic influences.

The most common sources (some of them more credible than others) for a literature review include, but are not limited to, the following: (1) standard reference materials, (2) computer-accessible databases, (3) the Internet, (4) books, (5) articles in professional journals, (6) personal interviews with authorities, (7) research reports and monographs, (8) presentations at conferences and symposia, (9) content of workshops, (10) public documents and records of public gatherings, (11) newspapers, (12) radio and television broadcasts, and (13) magazines and periodicals.

Standard Reference Materials

For relevant knowledge that is available in written form, the various abstracts publications (e.g., *Social Work Abstracts, Sociological Abstracts, Psychological Abstracts, Dissertation Abstracts International,* or *SAGE Urban Studies Abstracts)* are always a good place to start a literature search. Listing entries by topic area as well as by author, they provide a good overview of where recent publications on various topics can be found. Direct quotations from abstracts publications, however, should not be used in the literature review section of a research report (see Chapters 24 and 27). They are not meant to be a substitute for the original source. Abstracts are just a convenient way to learn about the existence of a publication that may, or may not, prove to be helpful.

Other standard reference materials actually contain facts and thus can themselves be cited in a research report that contains a "review of literature" section. Generally, they tend to possess higher credibility than, for example, data obtained from the Internet (see the following sections) because they have undergone a more thorough review and verification process. However, they often tend to be fairly general and can become dated fairly quickly. They may be called almanacs, encyclopedias, atlases, statistical abstracts, directories, annuals, yearbooks, compendia, or some similar title.

Two such sources commonly used by social workers to get their literature searches under way are the NASW publications *Encyclopedia of Social Work* (1995) and *Social Work Almanac* (1995). Such standard reference materials are a good place to begin a search of the literature, but, because of the breadth of topics covered, they rarely provide the depth of coverage needed. To accomplish the objectives of a literature review, it often is necessary to venture into other

areas of the literature that are more current or detailed, but also more suspect.

Computer-Accessible Databases

Progress in technology for the storage, retrieval, and transfer of information is rapidly increasing the amount of knowledge that is accessible to researchers. Technological sources can be excellent, often quite reliable, and are becoming ever more comprehensive.

Most university libraries now possess extensive databases that are electronically accessible through CD-ROMs. Although in the past these contained mostly descriptive data, such as census data, they are increasingly being expanded to contain much more, including the findings of research studies conducted almost anywhere on earth. CD-ROMs contain thousands of journal articles, book chapters, and dissertation abstracts within a given discipline. For example, the National Clearinghouse on Child Abuse and Neglect offers social service organizations a CD-ROM database on child abuse and neglect cases within the United States. There also are CD-ROM databases for certain government documents and major newspapers. CD-ROM databases are updated regularly, typically either yearly or quarterly.

CD-ROM databases are accessed electronically through computer terminals. Appropriate citations and abstracts are located through an electronic search process by specifying key words. Sources thus located are viewed on the computer screen and can be printed out as hard copy if desired. Conducting an electronic literature search is becoming a very user-friendly task. Although procedures vary somewhat by database and institution, generally once you have conducted one CD-ROM search, others are quite simple and can be highly productive. Like standard reference materials, computerized databases often are used early in the literature review process. They provide an excellent overview of what exists.

Even various abstracts publications (see the preceding discussion on standard reference material), such as *Social Work Abstracts* (SWAB), *Sociofile,* and *PsychLiT,* are now available on CD-ROM. There also are dozens of others that address particular specializations within social work and related disciplines.

The Internet

Increasingly, the Internet is proving a popular choice as a source of existing knowledge. Its easy accessibility and the breadth of information contained on it can greatly expedite a literature search. Unlike standard reference materials that often are out of date before they are in print, data on the Internet can be updated as frequently as is necessary. The ease with which knowledge can be put on the Internet is, at the same time, its greatest weakness. Individuals can put anything they want on it—no verification is required. Freedom of speech also permits freedom to play loosely with facts or to just plain fabricate.

If the Internet is so vulnerable to misinformation, why do we include it as a source of literature? Along with totally unreliable sources, it also contains some very useful ones for the social work researcher. Many of the other sources of literature described elsewhere in this chapter are now accessible via the Internet (for example, the *Congressional Record*); more undoubtedly will follow. Some websites are specifically dedicated to facilitating access to reliable knowledge for social workers. For example, a common place to begin searching the Web for resources related to social work practice or education is the frequently visited Social Work Access Network (SWAN). It is a popular link to many other Internet sites (also administered by dedicated social work practitioners and academicians) that are generally acknowledged to be reliable sources of knowledge. SWAN also offers a listing of websites for social work journals. The links include some sites that provide full text articles (from electronic journals) but also some that contain just abstracts or tables of contents.

Websites come and go rapidly on the Internet, and addresses are also subject to change. Thus, we will avoid the temptation to provide specific URLs. When this chapter was written, for example, UnCover was gaining in popularity among social work students and professors (Marson, 1999). It was free and very user-friendly. However, it will undoubtedly be replaced by other sites as they are developed and as older ones fall out of favor.

Books and Articles in Professional Journals

The professional literature of a field (for example, articles within refereed social work professional journals or the books published by major commercial publishers and reviewed in journals such as *Social Work* or *Journal of Social Work Education*) usually represent a sizable and important portion of the knowledge that is brought to bear on a research question. Generally, it has undergone a peer review process that, although no guarantee of scholarliness, at least suggests that others think that it is worthy of publication. However, even these sources cannot always be trusted and must be examined carefully.

Journals in social work and related fields have proliferated in recent years. Some publications that purport to be professional journals are not refereed; that is, they do not use a blind review process that ensures that the name of the author or a prestigious affiliation do not influence publication decisions. Some of the refereed journals receive so few manuscript submissions that they publish the majority of the ones they receive.

It sometimes seems as if the topic of a journal article on an issue that is popular or its use of a particular research method may have had more to do with its publication than its scholarliness. Sometimes the findings of a research study may be a major factor in the decision to publish the study in the first place. Undoubtedly some studies' findings are more popular than others—especially if they are consistent with popular opinion or seem to be supportive of our profession rather than critical of it.

Similarly, just because a fact is in a book in print, it cannot necessarily be construed as trustworthy. It may not have undergone rigorous review and scrutiny. Even major textbook publishers have to focus on potential sales and other factors when they make the decision to publish (or not to publish) a book. Checks on the accuracy of the content often are delegated to a few academicians who receive only minimal compensation for their reviews and who may be less than thorough in their efforts. There are also vanity presses that publish virtually any material in book form (including a professor's course notes and other writings) if the author is willing to pay enough to become a published author.

In certain forms of research, other considerations must be used so that the literature informs rather than misleads researchers and other readers of their reports. When a researcher is conducting a study with a different ethnic or cultural group or within a cross-cultural context, literature that helps the researcher to better understand the manifestation of the target problem or research issue within that particular cultural framework is especially useful. Additional effort may be required to locate literature written by indigenous social scientists, social work researchers, or practitioners who share an interest in the research topic.

If the literature is written in a foreign language, English translations will need to be found or undertaken if the work is considered critical to understanding the problem being investigated. Bilingual and bicultural students in the helping professions at nearby universities may be a good resource for both identifying relevant literature and for translation. International and ethnic-specific journals in the fields of social work, psychology, social welfare policy, education, health, family studies, and child welfare are excellent resources. Box 4.2 describes some of the best of these.

Personal Interviews with Authorities

All sources used for literature reviews should be approached with caution—some more than others, of course. Unless they are examined critically, researchers can be misled by assertions that are questionable, while simultaneously damaging the credibility of their own research efforts. Sometimes such assertions should be included, and other times they should be omitted. Often the questions must be asked: Where do I draw the line? and What constitutes usable knowledge and what does not?

As we mentioned in Chapter 1, authorities are one of the sources for our knowledge base. We described this method of knowing as somewhat untrustworthy for obvious reasons. So why would we include authorities as a possible source of knowledge? Because sometimes authorities *do* know something important. The principal problem surrounding content drawn from interviews with authorities is lack of consensus regarding who is an authority. Unfortunately, in some parts of

Western society, authority frequently has been assumed to reside in all individuals with certain academic credentials (or in anyone who travels a distance of more than fifty miles and carries a briefcase). For the social work researcher, an authority whose comments are worth quoting in a literature review is someone who has in-depth knowledge of some aspect of the research problem, preferably acquired through the use of the research method discussed in Chapter 1. This greatly limits the number of authorities who should be quoted in a report of a review of literature.

A researcher in colonial America, for example, might have had some justification for quoting a member of the clergy on virtually any topic, because the limited amount of available knowledge was concentrated within this profession. But today's researcher should not make any assumptions about any individual's claims to knowledge solely on the basis of academic or other formal credentials. There are no Renaissance folks alive today who have knowledge in virtually every area. It would be erroneous to assume that, for example, a quotation from any physician is appropriate on a medical research question or that one from a lawyer will provide needed knowledge on a legal research one.

The physician, for example, may see primarily older patients; hence, the doctor's position on a problem related to child rearing may have no empirical basis and may even be distorted through interaction with a biased sample of patients. The lawyer may specialize in contract law and may speak more out of personal opinion than out of knowledge in discussing needed changes in child abuse reporting laws. This is not an indictment of these or other professions; it is only a recognition that the base of knowledge within most professional fields (including social work) and even their subspecialties has grown dramatically during the past century, to the point where no one can possibly know everything.

Use of a few carefully chosen quotations from interviews with authorities in the review of literature section of a research report usually will not harm the credibility of the researcher's efforts. On the contrary, it may suggest balance and thoroughness in the final product. However, it might be wise to prevent any possible challenges to the credibility of authorities by including brief descriptions of the source of their

Scholarly Journals with Ethnic or Cross-Cultural Content

African Americans

- *Journal of Black Psychology.* Articles that promote the understanding of the experiences and behavior of black populations. This includes empirical research reports, discussion of current literature, and original theoretical analyses of data from research studies or programs in the areas of cognition, personality, social behavior, psychological functioning, child development, education, and clinical application. Sage Publications, Thousand Oaks, CA.

- *Journal of Black Studies.* Interdisciplinary journal of analytical discussions of issues related to persons of African descent in the United States, Africa, and the Caribbean, covering a wide range of social science questions. Sage Publications, Thousand Oaks, CA.

Asian, Pacific Islanders

- *Amerasia Journal.* National interdisciplinary journal of scholarship, criticism, and literature on Asian and Pacific Americans. Asian American Studies Center, University of California, Los Angeles.

- *Asian American and Pacific Islander Journal of Health.* Journal devoted to Asian/ Pacific-American health issues containing research reports written by scholars and practitioners. Asian American and Pacific Islander Health Promotion Center, Dublin, OH.

Hispanics

- *Aztlan-International Journal of Chicano Studies Research.* Biannual, interdisciplinary refereed journal that serves as a forum for research and essays related to the Mexican population. Its focus is critical analysis, research, theory, and methodology in the study of Mexicans in the United States and Mexico. UCLA Chicano Studies Research Center, University of California, Los Angeles.

Native Americans

- *Journal of American Indian Education.* Scholarly articles directly related to the education of North American Indians and Alaska Natives, with an emphasis on basic and applied research. Center for Indian Education, Arizona State University.

Cross-Cultural

- *International Journal of Intercultural Relations.* Quarterly journal dedicated to advancing knowledge and understanding of theory, practice, and research in intergroup relations. The contents encompass theoretical developments, field-based evaluations of training techniques, empirical discussions of cultural similarities and differences, and critical descriptions of new training approaches. Elsevier Science, Ltd., Kidlington, Oxford, UK.

- *Journal of Cross-Cultural Psychology.* Publishes papers that focus on the interrelationships between culture and psychological processes that result from either cross-cultural comparative research or results from other types of research concerning the ways in which culture (and related concepts such as ethnicity) affect the thinking and behavior of individuals, as well as how individual thought and behavior define and reflect aspects of culture. Sage Publications, Thousand Oaks, CA.

- *Journal of Ethnic and Cultural Diversity in Social Work.* Focuses on racial and ethnicity issues within the field of social work. The latest research and theory are provided on social work issues, practice, and problems. The journal is designed to help social work practitioners understand the underlying cultural issues involved in working with diverse ethnic groups. Haworth Press, Binghamton, NY.

---

expertise in the narrative. For example, a descriptive statement such as "one medical researcher, who has conducted National Institute of Mental Health (NIMH)-funded research on the possible relationship between the use of lithium and suicide among young men, has concluded that ..." would help to justify why that physician was cited in the literature review section of a research report.

Research Reports and Monographs

Research reports and monographs generally are intended to be honest communications of a researcher's methods and findings. Although the findings are only as good as the methods used to produce them, the fact that a researcher's methods are open to public critique and the possibility of replication increases the likelihood that a report or monograph will be credible. Of course, if the research study was funded by some organization or interest group that may have exerted undue influence over what was found and/or reported, such sources also cannot be trusted. For example, the credibility of research findings about the health effects of cigarette smoking is generally low when the research studies (that produced the findings) have been conducted by researchers employed by American cigarette manufacturers.

Presentations at Conferences and Symposia

There is a great amount of knowledge disseminated at conferences and symposia. There is also a great deal of unsubstantiated opinion and misinformation shared. A presentation may be selected using a blind review process, but this is not always the case. Often, the reputation of the presenter or the topic (if it is a popular one) is a major factor in its selection. Frequently, a conference presentation may have no empirical basis at all. Presentations may be little more than "show-and-tell" descriptions of what the presenters have done and why they think that what they have to say is good.

Most presentations at annual conferences, such as those sponsored by NASW, CSWE, or the Child Welfare League of America, have undergone a fairly rigorous screening procedure. Only a small percentage of proposals submitted are accepted for presentation. But the proposals usually consist of brief abstracts that are reviewed by volunteers who may have little interest in the topics and may not have the knowledge and skill to review their quality. These gatherings also give program space to invited speakers whose expertise in a subject area has been recognized by one or more members of their planning committee. Personal friendships, quid pro quos, or other political concerns sometimes enter into the decision to invite these professionals.

Many other professional gatherings that call themselves national and international conferences and symposia have far less credibility. (After all, any group can describe its conference as "national" or "international" if it chooses.) Some of the most suspect of these consist of small groups of individuals who share some specialized interest. They get together annually to present to each other (sometimes on the same topic as the previous year) at geographically desirable locations. Participants take turns hosting the annual gathering and inviting each other to present their work. Although some knowledge is undoubtedly shared, there also is a liberal amount of camaraderie, rest and recreation, and sightseeing

Presenting at conferences does not always require access to networks. Many national and especially international conferences that sound highly prestigious will accept nearly any program proposal submitted if the person submitting it agrees to show up and pay the registration fee. After all, conference registration fees represent a major source of revenue for some organizations.

Information acquired at regional, state, and local conferences and symposia also varies widely in the information's credibility. Before placing too much credence in knowledge presented at them, inquiries should be made as to the selection process for presentation and the credentials of the presenters. Of course, a critical assessment of the research methods used also should be made.

Content of Workshops

Workshop content may be based on empirical findings, or it may not. Frequently, workshop leaders have been contracted (paid) to deliver content in a way consistent with the wishes of whomever is paying for it (often a social service organization or some other type of organization). This leaves the knowledge contained therein vulnerable to influence and distortion. The researcher may need to explore whether what was said was based on the best knowledge available or was simply reflective of what the workshop's sponsoring organization wanted its participants to hear. If it is the former, workshop content may be appropriate for inclusion in a research literature review.

Public Documents and Records of Public Gatherings

Many good sources of information are available on request. Public documents and records of public gatherings (such as the minutes of public meetings) often are useful resources. For example, a researcher who wishes to understand the values and thinking that underlie current or pending legislation can learn a great deal by studying testimony of various individuals and interest groups that appears within the *Congressional Record*. Of course, because they are open to the public, these documents sometimes contain more posturing and efforts to appear politically correct than they do knowledge. Other public documents and records of public gatherings may also have undergone a certain sterilization process that leaves their credibility as a source of knowledge somewhat suspect.

Newspapers

Perhaps the most controversial sources that we have noted are those that depend on commercial success for their continued existence. People who publish newspapers, for example, may be more interested in how many newspapers they sell than the scientific accuracy of the papers' contents. Newspapers acquire some of what they publish from such generally credible sources as reports of government-sponsored research studies.

However, they also publish findings (sometimes selectively) from research of questionable quality and from what is referred to as simply "highly placed sources." They regularly publish what is openly identified as little more than opinion in the form of editorials and minimally screened positions of individuals under the heading of "Letters to the Editor." When a topic is believed to be of widespread interest, it sometimes seems that getting the facts is less important than getting out the story.

Except when a newspaper article can be determined to possess a carefully researched origin and contains only firsthand information, it probably is best to use knowledge drawn from newspapers with extreme caution. Often, they are best used to learn about the *existence* of the knowledge-building work of others. It is then possible to seek out the original source, obtain a full report, and evaluate its merits based on the description of the researcher's methods (see Chapter 21).

Radio and Television Broadcasts

Other media similarly offer sources of knowledge that run the gamut of scientific credibility. There is a great amount of knowledge and advice shared gratuitously by network radio and television talk show hosts and their "authority" guests. Very little of it, if any, would be likely either to enlighten the researcher or to convince others of the scholarliness of a literature review.

Some news specials and documentaries on both network and public radio and television are well researched and present excellent sources of information. However, the advent of certain types of television journalism and pseudo-news specials in the 1980s and the revelation in the 1990s that some findings reported on documentaries were manipulated have cast increasing doubt on the credibility of television news broadcasts. Frequently, they appear to be designed to entertain and to appeal to the lower interests of viewers and listeners. Special care and discretion should be used in separating knowledge from content that, if cited, would only weaken the literature review's credibility.

Magazines and Periodicals

This brings us to the bottom of our list (in many ways). Popular magazines and periodicals vary widely in how much knowledge they publish, as opposed to how much pure fiction they include in order to sell subscriptions and single copies in supermarkets and other outlets. Some newsmagazines and pop-science magazines seem to walk a thin line, attempting to appear scholarly and scientific while selecting topics and presentation formats (for example, short, topical articles featuring provocative pictures) that clearly reflect an eye on sales figures, rather than on the knowledge needs of their readers.

They may even reflect a pragmatic mixture within a single issue; for example, a scholarly article written by a respected researcher may be juxtaposed with another bit of "fluff" that would be an intellectual insult to anyone with more than a superficial knowledge of the topic. A social work researcher conducting a literature review on a research problem or question should obviously choose carefully in using such publications. You may subscribe to it, read it religiously, learn some things that are helpful to you in your work, and even display it on your coffee table without embarrassment. But that does not mean that every article in it is a potential source of knowledge that can be cited with confidence.

The popularity of a magazine or periodical is certainly no guarantee that its contents are the product of scientific inquiry or that they are worthy of citation in a literature review. In fact, we might speculate whether very high sales and financial success are not negatively correlated with the amount of scientific rigor that the publication employs.

Some magazines and periodicals make no pretense of scholarliness. Their readers, who may want to believe that they possess an inquiring mind, often seek nothing but recreational reading or amusing diversion. Consequently, they are less likely to purchase a periodical whose articles tend to be based on scientific research studies than ones that are based on the flimsiest of inquiry, if not outright fantasy. They would probably not buy (or read in the checkout line) a publication with a lead article entitled "Posttraumatic Stress Syndrome among Native Americans," but they might purchase the tabloid that promises a four-paragraph analysis of such fantasies as "Elvis Is Working as a Bartender in Cheektowaga" or "Despondent Twin Shoots Brother by Mistake."

Is there ever a place for acknowledging within a review of the literature such unscholarly publications that occur at the extreme end of the credibility continuum? Not in the usual way. However, these publications have one thing in common: high sales. Their owners and editors maintain high sales by maintaining a good pulse of what is of interest to the general public. A social problem that is in some form the topic of virtually every magazine at the supermarket checkout stand during a certain time period (for example, spouse battering or the activities of the press) can be assumed to have reached a certain level of public consciousness.

The observation that, during the week of August 8, 1998, nine of the ten most popular magazines in America carried at least one article on the increasingly chronic nature of HIV infections might be a useful contribution to a literature review, even though the sources cited might make some scholars cringe. The researcher would certainly not be saying that everything (or even anything) within the text of the articles can be construed as knowledge, only that the fact of their publication in popular magazines attests to the topic's popular interest.

We have chosen an extreme example of how far the researcher occasionally may go in seeking and using information for the review of literature. Obviously, even a single use of some of the more suspect sources of information that abound can seriously harm the researcher's credibility and others' assessment of the findings and recommendations generated by the researcher's methods. Such sources should be used rarely, if ever, and only for the limited purposes described. If more scholarly sources would accomplish the same purposes, they should be used instead. Our tongue-in-cheek examples, however, make an important point. Any source that relates to the research problem and to a research question *may* have the potential to inform the researcher in some way, even if the knowledge it contains may have no credibility whatsoever.

ORGANIZING THE LITERATURE REVIEW

After a search of existing knowledge, we usually find ourselves with a great amount of information. Typically it consists of a large stack of file cards with useful quotations on one side and the full citation (including all page numbers, volume numbers, and other necessary specifics) on the back. (A computer-assisted variation of the file card system is also popular.) A good first step in making sense out of the existing knowledge is to sort it into several broad topic areas. These may have been identified prior to embarking on the literature review, or they may simply suggest themselves during the sorting process. An example will help to illustrate how this can be done.

Suppose that you have conducted a literature review on the research question "What changes in the role of caregivers have been associated with the increasingly chronic nature of AIDS?" The variety of relevant knowledge that you have collected could be organized using an outline format like the following:

I. *Historical Responses to Terminal Illness*
    A. In-Hospital Services
    B. The Hospice Movement
    C. Family Roles and Responsibilities

II. *History of AIDS*
   A. Early Diagnostic Efforts
   B. Symptoms of the Disease
   C. Transmission
   D. Social and Political Responses
   E. Groups Most at Risk
   F. Past Treatment Approaches
   G. Efforts to Find a Cure or Vaccine
   H. Traditional Caregiver Roles
III. *Recent Developments and Changes*
   A. Incidence
   B. Descriptive Profile of Current Persons with AIDS
   C. Development of Life-Extending Drugs
   D. Changes in Life Quality
   E. Dependence on Caregivers

Organizing the products of a literature review into an outline containing broad topic areas can serve a number of useful purposes. Some knowledge that has been collected may not seem to fit perfectly within any of the areas. It may be concluded that it is not as relevant to the research problem or questions as had originally been assumed. Thus, it may be discarded. Or, if it seems to stand alone but clearly does enlighten some aspect of the research problem or questions, new subheadings may be added to incorporate it, and the information may have to be expanded upon with additional literature. It may be necessary to go back to the literature to seek out additional references.

If it appears that there is no logical sequence to the topics (note the logical progression of the preceding topics) when a broad outline is constructed, additional topics may be required to link those already identified. When all topic areas and their subtopics have been developed, they should reflect a logical flow, often from the more general to those most closely related to the current research question(s). The topics frequently are used as headings and subheadings when the report of the literature review is written.

WRITING THE LITERATURE REVIEW

What are the characteristics of a good literature review section of a research report? How can the compilation of existing knowledge be organized and presented so that it will be of maximum benefit to the reader? Chapter 24 presents a detailed discussion of how to write quantitative research reports while Chapter 27 discusses how to write qualitative ones.

Direction and Flow

As suggested earlier, the reader should expect to find topics (identified by subheadings) of general relevance to the research questions near its beginning. For example, in a research study seeking an answer to the broad research question "Is there a relationship between crack cocaine usage and adolescent suicide?" early sections of the literature review might be devoted to a historical overview of substance abuse, a summary of what is known about adolescent drug usage, and a description of statistical trends in the incidence of adolescent suicide in North America.

Knowledge that is more directly related to the research question—for example, a summary of the results of suicide autopsies conducted on recent cases of adolescent suicide or results of other studies that examined the relationship between other substance abuse and adolescent suicide—should appear later. Reports of studies that considered the same research questions, or very similar ones, should be summarized and discussed near the end of the review so that the current study will appear to be a logical extension of previous ones.

Good literature reviews reflect both direction and a logical progression. They demonstrate how other researchers have used existing knowledge to refine their thinking about their research problems and questions and how more specific questions and/or hypotheses have evolved from that knowledge. It also should be obvious just how researchers used the literature to draw conclusions about the most appropriate methods to use to study their research questions. Their thought processes should be obvious to the reader of the report. In this way, the reader can be convinced either that the researchers' conclusions are logical and justified or that they are not.

Use of Quotations and Citations

Direct quotations should be used sparingly in a literature review. It is the *substance* of what others have to say, rather than their specific words, that are important. Excessive use of quotations may mislead the reader because quotations are always taken out of context. In addition, because all writers have their own style, quotations can make the flow of the text uneven while providing more detail than the reader requires.

Citations are always appropriate within a literature review. They are used to explain how and why the researcher's thinking and conclusions have occurred. But, like quotations, they should be included only if the work cited truly contributed to the author's thinking, not simply as evidence that the researcher found a relevant source of knowledge.

There may be a natural tendency to want to include every bit of knowledge that has been discovered. After all, finding it took a considerable amount of effort! But, if ten articles present essentially the same position, there is no reason to cite them all—that would be overkill. One or two will make the point and will be less likely to disrupt the flow of the text.

How relevant should knowledge be in order to be cited? How much detail of others' work is needed or desirable? Daryl Bem (1991) has provided some useful guidelines to answer these questions:

> Cite only articles pertinent to the specific issues with which you are dealing; emphasize their major conclusions, findings, or relevant methodological issues and avoid unnecessary detail. If someone else has written a review article that surveys the literature on the topic, you can simply refer your own readers to the review and present only its most pertinent points in your own report. Even when you must describe an entire study, try to condense it as much as possible without sacrificing clarity. (453)

Are some types of citations better than others? Yes. But a good mix often is desirable. The best citations to use (all other factors being equal) may be those that refer to recent, rigorous scientific research (as opposed to those that may be a little dated or that are less empirically based). But it is perfectly acceptable to include some older citations (especially if the contribution was a major influence on subsequent thought on a topic or issue). Older citations can also be very useful for providing a historical perspective on a problem or event. They reflect the state of the art of knowledge, beliefs, and attitudes at a point in history.

It should be clear by now that the quotations and citations included in a literature review within a research report are there to help explain how the author went from Point A to Point B. Quotations and citations are not there to impress others with how much relevant information was examined. If anything should impress the reader of a good literature review contained within a research report, it should be the author's objectivity and open-mindedness.

Objectivity can be demonstrated in a number of ways. For example, it can be seen in a willingness to include the conflicting opinions and conclusions of other research studies which almost invariably exist. It is not unusual for two separate research reports to express beliefs and conclusions that are diametrically opposite to each other. The inclusion of references that reflect both sides of an argument may suggest that the author has produced a thorough and objective literature review.

The Role of the Researcher

We do not mean to suggest that the researcher should always remain well behind the scenes in a literature review or express no opinions or conclusions whatsoever. In fact, the opposite is true. Although biases should not be evident in a good literature review, *thought processes* should be both obvious and open to critique. The reader should be able to sense the presence of the author in the text. A good literature review is a carefully woven mixture of knowledge and the assimilation of it by the researcher.

It may be helpful to think of the researcher as a guide who has pulled together and organized what is of interest and value to save others' time and effort. But a guide does not *tell* others what to see or how it should be perceived or interpreted. Using the literature review, the reader is helped to navigate through existing, relevant knowledge, stopping along the way to pull together conclusions and to evaluate just where the literature seems to be leading. As a guide, the author tries not to exert too much influence on the reader, whenever possible letting the literature speak for itself. However, a well-written literature review will lead the reader to the same or similar conclusions as the author and to agree about what the literature has to say about the research questions and how best to study them. There will be no surprises. No conclusions will seem to come out of the blue.

If we perceive the researcher's role as that of guide, neither of the two problems that frequently characterize literature reviews is likely to occur. One fairly common problem occurs when the researcher's thinking dominates the literature review and appears to be invulnerable to influence by it. Scholarly development of thought is not in evidence. The reader is left with the suspicion that existing knowledge had little influence on the conclusions that were drawn. Even if a fair number of citations are present, they do not reflect balance. It appears that the researcher selectively used only that literature that would support existing biases and did not grow in an understanding of the research problem or questions. The researcher emerged from the literature review with unchanged beliefs. The reader, sensing this, is likely to doubt whether other stages of the research process were conducted in an unbiased manner.

Sometimes another problem can occur: The development of the researcher's thinking is barely evident in the literature review, but for a different reason. The literature review seems to be little more than a long series of quotations, included in the research report because they are expected to lend a scholarly appearance, but

with no other apparent purpose. There is no way for the reader to evaluate the researcher's thought processes. There is not enough evidence that the knowledge assembled by the researcher was even assimilated.

In either of these scenarios, the researcher has not made productive use of the literature accumulated. Credibility may be hopelessly damaged. But if the author assumes the role of guide, the proper mix of quotations reflecting relevant knowledge and the use of that knowledge to refine thinking about the research topic will be in evidence. The literature review will be a unified whole that seems to take the reader somewhere.

SUMMARY

The term "literature review" refers both to a step in the research process and to a product, namely a section or chapter of the research report. We made the point that a body of knowledge exists for any research question. We examined how the process of reviewing existing knowledge about a research question can shape our thinking about the question and its possible answer. We discussed the other reasons why we look at what is already known relative to a research question, that is, what the literature review is supposed to accomplish. The pros and cons of various sources of knowledge were discussed, with special focus on how the selection of a source can affect the credibility of the researcher and the research findings.

Practical suggestions also were given for organizing a wide array of knowledge into a logical and coherent report of what is known relative to a research topic. The role of the researcher was described as that of a guide for the reader to help in synthesizing existing knowledge and drawing a conclusion from it.

Approaches to Knowledge Development

The first two chapters of Part II present the two research approaches—the quantitative research approach (Chapter 5) and the qualitative research approach (Chapter 6)—that constitute the research method of knowing discussed in Part I. The following chapter (Chapter 7) then describes the relevance of gender, ethnicity, and race issues in the design and conduct of the research studies that were described in Chapters 5 and 6.

The Quantitative
Research Approach

Yvonne A. Unrau

Richard M. Grinnell, Jr.

Margaret Williams

5

The previous four chapters presented a brief discussion of why the generation of knowledge is best acquired through the use of the research method and the contexts and ethics contained within the research process. As we now know, the research method contains two complimentary approaches—the quantitative approach, which is the topic of this chapter—and the qualitative approach—the topic of the following chapter. No matter which approach we use to obtain our professional knowledge base, "knowing" something that resulted from either approach is much more objective than "knowing" that exact same something that was derived from the other four ways of knowing.

Before we discuss the quantitative approach to knowledge development you need to understand how this approach is embedded within the "positivist way of thinking" as illustrated in Figure 5.1 and Box 5.1.

RESEARCH STEPS WITHIN THE QUANTITATIVE APPROACH

The preceding discussion encompasses only the philosophy behind the quantitative research approach to knowledge building. With this philosophy in mind, we now turn our attention to the eight general sequential steps (in a more or less straightforward manner) that all quantitative researchers follow, as outlined in Figure 5.2. These steps yield a very useful format for obtaining knowledge in our profession.

The quantitative research approach as illustrated in Figure 5.2 is a "tried and tested" method of scientific inquiry. It has been used for centuries. As we now know, if data obtained within a research study are represented in the form of numbers, then this portion of the study is considered "quantitative." The numbers are then analyzed by descriptive and inferential statistics.

In a nutshell, most of the critical decisions to be made in a quantitative research study occur *before* the study is ever started. This means that the researcher is well aware of all the study's limitations before the study actually begins. It is possible, therefore, for a researcher to decide that a quantitative study has simply too many limitations and eventually decides not to carry it out.

Regardless of whether or not a proposed study is ever carried out, the process always begins with choosing a research topic and focusing the research question.

Steps 1 and 2: Developing the Research Question

As can be seen in Figure 5.2, the first two steps of the quantitative approach to knowledge development are to identify a general problem area to study (Step 1) and then to refine this general area into a research question that can be answered or a hypothesis that can be tested (Step 2). These studies are usually deductive processes; that is, they usually begin with a broad and general query about a general social problem and then pare it down to a specific research question or hypothesis. For instance, your general research problem may have started out with a curiosity about racial discrimination within public social service agencies. It could be written simply as:

> General Problem Area:
> Racial discrimination within public social service agencies

You may have noticed through your professional practice as a medical social worker in a local hospital, for example, that many of the patients within your hospital are from ethnic minority backgrounds, have high unemployment rates, have a large proportion of their members living under the poverty level, and have low levels of educational attainment. You believe that these four conditions alone should increase the likelihood of their utilizing the hospital's social service department where you work.

Conversely, and at the same time, you have also observed that there are more ethnic majorities than ethnic minorities who are seen in your hospital's social service department. Your personal observations may then lead you to question whether discrimination against ethic minorities exists when it comes to their having access to your hospital's social service department. You can easily test the possibility of such a relationship by using the quantitative research approach.

The next step in focusing your research question would be to visit the library and review the literature related to your two concepts:

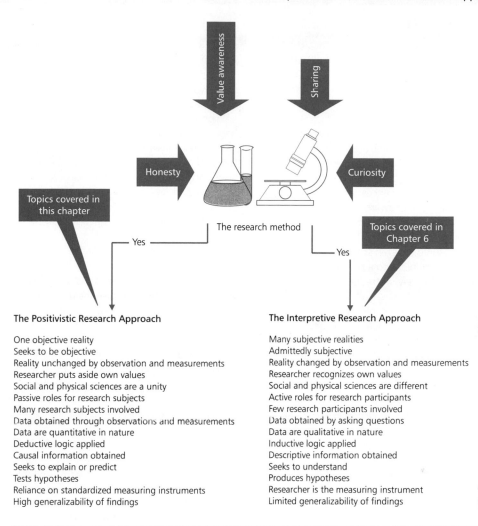

Figure 5.1   The Quantitative (Positivistic) and Qualitative (Interpretive) Research Approaches within the Research Method

- Racial discrimination within social service agencies (Concept 1)
- Access to social service (Concept 2)

You would want to read the literature related to the two main concepts within the general research question—racial discrimination within social service agencies and access to social services. You would want to learn about how various theories explain both of your main concepts in order to arrive at a meaningful research question. It may be, for example, that many

ethnic minority cultures are unlikely to ask "strangers" for help with life's personal difficulties.

Furthermore, you may learn that most social service programs are organized using bureaucratic structures, which require new potential clients to talk to several strangers (e.g., telephone receptionist, waiting-room clerk, intake worker) before they are able to access social services. Given that you know, via the literature, that ethnic minorities do not like talking with strangers about their personal problems and that social services are set up for people to deal with a series of strangers,

BOX 5.1

What Is the Positivist Way of Thinking?

The positivist way of thinking strives toward measurability, objectivity, the reducing of uncertainty, duplication, and the use of standardized procedures (see, for example, the left side of Figure 5.1).

Striving toward Measurability

The positivist way of thinking tries to study only those things that can be objectively measured, that is, knowledge gained through this belief is based on "objective measurements" of the real world, not on someone's opinions, beliefs, or past experiences. Conversely, and as you know from Chapter 1, knowledge gained through tradition or authority depends on people's opinions and beliefs and not on measurements of some kind. Entities that cannot be measured, or even seen, such as id, ego, or superego, are not amenable to a positivistic-oriented research study but rather rely on tradition and authority.

In short, a positivist principle is that the things you believe to exist must be measureable. However, at this point in our discussion, it is useful to remember that researchers doing studies within a positivistic framework believe that practically everything in life is measurable.

Striving toward Objectivity

The second ideal of the positivist belief is that research studies must be as "objective" as possible. The things that are being observed and/or measured must not be affected in any way by the person doing the observing or measuring. Physical scientists have observed inanimate matter for centuries, confident in the belief that objects do not change as a result of being observed. In the subworld of the atom, however, physicists are beginning to learn what social workers have always known. Things do change when they are observed. People think, feel, and behave very differently as a result of being observed. Not only do they change; they change in different ways depending on who is doing the observing and/or measuring.

There is yet another problem. Observed behavior is open to interpretation by the observer. To illustrate this point, let's take a simple example of a client you are seeing, named Ron, who is severely withdrawn. He may behave in one way in your office in individual treatment sessions, and in quite another way when his mother joins the interviews. You may think that Ron is unduly silent, while his mother remarks on how much he is talking. If his mother wants him to talk, perhaps as a sign that he is emerging from his withdrawal, she may perceive him to be talking more than he really is.

All folks who do research studies with the positivistic framework go to great lengths to ensure that their own hopes, fears, beliefs, and biases do not affect their

research results and that the biases of others do not affect them, either. Nevertheless, as discussed in later chapters, complete "objectivity" is rarely possible in social work, despite the many strategies that have been developed over the years to achieve it.

Suppose, for example, that a social worker is trying to help a mother interact more positively with her child. The worker, together with a colleague, may first observe the child and mother in a playroom setting, recording how many times the mother makes eye contact with the child, hugs the child, criticizes the child, makes encouraging comments, and so forth on a three-point scale (i.e., discouraging, neutral, encouraging). The social worker may perceive a remark that the mother has made to the child as "neutral," while the colleague thinks it was "encouraging."

As you will see throughout this book, in such a situation it is impossible to resolve the disagreement. If there were six objective observers, for example, five opting for "neutral" and only one for "encouraging," the one "encouraging observer" is more likely to be wrong than the five, and it is very likely that the mother's remark was "neutral." As you know from Chapter 1, as more people agree on what they have observed, the less likely it becomes that the observation was distorted by bias, and the more likely it is that the agreement reached is "objectively true."

As should be obvious by now, objectivity is largely a matter of agreement. There are some things—usually physical phenomena—about which most people agree. Most people agree, for example, that objects fall when dropped, water turns to steam at a certain temperature, sea water contains salt, and so forth. However, there are other things—mostly to do with values, attitudes, and feelings—about which agreement is far more rare.

An argument about whether Beethoven is a better composer than Bach, for example, cannot be "objectively" resolved. Neither can a dispute about the rightness of capital punishment, euthanasia, or abortion. It is not surprising, therefore, that physical researchers, who work with physical phenomena, are able to be more "objective" than social work researchers, who work with human beings.

Striving toward Reducing Uncertainty

Positivistic-oriented research studies try to totally rule out uncertainty. Since all observations and/or measurements in the social sciences are made by human beings, personal bias cannot be entirely eliminated, and there is always the possibility that an observation and/or measurement is in error, no matter how many people agree about what they saw or measured. There is also the pos-

BOX 5.1 *(continued)*

sibility that the conclusions drawn from even an accurate observation or measurement will be wrong. A number of people may agree, for example, that an object in the sky is a UFO when in fact it is a meteor. Even if they agree that it is a meteor, they may come to the conclusion—probably erroneously—that the meteor is a warning from an angry extraterrestrial person.

In the twentieth century, most people do not believe that natural phenomena have anything to do with extraterrestrial people. They prefer the explanations that modern researchers have proposed. Nevertheless, no researcher would say—or at least be quoted as saying—that meteors and extraterrestrial beings are not related for certain. When utilizing the research method of knowledge development, nothing is certain. Even the best-tested theory is only tentative and accepted as true until newly discovered evidence shows it to be untrue or only partly true. All knowledge gained through the research method is thus provisional. Everything presently accepted as true is true only with varying degrees of probability.

Striving toward Duplication

Positivistic researchers try to do research studies in such a way that the studies can be duplicated. Suppose, for a moment, you are running a 12-week intervention program to help fathers who have abused their children to manage their anger without resorting to physical violence. You have put a great deal of effort into designing your program and believe that your intervention (the program) is more effective than other interventions currently used in other anger-management programs. You develop a method of measuring the degree to which the fathers in your group have learned to dissipate their anger in nondamaging ways, and you find that, indeed, the group of fathers shows marked improvement.

Improvement shown by one group of fathers, however, is not convincing evidence for the effectiveness of your program. Perhaps your measurements were in error and the improvement was not as great as you hoped for. Perhaps the improvement was a coincidence, and the fathers' behaviors changed because they had joined a health club and each had vented his fury on a punching bag. In order to be more certain, you duplicate your program and measuring procedures with a second group of fathers. In other words, you replicate your study.

After you have used the same procedures with a number of groups and obtained similar results each time, you might expect that other social workers will eagerly adopt your methods. As presented in Chapters 1 and 2, tradi-

tion dies hard. Other social workers have a vested interest in their interventions, and they may suggest that you found the results you did only because you wanted to find them.

In order to counter any suggestion of bias, you ask another, independent social worker to use your same anger-management program and measuring methods with other groups of fathers. If the results are the same as before, your colleagues in the field of anger management may choose to adopt your intervention method (the program). Whatever your colleagues decide, you are excited about your newfound program. You wonder if your methods would work as well with women as they do with men, with adolescents as well as with adults, with Native Americans, Asians, or African Americans as well as with Caucasians, with mixed groups, larger groups, or groups in different settings. In fact, you have identified a lifetime project, since you will have to apply your program and measuring procedures repeatedly to all these different groups of people.

Striving toward the Use of Standardized Procedures

Finally, a true-to-the-bone positivist researcher tries to use well-accepted standardized procedures. For a positivistic-oriented research study to be creditable, and before others can accept its results, they must be satisfied that your study was conducted according to accepted scientific standardized procedures. The allegation that your work lacks "objectivity" is only one of the criticisms they might bring. In addition, they might suggest that the group of fathers you worked with was not typical of abusive fathers in general and that your results are not therefore applicable to other groups of abusive fathers. It might be alleged that you did not make proper measurements, or that you measured the wrong thing, or that you did not take enough measurements, or that you did not analyze your data correctly, and so on.

In order to negate these kinds of criticisms, over the years social work researchers have agreed on a set of standard procedures and techniques that are thought most likely to produce "true and unbiased" knowledge—which is what this book is all about. Certain steps must be performed in a certain order. Foreseeable errors must be guarded against. Ethical behavior with research participants and colleagues must be maintained, as outlined in Chapter 3. These procedures must be followed if your study is both to generate usable results and to be accepted as useful by other social workers.

you could develop a very simple quantitative research question:

> **Quantitative Research Question:**
> Do patients who come from ethnic minority backgrounds have difficulty accessing my hospital's social service department?

Your simple straightforward general problem area has become much more specific via the construction of a research question. In your research question, for example, you have identified a person's ethnicity and access to your hospital's social services as your two concepts of interest.

Developing Concepts

What are concepts, anyway? They are nothing more than ideas. When you speak of a client's ethnic background, for example, you have in mind the concept of *ethnicity*. When you use the word "ethnicity," you are referring to the underlying idea that certain groups of people can be differentiated from other groups on the basis of physical characteristics, customs, beliefs, language, and so on.

Take a female patient in your hospital, for example, who has just been referred to your social service department. She is a patient in the hospital, she is a woman, and she is now also your client. If she is married, she is a wife. If she has children, she is a mother. She may be a home owner, a committee member, an Asian, or a Catholic. She may be hostile, demanding, or compassionate. All of her characteristics are concepts. They are simply ideas that are all members of a society share—to a greater or lesser degree, of course.

Some concepts are perceived the same way by all of us. On the other hand, some concepts give rise to huge disagreements. The concept of being a mother, for example, involves the concept of children and, specifi-

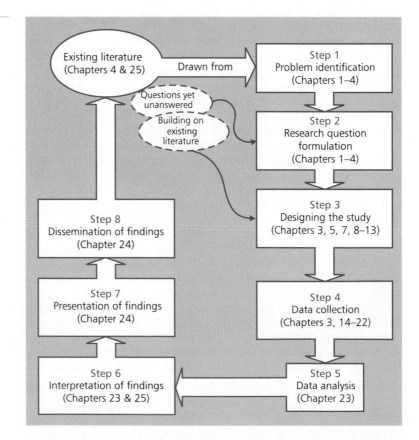

Figure 5.2 The Quantitative (Positivist) Research Approach to Knowledge Building

cally, the concept of having given birth to a child. Today, however, most people would agree that having given birth to a child is only *one* definition of a mother.

The idea of motherhood in Western society involves more than simply giving birth, however. Also involved in motherhood are the concepts of loving, of caring for the child's physical needs, of offering the child emotional support, of advocating for the child with others, of accepting legal and financial responsibility for the child, and of being there for the child in all circumstances and at all times. Some of us could easily argue that a woman who does all of these things is a mother, whether she has given birth or not. Others would say that the biological mother is the *only* real mother even if she abandoned her child at birth.

Like many other qualities of interest to social workers, ethnicity is a highly complex concept with many possible dimensions. Intelligence is another such concept, as are alienation, morale, conformity, cohesion, motivation, delinquency, prejudice, social status, and a host of others.

Identifying Variables within Concepts

You can now relate the concept of "the existence of different ethnic groups" to the patients who seek out your hospital's social service department. Some patients will belong to one ethnic group, some to another, some to a third, and so on. In other words, these folks *vary* with respect to which ethnic group they belong to. Any characteristic that can vary, logically enough, is called a *variable*.

Putting Value Labels on Variables

You now have a concept, ethnicity—and a related variable, ethnic group. Finally, you need to think about which particular ethnic groups will be useful for your study. Perhaps you know that Asians are patients within your hospital, and so are Caucasians, Hispanics, African Americans, and Native Americans. This gives you five categories, or *value labels*, of your ethnic group variable:

> Value Labels for Ethnicity Variable:
> Asian
> Caucasian
> Hispanic
> African American
> Native American

During your quantitative study, you will ask all of the hospital's patients which of the five ethnic groups they belong to; or perhaps these data will be recorded on the hospital's intake forms and you will not need to ask for them. In any case, the resulting data will be in the form of numbers or percentages for each value label. You will have succeeded in measuring the variable *ethnic group* by describing it in terms of five value labels, or categories.

Value labels do nothing more than describe a variable. You will note that these five categories only provide one possible description. You could also have included Pacific Islanders, for example, if there were any receiving medical treatment in your hospital, and then you would have had six value labels of your ethnic group variable instead of only five. If you were afraid that not all clients receiving medical treatment would fit into one of these categories, then you could include a miscellaneous category, *other*, to be sure you had accounted for everyone.

By reviewing the literature and your knowledge of your social service unit, you have more or less devised a direction for your study in relation to your ethnicity concept. You have come up with a concept, a variable, and five value labels for your variable, which are related as follows:

> **Concept:**   Ethnicity
> **Variable:**   Ethnic group
> **Variable Labels:** Asian
>   Caucasian
>   Hispanic
>   African American
>   Native American

As you know, ethnicity is not the only concept of interest in your study. There is also *access to social work services*, which is the idea that some people, or groups of people, are able to access social work services more readily than other people or groups.

BOX 5.2

The Importance of Variable Names

Operationalization is one of those things that is easier said than done. It is quite simple to explain to someone the purpose and importance of operational definitions for variables, and even to describe how operationalization typically takes place. However, until you've tried to operationalize a rather complex variable, you may not appreciate some of the subtle difficulties involved. Of considerable importance to the operationalization effort is the particular name that you have chosen for a variable. Let's consider an example from the field of urban planning.

A variable of interest to planners is citizen participation. Planners are convinced that participation in the planning process by citizens is important to the success of plan implementation. Citizen participation is an aid to planners' understanding of the real and perceived needs of a community, and such involvement by citizens tends to enhance their cooperation with and support for planning efforts. Although many different conceptual definitions might be offered by different planners, there would be little misunderstanding over what is *meant* by citizen participation. The name of the variable seems adequate.

However, if we asked different planners to provide very simple operational measures for citizen participation, we would likely find a variety among their responses that would generate confusion. One planner might keep a tally of attendance by private citizens at city commission and other local government meetings;

another might maintain a record of the different topics addressed by private citizens at similar meetings; a third might record the number of local government meeting attendees, as well as letters and phone calls received by the mayor and other pubic officials during a particular time period.

As skilled researchers, we can readily see that each planner would be measuring (in a very simplistic fashion) a different *dimension* of citizen participation: extent of citizen participation, issues that prompt citizen participation, and form of citizen participation. Therefore, the original *naming* of our variable, citizen participation, which was quite satisfactory from a conceptual point of view, proved inadequate for purposes of operationalization.

The precise and exact naming of variables is important in research. It is both essential to and a result of good operationalization. Variable names quite often evolve from an iterative process of forming a conceptual definition, then an operational definition, then renaming the concept to better match what can or will be measured.

This looping process continues (our example illustrates only one iteration), resulting in a gradual refinement of the variable name and its measurement until a reasonable fit is obtained. Sometimes the concept of the variable that you end up with is a bit different from the original one that you started with, but at least you are measuring what you are talking about, if only because you are talking about what you are measuring!

You might think of access simply in terms of how many of the patients receiving medical treatment within your hospital actually saw a social worker. Clients will *vary* with respect to whether they saw a social worker or not and so you have the variable—*saw social worker*—and two value labels of that variable:

- *yes*, the patient saw a social worker
- *no*, the patient did not see a social worker

You could, for example, ask each patient upon leaving the hospital a very simple question, such as:

Did you see a social worker while you were in the hospital?

- Yes
- No

If you wish to explore access in more depth, you might be interested in the factors affecting access. For example, perhaps your review of the literature has led you to believe that some ethnic groups tend to receive fewer referrals to social work services than other groups. If this is the case in your hospital, clients will vary with respect to whether or not they received a referral, and you immediately have a second variable—*referral*—and two value labels of that variable:

- *yes*, the patient was referred
- *no*, the patient was not referred

Once again, this variable can take the form of a very simple question, such as:

> When you were a patient within the hospital, were you at anytime referred to the hospital's social services department?
> - Yes
> - No

However, there is more to accessing hospital social work services than just being referred. Perhaps, according to the literature, certain ethnic groups are more likely to follow up on a referral than other groups because of cultural beliefs around the appropriateness of asking nonfamily members for help. In that case, you have a third variable, *follow-up of referral*, with two value labels of its own:

> - *yes*, the client followed up
> - *no*, the client did not follow up

This also can be put into a question form, such as:

> If you were referred to social work services while you were a patient in the hospital, did you follow up on the referral and actually see a social worker?
> - Yes
> - No

In addition, folks who do try to follow up on referrals may meet circumstances within the referral process that are more intimidating for some than for others. Perhaps they are obliged to fill out a large number of forms or to tell their stories to many unfamiliar people before they actually succeed in achieving an appointment with a social worker.

If this is the case, they *vary* with respect to how intimidating they find the process, and you have a fourth variable, *feelings of intimidation around the referal process*. The value labels here are not so immediately apparent, but you might decide on just three:

> - not at all intimidated
> - somewhat intimidated
> - very intimidated

This also can be put into the form of a simple question that you would ask all patients who were referred to social services:

> How intimidated were you when you were referred to the social services department within this hospital?
> - Not at all intimidated
> - Somewhat intimidated
> - Very intimidated

By reviewing the literature and your knowledge of your hospital's social service department, you have more or less devised a direction for your study in relation to your access concept. You have come up with a concept, four variables, and value labels for each one of the four variables, which are as follows:

Concept:	Access to social work services
First Variable:	Saw social worker?
Variable Labels:	• Yes
	• No
Second Variable:	Referral?
Variable Labels:	• Yes
	• No
Third Variable:	Follow-up of referral?
Variable Labels:	• Yes
	• No
Fourth Variable:	Feelings of intimidation around the referral process
Variable Labels:	• Not at all intimidated
	• Somewhat intimidated
	• Very intimidated

Defining Independent and Dependent Variables

A simple quantitative research study may choose to focus on the relationship between only two variables, called a *bivariate relationship*. The study tries to answer, in general terms: Does Variable X affect Variable Y? Or, how does Variable X affect Variable Y? If one variable affects the other, the variable that does the affecting is called an *independent variable*, symbolized by X. The variable that is affected is called the *dependent variable*, symbolized by Y. If enough is known about the topic and you have a good idea of what the effect will be, the question may be phrased: If *X* occurs, will *Y* result? If Variable *X* affects Variable *Y*, whatever happens to *Y* will depend on *X*.

No Independent or Dependent Variables.   Some quantitative research studies are not concerned with the effect that one variable might have on another. Perhaps it is not yet known whether two variables are even associated, and it is far too soon to postulate what the relationship between them might be. Your study might try to ascertain the answer to a simple question, such as "How intimidated do ethnic minority patients feel when they are referred to my hospital's social service department?" In this question, there is no independent variable; neither is there a dependent variable. There is only one variable—degree of intimidation felt by one group of people, the ethnic minorities. You could even include ethnic majorities as well and ask the question: How intimidated do *all* patients feel when they are referred to my hospital's social service department?

Constructing Hypotheses

There are many types of hypotheses, but we only briefly discuss two: (1) nondirectional, and (2) directional.

Nondirectional Hypotheses.   A nondirectional hypothesis (also called a two-tailed hypothesis), is simply a statement that says you expect to find a relationship between two or more variables. You are not willing, however, to "stick your neck out" as to the specific relationship between them. A nondirectional hypothesis for each one of your access variables could be, for example:

- **Nondirectional Research Hypothesis 1:** *Saw a Social Worker*
  Ethnic minorities and ethnic majorities see hospital social workers differentially.
- **Nondirectional Research Hypothesis 2:** *Referral*
  Ethnic minorities and ethnic majorities are referred to the hospital's social service department differentially.

- **Nondirectional Research Hypothesis 3:** *Follow-up*
  Ethnic minorities and ethnic majorities vary to the degree they follow up on referrals.
- **Nondirectional Research Hypothesis 4:** *Intimidation*
  Ethnic minorities and ethnic majorities feel differently about how intimidated they were by the referral process.

Directional Hypotheses.   Unlike a nondirectional hypothesis, a directional hypothesis (also called a one-tailed hypothesis) specifically indicates the "predicted" direction of the relationship between two or more variables. The direction stated is based on an existing body of knowledge related to the research question. You may have found out through the literature (in addition to your own observations), for example, that you have enough evidence to suggest the following directional research hypotheses:

- **Directional Research Hypothesis 1:** *Saw a Social Worker*
  Ethnic majorities see hospital social workers more than ethnic minorities.
- **Directional Research Hypothesis 2:** *Referral*
  Ethnic majorities are referred to the hospital's social service department more than ethnic minorities.
- **Directional Research Hypothesis 3:** *Follow-up*
  Ethnic majorities follow up with social service referrals more than ethnic minorities.
- **Directional Research Hypothesis 4:** *Intimidation*
  Ethnic minorities are more intimidated by the referral process than ethnic majorities.

Step 3: Designing the Research Study

As can be seen in Figure 5.2, Step 3 involves designing the research study a bit more. Having focused your general research question and, if appropriate, developed a hypothesis, you enter into the next phase of your study—designing the study. We begin with a word about sampling. One objective of your research study may be to generate findings that can be generalized beyond your study's sample. As you will see in Chapter 11, the "ideal" sample when this is the goal is one that has been randomly selected from a carefully defined population. The topic of sampling is discussed much more fully in Chapter 11.

As you shall see in this book, many research questions have at least one independent variable and one dependent variable. You could easily design your quantitative study where you have one independent variable, ethnicity (i.e., ethnic minority, ethnic majority), and

---

BOX 5.3

Constructing Good Hypotheses

Hypotheses have to be relevant, complete, specific, and testable.

Relevance

It is hardly necessary to stress that a useful hypothesis is one that contributes to the profession's knowledge base. Nevertheless, some social work problem areas are so enormously complex that it is not uncommon for people to get so sidetracked in reading the professional literature that they develop very interesting hypotheses totally unrelated to the original problem area they wanted to investigate in the first place.

The relevancy criterion is a reminder that, to repeat, the hypothesis must be directly related to the research question, which in turn must be directly related to the general research problem area.

Completeness

A hypothesis should be a complete statement that expresses your intended meaning in its entirety. The reader should not be left with the impression that some word or phrase is missing. "Moral values are declining" is one example of an incomplete hypothesis.

Other examples include a whole range of comparative statements without a reference point. The statement "Males are more aggressive," for example, may be assumed to mean "Men are more aggressive than women," but someone investigating the social life of animals may have meant "Male humans are more aggressive than male gorillas."

Specificity

A hypothesis must be unambiguous. The reader should be able to understand what each variable contained in the hypothesis means and what relationship, if any, is hypothesized to exist between them. Consider, for example, the hypothesis "Badly timed family therapy affects success." Badly timed family therapy may refer to therapy offered too soon or too late for the family to benefit, or to the social worker or family being late for therapy sessions, or to sessions that are too long or too

short to be effective. Similarly, "success" may mean resolution of the family's problems as determined by objective measurement, or it may refer to the family's—or the social worker's—degree of satisfaction with therapy, or any combination of these.

With regard to the relationship between the two variables, the reader may assume that you are hypothesizing a negative correlation. That is, the more badly timed the therapy, the less success will be achieved. On the other hand, perhaps you are only hypothesizing an association: Bad timing will invariably coexist with lack of success.

Be that as it may, the reader should not be left to guess at what you mean by a hypothesis. If you are trying to be both complete and specific, you may hypothesize, for example:

> Family therapy that is undertaken after the male perpetrator has accepted responsibility for the sexual abuse of his child is more likely to succeed in reuniting the family than family therapy undertaken before the male perpetrator has accepted responsibility for the sexual abuse.

This hypothesis is complete and specific. It leaves the reader in no doubt as to what you mean, but it is also somewhat wordy and clumsy. One of the difficulties in writing a good hypothesis is that specific statements need more words than unspecific or ambiguous statements.

Potential for Testing

The last criterion for judging whether a hypothesis is good and useful is the ease with which the truth of the hypothesis can be verified. Some statements cannot be verified at all with presently available measurement techniques. "Telepathic communication exists between identical twins" is one such statement. A hypothesis of sufficient importance often generates new data-gathering techniques, which will enable it to be eventually tested. Nevertheless, as a general rule, it is best to limit hypotheses to statements that can be tested immediately by current and available measurement methods.

one dependent variable, difficulty in accessing social services (i.e., yes or no). You could easily organize your variables in this way because you are expecting that a person's ethnicity is somehow related to his or her difficulty in accessing social services. It would be absurd to say the opposite—that the degree of difficulty that folks have in accessing social services influences their ethnicity. You could write your directional hypothesis as follows:

> **Directional Hypothesis:**
> Ethnic minorities have more difficulty than ethnic majorities in accessing my hospital's social service department

Having set out your hypothesis in this way, you can plainly see that your research design will compare two groups (i.e., ethnic minorities and ethnic majorities) in terms of whether or not (i.e., yes or no) each group had difficulty accessing your hospital's social service department. Your research design is the "blueprint" for the study. It is a basic guide to deciding how, where, and when data will be collected. How data are collected and where they are collected are determined by the data collection method you choose (Chapters 14–22). *When* data are collected is dictated by the specific research design you select (Chapters 12 and 13). Clearly, there are many things for you to consider when developing your research design.

Step 4: Collecting the Data

Data collection is one step within any research design. Data collection is the part of the study where you truly test out the operational definitions of your study's variables. There are three features of data collection that are key to all quantitative research studies:

1. All of your variables must be measurable. This means that you must precisely record the variable's frequency, and/or its duration, and/or its magnitude (intensity). Think about your ethnic minority variable for a minute. As noted earlier, you could simply operationalize this variable into two categories: ethnic minority and ethnic majority:

Are you an ethnic minority?
- Yes
- No

Here you are simply measuring the presence (ethnic minority) or absence (ethnic majority) of a trait for each research participant within your study. You also need to operationalize your difficulty in accessing the hospital's social services department variable. Once again, you could operationalize this variable in a number of ways. You may choose to operationalize it so that each person can produce a response to a simple question:

Did you have difficulty in accessing our hospital's social services department?
- Yes
- No

2. All of your data collection procedures must be objective. That is, the data are meant to reflect a condition in the *real* world and should not be biased by the person collecting the data in any way. In your quantitative study, the research participants will produce the data—not you, the researcher. That is, you will record only the data that each participant individually provides for both variables:

- "Ethnic Minority" **or** "Ethnic Majority" for the ethnicity variable
- "Yes" **or** "No" for the access to social service variable

3. All of your data collection procedures must be able to be duplicated. In other words, your data collection procedures that you use to measure the variables must be clear and straightforward enough so that other researchers could use them in their research studies.

In reference to Box 5.1, the three features of measurability, objectivity, and duplication within a quantitative research study are accomplished by using a series of standardized uniform steps that are applied consistently throughout a study's implementation. You must ensure that all of your research participants are measured in exactly the same way—in reference to their ethnicity and whether or not they had any difficulty in accessing hospital social services.

Steps 5 and 6: Analyzing and Interpreting the Data

There are two major types of quantitative data analyses: (1) descriptive statistics, and (2) inferential statistics.

Descriptive Statistics

As presented in Chapter 23, descriptive statistics describe your study's sample or population. Consider your ethnicity variable for a moment. You can easily describe your research participants in relation to their ethnicity by stating how many of them fall into each category label of the variable. Suppose, for example, that 50 percent of your sample are in the ethnic minority category and the remaining 50 percent are in the nonethnic minority category, as illustrated:

Variable Label:
• Ethnic Minority, 50%
• Ethnic Majority, 50%

These two percentages give you a "picture" of what your sample looks like with regard to ethnicity. A different picture could be produced where 10 percent of your sample were ethnic minorities and 90 percent were not, as illustrated:

Variable Label:
• Ethnic Minority, 10%
• Ethnic Majority, 90%

These data describe only one variable—ethnicity. A more detailed picture is given when data for two variables are displayed at the same time. Suppose, for example, that 70 percent of your research participants who were ethnic minorities reported that they had difficulty in accessing your hospital's social services, compared to 20 percent of those who were ethnic majorities:

Difficulty in Accessing Social Services?

Ethnicity	Yes	No
• Ethnic Minority	70%	30%
• Ethnic Majority	20%	80%

Other descriptive information about your research participants could include variables such as average age, percentages of males and females, average income, and so on. Much more is said about descriptive statistics in Chapter 23 when we discuss how to analyze quantitative data—that is, data that are in the form of numbers.

Inferential Statistics

Inferential statistics determine the probability that a relationship between the two variables within your sample also exists within the population from which the sample was drawn. Suppose that in your quantitative study, for example, you find a statistically significant relationship between your research participants' (your sample) ethnicity and whether they successfully accessed social services within your hospital setting. The use of inferential statistics will permit you to say whether or not the relationship detected in your study's sample exists in the larger population from which it was drawn—and the exact probability that your finding is in error. Much more is also said about inferential statistics in Chapter 23.

Steps 7 and 8: Presentation and Dissemination of Findings

Quantitative findings are easily summarized in tables, figures, and graphs. When data are disseminated to lay people, we usually rely on straightforward graphs and charts to illustrate our findings. As discussed in depth in Chapter 24, presentation of statistical findings is typically reserved for professional journals.

SUMMARY

This chapter briefly discussed the process of the quantitative research approach to knowledge development as outlined in Figure 5.2. The following chapter presents how the qualitative research approach can be used within the research method using the same example and format of this chapter.

The Qualitative
Research Approach

Margaret Williams

Yvonne A. Unrau

Richard M. Grinnell, Jr.

6

The preceding chapter presented a brief discussion of how the generation of social work knowledge is acquired through the use of research studies that gather quantitative data. This chapter is a logical extension of that one in that we now focus our attention on how knowledge is developed through the qualitative research approach.

As we know from the preceding chapter, the quantitative approach to knowledge development is embedded within the "positivist way of thinking, or viewing the world." In direct contract to the quantitative approach, the qualitative approach to knowledge development is embedded within the "interpretive way of thinking, or viewing the world." We now turn our attention to the "interpretive way of thinking" in detail.

WHAT IS THE INTERPRETIVE WAY OF THINKING?

The interpretive approach to knowledge development is the second way of obtaining knowledge in our profession (see the right side of Figure 5.1). It basically discards the positivist notion that there is only one external reality waiting to be discovered. Instead, the qualitative research approach is based on the interpretive perspective, which states that reality is defined by the research participants' interpretations of their own realities. In sum, it is the *subjective* reality that is studied via the qualitative research approach, rather than the *objective* one that is studied by the quantitative approach.

As you will see in Chapters 14–22, the differences between the philosophy of the quantitative approach and the qualitative approach to knowledge development naturally lead to different data collection methods. Subjective reality, for example, cannot be explored through the data collection method of observation. Empiricism—the belief that science must be founded on observations and measurements, another tenet of positivism—is thus also discarded. The qualitative approach says that the only real way to find out about the subjective reality of our research participants is to ask them, and the answer will come back in words, not in numbers. In a nutshell, qualitative research methods produce *qualitative* data in the form of text. Quantita-

tive research methods produce *quantitative* data in the form of numbers.

Multiple Realities

As you know, from a positivist standpoint, as presented in the preceding chapter, if you do not accept the idea of a single reality, which is not changed by being observed and/or measured, and from which you—the researcher—are "detached," then you are not a "real researcher" doing a "real research study." Thus, because you are a nonresearcher doing a nonresearch study, your findings are not thought to be of much use.

Many of the supposed "nonresearchers" whose views have not been thought to be valid were women and/or people who came from diverse minority groups. Feminists, for example, have argued that there is *not* only one reality—there are many realities. They contend that men and women experience the world differently and so they both exist in different realities, constructed by them from their own perceptions. Similarly, people from various cultural groups view the world from the perspective of their own beliefs and traditions and also experience different realities.

As for the idea that reality is not changed by being observed and/or measured, feminists have argued that a relationship of some kind is always formed between the researcher and the research participant (subject), resulting in yet another mutual reality constructed between the two of them. In any study involving human research participants, there are thus at least three realities:

1. the researcher's reality
2. the research participant's reality
3. the mutual reality they (researcher and research participant) both created and share

Moreover, all three realities are constantly changing as the study proceeds and as further interactions occur. The positivist idea of a single unchanged and unchanging reality, some feminists have argued, was typically a male idea, probably a result of the fact that men view human relationships as being less important than do women.

This is a low blow, which will quite properly be resented by the many men who do in fact ascribe importance to relationships. But, that aside, perhaps the problem lies less with phenomenalism (a single unchanged reality as opposed to multiple changing realities) than it does with scientism (the idea that the physical and social sciences can be approached in the same way).

Data versus Information

Here, it is worth pausing for a moment to discuss what is meant by *data*. Data are plural; the singular is *datum*, from the Latin *dare*, to give. A datum is thus something that is given, either from a quantitative observation and/or measurement or from a qualitative discussion with Ms. Smith about her experiences in giving birth at her home. A number of observations and/or measurements, in the quantitative approach, or a number of discussions, in the qualitative approach, constitute *data*.

Data are not the same thing as *information*, although the two words are often used interchangeably. The most important thing to remember at this point is that both approaches to the research method produce data. They simply produce different kinds of data.

Information is something you hope to get from the data once you have analyzed them—whether they are words or numbers. You might, for example, collect data about the home-birthing experiences of a number of women, and your analysis might reveal commonalties between them; perhaps all the women felt that their partners had played a more meaningful role in the birthing process at home than would have been possible in a hospital setting. The enhanced role of the partner is *information* that you, as a researcher, have derived from the interview *data*. In other words, data are pieces of evidence, in the form of words (qualitative data) or numbers (quantitative data), that you put together to give you information—which is what the research method is all about.

Subjects versus Research Participants

Having dealt with what data are (don't ever write "data *is*"), let's go back to the implications of collecting data about people's subjective realities. Because it is the research participant's reality you want to explore, the research participant is a very important data source. The

quantitative approach may seem to relegate the research participant to the status of an object or subject. In a study of caesarian births at a hospital during a certain period, for example, Ms. Smith will not be viewed as an individual within the quantitative approach to knowledge development, but only as the 17th woman who experienced such a birth during that period. Details of her medical history may be gathered without any reference to Ms. Smith as a separate person with her own hopes and fears, failings, and strengths. Conversely, a qualitative approach to caesarian births will focus on Ms. Smith's individual experiences. What *was* her experience? More important, what did it mean to her? How did she interpret it in the context of her own reality?

Values

In order to discover the truth of Ms. Smith's reality, however, you must be clear about the nature of your own reality. In Chapter 1 we discussed *value awareness* as one of the characteristics that distinguishes the research method from the other ways of knowledge development. As you know, value awareness is your ability to put aside your own values when you are conducting research studies or when you are evaluating the results obtained by other researchers. This is sometimes called *disinterestedness*. Researchers who are *disinterested* are ones who are able to accept evidence that runs against their own positions.

From a hard-line quantitative perspective, this putting aside of values seems more akin to sweeping them under the carpet and pretending they don't exist. Researchers engaged in quantitative studies will deny that their own values are important. They claim their values have nothing to do with the study. In a nutshell, their values cease to exist. On the other hand, qualitative researchers take a very different view. Their values are a part of their own realities and a part of the mutual reality that is constructed through their interaction with their research participants. A qualitative researcher's values therefore must be acknowledged and thoroughly explored so that the mutual shaping of realities that results from the interaction with their research participants may be more completely and honestly understood.

The term *value awareness*, while important to both research approaches, is thus understood in different ways. To quantitative researchers, it means putting values aside so that they don't affect the study. To qualitative researchers, it means an immersion in values so that their inevitable effect is understood and so that their research participants' realities emerge more clearly.

PHASES WITHIN THE QUALITATIVE APPROACH

Like quantitative researchers, qualitative researchers make a major commitment in terms of time, money, and resources when they undertake research studies. As can be seen in Figure 5.2, a quantitative study has eight basic sequential steps that must be followed to produce useful quantitative data. On the other hand, as can be seen in Figure 6.1, a qualitative study does not have these specific steps—the activities are more phases than steps, since many of the phases highly interact with one another.

As can be seen by comparing Figures 5.2 and 6.1, one of the major differences between the two research approaches is how they utilize the literature. In a quantitative study, for example, the literature is utilized mostly within the first three steps of the research method. In a qualitative study, the literature is heavily utilized in all of the phases.

The qualitative research approach is akin to exploring a "social problem maze" that has multiple entry points and paths. You have no way of knowing whether the maze will lead you to a place of importance, but you enter into it out of your own curiosity and, perhaps, even conviction. You enter the maze without a map or a guide; you have only yourself to rely on and your notebook to record important events, observations, conversations, and impressions along the way.

You will begin your journey of an interpretive inquiry by stepping into one entrance and forging ahead. You move cautiously forward, using all of your senses in an effort to pinpoint your location and what surrounds you at any one time. You may enter into dead-end rooms within the maze and have to backtrack. You may also

Figure 6.1 Phases of the Qualitative Research Process

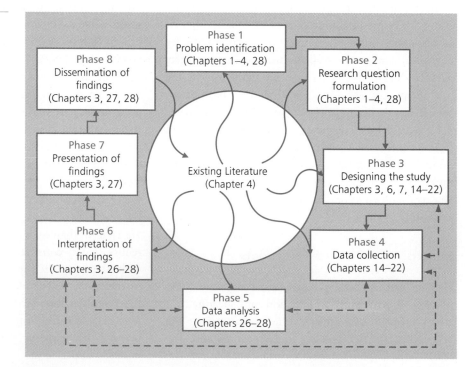

encounter paths that you did not think possible. In some cases, you may even find a secret passageway that links you to a completely different maze. Rothery, Tutty, and Grinnell (1996) present a few characteristics that most qualitative research studies have in common:

- They are conducted primarily in the natural settings where the research participants carry out their daily business in a "nonresearch" atmosphere.
- Variables cannot be controlled and experimentally manipulated (though changes in variables and their effect on other variables can certainly be observed).
- The questions to be asked are not always completely conceptualized and operationally defined at the outset (though they can be).
- The data collected are heavily influenced by the experiences and priorities of the research participants, rather than being collected by predetermined and/or highly structured and/or standardized measurement instruments.
- Meanings are drawn from the data (and presented to others) using processes that are more natural and familiar than those used in the quantitative method. The data need not be reduced to numbers and statistically analyzed (though counting and statistics can be employed if they are thought useful).

Phases 1 and 2: Problem Identification and Question Formulation

Qualitative studies are generally inductive and require you to reason in such a way that you move from a part to a whole or from a particular instance to a general conclusion. Let's return to the research problem introduced in the preceding chapter—racial discrimination within a hospital social services department. You begin the qualitative research process, once again, from your observations—ethnic minorities are among the groups with the highest unemployment and poverty rates and the lowest levels of education; however, ethnic majorities outnumber ethnic minorities in seeking assistance from social services.

You can focus your qualitative research question by identifying the key concepts in your question. These key concepts set the parameters of your research study—they are the "outside" boundaries of your maze. As in the quantitative research approach, you will want to visit the library and review the literature related to your key concepts. Your literature review, however, will take on a very different purpose. Rather than pinpointing "exact" variables to study, you will review the literature to see how your key concepts are generally described and defined by previous researchers.

Going with the maze example for the moment, you might learn whether your maze will have rounded or perpendicular corners, or whether it will have multiple levels. The knowledge you glean from the literature assists you with ways of thinking that you hope will help you move through the maze so that you arrive at a meaningful understanding of the problem it represents. Because you may never have been in the maze before, you must also be prepared to abandon what you "think you know" and accept new experiences presented to you along the way.

Let's revisit your research question—Do ethnic minorities have difficulty in accessing social services? In your literature review, you would want to focus on definitions and theories related to discrimination within the social services department. In the quantitative research approach, you reviewed the literature to search for meaningful variables that could be measured. You do not want, however, to rely on the literature to define key variables in your qualitative study. Rather, you will rely upon the qualitative research process itself to identify key variables and how they relate to one another.

On rare occasions, hypotheses can be used in a qualitative research study. They can focus your research question even further. A hypothesis in a qualitative study is less likely to be outright "accepted" or "rejected," as is the case in a quantitative study. Rather, it is a "working hypothesis" and is refined over time as new data are collected. Your hypothesis is changed throughout the qualitative research process on the basis of the reasoning of the researcher—not on a statistical test. So all of this leads us to ask the question "What do qualitative researchers actually do when they carry out a research study?" Neuman (2003) has outlined several activities that a qualitative researcher engages in when carrying out studies:

- Observes ordinary events and activities as they happen in natural settings, in addition to any unusual occurrences
- Is directly involved with the people being studied and personally experiences the process of daily social life in the field
- Acquires an insider's point of view while maintaining the analytic perspective or distance of an outsider
- Uses a variety of techniques and social skills in a flexible manner as the situation demands
- Produces data in the form of extensive written notes, as well as diagrams, maps, or pictures to provide detailed descriptions.
- Sees events holistically (e.g., as a whole unit, not in pieces) and individually in their social context
- Understands and develops empathy for members in a field setting and does not just record "cold," objective facts
- Notices both explicit and tacit aspects of culture
- Observes ongoing social processes without upsetting, disrupting, or imposing an outside point of view
- Is capable of coping with high levels of personal stress, uncertainty, ethical dilemmas, and ambiguity

Phase 3: Designing the Research Study

You can enter into a qualitative research study with general research questions or working hypotheses. However, you are far less concerned about honing in on specific variables. Because qualitative research studies are inductive processes, you do not want to constrain yourself with preconceived ideas about how your concepts or variables will relate to one another. Thus, while you will have a list of key concepts, and perhaps loosely defined variables, you want to remain open to the possibilities of how they are defined by your research participants and any relationships that your research participants may perceive.

A qualitative study is aimed at an in-depth understanding of a few cases, rather than a general understanding of many cases, or people. In other words, the number of research participants in a qualitative study is much smaller than in a quantitative one. As we will see in Chapter 11, sampling is a process of selecting the "best-fitting" people to provide data for your study. Nonprobability sampling strategies are designed for this task because they purposely seek out potential research participants. More is said about nonprobability sampling strategies in Chapter 11.

The qualitative research approach is about studying a social phenomenon within its natural context. As such, the "case study" is a major qualitative research design. A case can be a person, a group, a community, an organization, or an event. You can study many different types of social phenomena within any one of these cases.

Any case study design can be guided by different qualitative research methods. Grounded theory is a method that guides you in a "back and forth" process between the literature and the data you collect. Using grounded theory, you can look to the literature for new ideas and linkages between ideas that can bring meaning to your data. In turn, your data may nudge you to read in areas that you might not have previously considered.

Ethnography is a branch of interpretive research that emphasizes the study of a culture from the perspective of the people who live the culture. With your research example, you would be interested in studying the culture of social services, particularly with respect to how ethnic minorities experience it.

Phenomenology is another branch of interpretive research. It emphasizes a focus on people's subjective experiences and interpretations of the world. These subjective experiences include those of the researcher, as well as of the research participants. As a researcher in your discrimination study, you would want to keep a careful account of your reactions and questions to the events you observe and the stories you hear. Your task is to search for meaningful patterns within the volumes of data (e.g., text, drawings, pictures, video recordings).

Phase 4: Collecting the Data

Qualitative researchers are the principal instruments of data collection (Franklin & Jordan, 1997). This means that data collected are somehow "processed" through the person collecting them. Interviewing, for example, is a common data collection method that produces text data. Data collection in the interview is interactive; you can check out your understanding and interpretation of your participants' responses as you go along.

To collect meaningful text data, you want to be immersed in the context or setting of the study. You want to have some understanding, for example, of what it is like to be a client of social services before you launch into a dialogue with clients about their experiences of discrimination, if any, within the social services. If you do not have a grasp of the setting in which you are about to participate, then you run the risk of misinterpreting what is told to you.

Given that your general research question evolves in a qualitative study, the data collection process is particularly vulnerable to biases of the data collector. There are several principles to guide you in your data collection efforts:

- First, you want to make every effort to be aware of your own biases. In fact, your own notes on reactions and biases to what you are studying are used as sources of data later on, when you interpret the data (Chapter 26).
- Second, data collection is a two-way street. The research participants tell you their stories and, in turn, you tell them your understanding or interpretation of their stories. It is a process of checks and balance.
- Third, qualitative data collection typically involves multiple data sources and multiple data collection methods. In your study, you may see clients, workers, and supervisors as potential data sources. You may collect data from each of these groups using interviews, observation, and existing documentation (data collection methods).

Phases 5 and 6: Analyzing and Interpreting the Data

Collecting, analyzing, and interpreting qualitative data are intermingled. Let's say that, in your first round of data collection, you interview a number of ethnic minority clients about their perceptions of racial discrimination in the social services. Suppose they consistently tell you that to be a client of social services, they must give up many of their cultural values. You could then develop more specific research questions for a second round of interviews in an effort to gain more of an in-depth understanding of the relationship between holding certain cultural values and being a social service client.

Overall, the process of analyzing qualitative data is an iterative one. This means that you must read and reread the volumes of data that you collected. You simply look for patterns and themes that help to capture how your research participants are experiencing the social problem you are studying.

The ultimate goal is to interpret data in such a way that the true expressions of research participants are revealed. You want to explain meaning according to the beliefs and experiences of those who provided the data. The aim is to "walk the walk" and "talk the talk" of research participants and not to impose "outside" meaning to the data they provided. Much more is said about analyzing and interpreting qualitative data in Chapter 26.

Phases 7 and 8: Presentation and Dissemination of Findings

Qualitative research reports are generally lengthier than quantitative ones. The reason for this is that it is not possible to strip the context of a qualitative study and present only its findings. The knowledge gained from a qualitative endeavor is nested within the context in which it was derived. Furthermore, text data are more awkward and clumsy to summarize than numerical data. You cannot rely on a simple figure to indicate a finding. Instead, you display text usually in the form of quotes or summary notes to support your conclusions. Much more is said about the presentation and dissemination of qualitative studies in Chapter 27.

COMPARING THE QUANTITATIVE AND QUALITATIVE APPROACHES

Philosophical Differences

By comparing the philosophical underpinnings of quantitative and qualitative research approaches, you can more fully appreciate their important differences. Each approach offers you a unique method to studying a social work-related problem; the same research problem can be studied using either approach. (See Box 6.1.)

Suppose, for example, you are interested in a broad social problem such as racial discrimination. In particular, let's say you are interested in studying the social problem of racial discrimination within public social service programs. Let's now look at the major differences between the two approaches and see how your research problem, racial discrimination, could be studied under both approaches (Jordan & Franklin, 2003).

Perceptions of Reality

Quantitative   Ethnic minorities share similar experiences within the public social service system. These experiences can be described objectively; that is, a single reality exists outside any one person.

Qualitative   Individual and ethnic group experiences within the public social service system are unique. Their experiences can be described only subjectively; that is, a single and unique reality exists within each person.

Ways of "Knowing"

Quantitative   The experience of ethnic minorities within public social services is made known by closely examining specific parts of their experiences. Scientific principles, rules, and tests of sound reasoning are used to guide the research process.

Qualitative   The experience of ethnic minorities within public social services is made known by capturing the whole experiences of a few cases. Parts of their experiences are considered only in relation to the whole of them. Sources of knowledge are illustrated through stories, diagrams, and pictures that are shared by the people with their unique life experiences.

Value Bases

Quantitative   The researchers suspend all their values related to ethnic minorities and social services from the steps taken within the research study. The research participant "deposits" data, which are screened, organized, and analyzed by the researchers who do not attribute any personal meaning to the research participants or to the data they provide.

Qualitative   The researcher *is* the research process, and any personal values, beliefs, and experiences of the researcher will influence the research process. The researcher learns from the research participants, and their interaction is mutual.

Applications

Quantitative   Research results are generalized to the population from which the sample was drawn (e.g., other minority groups, other social services programs). The research findings tell us, on average, the experience that ethnic minorities have within the public social service system.

Qualitative   Research results tell a story of a few individuals' or one group's experience within the public social service system. The research findings provide an in-depth understanding of a few people. The life context of each research participant is key to understanding the stories he or she tells.

Similar Features

So far we have been focusing on the differences between the two research approaches. They also have many similarities. First, they both use careful and diligent research processes in an effort to discover and interpret knowledge. They both are guided by systematic procedures and orderly plans.

Second, both approaches can be used to study any particular social problem. The quantitative approach is more effective than the qualitative approach in reaching a specific and precise understanding of one aspect (or part) of an already well-defined social problem. The

Good Research Is Good Research

Fundamental to knowledge acquisition through quantitative and qualitative research studies is the idea that what we think should be rooted in and tested against good evidence and that sound articulated methods—systematic, disciplined inquiry—are necessary to bring this about. A good research study respects these essentials, regardless of the tradition within which it is conducted—quantitative or qualitative.

Bad research can also be found in both approaches. Qualitative case studies that pathologized women, and lower-income people as well, are abundant in the literature into the 1970s and beyond. Often, quantitative methods are now being used to repair the damage. Quantitative studies that evaluated social work interventions without recognizing their complexity or that dismissed the perceptions of the practitioners and their clients as subjective and therefore irrelevant did harm that qualitative researchers are working to correct.

Neither research approach can claim that its adherents have never done harm, and neither can deny that the other has made a genuine contribution. Neither deserves blind faith in its inherent virtues, and neither is innately perverse. As we discussed, however, differences do in fact exist. We now turn to a brief discussion of the implications of those differences as they relate to (1) our profession's knowledge base, (2) the social work practitioner, (3) gender, and (4) culture.

Research and the Profession's Knowledge Base

All approaches to research must generate and test the knowledge we need to be effective with our clients. Quantitative and qualitative approaches alike can contribute significantly in both ways. The main difference between the two is the kinds of knowledge they generate, which overlap but still tend to have different advantages and uses.

The cumulative effect of well-conducted quantitative research methods can be tremendously powerful in establishing client needs and documenting the effectiveness of our interventions. As examples, the steady accumulation in recent decades of evidence about the incidence of child abuse, sexual abuse, and AIDS, as well as about violence against women, has both changed the awareness of the public and professionals and had a wide-ranging impact on services to those populations. Indifference and skepticism about these issues have retreated as increasingly well-designed research has reinforced the message of earlier studies. Quantitative stud-

ies have an enviable ability to say, "This is true whether you want to believe it or not."

On the other hand, we need to know more than just the frequencies of the different forms of victimization, or how often a particular social work program produces particular outcomes for traumatized clients. When we want to understand the impacts of trauma in more depth and detail, when we want rich data about the experience of social workers and survivors working to ameliorate the effects of abuse, when we need to describe healing processes in ways that capture this human experience as something highly individual and sensitive to context—when these are our goals, the qualitative research approach is very useful.

The two approaches can contribute differently at different stages in the knowledge-building enterprise. When not much is known about a problem—in the early days of designing social programs for women who have been physically abused by their partners, for example—qualitative methods are well suited to providing exploratory data about possible needs and interventions. Once a reasonable understanding of such variables has been accumulated, quantitative methods can be efficiently used to provide more precise and generalizable data about the impacts that specific interventions have on needs. Qualitative researchers continue to contribute, however, by persisting in exploring issues, adding depth and texture to quantitative findings.

Considerations such as these lead us to believe that our profession would be foolish to reject the contribution to our knowledge base of either research approach. Irwin Epstein (1988) had a few strong words to say about the complementarity of the two research approaches more than a decade ago:

- Thus far we have maintained that quantitative and qualitative methods each have their special uses—it is only the uneducated person who states that one method is unequivocally better than the other. As a result, rather than asking which is best, it makes more sense for us to ask under what conditions each method is better than the other as a research strategy.
- To imply that we, as professional social workers, must make a choice between one or the other research method is senseless, idiotic, and simple-minded, to say the least. Both methods make meaningful contributions to our understanding of the social world and, when used together, can obviously augment it.

(continued)

BOX 6.1

(continued)

Research and the Practitioner

In recent years, some educators have suggested that front-line social workers should integrate quantitative research techniques into their practices. This was to be accomplished by educating students to become practitioner/researchers, that is, practitioners who regularly employ quantitative research methods to evaluate the effectiveness and efficiency of their practices.

Arguably, there is little evidence that the researcher/practitioner model has succeeded in winning significant numbers of adherents. One of the many reasons for this is that the quantitative research methods that were offered to practitioners for their consideration were too foreign to practice to be easily integrated into day-to-day activities. The tasks of administering standardized measuring instruments and collating, coding, and statistically analyzing client data are unnatural and intrusive when they are introduced into a practice setting. Additionally, and probably more important, they were too time consuming to use on a regular basis.

It has been hinted within the literature that qualitative research methods may be more promising than quantitative methods when it comes to evaluating the effectiveness of our treatment interventions. Unfortunately, it does not seem to us that this is likely, for reasons of feasibility: qualitative research remains a highly demanding exercise, and the time involved in preparing transcripts and subjecting them to a systematic qualitative analysis is no less formidable than the demands of quantitative research. A somewhat different issue is that of research utilization: Will practitioners find the data generated by either approach more accessible and relevant to their work? Only time will tell.

Research and Gender

There have been rumblings that there are gender issues associated with the quantitative and qualitative research approaches. The suggestion, in brief, is that since the quantitative approach strives for objectivity (read "distance") at all costs, dispassionate logic, and well-engineered and thought-out research designs, it is rooted in male values.

A more extreme extension of this argument is that quantitative researchers, subjecting the people in their studies to procedures imposed with no consultation or agreement and reducing peoples' experience to numbers, are acting in patriarchal ways. Therefore, some

believe that the quantitative research approach is inherently oppressive and morally inferior to the qualitative options. We know of women researchers with clear feminist commitments, however, who have had difficulty getting their work published because its quantitative approach was ideologically unpalatable.

The qualitative research approach, on the other hand, has been said to employ research methods that value relationships, egalitarianism, and empowerment of all research participants, sometimes called co-researchers. With their respect for individual experience, subjectivity, and subtlety, qualitative methods have been said to be more compatible with women's ways of knowing and experiencing the world.

Whatever the general validity of this position, it can easily be seriously overstated. While there appears to be current evidence that women and men are cognitively different, or have "different ways of knowing," the evidence also suggests that these differences are not particularly strong. Differences within the sexes are much greater than differences between them—men and women may experience life somewhat differently, but they do not inhabit separate cognitive worlds. For this reason, it is easy to identify well-known male qualitative researchers as well as female quantitative researchers who do very good research studies—regardless of research approach used.

As well, quantitative research studies and qualitative ones alike have been oppressively used. Practitioners who dismissed women's reports of sexual abuse as wish-fulfilling fantasy, for example, had solid support for their position in an extensive body of qualitative research findings beginning with the case studies of Sigmund Freud. To a large extent, quantitative studies have exposed this falsehood—an example of how this research approach had a liberating and empowering effect of considerable importance.

Research and Culture

Considerable concern has been expressed in recent years about research studies that involve people from diverse cultures. The concerns have indicated difficulties with both quantitative and qualitative approaches. Quantitative researchers have used standardized instruments developed in studies of one culture when studying others, without recognizing the problems this can create. A measure of social support employed with women who have been abused by their partners in a

(continued)

BOX 6.1

(continued)

Haitian community in Florida, for example, might be quite inappropriate if it was developed with white college students in New York.

Language, assumptions, and values implicit in an instrument's questions and the way they are interpreted may be foreign to research participants, making the process confusing or difficult and rendering the study's findings invalid. It is also possible that the lack of any meaningful relationship between the researcher and the research participant can be experienced as strange or even intimidating by someone from another culture. Many research studies conducted with diverse cultures have been qualitative in nature (the studies of cultural anthropologists, for example), and these have also been subject to criticism.

To the extent that qualitative researchers carry their own cultural assumptions into the field, they risk imposing a foreign frame of reference in interpreting the experience and meanings of the people they study. The problem is severe enough in the eyes of some critics that they have suggested that the only people who should study a culture should be members of that culture.

There are no easy answers to these complex problems. Quantitative researchers are working to develop methods and measures that are sensitive to cultural diversity. At the same time, some qualitative researchers are hopeful that their efforts to develop research approaches that are sensitive to social contexts and different ways of interpreting human experience will help them answer the concerns that have been raised.

In part, the issue will be less of a problem to the extent that members of different cultural groups develop ways of using both research approaches in the service of their own communities' agendas. As we have noted more than once, research in either tradition can be used oppressively. There is truth, however, in the cliché that knowledge is power, and there are certainly examples of culturally disadvantaged groups that are doing good research studies to further their legitimate aims.

---

quantitative approach seeks to answer research questions that ask about quantity, such as:

- Are women more depressed than men?
- Does low income predict one's level of self-concept?
- Does the use of child sexual abuse investigation teams reduce the number of times an alleged victim is questioned by professionals?
- Is degree of aggression related to severity of crimes committed among inmates?

A qualitative research approach, on the other hand, aims to answer research questions that provide you with a more comprehensive understanding of a social problem from an intensive study of a few people. This approach is usually conducted within the context of the research participants' natural environments (Rubin & Babbie, 1997). Research questions that would be relevant to the qualitative research approach might include:

- How do women experience depression as compared to men?

- How do individuals with low income define their self-concept?
- How do professionals on child sexual abuse investigation teams work together to make decisions?
- How do federal inmates describe their own aggression in relation to the crimes they have committed?

As you will see throughout this book, not only can both approaches be used to study the same social problem, but also they both can be used to study the same research question. Whichever approach is used clearly has an impact on the type of findings produced to answer a research question (or to test a hypothesis).

USING BOTH APPROACHES IN A SINGLE STUDY

Given the seemingly contradictory philosophical beliefs associated with the two research approaches, it is difficult to imagine how they could exist together in a single research study. As is stands, most research studies incorporate only one approach. The reason may, in part, relate to philosophy, but practical considerations of cost, time, and resources are also factors.

It is not unusual, however, to see quantitative data used within a qualitative study or qualitative data in a quantitative study. Just think that, if you were to use a quantitative approach, there is no reason why you could not ask research participants a few open-ended questions to allow them to more fully explain their experiences. In this instance, your quantitative research report would contain some pieces of qualitative data to help bring meaning to the study's quantitative findings.

Let's say you want to proceed with a qualitative research study to examine your research question about discrimination within the public social service system. Surely, you would want to identify how many research participants were included, as well as important defining characteristics such as their average age, the number who had difficulty accessing social services, or the number who were satisfied with the services they received.

While it is possible to incorporate qualitative research activity into a quantitative study (and quantitative research activity into a qualitative study) the approach you finally select must be guided by your purpose for conducting the study in the first place. Ultimately, all research studies are about the pursuit of knowledge. Just what kind of knowledge you are after is up to you.

WHAT DO YOU REALLY WANT TO KNOW?

As mentioned previously, both research approaches have their advantages and disadvantages, and both shine in different phases within the research method. Which approach you select for a particular study depends not on whether you are a positivist or an interpretivist but on what particular research question your study is trying to answer. Are you looking for descriptions or explanations? If the former, a qualitative study will be spot on; if the latter, a quantitative one will do the trick.

Human nature being what it is, we are always looking, in the end, for explanation. We want to know not only what reality is like but also what its interconnections are and what we can do to change it to make our lives more comfortable and safer. However, first things first. Description comes before explanation. Before you can know whether poverty is related to child abuse, for example, you must be able to describe both poverty and child abuse as fully as possible. Similarly, if you want to know whether low self-esteem in women contributes to spousal abuse, you must know what self-esteem is and what constitutes spousal abuse.

By now, because you are a social worker interested in people and not numbers, you may be ready to throw the whole quantitative research approach out the window. But let's be sure that you don't throw the baby out with the bath water. Social work values dictate that you make room for different approaches to knowledge development, different opinions, differing views on what reality really is. Believe us, the two different approaches each have value in their own way, depending on what kind of data (quantitative and/or qualitative) you hope to gain from a particular research study.

Example of Using Both Approaches in a Single Study

Suppose, for example, you have an assumption that caesarian operations are being conducted too often and unnecessarily for the convenience of obstetricians rather than for the benefit of mothers and their babies. In order to confirm or refute this hunch (it has yet to be proven), you would need data on the number of caesarian births in a particular time frame and on how many of them were justified on the basis of medical need. Numbers would be required—quantitative data. The questions about how many and how often could not be answered solely by descriptions of Ms. Smith's individual experiences.

On the other hand, Ms. Smith's experiences would certainly lend richness to the part of your study that asked how far the hospital's services took the well-being of mothers into account. Many of the best research studies use quantitative and qualitative methods within the same study. It is important to remember that the former provide the necessary numerical data, while the latter provide the human depth that allows for a richer understanding of the numbers in their particular context.

Sometimes, therefore, depending on the research question (assumption) to be answered, Ms. Smith will be seen as no more than a number. At other times, her individuality will be of paramount importance. If she is seen as a number, for example, her role will be passive. She will be one of a large number of persons. On the other hand, if she is seen as an individual, her part in the research method will be far more active. It is *her* reality that you are now exploring. She will be front and center in a research method that is driven by her and not the researcher. Even the language will change. She

is no longer a subject—or possibly an object—but a full and equal *participant*, along with the researcher.

SUMMARY

This chapter briefly discussed the qualitative research approach to knowledge building. We also highlighted a few differences and similarities between the two research approaches. These two complementary and respected research approaches are divergent in terms of their philosophical principles. Yet, they both share the following processes: choosing a general research topic, focusing the topic into a research question, designing the research study, collecting the data, analyzing and interpreting the data, and writing the report.

Gender, Ethnicity, and Race Matters

7

Antoinette Y. Rodgers-Farmer

Miriam Potocky-Tripodi

As we enter the 21st century, it is increasingly important that social workers become more competent in conducting research studies with culturally diverse populations, women, gays, and lesbians. The need to become more competent is dictated by the realization that traditional research paradigms, research methods, and data analytic strategies might not be appropriate for enhancing our understanding about the complex challenges that these populations face.

The aim of this chapter is to enhance the reader's awareness of the need to consider the issues of gender, ethnicity, and race in the planning and conduct of research studies. Using the phases of the research process as a conceptual framework presented in Chapter 1, this chapter examines how issues related to gender, ethnicity, and race can be incorporated into each phase of the research process. Before discussing each of these phases, however, the research paradigms that have influenced the research methodologies that we use are explored.

RESEARCH PARADIGMS

As we have seen in Chapters 1–6, social work research has historically been conducted from a positivist perspective, which can be succinctly summarized as follows (Chambers, Wedel, & Rodwell, 1992):

> There is a single tangible reality out there, independent of any observer and operating in a lawlike fashion. It is fragmentable into independent variables and processes, any of which can be studied independently of the others. From this position, the goal of social inquiry is to find the regularities and relationships, converging on reality until, finally, it can be predicted and controlled. This is possible because, in principle, it is always possible to discover the causes of social phenomena. (279)

Critics of this perspective argue that, having been developed by European men, it ignores the worldviews of women and persons from non-Western cultures. There is nothing in the positivist perspective that pro-

hibits one from examining issues related to gender, ethnicity, and race. However, it has been suggested that this perspective allows us to examine these issues only in a limited matter. For example, Barton (1998, p. 286) states that the positivist perspective merely allows us to examine the issues of gender, ethnicity, and race as "parameters to include in multivariate model specification."

Numerous alternatives to the positivist perspective have been suggested including the feminist, ecological, and empowerment perspectives. The feminist approach to research aims to "develop versions of reality that more accurately reflect the experience of women, versions that affirm women's strengths and value and can transform society itself" (Davis, 1994, p. 65). This approach is based on the assumption that the worldviews of women and other oppressed people are fundamentally different from those of the people in power. Feminist research emphasizes documenting the everyday lives of women so as to make their perspective visible (Swigonski, 1994).

The ecological perspective is embodied in constructivist research, which holds that reality can be understood accurately only in the context of the total person-in-environment situation. Like feminism, constructivism holds that there are multiple viewpoints among the people who live in a common environment. That is, there is not one single truth; rather, there are many truths. The aim of the constructivist approach is to articulate these differing viewpoints and, sometimes, to "co-construct" a mutually acceptable view of reality among the different participants in an environment (including research participants, researchers, and other stakeholders) so as to address social problems (Rodwell, 1998).

Finally, the empowerment perspective is embodied in participatory action research, which aims to enlist research participants as "co-researchers" who participate in defining the research questions, establishing methodology, and interpreting and applying the results. The purpose of participatory action research ultimately is social action on behalf of the population that is the focus of the study. By participating in all phases of the research process, the members of the population are able to influence the resultant social action and, thereby, are empowered (McNicoll, 1999).

The feminist, ecological, and empowerment research perspectives overlap in many ways. All aim to document the viewpoints of oppressed people with the ultimate goal of lessening their oppression. Researchers within each perspective often have advocated the use of qualitative methods (Chapter 6) as being more appropriate than quantitative methods (Chapter 5) to achieve the desired ends (Davis, 1994; Rodwell, 1998). Although some of us may argue that the two approaches are fundamentally incompatible with one another, many of us see the value in combining both approaches so as to achieve a greater understanding of the problem under investigation and greater relevancy of the study's findings (Padgett, 1998; Tutty, Rothery, & Grinnell, 1996).

PHASES OF THE RESEARCH PROCESS

This section highlights the seven major phases of the research process and pays particular attention to gender, ethnicity, and race issues within each phase: (1) problem formulation, (2) population definition, (3) research design, (4) data analysis, (5) data interpretation, and (6) reporting the results.

Problem Formulation

The formulation of the research problem is the initial phase in the research process. By the very name of this phase, it is implied that the researcher is operating from a "deficiency model." That is, the research questions or hypotheses may be stated in such a way as to focus on "problems" of minority groups (often in relation to the dominant group), rather than focusing on their strengths and resiliencies. For example, a research question addressing why there is a higher incidence of low-birth weight newborns in ethnic minority populations as compared to the white populations would focus on strengths.

In formulating the research problem, the researcher may be using his or her own experiences or interests and the findings of previous research studies (Hughes, Seidman, & Williams, 1993). Using these methods may lead to formulation of the "wrong problem" or errors in "conceptualization of the problem"

(Seidman, 1978). One way to avoid these errors in conceptualization of the problem is to have the participants define the research question.

Another issue that may arise in the problem formulation phase is that of sexism in research concepts. This occurs when behaviors, attributes, and/or traits are conceptualized as applying to only one gender when, in fact, they may be present in members of both genders (Eichler, 1988). For example, throughout the 1980s, the official AIDS definition was based on the symptoms typically observed in men with the disease. Women with AIDS do not present many of the same symptoms. As a result, these women were not diagnosed with AIDS and, therefore, were largely excluded from much of the research on the disease (Rosser, 1991).

Population Definition

When defining the population under investigation, one must carefully consider whose definition one plans to use—the U.S. Bureau of the Census's categorical definition or the person's self-definition. The choice has implications for the generalizability of the study's results. For example, research studies on black ethnic identity consistently has shown that "Blacks are not a monolithic group and that how individual Blacks see themselves, see other Blacks, and view non-Blacks reflects the extent to which they identify with their Blackness" (Thomas, Phillips, & Brown, 1998, p. 77).

Ignoring the fact that African Americans, Hispanics, and other ethnic groups are not monolithic has resulted in the continuation of culturally encapsulated research, which assumes that all persons within the group share the same norms and values and that they use and define concepts in the same manner (Pedersen, 1988). Such research results in overgeneralization of the findings obtained and ignores the diversity within the groups.

Research Design

During the past 18 years, the use of between-group designs to examine the differences between majority and minority groups has come under scrutiny (Phinney & Landin, 1998). Critics state that these designs focus on showing the differences between European Americans and African Americans, usually from a deficit perspective (Howard & Scott, 1981) and do not attempt to adequately explain why the differences found occurred (Hughes et al., 1993). On the other hand, supporters of the use of between-group designs (e.g., Azibo, 1992; Phinney & Landin, 1998) believe that these designs are helpful in demonstrating how cultural characteristics are related to different outcomes among various groups.

Within-group research designs also have been criticized. These designs have been criticized for their lack of generalizability. Despite this criticism, Hughes et al. (1993, p. 696) believe that these designs are appropriate when (1) the design question is solely oriented toward a within-culture understanding, (2) conceptual equivalence across cultures is not possible, or (3) conceptual equivalence exists, but measurement equivalence is not possible to achieve.

During this phase of the research process, the researcher should be concerned with three issues: (1) gaining access to the population of interest, (2) deciding who should collect the data, and (3) determining how the data should be collected (e.g., surveys, direct observations).

Gaining Access to the Population of Interest

Gaining access to the population of interest might be the most challenging phase of the data collection phase because of the historical relationship between the research community and the population of interest. It frequently has been the case that the exchange between researchers and research "subjects" has been one-way, benefiting only the researchers and exploiting the participants. To address this injustice, a social action model of research recently has been promoted that involves the research participants as co-investigators throughout the research process (Wagner, 1991). To start this active process, Becerra and Zambrana (1985) suggest several strategies for engaging members of minority communities. These include gaining the sponsorship of a well-known ethnic community social service program, explaining the purpose of the research to a variety of

appropriate community groups, and training indigenous personnel to participate as interviewers or in some other staff capacity.

Who Should Collect the Data

Some experts in the field of multicultural research argue that the researcher must be of the same ethnic/racial background as those being studied. Marin and Marin (1991) state that ethnic matching of the interviewer and the interviewee enhances the validity of responses to sensitive questions. On the other hand, Becerra (1997) argues that ethnic matching of the interviewer and the interviewer may result in biased responses. Furthermore, the use of ethnic matching of the interviewer and the interviewee may ignore other important variables that have implications for data collection, such as the trustworthiness of the interviewer and the interviewer's awareness of biases about the group under study.

Gender matching of the interviewer and the interviewee also must be considered when deciding who should collect the data. In a recent study that examined the effects of interviewer gender on mental health interviews, Pollner (1998) found that both male and female respondents interviewed by women reported more symptoms of depression, substance abuse, and conduct disorders than did respondents interviewed by men. He attributes his findings to women's creating a more conductive atmosphere for disclosure.

Because gender, ethnicity, and race of the interviewer have implications for the quality of the data obtained, we suggest that one should have a standardized procedure for training all interviewers. Once these interviewers have been trained, periodic retraining on the administration of the survey instrument also should be done to ensure that the interviewers still are administering the survey properly. The effects of gender, ethnicity, and race on the dependent variable also can be examined statistically once the data have been collected. One way in which to do this is to conduct a t-test or analysis of variance using gender, ethnicity, or race of the interviewer as the grouping variable. If it is detected that any of these variables had an effect on the dependent variable, then one should address this issue in the discussion section of the article with an emphasis on its implications for the findings obtained.

How the Data Should Be Collected

Data may be collected via standardized measures (Chapter 9), interviews (Chapter 16), direct observations (Chapters 14 and 15), or other methods. In conducting research with minority participants, however, it is critical that the researcher use measures that are culturally appropriate. The reason for this is that it is well documented that many assessment tools are biased against minority clients (Sue & Sue, 1990) because they have been normed on white middle-class respondents. Even though these measures are valid and reliable for that population, they might not be valid and reliable for minority participants (Hughes et al., 1993). Similar concerns have been raised about using measures normed in Western cultural settings with persons who are not from a Western culture (Ortega & Richey, 1998).

When conducting research studies with persons whose language is not English, the researcher is faced with the problem of trying to establish various types of equivalence, such as linguistic, semantic, and metric equivalence. Linguistic equivalence can be established by translating the instrument from English to the language of the respondents. Back-translation also is used to establish linguistic equivalence. For a detailed description of this procedure, see Brislin (1970). Semantic equivalence can be established after the measure has been translated or back-translated by determining whether the meaning of each item is congruent with the respondents' understanding of the phenomenon. Metric equivalence can be established by comparing the factor structure of the translated measure to the factor structure of the original measure. According to Burnett (1998), metric equivalence is used to determine whether the "observed indicators have the same relationships with the theoretical constructs across different cultures" (p. 77).

The need to establish metric equivalence also is important when conducting research studies with men and women. In examining the factor structure of the Beck Depression Inventory-II, Dozois, Dobson, and Ahnberg (1998) found that Factor 2 for Women (Somatic-Vegetative) represented Factor 1 for men and that Factor 1 for Women (Cognitive-Affective) represented Factor 2 for men. They also found differences in factor loadings. For example, they found that punishment feelings loaded on the Cognitive-Affective factor for women and on the Somatic-Vegetative factor for Men.

Data Analysis

Because most measures have been normed on white middle-class respondents, it is recommended that these measures be assessed for their psychometric adequacy when using them with minority populations (van de Vijver & Leung, 1997). Assessing these measures for their psychometric adequacy involves computing the reliability and the item statistics (e.g., item-total correlations, item means, item variances) and determining their construct validity. The item statistic can be used to determine whether there is a ceiling or floor effect (van de Vijver & Leung, 1997), whereas confirmatory factor analysis can be used to assess construct validity. For example, confirmatory factor analysis has been widely used for assessing the construct validity of the Center for Epidemiologic Studies Depression Scale for use in cross-cultural research (Ortega & Richey, 1998).

After determining the reliability and validity of the measure, one is faced with the challenge of deciding how the construct of ethnicity or race should be used in the data analysis. In examining the literature on adolescent development, for example, Steinberg and Fletcher (1998) found that ethnicity or race has been used in data analyses as a grouping variable, as a control variable, as a dynamic process, and as a moderator variable. Using ethnicity or race in any of the just-mentioned ways is not without its problems, both methodological and statistical.

For example, using ethnicity or race as a grouping variable may result in overlooking important demographic variables that covary with ethnicity or race and that may account for the findings obtained. In other words, using ethnicity or race as a grouping variable may lead one to wrongly conclude that there are ethnic or racial differences when none exists. For a more detailed description about the methodological issues related to the use of ethnicity or race as a control variable, as a dynamic process, and as a moderator variable, see Steinberg and Fletcher (1998).

In addition to dealing with the issue of ethnicity or race in the data analysis, one also has to deal with the issue of gender. Eichler (1988) notes that when it comes to dealing with the issue of gender in the data analysis, one usually does not analyze the data separately for men and for women. Therefore, the results of these analyses cannot be generalized to either group alone. To make the results generalizable, it is important that separate analyses be done for both men and women.

Data Interpretation

One of the hazards at this phase of the research process—data interpretation—is that of overgeneralization (Eichler, 1988). Data collected from one gender or one ethnic or racial group should not be generalized to apply to all persons. Another potential pitfall is in interpreting observed differences between diverse groups as indicative of "problems" or "deficiencies" in the minority members when, in fact, they are simply that—differences—and in many cases could be seen as strengths. For example, if ethnic minority or gay males were found to have elevated scores on the paranoia scale of the Minnesota Multiphasic Personality Inventory (MMPI), it would be erroneous to interpret this as indicative of psychopathology when, in fact, it is more likely indicative of a healthy survival skill in response to a hostile society (Sue & Sue, 1990).

Reporting the Results

In accordance with the social action model of research, study results and their implications should be shared with the research participants. Ideally, the results should be immediately usable by the community rather than having implications only for the future or for persons outside the community. Feedback from the research participants should be solicited to identify strengths and problems of the study and to suggest future directions. As a further component of the action research model, results should be used to influence policy and other activity at the macro level (Wagner, 1991).

SUMMARY

In this chapter, we have highlighted some of the issues that researchers must consider when conducting research studies with diverse populations, women, and gays and lesbians. With increased attention to these issues, we will begin to develop a body of knowledge that will help us to better understand the complex challenges that these populations face.

PART **III**

Measurement

· ·

Part III consists of three chapters that discuss

why we need to measure variables in social work

research. More specifically, Chapter 8 discusses

how validity and reliability are relevant to the

research process. Chapter 9 presents how to select

an existing measuring instrument to measure a

variable, and the final chapter discusses how to

design a measuring instrument if an existing one

cannot be found in the literature.

Gerald J. Bostwick, Jr.

Nancy S. Kyte

Measurement

8

This is the first chapter of this text that deals with the measurement of variables. At this point, it is assumed the reader will have read the previous chapters and has an appreciation of how both research approaches can be used to develop knowledge for our profession. As we have seen, both research approaches require measuring something or another, usually referred to as variables. Thus, this chapter provides a brief discussion of how variables can be measured, in addition to discussing the validity and reliability of the measurements used.

Measurement is a pervasive part of daily living. Our morning routine, for example, may include stepping on a scale, adjusting the water for a shower, and making breakfast. Not much thought needs to be given to these activities, but measurements are being taken of weight, water temperature, and food portions. The scale, a heat-sensitive finger, and a measuring cup or spoon are all measuring instruments.

What distinguishes this type of measurement from that engaged in by social workers is the nature of the measuring procedures used. For us, measurement is a systematic process that involves the assignment of symbols to properties of objects according to specified rules. These rules are designed to increase the probability that the world of concepts corresponds accurately to the world of reality.

The development of measurement procedures is an intricate process in the physical sciences, but it is even more complex in the social sciences. In physics, for example, measurement is concerned largely with such fundamental variables as weight, length, time, density, volume, and velocity. In social work, our interest is primarily in psychosocial variables such as racial conflict, social status, aggression, and group cohesion. We focus on the properties of individuals, families, groups, communities, and institutions, for which accurate measurement is always problematic.

DEFINITIONS AND FUNCTIONS OF MEASUREMENT

This chapter adopts a broad definition of measurement as the assignment of numerals to the properties or attributes of objects or events, according to rules.

Another way to understand measurement is in terms of the functions it serves.

Because the assignment of numerals carries a quantitative meaning, the terms "measurement" and "quantification" have often been used as if they were interchangeable. Recent efforts to develop a less restrictive view of measurement have produced broader definitions with less emphasis on quantification. These definitions have included the assignment of symbols to observations, the assignment of quantitative or qualitative values to attributes, and the assignment of numerals to either quantitative or qualitative response categories.

Common Characteristics of Measurement Definitions

Whether or not qualitative as well as quantitative components are included in these definitions, they all have in common three interrelated characteristics. First is the assignment of numerals (e.g., 1, 2, 3) or symbols (e.g., A, B, C), which are basically synonymous. When a numeral is used to identify something, it has no intrinsic quantitative meaning and is nothing more than a label. Thus, the numeral 1 is simply a symbol of a special kind, like a + is used to refer to addition or a $ used to refer to money. The letter A could be used just as easily. Measurement, however, has traditionally used numerals, which become numbers after they are assigned a quantitative meaning.

The second common characteristic of measurement definitions is that numerals or symbols are assigned to properties of objects rather than to the objects themselves. Put another way, objects are not measured per se; rather, their properties or characteristics are measured. To be even more precise, indicants of these properties are measured. This is important when measuring a complex concept where direct observation is impossible. Hostility, depression, and intelligence, for example, are concepts that cannot be directly observed. These properties must always be inferred from observations of their presumed variables (or indicants), such as fighting or crying.

The third characteristic is that numerals or symbols are assigned to (indicants of) properties of objects according to specified rules. The importance of these rules, often referred to as rules of correspondence or assignment, cannot be overemphasized (Kaplan, 1964). Measurement is a game played with objects and numerals. Games have rules, and rules can be good or bad. Other things being equal, good rules lead to good measurement, and bad rules lead to bad measurement. At its most basic level, then, a rule is a guide, method, or command that says what to do (Kerlinger, 1986).

Suppose a client is asked to identify five possible solutions to a problem and then rank-order them according to some criterion, such as probable effectiveness. A rule may be formulated that states that the range of numerals (1–5) should be assigned in such a manner that the highest (5) represents the solution the client judges to be the most effective and the lowest (1) represents the least effective solution. This rule clearly tells how to assign the range of numerals to the domain of problem-solving options that the client has identified.

While a definition of measurement stipulates the formulation of and adherence to rules, it does not restrict the kind of rules that can be used. Rules may be developed deductively, be based on previous experience, stem from common sense, or be pure hunches. Whatever the origin of the rules, the utility of any measure is contingent on its ability to explain adequately the variable being studied. Therefore, no measurement procedure is any better than its rules.

In summary, any endeavor that attempts to assign numerals or symbols to (indicants of) properties of objects according to specified rules qualifies as measurement, and measurement of anything is theoretically possible if rules can be set up on some rational or empirical basis. Whether that measurement is good or bad will depend on the formulation of clear, unambiguous rules of correspondence that can themselves be empirically tested.

Functions of Measurement

Measurement is not an end in itself. We can appreciate its usefulness only if we know what it is intended to do and what role and function it has in our profession. Its functions include correspondence, objectivity and standardization, quantification on different levels, and replication and communication.

Correspondence

Measurement theory calls for the application of rules and procedures to increase the correspondence between the real world and the world of concepts. The real world provides us with empirical evidence; the world of concepts provides us with a theoretical model for making sense out of that segment of the real world that we are trying to explain or predict. It is through measurement's rules of correspondence that this theoretical model can be connected with the world of reality.

Objectivity and Standardization

Measurement helps take some of the guesswork out of scientific observation; the observations are considerably more objective than, for example, personal judgments. The scientific principle that any statement of fact made by one person should be independently verifiable by another is violated if there is room for disagreement about observations of empirical events.

In the absence of a standardized measurement of narcissism, for instance, two social workers may disagree strongly about how narcissistic a particular client is. Obviously, then, we would find it impossible to make any empirical test of hypotheses derived from theories of narcissism. This, unfortunately, is frequently the case. We have myriad theories at our disposal, but because these theories often involve variables that cannot be adequately measured, the hypotheses they generate must remain untested. Thus, additions to our knowledge base depend on the extent to which it becomes possible to measure certain variables and theoretical constructs accurately.

Quantification

By allowing for the quantification of data, measurement increases not only the objectivity of our observations but also our ability to describe them precisely. Different types or levels of measurement result in different types of data. Classification, for example, makes it possible to categorize variables such as gender and religion into subclasses such as male-female and Protestant-Catholic-Jewish.

A second, higher level of measurement makes it possible not only to define differences between and among variable subclasses but also to determine greater-than and less-than relationships. Thus, a particular variable might be classified not only as occurring or not occurring but also as never, rarely, sometimes, often, or always occurring.

An even higher level makes it possible to rank-order certain variable characteristics and to specify the exact distances between the variable subclasses. This makes it possible to say that a family with an income of $13,000 has $5,000 more than a family with an income of $8,000, or a social service agency that employs 20 social workers has a professional staff that is twice as large as that of an agency that employs 10 social workers.

Each type of measurement provides important data that enable us to describe physical, psychological, or social phenomena empirically. The precision of the measurement increases as it moves from the lower (less sophisticated and refined) to the higher levels.

A related advantage of measurement is that it permits the use of powerful methods of statistical analysis. Once numbers are assigned, information can be analyzed with statistical techniques (Weinbach & Grinnell, 2004). Suppose we are conducting a study to determine what characteristics differentiate clients who continue in family therapy from those who drop out. We collect data from a variety of sources, such as clients, social workers, and independent judges, using questionnaires, in-person interviews, case records, and tape recordings of family therapy sessions. We must then be able to make some sense out of all these data in order to explain what is going on and why. The variables studied must be quantified, or reduced to numerical form so that our data can be analyzed with statistical techniques and the formulated hypotheses can be tested.

As seen throughout this text, when a hypothesis is supported in social work practice or research, the theory or theories from which it was derived are also supported, at least tentatively. Supporting a theory is tantamount to endorsing the explanations it provides for why certain events occur as they do. Measurement, therefore, facilitates the ability to discover and establish relationships among variables. When numbers are properly applied, the full range of mathematics can be used in constructing and testing theories aimed at explaining or predicting the phenomena of the real world.

Replication and Communication

The research process is concerned not only with conducting tests of theories but also with replicating and communicating the results. The more objective and precise the measurement procedures used in a particular study, the easier it will be for others to replicate the study and thereby to confirm or refute the results obtained. And the more rigorously measurement procedures have been specified, the greater the potential for increasing the effective communication of the study's findings.

MEASUREMENT VALIDITY AND RELIABILITY

The two most important considerations in choosing a measuring instrument are the validity and reliability of the instrument and, as a consequence, the validity and reliability of the data it generates. Where these two concepts have been referred to in preceding chapters, they have been identified only briefly and in simple terms. Validity has been described as the degree to which an instrument measures what it is supposed to, and reliability has been described as the degree of accuracy or precision of a measuring instrument.

The next three sections explore the meanings of validity and reliability in measurement more precisely. If we do not know how valid and reliable our measures are, we can put little faith in the results they obtain or the conclusions that are drawn from those results. In short, we cannot be sure of what we have measured.

VALIDITY OF MEASURING INSTRUMENTS

A measuring instrument is valid when it does what it is intended to do (Cronbach, 1970). To put it another way, valid measuring instruments measure what they are supposed to measure and yield scores whose differences reflect the true differences in the variable they are measuring.

An instrument such as a self-administered questionnaire, achievement test, personality inventory, or problem checklist is valid to the extent that it actually measures what it is meant to measure. An instrument that measures a variable such as dominance is valid only to the degree that it truly measures this trait—dominance. If the instrument actually measures some other variable, such as sociability, it is not a valid measure of dominance, but it may be a valid measure of sociability.

The definition of measurement validity has two parts: the extent to which an instrument actually measures the variable in question and the extent to which it measures that variable accurately. While it is possible to have the first without the second, the second cannot exist without the first. That is, a variable cannot be measured accurately if some other variable is being measured instead.

To establish the validity of a measuring instrument, therefore, we must think in terms not of its validity but rather of its validities. Validity refers broadly to the degree to which an instrument is doing what it is intended to do—and an instrument may have several purposes that vary in number, kind, and scope.

The various kinds of validity—content, criterion, and construct—relate to the different purposes of measurement. Each type has a specific purpose that dictates the type of evidence (logical or statistical) that is needed to demonstrate that the instrument is valid. The three types of validity (and face validity, a subtype) are listed in Table 8.1, along with the questions of validity each one can address.

Content Validity

Content validity is concerned with the representativeness or sampling adequacy of the content of the measuring instrument, such as the items or questions it contains. The instrument must provide an adequate sample of items (or questions) that represent the variables of interest, and it must measure the variable it is assumed to be measuring.

All variables being measured, therefore, must produce operational definitions (Nunnally, 1975). Moreover, the data gathered to measure the variables must be directly relevant and meaningful to these variables. If the properties of the measured variables are not all equally represented in the measuring instrument, a biased sample of responses will result, and the data will be meaningless and therefore useless.

Suppose, for example, we want to construct an instrument to measure students' general social work knowledge. The variable of general social work knowledge is operationally defined as including the following properties: knowledge about social welfare policy, social work research, casework, group work, and community organization. Before administering the instrument, several colleagues who are experts in these fields are

---

TABLE 8.1

Types of Measurement Validity and Questions Addressed by Each

Type	Question Addressed
Content Validity	Does the measuring instrument adequately measure the major dimensions of the variable under consideration?
(Face Validity)	Does the measuring instrument appear to measure the subject matter under consideration?
Criterion Validity	Does the individual's measuring instrument score predict the probable behavior on a second variable (criterion-related measure)?
Construct Validity	Does the measuring instrument appear to measure the general construct (element) it purports to measure?

asked to evaluate the instrument's contents—that is, to determine its content validity.

The community organization expert points out that no mention is made of several important functions of community organization, and the group work expert advises that there are no questions dealing with group cohesion and the normal phases of group development. Does the instrument have content validity? No, because its intended purpose—to measure general social work knowledge—will not be achieved.

Assuming that the other areas of the instrument are judged to be adequate, could the obtained data be used to validly determine a student's knowledge about casework, social work research, and social welfare policy? Here the answer is yes. Although there would be no justification for using the instrument to determine general social work knowledge, it could be used to assess knowledge about these three areas. Thus the instrument is content valid for one purpose but not for another.

Content validation is, by and large, a judgmental process; the colleagues asked to assess the instrument were also being asked to use their judgments to establish content validity. It may be assessed in the same instrument as high by one person but low by another. But if we had not asked for the judgments of colleagues or consulted with experts in each of the major areas of social work, the questions on the instrument might not have been representative of general social work knowledge. The resultant interpretations would have been open to question, to say the least.

Content validity also requires (at least in principle) specification of the universe of questions from which the instrument's questions are to be drawn. That is, the instrument must contain a logical sampling of questions from the entire universe of questions that are presumed to reflect the variable being measured. Further, the sampling of questions must correspond with the universe of questions in some consistent fashion. This is no easy task. There may be no consensus about the definition of the variable to be measured, and it may be difficult to identify the universe of questions. The potential number of representative questions to be included in the measuring instrument could approach infinity, particularly in measuring variables that are complex and multidimensional in nature.

The personal judgment of the person constructing the instrument determines how a variable is to be defined, how the universe of questions is to be identified, and how the sample of representative questions from that universe is to be drawn. Thus, the general content validity of any instrument rests to a large extent on the skill and the judgment of the person who constructs it. If poor judgment has been used—and this is always a possibility—the instrument is likely to have little, or no, content validity.

Face Validity

The terms "face validity" and "content validity" are often used interchangeably in the professional literature, but they are incorrectly thought of as synonymous. Technically, face validity is not a form of validation because it refers to what an instrument "appears to" measure rather than what it "actually" measures (that is, it appears relevant to those who will complete or administer it). Nevertheless, face validity is a desirable characteristic for a measuring instrument. Without it, there may be resistance on the part of respondents, and this can adversely affect the results obtained. Consequently, it is important to structure an instrument so that it not only accurately measures the variables under consideration (content validity) but also appears to be a relevant measure of those variables (face validity).

To assess the effects of a communication skills training course offered at a school of social work, for example, an assessment form is to be administered to each student at the beginning and the end of the course. A search of the literature locates a standardized instrument that measures the types of skills the course is designed to teach.

This instrument, however, was originally developed for use with upper- and middle-management personnel. If our students were presented with items reflecting the business world, they might well question how their responses could tell anything about how they work with clients. The items should be rephrased to reflect social work situations in order to increase the face validity of the instrument.

Criterion Validity

Criterion validity, which involves multiple measurement, is established by comparing scores of the measuring instrument with an external criterion known (or believed) to measure the variable being measured. Thus, there must be one or more external, or independent, criterion with which to compare the scores of the instrument.

In order to validate an instrument that has been constructed to predict our students' success in a BSW program, for example, the measuring instrument is administered to students entering their first semester. These test scores are then compared with their subsequent grade point averages. Here, the external criterion is grade point average. Other potential external criteria might be individual or combined ratings of academic and field practicum performance and graduation from the program.

The external criterion used, of course, should itself be reasonably valid and reliable. If a criterion that is inaccurate or undependable is chosen, the instrument itself will not be validated adequately. Unfortunately, valid and reliable criteria may not exist or may not have been thoroughly tested. In such a case, the one that seems most adequate (keeping in mind its limitations) should be chosen, supplemented, if possible, with other relevant criteria. The nature of the predictions and the techniques available for checking out criteria generally determine which ones are relevant.

Concurrent and Predictive Validity

Criterion validity may be classified as concurrent or predictive. Concurrent validity refers to the ability of a measuring instrument to predict accurately an individual's *current* status. An example of an instrument with concurrent validity is a psychopathology scale that is capable of distinguishing between adolescents who are *currently* in need of psychiatric treatment and those who are not.

Predictive validity denotes an instrument's ability to predict *future* performance or status from present performance or status. An instrument has predictive validity if it can distinguish between individuals who will *differ at some point in the future.* A psychopathology scale with predictive validity must be capable of differentiating not only those adolescents who need psychiatric treatment but those who will need it one year from now.

Both concurrent and predictive validity are concerned with prediction, and both make use of some external criterion that is purportedly a valid and reliable measure of the variable being studied. What differentiates the two is time. Concurrent validity predicts *current* performance or status, while predictive validity predicts *future* performance or status. Moreover, concurrent validity involves administering an instrument and comparing its scores with an external criterion at approximately the same time, or concurrently. In contrast, predictive validity entails comparative measurement at two different (present and future) points in time.

The major concern of criterion validity, however, is not whether an instrument is valid for concurrent or future discriminations. Rather, the concern is with the use of a second measure as an independent criterion to check the validity of the first measure.

Construct Validity

What sets construct validity apart from content and criterion validity is its preoccupation with theory, explanatory constructs, and the testing of hypothesized relationships between and among variables. Construct validity is difficult to understand because it involves determining the degree to which an instrument successfully measures a theoretical concept. The difficulty derives in part from the abstract nature of concepts.

A concept is a characteristic or trait that does not exist as an isolated, observable dimension of behavior. It cannot be seen, felt, or heard, and it cannot be measured directly—its existence must be inferred from the evidence at hand. Thus, the concept "hostility" may be inferred from observations of presumably hostile or aggressive acts; the concept "anxiety" may be inferred from test scores, galvanic skin responses, observations of anxious behaviors, and so on. Other typical concepts of concern to us are motivation, social class, delinquency, prejudice, and organizational conflict.

Construct validity is evaluated by determining the degree to which certain explanatory concepts account for variance, or individual differences, in the scores of an instrument. Put another way, it is concerned with the meaning of the instrument—that is, what it is measuring and how and why it operates the way it does. To assess the construct validity of the Rorschach inkblot test, for example, we would try to determine the factors, or concepts, that account for differences in responses on the test. Attempts might be made to determine if the test measures emotional stability, sociability, or self-control and whether it also measures aggressiveness. The question would be: What proportion of the total test variance is accounted for by the concepts of emotional stability, sociability, self-control, and aggressiveness?

With construct validity, there is usually more interest in the property, or concept, being measured than in the instrument itself. Thus, it involves validation not only of the instrument but also of the theory underlying it. To establish construct validity, the meaning of the concept must be understood, and the propositions the theory makes about the relationships between this and other concepts must be identified. We try to discover what predictions can be made on the basis of these propositions and whether the measurements obtained from the instrument will be consistent with those predictions. If the predictions are not supported, there is no clear-cut guide as to whether the shortcoming is in the instrument or in the theory.

Suppose a study is conducted to test the hypothesis that self-referred clients are more likely to have favorable attitudes toward treatment than those who come to the agency on some other basis. If the findings do not support the predicted relationship between self-referral and attitude toward treatment, should it be concluded that the measure is not valid or that the hypothesis is incorrect? In such a situation, the concept of attitude toward treatment and the network of propositions that led to this prediction should be reexamined.

Then the concept might be refined with more detailed hypotheses about its relationship to other concepts, and changes might be made in the instrument.

Construct validation makes use of data from a variety of sources. It is a painstaking building process much like theory construction—an attempt to ferret out the dimensions that an instrument is tapping and thereby to validate the theory underlying the instrument. This can be accomplished through a three-step process: (1) suggesting what concepts might account for performance on an instrument, (2) deriving hypotheses from the theory surrounding the concepts, and (3) testing these hypotheses empirically (Cronbach, 1970). The testing of the hypotheses can involve many procedures, including convergent-discriminant validation and factor analysis.

Convergent-Discriminant Validation

Convergent validity means that different measures of a concept yield similar results (i.e., they converge). Put another way, evidence gathered from different sources and in different ways leads to the same (or a similar) measure of the concept. If two different instruments, each alleging to measure the same concept, are administered to a group of people, similar responses or scores should be found on both instruments. And if one instrument is administered to groups of people in two different states, it should yield similar results in both groups. If it does not, the theory underlying the concept being measured should be able to explain why.

Discriminant validity means that a concept can be empirically differentiated (i.e., discriminated) from other concepts. The test is to see if an instrument is (or is not) related to other concepts from which, according to theory, it should differ. If it can be shown that an instrument measures a concept in the same way other instruments measure it, and that it is not related to any other concepts from which it should theoretically differ, it has both convergent and discriminant validity.

Factor Analysis

Another powerful method for determining construct validity is factor analysis, a statistical procedure in which a large number of questions or instruments (called factors) is reduced to a smaller number. The procedure is used to discover which factors go together (i.e., measure the same or similar things) and to determine what relationships exist between these clusters of factors.

Suppose we develop a measuring instrument and administer it, along with seven other different instruments, to a group of clients. Factor analysis would allow us to identify the concepts that are being measured by these eight instruments and to determine which instruments, if any, are essentially measuring the same concepts. The relationships of the new instrument to the other seven could be examined to determine which concept(s) it actually measures. Our understanding of that concept is improved by knowledge of the degree to which the other concepts are or are not related to the one measured in the new instrument.

Choosing the Best Approach

Content, criterion, and construct validity are three interrelated approaches to instrument validation. They are all relevant to any research situation. Because each type of validation functions in a different capacity, it is difficult to make any blanket generalizations about which is the best approach.

Three questions can be asked to discover how valid an instrument is (Thorndike & Hagen, 1969). They are:

1. How well does this instrument measure what it should measure?
2. How well does this instrument compare with one or more external criteria that purports to measure the same thing?
3. What does this instrument mean—what is it in fact measuring, and how and why does it operate the way it does?

The questions we choose to answer dictate which types of validation are of primary concern. The first requires content validity; the second, criterion validity; and the third, construct validity. Our objectives and our planned use of the instrument determine what kind of validity evidence is needed the most. When an instrument is employed for different purposes, it should be validated in different ways. If it is used for any purpose other

than that for which it was intended—or if it is used with a different client population or in a different setting—we have the responsibility to revalidate it accordingly.

RELIABILITY OF MEASURING INSTRUMENTS

The degree of accuracy, or precision, in the measurements an instrument provides is called reliability. Dependability, stability, consistency, predictability, reproducibility, and generalizability are all synonyms for reliability. A measuring instrument is reliable to the extent that independent administrations of the same instrument (or a comparable instrument) consistently yield similar results.

In its broadest sense, an instrument's reliability indicates the degree to which individual differences in scores are attributable to "true" differences in the property being measured or to errors of measurement. As is discussed in a later section of this chapter, errors of measurement involving reliability are random, rather than constant. They are the product of causes and conditions, such as fatigue and fluctuations of memory or mood, that are essentially irrelevant to the purpose of the instrument. Scores on an instrument therefore tend to lean now this way, now that.

Since random errors are present in all measurement, no instrument is 100 percent reliable. The data yielded by an instrument are dependable only to the extent that the instrument is relatively free from errors of measurement. Consequently, every instrument should be tested for reliability before it is formally administered, rather than after.

The term "reliability" is frequently used to refer to three different but interrelated concepts: (1) stability, (2) equivalence, and (3) homogeneity. Underlying each of these is the notion of consistency.

- Stability, also called temporal stability, refers to an individual's responses from one administration of an instrument to another. It is determined by the test-retest method, which compares the results of repeated measurements.
- Equivalence concerns an individual's responses on different instruments intended to measure the

TABLE 8.2

Types of Measurement Reliability and Questions Addressed by Each

Type	Question Addressed
Test-Retest Method	Does an individual respond to a measuring instrument in the same general way when the instrument is administered twice?
Alternate-Forms Method	When two forms of an instrument that are equivalent in their degree of validity are given to the same individual, is there a strong convergence in how that person responds?
Split-Half Method	Are the scores on one-half of the measuring instrument similar to those obtained on the other half?

same thing. It can be established using alternate, or parallel, forms.

• Homogeneity focuses on the internal consistency of an instrument and can be determined with the split-half method.

All three concepts and procedures essentially involve establishing the degree of consistency or agreement between two or more independently derived sets of scores. The three general methods for establishing the reliability of a measuring instrument are listed in Table 8.2, along with the measurement reliability question addressed in each.

The Test-Retest Method

A common approach to establishing reliability is through repeated measurement. The same instrument is administered to the same group of individuals on two or more separate occasions. Then the results are compared by correlating the sets of scores and calculating what is known as a reliability coefficient, which indicates the extent of the relationship between the scores. If this coefficient is high, it can be concluded that the instrument has good test-retest reliability.

Test-retest reliability thus estimates the stability of an instrument by permitting it to be compared with itself and by showing the extent to which its scores are consistent over time. The higher the reliability, the less

susceptible the scores are to random daily changes in the condition of the individual (e.g., fatigue, emotional strain, worry) or the testing environment (e.g., noise, room temperature). And the less susceptible the instrument is to such extraneous influences, the more reliable it is.

Effects of Retesting

To determine if a difference between measurements of the same measuring instrument is due to extraneous factors or to a genuine change in the variable being measured, the first consideration is the possibility that the first testing has influenced the second. The very process of remeasuring may have increased the influence of extraneous factors. Individuals may be less interested, less motivated, and less anxious during the second testing because they are already familiar with the instrument, for example. If the time interval between retests is fairly short, they may remember their answers and simply repeat many of the responses they provided the first time.

Another possibility is that the first testing has actually changed the variable being measured. For instance, a self-administered questionnaire assessing attitudes toward the elderly may raise questions people have never thought about before, so their interest in the issue is heightened and they form definite opinions. Thus, a "do not know" response on the first testing may be replaced by a "definitely agree" or "definitely disagree" response on the second. It is also possible that a genuine change due to influences unrelated to the testing has occurred.

Because test-retest reliability is subject to a number of biases caused by the effects of recall, practice, or repetition, measuring instruments that are appreciably affected by memory or repetition do not lend themselves to this method. If the measures obtained on an instrument will not be appreciably affected by a repeat testing, the test-retest method can be used, but careful consideration must be given to the time interval between tests. The shorter this interval, the more likely it is that the first testing will have an effect on the second one; the longer the interval, the more likely it is that real change will have occurred. A shorter interval increases the likelihood of erring in the direction of overestimating reliability, and a longer interval may result in underestimating reliability.

There are no hard and fast rules for judging the optimal time interval between tests. A two- or four-week interval is generally considered suitable for most psychological measures, and the waiting period should rarely exceed six months. On a general level, wait long enough for the effects of the first testing to wear off, but not long enough for a significant amount of real change to occur. If an IQ test is administered to a group of children on two separate occasions, approximately one month apart, for example, changes in scores are not likely, but an interval of five years can be expected to produce significant changes.

An example of the use of the test-retest method in social work practice involves a series of instruments to assess the extent of clients' problems and to obtain evaluative feedback on therapeutic progress (Nurius & Hudson, 1993). Clients complete them every week or two weeks, and we can use their scores to monitor and guide the course of our treatment. The test-retest reliability of these scales was established by asking a group of clients to complete them at one sitting, wait a minimum of 2 hours and a maximum of 24 hours, and complete them again. The resultant reliability coefficients were high. In clinical applications, the reliability of these measures has not appeared to change markedly as a result of repeated administrations.

The Alternate-Forms Method

One way to avoid some of the problems encountered with test-retest reliability is to use alternate (or parallel) forms. The alternate-forms method involves administering, in either immediate or delayed succession, supposedly equivalent forms of the same instrument to the same group of individuals. The reliability coefficient obtained indicates the strength of the relationship between the two alternate forms.

Alternate forms can be thought of as instruments with equivalent content that are constructed according to the same specifications. The forms contain questions that are different (thus eliminating exact recall) but are intended to measure the same variable equally. Form A and Form B of a reading comprehension test, for example, should contain passages of equal difficulty and should ask similar types of questions. If Form A uses a passage from a novel and Form B uses an excerpt from a research text, the levels of difficulty can be expected to be quite different. Any observed differences, then, could be explained as a result of the test's content, not differing levels of reading comprehension.

Use of the alternate-forms method requires both appropriate time intervals and equivalent sets of questions. Each alternate form must contain a sampling of questions that is truly representative. Questions must be randomly drawn from the universal pool of potential questions in such a way that if the same procedure were followed a second or even a third time, essentially equivalent sets of questions would result each time. Each set would then qualify as an alternate form of the instrument. In addition to content-equivalent questions, alternate forms should contain the same number of questions, questions expressed in a similar form, and questions of equal difficulty, and they should have comparable instructions, formats, illustrative examples, and time limits.

Considerable time and effort are needed to develop and administer truly equivalent forms. All the problems of measuring social and psychological phenomena are compounded by the need to construct two instruments.

The Split-Half Method

The split-half method of establishing reliability involves administering an instrument to a group of people, with the questions divided into comparable halves, and comparing the scores on the two parts to determine the extent to which they are equivalent. This is in many ways analogous to alternate-forms reliability because each half is treated as if it were a parallel form of the same instrument.

If the two halves are not equivalent, the instrument may not have a representative sampling of questions, and an individual's score may be influenced more by the questions than by the variable being measured. If the scores obtained from the two halves are similar, it can be assumed that the individual's performance is not appreciably affected by the sampling of questions in either half of the instrument.

One of the main problems with split-half reliability is how to divide the instrument into equivalent halves. The first thought might be to divide the instrument in half by counting the total number of questions and dividing by two; a 30-question instrument would be split so that Questions 1 through 15 would make up the first half and Questions 16 through 30 the second

half. But what happens if the nature or level of difficulty of the questions is different at the beginning and end of the instrument? And how can such extraneous factors as fatigue and boredom, which may influence responses at the beginning and the end of the instrument differently, be controlled for?

One answer is the odd-even procedure, whereby all the even-numbered questions are assigned to one group and all the odd-numbered questions to the other group. Then the scores from the two groups are compared.

THE VALIDITY-RELIABILITY RELATIONSHIP

Although validity and reliability have been treated as separate properties of a measuring instrument, they are clearly related. There cannot be validity without reliability, but there can be reliability without validity. Put simply, high reliability does not guarantee validity. Reliability can show only that something is being measured consistently, but that "something" may or may not be the variable that is to be measured. Thus, an instrument that is reliable may not be valid. However, it is not possible to have an instrument that is valid but not reli-

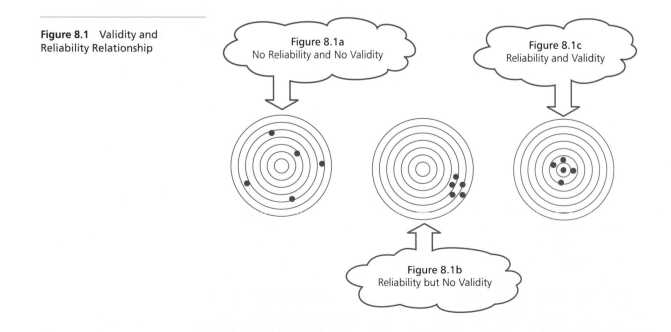

Figure 8.1 Validity and Reliability Relationship

Figure 8.1a
No Reliability and No Validity

Figure 8.1c
Reliability and Validity

Figure 8.1b
Reliability but No Validity

able. If an instrument measures what it says it measures, then by definition it must be reliable.

The relationship between validity and reliability can be illustrated with an analogy. Suppose a new rifle is used in a sharpshooter contest, but first the new sight and overall accuracy of the weapon must be checked out. A target is set up and five rounds are fired. As Figure 8.1a shows, the shots are scattered all over; not one has hit the target, let alone the bull's-eye.

Luckily, another shooter notices that the rifle is jerked when fired, which could account for the scattering of shots. The rifle is then put on a stand to minimize this effect, and on the next try five rounds are fired. As Figure 8.1b illustrates, all five shots are grouped together in a pattern, which seems to indicate that the inconsistency on the first attempt was caused by the jerking of the rifle and not by a problem with the rifle itself. However, the shots are still off target.

The problem must be the new rifle sight; the target is not being hit where the rifle is aimed. After realigning the sight, another five rounds are fired, and this time they hit the bull's-eye every time (Figure 8.1c). This analogy shows that it is possible to have an instrument that is both unreliable and invalid (Figure 8.1a), that has high reliability and no validity (Figure 8.1b), or that has high reliability and high validity (Figure 8.1c).

SOURCES OF MEASUREMENT ERROR

Measurement error is any variation in responses on a measuring instrument—such as answers on a questionnaire or ratings made by an independent observer—that cannot be attributed to the variable being measured. Thus, measurement error is inversely related to the validity and reliability of an instrument. The greater the variation due to extraneous factors, the lower the validity and reliability of the measurements taken.

Our goal, therefore, is to develop or locate a measuring instrument that is as free as possible from outside, unwanted influences. However, most measurement occurs in more or less complex situations in which numerous factors may affect both the variable being measured and the process of measurement. As a result,

it is virtually impossible to construct a perfectly valid and reliable instrument.

Because measurements are never totally free of error, we must identify potential sources of error and then control or lessen their impact. Put simply, the aim is to minimize error and maximize accuracy. Of the myriad extraneous influences that could be operating in any measurement situation as sources of error, only the most common are reviewed in this section. There are basically two categories of factors that may have unwanted influence on a measurement so that they obscure the "true" differences in the variable being measured—constant (systematic) and random (variable) sources of error.

Constant Error

Constant, or systematic, error refers to those factors that consistently or systematically affect the variable being measured. By their nature, these factors are concerned with relatively stable qualities of the respondents to the measuring instruments. Demographic characteristics and personal style are the two most common sources of constant error.

Demographic variables that could influence an individual's responses include intelligence, education, socioeconomic status, race, culture, and religion. Suppose an assessment is to be made of the job satisfaction of a group of young people who dropped out of high school and enrolled in a job training program. The measuring instrument (a self-administered job satisfaction questionnaire) requires an ability to read at the eighth-grade level.

If the measuring instrument is administered to the trainees without determining their reading levels in advance, it is likely to produce a set of confounded scores. That is, the scores will reflect not their job satisfaction, either before or after completing the program, but rather their ability to read and understand the questions. It cannot be assumed that the respondents represent a homogeneous group with respect to demographic characteristics or that these characteristics exert little influence on the measurements. In this example, there would be no justification for assuming that, since all of the trainees had dropped out of high school, they can all read at the eighth-grade level.

Personal Styles or Response Sets

Test constructors and research methodologists have devoted the most attention to the personal styles of the respondents as a source of error. This is partly because different personal styles, or response sets, have come to be viewed as indicants of personality traits. Some of the common personal styles that can consistently affect the responses of individuals or the reactions of observers are listed in Box 8.1.

There is some controversy about the actual biasing or error effects of response sets. Some maintain that they explain only a small portion of the variance in measurement and do not apply to all types of instruments. Ideally, however, every measurement situation

would be examined for such sources of error and appropriate steps would be taken to reduce their confounding effects. Control procedures for errors due to personal styles of respondents include development of subtle or socially neutral questions and items, incorporation of various response-set or "faking" indicators, and concealment of the instrument's true purpose. Control efforts to minimize observers' reactions include careful training of observers and use of multiple observers.

Random Error

Random error (or variable error), refers to unknown or uncontrolled factors that affect the variable being measured and the process of measurement in an inconsistent (variable) fashion. Unlike constant error, random error effects have no uniform trend or direction. Measurements are affected in such a way that both overestimates and underestimates of the "true" differences in the variable being measured may result.

These errors therefore are self-compensating; that is, they tend to cancel each other out, especially where there is a relatively large sample of respondents. Nevertheless, it is advisable to try to minimize their potential effects. The ideal situation is one in which the respondent's physical or emotional state, the testing environment, and the procedures used to administer the instrument all exert little or no influence on the measurement process.

The types of random errors reflect three criteria: (1) the transient qualities of the respondent, (2) situational factors in the measurement, and (3) factors related to the administration of the instrument. The transient qualities of respondents to a measuring instrument are those that can vary from day to day—indeed, from moment to moment. These include physical or mental health, mood, motivation, and degree of alertness, boredom, or fatigue. We must consider each quality separately and make a judgment as to how germane or influential it may be in a particular measurement situation.

External, or situational, factors also can introduce unwanted sources of variation into the measures. These include factors in the physical setting, such as seating

---

BOX 8.1

Response-Set Sources of Error

Errors Due to Personal Styles of Respondents

- Social desirability—A tendency to try to give a favorable impression of oneself in one's responses
- Acquiescence—A tendency to agree with statements regardless of their content
- Deviation—A tendency to give unusual or uncommon responses

Errors Due to Reactions of Observers

- Contrast error—A tendency to rate others as opposite to oneself in regard to a particular trait or characteristic
- Halo effect—A tendency to be unduly influenced by a single favorable trait or to let one's general impression affect one's ratings of a single trait or characteristic
- Error of leniency—A tendency to rate too high or to always give favorable reports
- Error of severity—A tendency to rate too low or to always give unfavorable reports
- Error of central tendency—A tendency to rate in the middle, thus avoiding any extreme positions

arrangements, work space, noise, lighting, or the presence of a tape recorder, as well as factors in the social setting, such as the degree of anonymity afforded respondents and the presence or absence of peers. It would not be surprising, for example, to find that adolescents provide different responses to questions about gang behavior when interviewed on the street or at a police station, as a group or individually, or in the presence or absence of family members.

Random error attributable to the administration of the measuring instrument often stems from a lack of uniformity in applications. For instance, interviewers without adequate training might add or omit material or change the wording of questions; group administrators might improvise their own instructions; observers might use different criteria or types of information to classify behaviors. Standardization helps minimize the amount of subjectivity influencing the measurement process and maximize the comparability and objectivity of measurements.

The administrator of the instrument also can be a source of error. It has been found, for example, that an administrator's demeanor and physical appearance, as well as such characteristics as race, gender, age, and socioeconomic status, can affect how an individual will respond. Administrators of measuring instruments must be aware of the image they present and try to minimize the effects of demographic dissimilarities between themselves and respondents.

Administrative factors have a good deal to do with controlling or reducing all three types of random errors. One way is for the administrator to foster rapport with the respondents by arousing interest in the instrument, eliciting cooperation, spending time getting acquainted, increasing motivation, reducing anxiety, and making sure the respondents are capable of completing the tasks required. Another is to select a setting that is conducive to the types of responses needed, such as separate interviews for husbands and wives to determine their attitudes toward their marriages. The use of clear, standardized instructions and the advance preparation of interviewers, observers, and administrators with rehearsals or trial runs will further reduce administrative errors.

SUMMARY

Measurement is a necessary part of social work research that facilitates the correspondence between the world of concepts and the world of observations. It has a meaningful role not only in the selection of appropriate methods of data collection but also in the operationalization of variables and the testing of hypotheses. Through its rules of correspondence, measurement serves to increase the objectivity of observations, the potential duplication of research studies, and the effective communication of findings.

Validity and reliability are the most important characteristics to be considered in selecting a measuring instrument. Validity refers to the degree to which an instrument measures what it is supposed to measure. An instrument may have several purposes that vary in number, kind, and scope, for each of which validity must be established. There are three types of validity: content, criterion, and construct. Measurement reliability refers to the accuracy or precision of an instrument. There are three general methods for establishing reliability: the test-retest, alternate-forms, and split-half methods. Reliability and validity are highly interrelated.

Measurement error refers to variations in instrument scores that cannot be attributed to changes in the variable being measured. Basically, all measurement errors can be categorized as constant (systematic) error or random (variable) error. While measurement errors can never be completely eliminated, all possible steps must be taken to minimize their impact, since the validity and the reliability of the instrument decrease as the measurement error increases.

The next two chapters deal with the basic types of measuring instruments. A thorough treatment of standardized instruments, describing how they are constructed and used, is given in Chapter 9, and instruments designed by a social worker for a specific purpose are discussed in Chapter 10. The choice between these two types is usually moot; if a standardized measuring instrument is available that will provide valid and reliable measures of the variables under consideration, it is almost always used.

Measuring Instruments

Catheleen Jordan

Cynthia Franklin

Kevin Corcoran

9

A great variety of standardized measuring instruments is available to cover most of our research needs. The selection of an appropriate instrument(s) for a specific measurement purpose requires a thorough understanding of how standardized instruments are constructed and used. Only with this knowledge can we evaluate competing instruments and choose the one(s) that will provide the most valid and reliable data for a particular purpose. Measuring instruments are standardized through rigorous research procedures aimed at empirically verifying their characteristics, results, and applicability. The level of their development varies from minimal to extensive. A well-developed instrument is better than a less-developed instrument.

ADVANTAGES OF STANDARDIZED MEASURING INSTRUMENTS

Every person to whom a particular standardized measuring instrument is administered should be treated in exactly the same way. In theory, the only reason individuals should score differently on the instrument is that they differ on the variable that is being measured. By providing uniform administration and scoring procedures and normative data that can be used as a basis for comparison, standardized measuring instruments help ensure that the data collected will be valid and reliable measures.

Uniform Administration and Scoring

In standardized measuring instruments, measurement conditions and outcomes are clearly specified to ensure comparability across respondents and across research situations. Detailed instructions about how the instrument is to be administered, to whom it is to be administered, and the exact meaning of the results usually are included in a technical manual that accompanies the instrument. Specifications include the materials to be used, the oral instructions to be given while administering the instrument, preliminary demonstrations, scoring methods, and the meaning of the scores produced.

These directions must be followed explicitly in order to reduce the sources of measurement error. With any instrument, care must be taken that constant errors, such as personal style and demographic characteristics, and random errors, such as changeable qualities of the respondents and situational and administrative factors, do not affect the measurements taken (see Chapter 8).

Generation of Normative Data

Normalization, or the establishment of normative data (norms), is essential to the scoring and interpretation of a standardized instrument. Norms are group standards, usually based on a group's average or mean score on a measuring instrument. By giving information on the typical (or average) performance of a particular group, norms provide a point of comparison that can be used to interpret individual scores (Sattler, 1988; Graham & Lilly, 1984). Norms also empirically define the limits and applicability of the measuring instrument by establishing data such as the means and standard deviations of the measures and by identifying types of groups for which the instrument is appropriate.

Norms are developed by administering the instrument to a large representative sample (the normalization or norm group) whose demographic characteristics are known. Descriptive statistics are computed for the sample, and an individual's score on an instrument can then be compared to the norms established by the representative sample group.

The raw score of a respondent also can be converted into a derived score, which can be directly compared to the average score achieved by the sample to determine the respondent's standing in relation to the normalization group. Examples of derived scores used in normative measurement include clinical cutting points (such as "A score of 30 or above is considered clinically significant") and age-grade equivalents. Statistical concepts such as standard scores (for example, a T-score with a mean of 50 and a standard deviation of 10) and percentile ranks are also derived scores. Jerome Sattler (1988) provides three guidelines for evaluating the norms of a standardized instrument:

1. The norm group (the sample) should have the same characteristics as the potential respondents. For example, if Asian students are to be assessed

to determine why they consistently score high in academic programs, an instrument for which few or no Asians had been included in the sample should not be used.

2. The larger and more representative the norm group, the better. As a general rule, the sample should consist of at least 100 individuals with similar characteristics.

3. The relevance of a particular norm group to the population to be studied must be determined. Many standardized measuring instruments provide several different norm groups ranked by characteristics, from which the group that best characterizes the one to be measured can be chosen.

VALIDITY OF STANDARDIZED INSTRUMENTS

It is through standardization that the validity of the measuring instrument is established. This concept has been defined as the extent to which the instrument actually measures what it is intended to measure. The scores on a measuring instrument should reflect the true differences of the variable they are measuring. The definition therefore includes not only the extent to which an instrument actually measures the variable in question but also the extent to which it measures that variable accurately.

Three types of validity for measuring instruments were identified in the previous chapter: content, criterion, and construct. Some guidelines for establishing each of these validities in evaluating standardized instruments are briefly discussed in this section. Each type of validity is related to a different purpose of measurement, and no one type is appropriate for every measurement situation. Validity, therefore, must be verified with reference to the intended use of a particular standardized instrument. In other words, potential users of an instrument must ask what it is valid for and for whom it is valid. Let us now turn to the three types of validity.

Content Validity

To ensure content validity, a measuring instrument must include an adequate sample of the universe of questions or items that represent the variable under consideration. This type of validity represents the extent to which the content of a measuring instrument reflects the variable that is being measured and in fact measures that variable and not another. Eight general guidelines have been proposed for the establishment of content validity in a standardized measuring instrument. Many of these points are discussed further in Chapter 10 in relation to the design and construction of a measuring instrument for specific purposes. We need to consider the following points when it comes to adopting a standardized measuring instrument:

1. Each question or item must represent an aspect of the variable being measured. ("Question" is the term used to designate the item to be rated or responded to, although it could be in the form of a statement.)

2. Questions should be empirically related to the construct being measured.

3. Questions must differentiate among individuals at different points in the dimension being measured. In other words, the instrument should discriminate between individuals at low and high extremes and in the middle.

4. Double-barreled questions or otherwise ambiguous interpretations should be avoided (see Chapter 10).

5. Some questions should be worded positively and others negatively so that the variable being measured can be indicated by a yes or agree response approximately half the time and by a no or disagree response half the time. Alternating positive and negative wording for questions breaks up the social desirability response set (see Chapter 10).

6. Short questions should be used when possible.

7. Negative questions should be avoided.

8. Biased questions should be avoided, including derogatory statements, slang terms, and prejudicial or leading questions.

The two principal methods used in selecting questions for a measuring instrument so as to ensure content validity—the rational-intutitive and the empirical methods—are discussed later in this chapter.

Criterion Validity

Criterion validity has been defined as a process of comparing scores on a measuring instrument with an external criterion. Some criteria that can be used to establish criterion validity for standardized measuring instruments are described in this section (Anastasi, 1988).

One criterion is performance in school or training programs. Independent criteria against which instrument scores can be compared include grades, commendations, and credits earned. This method is used for all types of achievement and diagnostic measuring instruments.

Another criterion involves contrast groups. The scores of one group may be compared with those of another that is assumed to be different, such as the scores of salespersons and accountants, or the scores of an individual may be compared with those of a group. This method is used in the development of personality, interest, and aptitude inventories.

Psychiatric diagnoses also can be used as an external criterion. This involves comparing an individual's performance on a measuring instrument with the psychiatric diagnosis of the person. As a basis of test validity, a psychiatric diagnosis is often used to validate personality instruments and other diagnostic measuring instruments. The validity of a psychiatric diagnosis should be checked before it is used as an indicator or predictor in this way, however.

Other measuring instruments for which criterion validity has been established are often used to establish an instrument's validity. Comparing scores on these instruments with those of the instrument under consideration is a validation method that can be used with all types of measuring instruments.

Other criteria are provided through ratings by observers. Ratings of children's behavior by teachers, parents, or peers and ratings of employees' attitudes by supervisors, coworkers, or others are frequently used in the development of personality measuring instruments.

Construct Validity

Construct validity has been defined as the degree to which an instrument successfully measures a theoretical construct, or an unobservable characteristic or trait. There is more interest in the construct being measured than in the measuring instrument or the scores it generates. The ability to predict developmental changes in children, for example, is a traditional criterion for the construct of IQ scores, which should increase as children get older (Anastasi, 1988). Developmental changes reflected in test scores may be taken as evidence of the measuring instrument's construct validity.

Another way to establish construct validity suggested by Anastasi is to use other measuring instruments with proven construct validity to validate new instruments for measuring related constructs. Scores on the new instrument should correlate highly with those on the other one, but not too highly. There might not be a good reason for developing the new measuring instrument if it does not improve on already available instruments in some way.

Statistical techniques and hypothesis testing procedures such as factor analysis and the establishment of convergent-discriminant validation (see Chapter 8) also can be used to establish construct validity. Factor analysis is particularly relevant because it identifies underlying dimensions of traits or behaviors, as well as the common factors that exist in or between measuring instruments. Convergent-discriminant validation concerns the extent to which measures of a construct from different instruments yield similar results, or converge, and the extent to which constructs tested can be empirically discriminated, or differentiated, from other constructs.

The constructs of a measuring instrument also can be validated with experimental interventions, as in the one-group pretest-posttest research design described in Chapter 13. For example, we might be given a pretest in the form of an anxiety-measuring instrument, be subjected to some type of anxiety-raising stimulus such as having to meet higher productivity levels, and then be retested to see if our anxiety scores have risen. In this case, a rise in scores could be taken as evidence of the measuring instrument's ability to reflect our current anxiety levels.

CONSTRUCTION OF STANDARDIZED INSTRUMENTS

A standardized measuring instrument that lacks both validity and reliability would not be a good candidate for selection. Constructors of standardized instruments, therefore, seek to develop instruments that are as valid and reliable as possible. After questions have been selected to maximize content validity, the principal concerns are with the response categories for each question and the length of the instrument.

Question Selection

Two basic methods of selecting questions so as to enhance the content validity of a measuring instrument are the rational-intuitive and the empirical methods (Fairweather & Tornatsky, 1977).

The rational-intuitive method involves choosing questions in a logical manner. A group of experts, such as clinical social workers, for example, might be asked to suggest questions for determining the presence of a high-risk suicidal behavior. Similar questions suggested might be included, while dissimilar questions would be excluded. Questions selected would then be arranged in groups that logically appear to measure the same variable. Questions related to level of impulse control, such as drug usage and temper tantrums, might be grouped together, and questions related to the immediate danger of suicidal action, such as having a clear plan of doing the act and the means to do it, might form another group.

In the empirical method of establishing content validity, statistical techniques are used to select questions. In the development of a service satisfaction measuring instrument for a social work agency, for example, we might conduct a simple exploratory study and sample the agency's records to determine all the different services offered by the agency. The various types of services offered would then guide the types of questions to be included on the satisfaction questionnaire. A combination of the rational-intuitive and the empirical methods is often used in the development of measuring instruments. Questions are generated utilizing experts (rational-intuitive method) and later tested using factor analysis techniques (empirical method).

Response Category Selection

Once the questions have been developed for a standardized instrument, the possible responses for each question are assigned. This provides some notion of the magnitude of the variable being measured for an individual respondent. One logical way is to assign a value for each response, with a low value indicating a low level of the variable being measured and a larger value indicating a higher level.

Values can be thought of as being situated on a continuum of degree, intensity, or magnitude. An example of a question with five responses (i.e., never, rarely, occasionally, frequently, very frequently) and their respective values (i.e., 1, 2, 3, 4, 5) is:

I often get angry at my spouse.
(Circle one number below.)

1. Never
2. Rarely
3. Occasionally
4. Frequently
5. Very frequently

Number of Categories

The next decision concerns the number of response categories for a particular variable. Should 5 responses be included, as in the example above, or should as many as 10 or 20 be used?

As a general rule, the number of response categories should be large enough to allow for some variance in responses but small enough so that appropriate discriminations can be made between the levels. If there are too many response categories, the difference between one level and the next may not be clear. The Subjective Units of Disturbance Scale has 100 possible deviations, and respondents rate their anxiety along a 100-point continuum (Barlow, Hayes, & Nelson, 1984). The problem is to determine the meaningfulness of a score of, say, 85, compared to a score of 90. The opposite is true if an instrument uses only three or four response categories; not enough latitude is allowed to determine the true differences in responding. Including between five and nine response categories is generally the most appropriate and reliable method for standardized instruments.

A choice also must be made between using an odd or an even number of categories. If an odd number is chosen, respondents may choose the middle-of-the-road responses to avoid revealing their true feelings. An example of a question with an odd number of response categories is:

The bus service in this city is adequate.
(Circle one number below.)

1. Strongly disagree
2. Disagree
3. Neither agree nor disagree
4. Agree
5. Strongly agree

If an even number of categories is chosen, however, there is no middle road, so respondents are forced to respond one way or the other. Then the problem is that they may develop a response set favoring one side or the other or refuse to answer questions at all. An example of a question with an even number of response categories is:

The bus service in this city is adequate.
(Circle one number below.)

1. Strongly disagree
2. Disagree
3. Agree
4. Strongly agree

Unfortunately, there are no guidelines for determining the ideal number of response categories or the advantages of an odd or an even number of categories. The choice is left to the discretion of the instrument's developer.

The Response-Value Continuum

Defining the response-value continuum involves decisions about how respondents should be rated—according to frequencies or to agree-disagree, true-false, or yes-no dichotomies. Hudson (1981) suggests that in rating human or social problems, an appropriate approach is to first write questions so that a yes-no or true-false answer indicates that the problem is either present or absent and then to scale the responses to get some idea of their magnitude.

Determination of Instrument Length

Ordinarily, the longer the measuring instrument, the greater its reliability. However, lengthy instruments are cumbersome to use and difficult to administer and score. The general rule is that the instrument should include as many questions as necessary to establish its content validity. A minimum of five questions is usually needed.

BASIC TYPES OF INSTRUMENTS

There are three basic types of measuring instruments: (1) rating scales, (2) summated scales, and (3) modified scales. All three aim to measure variables; the difference lies in the scaling techniques they use. Rating scales use judgments by self or others to assign an individual a single score (or value) in relation to the variable being measured. Questionnaire-type scales combine the responses of all the questions within an instrument to form a single overall score for the variable being measured. Modified scales do not fit into either of these classifications.

Rating Scales

The common feature in the various types of rating scales is the rating of individuals, objects, or events on various traits or characteristics at a point on a continuum or a position in an ordered set of response categories. In order to rate the person or thing, numerical values are assigned to each category.

Rating scales for individuals may be completed by the person being evaluated (self-rating) or by some significant other, such as a parent, supervisor, spouse, or social worker. Sometimes a client and a significant other are asked to complete the same rating scale in order to provide us with two different views. A wife and her husband might each rate the latter's openness to communication and other characteristics, for example. Self-ratings are helpful because individuals can evaluate their own thoughts, feelings, and behaviors accurately, provided they are self-aware and willing to be truthful.

Four types of rating scales—graphic rating, itemized rating, comparative rating, and self-anchored scales—are discussed in this section.

Graphic Rating Scales

In graphic rating scales, a variable is described on a continuum from one extreme to the other, such as low to high or most to least. The points of the continuum are ordered in equal intervals and are assigned numbers. Most points have descriptions to help respondents locate their correct positions on the scale. The example below is a "feeling thermometer" on which children are asked to rate, via a check mark, their level of anxiety from very anxious to very calm:

___ 100 Very anxious
___ 90
___ 80
___ 70
___ 60
___ 50 Neither anxious nor calm
___ 40
___ 30
___ 20
___ 10
___ 0 Very calm

Another example is a scale on which clients are asked to rate their individual therapy sessions from not productive to very productive:

Please circle the number that comes closest to describing your feelings about the session you just completed.

1	2	3	4	5
Not productive		Moderately productive		Very productive

The major advantage of graphic rating scales is that they are easy to use, though care should be taken in the development of appropriate descriptive statements. End statements that are excessive, such as "extremely hot" or "extremely cold," should not be used.

Itemized Rating Scales

Itemized rating scales offer a series of statements designed to rank different positions on the variable being measured. Respondents may be asked to check all the statements with which they agree, or only the one statement that is closest to their own position. On the following itemized rating scale, for example, clients are asked to prioritize questions related to self-image (Warwick & Lininger, 1975):

If someone asked you to describe yourself, and you could tell only one thing about yourself, which of the following answers would you be most likely to give? (Put a 1 in the space to the left of that question.)

___ I come from (home state)
___ I work for (employer)
___ I am a (my occupation or type of work)
___ I am a (my church membership or preference)
___ I am a graduate of (my school)

Itemized rating scales vary according to the number of statements given and the specificity of the descriptive statements. Higher scale reliability is associated with clear definitions of categories. Even the use of precise categories, however, cannot obviate the fact that clients respond differentially, because of their individual frames of reference. The less homogeneous the group of respondents, the less suitable is an itemized rating scale.

Comparative Rating Scales

In comparative rating scales, respondents are asked to compare an individual (or object) being rated with others. An often-cited example is the ratings that professors are asked to give for students applying to enter graduate school. They may be asked to compare a student with others they have known and then to rate the individual in the top 10 or 20 percent of students.

A variation of the comparative rating scale is the rank-order scale, in which the rater is asked to rank individuals (or objects or events) in relation to one another on some characteristic. Below is an example of a rank-order scale on which a social work supervisor is asked to rank-order four workers who have been recommended for promotion:

*Below are the four individuals that your
department has recommended for promotion.
Please rank-order these individuals from highest to lowest.*

___ Mary Smith
___ Mike Jones
___ Jane Johnson
___ Jim Jackson

The assumption that underlies comparative rating scales is that the rater has some knowledge of the comparison groups. If a small, select group such as the one in the example is being ranked, the scale would have little usefulness in other settings or with other groups.

Self-Anchored Rating Scales

Self-anchored rating scales are similar to others in that respondents are asked to rate themselves on a continuum, usually a seven- or nine-point scale from low to high. However, the specific referents for each point on the continuum are defined by the respondent. This type of scale is often used to measure such attributes as intensity of feeling or pain. Clients who have difficulty in being honest in group therapy sessions, for example, could complete the following question, which is intended to measure their own perceptions of their honesty. The advantage is that they do not have to attempt to compare themselves with any external group.

*Extent to which you feel you can be honest in
the group:*

1   2   3   4   5   6   7   8   9
Can never   Can sometimes   Can always be
be honest   be honest   completely honest

Summated Scales

Whereas rating scales require judgments on the part of a respondent who is asked to make a single judgment about the topic of interest, summated scales include multiple questions that the respondent is asked to answer. Then a total composite score of all the questions is obtained to indicate the individual's position on the variable of interest.

Summated scales are widely used for assessing individual or family problems, for needs assessment, and for other types of program evaluation. In the summated scale, respondents indicate the degree of their agreement or disagreement with each question. Response categories may include strongly agree, agree, neutral, disagree, or strongly disagree. Two examples of summative scales are presented in Figures 9.1 and 9.2.

Modified Scales

Modified scales such as the semantic differential scale and the Goal Attainment Scale have been developed to elicit responses that are not ordinarily included in a rating scale or questionnaire-type scale.

Semantic Differential Scales

The semantic differential scale rates the respondent's perception of three dimensions of the concept under study: evaluation (bad-good), potency (weak-strong), and activity (slow-fast). Each dimension includes several questions scored on a 7- or 11-point continuum on which only the extreme positions are identified. Below are a few questions taken from a scale designed to measure patients' feelings toward the nursing home in which they live (Atherton & Klemmack, 1982):

*Below are 29 pairs of words that can be used
to describe nursing homes in general. For each
pair of words, we would like you to circle the
number that comes closest to your feelings
about nursing homes. For example, if you feel
that nursing homes are more good than bad,
circle a number closer to good. The closer the
number you circle is to good, the more good
and less bad you feel nursing homes in general
to be. Continue with each pair.*

Good	1	2	3	4	5	6	7	Bad
Beautiful	1	2	3	4	5	6	7	Ugly
Rigid	1	2	3	4	5	6	7	Flexible
Dirty	1	2	3	4	5	6	7	Clean
Happy	1	2	3	4	5	6	7	Sad

INDEX OF SELF-ESTEEM

Name: _____ Today's Date:_ _____

Context: _____

This questionnaire is designed to measure how you see yourself. It is not a test, so there are no right or wrong answers. Please answer each item as carefully and as accurately as you can by placing a number beside each one as follows:

    1 = None of the time
    2 = Very rarely
    3 = A little of the time
    4 = Some of the time
    5 = A good part of the time
    6 = Most of the time
    7 = All of the time

---

1. _____ I feel that people would not like me if they really knew me well.
2. _____ I feel that others get along much better than I do.
3. _____ I feel that I am a beautiful person.
4. _____ When I am with others I feel they are glad I am with them.
5. _____ I feel that people really like to talk with me.
6. _____ I feel that I am a very competent person.
7. _____ I think I make a good impression on others.
8. _____ I feel that I need more self-confidence.
9. _____ When I am with strangers I am very nervous.
10. _____ I think that I am a dull person.
11. _____ I feel ugly.
12. _____ I feel that others have more fun than I do.
13. _____ I feel that I bore people.
14. _____ I think my friends find me interesting.
15. _____ I think I have a good sense of humor.
16. _____ I feel very self-conscious when I am with strangers.
17. _____ I feel that if I could be more like other people I would have it made.
18. _____ I feel that people have a good time when they are with me.
19. _____ I feel like a wallflower when I go out.
20. _____ I feel I get pushed around more than others.
21. _____ I think I am a rather nice person.
22. _____ I feel that people really like me very much.
23. _____ I feel that I am a likeable person.
24. _____ I am afraid I will appear foolish to others.
25. _____ My friends think very highly of me.

Figure 9.1 Hudson's Index of Self-Esteem. Copyright © 1993 Walter W. Hudson.

The semantic differential scale correlates well with, and appears more direct than, some other scales. However, the scale is not completely comparable across variables. Much depends on the variable being measured and whether or not the three dimensions—evaluation, potency, and activity—are the best ways to measure a particular variable.

Goal Attainment Scales

Goal Attainment Scaling (GAS) is used widely to evaluate client or program outcomes. Specific areas of change are described and the range of possible outcomes, which usually consists of most unfavorable to best anticipated or most favorable outcomes, is

---

SOCIAL SERVICE SATISFACTION SCALE

Using the scale from one to five described below, please indicate on the line to the left of each item the number that comes closest to how you feel.

1 Strongly agree
2 Agree
3 Undecided
4 Disagree
5 Strongly disagree

_____

- _____ 1. The social worker took my problems very seriously.
- _____ 2. If I had been the social worker, I would have dealt with my problems in just the same way.
- _____ 3. The worker I had could never understand anyone like me.
- _____ 4. Overall the agency has been very helpful to me.
- _____ 5. If friends of mine had similar problems I would tell them to go to the agency.
- _____ 6. The social worker asks a lot of embarrassing questions.
- _____ 7. I can always count on the worker to help if I'm in trouble.
- _____ 8. The agency will help me as much as it can.
- _____ 9. I don't think the agency has the power to really help me.
- _____ 10. The social worker tries hard but usually isn't too helpful.
- _____ 11. The problem the agency tried to help me with is one of the most important in my life.
- _____ 12. Things have gotten better since I've been going to the agency.
- _____ 13. Since I've been using the agency my life is more messed up than ever.
- _____ 14. The agency is always available when I need it.
- _____ 15. I got from the agency exactly what I wanted.
- _____ 16. The social worker loves to talk but won't really do anything for me.
- _____ 17. Sometimes I just tell the social worker what I think she wants to hear.
- _____ 18. The social worker is usually in a hurry when I see her.
- _____ 19. No one should have any trouble getting some help from this agency.
- _____ 20. The worker sometimes says things I don't understand.
- _____ 21. The social worker is always explaining things carefully.
- _____ 22. I never looked forward to my visits to the agency.
- _____ 23. I hope I'll never have to go back to the agency for help.
- _____ 24. Every time I talk to my worker I feel relieved.
- _____ 25. I can tell the social worker the truth without worrying.
- _____ 26. I usually feel nervous when I talk to my worker.
- _____ 27. The social worker is always looking for lies in what I tell her.
- _____ 28. It takes a lot of courage to go to the agency.
- _____ 29. When I enter the agency I feel very small and insignificant.
- _____ 30. The agency is very demanding.
- _____ 31. The social worker will sometimes lie to me.
- _____ 32. Generally the social worker is an honest person.
- _____ 33. I have the feeling that the worker talks to other people about me.
- _____ 34. I always feel well treated when I leave the agency.

Figure 9.2   Reid-Gundlach Social Service Satisfaction Scale

identified. These scales can be completed by clients, independent judges, social workers, or other interested persons. Figure 9.3 is an example of a GAS for a nine-year-old boy with three problem areas: being overweight, spending too much time alone, and exhibiting behavior problems in school.

SELECTION OF A STANDARDIZED INSTRUMENT

The selection of a standardized measuring instrument for a particular social work research study is dependent on how the research question has been conceptualized and operationalized. It is through operational definitions of the variables being measured that the independent and dependent variables in a research hypothesis are quantified. If it is asserted in a single-system research design, for example, that a particular intervention (independent variable) causes a particular change in a client's target problem (dependent variable), both the intervention and the client's problem must be operationalized in such a way that they can be objectively measured. The operational definitions of the variables determine the field of available standardized measuring instruments that is capable of measuring them.

There are three general considerations in the selection of a measuring instrument: determining measurement need (why, what, who, which type, where, and when), locating measuring instruments capable of measuring the variables, and evaluating the alternatives among the instruments that are available.

Determining Measurement Need

The first consideration in selecting an appropriate standardized measuring instrument is to determine measurement need as specifically as possible. In order to do this, we need to know precisely why we want to measure a particular variable, who would complete the instrument, which type of measurement format is acceptable, which type should be used in a specific setting or environment, and how often the instrument is to be administered. The six critical questions listed here are guides that can be used to determine measurement need:

1. *Why will the measurement occur?*
   a. Research
   b. Assessment/diagnosis
   c. Evaluation
2. *What will be measured?*
   Specify_____

3. *Who is appropriate for making the most direct observations?*
   a. Research participant/client
   b. Practitioner or researcher
   c. Relevant other
4. *Which type of format is acceptable?*
   a. Inventories and surveys
   b. Indexes
   c. Scales
   d. Checklists and rating systems
5. *Where will the measurement occur?*
   a. General setting
   b. Situation-specific environment
6. *When will the measurement occur?*
   a. Random
   b. Posttest only
   c. Repeated over time

Why Is the Measurement Needed?

Standardized measuring instruments are used for three general purposes, each with different measurement requirements. Some measuring instruments are more appropriate than others, depending on the purpose of the research study: applied research, assessment and diagnosis, or evaluation of practice effectiveness (Sunberg, 1977). In an applied research study where participation is involuntary, for example, participants may have little investment in completing an instrument, so shorter instruments are preferable. In single-system research designs, both the social worker and the client often are more interested in treating feelings, behaviors, or cognitions than in measuring them, so short instruments that can measure specific presenting problems or treatment goals are needed (Barlow & Hersen, 1984).

The purpose of a research study also has an influence on how stringent the psychometric properties (mental measurement techniques) of the instrument must be. Requirements for validity and reliability may be less rigid if the purpose is applied or theoretical research, where the resulting theory will be tentative. These requirements are more rigid in testing a hypothesis or if the results will impact on a person's life. The most rigid requirements apply to measuring instruments used for assessment and diagnostic purposes and to those used in

Outcomes	Scale 1 Overweight	Scale 2 Spending Time Alone	Scale 3 Behavior Problems in School
Most unfavorable outcome thought likely (Score −2)	Gain of 3 lbs.	Spends 12 hours or more in own room	School contract indicates fighting and time in isolation
Less favorable outcome (Score −1)	Loss of 1 lb.	Spends 10 hours in own room	School contract indicates fighting
Expected outcome (Score 0)	Loss of 5 lbs.	Goes to activity room on staff suggestion	School contract shows point loss for behavior modification
More favorable outcome (Score +1)	Loss of 7 lbs.	Spends time in activity room on own initiative	School contract shows no point loss
Most favorable outcome thought likely (Score +2)	Loss of 10 lbs.	Participates in some activities	School contract gives points for cooperation

Figure 9.3   Example of a Goal Attainment Scale

single-system studies where the results can affect termination, referral, or third-party reimbursement.

What Is to Be Measured?

The second question is what is to be measured. Many measuring instruments are used to collect data about a variable such as thoughts, feelings, or behaviors. The variable may be covert and known only to the research participants, or it may be overt and observable. The guiding principle in determining what to measure is the degree of specificity required, which is less when there is an interest in a broad trait or characteristic and greater when an explicitly defined variable is being measured. Measurement instruments for global, or broad, variables, which are called wideband instruments, assess variables in a general sense but lack specificity. Measures for more narrowly focused variables, which are called narrowband instruments, provide more precision in measuring the variable but few meaningful overall data.

Who Could Make Direct Observations?

Measurement need also depends on who could make the most reliable direct observations to complete the instrument. There are three sources of observers: outside observers, usually professionals; indigenous observers, including relevant others (such as family members or peers) and collaterals (such as staff members); and self-observers, the research participants themselves. The instrument chosen must allow use of the type of observer that we consider most effective.

A school social worker, for example, may want to evaluate how an interpersonal skills training program affects the quality of the social relationships among students and teachers. An instrument that can be used for self-reports by students or teachers or one that calls for students and teachers to rate one another might be selected. Since both of these sources may be biased, however, the observations could be made by some other relevant person, such as a school principal (Hops & Greenwood, 1981).

The decision about which source to use must always be made on the basis of who will provide the most accurate and objective assessment. If at all possible, more than one source of observations should be used in order to increase the reliability of the observations.

Which Type of Format Is Most Acceptable?

The fourth question concerns the format of the measuring instrument to be used. The choice among inventories, surveys, indexes, scales, checklists, or rating systems is based on consideration of the variable being measured and who is to complete the instrument.

In general, inventories and surveys are multidimensional, wideband instruments. The questions may take on a variety of formats, such as true-false or ratings of intensity or frequency. Traditionally, inventories and surveys have been fairly lengthy; an example is the Minnesota Multiphasic Personality Inventory. Scales and indexes generally are unidimensional and fairly short, with no more than 50 questions. Scales and indexes can be defined as narrowband measuring instruments that assess a particular variable at an interval or ratio level of measurement (Weinbach & Grinnell, 2004).

These distinctions among formats are fairly arbitrary. Inventories, surveys, indexes, and scales are similar in that they can be used when the variable is observable only to the respondent. When a relevant other can observe the variable, an option is to use a rating system or checklist. These instruments also have a variety of formats; in fact, some self-report types may be checklists, such as the Symptom Checklist (Derogates, Rickles, & Rock, 1976). Examples of rating systems include the Discharge Readiness Inventory, which is multidimensional (Hogerty & Ulrich, 1972), and the Behavior Rating Scale, which is unidimensional (Cowen et al., 1970). In sum, there are many formats from which to choose. The choice should always be based on which format will collect the most valid and reliable data.

Where Will the Measurement Be Done?

Measurement can be done in various settings and can reflect behaviors or feelings that are specific to an environment (Wicker, 1981). Moreover, observations in one situation may not necessarily generalize to others (Bellack & Hersen, 1977; Mischel, 1968). Determination of measurement need therefore depends on the setting where the measuring instrument is to be completed and the environment the observations represent.

Many variables of interest to us are situation-specific; that is, the variable may be observable only in certain environments and under certain circumstances or with particular people. When a measuring instrument is needed for a situation-specific variable, it is best to choose one that can be completed in that environment (Nelson & Barlow, 1981). It is more valuable to have a parent complete a checklist of a child's problems at home where the trouble occurs than in a social worker's office, for example (Goldman, Stein, & Guerry, 1983). If the variable is not situation-specific (that is, it is assumed to be a trait manifested in a variety of settings), an instrument can be chosen that can be completed in any environment that does not influence the respondent's observations (Anastasi, 1988).

When Will the Measurements Be Taken?

The final question to be considered in determining measurement need is the time frame for administering the instrument. Ideally, the instrument chosen will allow the measurement to be made after the independent variable has been introduced so that the change to be measured (the dependent variable) has occurred. In many single-system research designs, for example, target problems are measured both before and after the intervention has been introduced. The instrument should also allow for the instrument to be administered as closely as possible to the occurrence of a change in behavior or feeling. Observing these two principles increases the accuracy and reliability of the observations.

An additional consideration is how often the measurement will be taken. As we will see in Chapter 12, a case-level research design such as the *ABAB* design requires two administrations of the instrument over a period of time, whereas group designs such as the one-group posttest-only design require only one administration. When a measuring instrument is to be administered more than once, the internal validity of the results may be threatened by the effects of retesting (see Chapter 13). Respondents' answers on a posttest may be affected by their ability to recall questions or responses on a pretest, or they may be less interested, less motivated, or less anxious during the second testing.

Locating Standardized Instruments

Once the measurement need has been established, the next consideration is locating appropriate standardized measuring instruments from which to choose. The two general sources for locating such instruments are commercial or professional publishers and the professional literature.

Publishers

Numerous commercial and professional publishing companies specialize in the production and sale of standardized measuring instruments for use in social work research and practice. The cost of instruments purchased from a publisher varies considerably, depending on the instrument, the number of copies needed, and the publisher. The instruments generally are well developed, and their psychometric properties are supported by the results of several research studies. Often they are accompanied by normative data.

Publishers are expected to comply with professional standards such as those established by the American Psychological Association. These standards address the claims made about the instrument's rationale, development, psychometric properties, and administration and about interpretation of results.

Standards for the use of some instruments have been developed to protect the integrity of research participants, clients, respondents, and the social work profession. Consequently, purchasers of instruments may be required to have certain qualifications, such as a college course in testing and measurement or an advanced degree in a relevant field. A few publishers require membership in particular professional organizations. Most publishers will accept an order from a student if it is cosigned by a qualified person, such as an instructor, who will supervise the use of the instrument. A selected list of publishers of measuring instruments can be found in Jordan, Franklin, and Corcoran (1997).

Journals and Books

Standardized measuring instruments are most commonly reproduced in professional research journals; in fact, most commercially marketed instruments appear first in one of these publications. The instruments usually are supported by evidence of their validity and reliability, although they often require cross-validation and normative data from more representative samples.

Locating instruments in journals or books is not easy. Of the two methods used most often, computer searches of data banks and manual searches of the literature, the former is faster, unbelievably more thorough, and easier to use. This is especially true when the research question combines several important variables, such as the effects of poverty on the self-esteem of minority youth from rural and urban areas. Moreover, the data banks used in computer searches are updated regularly.

Financial support for the development of comprehensive data banks has been limited and intermittent, however. Another disadvantage is that many articles on instruments are not referenced with the appropriate indicators for computer retrieval. These limitations are being overcome by the changing technology of computers and information retrieval systems. Several services allow for a complex breakdown of measurement need. Data banks that include references from more than 1,300 journals, updated monthly, are now available from a division of Psychological Abstracts Information Services.

Evaluating Standardized Instruments

A literature search should produce several standardized instruments that would be suitable for use in measuring a particular variable. The choice of one instrument over others depends on the strength of the quantitative data the instrument provides and its practicality in application. These two dimensions can be evaluated by finding answers to a number of questions that focus on the population or sample to be used, the validity and reliability of the instrument, and the practicality of administering the instrument:

1. *The Sample from Which Data Were Drawn*
   a. Are the samples representative of pertinent populations?
   b. Are the sample sizes sufficiently large?
   c. Are the samples homogeneous?
   d. Are the subsamples pertinent to respondents' demographics?
   e. Are the data obtained from the samples up to date?
2. *The Validity of the Instrument*
   a. Is the content domain clearly and specifically defined?
   b. Was there a logical procedure for including the items?
   c. Is the criterion measure relevant to the instrument?
   d. Was the criterion measure reliable and valid?
   e. Is the theoretical construct clearly and correctly stated?
   f. Do the scores converge with other relevant measures?
   g. Do the scores discriminate from irrelevant variables?
   h. Are there cross-validation studies that conform to these concerns?
3. *The Reliability of the Instrument*
   a. Is there sufficient evidence of internal consistency?
   b. Is there equivalence between various forms?
   c. Is there stability over a relevant time interval?
4. *The Practicality of Application*
   a. Is the instrument an appropriate length?
   b. Is the content socially acceptable to respondents?
   c. Is the instrument feasible to complete?
   d. Is the instrument relatively direct?
   e. Does the instrument have utility?
   f. Is the instrument relatively nonreactive?
   g. Is the instrument sensitive to measuring change?
   h. Is the instrument feasible to score?

The questions related to the validity and the reliability of both the instrument and the data collected with it are concerned with issues discussed in Chapter 8. These issues are the most crucial concerns in evaluating any standardized measuring instrument.

Representativeness of the Sample

Another major concern in the evaluation of standardized instruments is the extent to which the data collected in setting the norms for the instrument represent the population from which the sample is to be drawn for the proposed study (see Chapter 11). If the instrument being considered, for example, was formulated and tested on a sample drawn from a population of white Anglo-Saxon males, it might give perfectly valid results when administered to white Anglo-Saxons males but not when administered to Native Americans, African Americans, or females.

In general terms, the samples used in setting the norms for an instrument must reflect a population that is pertinent to the respondents who will complete the instrument. Subsamples of demographic characteristics such as age, gender, race, and socioeconomic status must be considered. Thus, if the sample on which the norms were established consisted of middle-class African Americans, the instrument's applicability to a sample of inner-city African Americans would be suspect.

Another consideration is the size of the sample, which affects sampling error. As pointed out in Chapter 11, sampling error is reduced to the extent that the sample is sufficiently large and homogeneous. The larger the sample, and the less variance there is in the population from which the sample has been drawn, the smaller the standard error will be.

When the data were collected from the sample is another concern. Data based on samples gathered 20 years ago may not be an adequate basis for accepting the instrument as psychometrically sound for today's use. One popular measure of social desirability developed more than 30 years ago, for example, includes questions that pertain to the social status derived from owning an automobile (Crowne & Marlowe, 1960). Predicted responses would be substantially different today.

Practicality of Application

Consideration of the practicality of application in social work research and practice involves implementation of the instrument and analysis of the data it generates. The first three practicality questions (i.e., 4a–c) concern the likelihood that research participants will complete the instrument. Even the most valid and reliable instrument has no practical utility if it is left unanswered because it is too long, it is not socially acceptable to the respondent, or the respondent does not understand the instructions or questions.

While a longer instrument is usually more reliable than a shorter one (Allen & Yen, 1979), it is also more time-consuming and may not be completed. This is especially important in single-case research designs where multiple measures are needed and in survey research where the response rate is critical.

The social acceptability of a measuring instrument concerns the respondent's evaluation of the appropriateness of the content (Haynes, 1983). The perceived appropriateness of the content as a measure of the variable of interest—not what the instrument measures but what it appears to measure—is referred to as face validity (see Chapter 8). An instrument that is offensive or insulting to respondents will not be completed. Instruments also should be easy for respondents to complete, with content and instructions that are neither above nor below their typical functioning level and questions that can be answered easily.

The other five practicality questions (i.e., 4d–h) concern the meaning or interpretation of the results provided by the instrument. Interpretation is easiest and most practical when the instrument provides direct measurements, has utility, is nonreactive, is sensitive to small changes, and is easy to score.

Variables that can be measured directly include physical ones such as height, weight, and age. Other variables, such as self-esteem or depression, can be measured only indirectly. An instrument is considered to have utility if the results provide some practical advantage or useful data. The results of an instrument are influenced by whether the instrument is obtrusive, or reactive, or is unobtrusive. An instrument is said to be reactive if administration of it can affect the respondent or alter the variable being measured. The self-monitoring of cigarette smoking, for example, actually influences this behavior. The degree of internal and external validity depends on minimizing the reactive effects that completing an instrument can have by selecting instruments that are unobtrusive, or nonreactive.

The instrument also has to be sensitive enough to pick up small changes in the variable being measured. If the research purpose is assessing client change, for example, the instrument must be sensitive to changes in the dependent variable that could occur from one administration to the next.

What is done with the instrument after it has been completed is also a practicality consideration. It may seem self-evident that if an instrument is to provide meaningful information, it must be possible to score it. However, many instruments have scoring procedures that are too complicated and time-consuming to be practical in social work research and practice situations. Even though they are psychometrically sound, they should be eliminated in favor of others that can be scored more easily.

NONSTANDARDIZED MEASURING INSTRUMENTS

Wherever possible, we should select a standardized measuring instrument, not only because it has been developed and tested by someone else—which saves us an inestimable amount of time and trouble—but also because of the advantages it has with regard to uniformity of content, administration, and scoring. There will be occasions, however, when no standardized instrument seems to be right for our particular purpose. Some standardized instruments are excessively long, complicated, and difficult to score and interpret: That is, they do not meet the criteria for practicality previously mentioned.

Let us take an example from a practice perspective on how to use nonstandardized instruments. No standardized instrument may enable us to discover how Ms. Yen feels about her daughter's marriage. The only way to get this information is to ask Ms. Yen; if we want to keep on asking Ms. Yen—if the object of our intervention, say, is to help her accept her daughter's marriage—it will be best to ask the questions in the same way every time, so that we can compare the answers and assess her progress with some degree of certainty.

In other words, we will have to develop our own measuring instrument. Perhaps we might begin by asking Ms. Yen to list the things that bother her about her daughter's marriage; that is, we might ask her to develop an inventory. Or, if we do not think Ms. Yen is up to making a list, we might develop our own checklist of possibly relevant factors and ask her to check off all that apply.

Once we know what the factors are, we might be interested in knowing to what degree each one bothers Ms. Yen. Perhaps her daughter's marriage will involve her moving to a distant town with her new husband, and it is this that is most important to Ms. Yen. Or perhaps her daughter's prospective husband has characteristics that Ms. Yen perceives as undesirable: He may be non-Asian, while Ms. Yen is Asian, or he may hold unacceptable religious or political views or come from the "wrong" social or occupational class, and so on.

With Ms. Yen's help, we might develop a simple scale, running from "very bothersome" to "not at all bothersome." Perhaps, we might settle on something like the following:

Here are a number of statements about your daughter's marriage. Please show how bothersome you find each statement to be by writing the appropriate number in the space to the left of each statement.

1 = Not at all bothersome
2 = A little bothersome
3 = Quite bothersome
4 = Very bothersome

_____ My daughter will move away after her marriage.
_____ My daughter's husband is non-Asian.
_____ My daughter's husband has been married before.
_____ I don't like my daughter's husband's family.
_____ My daughter's husband is unemployed.
_____ . . .

We then assess Ms. Yen's total botherment by adding up her scores on the individual items.

Sometimes we will stumble across an existing instrument that has not been standardized. Box 9.1 presents a checklist of some questions to ask when trying to determine if a specific nonstandardized instrument should be used.

Advantages

The major advantage of a nonstandardized instrument is that it is customized, that is, it is totally pertinent and appropriate to a particular client because it was designed with the client in view; possibly it was even designed by the client or at least with the client's help. We are not worried, as we would be with a standardized instrument, that the instrument was developed with a population different from the client's or that the sample used for development and testing was not representative of the population from which it was drawn.

This advantage is more likely to apply if we have developed our own instrument than if we have borrowed one from a colleague who happens to have a similar client in a similar situation. Our colleague's client is not our client, and so we do not really know how appropriate the instrument will be. Neither can we be sure that we are administering or scoring the instrument in the same way as did our colleague, since the administration and scoring instructions are unlikely to be written down.

If we develop our own instrument, it will probably be simple to administer and score because we knew when we designed it that we would personally have to administer and score it. Most of the previous questions about an instrument's practicality will have been answered in the affirmative. We know that the instrument provides useful information and that it is relatively direct, of an appropriate length, feasible to complete, and acceptable to the client. We do not know, however, whether it is sensitive to real, small changes and to what degree it is nonreactive.

The main advantage, then, of using nonstandardized measures is that they can be constructed for an individual measurement purpose. We could use an instrument like the one displayed in Figure 9.4, however. Here, we are interested in ascertaining the perceptions of people who live in a specific community.

Disadvantages

Because the instrument is nonstandardized, we do not know to what degree it is valid and reliable. With respect to reliability, we do not know whether a difference in score from one administration to the next means that Ms. Yen's attitudes toward her daughter's marriage have really changed or whether the difference is a result of the instrument's instability over time or measurement error. With respect to validity, we do not know to what degree the instrument is content valid, that is, to what degree the items on our instrument include every aspect of Ms. Yen's feelings about the marriage. Perhaps what is really bothering her is that she believes her daughter suffers from an emotional disorder and is in no fit state to marry anyone. She has not mentioned this, there is no item on the instrument that would reveal it, and so we will never be able to discuss the matter with her.

In other words, we are not sure to what degree our instrument is providing a reliable and valid measure of Ms. Yen's attitudes toward her daughter's marriage. Perhaps the instrument focuses too much on the prospective husband and it is really Ms. Yen's attitudes toward the husband that we are measuring, not her attitudes toward the marriage.

Unless we have a real interest in the development of measuring instruments, however, we are unlikely to run validity and reliability checks on instruments we have developed ourselves. Our nonstandardized instruments may therefore be somewhat lacking with respect to validity and reliability. We will not be able to use them to evaluate our own practice or to compare our client's scores

---

BOX 9.1

Checklist for Assessing Existing Nonstandardized Measuring Instruments

1. Will the responses to the questionnaire provide the data needed to answer the research question?
2. Does the questionnaire address the same types of variables that are to be studied (i.e., value, attitude, personality traits, behavior, knowledge, skill, perception, judgment)?
3. Is the level of measurement appropriate for the intended statistical analyses?
4. Is the format of the items appropriate to the level of inquiry?
5. Does the questionnaire have known reliability? Are the circumstances in which reliability was established known?
6. Does the questionnaire have known validity?
7. Have there been other applications of the instrument? Or has the instrument been reviewed by other professionals in journals, books, or other publications?
8. Is the language of the questionnaire appropriate for the sample or population?
9. Are the instructions clear and easy to follow?
10. Do the items meet standards for item construction (i.e., clear, precise, not double-barreled or biased)?
11. Is the flow of the questionnaire logical and easy to follow?
12. Is the questionnaire the appropriate length for the time available for data collection, the attention span of intended respondents, and other circumstances related to the design?

---

with the scores of other similar people in similar situations. We will, however, be able to use them both to help determine the problem and to assess the client's progress in solving the problem. And a nonstandardized instrument is sometimes better than no instrument at all.

SUMMARY

Standardized measuring instruments are designed to quantify the variables being measured. They have the advantages of uniform administration and scoring and the generation of normative data. Constructors of stan-

PROBLEMS IN YOUR COMMUNITY?

This part of the survey is to learn more about your perceptions of these problems in the community. Listed below are a number of problems some residents of Northside have reported having.

Please place a number from 1 to 3 on the line to the right of the question that represents how much of a problem they have been to you within the last year:

1. No problem (or not applicable to you)
2. Moderate problem
3. Severe problem

Questions		Responses		
1. Finding the product I need	1	2	3	_____
2. Impolite salespeople	1	2	3	_____
3. Finding clean stores	1	2	3	_____
4. Prices that are too high	1	2	3	_____
5. Not enough Spanish-speaking salespeople	1	2	3	_____
6. Public transportation	1	3	3	_____
7. Getting credit	1	2	3	_____
8. Lack of certain types of stores in Northside	1	2	3	_____
9. Lack of an employment assistance program	1	2	3	_____
10. Finding a city park that is secure	1	2	3	_____
11. Finding a good house	1	2	3	_____

Figure 9.4 Example of a Nonstandardized Survey Measuring Instrument

dardized measures seek to develop instruments that are as valid and reliable as possible. The major considerations are the selection of questions that will maximize content validity, the number of response categories, and the length of the instrument. The difference among the three major types of measuring instruments (i.e., rating scales, summative scales, and modified scales) is the scaling techniques used. Rating scales use judgments by self or others to assign an individual a single score (or value) in relation to the variable being measured. Summative scales combine the responses on several questions to form a single overall score on the variable of interest for each respondent. Modified scales do not fit either of these classifications.

The selection of a standardized measuring instrument for a particular research study depends on how the research question has been conceptualized and how the variables represented in it have been operationally defined. The three general considerations are determin-

ing measurement need, locating a number of measuring instruments capable of measuring the variables, and evaluating the alternatives among the instruments available. Measurement need is related to our purpose, the research question, and the circumstances in which the instrument is to be administered.

Instruments that satisfy these needs can be selected from the two principal sources: publishing houses and the professional literature. They can be evaluated by considering questions that focus on the sample used in developing each instrument, the instrument's validity and reliability, and practicality issues such as the likelihood that respondents will complete the instrument and interpretation of the results.

The following chapter completes the discussion of measurement by describing how we can design and construct a measuring instrument to fit a particular research need in the event that a suitable standardized instrument cannot be located.

Charles H. Mindel

Designing
Measuring
Instruments

10

If an appropriate standardized measuring instrument is not available for a particular research purpose, we need to know how to design and construct one. While, as noted in Chapter 9, a standardized measuring instrument is rarely unavailable, knowledge of how valid and reliable instruments are designed not only is useful in certain research situations but also improves understanding of measurement principles.

The type of measuring instrument used as an example in this chapter is applicable primarily to survey research (Chapter 17), one of the data collection methods discussed in Part V of this text. The principles of design and construction described in this chapter, therefore, are most appropriate to survey instruments, but they generally apply to most other types of measuring instruments as well.

In our discussion of how we can design and construct measuring instruments, our two guiding principles are based on sampling procedures (described in Chapter 11) and measurement validity and reliability (described in Chapters 8 and 9).

- First, the design and construction of our instrument should attempt to maximize the response rate of individuals in our sample or population.
- Second, our instrument should minimize the amount of measurement error in the responses of individuals.

An instrument that embodies these two principles is well constructed. The product of the research process, particularly in quantitative research studies, is data that have been gathered with some type of measuring instrument so that they can be quantified and analyzed. In survey research, the instrument utilized to collect data is called a self-administered questionnaire. When data are collected by means of face-to-face interviews or telephone surveys, the data collection instrument is referred to as an interview schedule. In this text, a measuring instrument is considered to be any type of data collection device or procedure designed to gather data in any research study.

SOCIAL WORKERS' USE OF SURVEY RESEARCH

The survey is a popular form of data collection because it provides a useful and convenient way to acquire large amounts of data about individuals, organizations, or communities. It can be used to determine what people know, believe, or expect about a research question. It also can provide data on how they feel, what they want, what they intend to do, what they have done, and why.

One of the most important uses of survey research is to determine certain kinds of facts about individuals or other units of analysis. Social service agencies, for example, undertake surveys to collect facts about people in order to gather such data as the number and characteristics of individuals who request our services.

Survey research also is useful for gathering reports about people's behavior, both past and present. These kinds of data are often needed in our profession, particularly in service utilization studies. Clients might be asked how many times they have visited a physician in the past year or the past month, for example. The potential problem with these types of data is their accuracy. The instrument must not require individuals to reconstruct events from so far in the past that they cannot remember them accurately. It is much better to ask specific questions about events within a reasonable time frame than to ask global, general questions that range over a long period.

Determining Beliefs, Feelings, and Ethical Standards

Surveys are particularly useful in helping to investigate unobservable variables such as attitudes, beliefs, feelings, and ethical standards. The distinction between what the facts are and what people believe them to be is often important. A social service agency, for example, might want to investigate why it is having difficulty recruiting staff or serving an intended population. A study might show that the beliefs of individuals in the community about that agency (whether or not they are based on fact) are quite negative.

In program planning, the existence of a certain social problem may or may not coincide with the attitudes in the community toward the existence of that problem. At one time, for example, African American families were considered dysfunctional by outside observers, but many African Americans disputed this evaluation and maintained that their family form worked well for them. Difficulties are inevitable if an agency attempts to organize a program to address a social problem that the community does not recognize. An important part of a community needs assessment therefore is to determine the beliefs of individuals and constituencies about it.

Measuring instruments also explore individuals' feelings and desires. We often need to measure our clients on a variety of feelings or states, such as anxiety or marital satisfaction. Many well-established, standardized instruments that explore feelings are available. Instruments also can probe individuals' ethical standards or their attitudes toward what should be done or what can feasibly be done with respect to certain social policies. Many instruments have examined attitudes toward abortion, women's rights, and education, for example. Ethical standards are also represented in questions that explore what individuals would do in certain situations. Questions that explore what people should or would do do not necessarily indicate what they actually do, however. Attitudes are not the same as behavior (LaPiere, 1934).

We can also use survey research to try to ascertain why people behave, believe, or feel the way they do. Instruments often contain questions that explore this. In a research study on elderly parents who live with their adult children, for example, one question asked why and under what circumstances this family arrangement had been formed. The history of the event, the types of reactions individuals felt at the time this event occurred, and the process at work were all relevant.

VALIDITY FACTORS IN INSTRUMENT DESIGN

The most crucial considerations in the construction of a measuring instrument by a social worker are the same as those in the development of a standardized instrument—validity and reliability. Applications of these concepts to measurement and the evaluation of standardized measuring instruments were examined in the two preceding chapters. Chapter 8 defines reliability as

the accuracy or precision of the results the instrument produces and validity in terms of content, criterion, and construct validities.

This chapter adopts the external and internal validity terms used in Chapter 13 on group research designs. Internal validity refers to the degree to which the instrument actually measures the concept being studied and, moreover, measures that concept accurately. External validity goes a step further to consider the degree to which the answers to the questions given by the individuals in the sample can be generalized to a larger population or a different research setting. Some methods we can use to improve the external and internal validities of the instruments we construct are reviewed in the following sections.

Maximizing External Validity

There are several reasons why an instrument will fail to achieve an adequate response rate, thus affecting the degree to which responses to the questions can be generalized to a larger population or a different population or setting. The suggestions that follow for design and construction of the instrument, including those that relate to the choice and wording of questions and their format and layout, can help to achieve external validity and ensure generalizability. The external validity of an instrument we construct may be compromised, however, by the fact that there are no normative data to compare scores against and that uniform administration procedures are not specified, as in standardized instruments (see Chapter 9).

Clearly State the Purpose of the Study

One way to ensure an adequate response rate is to be explicit in explaining to potential respondents why a study is being undertaken. If they feel it is being used for purposes other than those stated, or if they have other misgivings about the study or the person conducting the study, their responses may be inhibited or inaccurate. One way to offer this explanation is with a cover letter to respondents or research participants describing the study, written under the official letterhead of the sponsoring organization (see Figure 16.3).

Public knowledge that the study is to take place also helps.

Feelings of being exploited by research studies are most common among minority group members. One way to counter this attitude is to demonstrate that there is something of value to the group or individuals that justifies their participation. This might involve meetings with community members to discuss the purposes of the study and its value to them or hiring minority group members as staff.

Keep Sensitive Questions to a Minimum

Some individuals may feel that a particular research study would invade their privacy. The instrument may include personal questions in sensitive areas, and respondents often believe that participants can be identified. These fears can be alleviated by omitting or reducing personal or sensitive questions and by ensuring anonymity or confidentiality. On many mailed questionnaires, however, some form of identification of participants is necessary so that a follow-up can be sent in order to ensure an adequate response.

Sensitive questions will also be disregarded if their content or wording causes them to be perceived by respondents as insulting or offensive. As pointed out in Chapter 8, the face validity of an instrument (not what it does but what it appears to do) often determines whether or not it will be completed.

Avoid Socially Desirable Responses

The tendency of respondents to adopt the social desirability response set and answer in a way they think will make them look good is another threat to achieving a valid and reliable response. With direct-service questionnaires, particularly, respondents are likely to be unsophisticated and unfamiliar with the types or format of questions used. University students may be used to taking tests and filling out answer sheets, but others will be at a loss as to how to complete an instrument. If they answer as they think they should, the possibility of measurement error is increased and the generalizability of the results is reduced. The constructor of the instrument therefore must word questions sensitively and assure respondents that there are no right or wrong answers.

Ask Only Relevant Questions

The relevance of questions is particularly important in social work policy studies, where the population being studied often consists of professionals who face time constraints and who may not feel justified in responding to numerous or lengthy questions. The importance of the research question under study and of their responses should be emphasized, and the instrument must not be too long or vague. No item should be included that is not relevant to the study's research question. Sending professionals a questionnaire that is too long or too general demonstrates that the person doing the study is unsophisticated in using the research process, and potential respondents are likely to ignore the instrument.

Maximizing Internal Validity

Internal validity is basically concerned with reducing or eliminating measurement error in the content of the instrument. The paragraphs that follow constitute a checklist of procedures to be used in selecting and presenting effective questions. As in the preceding chapter, "question" is the general term used to refer to the items, statements, or questions that, together with the accompanying response categories, make up the instrument.

Make Questions Clear

Aside from the fact that all questions on an instrument must be relevant to the research question being investigated, the most important factor in wording questions to avoid measurement error is clarity. The words used must not mean different things to different individuals; this applies to ambiguous or vague words, as well as to slang terms or colloquial expressions that may be familiar to certain groups but not to others. Meanings can vary across age levels, ethnic groups, social classes, and regions. We can become so close to the studies we are doing that questions that are perfectly clear to us are not clear at all to others. Consider the following example:

What is your marital status? (Circle one number below.)

1. Married
2. Divorced
3. Separated
4. Widowed
5. Never Married

It is not clear whether "marital status" refers to *present* status or whether the respondents are being asked if they were *ever* married, divorced, separated, or widowed. The way the question is stated, a person might in fact fit into the first four of the five categories. This question is more accurately stated: What is your present marital status?

Other problems with ambiguity are likely to occur when we are not familiar with the population being studied, such as elderly people, a racial or ethnic minority group, or professionals. Questions with little or no meaning to respondents can result.

Use Simple Language

The language used in questions may also be much too complicated for a respondent. The wording must be simple enough for the least educated person, while at the same time it must not insult the intelligence of anyone who could be presented with the instrument. If we were interested in the types of health care services utilized by individuals, for example, we might provide a checklist that includes such medical specialties as ophthalmology, otolaryngology, and dermatology. A list more likely to be understood by all respondents would call these specialists eye doctors; ear, nose, and throat doctors; and doctors for skin diseases.

Ask Questions That Respondents Are Qualified to Answer

Some measuring instruments ask individuals to respond to questions to which they have not given much thought or that they may not be competent to answer. In a public opinion poll, for example, an unknowledgeable research sample might be asked to provide opinions about psychotherapeutic techniques or needs

tests in social welfare. We run the risk of being misled by the responses if the respondents are not qualified to answer such a question.

Avoid Double-Barreled and Negative Questions

Double-barreled questions contain two questions in one. A simple example of such a question is:

> Do you feel that the federal government should make abortion or birth control available to women in households that receive welfare benefits?

The problem with this question is that some respondents might agree to tax support for birth control but not for abortion, or for abortion but not for birth control. The way the question is worded, we can never know which position the respondents are taking. The solution, of course, is to present the two questions separately. A clue to double-barreled questions is the presence of an "and" or an "or." Such questions should be reexamined to see whether they include two questions.

Another type of question to be avoided is negative questions, such as asking whether respondents agree or disagree with a negative statement. An example is:

> Federal funds should not be used to pay for abortions for women who receive welfare benefits.

The word "not" is often overlooked in these kinds of questions, and the error that is therefore introduced can be considerable. This question should be rephrased in one of these two ways:

> The federal government should pay for abortions for women receiving welfare benefits.
>
> —or—
>
> Abortions for women receiving welfare benefits should only be paid for by nongovernmental sources.

Keep Questions Short

Questions that are kept short get to the point quickly, so respondents will be more likely to read them and complete them. Keeping questions short and to the point helps maintain the relevance, clarity, and precision of the instrument.

Pretest the Instrument

The traditional way in which the clarity of questions (and consequent internal validity) is examined is by pretesting the instrument on a sample of individuals who will not take part in our final study. Our pretest is concerned not with the answers to the questions per se but rather with the difficulties respondents may have in answering the questions. Are the questions clear and unambiguous, and do respondents understand what our instrument is trying to accomplish?

The pretest should be followed by a debriefing to uncover any difficulties. Pretesting is discussed further in the last section of this chapter.

OPEN- AND CLOSED-ENDED QUESTIONS

When constructing a measuring instrument, we must take into account differences not only in the wording of questions but in the kinds of responses asked for. There are two general categories: open-ended questions, in which the response categories are not specified in detail and are left unstructured, and closed-ended or fixed-alternative questions, in which respondents are asked to select one (or more) of several response categories provided in the instrument. Each of these methods for responding has particular purposes, as well as certain strengths and disadvantages.

Open-Ended Questions

Open-ended questions are designed to permit free responses; they do not incorporate any particular structure for replies. An example is:

> We would like to know some of your feelings about your job as an employee of the Department of Social Services:
> 1. What types of duties are most satisfying to you?
> 2. What types of duties are most dissatisfying to you?

These open-ended questions ask for much information and considerable thought, since they deal with a complex issue that can involve several dimensions of feeling.

If we are unaware of the various sources of satisfaction and dissatisfaction in the department, answers to the two open-ended questions will produce some clues. Open-ended questions are often used when all of the possible issues (and responses) involved in a question are not known or when we are interested in exploring basic issues and processes in a situation. Such questions are usually used in a preliminary phase of the study. Responses to open-ended questions, however, may be used in constructing questions for use in a later phase. An important function of open-ended questions, in fact, is their use in the development of closed-ended questions.

An additional advantage of open-ended questions is that they put few constraints on individuals' statements of their feelings. A closed-ended question might list various sources of satisfaction and ask individuals to check how they feel about them. Open-ended questions allow respondents to go into detail and to express greater depth in their answers. Respondents are not forced to choose among alternatives we developed but can express their feelings on a matter more precisely. If an interviewer administers the instrument, it is possible to probe responses and elicit them by using appropriate attending behaviors. These techniques encourage respondents to provide fuller, more thoughtful answers.

There are also some distinct disadvantages; open-ended questions may lead to a lower response rate and decrease external validity. A measuring instrument with many open-ended questions takes considerable time to complete, and a long questionnaire can discourage potential respondents. Some people may be discouraged from replying to an instrument composed of open-ended questions because they are not articulate enough to provide their own responses, particularly if they must express themselves in writing. Only those with high levels of education may respond to such questions. In a study with a population that is homogeneous with respect to education, this is less of a problem. With a well-educated population, it may even be advisable to take advantage of the respondents' expertise by using open-ended questions.

Internal validity can also be a consideration with respect to open-ended questions, which introduce an element of subjectivity to the responses. Suppose 100 social workers on the staff of a department of social services complete a measuring instrument that asks for a paragraph describing why they are satisfied with the agency. In order to analyze the data, we need to code these individual replies into meaningful categories.

From answers to the question "Are you satisfied working in the department?" a list of different sources of satisfaction could be deduced. The problem is that different individuals may state the same kind of satisfaction in different ways. One respondent, for example, may say: "I like the personal autonomy that is provided by this agency," and another might say, "They leave me alone here, and the supervisor does not bother me very much." It is our responsibility to decide whether or not such answers fall in the same category. The potential for error is the miscoding of responses, or lack of interrater reliability.

Interrater reliability can be achieved by having more than one person (usually called a rater) code the responses. When several raters code the same responses and develop their own sets of categories, a measure of interrater reliability, such as the percentage of responses for which the raters agree on an appropriate code, can be calculated. When low interrater reliability is found for the response to a particular question, we should try to ascertain the reasons why. If it is impossible to solve this problem, serious consideration should be given to eliminating the question, because it is useless to include a question that different respondents will interpret in different ways.

Closed-Ended Questions

In closed-ended questions, responses can be selected from a number of specified choices: expressing a simple yes or no, selecting degrees of agreement, or choosing one or more of a list of response categories. Two examples of closed-ended questions are:

1. *If the abused child is out of the home, which situation best describes your current plan of action? (Circle one number below.)*

   1. Return child to intact family
   2. Return child if abuser remains out of home
   3. Continue foster care
   4. Seek adoptive placement
   5. None of the above
   8. Not applicable
   9. Do not know

2. *Did the mother deny having knowledge of sexual abuse? (Circle one number below.)*

   1. Yes
   2. No
   8. Not applicable
   9. Do not know

The advantages of fixed-alternative questions are fairly obvious. These kinds of questions can be presented in such a way as to attract and maintain reliable responses from individuals. Answers are easily compared from person to person, and there is no need for time-consuming coding procedures such as those involved with open-ended questions. Because choices are provided, respondents are less likely to leave certain questions blank or to choose a "do not know" response. Missing data can be a serious problem when analyzing the data collected for a study, particularly if the response rate is low.

Closed-ended questions can elicit data on topics that would be difficult to obtain by other methods. It is difficult to get responses to an open-ended question on sexual behavior, for example. A series of short, closed-ended questions inquiring whether respondents agree or disagree with a statement or whether they participate in a certain behavior to a greater or lesser extent is much more likely to be answered. Moreover, a variable such as income level, for example, can be difficult to measure when asked as an open-ended question, such as:

• What is your present income?
• How much money did you make last year?

It is much more effective to ask individuals to place themselves in a set of categories containing a range of income levels, such as $10,000–$20,000.

Respondents may also be reluctant to answer questions about their age; this may or may not be a sensitive topic, depending on the study's population. As a rule, however, data on variables such as age, which are measured primarily at the interval or ratio level (such as years of education, income level, number of children in the home, or number of years married), should be gathered with open-ended questions. Thus, a more precise answer will be provided by an open-ended question on age that uses the following form:

> *What was your age at your last birthday?*
> *(Place number on line below.)*

> _____

Less usable data will be provided by a closed-ended question with a range of responses, such as:

> *What is your age? (Circle one number below.)*

> 1. 1 to 5 years
> 2. 6 to 10 years
> 3. 11 to 15 years
> 4. 16 to 20 years
> 5. More than 20 years

Only when questions about these kinds of variables are sensitive and there is reason to believe that there will be a low or mistaken response to them should the responses be grouped into categories. By grouping, we are throwing away important data; putting a child who is ten years old into the same category as one who is six years old, for example, is needlessly inexact.

There are other problems with closed-ended questions. Respondents may not feel that the alternatives provided are appropriate to their answers. They also may be tempted to give an opinion on something they have never thought about before; the tendency to simply circle a fixed alternative is much greater than the tendency to answer an open-ended question where it is necessary to write something down. When closed-ended questions used in interview situations, respondents who do not want to appear ignorant or who want to give socially desirable answers may say they do not know.

Comparison of the Two Types of Questions

As the preceding sections have shown, both open- and closed-ended questions have advantages and disadvantages, and each serves purposes that make it most appropriate for certain usages. One type of question therefore cannot be said to be better than the other. Open-ended questions are appropriate in exploratory studies with complex research questions, especially when all the alternative choices are not known. Closed-ended questions are preferable when the choices are all known or limited in number or when respondents have clear opinions on specific issues and feelings.

An important consideration in the choice of open- or closed-ended questions is the time required to measure the responses. Open-ended questions are time-consuming to code, introduce error, and require more personnel for data processing. Closed-ended questions can be designed so that they do not require extensive coding and can go to the data processing stage quickly.

The type of question to be used is not necessarily an either/or choice; a measuring instrument can easily include both open- and closed-ended questions. It is possible to analyze the responses to open-ended questions individually and to have the responses to a series of closed-ended questions processed and analyzed by a computer.

INSTRUMENT CONSTRUCTION AND APPEARANCE

A list of questions is not a measuring instrument. How an instrument is constructed and what it looks or sounds like also determine whether or not those to whom it is sent or administered will respond. Those who receive a measuring instrument in the mail or in person or who interact with an interviewer face-to-face or on the telephone must be given the impression that completing the questionnaire or being interviewed is worthwhile and will not be too difficult or time-consuming. This is particularly the case with a mailed instrument, which can easily be discarded. To ensure an adequate response rate, a written instrument should be designed to provide immediate positive impressions about its importance, difficulty, and length. Each of these factors can be manipulated by careful attention to detail.

To some extent it is possible to indicate the importance of an instrument by a professional appearance, and the difficulty can be indicated by how the questions are ordered. The length can be controlled by structuring the questions to save space or by including only those questions that are absolutely necessary for studying the research question.

Somewhat different methods are necessary when the instrument is to be used in interviewing respondents face-to-face or on the telephone. Procedures for developing an interview schedule for use in these cases are described in Chapters 16 and 17.

General Impression

Appearance, or how the instrument looks to potential respondents, often is affected by cost constraints. If these considerations can be overlooked, we can think in terms of the best way to present the instrument to make a good appearance.

The brief description of the design of a printed measuring instrument in this section is based on Donald Dillman's (1999) total design method for survey instruments. This is an expensive design to execute, but it illustrates the preferred method. The instrument is printed as a booklet. It consists of 8¼" by 12¼" sheets of paper folded in the middle and, if more than one sheet is used, stapled to form a booklet with the dimensions 8¼" by 6⅛".

No questions are included on the front or back pages, which should stimulate the interest of recipients of the instrument. Pages are typed on a word processor using 12-point (Elite) type in a 7" by 9½" space on regular 8" by 11" paper. To fit the booklet format, the pages are photographically reduced to 70 percent of the original size. They are reproduced on white or off-white paper by a printing method that produces quality work.

This format has several advantages. Photographically reducing the size of the page makes the questionnaire appear shorter and uses less paper; it also lowers postage costs if the questionnaire is to be mailed. The booklet format and the use of a cover page give the appearance of a professionally produced document, which lends the impression that considerable thought has gone into the process. In contrast, instruments that are typed, photocopied, and held together with a single staple in the upper-left corner present an uneven and unprofessional appearance. Particularly to be avoided is a form that consists of several 8½" by 14"

sheets of legal-size paper, folded several times to fit into a business envelope. Though this design probably saves money, the larger size and unattractive appearance are likely to discourage respondents.

Page Layout

In addition to how the questions in an instrument are presented in type, the design format determines how they are laid out on the page. This is an important consideration in producing a professional-appearing instrument that will encourage a high response rate. The instrument must be constructed so that respondents decide to complete it and do not overlook any question or section.

To keep sections of questions together and separated from other sections, various levels of spacing are used. If possible, questions and response categories should not start on one page and continue on another. Questions in a series, particularly, should be kept together or clearly follow one another. Confusion and mistakes often result when parts of questions or questions and responses become separated. Nevertheless, large blank spaces should be avoided when possible, for economy, as well as for appearance.

Typographical considerations in the layout of the instrument also can facilitate data processing by making answers easier to locate and to score. Careful design and planning with respect to how the instrument is to be processed once the questions have been answered can save much time, energy, and money.

Question Order

The ordering of questions in measuring instruments has been a topic of debate, but there appears to be some consensus on certain aspects. It is generally agreed, for example, that instruments should begin with questions that are interesting to the respondent and relevant to the purpose of the study, as stated in either the cover letter that accompanies the mailed instrument or the introductory statement delivered by an interviewer.

To begin by asking for demographic data such as gender, age, or educational level can irritate respondents, who may regard the instrument as an application or evaluation form of some kind. Questions should be ordered along a descending gradient of social useful ness or importance. That is, questions that are judged to be the most important to the research question should be stated first. Demographic data should appear at the end of the instrument.

Potentially sensitive or objectionable questions also should be positioned later. It would not be wise, for example, to begin by asking how many times respondents had engaged in sexual intercourse in the previous week.

Another principle of ordering is that questions should be arranged by content area. Respondents should not be forced to constantly switch their train of thought by having to consider a question on one topic and then being asked to respond to another question on a totally different topic. Some of us maintain that forcing respondents to switch from one topic to another reduces their tendency to try to structure answers so that they appear consistent. In fact, however, respondents are likely to give more thought to their answers if the instrument presents consecutive questions on a single general topic. Much less mental effort is required to respond to an instrument if the questions are organized by topic or content area.

Within the content areas, questions should be grouped by type of question (closed- versus open-ended). This means that questions that require a simple yes or no answer or those for which responses are sought on a range of agreement to disagreement should appear together. This not only eases the mental effort required to respond to the questions but also makes the instrument appear more logically constructed. At times, of course, compromises must be made in question ordering; it is not always possible to follow all these principles. For example, we may not be able to sort the questions by content area and then sort them again by type of question in such a way as to give the appearance of a well-thought-out instrument. The goal always is to try to strike a satisfactory balance.

Presentation of Questions and Responses

One of the most common reasons for mistakes in constructing questionnaires is the mistaken assumption that the average person will know how to complete the instrument. Procedures that we take for granted can be mysteries to respondents, and detailed directions on how to answer the questions often are needed. In face-to-face or telephone interviews, explanations can be given verbally. But in a mailed questionnaire, or for those that respondents are to complete on their own, questions that are not understood can be a source of serious error.

Figure 10.1 shows both unacceptable and acceptable ways of asking five typical questions in a survey instrument. In a question where the appropriate answer is to be circled, for example, unless this is explicitly stated in the instructions, respondents may circle more than one response. For each question, directions such as "Circle one number below" must be given (see Questions 1–5 in Section B).

Response categories should not appear on the same line as the question but should be placed on the line below, and questions should not be squeezed onto a page with little room between items or between a question and its response categories. This not only produces a very cluttered and unsightly appearance but also increases the likelihood that respondents will overlook questions or make mistakes in answering.

Precoding Responses

There are several ways to provide for questions to be answered, such as blank lines to be filled in or boxes to be checked. A better technique is precoding, or numbering the categories on the left and asking respondents to circle the appropriate number. This technique aids in data analysis because a number is preassigned to each alternative or response, as in Section B of Figure 10.1. Having respondents circle the number when they answer the question eliminates an additional step in data processing and another potential source of error. The number for each response should be placed at the left of the answer rather than at the right or anywhere else because responses could have different lengths (see Question 4 in Section B in Figure 10.1).

As an aid to both respondents and coders, it is helpful if certain numerical values are always used for the same types of responses. If there are numerous questions

---

A. UNACCEPTABLE QUESTION FORMS

1. Sex: M _____   F _____

2. Number of children at home
   0–1 ____   2–3 _____   4–5 _____   6 or more _____

3. Do you own your own home?   Y _____   N _____

4. Religious preference:
   Protestant _____
   Catholic _____
   Jewish _____

5. Health: Good _____   Fair _____   Poor _____

B. ACCEPTABLE QUESTION FORMS

1. What is your gender? (Circle one number below.)
   0. Male
   1. Female

2. How many of your children live at home with you? (Place number on line below.)

   _____

3. Do you own your own home? (Circle one number below.)
   0. No
   1. Yes
   8. Not applicable
   9. Do not know

4. What is your religious preference? (Circle one number below.)
   1. Protestant
   2. Catholic
   3. Jewish
   4. None
   5. Other (please specify) _____

5. How would you describe your physical health? (Circle one number below.)
   1. Poor
   2. Fair
   3. Good
   9. Do not know

Figure 10.1   Unacceptable and Acceptable Survey Questions

---

asking for yes or no responses, for example, the same value should be used for all the yes answers and another value for all the no answers. Thus, a value of 0 might be used for "no" and a value or 1 for "yes" throughout the instrument. A single value can also be used for the "missing data" category, so that all "Do not know," "No opinion," and "Not applicable" answers have the same value. Thus, in Section B, 9 is the value for the "Do not know" answers in Questions 3 and 5, and 8 is the value for the "Not applicable" response in Question 3.

Precoded questions should be arranged one below the other, and response categories also should be in vertical order, rather than side by side. If there are several choices of response categories on the same line, respondents may circle the wrong number or overlook some responses.

Edge-Coding Responses

In edge coding, another technique that aids in data processing, a series of blanks is added at the right side of the instrument (see Figure 9.4). Respondents are instructed not to write on these lines; they are utilized by us to transfer the response number circled by the respondent over to the blank line allocated for each question. This simple procedure eliminates the preparation of coding sheets, onto which responses otherwise are transferred after being converted into numbers. The inclusion of edge-coding lines may be distracting on the page, but the lines need not be obtrusive. Considering the savings of time and effort they provide, the possible disadvantages are minimal.

Organization of Content

In the two principal ways of organizing the contents of a questionnaire, respondents are asked to respond to a series of questions or to rank-order their responses. With a series of questions, respondents may be asked, for example, to choose whether they strongly agree, disagree, or strongly disagree on several questions. If the guidelines given earlier for question and response presentation have all been followed, this type of scale will likely take up a large amount of space, as well as being needlessly repetitive. There are special ways to handle a series of questions in a small amount of space so that the instrument appears less cluttered and easier to follow.

Figure 9.4, for example, is an example of a needs assessment in a specific community. Rather than asking 11 separate questions regarding the severity of problems in the community, the questions have been set up in a multiquestion format. First, there is an opening statement briefly that describes the purpose of the questionnaire and provides directions for answering the series of questions. Respondents are requested to circle the number that represents how they feel, and the three choices are given with their appropriate values (e.g., 1, 2, 3). The questions are listed consecutively on the left side of the page. The values appear in columns at the right of the 11 statements, and at the far right are the edge-coding lines.

Other techniques can be used when the same data are needed about a number of different people, such as collapsing questions into a single matrix. In the example presented in Figure 10.2, respondents are requested to state the occupational categories of their fathers and mothers. Rather than presenting the list of occupational categories twice, it is given once, and the same series of values is repeated for father and for mother in separate columns. The values must appear in both columns, and clear instructions must be given to circle only one number in each column.

An alternative way of presenting questions is the use of rank-ordering. Respondents might be asked to consider the 11 problems listed in Figure 9.4, for example, and to rank them in terms of the severity each problem represents for them.

This form of question is not recommended, for several reasons. It is very difficult to consider more than three or four different concepts at once for rank-ordering purposes. If the list consists of 11 or more problems (as in Figure 9.4), it will be virtually impossible to give adequate thought to the severity of each problem. In addition, rank-ordering usually takes more time than considering each question on an individual basis. And, for data analysis purposes, rank-ordering restricts the type of analyses that can be carried out with the question.

If a series of questions is used, we can rank-order the responses and carry out other analyses, as well. By calculating the mean score for each of the 11 questions listed in Figure 9.4 and then rank-ordering these means, for example, we can achieve the same result as if we had been asked to rank-order the questions themselves. In addition, using a series of questions makes it possible to create an index or scale and calculate its reliability, which could not be done if rank-orders were used.

Transition Statements

Transition statements are used for several purposes. First, by speaking directly to the respondents, they lend informality to the instrument and reduce monotony. This type of statement helps respondents answer the questions and become involved in the task. An example is:

> In this section of our survey we would like to develop a sort of thumbnail sketch of your everyday life, the things you do, the things that worry

Into which occupational category do your father and mother presently fall? (Circle one number in each column below.)

	Relationship	
Occupational Category	Father	Mother
Professional	1	1	_____
Manager	2	2	_____
Sales worker	3	3	_____
Clerical worker	4	4	_____
Craftsperson	5	5	_____
Equipment operator	6	6	_____
Laborer	7	7	_____
Farmer	8	8	_____
Service	9	9	_____
Unemployed	10	10	_____
Do not know	88	88	_____
Deceased (not applicable)	99	99	_____
Other (specify)	13	13	_____

Figure 10.2 Single-Questionnaire Format for Dual Responses

or concern you, and the things that make you happy.

Transition statements are also used when the instrument introduces a new line of questioning. They tell people that they will be changing directions and forewarn them not to be surprised when they get to the next section. An example is:

Now I would like to ask you a few questions concerning recreational activities.

A third type of transition statement occurs toward the end of the questionnaire. The section that asks for demographic data should be introduced with a statement such as the following:

Finally, we would like to ask you a few questions about yourself for statistical purposes.

This kind of statement indicates the approaching end of the instrument. Transition statements are important, but they can be overdone. Overly long statements and those that may inadvertently bias the response by pressuring the respondent toward a certain kind of answer should be avoided. Moreover, the approach

should not be so didactic that it alienates respondents or makes them appear ignorant or foolish.

EVALUATING AND PRETESTING THE INSTRUMENT

A measuring instrument should be evaluated before it is administered. This can be done by providing answers to the questions presented in Chapter 9. The instrument also should be pretested to determine whether the respondents understand the questions and have a favorable impression of the appearance and utility of the instrument. Beginning researchers often conduct pretests as an afterthought, as something that must be done as part of the research process. This does not fulfill the real purposes of a pretest, which, according to Dillman (1978), should provide answers to eight specific questions about the measuring instrument:

1. Is each question measuring what it is intended to measure?
2. Are all the words understood?
3. Are questions interpreted similarly by all individuals?

4. Does each closed-ended question have a response category that applies to each person?
5. Does the questionnaire create a positive impression, one that motivates people to answer it?
6. Can the questions be answered correctly?
7. Are some questions missed? Do some questions elicit uninterpretable answers?
8. Does any aspect of the instrument suggest bias on the part of the investigator?

Answers can be found for some of these questions by mailing out the questionnaire to a sample of individuals who are similar to the study's sample or population. What we are really concerned with, however, is feedback from these individuals, and this can best be gathered by direct interaction with them.

Essentially, a sample of respondents from three types of groups is preferable for use in a pretest of a measuring instrument: colleagues, the potential users of the data, or individuals drawn from the population to be surveyed. Each of these groups can provide a different type of feedback to the instrument designer. Colleagues may be fellow students, instructors, or associates. All should have specialized experience and understand the study's purpose. Potential users of the data—agency personnel, policy makers, clients, professionals—can indicate whether any of the questions are irrelevant to their purposes or reveal a lack of knowledge on our part. People who might be the focus of the study can provide information as to the clarity and difficulty of the questions, the appropriateness of the response categories, and so on.

To gather this feedback, perhaps the best method is to administer the instrument to representatives of one of these types of groups, individually or together, and follow with a debriefing session. This gives the pretest respondents an opportunity to discuss with us what they did and did not like about the instrument, what kinds of problems they had with it, and how they felt about the experience.

SUMMARY

We can construct measuring instruments when standardized instruments are simply not available. We can use them to determine and quantify facts about people and their behaviors, beliefs, feelings, and ethical standards.

The validity and reliability of the instrument are the most crucial concerns in the design and construction of a measuring instrument. External validity can be maximized by ensuring an adequate response rate. This can be done by clearly stating the purpose of the study, avoiding sensitive questions and socially desirable answers, and asking only relevant questions. Internal validity can be maximized by reducing or eliminating measurement error in the content of the instrument. The principal concern in achieving internal validity is to make the questions clear and understandable.

The constructor of an instrument must take into account not only the content of the questions but also the kinds of responses asked for. The two principal types of questions and response categories are open-ended questions, for which respondents supply their own responses, and closed-ended questions, for which they can select responses from a number of specified choices.

A measuring instrument should give an immediate positive impression to potential respondents. This can be achieved by attention to the appearance of the instrument, the order of questions, the manner of presenting questions and responses, the organization of questions in a series or rank-ordering format, and the use of transition statements.

The principles of measurement set forth in Chapter 8, the help given in Chapter 9 for understanding and evaluating measuring instruments, and the concrete suggestions for constructing instruments given in this chapter have laid a solid foundation for the next phase of the research process—selecting an appropriate sample and a corresponding research design.

The Logic of
Research Design

Part IV consists of three chapters that present

the logic of research designs. More specifically,

Chapter 11 discusses how sampling is used in the

research process. Chapter 12 discusses the various

research designs that can be utilized when doing a

research study with a single case, while Chapter 13

presents the various designs that can be utilized

when doing a research study with groups of

people.

Sampling

11

Russell K. Schutt

A common technique in journalism is to put a "human face" on a story. A reporter for the *New York Times,* for example, went to an emergency assistance unit near Yankee Stadium to ask homeless mothers about new welfare policies that required recipients to work. One woman with three children suggested, "If you work a minimum wage job, that's nothing. . . . Think about paying rent, with a family." In contrast, another mother with three children remarked, "It's important to do it for my kids, to set an example."

A story about deportations of homeless persons in Moscow focused on the case of one 47-year-old Russian laborer temporarily imprisoned in Social Rehabilitation Center Number 2. He complained that in the town to which he would have to return, "I have no job, no family, no home" (Swarns, 1996, p. A1).

These are interesting comments in effective articles, but we do not know whether they represent the opinions of most homeless persons in the United States and Russia, of most homeless persons in New York City and Moscow, of only persons found in the emergency assistance unit near Yankee Stadium and in Social Rehabilitation Center Number 2—or of just a few people in these locations who caught the eye of these specific reporters.

In other words, we don't know how generalizable these comments are, and if we don't have confidence in their generalizability, their validity is suspect. Because we have no idea whether these opinions are widely shared or quite unique, we cannot really judge what they tell us about the real social world.

DESIGNING A SAMPLING STRATEGY

Whether we are designing a sampling strategy for a particular research study or are evaluating the generalizability of the findings from someone else's research study, we have to understand how and why social work researchers decide to sample in the first place. Sampling is very common in research studies, but sometimes it isn't necessary.

Defining the Sample Components and the Population

Let's say we are designing a research study on a topic that requires us to involve a lot of people (or other entities). These people are called *elements*. Also, we don't have the time or resources to study the entire population of all these people, so we take a subset of the population, which is called a *sample*.

We may collect our data directly from the people in our sample. Some research studies, however, are not so simple. The entities we can easily reach to gather data may not be the same as the entities from whom we really want the data. So we may collect data about the elements from another set of entities, which is called the *sampling units*. For example, if we interview mothers to learn about their families, the families are the elements and the mothers are the sampling units. If we survey department chairpersons to learn about college departments, for example, the departments are the elements and the chairpersons are the sampling units. In a study in which individual people are sampled and are the focus of the study, the sampling units are the same as the elements. (See Figure 11.1.)

One key issue with selecting or evaluating a sample's components is understanding exactly what population the sample is supposed to represent. In a survey of "adult Americans," for example, the general population may reasonably be construed as all residents of the United States who are at least 21 years of age. But always be alert to ways in which the population may have been narrowed by the sample selection procedures. Perhaps only English-speaking adult residents of the continental United States were actually sampled. The population for a study is the aggregation of elements that we actually focus on and sample from, not some larger aggregation that we really wish we could have studied.

Some populations, such as the homeless, are not identified by a simple criterion such as a geographic boundary or an organizational membership. A clear definition of such a population is difficult but quite necessary. Anyone should be able to determine just what population was actually studied. However, studies of homeless persons in the early 1980s "did not propose definitions, did not use screening questions to be sure that the people they interviewed were indeed homeless, and

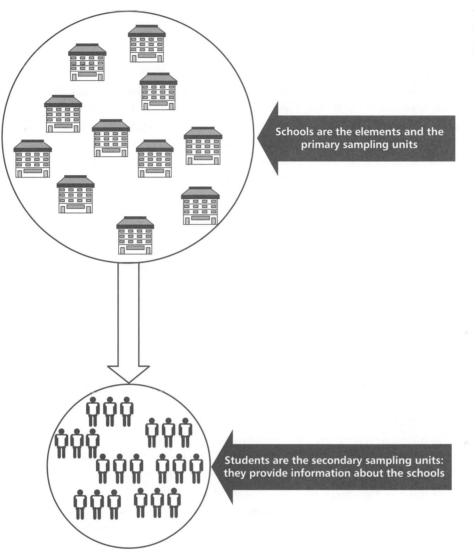

Figure 11.1 Sampling Components in a Two-Stage Study

Schools are the elements and the primary sampling units

Students are the secondary sampling units: they provide information about the schools

did not make major efforts to cover the universe of homeless people." (Perhaps just homeless persons in one shelter were studied.) The result was "a collection of studies that could not be compared" (Burt, 1996, p. 15).

Several studies of homeless persons in urban areas addressed the problem by employing a more explicit definition of the population (Burt, 1996):

> People are homeless if they have no home or permanent place to stay of their own (renting or owning) and no regular arrangement to stay at someone else's place. (15)

Even this more explicit definition still leaves some questions unanswered: What is a "regular arrangement"? How permanent does a "permanent place" have to be? In a study of homeless persons in Chicago, for example, Michael Sosin and his colleagues (1988) answered these questions in their definition of the population of interest:

> We define the homeless as: those current[ly] residing for at least one day but for less than fourteen with a friend or relative, not paying rent, and not sure that the length of stay will surpass

fourteen days; those currently residing in a shelter, whether overnight or transitional; those currently without normal, acceptable shelter arrangements and thus sleeping on the street, in doorways, in abandoned buildings, in cars, in subway or bus stations, in alleys, and so forth; those residing in a treatment center for the indigent who have lived at the facility for less than 90 days and who claim that they have no place to go, when released. (22)

This definition reflects accurately Sosin et al.'s concept of homelessness and allows researchers in other locations or at other times to develop procedures for studying a comparable population. The more complete and explicit the definition of the population from which a sample is drawn, the more precise the generalizations of the study's findings can be.

Evaluating the Sample's Generalizability

Once we have clearly defined the population from which a sample will be drawn, we need to determine the scope of the generalizations we wish to make from our sample; that is, can the findings from a sample be generalized to the population from which the sample was drawn? This is really the most basic question to ask about a sample, and social work research methods provide many tools with which to address it.

Sample generalizability depends on sample quality, which is determined by the amount of sampling error. Sampling error is the difference between the characteristics of a sample and the characteristics of the population from which the sample was selected. The larger the sampling error, the less representative the sample—and thus the less generalizable are the study's findings. To assess sample quality when you are planning or evaluating a research study, ask yourself three questions:

1. From what population were the cases selected?
2. What sampling method was used to select cases from this population?
3. Do the cases that were selected—and thus studied—represent, in the aggregate, the population from which they were drawn?

But researchers often project their study's findings onto groups or populations much larger than, or simply different from, those they have actually studied. The population to which generalizations are made in this way is called a *target population*. A target population is a set of elements larger than, or different from, the population that was sampled and to which the researcher would like to generalize the study's findings. When we generalize a study's findings to a target population, for example, we must be somewhat speculative. We must carefully consider the validity of the claim that a study's findings can be applied to other groups, to other geographic areas, to other cultures, and to other times.

Assessing the Diversity of the Population

Sampling is unnecessary if all the units in the population are identical. Physicists don't need to select a representative sample of atomic particles to learn about basic physical processes. They can study a single atomic particle, since it is identical to every other particle of its type. Similarly, biologists don't need to sample a particular type of plant to determine whether a given chemical has a toxic effect on it. The idea is, "If you've seen one, you've seen 'em all."

What about people? Certainly all people are not identical (nor are other animals in many respects). Nonetheless, if we are studying physical or psychological processes that are *exactly the same* among all people, sampling is not needed to achieve generalizable findings. Psychologists and social psychologists often conduct experiments on college students to learn about processes that they think are identical across individuals. They believe that most people would have the same reactions as the college students if they were to experience the same experimental conditions. Field researchers who observe group processes in small communities sometimes make the same assumption.

There is a potential problem with this assumption, however: There is no way to know for sure if the processes being studied are identical across all people. In fact, experiments can give different results depending on the type of people who are studied or the conditions for the experiment. Stanley Milgram's (1965) classic experiments on obedience to authority, among the most replicated (repeated) experiments in the history of social psychological research, illustrate this point very well. The Milgram experiments tested the willingness of male volunteers in New Haven, Connecticut, to comply with the instructions of an authority figure to give "electric shocks" to someone else, even when these shocks seemed to harm the person receiving them. In most cases, the volunteers complied. Milgram concluded that people are very obedient to authority.

Were these results generalizable to all men, to men in the United States, or to men in New Haven? Similar results were obtained in many replications of the Milgram experiments when the experimental conditions and subjects were similar to those studied by Milgram. Other studies, however, showed that some groups were less likely to react so obediently. Given certain conditions, such as another "subject" in the room who refused to administer the shocks, subjects were likely to resist authority.

So what do the experimental results tell us about how people will react to an authoritarian movement in the real world, when conditions are not so carefully controlled? In the real social world, people may be less likely to react obediently, as well. Other individuals may argue against obedience to a particular leader's commands, or people may see on TV the consequences of their actions. Alternatively, people may be even more obedient to authority than the experimental subjects as they get swept up in mobs or are captivated by ideological fervor. Milgram's research gives us insight into human behavior, but there's no guarantee that what he found with particular groups in particular conditions can be generalized to the larger population (or to any particular population) in different settings.

Generalizing the results of experiments and of participant observation is risky, because such types of research studies often involve a small number of people who don't represent any particular population. Researchers may put aside concerns about generalizability when they observe the social dynamics of specific clubs, college dorms, and the like or in a controlled experiment when they test the effect of, say, a violent movie on feelings for others. But we have to be cautious about generalizing the results of such studies.

The larger point is that social scientists rarely can skirt the problem of demonstrating the generalizability of their studies' findings. If a small sample has been studied in an experiment or field research project, the study should be replicated in different settings or, preferably, with a representative sample of the population to which generalizations are sought (see Figure 11.2). The social world and the people in it are just too diverse to be considered "identical units." Social psychological experiments and small field studies have produced good research studies, but they need to be replicated in other settings with other subjects to claim any generalizability. Even when we believe that we have uncovered basic social processes in a laboratory experiment or field observation, we should be very concerned with seeking confirmation in other samples and in other research studies.

In short, a representative sample "looks like" the population from which it was drawn in all respects that are potentially relevant to the study. Thus, the distribution of the characteristics among the elements of a representative sample is the same as the distribution of those characteristics among the total population from which the sample was drawn. As can be seen in Figure 11.2, in an unrepresented sample, some characteristics are overrepresented or underrepresented.

Considering a Census

In some circumstances, it may be feasible to skirt the issue of generalizability by conducting a *census*—studying the entire population of interest—rather than by drawing a sample from the population. This is what the federal government does every 10 years with the U.S. Census. Censuses may include studies of all the employees (or students) in small organizations, studies that compare all 50 states, and studies of the entire population of a particular type of organization in some area. However, in all of these instances, except for the U.S. Census, the population that is studied is relatively small.

The reason that social work researchers don't often attempt to collect data from all the members of some large population is simply that doing so would be too expensive and time-consuming (and they can do almost as well with a sample). Some do, however, conduct research studies with data from the U.S. Census,

Figure 11.2   Representative and Unrepresentative Samples

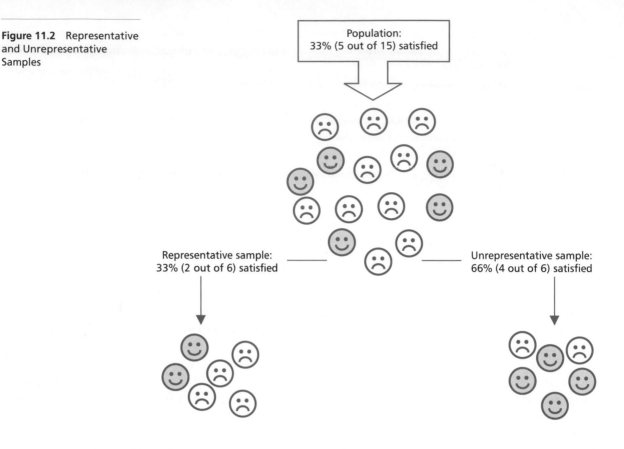

Population: 33% (5 out of 15) satisfied

Representative sample: 33% (2 out of 6) satisfied

Unrepresentative sample: 66% (4 out of 6) satisfied

but it's the government that collects the data, and your tax dollars pays for the effort. For the 1990 census, for example, the Bureau of the Census needed more than 300,000 employees just to follow up on the households that did not return their census forms in the mail (Navarro, 1990). The entire 1990 census effort cost $2.6 billion (Holmes, 1994).

Even if the population of interest for a survey is a small town of 20,000 or students in a university of 10,000, researchers will have to sample. The costs of surveying "just" thousands of individuals exceeds by far the budgets for most research projects. In fact, even the U.S. Bureau of the Census cannot afford to have everyone answer all the questions that should be covered in the census. So it draws a sample. Every household must complete a short version of the census (it had 14 questions in 1990), and a sample consisting of one in six households must complete a long form (it had 45 additional questions in 1990).

Another costly fact is that it is hard to get people to complete a survey. Federal law requires all citizens to complete their census questionnaires, but other researchers have no such authority. So most researchers must make multiple efforts to increase the rate of response to their surveys.

Even the U.S. Bureau of the Census, with all its resources, is failing to count all the nation's households. The U.S. General Accounting Office estimates that almost 10 million people were not included in the 1990 census and 4.4 million were counted twice (Holmes, 1994). Difficulties with the 1990 census included (Gleick, 1990):

too many doors to knock on, and too many people living without doors, [and] a rate of noncooperation that exceeded the estimates of even the most severe critics. . . . Those overcounted . . . tend to be wealthier and more rural than those undercounted. In poor urban neighborhoods, field workers are often afraid to enter tenements and housing projects. (22–23, 26)

Because of these problems, many statisticians recommend that the U.S. Census survey a large sample of Americans rather than the complete population, and the Bureau of the Census has tested the feasibility of focusing follow-up efforts on a sample of those who do not return their census form in the mail nor respond to phone interview attempts or door-to-door visits (Holmes, 1994). The basic idea is to invest more resources in increasing the rate of response of a representative sample of persons who do not respond easily, rather than spreading even the government's substantial resources thinly over the total respondent pool (Stout, 1997a). These statisticians believe it is "Better to hound 1 in 10 than 10 in 10" (Holmes, 1996, p. A18). Some argue that the U.S. Constitution requires a complete census, but a well-designed sample may still be preferable (Stout, 1997b, p. 31).

One final caution about census studies: Be sure you know exactly what population has been studied. James Wright and Eleanor Weber (1987) undertook a massive study of homeless persons as part of the national Health Care for the Homeless program (HCH). Teams that included doctors, nurses, and social workers filled out a contact form each time they delivered services to a homeless person in a variety of sites in 19 cities. After about a year, the resulting HCH database included data on about 34,035 clients obtained on 90,961 contact forms.

This database is a complete census of persons who receive care from HCH clinics. But the program operated in only 19 large U.S. cities, only 18 of the cities provided usable data, and the number of HCH clients appeared to include only between one-quarter and one-third of the total homeless population in these cities (Wright & Weber, 1987). Thus, the study was a census of the population of HCH clients in 18 cities, not at all a census of the entire homeless population in the nation. We might think it likely that the HCH population is similar to the general homeless population, but we won't know until we figure out how well the HCH population represents all those who are homeless.

SAMPLING METHODS

We now discuss the features of samples that make it more or less likely that they will represent the population from which they are selected. The most important distinction that needs to be made about samples is whether they are based on a probability sampling method or a nonprobability sampling method.

Probability sampling methods allow us to know in advance how likely it is that any element within a population will be selected for the sample. Nonprobability sampling methods do not let us know of this likelihood in advance.

Probability sampling methods rely on random, or chance, selection procedures. This is the same principle as flipping a coin to decide which one of two people "wins" and which one "loses." Heads and tails are equally likely to turn up in a coin toss, so both folks have an equal chance to win. That chance (a person's probability of being selected) is 1 out of 2, or .5.

Flipping a coin is a fair way to select one of two people because the selection process harbors no systematic bias. You might win or lose the coin toss, but you know that the outcome was due simply to chance, not to bias. For the same reason, a roll of a six-sided die is a fair way to choose one of six possible outcomes (the odds of selection are 1 out of 6, or .17). Dealing out a hand after shuffling a deck of cards is a fair way to allocate sets of cards in a card game (the odds of each person getting a particular outcome, such as a full house or a flush, are the same). Similarly, state lotteries use a random process to select winning numbers. Thus, the odds of winning a lottery, the probability of selection, are known, even though they are very much smaller (perhaps 1 out of 1 million) than the odds of winning a coin toss.

There is a natural tendency to confuse the concept of random sampling, in which cases are selected only on the basis of chance, with a haphazard method of sampling. On first impression, "leaving things up to chance" seems to imply not exerting any control over the sampling method. But to ensure that nothing but chance influences the selection of cases, the researcher must proceed very methodically, leaving nothing to chance except the selection of the cases themselves. The researcher must follow carefully controlled procedures if a purely random process is to occur. In fact, when reading about sampling methods, do not assume that a random sample was obtained just because the researcher used a random selection method at some point in the sampling process. Look for these two major particular problems:

1. Selecting a sample from an incomplete list of the total population from which the sample was selected
2. Failing to obtain an adequate response rate

If the sampling frame (the list from which the elements of the population were selected) is incomplete, a sample selected randomly from that list will not really be a random sample of the population from which it was drawn. You should always consider the adequacy of the sampling frame. Even for a simple population like a university's student body, the Registrar's list is likely to be at least a bit out of date at any given time. For example, some students will have dropped out, but their status will not yet be officially recorded. Although you may judge the amount of error introduced in this particular situation to be negligible, the problems are greatly compounded for larger populations. The sampling frame for a city, state, or nation, for example, is always likely to be incomplete because of constant migration into and out of the area. Even unavoidable omissions from the sampling frame can bias a sample against particular groups within a population.

A very inclusive sampling frame may still yield systematic bias if many sample members cannot be contacted or refuse to participate. Nonresponse is a major hazard in survey research because nonrespondents are likely to differ systematically from those who take the time to participate. You should not assume that findings from a randomly selected sample will be generalizable to the population from which the sample was selected if the rate of nonresponse is considerable (certainly not if it is much above 30 percent).

Probability Sampling Methods

Probability sampling methods are those in which the probability of an element's being selected is known in advance. These methods randomly select elements and therefore have no systematic bias; nothing but chance determines which elements are included in the sample. This feature of probability samples makes them much more desirable than nonprobability samples when the goal of a research study is to generalize its findings to a larger population.

Even though a random sample has no systematic bias, it will certainly have some sampling error due to chance. The probability of selecting a head is .5 in a single toss of a coin and in 20, 30, and however many tosses of a coin you like. But it is perfectly possible to toss a coin twice and get a head both times. The random "sample" of the two sides of the coin is selected in an unbiased fashion, but it still is unrepresentative. Imagine selecting randomly a sample of 10 people from a population comprising 50 men and 50 women. Just by chance, can't you imagine finding that these 10 people include 7 women and only 3 men? Fortunately, we can determine mathematically the likely degree of sampling error in an estimate based on a random sample, assuming that the sample's randomness has not been destroyed by a high rate of nonresponse or by poor control over the selection process.

In general, both the size of the sample and the homogeneity (sameness) of the population from which the sample was drawn affect the degree of error due to chance; the proportion of the population that the sample does not represent. To elaborate:

- The larger the sample, the more confidence we can have in the sample's representativeness. If we randomly pick 5 people to represent the entire population of our city, for example, our sample is unlikely to be very representative of our city's entire population in terms of age, gender, race, attitudes, and so on. But if we randomly pick 100 people, the odds of having a representative sample of our city's entire population are much better; with a random sample of 1,000, the odds become very good indeed.
- The more homogeneous the population, the more confidence we can have in the representativeness of a sample of any particular size. Let's say we plan to draw samples of 50 families from each of two communities to estimate "average

family income." One community is very diverse, with family incomes varying from $12,000 to $85,000. In the other, more homogeneous community, family incomes are concentrated in a narrow range, from $41,000 to $64,000. The estimate of average family income based on the sample from the homogeneous community is more likely to be representative than is the estimate based on the sample from the more heterogeneous community. With less variation to represent, fewer cases are needed to represent the homogeneous community.

- The fraction of the total population that a sample contains does not affect the sample's representativeness, unless that fraction is large. We can regard any sampling fraction under 2 percent with about the same degree of confidence (Sudman, 1976). In fact, sample representativeness is not likely to increase much until the sampling fraction is quite a bit higher. Other things being equal, a sample of *1,000* from a population of 1 million (with a sampling fraction of 0.001, or 0.1 percent) is much better than a sample of 100 from a population of *10,000* (although the sampling fraction is 0.01, or 1 percent, which is 10 times higher). The size of a sample is what makes representativeness more likely, not the proportion of the whole that the sample represents.

Polls to predict presidential election outcomes illustrate both the value of random sampling and the problems that it cannot overcome. In most presidential elections, pollsters have predicted accurately the outcomes of the actual final vote by using random sampling and, these days, phone interviewing to learn whom likely voters intend to vote for. Table 11.1 shows how close these sample-based predictions have been in the past 10 contests. The big exception, however, was the 1980 election, when a third-party candidate had an unpredicted effect. Otherwise, the small discrepancies between the votes predicted through random sampling and the actual votes can be attributed to random error.

But election polls have produced some major errors in prediction. The reasons for these errors illustrate some of the ways in which unintentional systematic bias can

TABLE 11.1

Election Outcomes: Predicted[1] and Actual

Winner	Year	Polls	Results
Kennedy	1960	49%	50%
Johnson	1964	64%	61%
Nixon	1968[2]	44%	43%
Nixon	1972	59%	61%
Carter	1976	49%	50%
Reagan	1980[2]	42%	51%
Reagan	1984	57%	59%
Bush	1988	50%	53%
Clinton	1992[2]	41%	43%[3]
Clinton	1996[2]	52%[4]	46%[5]

[1]Polls one week prior to election.
[2]There was also a third-party candidate.
[3]Outcome from *Academic American Encyclopedia,* on-line version.
[4]Source of 1996 poll data: Gallup poll (http:www.gallup.com/poli/data/96prelec.html).
[5]Outcome from Mediacity.com Web pages E6, 8/30/97.
  Source: 1960–1992 data, Gallup poll (Loth, 1992).

influence sample results. In 1936, for example, a *Literary Digest* poll predicted that Alfred M. Landon would defeat President Franklin D. Roosevelt in a landslide, but instead Roosevelt took 63 percent of the popular vote. The problem? The *Digest* mailed out 10 million mock ballots to people listed in telephone directories, automobile registration records, voter lists, and so on. But in 1936, the middle of the Great Depression, only relatively wealthy people had phones and cars, and they were more likely to be Republican. Furthermore, only 2,376,523 completed ballots were returned, and a response rate of only 24 percent leaves much room for error. Of course, this poll was not designed as a random sample, so the appearance of systematic bias is not surprising. Unlike the *Literary Digest* poll, George Gallup was able to predict the 1936 election results accurately with a randomly selected sample of just 3,000 (Bainbridge, 1989).

In 1948, pollsters mistakenly predicted that Thomas E. Dewey would beat Harry S. Truman. They relied on the random sampling method that Gallup had used successfully since 1934. The problem? Pollsters stopped collecting data several weeks before the election, and in those weeks many people changed their minds (Kenney, 1987). So the sample was systematically biased by underrepresenting shifts in voter sentiment just before the election.

The year 1980 was the only year in the preceding 32 that pollsters had the wrong prediction in the week prior to the election. With Jimmy Carter ahead of Ronald Reagan in the polls by 45 percent to 42 percent, Gallup predicted a race too close to call. The outcome: Reagan 51 percent, Carter 42 percent. The problem? A large bloc of undecided voters, an unusually late debate with a strong performance by Reagan, and the failure of many pollsters to call back voters whom interviewers had failed to reach on the first try (these harder-to-reach voters were more likely to be Republican-leaning) (Dolnick, 1984; Loth, 1992). In this case, the sample was systematically biased against voters who were harder to reach and those who were influenced by the final presidential debate. The presence in the sample of many undecided voters was apparently an accurate representation of sentiment in the general population, so the problem would not be considered "sample bias." It did, however, make measuring voting preferences all the more difficult.

Because they do not disproportionately exclude or include particular groups within the population, random samples that are successfully implemented avoid systematic bias. Random error can still be considerable, however, and different types of random samples vary in their ability to minimize it. The four most common methods for drawing random samples are (1) simple random sampling, (2) systematic random sampling, (3) stratified random sampling, and (4) cluster random sampling.

Simple Random Sampling

Simple random sampling requires some procedure that generates numbers or otherwise identifies cases strictly on the basis of chance. As you know, flipping a coin and rolling a die both can be used to identify cases strictly on the basis of chance. These procedures, however, are not very efficient tools for drawing samples. A random numbers table simplifies the process considerably. The researcher numbers all the elements in the sampling frame (the population) and then uses a systematic procedure for picking corresponding numbers from the random numbers table. Alternatively, a researcher may use a lottery procedure. Each case number is written on a small card. Then the cards are mixed up and a sample is selected from the cards.

When a large sample must be generated, these procedures are very cumbersome. Fortunately, a computer program can easily generate a random sample of any size. The researcher must first number all the elements to be sampled (the sampling frame) and then run the computer program to generate a random selection of the numbers within the desired range. The elements represented by these numbers are the sample.

Organizations that conduct phone surveys often draw random samples with another automated procedure, called random digit dialing. A machine dials random numbers within the phone prefixes corresponding to the area in which the survey is to be conducted. Random digit dialing is particularly useful when a sampling frame is not available. The researcher simply replaces any inappropriate telephone numbers (those that are no longer in service or that are for businesses, for example) with the next randomly generated phone number.

The probability of selection in a true simple random sample is equal for each element. If a sample of 500 is selected from a population of 17,000 (that is, a sampling frame of 17,000), then the probability of selection for each element is 500/17,000, or .03. Every element has an equal chance of being selected, just like the odds in a toss of a coin (1/2) or a roll of a die (1/6).

Simple random sampling can be done either with or without replacement sampling. In replacement sampling, each element is returned to the sampling frame after it is selected so that it may be sampled again. In sampling without replacement, each element selected for the sample is then excluded from the sampling frame. In practice, it makes no difference whether sampled elements are replaced after selection, as long as the population is large and the sample is to contain only a small fraction of the population.

In a study involving simple random sampling, for example, Bruce Link and his associates (1996) used random digit dialing to contact adult household members in the continental United States for an investigation of public attitudes and beliefs about homeless people. Sixty-three percent of the potential interviewees responded. The sample actually obtained was not exactly comparable to the population from which his sample was drawn: Compared to U.S. Census figures, his sample overrepresented women, people ages 25 to 54, married people, and those with more than a high school education. It also underrepresented Latinos.

How does this sample strike you? Let's assess sample quality using the questions posed earlier in the chapter:

1. *From what population were the cases selected?* There is a clearly defined population: the adult residents of the continental United States (who live in households with phones).
2. *What method was used to select cases from this population?* The case selection method is a random selection procedure, and there are no systematic biases in the sampling.
3. *Do the cases that were studied represent, in the aggregate, the population from which they were selected?* The findings are very likely to represent the population sampled, because there were no biases in the sampling and a very large number of cases was selected. However, 37 percent of those selected for interviews could not be contacted or chose not to respond. This rate of nonresponse seems to create a small bias in the sample for several characteristics.

We also must consider the issue of cross-population generalizability: Do findings from this sample have implications for any larger group beyond the population from which the sample was drawn? Because a representative sample of the entire U.S. adult population was drawn, this question has to do with cross-national generalizations. Link and his colleagues don't make any such generalizations. There's no telling what might occur in other countries with different histories of homelessness and different social policies.

Systematic Random Sampling

Systematic random sampling is a variant of simple random sampling. The first element is selected randomly from a list or from sequential files, and then every *n*th element is selected. This is a convenient method for drawing a random sample when the population elements are arranged sequentially. It is particularly efficient when the elements are not actually printed (that is, there is no sampling frame) but instead are repre-

sented by folders in filing cabinets. For example, at a homeless shelter in Boston, a colleague and I drew a systematic random sample of intake records (Garrett & Schutt, 1990).

Systematic random sampling requires three steps:

Step 1.   The total number of cases in the population is divided by the number of cases required for the sample. This division yields the sampling interval, the number of cases from one sampled case to another. If 50 cases are to be selected out of 1,000, for example, the sampling interval is 20 (1000/50); every 20th case is selected.

Step 2.   A number from 1 to 20 (or whatever the sampling interval is) is selected randomly. This number identifies the first case to be sampled, counting from the first case on the list or in the files.

Step 3.   After the first case is selected, every *n*th case is selected for the sample, where *n* is the sampling interval. If the sampling interval is not a whole number, the size of the sampling interval is varied systematically to yield the proper number of cases for the sample. For example, if the sampling interval is 30.5, the sampling interval alternates between 30 and 31.

In almost all sampling situations, systematic random sampling yields what is essentially a simple random sample. The exception is a situation in which the sequence of elements is affected by periodicity—that is, the sequence varies in some regular, periodic pattern. For example, the houses in a new development with the same number of houses on each block (eight, for example) may be listed by block, starting with the house in the northwest corner of each block and continuing clockwise. If the sampling interval is 8, the same as the periodic pattern, all the cases selected will be in the same position (see Figure 11.3). But in reality, periodicity and the sampling interval are rarely the same.

Stratified Random Sampling

Although all probability sampling methods use random sampling, some add additional steps to the sampling

Figure 11.3 The Effect of Periodicity on Systematic Random Sampling

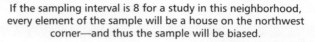

If the sampling interval is 8 for a study in this neighborhood, every element of the sample will be a house on the northwest corner—and thus the sample will be biased.

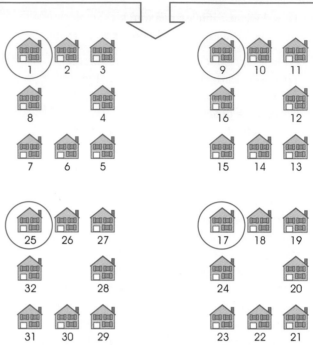

process in order to make sampling more efficient or easier. A particular sample is more efficient than another when it is easier to obtain without sacrificing confidence that its sample statistics are representative of the population from which it was drawn. Samples are easier to collect when they require less time, less money, and less prior information.

Stratified random sampling uses information known about the total population prior to sampling to make the sampling process more efficient. First, all elements in the population (that is, in the sampling frame) are distinguished according to their value on some relevant characteristic. That characteristic forms the sampling strata. Next, elements are sampled randomly from within these strata. For example, race may be the basis for distinguishing individuals in some population of interest. Within each racial category, individuals are then sampled randomly.

Why is this method more efficient than drawing a simple random sample? Imagine that you plan to draw a

sample of 500 from an ethnically diverse neighborhood. The neighborhood's population is as follows:

black	15%
Hispanic	10%
Asian	5%
white	70%

If you drew a simple random sample, you might end up with disproportionate percentages (or numbers) for each group. But if you created sampling strata based on race and ethnicity, you could randomly select cases from each stratum:

blacks	(15% of the sample)	75 cases selected	(500 × .15)
Hispanics	(10% of the sample)	50 cases selected	(500 × .10)
Asians	(5% of the sample)	25 cases selected	(500 × .05)
whites	(70% of the sample)	350 cases selected	(500 × .70)

By using proportionate stratified sampling, you would eliminate any possibility of error in the sample's distribution of ethnicity. Each stratum would be represented exactly in proportion to its size in the population from which the sample was drawn (see Figure 11.4).

In disproportionate stratified sampling, the proportion of each stratum that is included in the sample is intentionally varied from what it is in the population. In the case of the sample stratified by ethnicity, you might select equal numbers of cases from each racial or ethnic group:

125 blacks	(25% of the sample)
125 Hispanics	(25% of the sample)
125 Asians	(25% of the sample)
125 whites	(25% of the sample)

In this type of sample, the probability of selection of every case is known but unequal between strata. You know what the proportions are in the population, and so you can easily adjust your combined sample statistics to reflect these true proportions. For instance, if you want to combine the ethnic groups and estimate the average income of the total population, you have to "weight" each case in the sample. The weight is a number you multiply by the value of each case based on the stratum it is in. For example, you would multiply the incomes of all:

blacks in the sample by 0.6	(75/125)
Hispanics in the sample by 0.4	(50/125)
Asians in the sample by 0.2	(25/125)
whites in the sample by 2.8	(350/125)

Weighting in this way reduces the influence of the oversampled strata and increases the influence of the

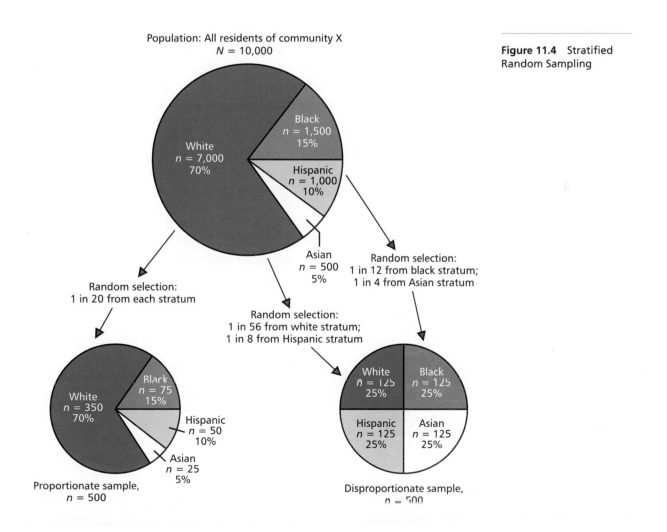

Figure 11.4   Stratified Random Sampling

undersampled strata to just what they would have been if pure probability sampling had been used.

Why would anyone select a sample that is so unrepresentative in the first place? The most common reason is to ensure that cases from smaller strata are included in the sample in sufficient numbers to allow separate statistical estimates and to facilitate comparisons between strata. Remember that one of the determinants of a sample's quality is its size. The same is true for subgroups within samples. If a key concern in a research project is to describe and compare the incomes of people from different racial and ethnic groups, then it is important that the researchers base the average income of each group on enough cases to ensure a valid representation. If few members of a particular minority group are in the population, they need to be oversampled. Such disproportionate sampling may also result in a more efficient sampling design if the costs of data collection differ markedly between strata or if the variability (heterogeneity) of the strata differs.

Cluster Random Sampling

Stratified sampling requires more information than usual prior to sampling (about the size of strata in the population); cluster sampling, on the other hand, requires less prior information. Specifically, cluster sampling can be useful when a sampling frame is not available, as often is the case for large populations spread out across wide geographic areas or among many different organizations.

A cluster is a naturally occurring mixed aggregate of elements of the population, with each element appearing in one and only one cluster. Schools could serve as clusters for sampling students, blocks could serve as clusters for sampling city residents, counties could serve as clusters for sampling the general population, and businesses could serve as clusters for sampling employees.

Drawing a cluster sample is at least a two-stage procedure. First, the researcher draws a random sample of clusters. A list of clusters should be much easier to obtain than a list of all the individuals in each cluster in the population. Next, the researcher draws a random sample of elements within each selected cluster. Because only a fraction of the total clusters are involved, obtaining the sampling frame at this stage should be much easier.

In a cluster sample of city residents, for example, blocks could be the first-stage clusters. A research assistant could walk around each selected block and record the addresses of all occupied dwelling units. Or, in a cluster sample of students, a researcher could contact the schools selected in the first stage and make arrangements with the Registrar to obtain lists of students at each school. Cluster samples often involve multiple stages (see Figure 11.5).

How many clusters and how many individuals within clusters should be selected? As a general rule, cases in the sample will be closer to the true population value if the researcher maximizes the number of clusters selected and minimizes the number of individuals within each cluster. Unfortunately, this strategy also maximizes the cost of obtaining the sample. The more clusters selected, the higher the travel costs. It also is important to take into account the homogeneity of the individuals within clusters—the more homogeneous the clusters, the fewer cases needed per cluster.

Cluster sampling is a very popular method among survey researchers, but it has one drawback: Sampling

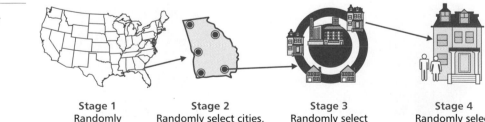

Figure 11.5 Cluster Sampling

Stage 1
Randomly select states

Stage 2
Randomly select cities, towns, and counties within those states

Stage 3
Randomly select dwellings within those cities and towns

Stage 4
Randomly select individuals within each dwelling

TABLE 11.2

Chicago Shelter Universe and Shelter Samples, Fall and Winter Surveys

		Fall	Winter
A. Shelter Universe and Samples			
Eligible shelters in universe		28	45
Universe bed capacities		1,573	2,001
Shelters drawn in sample		22	27

B. Details of Winter Shelter Sample

Shelter Size Classification	Number in Universe	Number in Sample	Occupant Sampling Ratio
Large (37 or more beds)	17	17	0.25
Medium (18–33 beds)	12	6	0.50
Small (under 18 beds)	16	4	1.00

Note: Shelters were drawn with probabilities proportionate to size, with residents sampled disproportionately within shelters to form a self-weighting sample. Sampling ratios for the phase two samples are given in Panel B.
Source: Rossi, 1989, p. 225.

---

error is greater in a cluster sample than in a simple random sample. This error increases as the number of clusters decreases, and it decreases as the homogeneity of cases per cluster increases.

Many professionally designed surveys use multistage cluster samples or even combinations of cluster and stratified probability sampling methods. For example, Peter Rossi (1989) drew a disproportionate stratified cluster sample of shelter users for his Chicago study (see Table 11.2). The shelter sample was stratified by size, with smaller shelters having a smaller likelihood of selection than larger shelters. In fact, the larger shelters were all selected; they had a probability of selection of 1.0. Within the selected shelters, shelter users were then sampled using a systematic random selection procedure (except in the small shelters, in which all persons were interviewed). Homeless persons living on the streets were also sampled randomly. In the first stage, city blocks were classified in strata on the basis of the likely concentration of homeless persons (estimated by several knowledgeable groups). Blocks were then picked randomly within these strata and, on the survey night between 1 a.m. and 6 a.m., teams of interviewers screened all people found outside on that block for their homeless status. Persons identi-

fied as homeless were then interviewed (and given $5 for their time). The rate of response for two different samples (fall and winter) in the shelters and on the streets was between 73 percent and 83 percent.

How would we evaluate the Chicago homeless sample (Table 11.2), using the sample evaluation questions?

1. *From what population were the cases selected?* The population was clearly defined for each cluster.
2. *What method was used to select cases from this population?* The random selection method was carefully described.
3. *Do the cases that were studied represent, in the aggregate, the population from which they were selected?* The unbiased selection procedures make us reasonably confident in the representativeness of the sample, although we know little about the nonrespondents and therefore may justifiably worry that some types of homeless persons were missed.

Cross-population generalization seems to be reasonable with this sample, since it seems likely that the findings reflect general processes involving homeless persons. Rossi clearly thought so, because his book's title referred to homelessness in America, not just in Chicago.

Nonprobability Sampling Methods

Four nonprobability sampling methods are used with some frequency: (1) availability sampling, (2) quota sampling, (3) purposive sampling, and (4) snowball sampling. Because they do not use random selection procedures, we cannot expect samples selected with any of these methods to yield representative samples for the populations from which they were drawn. Nonetheless, these methods may be useful when random sampling is not possible, for research questions that do not concern large populations, or for qualitative research studies.

Availability Sampling

Elements are selected for availability sampling because they're available and/or easy to find. Thus, this sampling method is also known as a haphazard, accidental, or convenience sample. News reporters often use person-on-the-street interviews—availability samples—to inject color into a news story and to show what ordinary people think.

An availability sample is often appropriate in social work research, for example, when a field researcher is exploring a new setting and is trying to get some sense of prevailing attitudes, or when a survey researcher conducts a preliminary test of a new set of questions. And there are many ways to select elements for an availability sample: standing on street corners and talking to whoever walks by; asking questions of employees who come to pick up their paychecks at a personnel office and who have time to talk to a researcher; surveying merchants who happen to be at work when the researcher is looking for research participants. For example, when Philippe Bourgois and his colleagues (1997) studied homeless heroin addicts in San Francisco, they immersed themselves in a community of addicts living in a public park. These addicts became their availability sample.

But now I'd like you to answer the three sample evaluation questions with person-on-the-street interviews of the homeless in mind. If your answers are something like "The population was unknown," "The method for selecting cases was haphazard," and "The cases studied do not represent the population," you're

right! There is no clearly definable population from which the respondents were drawn, and no systematic technique was used to select the respondents. There certainly is not much likelihood that the interviewees represent the distribution of sentiment among homeless persons in the Boston area or of welfare mothers or of impoverished rural migrants to Moscow or of whatever we imagine the relevant population is. Perhaps person-on-the-street comments to news reporters do suggest something about what homeless persons think. Or maybe they don't; we can't really be sure.

But let's give reporters their due: If they just want to have a few quotes to make their story more appealing, nothing is wrong with their sampling method. However, their approach gives us no basis for thinking that we have an overview of community sentiment. The people who happen to be available in any situation are unlikely to be just like those who are unavailable. We shouldn't kid ourselves into thinking that what we learn can be generalized with any confidence to a larger population of concern.

Availability sampling often masquerades as a more rigorous form of research. Popular magazines periodically survey their readers by printing a questionnaire for readers to fill out and mail in. A follow-up article then appears in the magazine under a title like "What You Think about Intimacy in Marriage." If the magazine's circulation is large, a large sample can be achieved in this way. The problem is that usually only a tiny fraction of readers return the questionnaire, and these respondents are probably unlike other readers who did not have the interest or time to participate. So the survey is based on an availability sample. Even though the follow-up article may be interesting, we have no basis for thinking that the results describe the readership as a whole—much less the population at large.

Quota Sampling

Quota sampling is intended to overcome the most obvious flaw of availability sampling—that the sample will just consist of whomever or whatever is available, without any concern for its similarity to the population of interest. The distinguishing feature of a quota sample is that quotas are set to ensure that the sample represents certain characteristics in proportion to their prevalence in the population from which it is to be drawn.

Suppose, for example, that you wish to sample adult residents of a town to ascertain their support for a tax increase to improve the town's schools. You know from the town's annual report what the proportions of town residents are in terms of gender, race, age, and number of children per family. You think that each of these characteristics might influence support for new school taxes, so you want to be sure that the sample includes men, women, whites, blacks, Hispanics, Asians, older people, younger people, big families, small families, and childless families in proportion to their numbers in the town's population.

This is where quotas come in. Let's say that the town is composed of:

48% men
52% women

60% white
15% black
10% Hispanic
15% Asian

These percentages and the percentages that correspond to the other characteristics become the quotas for the sample. If you plan to include a total of 500 residents in your sample:

240 must be men	(48% of 500)
260 must be women	(52% of 500)
300 must be white	(60% of 500)
75 must be black	(15% of 500)
50 must be Hispanic	(10% of 500)
75 must be Asian	(15% of 500)

You may even set more refined quotas, such as certain numbers of white women, white men, and Asian men.

With the quota list in hand, you (or your research staff) can now go out into the community looking for the right number of people in each quota category. You may go door to door, go bar to bar, or just stand on a street corner until you have surveyed 240 men, 260 women, and so on.

Some features of quota sampling may appear in what are primarily availability sampling strategies. For

instance, Doug Timmer and his colleagues (1993) interviewed homeless persons in several cities and other locations for their book on the sources of homelessness. Persons who were available were interviewed, but the researchers paid some attention to generating a diverse sample. They interviewed 20 homeless men who lived on the streets without shelter and 20 mothers who were found in family shelters. About half of those the researchers selected in the street sample were black, and about half were white. Although the researchers did not use quotas to try to match the distribution of characteristics among the total homeless population, their informal quotas helped to ensure some diversity in key characteristics.

Even when we know that a quota sample is representative of the particular characteristics for which quotas have been set, we have no way of knowing whether the sample is representative in terms of any other characteristics. In Figure 11.6, for example, quotas have been set for gender only. Under the circumstances, it's no surprise that the sample is representative of the population only in terms of gender, not in terms of race. Interviewers are only human; they may avoid potential respondents with menacing dogs in the front yard, or they could seek out respondents who are physically attractive or who look like they'd be easy to interview. Realistically, researchers can set quotas for only a small fraction of the characteristics relevant to a study, so a quota sample is really not so much better than an availability sample (although following careful, consistent procedures for selecting cases within the quota limits always helps).

This last point leads to another limitation of quota sampling: You must know the characteristics of the entire sample to set the right quotas. In most cases, researchers know what the population looks like in terms of no more than a few of the characteristics relevant to their concerns. And in some cases they have no such information on the entire population.

Purposive Sampling

In purposive sampling, each sample element is selected for a purpose because of the unique position of the sample elements. Purposive sampling may involve studying the entire population of some limited group (directors

Figure 11.6   Quota Sampling

Population
50% male, 50% female
70% white, 30% black

Quota sample
50% male, 50% female

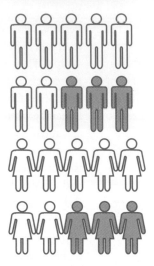

Representative of gender distribution
in population, not representative of
race distribution.

of shelters for homeless adults) or a subset of a population (mid-level managers with a reputation for efficiency). Or a purposive sample may be a "key informant survey," which targets individuals who are particularly knowledgeable about the issues under investigation.

Herbert Rubin and Irene Rubin (1995) suggest three guidelines for selecting informants when designing any purposive sampling strategy. Informants should be:

• Knowledgeable about the cultural arena or situation or experience being studied
• Willing to talk
• Represent(ative of) the range of points of view

In addition, they suggest continuing to select interviewees until you can pass two tests:

• *Completeness.* What you hear provides an overall sense of the meaning of a concept, theme, or process.
• *Saturation.* You gain confidence that you are learning little that is new from subsequent interview(s).

Adhering to these guidelines will help to ensure that a purposive sample adequately represents the setting or issues studied.

Of course, purposive sampling does not produce a sample that represents some larger population, but it can be exactly what is needed in a case study of an organization, a community, or some other clearly defined and relatively limited group. In an intensive organizational case study, for example, a purposive sample of organizational leaders might be complemented with a probability sample of organizational members. Before designing her probability samples of hospital patients and homeless persons, Dee Roth (1990) interviewed a purposive sample of 164 key informants from organizations that had contact with homeless people in each county she studied.

Snowball Sampling

For snowball sampling, you identify one member of the population and speak to him or her, then ask that person to identify others in the population and speak to them, then ask them to identify others, and so on. The sample thus "snowballs" in size. This technique is useful for hard-to-reach or hard-to-identify, interconnected populations (at least some members of the population know each other), such as drug dealers, prostitutes, practicing criminals, participants in Alcoholics Anonymous groups, gang leaders, and informal organizational leaders. It also may be used for charting the relationships among members of some group (a sociometric study), for exploring the population of interest prior to developing a formal sampling plan, and for developing what becomes a census of informal leaders of small organizations or communities. However, researchers who use snowball sampling normally cannot be confident that their samples represent the total populations of interest, so their generalizations must be tentative.

Rob Rosenthal (1994) used snowball sampling to study homeless persons living in Santa Barbara, California:

> I began this process by attending a meeting of homeless people had heard about through my housing advocate contacts. . . . One homeless, woman . . . invited me to . . . where she promised to introduce me around. Thus a process of snowballing began. I gained entree to a group through people I knew, came to know others, and through them I gained entree to new circles. (178, 180)

One problem with this technique is that the initial contacts may shape the entire sample and foreclose access to some members of the population of interest (Rosenthal, 1994):

> Sat around with [my contact] at the Tree. Other people come by, are friendly, but some regulars, especially the tougher men, don't sit with her. Am I making a mistake by tying myself too closely to her? She lectures them a lot. (181)

More systematic versions of snowball sampling can reduce this potential for bias. The most sophisticated, termed "respondent-driven sampling," gives financial incentives to respondents to recruit peers (Heckathorn, 1997). Limitations on the number of incentives that anyone respondent can receive increase the sample's

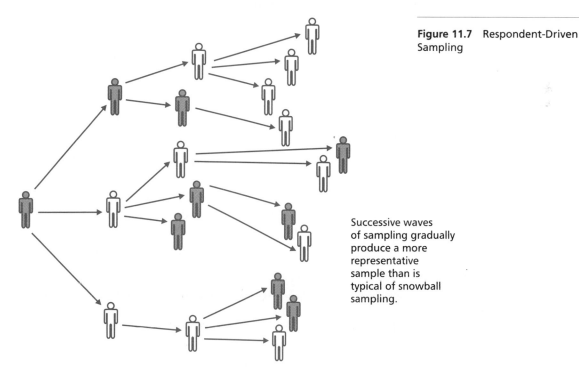

Figure 11.7   Respondent-Driven Sampling

Successive waves of sampling gradually produce a more representative sample than is typical of snowball sampling.

Instructions to respondents:
"We'll pay you $5 each for up to three names, but only one of those names can be somebody from your own town. The others have to be from somewhere else."

diversity. Targeted incentives can steer the sample to include specific subgroups. When the sampling is repeated through several waves, with new respondents bringing in more peers, the composition of the sample converges on a more representative mix of characteristics. Figure 11.7 shows how the sample spreads out through successive recruitment waves to an increasingly diverse pool (Heckathorn, 1997).

LESSONS ABOUT SAMPLE QUALITY

Some lessons are implicit in the evaluations of the samples in this chapter:

- We can't evaluate the quality of a sample if we don't know what population it is supposed to represent. If the population is unspecified because the researchers were never clear about just what population they were trying to sample, then we can safely conclude that the sample itself is no good.
- We can't evaluate the quality of a sample if we don't know just how cases in the sample were selected from the population. If the method was specified, we then need to know whether cases were selected in a systematic fashion and on the basis of chance. In any case, we know that a haphazard method of sampling (as in person-on-the-street interviews) undermines the generalizability of the study's findings.
- Sample quality is determined by the sample actually obtained, not just by the sampling method itself. If many of the people selected for our sample are nonrespondents or people (or other entities) who do not participate in the study although they have been selected for the sample, the quality of our sample is undermined—even if we chose the sample in the best possible way.
- We need to be aware that even researchers who obtain very good samples may talk about the implications of their findings for some other groups that are larger than or just different from the population they actually sampled. For example, findings from a representative sample of students in one university often are discussed as if they tell us about university students in general. And maybe they do; we just don't know.

DETERMINING SAMPLE SIZE

Now that you know that more confidence can be placed in the generalizability of statistics from larger samples, you may be eager to work with random samples that are as large as possible. Unfortunately, researchers often cannot afford to sample a very large number of cases. They therefore try to determine during the design phase of their studies how large a sample they must have to achieve their purposes. They have to consider the degree of confidence desired, the homogeneity of the population, the complexity of the analysis they plan, and the expected strength of the relationships they will measure:

- The less sampling error desired, the larger the sample size must be.
- Samples of more homogeneous populations can be smaller than samples of more diverse populations. Stratified sampling uses prior information on the population to create more homogeneous population strata from which the sample can be selected, so the sample can be smaller than if simple random sampling were used.
- If the only analysis planned for a survey sample is to describe the population in terms of a few variables, a smaller sample is required than if a more complex analysis involving sample subgroups is planned.
- When the researchers will be testing hypotheses and expect to find very strong relationships among the variables, they will need smaller samples to detect these relationships than if they expect weaker relationships.

Researchers can make more precise estimates of the sample size required through a method termed "statistical power analysis" (Kraemer & Thiemann, 1987). Statistical power analysis requires a good advance estimate of the strength of the hypothesized relationship in the population. In addition, the math is complicated, so it helps to have some background in mathematics or to be able to consult a statistician. For these reasons, many researchers do not conduct formal power analyses when deciding how many cases to sample.

You can obtain some general guidance about sample sizes from the current practices of social scientists. For professional studies of the national population in which only a simple description is desired, professional social science studies typically have used a sample size of between 1,000 and 1,500, with up to 2,500 being included if detailed analyses are planned. Studies of local or regional populations often sample only a few hundred people, in part because these studies lack sufficient funding to draw larger samples. Of course, the sampling error in these smaller studies is considerably larger than in a typical national study (Sudman, 1976).

SUMMARY

Sampling is a powerful tool for social work research. Probability sampling methods allow a researcher to use the laws of chance, or probability, to draw samples from which population parameters can be estimated with a high degree of confidence. A sample of just 1,000 or 1,500 individuals can be used to estimate reliably the characteristics of the population of a nation comprising millions of individuals.

But researchers do not come by representative samples easily. Well-designed samples require careful planning, some advance knowledge about the population to be sampled, and adherence to systematic selection procedures—all so that the selection procedures are not biased. And even after the sample data are collected, the researcher's ability to generalize from the sample's findings to the population from which it was drawn is not completely certain.

The alternatives to random, or probability-based, sampling methods are almost always much less palatable, even though they typically are much cheaper. Unless the researcher's method of selecting cases is likely to yield a sample that represents the population in which the researcher is interested, research findings will have to be carefully qualified. Unrepresentative samples may help researchers understand which aspects of a social phenomenon are important, but questions about the generalizability of this understanding are left unanswered.

Case-Level Designs

Margaret Williams

Richard M. Grinnell, Jr.

Yvonne A. Unrau

12

In the preceding chapter, we discussed how to select research participants for research studies. This chapter is a logical extension of the pervious one in that we now look at the different ways of designing or setting up our studies in which research participants are included. On a basic level, a research design is essentially a plan for conducting the entire research study from beginning to end. All research plans—interpretive or positivistic—are formulated in order to answer the following basic questions:

- When, or over what period, should the research study be conducted?
- What variables need to be measured?
- How should the variables be measured?
- What other variables need to be accounted for or controlled?
- From whom should the data be collected?
- How should the data be collected?
- How should the data be analyzed?
- How should the results of the study be disseminated?

As you should know by now, these questions are highly interrelated and are directly related to the question we are trying to answer or the hypothesis we are testing. If you are exploring the concept of bereavement, for example, you will collect data from bereaved people and perhaps involved social workers, and you will need to measure variables related to bereavement, such as grief, anger, depression, and levels of coping. You might need to measure these variables over a period of months or years, and the way you measure them will suggest appropriate methods of how you will analyze your data. Decisions about how best to accomplish these steps depends on how much we already know about the bereavement process: that is, where your bereavement research questions fall on the knowledge level continuum as presented in Figure 1.5.

Over the years, researchers have developed a kind of shorthand, representing research designs in terms of letters and numbers, dividing them into categories, and giving them names. Let us now look at how this research shorthand is applied to research questions that can be loosely classified as case-level designs. They are also called *single-subject designs, single-case experimentations*, or *idiographic research*. They are used to fulfill the major purpose of social work practice: to improve the situation of a client system—*an* individual client, *a* couple, *a* family, *a* group, *an* organization, or *a* community. Any of these client configurations can be studied with a case-level design. In short, they are used to study *one* individual or *one* group intensively.

CASE-LEVEL RESEARCH DESIGNS

Some research studies are conducted in order to study one individual, or case, some to study groups of people (including families, organizations, and communities), and some to study social artifacts (such things as birth practices or divorces). The individual, group, or artifact being studied is called the *unit of analysis*. If you are exploring the advantages and disadvantages of home birth, for example, you might be asking questions from women who have experienced homebirth, but the thing you are studying—the *unit of analysis*—is the social artifact, home birth. Conversely, if you are a social work practitioner studying the impact of home birth on a particular client, the unit of analysis is the client or individual; if you are studying the impact on a group of women, the unit of analysis is the group of women.

Case-level designs can provide information about how well a treatment intervention is working, so that alternative or complementary interventive strategies can be adopted if necessary. They can also indicate when a client's problem has been resolved. Single-case studies can be used to monitor client progress up to, and sometimes beyond, the point of termination.

They can also be used to evaluate the effectiveness of a social work program as a whole by aggregating or compiling the results obtained by numerous social workers serving their individual clients within the program. A family therapy program might be evaluated, for example, by combining family outcomes on a number of families that have been seen by different social workers.

A *case-level* design is represented in terms of the letters *A, B, C,* and *D.* Let us see how this works, first in relation to exploratory research questions.

EXPLORATORY CASE-LEVEL DESIGNS

Suppose you have a client—Celia—whose underlying problem, you believe, is poor self-esteem. She will be the "case" in your case-level design. Before you go ahead with an intervention designed to increase her self-esteem—Celia doesn't need your intervention if your belief is wrong—you will have to answer the simple question "Does Celia really have a clinically significant problem with self-esteem?" In other words, does the self-esteem problem you think she has in fact really exists in the first place?

In order to answer this question, you select a measuring instrument to measure self-esteem that is valid, reliable, sensitive, nonreactive, and useful in this particular situation. Say you choose Hudson's Index of Self-Esteem (see Figure 9.1), which has a clinical cutting score of 30 (plus or minus 5). You administer it to Celia, and she scores 37. On the Hudson scale, scores above the clinical cutting score indicate a clinically significant problem. You might think, "Ah-Hah! She has a problem!" and hurry forward with your intervention.

On the other hand, any social work intervention has the potential to harm as well as help (in the same way that

any medication does), and you might first want to be sure that this is a persisting problem and not just a reflection of Celia's poor self-esteem today. You might also want to be sure that her low self-esteem problem will not go away by itself. Doctors usually do not treat conditions that resolve themselves, given time, and the same is true for social workers.

In order to see whether Celia meets these two criteria for treatment—first, the problem is persisting and, second, it is either stable at an unacceptable level or getting worse—you will need to administer the same measuring instrument two or three times more at intervals of, say, a week. You might then graph your results as shown in Figure 12.1. This figure constitutes a baseline measure of Celia's self-esteem and is a very simple example of an A design.

A Design

At the risk of sounding a bit ridiculous, the letter A simply designates "a research study" where the intention is to establish, via measurement, a baseline for an individual client's problem. Perhaps "research study" is a grandiose term to describe a routine assessment, but the

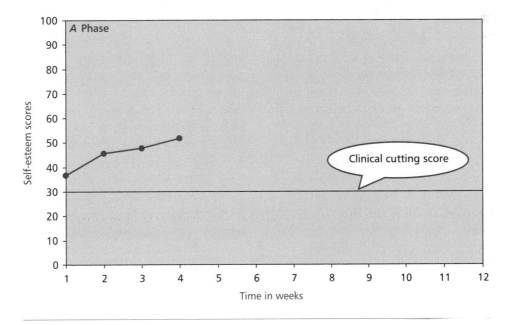

Figure 12.1 *A* Design: Celia's Self-Esteem Scores for the First Four Weeks without Intervention

word *re-search* does mean *to look again,* and you are indeed looking again at Celia's potential problem in order to see if her problem exists in the first place.

Figure 12.1 contains four data points. Three is the minimum number needed to show any kind of trend, and some experts maintain that you need no fewer than seven. However, in a clinical situation the client's need for intervention is the primary factor, and you will have to use your judgment to decide how long you ought to continue to gather baseline data before you intervene.

Figure 12.1 indicates a worsening problem that requires intervention, since each score is higher than the last. Remember, higher scores mean higher levels of the problem. Had each score been lower than the preceding one, the problem would have been improving by itself and no intervention would be indicated. If the scores had fallen more or less on a horizontal line, intervention would have been indicated if the line was above the clinical cutting score and not if the line was below it.

Before we proceed from *A* designs to *B* designs, a word is in order about graphs. If math is but a dim and nasty memory for you, the following points might be worthy to note:

* The horizontal line in Figure 12.1 is called the *x*-axis, or abscissa.
* The vertical line is called the *y*-axis, or ordinate.
* The dotted horizontal line indicates the clinical cutting score. It is important to include this, since your objective with Celia when you intervene will be to get her score below the clinical cutting score line.
* Both axes must be labeled. In Figure 12.1 the *y*-axis shows self-esteem level and the *x*-axis shows time in weeks. By convention, the dependent variable is placed on the *y*-axis and the independent variable on the *x*-axis. In our simple study, there are not yet any dependent and independent variables, but you might hope to show later on that Celia's self-esteem level has been affected by your intervention. If this were the case, self-esteem level would be the dependent variable, since it is the thing being changed, and the intervention over time would be the inde-

pendent variable, since it is the thing doing the changing

B Design

The second type of exploratory single-case research design is the *B* design. As we have seen, an *A* design answers the question "Does the problem exist?" The *A* design also answers another type of exploratory question: "Does the problem exist at different levels over time?" In other words, "Is the problem changing *by itself?*"

A *B* design also addresses the question "Is the problem changing?," but here we want to know whether the problem is changing *while an intervention is being applied.* Let's forget Celia for a moment—we have not abandoned her; we will return to her in due course—and consider Bob instead.

Bob has come to you complaining that he experiences a great deal of anxiety in social situations. He is nervous when he speaks to his boss or when he meets people for the first time, and the prospect of giving public presentations at work appalls him. You decide that you will measure Bob's anxiety level using a standardized measuring instrument called the Interaction and Audience Anxiousness Scale (*IASS*). On this particular measuring instrument, higher scores indicate higher anxiety levels, the clinical cutting score for the *IASS* is 40, and Bob scores 62. This one score is more of a base point rather than a base line, but you decide that it would be inappropriate to collect baseline data over time in Bob's case, as he is experiencing a great deal of discomfort at work, is highly nervous in your presence (you are a stranger, after all), and probably will not be able to bring himself to seek help in the future if he does not receive some kind of intervention now.

You therefore begin your intervention, engaging Bob to the extent that he returns the following week, when you administer the *IASS* again. Now he scores 55. In the third week, he scores 52, as shown in Figure 12.2.

Figure 12.2 is an example of a *B* design, in which you track change in the problem level at the same time as you are intervening. You do not know, from this graph, whether your intervention *caused* the change you see. Anything else could have caused it. Perhaps Bob

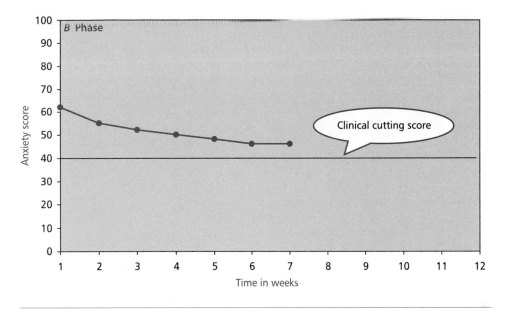

Figure 12.2 *B* Design: Bob's Anxiety Scores for the First Seven Weeks with Intervention

is having a weekly massage to reduce muscle tension, or his boss has been fired, or the public presentation that he was suppose to do has been postponed. Therefore, you cannot use this design to answer explanatory research questions, which come quite high on the knowledge continuum (refer to Figure 1.5).

BB_1 *Design*

Figure 12.2 shows that Bob's anxiety level has improved, but it has not fallen below the clinical cutting score. Moreover, it does not look as though it will because it has been relatively stable around 46 for the past three weeks. It may be that Bob is a naturally anxious person and that no intervention, however inspired, will reduce his problem to below significant levels. On the other hand, you might make the clinical decision that it is worth trying a variation on your intervention: you might apply it more *frequently* by having Bob come twice a week instead of once, or you might apply it more *intensively* by increasing the amount of time Bob is expected to spend each evening on relaxation exercises. You can graph the changes that occur while you are applying the variation, as shown in Figure 12.3.

Figure 12.3 shows two *phases*: the *B* phase and the B_1 phase, separated by the vertical dotted line that runs between Weeks 7 and 8. Week 7 marks the end of your original intervention, designated by the *B* intervention, and all the scores obtained by Bob while you were applying the *B* intervention constitute the *B* phase. (If it seems odd to call the first intervention *B* instead of *A*, remember that *A* has been used already to designate baseline scores.) Week 8 marks the beginning of the variation on your original intervention, designated B_1, and all the scores obtained by Bob while you were applying the variation constitute the B_1 phase. The *B* and B_1 phases together constitute the BB_1 *design*. You will note that the *B* phase shown in Figure 12.3 has been copied from Figure 12.2. in order to illustrate the BB_1 design.

When you look at the score of 38 that Bob achieved by Week 12, you might be tempted to think, "Hallelujah! My specific intervention *did* work. All Bob needed was a bit more of it." However, the same considerations apply to the BB_1 design as apply to the *B* design. You cannot be sure that there is any relationship between your intervention and Bob's decreased anxiety, far less that one was the cause of the other.

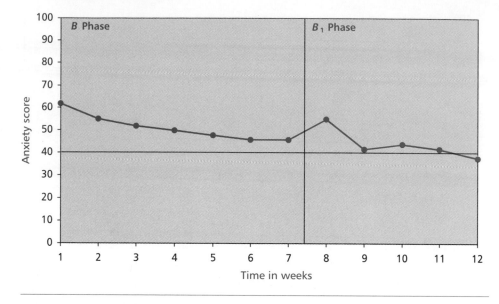

Figure 12.3 *BB₁* Design: Bob's Anxiety Scores for *B* Phase and *B₁* Phase

---

BC Design

The final exploratory case-level research design is the *BC* design. Let us go back in time, to the point where you decided that it was worth trying a variation on your *B* intervention. Suppose you had decided instead to try an entirely different intervention, designated as *C* because it is a *different* intervention, following immediately after *B*. Now you implement the *C* intervention, administering the *IASS* every week, graphing your results, and creating a *C* phase after the *B* phase as shown in Figure 12.4.

Again, the *B* phase in Figure 12.4 is copied from Figure 12.2, and after the *C* intervention you see that Bob has succeeded in reducing his anxiety level to below the clinical cutting score. Repressing your hallelujahs, you realize that there is still no sure relationship between your intervention and Bob's success. Indeed, the waters are becoming more murky because even if your intervention were in fact related to Bob's success, you would still not know whether it was the *C* intervention that did the trick, or a delayed reaction to *B*, or some combination of *B* and *C*.

DESCRIPTIVE CASE-LEVEL DESIGNS

There are two kinds of case-level research designs that center around answering descriptive research questions: (1) *AB* designs, and (2) *ABC* and *ABCD* designs.

AB Design

An *AB* design is simply an *A*—or baseline phase—followed by a *B* or intervention phase. Returning to Celia, you have already completed a baseline phase with her, as shown in Figure 12.1, and that phase alone answered the two simple exploratory questions "Does the problem exist?" and "Does the problem exist at different levels over time?" Now you implement a *B* intervention and find, to your pleasure, that Celia's self-esteem level approaches the clinical cutting score of 30 and falls below it at Weeks 9 and 10. Celia's progress is illustrated in Figure 12.5.

What you really want to know, of course, is whether there is any relationship between your *B* intervention and Celia's success. You are now in a better position to hypothesize that there is, since you know that Celia was getting worse during the four weeks of the baseline phase and

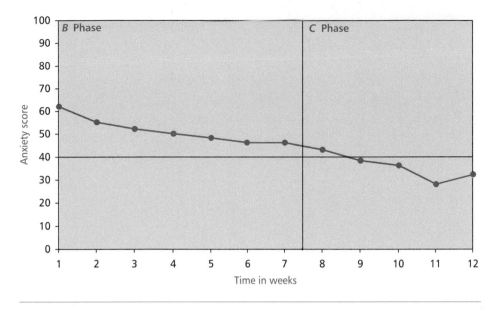

Figure 12.4   *BC* Design: Bob's Anxiety Scores for *B* Phase and *C* Phase

began to improve the week after you started your intervention. *Something* happened in Week 5 to set Celia on the road to recovery, and it would be very coincidental if that something were not your intervention.

However, coincidences do happen, and you cannot be certain that your intervention *caused* the change you see unless you can eliminate all the other coincidental happenings that might have caused it. Hence, the *AB* design cannot answer explanatory research questions, but the change between the baseline data (getting worse) and the intervention data (getting better) is enough to indicate that there may be some relationship between your intervention and Celia's improvement. The moral to the story is *always collect baseline data if you can,* since social work ethics requires you to be reasonably sure an intervention is effective before you try it again with another client.

ABC and *ABCD* Designs

As discussed earlier, you can always follow a *B* phase with a *C* phase if the *B* intervention does not achieve the desired result. An *A* phase followed by a *B* phase followed by a *C* phase constitutes an *ABC* design, and if

there is a *D* intervention as well, you have an *ABCD* design. So long as there is a baseline, you can conclude fairly safely that there is a relationship between the results you see and the intervention you implemented.

However, if you have more than one intervention, you will not know which intervention—or combination of interventions—did the trick, and the more interventions you try the more murky the waters become. Since a single intervention often comprises a package of practice techniques (e.g., active listening plus role play plus relaxation exercises), it is important to write down exactly what you did so that later on you will remember what the *B* or *C* or *D* interventions were.

EXPLANATORY CASE-LEVEL DESIGNS

As we have seen, if you want to show that a particular intervention caused an observed result, you must eliminate everything else that may have caused it: in other words, you must control for intervening variables. There are two types of case-level designs that can answer causality, or explanatory research questions: (1) reversal designs, and (2) multiple baseline designs.

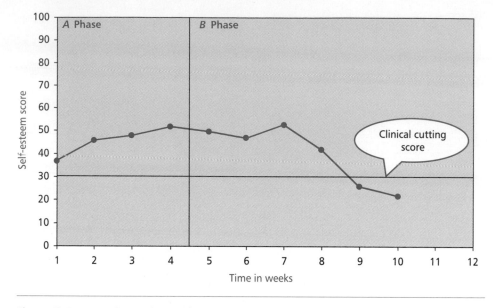

Figure 12.5 *AB* Design: Celia's Self-Esteem Scores for *A* Phase and *B* Phase

Reversal Designs

The first type of explanatory case-level designs are the reversal designs. There are three kinds of case-level reversal designs: (1) *ABA* and *ABAB* designs, (2) *BAB* designs, and (3) *BCBC* designs.

ABA and ABAB Designs

Look at Figure 12.5, which illustrates Celia's success in getting her self-esteem score below the clinical cutting score in Weeks 9 and 10. In Week 11, you decide that you will withdraw your intervention related to Celia's self-esteem since she seems to be doing well, but you will continue to monitor her self-esteem levels to ensure that treatment gains are maintained. Ongoing monitoring of problems that appear to be solved is something of a luxury in our profession. Too often our approach is crisis-oriented; follow-up tends to be ignored in the light of other, more pressing problems, and the result may well be a recurrence of the original problem because it had not been solved to the extent that the social worker thought.

However, with Celia you follow up. In Week 11, as shown in Figure 12.6, the score hovers at the clinical cutting score. In Week 12, it goes up a little; in Week 13, it jumps; and in Weeks 14 and 15, it is no better.

Figure 12.6 illustrates an *ABA* design where the client's scores are displayed first without an intervention (the first *A* phase), then with an intervention (the *B* phase), then without an intervention again (the second *A* phase). The scores are not as high in the second *A* phase as they were in the first *A* phase, and this is to be expected, since some of the strategies Celia learned in the *B* phase should remain with her even though the intervention has stopped. However, from a research point of view, the very fact that her scores increased again when you stopped the intervention makes it more certain that it was your intervention that caused the improvement you saw in the *B* phase. Celia's improvement when the intervention started might have been a coincidence, but it is unlikely that her regression when the intervention stopped was also a coincidence.

Your certainty with respect to causality will be increased even further if you reintroduce the *B* inter-

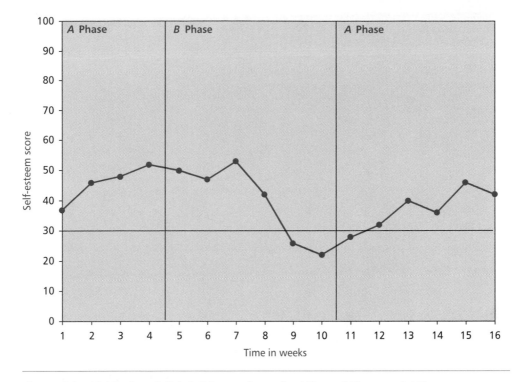

Figure 12.6   *ABA* Design: Celia's Self-Esteem Scores for *A* Phase, *B* Phase, and *A* Phase

vention in Week 16 and Celia's score begins to drop again as it did in the first *B* phase. Now you have implemented two *AB* designs one after the other with the same client to produce an *ABAB* design. This design is illustrated in Figure 12.7. It is sometimes called a *reversal* design or a *withdrawal* design.

Causality is established with an *ABAB* design because the same intervention has been shown to work twice with the same client and you have baseline data to show the extent of the problem when there was no intervention.

BAB Design

Let's now return to Bob, with whom you implemented a *B* intervention to reduce his social anxiety, as shown in Figure 12.2. When Bob's social anxiety level has fallen beneath the clinical cutting score, you might do the same thing with Bob as you did with Celia: withdraw the intervention and continue to monitor the

problem, creating an *A* phase after the *B* phase. If the problem level worsens during the *A* phase, you intervene again in the same way as you did before, creating a second *B* phase and an overall design of *BAB*.

We have said that causality is established with an *ABAB* design because the same intervention has worked twice with the same client. We cannot say the same for a *BAB* design, however, as we do not really know that our intervention "worked" the first time. Since there were no initial baseline data (no first *A* phase), we cannot know whether the resolution of the problem on the first occasion had anything to do with the intervention.

The problem may have resolved itself, or some external event (intervening variable) might have resolved it. Nor can we know the degree to which the problem changed during the first *B* phase (intervention), since there were no baseline data with which to compare the final result. An indication of the amount of change can be obtained by comparing the first and last scores in the *B* phase, but the first score may have

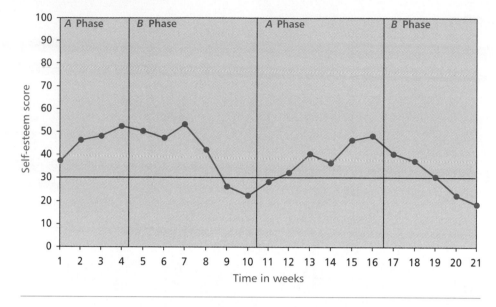

Figure 12.7   *ABAB* Design: Celia's Self-Esteem Scores for Two *A* Phases and Two *B* Phases

been an unreliable measure of Bob's problem. Bob may have felt less or more anxious that day than usual, and a baseline is necessary to compensate for such day-to-day fluctuations.

Since the effectiveness of the intervention on the first occasion is unknown, there can be no way of knowing whether the intervention was just as effective the second time it was implemented, or less or more effective. All we know is that the problem improved twice, following the same intervention, and this is probably enough to warrant using the intervention again with another client.

BCBC Design

A *BCBC* design, as the name suggests, is a *B* intervention followed by a *C* intervention implemented twice in succession. The point of doing this is to compare the effectiveness of two interventions—*B* and *C*. It is unlikely that a social worker would implement this design with a client since, if the problem improved sufficiently using *B*, you would not need *C*, and, if you did need *C*, you would hardly return to *B* whether or not *C* appeared to do the trick. However, if the problem has nothing to do with a client's welfare but is concerned

instead with a social work program's organizational efficiency, say, as affected by organizational structure, you might try one structure *B* followed by a different structure *C* and then do the same thing again in order to show that one structure really has proved more effective in increasing efficiency when implemented twice *under the same conditions*.

Multiple Baseline Designs

The second type of explanatory case-level designs are the multiple baseline designs. Multiple baseline designs are like *ABAB* designs in that the *AB* design is implemented more than once. However, whereas *ABAB* designs apply to one case with one problem in one setting, multiple baseline designs can be used with more than one case, with more than one setting, or with more than one problem.

More Than One Case

Suppose that, instead of Bob with his social anxiety problem, you have three additional clients, Breanne, Warren, and Alison, with anxiety problems. All three are residents in the same nursing home. You use the same

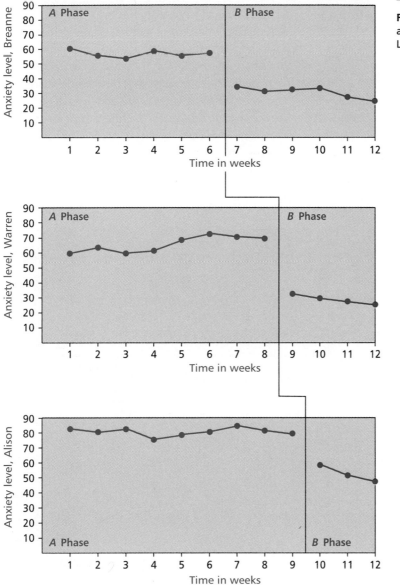

Figure 12.8   Multiple-Baseline Design across Clients: Magnitude of Anxiety Levels for Three Clients

measuring instrument to measure anxiety (the *IASS*) in all three cases, and you give all three clients the same intervention. However, you vary the number of weeks over which you collect baseline data, allowing the baseline phase to last for six weeks in Breanne's case, eight weeks in Warren's case, and nine weeks for Alison. You plot your results as shown in Figure 12.8.

Breanne starts to show improvement in Week 7, the week you began your intervention. Had that improve-

ment been due to some intervening variable—for example, some anxiety-reducing change in the nursing home's routine—you would expect Warren and Alison to also show improvement. The fact that their anxiety levels continue to be high indicates that it was your intervention, not some other factor, that caused the improvement in Breanne. Causality is demonstrated again in Week 9 when you begin to intervene with Warren and Warren improves but Alison does not. Your triumph is complete when Alison, given the same intervention, begins to improve in Week 10.

More Than One Setting

Another way to conduct a multiple baseline study is with one client in a number of settings. Suppose that your objective is to reduce the number of a child's temper tantrums at home, in school, and at the daycare center where the child goes after school. The same intervention is offered by the parents at home, by the teacher in school, and by the worker at the daycare center. They are also responsible for measuring the number of tantrums that occur each day. The baseline phase continues for different lengths of time in each setting as shown in Figure 12.9. If the child improves at home after the intervention begins in Week 7 but continues to throw numerous tantrums in school and at daycare,

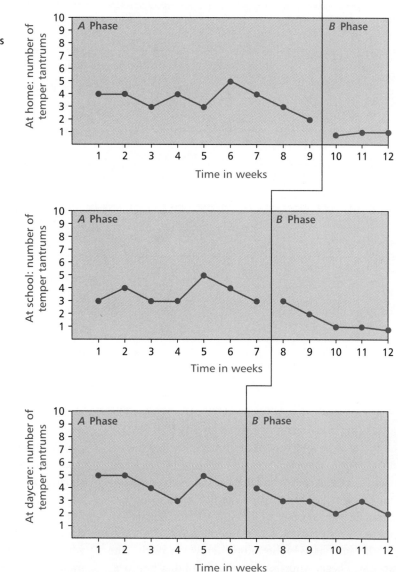

Figure 12.9 Multiple-Baseline Design across Settings: Number of Temper Tantrums for One Client in Three Settings

the indication is that it was not the intervention that caused the improvement at home. If the intervention was the causal agent, then improvement would occur in all settings.

More Than One Problem

A third way to conduct a multiple-baseline study is to use the same intervention to tackle different target problems. Suppose that Joan is having trouble with her daughter, Anita. In addition, Joan is having trouble with her in-laws and with her boss at work. After exploration, a worker may believe that all these troubles stem from her lack of assertiveness. Thus, the intervention would be assertiveness training. Progress with Anita might be measured by the number of times each day she is flagrantly disobedient. Progress can be measured with Joan's in-laws by the number of times she is able

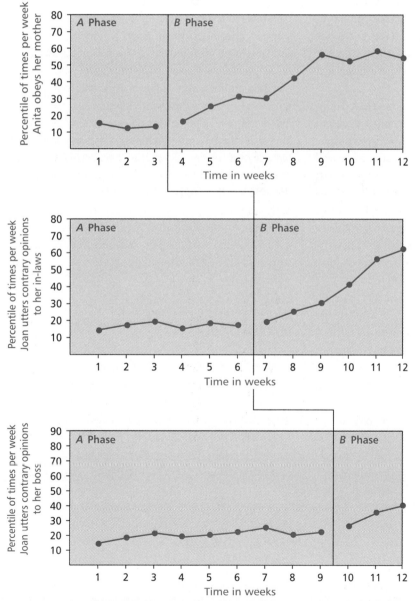

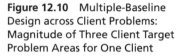

Figure 12.10   Multiple-Baseline Design across Client Problems: Magnitude of Three Client Target Problem Areas for One Client

to utter a contrary opinion, and so on. Since the number of occasions on which Joan has an opportunity to be assertive will vary, these figures might best be expressed in percentiles. Figure 12.10 illustrates an example of a multiple-baseline design that was used to assess the effectiveness of Joan's assertiveness training in three problem areas.

Whether it is a reversal design or a multiple-baseline design, an *ABAB* explanatory design involves establishing a baseline level for the client's target problem. This is not possible if the need for intervention is acute, and sometimes the very thought of an *A*-type design has to be abandoned. It is sometimes possible, however, to construct a retrospective baseline—that is, to determine what the level of the problem was before an intervention was implemented.

The best retrospective baselines are those that do not depend on the client's memory. If the target problem occurs rarely, memories may be accurate. For example, Tai, a teenager, and his family may remember quite well how many times he ran away from home during the past month. They may not remember nearly so well if the family members were asked how often he behaved defiantly. Depending on the target problem, it may be possible to construct a baseline from archival data: that is, from written records, such as school attendance sheets, probation orders, employment interview forms, and so forth.

Although establishing a baseline usually involves making at least three measurements before implementing an intervention, it is also acceptable to establish a baseline of zero, or no occurrences of a desired event. A target problem, for example, might focus upon the client's reluctance to enter a drug treatment program. The baseline measurement would then be that the client did not go (zero occurrences), and the desired change would be that the client did go (one occurrence). A social worker who has successfully used the same tactics to persuade a number of clients to enter a drug treatment program has conducted a multiple-baseline design across clients.

As previously discussed, a usable baseline should show either that the client's problem level is stable or that it is growing worse. Sometimes an *A*-type design can be used even though the baseline indicates a slight improvement in the target problem. The justification must be that the intervention is expected to lead to an improvement that will exceed the anticipated improvement if the baseline trend continues.

Perhaps a child's temper tantrums are decreasing by one or two a week, for example, but the total number per week is still 18 to 20. If a worker thought the tantrums could be reduced to four or five a week, or they could be stopped altogether, the worker would be justified in implementing an intervention even though the client's target problem was improving slowly by itself.

In a similar way, a worker may be able to implement an *A*-type design if the client's baseline is unstable, provided that the intervention is expected to exceed the largest of the baseline fluctuations. Perhaps the child's temper tantrums are fluctuating between 12 and 20 per week in the baseline period, and it is hoped to bring them down to less than 10 per week.

Nevertheless, there are some occasions when a baseline cannot be established or is not usable, such as when a client's behaviors involve self-injurious ones. Also, sometimes the establishment of a baseline is totally inappropriate.

SUMMARY

Exploratory designs are used when little is known about the field of study and data are gathered in an effort to find out "what's out there." These ideas are then used to generate hypotheses that can be verified using more rigorous designs. No design is inherently inferior or superior to the others. Each has advantages and disadvantages in terms of time, cost, and the data that can be obtained.

Group-Level Designs

Richard M. Grinnell, Jr.

Yvonne A. Unrau

Margaret Williams

· ·

13

Now that we know how to draw samples for qualitative and quantitative research studies, we turn our attention to the various group-level designs that research studies can take. The two most important factors in determining what design to use in a specific study are (1) what the research question is, and (2) how much knowledge about the problem area is available. If there is already a substantial knowledge base in the area, we will be in a position to address very specific research questions, the answers to which could add to the explanation of previously gathered data. If less is known about the problem area, our research questions will have to be of a more general, descriptive nature. If very little is known about the problem area, our questions will have to be even more general, at an exploratory level.

Research knowledge levels are arrayed along a continuum, from exploratory at the lowest end to explanatory at the highest (see Figure 1.5). Because research knowledge levels are viewed this way, the assignment of the level of knowledge accumulated in a problem area prior to a research study, as well as the level that might be attained by the research study, is totally arbitrary. There are, however, specific designs that can be used to provide us with knowledge at a certain level.

At the highest level are the explanatory designs, also called experimental designs or "ideal" experiments. These designs have the largest number of requirements (examined in the following section). They are best used in confirmatory research studies where the area under study is well developed, theories abound, and testable hypotheses can be formulated on the basis of previous work or existing theory. These designs seek to establish causal relationships between the independent and dependent variables.

In the middle range are the descriptive designs, sometimes referred to as quasi-experimental. A quasi-experiment resembles an "ideal" experiment in some aspects but lacks at least one of the necessary requirements.

At the lowest level are the exploratory designs, also called pre-experimental or nonexperimental, which explore only the research question or problem area. These designs do not produce statistically sound data or conclusive results; they are not intended to. Their purpose is to build a foundation of general ideas and tentative theories, which can be explored later with more precise and hence more complex research designs and their corresponding data-gathering techniques.

The research designs that allow us to acquire knowledge at each of the three levels are described in a later section of this chapter. Before considering them, however, it is necessary to establish the characteristics that differentiate an "ideal" experiment, which leads to explanatory knowledge, from other studies that lead to lower levels of knowledge.

CHARACTERISTICS OF "IDEAL" EXPERIMENTS

An "ideal" experiment is one in which a research study most closely approaches certainty about the relationship between the independent and dependent variables. The purpose of doing an "ideal" experiment is to ascertain whether it can be concluded from the study's findings that the independent variable is, or is not, the only cause of change in the dependent variable. As pointed out in previous chapters, some social work research studies have no independent variable—for example, those studies that just want to find out how many people in a certain community wish to establish a community-based halfway house for people who are addicted to drugs.

The concept of an "ideal" experiment is introduced with the word "ideal" in quotation marks because such an experiment is rarely achieved in social work research situations. On a general level, in order to achieve this high degree of certainty and qualify as an "ideal" experiment, an explanatory research design must meet six conditions:

1. The time order of the independent variable must be established.
2. The independent variable must be manipulated.
3. The relationship between the independent and dependent variables must be established.
4. The research design must control for rival hypotheses.
5. At least one control group should be used.
6. Random assignment procedures (and if possible, random sampling from a population) must be

employed in assigning research participants (or objects) to groups.

Controlling the Time Order of Variables

In an "ideal" experiment, the independent variable must precede the dependent variable in time. Time order is crucial if our research study is to show that one variable causes another, because something that occurs later cannot be the cause of something that occurred earlier.

Suppose we want to study the relationship between adolescent substance abuse and gang-related behavior. The following hypothesis is formulated after some thought:

> Adolescent substance abuse causes gang-related behavior.

In this hypothesis, the independent variable is adolescent substance abuse, and the dependent variable is gang-related behavior. The substance abuse must come *before* gang-related behavior because the hypothesis states that adolescent drug use causes gang-related behavior. We could also come up with the following hypothesis, however:

> Adolescent gang-related behavior causes substance abuse.

In this hypothesis, adolescent gang-related behavior is the independent variable, and substance abuse is the dependent variable. According to this hypothesis, gang-related behavior must come *before* the substance abuse.

Manipulating the Independent Variable

Manipulation of the independent variable means that we must do something with the independent variable in terms of at least one of the research participants in the study. In the general form of the hypothesis "if X occurs, then Y will result," the independent variable (X) must be manipulated in order to effect a variation in the dependent variable (Y). There are essentially three ways in which independent variables can be manipulated:

1. *X present versus X absent.* If the effectiveness of a specific treatment intervention is being evaluated,

an experimental group and a control group could be used. The experimental group would be given the intervention; the control group would not.

2. *A small amount of X versus a larger amount of X.* If the effect of treatment time on client's outcomes is being studied, two experimental groups could be used, one of which would be treated for a longer period of time.

3. *X versus something else.* If the effectiveness of two different treatment interventions is being studied, Intervention X_1 could be used with Experimental Group 1 and Intervention X_2 with Experimental Group 2.

There are certain variables, such as the gender or race of our research participants, that obviously cannot be manipulated because they are fixed. They do not vary, so they are called constants, not variables, as was pointed out in Chapter 5. Other constants, such as socioeconomic status or IQ, may vary for research participants over their life spans, but they are fixed quantities at the beginning of the study, probably will not change during the study, and are not subject to alteration by the one doing the study.

Any variable we can alter (e.g., treatment time) can be considered an independent variable. At least one independent variable must be manipulated in a research study if it is to be considered an "ideal" experiment.

Establishing Relationships between Variables

The relationship between the independent and the dependent variables must be established in order to infer a cause-effect relationship at the explanatory knowledge level. If the independent variable is considered to be the cause of the dependent variable, there must be some pattern in the relationship between these two variables. An example is the hypothesis "The more time clients spend in treatment (independent variable), the better their progress (dependent variable)."

Controlling Rival Hypotheses

Rival hypotheses must be identified and eliminated in an "ideal" experiment. The logic of this requirement is extremely important, because this is what makes a cause-effect statement possible.

The prime question to ask when trying to identify a rival hypothesis is "What other extraneous variables might affect the dependent variable?" (What else might affect the client's outcome besides treatment time?) At the risk of sounding redundant, "What else besides X might affect Y?" Perhaps the client's motivation for treatment, in addition to the time spent in treatment, might affect the client's outcome. If so, motivation for treatment is an extraneous variable that could be used as the independent variable in the rival hypothesis "The higher the clients' motivation for treatment, the better their progress."

Perhaps the social worker's attitude toward the client might have an effect on the client's outcome, or the client might win the state lottery and ascend abruptly from depression to ecstasy. These extraneous variables could potentially be independent variables in other rival hypotheses. They must all be considered and eliminated before it can be said with reasonable certainty that a client's outcome resulted from the length of treatment time and not from any other extraneous variables.

Control over rival hypotheses refers to efforts on our part to identify and, if at all possible, to eliminate the extraneous variables in these alternative hypotheses. Of the many ways to deal with rival hypotheses, three of the most frequently used are to keep the extraneous variables constant, use correlated variation, or use analysis of covariance.

Holding Extraneous Variables Constant

The most direct way to deal with rival hypotheses is to keep constant the critical extraneous variables that might affect the dependent variable. As we know, a constant cannot affect or be affected by any other variable. If an extraneous variable can be made into a constant, then it cannot affect either the study's real independent variable or the dependent variable.

Let us take an example to illustrate this point. Suppose, for example, that a social worker who is providing counseling to anxious clients wants to relate client outcome to length of treatment time, but most of the clients are also being treated by a consulting psychiatrist

with antidepressant medication. Because medication may also affect the clients' outcomes, it is a potential independent variable that could be used in a rival hypothesis. However, if the study included only clients who have been taking medication for some time before the treatment intervention began, and who continue to take the same medicine in the same way throughout treatment, then medication can be considered a constant (in this study, anyway).

Any change in the clients' anxiety levels after the intervention will, therefore, be a result of the intervention with the help of the medication. The extraneous variable of medication, which might form a rival hypothesis, has been eliminated by holding it constant. In short, this study started out with one independent variable, the intervention, then added the variable of medication to it, so the final independent variable is the intervention plus the medication.

This is all very well in theory. In reality, however, a client's drug regime is usually controlled by the psychiatrist and may well be altered at any time. Even if the regime is not altered, the effects of the drugs might not become apparent until the study is under way. In addition, the client's level of anxiety might be affected by a host of other extraneous variables over which the social worker has no control at all: for example, living arrangements, relationships with other people, the condition of the stock market, or an unexpected visit from an IRS agent. These kinds of pragmatic difficulties tend to occur frequently in social work practice and research. It is often impossible to identify all rival hypotheses, let alone eliminate them by keeping them constant.

Using Correlated Variation

Rival hypotheses can also be controlled with correlated variation of the independent variables. Suppose, for example, that we are concerned that income has an effect on a client's compulsive behavior. The client's income, which in this case is subject to variation due to seasonal employment, is identified as an independent variable. The client's living conditions—a hotel room rented by the week—are then identified as the second independent variable that might well affect the client's level of compulsive behavior. These two variables, however, are correlated, since living conditions are highly dependent on income.

Correlated variation exists if one potential independent variable can be correlated with another. Then only one of them has to be dealt with in the research study.

Using Analysis of Covariance

In conducting an "ideal" experiment, we must always aim to use two or more groups that are as equivalent as possible on all important variables. Sometimes this goal is not feasible, however. Perhaps we are obliged to use existing groups that are not as equivalent as we would like. Or, perhaps during the course of the study we discover inequivalencies between the groups that were not apparent at the beginning.

A statistical method called *analysis of covariance* can be used to compensate for these differences. The mathematics of the method is far beyond the scope of this text, but an explanation can be found in most advanced statistics texts.

Using a Control Group

An "ideal" experiment should use at least one control group in addition to the experimental group. The experimental group may receive an intervention that is withheld from the control group, or equivalent groups may receive different interventions or no interventions at all.

A social worker who initiates a treatment intervention is often interested in knowing what would have happened had the intervention not been used or had some different intervention been substituted. Would members of a support group for alcoholics have recovered anyway, without the social worker's efforts? Would they have recovered faster or more completely had family counseling been used instead of the support group approach?

The answer to these questions will never be known if only the support group is studied. But, what if another group of alcoholics is included in the research design? In a typical design with a control group, two equivalent groups, 1 and 2, would be formed, and both would be administered the same pretest to determine the initial level of the dependent variable (e.g., degree of alcoholism). Then an intervention would be initiated with

Group 1 but not with Group 2. The group treated—Group 1, or the experimental group—would receive the independent variable (the intervention). The group not treated—Group 2, or the control group—would not receive it.

At the conclusion of the intervention, both groups would be given a posttest (the same measure as the pretest). Both the pretest and the posttest consist of the use of some sort of data-gathering procedure, such as a survey or self-report measure, to measure the dependent variable before and after the introduction of the independent variable. There are many types of group research designs and there are many ways to graphically display them. In general, group designs can be written in symbols as shown in Figure 13.1, where

R_s	=	Random selection from a population
R_a	=	Random assignment to a group
O_1	=	First measurement of the dependent variable
X	=	Independent variable, or intervention
O_2	=	Second measurement of the dependent variable

The R_a in this design indicates that the research participants were randomly assigned to each group. The symbol X, which, as usual, stands for the independent variable, indicates that an intervention is to be given to the experimental group after the pretest (O_1) and before the posttest (O_2). The absence of X for the control group indicates that the intervention is not to be given to the control group. This design is called a classical experimental design because it comes closest to having all the characteristics necessary for an "ideal" experiment.

Randomly Assigning Research Participants to Groups

Once a sample has been selected (see previous chapter), the individuals (or objects or events) in it are randomly assigned to either an experimental or a control group in such a way that the two groups are equivalent. This procedure is known as random assignment or randomization. In random assignment, the word "equivalent" means equal in terms of the variables that are

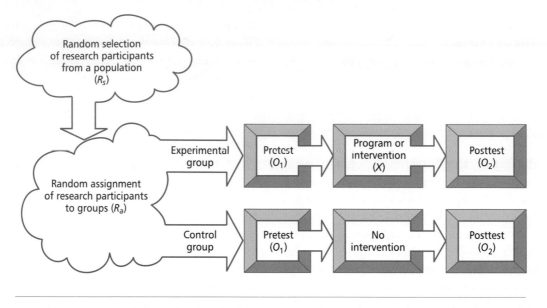

Figure 13.1   True Experimental Research Design

important to the study, such as the clients' motivation for treatment, or problem severity.

If the effect of treatment time on clients' outcomes is being studied, for example, the research design might use one experimental group that is treated for a comparatively longer time, a second experimental group that is treated for a shorter time, and a control group that is not treated at all. If we are concerned that the clients' motivation for treatment might also affect their outcomes, the research participants can be assigned so that all the groups are equivalent (on the average) in terms of their motivation for treatment.

The process of random sampling from a population followed by random assignment of the sample to groups is illustrated in Figure 13.2.

Let us say that the research design calls for a sample size of one-tenth of the population. From a population of 10,000, therefore, a random sampling procedure is used to select a sample of 1,000 individuals.

Then random assignment procedures are used to place the sample of 1,000 into two equivalent groups of 500 individuals each. In theory, Group A will be equivalent to Group B, which will be equivalent to the random sample, which will be equivalent to the population in respect to all important variables contained within the research sample.

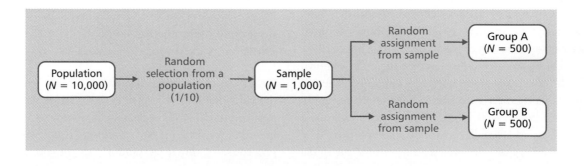

Figure 13.2   Random Sampling from a Population and Random Assignment to Groups

Matched Pairs

Another, more deliberate method of assigning people or other units to groups, a subset of randomization, involves matching. The matched-pairs method is suitable when the composition of each group consists of variables with a range of characteristics. One of the disadvantages of matching is that some individuals cannot be matched and so cannot participate in the study.

Suppose a new training program for teaching parenting skills to foster mothers is being evaluated, and it is important that the experimental and control groups have an equal number of highly skilled and less-skilled foster parents before the training program is introduced. The women chosen for the sample would be matched in pairs according to their parenting skill level; the two most skilled foster mothers would be matched, then the next two, and so on. One person in each pair of approximately equally skilled foster parents would then be randomly assigned to the experimental group and the other placed in the control group.

Let us suppose that in order to compare the foster mothers who have been exposed to the new training program with women who have not, a standardized measuring instrument that measures parenting skill level (the dependent variable) is administered to a sample of 10 women. The scores can range from 100 (excellent parenting skills) to zero (poor parenting skills). Then their scores are rank-ordered from the highest to the lowest, and out of the foster mothers with the two highest scores, one is selected to be assigned to either the experimental group or the control group. It does not make any difference to which group our first research participant is randomly assigned, as long as there is an equal chance that she will go to either the control group or the experimental group. In this example, the first person is randomly chosen to go to the experimental group, as illustrated:

Rank Order of Parenting Skills Scores (in parentheses)

First Pair
- — (99) Randomly assigned to the experimental group
- — (98) Assigned to the control group

Second Pair
- — (97) Assigned to the control group
- — (96) Assigned to the experimental group

Third Pair
- — (95) Assigned to the experimental group
- — (94) Assigned to the control group

Fourth Pair
- — (93) Assigned to the control group
- — (92) Assigned to the experimental group

Fifth Pair
- — (91) Assigned to the experimental group
- — (90) Assigned to the control group

The foster parent with the highest score (99) is randomly assigned to the experimental group, and this person's "match," with a score of 98, is assigned to the control group. This process is reversed with the next matched pair, where the first person is assigned to the control group and the match is assigned to the experimental group. If the assignment of research participants according to scores is not reversed for every other pair, one group will be higher than the other on the variable being matched.

To illustrate this point, suppose the first participant (highest score) in each match is always assigned to the experimental group. The experimental group's average score would be 95 (99 + 97 + 95 + 93 + 91 = 475/5 = 95), and the control group's average score would be 94 (98 + 96 + 94 + 92 + 90 = 470/5 = 94). If every other matched pair is reversed, however, as in the example, the average scores of the two groups are closer together; 94.6 for the experimental group (99 + 96 + 95 + 92 + 91 = 473/5 = 94.6) and 94.4 for the control group (98 + 97 + 94 + 93 + 90 = 472/5 = 94.4). In short, 94.6 and 94.4 (difference of 0.2) are closer together than 95 and 94 (difference of 1).

INTERNAL AND EXTERNAL VALIDITY

We must remember that the research design we finally select should always be evaluated on how close it comes to an "ideal" experiment in reference to the characteristics presented at the beginning of this chapter. As stressed throughout this book, most research designs used in social work do not closely resemble an "ideal" experiment. The research design finally selected needs to be evaluated on how well it meets its primary objective—adequately answering a research question or testing a hypothesis. In short, a research design will be evaluated on how well it controls for:

- Internal validity (Box 13.1)—the ways in which the research design ensures that the introduction of the independent variable (if any) can be identified as the *sole cause* of change in the dependent variable.
- External validity (Box 13.2)—the extent to which the research design allows for generalization of the study's findings to other groups and other situations.

Both internal and external validity are achieved in a research design by taking into account various threats that are inherent in all research efforts. A design for a study with both types of validity will recognize and attempt to control for potential factors that could affect the study's outcome or findings. All research studies try to control as many threats to internal and external validity as possible.

GROUP RESEARCH DESIGNS

While, in some situations, a group research design may need to be complex to accomplish the purpose of the study, a design that is unnecessarily complex costs more, takes more time, and probably will not serve its purpose nearly as well as a simpler one. In choosing a research design (whether a single case [see preceding chapter] or group), therefore, the principle of parsimony must be applied: The simplest and most economical route to the objective is the best choice.

Exploratory Designs

At the lowest level of the continuum of knowledge that can be derived from research studies are exploratory group research designs. An exploratory study explores a research question about which little is already known in order to uncover generalizations and develop hypotheses that can be investigated and tested later with

more precise and, hence, more complex designs and data-gathering techniques.

The four examples of exploratory designs given in this section do not use pretests; they simply measure the dependent variable only after the intervention has been introduced. Therefore, they cannot be used to determine whether changes took place in the study's research participants; these designs simply describe the state of the research participants after they have received the intervention (see Box 13.3).

One-Group Posttest-Only Design

The one-group posttest-only design is sometimes called the one-shot case study or cross-sectional case study design. Suppose in a particular community, Rome, Wisconsin, there are numerous parents who are physically abusive toward their children. The city decides to hire a school social worker, Antonia, to implement a program that is supposed to reduce the number of parents who physically abuse their children. She conceptualizes a 12-week child abuse prevention program (the intervention) and offers it to parents who have children in her school who wish to participate on a voluntary basis. A simple research study is then conducted to answer the question "Did the parents who completed the program stop physically abusing their children?" The answer to this question will determine the success of the intervention.

There are many different ways in which this program can be evaluated. For now, and to make matters as simple as possible, we are going to evaluate it by simply calculating the percentage of parents who stopped physically abusing their children after they attended the program.

At the simplest level, the program could be evaluated with a one-group posttest-only design. The basic elements of this design can be written as shown in Figure 13.3, where:

X = Child Abuse Prevention Program, or the intervention (see Box 13.3)

O_1 = First and only measurement of the dependent variable (percentage of parents who stopped physically abusing their children, the program's outcome, or program objective)

BOX 13.1

Threats to Internal Validity

In any explanatory research study, we should be able to conclude from our findings that the independent variable is, or is not, the only cause of change in the dependent variable. If our study does not have internal validity, such a conclusion is not possible, and the study's findings can be misleading.

Internal validity is concerned with one of the requirements for an "ideal" experiment—the control of rival hypotheses, or alternative explanations for what might bring about a change in the dependent variable. The higher the internal validity of any research study, the greater the extent to which rival hypotheses can be controlled; the lower the internal validity, the less they can be controlled. Thus, we must be prepared to rule out the effects of factors other than the independent variable that could influence the dependent variable.

History

The first threat to internal validity, history, refers to any outside event, either public or private, that may affect the dependent variable and that was not taken into account in our research design. Many times, it refers to events that occur between the first and the second measurement of the dependent variable (the pretest and the posttest). If events occur that have the potential to alter the second measurement, there is no way of knowing how much (if any) of the observed change in the dependent variable is a function of the independent variable and how much is attributable to these events.

Suppose, for example, we are investigating the effects of an educational program on racial tolerance. We may decide to measure the dependent variable, racial tolerance in the community, before introducing the independent variable, the educational program.

The educational program is then implemented. Since it is the independent variable, it is represented by X. Finally, racial tolerance is measured again, after the program has run its course. This final measurement yields a posttest score, represented by O_2. The one-group pretest-posttest study design is presented in Figure 13.12.

The difference between the values O_2 and O_1 represents the difference in racial tolerance in the community before and after the educational program. If the study is internally valid, $O_2 - O_1$ will be a crude measure of the effect of the educational program on racial tolerance, and this is what we were trying to discover. Now suppose that before the posttest could be administered, an outbreak of racial violence, such as the type that occurred in Los Angeles in the summer of 1992,

occurred in the community. Violence can be expected to have a negative effect on racial tolerance, and the posttest scores may, therefore, show a lower level of tolerance than if the violence had not occurred. The effect, $O_2 - O_1$, will now be the combined effects of the educational program *and* the violence, not the effect of the program alone, as we intended.

Racial violence is an extraneous variable that we could not have anticipated and did not control for when designing the study. Other examples might include an earthquake, an election, illness, divorce, or marriage—any event, public or private, that could affect the dependent variable. Any such variable that is unanticipated and uncontrolled for is an example of history.

Maturation

Maturation, the second threat to internal validity, refers to changes, both physical and psychological, that take place in our research participants over time and that can affect the dependent variable. Suppose that we are evaluating an interventive strategy designed to improve the behavior of adolescents who engage in delinquent behavior. Since the behavior of adolescents changes naturally as they mature, the observed changed behavior may have resulted as much from their natural development as from the intervention strategy.

Maturation refers not only to physical or mental growth, however. Over time, people grow older, more or less anxious, more or less bored, and more or less motivated to take part in a research study. All these factors and many more can affect the way in which people respond when the dependent variable is measured a second or third time.

Testing

The third threat to internal validity, testing, is sometimes referred to as the initial measurement effect. Thus, the pretests that are the starting point for many research designs are another potential threat to internal validity. One of the most utilized research designs involves three steps: measuring some dependent variable, such as learning behavior in school or attitudes toward work; initiating a program to change that variable; then measuring the dependent variable again at the conclusion of the program.

The testing effect is the effect that taking a pretest might have on posttest scores. Suppose that Roberto, a

(continued)

BOX 13.1   (continued)

research participant, takes a pretest to measure his initial level of racial tolerance before being exposed to a racial tolerance educational program. He might remember some of the questions on the pretest, think about them later, and change his views on racial issues before taking part in the educational program. After the program, his posttest score will reveal his changed opinions, and we may incorrectly assume that the program was responsible, whereas the true cause was his experience with the pretest.

Sometimes, a pretest induces anxiety in a research participant, so that Roberto receives a worse score on the posttest than he should have; or boredom caused by having to respond to the same questions a second time may be a factor. In order to avoid the testing effect, we may wish to use a design that does not require a pretest.

If a pretest is essential, we then must consider the length of time that elapses between the pretest and posttest measurements. A pretest is far more likely to affect the posttest when the time between the two is short. The nature of the pretest is another factor. Questions that deal with factual matters, such as knowledge levels, may have a larger testing effect because they tend to be more easily recalled.

Instrumentation Error

The fourth threat to internal validity is instrumentation error, which refers to all the troubles that can afflict the measurement process. The instrument may be unreliable or invalid, as presented in Chapters 9 and 10. It may be a mechanical instrument, such as an electroencephalogram (EEG), that has malfunctioned. Occasionally, the term "instrumentation error" is used to refer to an observer whose observations are inconsistent or to measuring instruments, such as the ones presented in Chapter 9, that are reliable in themselves but that have not been administered properly.

"Administration," with respect to a measuring instrument, means the circumstances under which the measurement is made: where, when, how, and by whom. A mother being asked about her attitudes toward her children, for example, may respond in one way in the social worker's office and in a different way at home when her children are screaming around her feet.

A mother's verbal response may differ from her written response, or she may respond differently in the morning than she would in the evening, or differently alone than she would in a group. These variations in situational responses do not indicate a true change in the feelings, attitudes, or behaviors being measured, but are only examples of instrumentation error.

Statistical Regression

The fifth threat to internal validity, statistical regression, refers to the tendency of extremely low and extremely high scores to regress, or move toward the average score for everyone in the research study. Suppose that a student named Maryanna has to take a multiple-choice exam on a subject she knows nothing about. There are many questions, and each question has five possible answers. Since, for each question, Maryanna has a 20 percent (one in five) chance of guessing correctly, she might expect to score 20 percent on the exam just by guessing. If she guesses badly, she will score a lot lower; if well, a lot higher. The other members of the class take the same exam, and, since they are all equally uninformed, the average score for the class is 50 percent.

Now suppose that the instructor separates the low scorers from the high scorers and tries to even out the level of the class by giving the low scorers special instruction. In order to determine whether the special instruction has been effective, the entire class then takes another multiple-choice exam. The result of the exam is that the low scorers (as a group) do better than they did the first time, and the high scorers (as a group) do worse. The instructor believes that this has occurred because the low scorers received special instruction and the high scorers did not.

According to the logic of statistical regression, however, both the average score of the low scorers (as a group) and the average score of the high scorers (as a group) would move toward the total average score for both groups (i.e., high and low).

Even without any special instruction and still in their state of ignorance, the low scorers (as a group) would be expected to have a higher average score than they did before. Likewise, the high scorers (as a group) would be expected to have a lower average score than they did before.

It would be easy for the research instructor to assume that the low scores had increased because of the special instruction and the high scores had decreased because of the lack of it. Not necessarily so, however; the instruction may have had nothing to do with it. It may all be due to statistical regression.

Differential Selection of Research Participants

The sixth threat to internal validity is differential selection of research participants. To some extent, the participants selected for a research study are different from one another to begin with. "Ideal" experiments, however, require random sampling from a population (if at all possible) and random assignment to groups.

BOX 13.1   *(continued)*

This assures that the results of a study will be generalizable to a larger population, thus addressing threats to external validity. In respect to differential selection as a threat to internal validity, "ideal" experiments control for this, since equivalency among the groups at pretest is assumed through the randomization process.

This threat, however, is present when we are working with preformed groups or groups that already exist, such as classes of students, self-help groups, or community groups. In terms of the external validity of such designs, because there is no way of knowing whether the preformed groups are representative of any larger population, it is not possible to generalize the study's results beyond the people (or objects or events) that were actually studied. The use of preformed groups also affects the internal validity of a study, though. It is probable that different preformed groups will not be equivalent with respect to relevant variables and that these initial differences will invalidate the results of the posttest.

A child abuse prevention educational program for children in schools might be evaluated by comparing the prevention skills of one group of children who have experienced the educational program with the skills of a second group who have not. In order to make a valid comparison, the two groups must be as similar as possible with respect to age, gender, intelligence, socioeconomic status, and anything else that might affect the acquisition of child abuse prevention skills.

We would have to make every effort to form or select equivalent groups, but the groups are sometimes not as equivalent as might be hoped—especially if we are obliged to work with preformed groups, such as classes of students or community groups. If the two groups were different before the intervention was introduced, there is not much point in comparing them at the end.

Accordingly, preformed groups should be avoided whenever possible. If it is not feasible to do this, rigorous pretesting must be done to determine in what ways the groups are (or are not) equivalent, and differences must be compensated for with the use of statistical methods.

Mortality

The seventh threat to internal validity is mortality, which simply means that individual research participants may drop out before the end of the study. Their absence will probably have a significant effect on the study's findings because people who drop out are likely to be different in some ways from the other participants who stay in the study. People who drop out may be less motivated to participate in the intervention than people who stay in, for example.

Since dropouts often have such characteristics in common, it cannot be assumed that the attrition occurred in a random manner. If considerably more people drop out of one group than out of the other, the result will be two groups that are no longer equivalent and cannot be usefully compared. We cannot know at the beginning of the study how many people will drop out, but we can watch to see how many do. Mortality is never problematic if dropout rates are 5 percent or less *and* if the dropout rates are similar for the various groups.

Reactive Effects of Research Participants

The eighth threat to internal validity is reactive effects. Changes in the behaviors or feelings of research participants may be caused by their reaction to the novelty of the situation or to the knowledge that they are participating in a research study. A mother practicing communication skills with her child, for example, may try especially hard when she knows the social worker is watching. We may wrongly believe that such reactive effects are the result of the intervention.

The classic example of reactive effects was found in a series of studies carried out at the Hawthorne plant of the Western Electric Company, in Chicago, many years ago. Researchers were investigating the relationship between working conditions and productivity. When they increased the level of lighting in one section of the plant, productivity increased; a further increase in the lighting was followed by an additional increase in productivity.

When the lighting was then decreased, however, production levels did not fall accordingly but continued to rise. The conclusion was that the workers were increasing their productivity not because of the lighting level but because of the attention they were receiving as research participants in the study.

The term "Hawthorne effect" is still used to describe any situation in which the research participants' behaviors are influenced not by the intervention but by the knowledge that they are taking part in a research project. Another example of such a reactive effect is the placebo given to patients, which produces beneficial results because the patients believe it is medication.

Reactive effects can be controlled by ensuring that all participants in a research study, in both the experimental

(continued)

BOX 13.1 (*continued*)

and the control groups, appear to be treated equally. If one group is to be shown an educational film, for example, the other group should also be shown a film—some film carefully chosen to bear no relationship to the variable being investigated. If the study involves a change in the participants' routine, this in itself may be enough to change behavior, and care must be taken to continue the study until novelty has ceased to be a factor.

Interaction Effects

Interaction among the various threats to internal validity can have an effect of its own. Any of the factors already described as threats may interact with one another, but the most common interactive effect involves differential selection and maturation.

Let us say we are studying two preformed groups of clients who are being treated for depression. The intention was for these groups to be equivalent, in terms of both their motivation for treatment and their levels of depression. It turns out that Group A is more generally depressed than Group B, however. Whereas both groups may grow less motivated over time, it is likely that Group A, whose members were more depressed to begin with, will lose motivation more completely and more quickly than Group B. Inequivalent preformed groups thus grow less equivalent over time as a result of the interaction between differential selection and maturation.

Relations between Experimental and Control Groups

The final group of threats to internal validity has to do with the effects of the use of experimental and control groups that receive different interventions. These effects include (1) diffusion of treatments, (2) compensatory equalization, (3) compensatory rivalry, and (4) demoralization.

Diffusion of Treatments

Diffusion, or imitation, of treatments may occur when members of the experimental and control groups talk to each other about the study. Suppose a study is designed that presents a new relaxation exercise to the experimental group and nothing at all to the control group. There is always the possibility that one of the participants in the experimental group will explain the exercise to a friend who happens to be in the control group. The friend explains it to another friend, and so on. This might be beneficial for the control group, but it invalidates the study's findings.

Compensatory Equalization

Compensatory equalization of treatment occurs when the person doing the study and/or the staff member administering the intervention to the experimental group feels sorry for people in the control group who are not receiving it and attempts to compensate them.

A social worker might take a control group member aside and covertly demonstrate the relaxation exercise, for example. On the other hand, if our study has been ethically designed, there should be no need for guilt on the part of the social worker because some people are not being taught to relax. They can be taught to relax when our study is "officially" over.

Compensatory Rivalry

Compensatory rivalry is an effect that occurs when the control group becomes motivated to compete with the experimental group. For example, a control group in a program to encourage parental involvement in school activities might get wind that something is up and make a determined effort to participate, too, on the basis that "anything they can do, we can do better." There is no direct communication between groups, as in the diffusion of treatment effect—only rumors and suggestions of rumors. However, rumors are often enough to threaten the internal validity of a study.

Demoralization

In direct contrast with compensatory rivalry, demoralization refers to feelings of deprivation among the control group that may cause them to give up and drop out of the study, in which case this effect would be referred to as mortality. The people in the control group may also get angry.

BOX 13.2

Threats to External Validity

External validity is the degree to which the results of a research study are generalizable to a larger population or to settings outside the research situation or setting.

Pretest-Treatment Interaction

The first threat to external validity, pretest-treatment interaction, is similar to the testing threat to internal validity. The nature of a pretest can alter the way research participants respond to the experimental treatment, as well as to the posttest.

Suppose, for example, that an educational program on racial tolerance is being evaluated. A pretest that measures the level of tolerance could well alert the participants to the fact that they are going to be educated into loving all their neighbors, but many people do not want to be "educated" into anything. They are satisfied with the way they feel and will resist the instruction. This will affect the level of racial tolerance registered on the posttest.

Selection-Treatment Interaction

The second threat to external validity is selection-treatment interaction. This threat commonly occurs when a research design cannot provide for random selection of participants from a population. Suppose we wanted to study the effectiveness of a family service agency staff, for example. If our research proposal was turned down by 50 agencies before it was accepted by the fifty-first, it is very likely that the accepting agency differs in certain important aspects from the other 50. It may accept the proposal because its social workers are more highly motivated, more secure, more satisfied with their jobs, or more interested in the practical application of the study than the average agency staff member.

As a result, we would be assessing the research participants on the very factors for which they were unwittingly (and by default) selected—motivation, job satisfaction, and so on. The study may be internally valid, but, since it will not be possible to generalize the results to other family service agencies, it will have little external validity.

Specificity of Variables

Specificity of variables has to do with the fact that a research project conducted with a specific group of people at a specific time and in a specific setting may not always be generalizable to other people at different times and in different settings.

For example, a measuring instrument developed to measure the IQ levels of upper-socioeconomic-level Caucasian suburban children does not provide an equally accurate measure of IQ when it is applied to lower-socioeconomic-level children of racial minorities in the inner city.

Reactive Effects

The fourth threat to external validity is reactive effects, which, as with internal validity, occur when the attitudes or behaviors of the research participants are affected to some degree by the very act of taking a pretest. Thus, they are no longer exactly equivalent to the population from which they were randomly selected, and it may not be possible to generalize the study's results to that population. Because pretests affect research participants to some degree, the study results may be valid only for those who were pretested.

Multiple-Treatment Interference

The fifth threat to external validity, multiple-treatment interference, occurs when a research participant is given two or more interventions in succession so that the results of the first intervention may affect the results of the second one. A client who attends treatment sessions, for example, may not seem to benefit from one therapeutic technique, so another is tried. In fact, however, the client may have benefited from the first technique but the benefit may not become apparent until the second technique has been tried. As a result, the effects of both techniques become commingled, or the results may be erroneously ascribed to the second technique alone.

Because of this threat, interventions should be given separately if possible. If the research design does not allow this, sufficient time should be allowed to elapse between the two interventions in an effort to minimize the possibility of multiple-treatment interference.

Researcher Bias

The final threat to external validity is researcher bias. Researchers, like people in general, tend to see what they want to see or expect to see. Unconsciously and without any thought of deceit, they may manipulate a study so that the actual results agree with the anticipated results. A practitioner may favor an intervention so strongly that the research study is structured to support it, or the results may be interpreted favorably.

(continued)

All that this design provides is a single measure (O_1) of what happens when one group of people is subjected to one treatment or experience (X). The program's participants were not randomly selected from any particular population, and, thus, the results of the findings cannot be generalized to any other group or population.

It is safe to assume that all the members within the program had physically abused their children before they enrolled, since people who do not have this problem would not have enrolled in such a program. But, even if the value of O_1 indicates that some of the parents did stop being violent with their children after the program, it cannot be determined whether they quit because of the intervention (the program) or because of some other rival hypothesis. Perhaps a law was passed that made it mandatory for the police to arrest anyone who behaves violently toward his or her child, or perhaps the local television station started to report such incidents on the nightly news, complete with pictures of the abusive parent. These or other extraneous variables might have been more important in persuading the parents to cease their abusive behavior toward their children than their voluntary participation in the program.

In sum, this design does not control for many of the threats to either internal or external validity. In terms of internal validity, the threats that are not controlled for in this design are history, maturation, differential selection, and mortality.

Cross-Sectional Survey Design

Let us take another example of a one-group posttest-only design that *does not* have an intervention of some kind. In survey research, this kind of a group research design is called a cross-sectional survey design.

In doing a cross-sectional survey, we survey *only once* a cross-section of some particular population. In addition to running her child abuse prevention program geared for abusive parents, Antonia may also want to start another program geared for all the children in the school

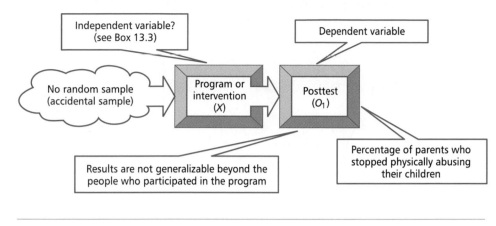

Figure 13.3 One-Group Post-Test Only Design

(whether they come from abusive families or not)—a child abuse educational program taught to children in the school.

Before Antonia starts her educational program geared for the children, however, she wants to know what parents think about the idea. She may send out questionnaires to all the parents, or she may decide to personally telephone every second parent, or every fifth or tenth, depending on how much time and money she has. The results of her survey constitute a single measurement, or observation, of the parents' opinions of her proposed educational program (the one for the children) and may be written as shown in Figure 13.4.

The symbol O represents the entire cross-sectional survey design since such a design involves making only a single observation, or measurement, at one time period. Note that there is no X, since there is really no intervention. Antonia wants only to ascertain the parents' attitudes toward her proposed program—nothing more, nothing less.

Multigroup Posttest-Only Design

The multigroup posttest-only design is an elaboration of the one-group posttest-only design in which more than one group is used. To check a bit further into the effectiveness of Antonia's program for parents who have been physically abusive toward their children, for example, she might decide to locate several more groups of parents who have completed her program and see how many of them have stopped abusing their children—and so on, with any number of groups. This design can be written in symbols as shown in Figure 13.5, where:

$X =$ Child Abuse Prevention Program, or the intervention (see Box 13.3)

Figure 13.4 Cross-Sectional Survey Design

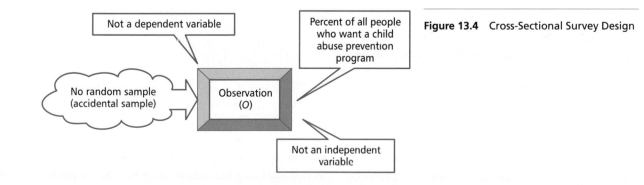

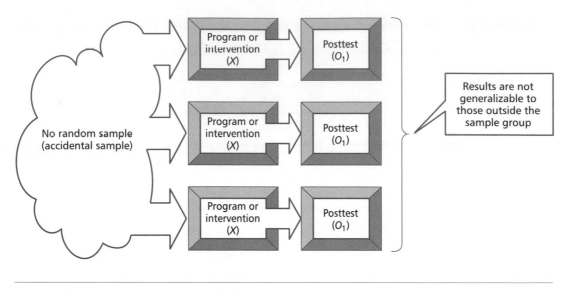

Figure 13.5 Multi-Group Posttest-Only Design

O_1 = First and only measurement of the dependent variable (percentage of parents who stopped physically abusing their children, the program's outcome or program objective)

With the multigroup design it cannot be assumed that all three Xs are equivalent because the three programs might not be exactly the same; one group might have had a different facilitator, the program might have been presented differently, or the material could have varied in important respects.

In addition, nothing is known about whether any of the research participants would have stopped being violent anyway, even without the program. It certainly cannot be assumed that any of the groups were representative of the larger population. Thus, as in the case of the one-group posttest-only design, the same threats to the internal and the external validity of the study might influence the results of the multigroup posttest-only design.

Longitudinal Case Study Design

The longitudinal case study design is exactly like the one-group posttest-only design, except that it provides

for more measurements of the dependent variable (Os). This design can be written in symbols as shown in Figure 13.6, where:

X = Child Abuse Prevention Program, or the intervention (see Box 13.3)

O_1 = First measurement of the dependent variable (percentage of parents who stopped physically abusing their children, the program's outcome or program objective)

O_2 = Second measurement of the dependent variable (percentage of parents who stopped physically abusing their children, the program's outcome or program objective)

O_3 = Third measurement of the dependent variable (percentage of parents who stopped physically abusing their children, the program's outcome or program objective)

Suppose that, in our example, Antonia is interested in the long-term effects of the child abuse prevention program. Perhaps the program was effective in helping some people to stop physically abusing their children, but will they continue to refrain from abusing their children? One way to find out is to measure the percentage of parents

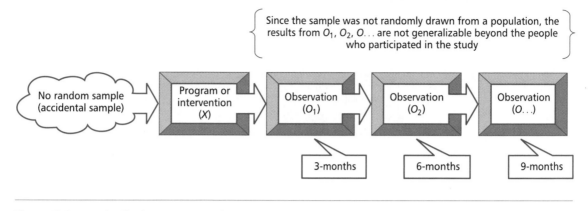

Since the sample was not randomly drawn from a population, the results from O_1, O_2, O... are not generalizable beyond the people who participated in the study

No random sample (accidental sample) → Program or intervention (X) → Observation (O_1) → Observation (O_2) → Observation (O...)

3-months   6-months   9-months

Figure 13.6   Longitudinal One-Group Only Posttest Design

who physically abuse their children at intervals—say at the end of the program, three months after the program, three months after that, and every three months for the next two years.

This design can be used to monitor the effectiveness of treatment interventions over time and can be applied not just to groups but also to single-client systems, as described in Chapter 12. However, all of the same threats to the internal and external validity that were described in relation to the previous two exploratory designs also apply to this design.

Longitudinal Survey Design

Unlike cross-sectional surveys, where the variable of interest (usually the dependent variable) is measured at one point in time, longitudinal surveys provide data at various points in time so that changes can be monitored over time. They can be broken down into two general types: (1) trend studies and (2) cohort studies.

Trend Studies.   A trend study is used to find out how a population, or sample, changes over time. Antonia, the school social worker mentioned previously, may want to know whether parents of young children enrolled in her school are becoming more receptive to the idea of the school teaching their children child abuse prevention education in the second grade (Williams, Tutty, & Grinnell, 1995). She may survey all the parents

of Grade 2 children this year, all the parents of the new complement of Grade 2 children next year, and so on until she thinks she has sufficient data.

Each year the parents surveyed will be different, but they will all be parents of Grade 2 children. In this way, Antonia will be able to determine whether parents are becoming more receptive to the idea of introducing child abuse prevention material to their children as early as Grade 2. In other words, she will be able to measure any attitudinal trend that is, or is not, occurring. The research design can still be written as shown in Figure 13.7, where:

$O_1 =$ First measurement of a variable **in Sample 1**

$O_2 =$ Second measurement of a variable **in Sample 2**

$O_3 =$ Third measurement of a variable **in Sample 3**

Cohort Studies.   Cohort studies are used over time to follow a single group of people who have shared a similar experience—for example, AIDS survivors, sexual abuse survivors, or parents of grade-school children. In a cohort study, the *same individuals* are followed over a period of time. Antonia might select one particular sample of parents, for example, and measure their attitudes toward child abuse prevention education in successive years. Again, the design can be written as shown in Figure 13.8, where:

Figure 13.7 Trend Research Studies

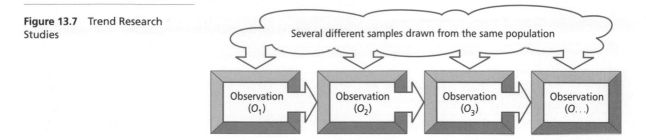

Several different samples drawn from the same population

O_1 = First measurement of some variable for a **sample of individuals**

O_2 = Second measurement of some variable **for the same sample of individuals one year later**

O_3 = Third measurement of some variable **for the same sample of individuals after two years**

Descriptive Designs

At the midpoint on the knowledge continuum are descriptive designs, which have some but not all of the requirements of an "ideal" experiment. They usually require specification of the time order of variables, manipulation of the independent variable, and establishment of the relationship between the independent and dependent variables.

They may also control for rival hypotheses and use a second group as a comparison (not as a control). The requirement that descriptive designs lack most frequently is the random assignment of research participants to two or more groups.

We are seldom in a position to randomly assign research participants to either an experimental or a con-trol group. Sometimes the groups to be studied are already in existence; sometimes ethical issues are involved. It would be unethical, for example, to assign clients who need immediate help to two random groups, only one of which is to receive the intervention. Since a lack of random assignment affects the internal and external validities of the study, the descriptive research design must try to compensate for this.

Randomized One-Group Posttest-Only Design

The distinguishing feature of the randomized one-group posttest-only design is that members of the group are randomly selected for it. Otherwise, this design is identical to the exploratory one-group posttest-only design. The randomized one-group posttest-only design is written as shown in Figure 13.9, where:

R_s = Random selection from a population

X = Program, or the intervention (see Box 13.3)

O_1 = First and only measurement of the dependent variable

In the example of the child abuse prevention program, the difference in this design is that the group does

Figure 13.8 Cohort Research Studies

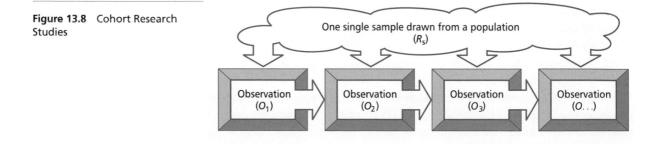

One single sample drawn from a population (R_s)

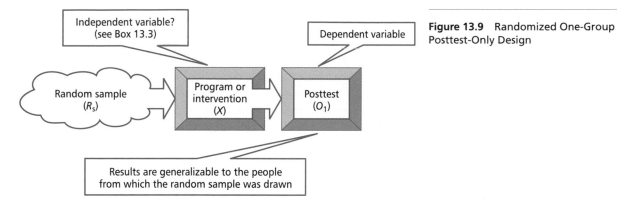

Figure 13.9 Randomized One-Group Posttest-Only Design

not accidentally assemble itself by including anyone who happens to be interested in volunteering for the program. Instead, group members are randomly selected from a population, say, of all the 400 parents who were reported to child welfare authorities for having physically abused a child in Rome, Wisconsin, in 2005 and who wish to receive voluntary treatment. These 400 parents comprise the population of all the physically abusive parents who wish to receive treatment in Rome, Wisconsin.

The sampling frame of 400 people is used to select a simple random sample of 40 physically abusive parents who voluntarily wish to receive treatment. The program (X) is administered to these 40 people, and the percentage of parents who stop being abusive toward their children after the program is determined (O_1). The design can be written as shown in Figure 13.10, where:

R = Random selection of 40 people from the population of physically abusive parents who voluntarily wish to receive treatment in Rome, Wisconsin

X = Child Abuse Prevention Program, or the intervention (see Box 13.3)

O_1 = Percentage of parents in the program who stopped being physically abusive to their children

Say that the program fails to have the desired effect, and 80 percent of the people continue to physically harm their children after participating in the program. Because the program was ineffective for the sample and the sample was randomly selected, it can be concluded that the program would be ineffective for the physically abusive

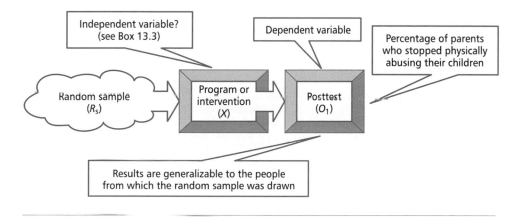

Figure 13.10 Randomized One-Group Posttest-Only Design

parent population of Rome, Wisconsin—the other 360 who did not go through the program. In other words, because a representative random sample was selected, it is possible to generalize the program's results to the population from which the sample was drawn.

Since no change in the dependent variable occurred, it is not sensible to consider the control of rival hypotheses. Antonia need not wonder what might have caused the miniscule change—X, her program, or an alternative explanation. If her program had been successful, however, it would not be possible to ascribe her success *solely* to the program.

Randomized Cross-Sectional Survey Design

As discussed earlier, a cross-sectional survey obtains data only once from a sample of a particular population. If the sample is a random sample—that is, if it represents the population from which it was drawn—then the data obtained from the sample can be generalized to the entire population. A cross-sectional survey design using a random sample can be written as shown in Figure 13.11, where:

R_s = Random sample drawn from a population
O_1 = First and only measurement of the dependent variable (see Box 13.3)

Explanatory surveys look for associations between variables. Often, the suspected reason for the relationship is that one variable caused the other. In Antonia's case, she has two studies going on: the child abuse prevention program for parents who have physically abused their children, and her survey of parental attitudes toward the school that is teaching second-grade children child abuse

prevention strategies. The success of the child abuse prevention program (her program) may have caused parents to adopt more positive attitudes toward the school in teaching their children child abuse prevention (her survey). In this situation, the two variables, the program and survey, become commingled. Demonstrating causality is a frustrating business at best because it is so difficult to show that nothing apart from the independent variable could have caused the observed change in the dependent variable.

One-Group Pretest-Posttest Design

The one-group pretest-posttest design is also referred to as a before-after design because it includes a pretest of the dependent variable, which can be used as a basis of comparison with the posttest results. It is written as shown in Figure 13.12, where:

O_1 = First measurement of the dependent variable
X = Program, or the intervention (see Box 13.3)
O_2 = Second measurement of the dependent variable

The one-group pretest-posttest design, in which a pretest precedes the introduction of the intervention and a posttest follows it, can be used to determine precisely how the intervention affects a particular group. The design is used often in social work decision making. It does not control for many rival hypotheses. The difference between O_1 and O_2, on which these decisions are based, could be due to many other factors rather than to the intervention.

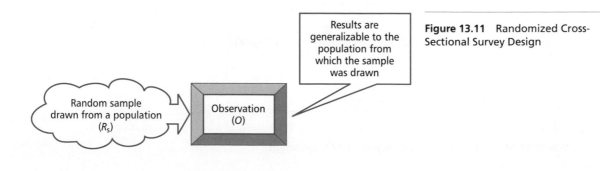

Results are generalizable to the population from which the sample was drawn

Random sample drawn from a population (R_s)

Observation (O)

Figure 13.11 Randomized Cross-Sectional Survey Design

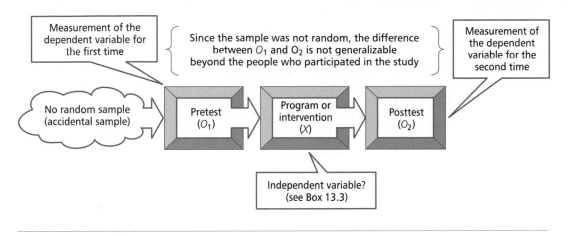

Figure 13.12   One-Group Pretest-Posttest Design

Let us take another indicator of how Antonia's child abuse prevention program could be evaluated. Besides counting the number of parents who stopped physically abusing their children as the only indicator of the program's success, she could have a second outcome indicator such as a reduction in the parents' risk for abusive and neglecting parenting behaviors. This dependent variable could be easily measured by an instrument that measures their attitudes toward physical punishment of children.

Let us say that Antonia had the parents complete the instrument *before* participating in the child abuse prevention program (O_1) and *after* completing it (O_2). In this example, history would be a rival hypothesis or threat to internal validity because all kinds of things could have happened between O_1 and O_2 to affect the participants' behaviors and feelings—such as the television station's deciding to publicize the names of parents who are abusive to their children. Testing also could be a problem. Just the experience of taking the pretest could motivate some participants to stop being abusive toward their children. Maturation—in this example, the children becoming more mature with age so that they became less difficult to discipline—would be a further threat.

This design controls for the threat of differential selection, since the participants are the same for both pretest and posttest. Second, mortality would not affect the outcome, because it is the differential drop-out between groups that causes this threat, and, in this example,

ple, there is only one group (Williams, Tutty, & Grinnell, 1995).

Comparison Group Posttest-Only Design

The comparison group posttest-only design improves on the exploratory one-group and multigroup posttest-only designs by introducing a comparison group that does not receive the independent variable but is subject to the same posttest as those who do (the comparison group). The group used for purposes of comparison is usually referred to as a comparison group in an exploratory or descriptive design and as a control group in an explanatory design. While a control group is always randomly assigned, a comparison group is not. The basic elements of the comparison group posttest-only design are as shown in Figure 13.13, where:

X = Independent variable, or the intervention
O_1 = First and only measurement of the dependent variable

In Antonia's child abuse prevention program, if the January, April, and August sections are scheduled but the August sessions are canceled for some reason, those who would have been participants in that section could be used as a comparison group. If the values of O_1 on the measuring instrument were similar for the experimental and comparison groups, it could be concluded that the

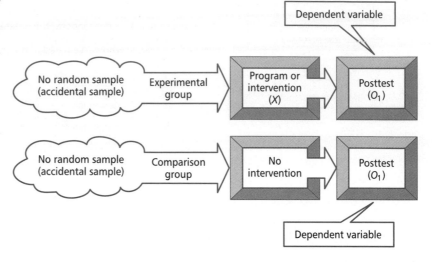

Figure 13.13 Comparison Group Posttest-Only Design

program was of little use, since those who had experienced it (those who had received X) were not much better or worse off than those who had not.

A problem with drawing this conclusion, however, is that there is no evidence that the groups were equivalent to begin with. Selection, mortality, and the interaction of selection and other threats to internal validity are, thus, the major difficulties with this design. The comparison group does, however, control for such threats as history, testing, and instrumentation.

Comparison Group Pretest-Posttest Design

The comparison group pretest-posttest design elaborates on the one-group pretest-posttest design by adding a comparison group. This second group receives both the pretest (O_1) and the posttest (O_2) at the same time as the experimental group, but it does not receive the independent variable. This design is written as shown in Figure 13.14, where:

$O_1 =$ First measurement of the dependent variable, the parents' scores on the measuring instrument
$X =$ Independent variable, or the intervention
$O_2 =$ Second measurement of the dependent variable, the parents' scores on the measuring instrument

The experimental and comparison groups formed under this design will probably not be equivalent, because members are not randomly assigned to them. The pretest scores, however, will indicate the extent of their differences. If the differences are not statistically significant but are still large enough to affect the posttest, the statistical technique of analysis of covariance can be used to compensate for this. As long as the groups are equivalent at pretest, then, this design controls for nearly all of the threats to internal validity. But, because random selection and assignment were not used, the external validity threats remain.

Interrupted Time-Series Design

In the interrupted time-series design, a series of pretests and posttests are conducted on a group of research participants over time, both before and after the independent variable is introduced. The basic elements of this design are shown in Figure 13.15, where:

$O_s =$ Measurements of the dependent variable
$X =$ The intervention (see Box 13.3)

This design takes care of the major weakness in the descriptive one-group pretest-posttest design, which does not control for many rival hypotheses. Suppose, for example, that a new policy is to be introduced into an agency whereby all promotions and raises are to be

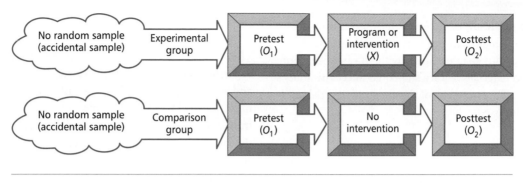

Figure 13.14   Comparison Group Pretest-Posttest Design

tied to the number of educational credits acquired by social workers. Since there is a strong feeling among some workers that years of experience should count for more than educational credits, the agency's management decides to examine the effect of the new policy on morale.

Because agency morale is affected by many things and varies normally from month to month, it is neces-

sary to ensure that these normal fluctuations are not confused with the results of the new policy. Therefore, a baseline is first established for morale by conducting a number of pretests over, say, a six-month period before the policy is introduced. Then, a similar number of posttests is conducted over the six months following the introduction of the policy.

The same type of time-series design can be used to

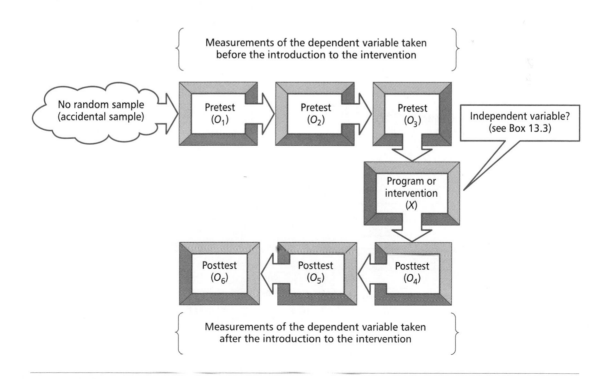

Figure 13.15   Interrupted Time Series Design

evaluate the result of a treatment intervention with a client or client system, as in case-level designs described in the previous chapter. Again, without randomization, threats to external validity still could affect the study's generalizability, but most of the threats to internal validity are addressed.

Explanatory Designs

Explanatory group research designs approach the "ideal" experiment most closely. They are at the highest level of the knowledge continuum, have the most rigid requirements, and are most able to produce results that can be generalized to other people and situations. Explanatory designs, therefore, are most able to provide valid and reliable research results that can serve as additions to our professions' knowledge base.

The purpose of an explanatory design is to establish a causal connection between the independent and dependent variable. The value of the dependent variable could always result from chance rather than from the influence of the independent variable, but there are statistical techniques for calculating the probability that this will occur.

Classical Experimental Design

The classical experimental design is the basis for all the experimental designs. It involves an experimental group and a control group, both created by a random assignment method (and, if possible, by random selection from a population). Both groups take a pretest (O_1) at the same time, after which the independent variable (X) is given only to the experimental group, and then both groups take the posttest (O_2). This design is written as shown in Figure 13.16, where:

R = Random selection from a population and random assignment to group
O_1 = First measurement of the dependent variable
X = Independent variable, or the intervention
O_2 = Second measurement of the dependent variable

Because the experimental and control groups have been randomly assigned, they are equivalent with respect to all important variables. This group equivalence in the design helps control for rival hypotheses, because both groups will be affected by them in the same way.

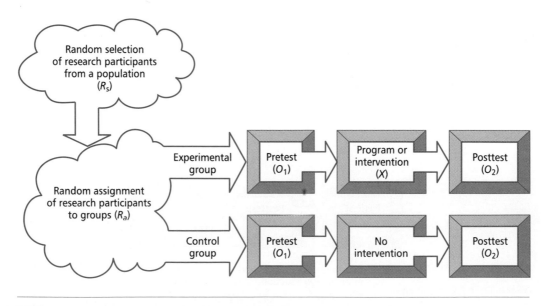

Figure 13.16   Pretest-Posttest Control Group Design (Classical Experimental Design)

Randomized Posttest-Only Control Group Design

The randomized posttest-only control group research design is identical to the descriptive comparison group posttest-only design, except that the research participants are randomly assigned to two groups. This design, therefore, has a control group, rather than a comparison group.

The randomized posttest-only control group research design usually involves only two groups, one experimental and one control. There are no pretests. The experimental group receives the independent variable and takes the posttest; the control group only takes the posttest. This design can be written as shown in Figure 13.17, where:

R = Random selection from a population and random assignment to group

X = Independent variable, or the intervention

O_1 = First and only measurement of the dependent variable

In addition to measuring change in a group or groups, a pretest also helps to ensure equivalence between the control and the experimental groups. As you know, this design does not have a pretest. The groups have been randomly assigned, however, as indicated by R, and this, in itself, is theoretically enough to ensure equivalence without the need for a confirmatory pretest. This design is useful in situations where it is not possible to conduct a pretest or where a pretest would be expected to strongly influence the results of the posttest because of the effects of testing. This design also controls for many of the threats to internal validity.

SUMMARY

Group research designs are conducted with groups of cases rather than on a case-by-case basis. They cover the entire range of research questions and provide designs that can be used to gain knowledge on the exploratory, descriptive, and explanatory levels.

Exploratory designs are used when little is known about the field of study and data are gathered in an effort to find out "what's out there." These ideas are then used to generate hypotheses that can be verified using more rigorous research designs. Descriptive designs are one step closer to determining causality. Explanatory designs are useful when considerable preexisting knowledge is available about the research question under study and a

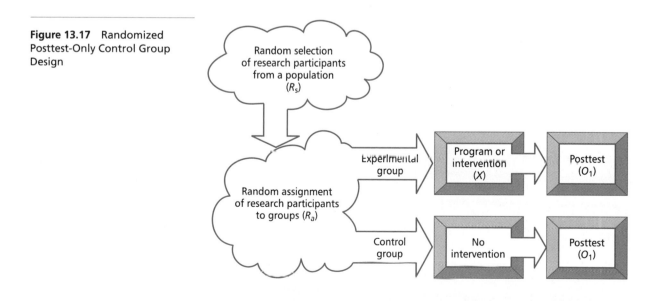

Figure 13.17 Randomized Posttest-Only Control Group Design

testable hypothesis can be formulated on the basis of previous work. They have more internal and external validity than exploratory and descriptive designs, so they can help establish a causal connection between two variables.

No one group research design is inherently inferior or superior to the others. Each has advantages and disadvantages. Those of us who are familiar with all three categories of group research designs will be equipped to select the one that is most appropriate to a particular research question.

PART V

Collecting Original Data

· ·

Part V discusses the three main obtrusive data collection methods that collect original data for social work research studies—observation, interviewing, and the use of survey questionnaires. Chapter 14 focuses on how observational methods can be used as a data collection method, and the following chapter (Chapter 15) expands on this content by presenting how observations can be used in participant observation. Chapter 16 then goes on to discuss how to conduct research interviews, while Chapter 17 presents how to construct and execute surveys.

All four chapters in Part V present obtrusive data collection methods; that is, they all require an interaction of some kind between the researcher and the research participant. In contrast to Part V, Part VI presents unobtrusive data collection methods that require no involvement of the research participant and that collect data that already exist.

Jeane W. Anastas

Observation

. . . .

14

In some ways, all research studies are based on some form of observation. As we know, the research process is empirical. And, by definition, "empirical" means perceived through the senses, that is, observed. In research terminology, however, the term "observation" has come to mean something more restricted; it refers to the data collected by a researcher who directly observes a study's research participant(s). Observational data-collection methods are underutilized in social work and human services research. Nevertheless, they are great ways to collect original data and have been widely used in psychology in such topic areas as infant and child development. Observational data-collection methods have been used to study social processes in formal organizations, informal groups, and even households.

In most cases, the person whose characteristic(s) are observed (the research participants) and the person doing the observing (the researcher) are different people. For this reason, observational data-collection methods are often assumed to be less biased than other methods of data collection, such as self-reports. Stem (1985), for example, has commented that we live in an age in which observations are often the preferred form of evidence.

There is something quite compelling about observational data. Critics may object to the manner in which they were collected or to the interpretations that the researcher made from them. Even the most skeptical critic of a study's findings based on observational data, however, is unlikely to totally discount data that were "seen." In the research enterprise where evidence is everything, observational evidence is often considered the most valuable of all, as it can be "seen."

None of the social sciences can lay claim to having a special expertise in using observations as a data-collection method. As we know from Chapter 1, observations are a form of measurement and are as old as science itself. What the social sciences can lay claim to, however, is their refinement of this data-collection method over time in measuring abstract phenomena, or variables. This refinement has been no easy task. The social sciences typically study variables that do not exist apart from the conceptual and social judgments about them. This statement is especially true of the helping professions, which tend to study variables when there is a socially defined need to do so.

Consider, for a moment, the act of striking a child. Once considered a proper discipline approach in school and home settings, this act is now regarded as abusive. It is relatively easy for someone who is present at the time to decide whether or not a child is being hit. It may be less easy, however, to decide whether or not a bruise (or other mark observed on a child's body) is evidence of having been hit. It is even more difficult to decide what is good discipline in general and what is not.

Even legal definitions of child abuse may be difficult to tie unambiguously to observational data. In our profession, for example, definitions of key variables change over time and in different contexts. The kind of data needed to provide irrefutable evidence even of an often-defined concept like child abuse may be hard to provide unambiguously. For example, Southeast Asian American women may use "cupping" and burning as folk cures for colds—remedies and acts of caring that are standard and readily accepted in their cultures. The marks these practices may leave on the body of the child, however, may be seen as "evidence of abuse." The same evidence would be labeled by others in their own communities as "evidence of nurturance" (Landrine, Klonoff, & Brown-Collins, 1992).

This chapter provides a brief overview of how to use observation as a data-collection method. In qualitative research studies (a flexible research approach), the observations made are formative of the understandings and explanations generated. By contract, in quantitative research studies (a fixed research approach), the variables to be observed are specified and defined before data collection begins. Thus, the quantitative-observational process is structured in light of those specifications and definitions. In fact, the observational traditions in the quantitative research approach and in the qualitative research approach are based on sharply divergent assumptions about the research enterprise, the nature of useful evidence, and the role of the researcher in the observational process. What observation has in common in both research approaches, however, is its focus on non-verbal visual data and the quandaries that are raised by the observation process itself.

BASIC PRINCIPLES OF OBSERVATION

In the helping professions, observational methodologies have largely been developed and refined by clinicians and researchers working within the behavioral tradition. This connection is not surprising, as behavioral theorists traditionally have held that practitioners should address what can be seen, that is, overt behavior. As a consequence, their measurement methods—largely directed toward assessing the observable—have been predominantly observational ones. Thus, it is no surprise that behavioral research has generally followed the traditional quantitative approach to knowledge building. In traditional behavioral terms, observation is a process by which a measuring instrument is used to calibrate certain predefined properties of an observable variable. The measuring instrument of observation may be mechanical (e.g., a machine to measure galvanic skin response, reflecting perspiration as an index of physiological anxiety). Actually, the term "detection" rather than "observation" should be used when instruments function to record variables that would ordinarily be unnoticeable.

More often than not, however, the instrument of observation is a person, and any instrument used, such as a videotape recorder, functions only to make a record of what human senses would perceive. However, when people function as observers in the behavioral tradition, they are instructed do so as precisely and objectively as a machine. That is, the human observers make a record of what they observe by rules that must be invariantly applied. The observers also must minimize their impact on, or interaction with, those whom they are observing. This must be done above and beyond what may be inherent in the act of observation itself.

To some extent, however, observation involves making judgments. Traditionally, observers are therefore trained in applying some clear rules to their observational techniques they employ. These rules specify:

1. The circumstances of observation, when and where observations will take place, and how much control will be exercised over the observational context

2. The period of time over which observations will be made and with what frequency, including whether and how to sample times of observation
3. Precisely who will be observed and what will be observed about each person
4. How the observations will be recorded

Even when observations are less structured, such as those in a qualitative research study, decisions are made about each of these four dimensions. Participant observational research, however, is opportunistic (Jorgensen, 1989). This means that the four decisions on how to observe a variable are often made in the field and adjusted as the process unfolds. In contract, in quantitative studies, decisions about these rules are made before data collection ever begins. Nevertheless, whatever the research approach, the guiding principle used when answering these questions is the purpose of the research study.

Context and Circumstance

With respect to the question of when observations should be made, the optimal circumstances of observation within the qualitative research study are whatever ones present themselves in the setting that are relevant to the study's research question(s). The principle of prolonged engagement indicates that observations are often made over an extended period of time (Padgett, 1998). In the quantitative approach, the question of when to observe is essentially a matter of deciding on the context(s) in which the variable of interest can best be assessed.

The question of how long to observe really breaks down into two different questions depending on whether the researcher intends to observe a few people over an extended period of time or many people at one or only a few points in time. In the first case, the question remains how long these few people should be observed. In the second scenario, the question becomes how many people to observe; since each person will be observed for a roughly equivalent amount of time, the total amount of observation time will be determined by the number of different people observed.

In qualitative studies, it is not possible to specify for certain how much observation will be enough before the fact. Leaving such matters open is inherent in this research approach, since the method must remain flexible enough to respond to the data as they come in. With qualitative studies, then, the answer to the question of how long to collect observations is at the same time simple and demanding: until enough data have been gathered to answer the study's research question—to be addressed with convincing data to defend the answer—or at least until additional observation time is yielding little or no new meaningful data or insights. That is why it is impossible to predict beforehand how much observation will be enough in qualitative studies.

This inability to specify before the fact how much observation will be enough—which is inherent in the qualitative research approach—is also inherent in quantitatively oriented case-level studies (see Chapter 12). As we know, many case-level designs set out to document specific changes in the dependent variable. In these designs, the length of time over which data must be collected is determined not a priori but rather by the form the data are taking as they occur: Data collection in case-level designs must continue until the response to the intervention becomes clear.

And, while sometimes there is an immediate and dramatic reaction to an intervention, more often than not data collection must continue for some period of time until any trends or changes in the dependent variable can be adequately documented. In both quantitative case-level designs and qualitative studies, then, the answer to the question "How much should I observe" is the same: You should observe until you have an answer to the question or hypothesis you set out to address and until you have data in hand that you can present to others that will give them reason to believe the study's conclusions.

The question of how long to observe can be answered before the fact easily in descriptive and explanatory studies. The question really is a conceptual one that boils down to whether or not the variable being studied requires a longitudinal approach to answer the question or whether a cross-sectional study can serve the purpose.

Time is only one element of an observational context. The circumstances or settings in which the observations will take place must be considered, as well. In any type of research study, the researcher must decide before initiating the observations what the observational circumstances will be.

Therefore, whether planning a quantitative or qualitative research study, researchers often do preliminary work to determine which of several alternative available observational circumstances may present the best ones for the research effort. In field research, for example, this work typically involves finding naturally occurring settings where the behavior of interest is likely to occur and that will accommodate the observation process. In quantitative studies, for example, the goal may also be to identify or arrange a setting that will remain sufficiently stable and available to allow making meaningful comparisons of behavior across repeated observations made in it.

Since quantitative studies are often directed toward making some form of comparison, they frequently require repeated observations either over time or across people. When comparing what is observed in these repeated observations, the observational context must remain the same or at least be equivalent. If constancy or at least equivalence of the observational context is not maintained, what is observed can be expected to literally look different—not because it is in fact different in some intrinsic way but rather because the circumstances under which it is being studied have changed.

Since comparability of observational settings can be so important in quantitative studies, sometimes the researcher decides to create the observational circumstance rather than use a naturally occurring one. Consistency in the observational context can be arranged either within or outside the laboratory. When it is arranged within the laboratory, for example, the form of the observation is typically called "controlled," because the researcher is controlling not what the people being observed are doing but the circumstances within which the participants can do whatever they are doing. When it is arranged outside the laboratory, it is called "contrived." There is no functional difference between controlled and contrived observation: Both involve standardizing the observational context. The difference between them is that controlled observations take place within a laboratory and therefore always with the knowledge of the person being observed. Contrived observations take place outside the laboratory and therefore potentially without the knowledge of the person being observed (see Chapter 3).

One example of a controlled observational context can be found in attachment research by Ainsworth and her colleagues (1978). Their strange-situation procedure was carefully designed to assess the attachment of one-year-old babies to their primary caretaker, the mother. Using a one-way mirror, the researchers observed the mother. Two chairs for adults, one for the child, and some toys were arranged in a standardized way in an office-like room. A fixed sequence of events took place. First, the mother and baby were alone in the room; then a stranger entered and approached the baby and then left; then the mother left and the stranger returned; and then the mother returned. Babies reacted in quite different ways to this sequence of events. Their contact with the adults, their movement around the room, and their affect were all observed by two people who were not in the room. A system of categories was developed to describe the various styles of reactions that babies displayed in this standardized set of circumstances. This classification system for styles of attachment in infancy, in turn, has subsequently been studied as a predictor of many aspects of later development. This is only one example of how controlled observational circumstances have been used in the study of infant and child behavior and development.

Whom and What to Observe

Whom to observe may, at first, seem quite straightforward: Certainly the people chosen to be participants in the study should be observed. As you know from Chapter 11, these participants should be the ones in whom the dependent variable is expected to appear. Given this, the question becomes "Who else should be observed?" When the research question involves inquiry into the context surrounding the primary research participant's behavior, for example, it is often appropriate to observe people other than the primary study participant, as well. From this perspective, these other people become important as potentially interesting features of the interpersonal context for the primary participant's observed behavior. These other people then become part of the "what" that is observed.

The behavioral tradition has given rise to a form of observation in which the observer and the observed are one and the same person. This form of observation is called *self-monitoring* or *self-observation*. Typically self-monitoring can be used with two types of variables:

- *First,* they can be variables that are easily defined and counted, such as the number of cigarettes smoked each day.
- *Second,* they can be variables that are the subjective experiences that are otherwise inaccessible to outside observers, such as the number of self-critical thoughts one has while smoking a cigarette.

This chapter, however, focuses on observation by a third type of variable and thus on how to capture behavior and interactions—those things that are observable—by someone else. Of the several questions that must be answered when designing or choosing an observational strategy, it is the "what" question that has received the most careful attention. This attention, however, has tended to be technical. Much has been written about characteristics that distinguish between variables that can be observed successfully and those that cannot be observed successfully. In general, physical objects, nonverbal behaviors, facial expressions, gestures, and social interactions lend themselves best to observation. On the other hand, subjective experiences, ideas, meanings, and other intangibles can only be inferred from observational data. When this is the case, other data-collection methods may be preferable for measuring such variables. However, children and others who cannot give a verbal account of themselves that is understandable to the observer cannot be interviewed, and observation is often used to study them, instead. In addition, what people do and what they know or say they do may differ markedly. Much social and interactive behavior may be unconscious and unexamined by the participants, and observational methods can be more effective for studying them than relying on some form of self-report.

A major challenge in observing an abstract variable of some kind is the development of an operational definition for the variable that discriminates between when that variable is and is not present. In quantitative studies, it is assumed that the variable to be observed has been adequately defined, at least at a conceptual level. It should be remembered, however, that the nature of the operational definition critically and indelibly influences the nature of the data subsequently collected. As is always the case in data collection, "what variable is being measured" can never be assumed to be correct only on the basis of "how the variable is being measured."

Observational data describing well-defined, observable variables, however, only *seem* self-evident; the complexity of the act of observation has traditionally been overlooked. The logical positivist tradition has maintained that observers see what they are observing in an objective and undistorted fashion. Moreover, it has assumed that when the observers make their observations, what they see is reality. Thus, what they believe they see reflects what is objectively really there.

This belief reflects two underlying assumptions. The first is that human observers can be made to function as reliably and predictably as a mechanical recorder, that human observers can be trained well enough so that they will perform just like a reliable thermometer. This assumption turns out to be true only sometimes. In quantitative studies, it has been shown that human observers are reliable only when rigorous design guidelines are followed in both the development and the application of whatever observational methodology is being used.

There is a second assumption embedded in the logical positivist tradition, however, which turns out to be much more problematic: Human observers can be passive receptors of their external worlds. Observations are only what the observers make of them. Stem (1985), for example, speaks of the "observed infant" described in developmental psychology as "a special construct, a description of capacities that can be observed directly" (p. 17). Such a view of the infant is formed both by what the observer notices and by what the observer *can* notice; the infant's subjective experience, for example, can only be inferred from one's observations of the infant.

The way in which observations are processed influences what is seen. This effect is more subtle, but its impact is more profound. For a moment, force your attention away from the words you are reading in this chapter. Without changing positions, let your eyes move around the space in front of you. No matter where you are sitting, there will be a great number of objects and surfaces before you. Had you noticed them when you were reading this chapter? Probably not. The point is that when we observe, we engage in a process similar to the one you are using when reading this chapter: You will see only a portion of what is in front of you, the parts you choose to focus on.

It is easy to see how this form of perceptual selection bias could exist when one is evaluating a very focused and specific observational recording system. In fact, there is some reason to believe that the more focused an observational system is, the less possible it is to notice phenomena that were "unexpected." In a nutshell, defining what is to be observed places constraints on what can be observed. Observers are unlikely to see what they are not looking for and to see what they are looking for.

Decisions about what variables to observe, then, are of profound importance. They must be made so that the observational recording system chosen will be consistent in principle with the properties of the research design. In qualitative studies, for example, observational systems must start out as very unfocused. The observations used within qualitative studies are always guided by a general notion of what is being looked for. To have specific notions of what will form the variable of interest would likely preclude the observer's being sensitive to the unexpected. As we know, qualitative studies have as their intent of understanding variables that are poorly or incompletely understood. This in turn implies seeing the unexpected, and an observational system with preconceived parameters would not work.

At this point, it should come as no surprise that it may be easier to conduct observations within descriptive and explanatory studies than in exploratory ones. Descriptive and explanatory research designs all require that one specify how observational data are to be gathered before the data are in hand. It follows, then, that the specific variables that will be observed should be specified and operationally defined before the study begins.

Recording Observations

The question of how observations should be recorded is, of course, a technical one with a general answer that applies in all cases, regardless of the research approach used or the observational strategy that is used to collect the data. The method that preserves as much of the available relevant data as possible with the greatest degree of accuracy and permanency, and the least degree of intrusion on the data preserved, is the one that should be used. Since most observations are collected and recorded by human observers, we have grown accustomed to collapsing the several stages in an observe-record-code complex into one in our thinking, but they are really separate stages, each of which merits attention.

Consider the situation in which observation is accomplished by a video camera. When the camera is running, observations are taking place in the situation, even if there is a mechanical problem that precludes making a record of what is observed. If there is no mechanical failure, there will be a record on the tape. However, what will be recorded will be limited to the times when the camera was running and the part of the scene on which the camera was focused. In addition, not until those data are coded, or translated into meaning units in some fashion, will the observation of them be complete. It clarifies the issues involved in the observation-record-code complex to consider each of the facets in it separately.

The recording process refers to the technology used to make a permanent record of what is observed. This technology is most clearly illustrated by the photographic methodology of video cameras when video observation is used or the magnetic recording processes of audio recorders when audio observation is used. Often, however, the recording methodology involves arranging for a human being to serve in the role of an audio and/or video recorder by providing that human observer with a set of rules that indicate what record to make when a certain event is observed to occur.

There is a clear analogue between the mechanical and the human processes in observation. Mechanical technology works by virtue of the translation of data from one form to another. In the case of audiotape recordings, for example, sounds issued within a certain frequency range and at greater than a certain volume will be recorded by a machine that enters electrical impulses onto magnetic tape. This then becomes a symbolic representation of the event that transpired. In like fashion, when human observers make records of what they observe, they follow a set of rules that results in their

entering symbols, usually onto paper, such that these symbols are recognized as representing the event recorded.

In some circumstances, researchers prefer to use mechanical rather than human observers. With human observers there can be lapses in attention or motivation and misunderstandings or differences of interpretation about how to implement the recording rules. In addition, human recorders have been shown to change over time: As they observe a certain variable more often, they can become immune to noticing minor instances of it, which has been termed "calibration shift" (Kent & Foster, 1977).

Unlike humans, mechanical recorders are consistent. However, mechanical recorders lack some capacities that make human recorders an indispensable part of the data recording and data reduction processes. The capacities of human observers include:

- Selectivity in recording what is observed
- Sensitivity to what was not expected to be observed
- Flexibility in changing focus when needed
- The capacity for following recording rules that involve the higher-order processing of information

Machines record indiscriminately. For example, a machine can record an entire conversation. A human observer, on the other hand, can be instructed and trained to record only those parts of a conversation that are characterized by a certain content, for example, only those parts that are relevant to the expression of affection.

Research questions often concern complex variables that are difficult to define in a straightforward manner. Quite often, determining whether the variable has occurred in a given situation requires making complex judgments. Machines will record only what they are sensitive to recording. An audiotape, for example, will miss whatever nonverbal communication is taking place, and a video camera will record only what it is focused on and only for the period specified. Human recorders, on the other hand, do not lose their more general awareness when following a set of recording rules. Unexpected or complex phenomena that strike the human recorder as important can be noted, observed, and passed on to the researcher.

The process of coding is always a human activity. It involves selecting specific features of the observation record to classify conceptually. Observational systems that rely on human observers typically complete the record and encode components of the observation-record-code complex simultaneously; in fact, typically only codable features of what is observed are recorded as part of the observation process. Observational systems that rely on mechanical recorders, on the other hand, accomplish the recording and encoding components separately. The first is handled mechanically, while the second is managed by a person after the fact.

THE OBSERVER AND THE OBSERVED

There is a final critical feature of observation that must be addressed: the relationship between the observer and the observed. In the traditional view, observation implies that there is no relationship between the observer and the observed—observers are related to the observed only through the passive receiving and accurate recording of data about the behavior of those being observed. There are, of course, very few observational circumstances that approximate this situation.

Consider what may happen when one is making observations of two children interacting with a parent. The observer's role may involve sitting quietly in a corner, clipboard and pencil in hand, observing and recording any event that seems important in understanding the parent-child interaction. The children have a different take on the circumstance, however. The children do not allow the observer to remain in the role of a passive, uninvolved, and environmental feature. Questions ranging from "Who are you?" to "What are you writing?" are asked continuously by the children. When the questions go unanswered, the observer is subjected to nose pulls, shin kicks, and lap climbs. Under such circumstances, an observer will usually find it impossible to maintain a totally passive stance.

Reactivity

In general, the process of observation involves introducing something into a situation that would not oth-

erwise be there. As has been mentioned many times, the introduction of this feature constitutes making a change in the circumstances surrounding the variable to be researched. And since we are typically interested in studying variables in people who are responsive to their environments, the process of observation can be expected to affect the person being observed and often the feature(s) of interest in the person being observed. This effect is termed "reactivity"; it refers to change induced in what is observed by the process of observing it. The reactivity inherent in observation troubles many researchers: All researchers do not like to think that they are getting invalid pictures of what they are studying. It is distress over this nettling reality that has led some researchers to use "concealed observational methods."

An example of such concealed observation is presented by the work of Humphreys (1970), who entered public restroom facilities to systematically gather data on the activities of the men who came there to engage in impersonal acts of homosexual sex. People observed in the rest room were traced by means of their auto license plate numbers and found to include middle-class, married members of the community. The use of a concealed observational method was defended on the basis of reactivity: Given the nature of the behavior being observed, the phenomenon studied would never have been evidenced in the presence of a known observer. Humphreys took on a role in the setting—of lookout—that justified his presence as an otherwise nonparticipating observer, a strategy he defended as "passing as deviant to avoid disrupting the behavior he wished to observe" but not for the purpose of gaining access to a space that was private, since he was already entitled to access (Golden, 1976).

This study presents a dramatic and controversial example that highlights the troubling ethical issues raised by the question of whether researchers ever have the right to observe others without their knowledge and informed consent. Most institutional review boards believe that such observation is permissible only when one is studying innocuous behaviors as they naturally occur in very public situations and when the persons observed are not identified or affected by the observers. Concealed observation in other cases is more controversial and represents a clear example of the important role that institutional review boards play. The researcher should also consult with community members and colleagues not invested in the research study.

The observer-observed relationship distills into a single question: How much and what kinds of interactions will occur within it? Some observational systems try to minimize or standardize them. In these systems, the observer is to function in a manner analogous to a mechanical instrument. As much as possible, the observer is to be affected by, but not to affect, the observed. Any effect is to be only temporary and is to extend only as far as is necessary to make a record of whatever observed event was just noticed. However, other observational systems make good use of observer-observed interactions to further the research study. One such form of observation is called "participant observation," which is discussed briefly in the next section and presented in depth in the following chapter.

EXAMPLES OF OBSERVATION IN USE

In recent decades, the use of observation has revolutionized the field of early infant research and the theoretical understanding of psychological development in infancy. Fraiberg's (1970) research on blind infants illustrates the use of observation in developmental research. Stern (1985) describes the new developments in infant research as follows:

> The revolution in research consisted of turning the situation on its head, by asking not, what is a good question to pose to an infant? But what might an infant be able to do (like sucking) that would serve as an answer? With this simple turnaround, the search for infant abilities that could be made into answers (response measures) began, and the revolution was set in motion. . . . Good infant "answers" have to be readily observable behaviors that are frequently performed, that are under voluntary muscular control, and that can be solicited during alert inactivity. Three such behavioral answers immediately qualify, beginning at birth: head-turning, sucking, and looking. (38–39)

Infants, for example, have been shown, using electronically wired pacifiers, to be especially interested in the human voice as compared to other sounds of the same pitch and loudness. They also demonstrate by turning their heads that they prefer the smell of their own mother's milk to the milk of another woman (Stern, 1985). From the accumulation of many such observational studies of infants' early abilities, preferences, and interests, new theoretical understandings of infant development and parent-child interactions have emerged.

Infant research is not the only area in which observational data are useful. Hochschild's (1989) study of how two-career couples handle the work of caring for both a home and young children used in-home observations to supplement the extensive data collected through interviewing. The purpose of Hochschild's study was to explore whether married men were contributing any more to household work than the early studies in the 1960s and 1970s had shown. She also explored the various tensions that couples experienced because of class norms and ideologies about how things "should" be that didn't match with day-to-day necessity and the effects of earnings differentials in couples on how work at home was shared.

In particular, she wished to examine how well people's accounts of themselves and how they shared domestic responsibilities meshed with reality. She accomplished this in part by interviewing both members of the couples, but she also observed selected couples at home (Hochschild, 1989):

> I also watched daily life in a dozen homes during a weekday evening, during the weekend, and during the months that followed, when I was invited on outings, to dinner, or just to talk. I found myself waiting on the front doorstep as weary parents and hungry children tumbled out of the family car. . . . I sat on the living room floor and drew pictures and played with the children. I watched as parents gave them baths, read stories, and said goodnight. Most couples tried to bring me in to the family scene, inviting me to eat with them and talk. I responded if they spoke to me, from time to time asked questions, but I rarely

initiated conversations. I tried to become as unobtrusive as the family dog. (6–7)

Note that this brief description offers a sense of the "time sampling" attempted with each family. It also speaks to the particular role that Hochschild, as observer, elected to play in each setting.

What did such an observational strategy yield? In many cases, the subtle effects of the strains and tensions between husbands and wives about housework (and other issues) that they might not even be aware of became evident. A brief vignette from one family may illustrate this point (Hochschild, 1989):

> After a long day, mother, father, and son sit down to dinner. Evan and Nancy get the first chance of the day to talk to each other, but both turn anxiously to Joey, expecting his mood to deteriorate. Nancy asks him if he wants celery with peanut butter on it. Joey says yes. "Are you sure that's how you want it?" "Yes." Then the fidgeting begins. "I don't like the strings on my celery." "Celery is made up of strings." "The celery is too big." Nancy grimly slices the celery. A certain tension mounts. Every time one parent begins a conversation with the other, Joey interrupts. "I don't have anything to drink." . . . By the end of the meal, no one has obstructed Joey's victory. (35)

If nothing else, such observations illustrate vividly the vicissitudes of daily life in the family. Hochschild uses such data to make the point that inequities in the division of child care and housework responsibilities set up complicated dynamics among all family members that help to perpetuate whatever arrangement exists. From the interview data, the researcher observed that the mother and the father in this family had wholly different explanations for "Joey's problem," that he wouldn't go to bed at night as "normal" stage-related behavior. Whatever the framework that might be used to explain the observed interactions, the observational data make the nature of them quite vivid and clearly suggest—on the basis of an interpretation by the observer—that Joey's behavior is related to dynamics between his mother and his father. Thus, observational

data can reveal aspects of a situation that even the participants in it may not see or articulate clearly.

DEVELOPING OR SELECTING AN OBSERVATIONAL MEASURING INSTRUMENT

As is true with all data-collection methods, researchers have two options when planning quantitative studies that employ the use of observational data as the data-gathering technique: They may choose to employ existing measuring instruments such as those previously developed by other investigators, or they may choose to develop new observational systems specifically tailored to the requirements of their research circumstances. Chapter 9 discusses how to locate and select existing measures.

Naturally, whenever a qualitative study is developed, the form of the research study requires developing the observational system as the research process goes along. Hochschild (1989), for example, found that talking to a family's babysitters and child-care providers—and even doing some observation with them—was an unexpected and useful source of data. She then added these two groups of people to her data-collection plan for each family. A skilled researcher, then, should know how to invent an observational methodology. A consideration of how a new observational system has to be developed clarifies many of the issues that should be attended to when deciding whether someone else's existing system is good enough to use.

Developing an Observational System

The first step in observation is specifying the purpose of the observation, that is, what research question(s) the observation is supposed to inform. In qualitative methods, this purpose is usually to define and understand the variable of interest more clearly. In other forms of research, this purpose is to describe and/or show connections between some already well-defined variables. In the second case, this first step requires that one clearly specify the definition of the dependent variable to be observed. In the beginning of the research process, this definition properly remains an abstract and conceptual one; later on, the definition will be narrowed to an operational one, that is, to a set of rules for deciding whether or how much of a variable has been seen in response to what is observed.

It may be of interest in this context to note that developing a new observational system for any research purpose often requires conducting what might most easily be described as a qualitative research study at the outset. While there is a general idea of what is to be observed, an idea that is used to guide the observation process, specific notions of what is to be noticed are left open until the data are given an opportunity to inform and shape them. The Fraiberg (1970) research study of the development of infants blind from birth illustrate this evolution well. Fraiberg used her observations of a particular case to shape her later observations of a group of blind babies. Any research study takes place in a specific context. That is, the question or hypothesis is posed not in the abstract but under some narrowed or restricted set of circumstances. These circumstances must also be defined at the outset of developing an observational system. Just as the research purpose guides what is to be observed, the context defines the circumstances under which observations will be made.

Practical considerations enter into the selection of an observational context, as well. Suppose, for example, we are interested in studying intimacy. Optimal circumstances for making observations relevant to this construct would most probably be private (i.e., intimate) ones. However, short of developing a mechanical observation system that can run continuously in such circumstances (and this procedure has in fact been used), arranging observations in private circumstances is quite difficult and can raise important ethical questions.

Once the researcher has specified the purpose of the observation, including an explicit conceptual definition of the variable to be observed and the circumstances under which observations will be made, unstructured observations should take place. In unstructured observations, the researcher enters the observational situation armed only with a clipboard and a pen or pencil or a portable computer and the guiding notion of the study's purpose. The observer's initial task is to literally observe, to notice everything taking place in the circumstance that seems even remotely related to the study's purpose as

stated, and to record as completely as possible a narrative description of what he or she sees.

The observer's task does not involve interpreting or making sense of what is noticed at this point. As much as possible, the observer is to function as a probe, an instrument of observation sufficiently sensitive to notice whatever there is of importance to be observed. Preconceived notions and theoretical biases should exert as minimal an influence as possible on what is noticed.

There is no such thing as a "naive observer." Without some sophistication, an observer would be incapable of discriminating between what data are important to attend to and what data are not. Observers necessarily have different perspectives, and sometimes these perspectives can be dictated strongly by preconceived notions. To the extent that they are, the observers become biased, that is, they become predispositioned to "see" events in certain ways. When a research study is done by a team, it is always a good idea for the person directing the study, who may have the strongest preconceptions about what should or will be seen, to conduct some of this informal observation, as well.

In the quantitative research approach, the data obtained are regarded not as an end in themselves but instead as preliminary. The records from these observations must be studied carefully to identify observations that are concrete instances of the study's variable(s) to be studied. The descriptions of these observed events are then used to derive statements that identify how to recognize instances of the researched variable and how to distinguish between observed events that are instances of it and similar events that are not.

For example, suppose a quantitative study focused on observing "aggression." A conceptual definition for this study's variable might be "actions with the apparent primary intent of coercing another or expressing anger toward them." While this conceptual definition might be acceptable to a variety of researchers studying aggression in a variety of contexts, concrete definitions of aggression would be expected to vary widely across subject types and observational situations. Aggressive behavior among four-year-olds, for example, is quite different from aggressive behavior in adults. Similarly, the form that adult aggression may take at work typically differs from the form that adult aggression may take at home.

Variations in concrete definitions might also arise because of differences in theoretical or political perspectives; what appears to be aggression from one person's perspective might appear to be self-defense from another. Sorting through narrative records from unstructured observations, then, allows a quantitative researcher to clarify what the distinguishing features of the dependent variable are, given his or her interpretation of the conceptual definition and given the people and setting that will be observed.

Once these distinguishing features are identified, the statements describing them become the variable's operational definition. These definitions then form the basis of what observers will be trained and expected to recognize. The purpose of the initial unstructured observations is to generate data that will allow the researcher to create an informed system for structured observations. In this way, an observational system can be tailor-made to fit the observational circumstances, making it more likely that the structured system will be sensitive to the research phenomenon as it is conceptually defined and as it is manifested in the particular circumstances that will be studied.

Once the definition has been clearly stated, the technology surrounding how the defined phenomenon will be observed, recorded, and coded must be specified. The observation technology will typically be either mechanical or human. Sometimes the phenomenon can be operationally defined such that a mechanical device can reliably detect it (e.g., defining making too much noise in the house as "sound episodes or events that exceed 70 decibels for three or more seconds"). In such a case, if the appropriate mechanical apparatus is both available and acceptable to those who will be observed, then a mechanical observational system is often preferable.

Sometimes, however, the phenomenon as operationally defined is either too subtle or too complex to be mechanically detected. This is particularly likely to be the case in two circumstances. First, many psychological phenomena are difficult to detect mechanically; these phenomena are typically quite subtle, and their indicators can vary widely across different people or even within the same person at different points in time. Second, many interpersonal phenomena can be detected only by human observers, since recognition of the occurrence of

such phenomena typically cannot occur without a knowledge and understanding of the interactional context within which particular events are occurring.

Where a mechanical observational system can be arranged, developing the observe-record-code complex is straightforward. The apparatus is positioned optimally, that is, so as to have most complete access to the circumstances of observation, and an observation schedule is set. The observation schedule can be continuous, which is most appropriate when a research phenomenon both rarely occurs and is no more likely to occur at certain times than others. If one were studying how two-worker families with school-age children manage morning tasks, however, it would be inefficient to record all day—continuously—rather than just during the morning hours when the research phenomenon is present. But if one were researching all the ways in which such parents coped with both work and family responsibilities, it would be optimal to record continuously at various times in the day except, of course, when both were at work, as Hochschild (1989) did.

Sampling Observational Periods

In general, with any circumstance where the dependent variable appears often, observations can be conducted on a schedule, rather than all the time; they can be sampled. The assumption under these circumstances, of course, is that the times that are observed give a representative picture of what happens during the times that are not observed. This assumption is similar to the assumption that is always made whenever a sample is used to draw conclusions about a larger population from which the sample was drawn. In other words, study participants are not the only feature sampled in research designs; occasions for observation may be another. In this case, the assumption is that what is observed during the times that observation takes place represents fairly what would have been observed at other times that observation might or could have taken place.

As in sampling individuals, when the interest is in generalizing from the sample observations to some larger population of observations, the only or at least primary determinant of when observations occur should be chance. Optimally, then, one would decide on the duration of single observation sessions (for instance, 45 minutes), write each possible 45-minute observation period on a slip of paper, and then randomly select slips to determine when observations will be made each day.

Practical constraints typically impinge on this ideal. Especially with human observers, schedules must be at least as influential a determinant of when observation sessions take place as is chance. And in certain settings, such as schools, hospitals, nursing homes, or homeless shelters, there are organizational schedules that dictate when observations can be made. Letting these practical considerations, rather than chance, determine when observations occur does not necessarily lead to bad research. But the conclusions drawn from studies in which observation schedules were determined by practical considerations must take into account the limits of these practical features on the generalizability of what was found.

Most quantitative observational systems specify short time periods during which the observer will work, followed by short time periods during which the observer will make a record of what was just seen. The length of both these intervals varies. The length of the observation cycle will depend on how much observation time is required to see enough of what is going on to be able to detect the research phenomenon, the dependent variable, as defined. This length of time will obviously be longer for phenomena that themselves take longer to occur, as well as for phenomena that cannot be identified without knowledge of what else is going on when they do or do not occur. Someone observing compliance with authority figures, for example, would be unable to code a particular action as an instance of compliance without knowing whether or not the action had been preceded by an authority figure's request that the subject perform it. Recording cycles are usually short. They need only be long enough to permit the observer to make a record of whether the observation target events did or did not occur.

Recording Data

An observation record can be either mechanically or humanly produced. In the case of mechanical observa-tion, the record will of course be made mechanically. A video recorder will produce a videotape record, an audio recorder will produce an audiotape record, and a polygraph will produce a written polygram.

In the case of human observation, the record can be made either with or without the assistance of mechanical aids. In the simplest case, the human observer will keep track of what was observed by making marks on an observation sheet. A set of codes will be used for each observation period or cycle. At the end of each cycle, the observer will mark various codes to reflect which of the observed behaviors did and did not occur during each of the observation intervals. If available, mechanical or computerized recording methods can be used to facilitate this process.

When observations have been made by humans, the observe-record-code complex has been completed with the creation of the record. This assumes that the recording system involved making a record. A record is made by coding whether a specific predefined variable was or was not observed during the observation cycle. Thus, in structured observation systems, to record *is* to code. When unstructured observations are made mechanically, however, the observation record, such as a videotape, will itself typically require review and coding by a human observer. In other words, only the "observe" and "record" parts of the observe-record-code sequence will have occurred.

Having a videotape certainly provides certain research advantages. It is no small contribution, for example, to have a permanent record of the events of interest that can be examined and reexamined, permitting a greater degree of depth in what is understood about them. Alongside this decided advantage is a disadvantage. The videotape record is no more informative than were the events as they originally occurred. Usually, then, mechanical observation requires a human observer who must later execute the "observe" and "code" components of the observe-record-code complex during a coding process.

Whether a mechanically assisted observation technology is used or one that relies only on human observers, the end product of the observe-record-code complex are data about whether the defined variable did or did not occur during each of a series of observation intervals. These data are typically translated into a frequency score, reflecting the number of times the dependent variable was seen during the observation period. As with any structured data-collection method, the resulting data are then analyzed for reliability and validity, as described in Chapter 8.

The advantages of developing a new observational system are clear: The system can be tailored to conform exactly to the new investigator's conception of the researched phenomenon, as well as to the specific research circumstances involved. But this luxury comes at some cost: It takes a lot of effort to develop an observational system, as is the case with any new measure.

Using an Existing Observational Measure

Having learned about the steps that one must go through to create a good structured observational measuring instrument, the reader may think it obvious why many quantitative research studies often use existing measures. First, the quality of the observational system, in terms of its reliability and validity when used in previous studies, will already have been established. It is generally easier to demonstrate a measuring instrument's usefulness in a new context than to demonstrate the reliability and validity of one that has never been used before.

There is a second reason for using existing observational systems: Doing so allows comparisons of results across research studies. Using a pre-established observational measure creates a connection between a new study and others that have used the same measuring instrument. It is this interlocking of method that makes research a collaborative rather than an isolated activity across investigators. Familiar data-collection methods yield results more easily interpretable by other researchers.

How to find and select among existing measures is covered in detail in Chapter 9. In general, there is little difference between selecting an existing measure for observation and choosing an interview (Chapter 16) or questionnaire (Chapters 10 and 17) measure. However, there are a couple of additional points to consider. The first is that, in addition to the content of the observations, the observe-record-code complex must also be suited to the circumstances of the present study. The observational

recording system in particular deserves review; some may be too demanding or complex for easy use in all settings. The training requirements for observers should also be considered. In general, when multiple observers are used, a rate of interobserver agreement of 85 percent is considered minimally acceptable.

As with all preexisting measures, the reliability and validity of any observational measure adopted for a study must be established in the new research context. It also has to be checked throughout the duration of the data gathering. In addition, it is also useful to arrange checks on what has traditionally been called "calibration slippage," which refers to the fact that observers may unintentionally alter their standards of observation over time. This sort of slippage occurs, for example, when there is a certain event that strikes observers as a blatant example of what is being observed when the study first begins but as not a real example of what is being observed after they have watched things for a while; observers risk becoming "jaded," or "desensitized" to what they see.

Of course, it is not always possible to use a previously developed and existing observational system. Sometimes one is not available. Sometimes the ones available do not suit the circumstances, sample, or conceptual base of the proposed research study. In this circumstance, sometimes the existing system can be modified to make it acceptable: Observation intervals can be lengthened, recording technologies can be added, and so forth. Whenever such changes are made, however, the observational method is in reality a new one, and its reliability and validity should be again examined and reported.

RELIABILITY AND VALIDITY IN OBSERVATION

It is interesting to note that, because observational data can *seem* so inherently credible, the reliability and validity of observational data-collection systems have not always been examined as carefully as other types. This failure is unfortunate in that every data-collection method must be shown to be good and not assumed to be so.

The most usual form of reliability examined with observational data collection is called *interrater reliabil-*

ity or *interobserver agreement.* This kind of reliability requires demonstrating that different raters (or observers) are making (or would make) the same recordings about the same events. Most often, interrater reliability is demonstrated by arranging for two or more observers to make records of the same situations or events. In the case of live observations, for example, this would involve being in the same place at the same time, as Fraiberg (1970) and her co-investigators were in their study. When working with audio- or videotapes, the observers need not be working at the same time.

In quantitative studies, double coding by observers in order to assess interobserver reliability must be done independently. That is, the two observers should not be influenced in their ratings by seeing how the other observer has classified a particular event. Given this requirement, mechanical records have a clear advantage in that it is easy to make sure observers are not working together when they are coding.

After each observer has prepared his or her observation record, the records are compared to see how much agreement there is between them. If there is a high level of agreement, the system can be regarded as reliable. If agreement is not good, the operational definitions provided for the observers may not have been not clear enough, the observational task may have been too demanding (the observers may have been expected to notice too many different things at once), or the observer may not have been trained adequately. Each of these problems is of course correctable. Unless the problem is fixed, the resulting observational data cannot be regarded as trustworthy or repeatable.

Observer agreement can be calculated in several ways. The simplest involves counting the number of observation intervals during which the observers agree and dividing that number by the total number of observation intervals in the study. This method is generally regarded as acceptable when whatever is being observed occurs about half the time. However, when the phenomenon to be observed occurs either very often or very rarely, this method will make it look like observers are agreeing very closely when in fact they may not be agreeing at all.

Consider, for example, the following situation. Suppose two observers observe a child for 20 observation intervals, and suppose the first observer records a single instance of the variable in the third interval, while the second observer records a single instance of the observed phenomenon during the seventeenth interval. Computing their agreement by counting the number of agreements by the number of agreements and disagreements would produce a very high agreement index: They produced the same record 18 times (agreeing that the observation target was not seen in intervals 1, 2, 4, 5, 6, 7, 8, 9, 10, 11, 12, 13, 14, 15, 16, 18, 19, and 20) and different records twice (intervals 3 and 17). Their coefficient of agreement, then, would be 18 divided by 20, or 90 percent, but in reality they would have had absolutely no agreement at all on when the phenomenon occurred. Coefficients of rater agreement must be calculated in such as way as to genuinely reflect the degree of agreement between the two observers.

With observational data, interrater reliability is generally regarded as the most important form of reliability to demonstrate. When it has been demonstrated, the researcher can legitimately argue that the dependent variable, as operationally defined, is being observed similarly by two (or more) independent raters. Other forms of reliability, such as demonstrating consistency across times or across settings, may also be examined. Consistency in observation must be demonstrated and not assumed.

When the conceptual and operational definitions that guide the observation have been carefully developed and articulated, observational data are generally regarded as easily having face and content validity (see Chapter 8). Of course, neither face nor content validity involves an empirical demonstration of the meaning of a score. However, criterion-related and more general construct validity must be empirically demonstrated for new observational systems, just as they must for any new measurement procedure (see Chapter 8).

Particularly if an observational system is to be used in additional research studies by other researchers, it is important to demonstrate the criterion and/or construct validity of the observational method. Past demonstrations of interrater reliability, for example, may show that the observational system *can* be used reliably in previous studies, not that it *is* being used reliably in the current study. Thus, it is necessary to demonstrate interrater reliability with each new application of the observational system, in part because the system itself is only one component of the observational methodology. The observers are also an integral component of the methodology. There is no guarantee that new observers will perform reliably using the same system that other observers were able to use successfully.

It is also wise to collect evidence that bears on an observational system's validity, and most well-designed studies will afford these data as a matter of course. Random error in measurement is inevitable. Therefore, it is often prudent to include multiple measures of dependent variable in any study. To the extent that important findings are replicated across different measures, a more compelling argument can be made for the apparently significant result.

Well-designed quantitative studies, then, often include more than one measure, or operationalization, for the dependent variable. These several measures, while not properly interchangeable, should be meaningfully related; it follows that scores from them should be significantly correlated. To the extent that scores on an observational measure are correlated with scores on other measures of the same dependent variable, the observational measure can be regarded as a valid indicator of the dependent variable, or phenomenon, under study.

PARTICIPANT OBSERVATION

Participant observation is widely used to examine social interactions, small groups, and organizational or community life. It involves the observer's becoming a part of—and a participant in—the groups and communities being observed so that the role taken with those observed is less distant and more "inside." Participant observation includes the same basic processes of seeing, recording, and coding or analyzing what is seen, although adapted to the role the observer takes in the research setting.

Observation, however, is often only one part of the participant observational process. For example, ethnomethodological studies, and others, typically gather data through both observation and intensive interviewing (see Chapter 16) for the purpose of understanding the culture of a particular group or society. Beyond formal interviewing, asking and listening take place as the observations are made. Documents and other artifacts may be collected at the site, as well. Participant observation is above all opportunistic (Jorgensen, 1989); therefore, observation is not as clearly separated from other methods of data gathering as in other kinds of research.

Participant observation as a method is defined by the fact that the researcher is both a participant and an actor in the situation being studied and an observer of it. However, the participant-observer role can be thought of as a continuum (Williamson et al., 1982), as can be seen in Figure 15.1.

Jorgensen (1989), for example, discusses three styles of participant observation: (1) the active participant, who has a job or other social role in the setting in addition to performing the research study; (2) the privileged observer, who is known and trusted and who has access to private information; and (3) the limited observer, the most common type, who has no role other than researcher and who works to build trust in the setting over time. When multiple roles are occupied, as in the first two styles, managing and negotiating them can be challenging.

In fact, major issues in all participant observational studies concern how the observers will gain access to and enter the groups or social systems that they will be observing, whether and how the studies will be represented to others, and what role(s) the observers will engage in the settings. In general, observations and other data-gathering activities in the setting go from being very unfocused in the beginning to being more focused as data accumulate and potential answers to the research questions begin to emerge (Jorgensen, 1989).

Participant observation research uses reactivity as a tool in the research process. How those who are being observed react to the research and/or to the observer form part of what is learned about them, their social systems, and their view of the world. The personal reactions of the researchers to those they observe are also data that inform them about the people and situations they study. For example, like any traveler, a newcomer to a group or social setting will notice patterns of behavior that seem odd at first but that to a group member are so familiar and taken for granted that they would never be commented on as being unique or of any importance.

Like other forms of observation, participant observation is an expensive data-collection method. It requires long periods of contact with the groups being studied, in part because over time initial atypical responses that are a response to the presence of an outsider fade as the "outsider" becomes an "insider." Although there is much to gain in knowledge from such familiarity, there is a risk that the researcher will begin adopting uncritically the views and perspectives of those who are studied and will fail to take adequate notice of things about which the observer is no longer naive.

As you will see in the following chapter, during the course of a participant observation study, an observer is typically exposed to many sources of data and to many informants. Often, for example, a key informant serves as a guide or a person who can help the researcher gain access to a particular group or social setting. Williams (1992) reports having such a "guide" in his study of crack houses in New York. The researcher-key informant relationship requires careful nurture and can be quite rewarding to both parties. However, no one informant can be assumed to be typical of a group in every way, and no one informant can be assumed to be trustworthy and nonpartisan at all times and on all issues.

As you will see in Chapter 26, triangulating data obtained on different occasions and from different sources is an important technique that can both validate data obtained and, when data are discrepant, suggest new dimensions of inquiry to pursue in order to explain apparent inconsistencies (Fetterman, 1989). Seeking out and using multiple contacts and sources of information in the setting is thus an important step in determining which data are credible and worthy to report. Given the complexities involved when any individual enters, negotiates roles in, and leaves the field of study, the use of multiple data sources to validate information is much more common in participant observation than is the use of multiple observers.

Recording the observations that were made is essential. Sometimes recording in the form of note taking can go on in the setting, and sometimes it cannot. In either case, the researcher must plan adequate time for preparing the narrative records, generally called field notes, of what has been observed (Taylor & Bogdan, 1984). These field notes should contain as much detail as possible about who participated in the recorded events and where they took place, as well as about the events themselves. There is always a great deal of detail observed in any interaction, and it may take a great amount of time before it is possible to distinguish important and relevant information from the unimportant. In fact, the analysis stage may be well under way by then.

Recording data is generally less compelling and interesting than collecting them, but keeping the record complete and up-to-date is an essential discipline in participant observation research. While the notes must be as complete as possible in describing the events observed, they usually include interpretive material, as well. Recording the subjective reactions of the observer brings them into awareness and makes them a part of the data to be used in understanding the events studied. Thus, the observer and the observed not only interact with each other; they are both "inside the frame" of the research study itself.

SUMMARY

Observation is involved whenever a recorder, human or mechanical, observes events for the purpose of collecting data about and making a permanent record of them. This is a broad definition, for observation is a versatile data-collection method. Observation can be used as the data-collection method in both quantitative and qualitative studies. In fact, its use illustrates extremes in assumptions and styles of the research enterprise. It can appear as the most "objective" or as the most "subjective" and reactive form of data gathering. Because visual data are so compelling, however, observational data-collecting methods have been essential to knowledge building in many important areas of inquiry.

In some senses, observation captures the spirit of true empiricism. The greatest limitation of observation is probably practical: Done correctly, it is expensive and time-consuming. Standing alongside this limitation is great strength: Done correctly, it produces highly credible data especially when data about nonverbal and social behavior are needed.

As we know, using direct observations as a form of data collection is obtrusive; that is, the researcher intrudes into the research participants' lives in some form or another. The following chapter continues our discussion of conducting observations within an obtrusive data-collection method known as participant observation.

Participant
Observation

Gayla Rogers

Elaine Bouey

15

The preceding chapter ended with a brief discussion of how participant observation can be used to collect original data. This chapter continues the discussion of participant observation and discusses this data-collection method in much more detail. Like all the other data-collection methods presented in this book, its appropriateness for any particular research study is directly related to the study's research question. This chapter provides a definition and description of participant observation and discusses its practical application to social work research.

DEFINITION

It is difficult to provide an exact definition of participant observation, since there are many different ways of defining it depending on the discipline of the definer and how it has been applied to research situations over the past 80 years. Participant observation as a data-collection method began with early anthropological ethnomethodology studies in the 1920s. Since then, it has undergone a radical transformation as a result of an effort to look for new ways to obtain useful, reliable, and valid data from research participants. Currently, participant observation is viewed as more of a mind-set (or an orientation) toward research rather than as a set of specific, applied data-collection techniques (Neuman, 2003). Further, the terms "field research," "ethnographic research," and "ethnography" are often used interchangeably with "participant observation."

Distinguishing Features

Participant observation is an obtrusive data-collection method, because it requires the one doing the study, the participant observer, to undertake roles that involve establishing and maintaining ongoing relationships with research participants who are often in field settings.

The passage of time is also an integral part of participant observation. We need to consider, for example, the sequences of events (and to monitor processes) over time so that research participants' relationships and the meanings of what they are experiencing can be discovered. We gather data primarily through direct observation, supplemented with other data-gathering methods such as interviewing (Chapter 16), using existing documents (Chapters 18–21), and using our own personal experiences.

Participant observation is an excellent way to gather data for understanding how other people see or interpret their experiences (Spradley, 1980). It represents a unique opportunity to see the world from *other* points of view, often at the sites where the activities or phenomena occur. It is also compatible with the "reflective practitioner" model of social work practice, as part of the process involves examining our personal insights, feelings, and perspectives in order to understand the situations we are studying (Papell & Skolnik, 1992; Schön, 1983).

A key factor in participant observation is its emphasis on the use of *relatively unstructured* data-gathering methods, such as observing everyday events in natural settings in an effort to understand how other people see or interpret their experiences and then stepping outside that perspective to add a "more objective" viewpoint (Neuman, 1994). In practice, however, it is often a back-and-forth (or recursive) process. Through observations and interactions with research participants over time (e.g., weeks, months, years), we can learn great deal about them—their histories, habits, and hopes, and their cultures, values, and idiosyncrasies, as well. These observations and interactions can be fascinating and fun as well as time-consuming, costly, and emotionally draining.

As we know, data derived from a participant observation study can easily be augmented with survey research data. In addition, they can be used with both research approaches—quantitative and qualitative. The use of several data-gathering methods, such as participant observation and survey research, in addition to the use of supplemental data sources such as existing documents, as well as the observation of people in different roles, creates the potential for a fuller understanding of the phenomena being studied.

Participant observation is an excellent data-collection method for exploring a wide variety of social settings and subcultures and most aspects of social life. It is valuable, for example, in studying deviant behavior (e.g., prostitution, drug use), unusual or traumatic circumstances (e.g., spinal cord injury, rape), and important life events (e.g., birth, divorce, death). It can be used to study entire communities in a range of settings or relatively small groups that interact on a regular basis in a fixed setting. Some examples include studies of women's emergency shelters, the workings of social service agencies from the perspective of the members in those settings, or an immigrant group living in a particular neighborhood. Participant observation can also be used to study social experiences that are not fixed in a place but for which in-depth interviewing and direct observation are the only ways to gain access to the experience—for example, the feelings of women who have left violent relationships.

Researchers who participate in these settings can also occupy other roles, including social worker, volunteer, English as a Second Language tutor, program aide, or administrative assistant. The more roles we assume, the better our understanding of the situation because we come to understand different points of view.

When to Use Participant Observation

Participant observation as a data-collection method is well suited to situations where we wish to better understand how people see their own experiences, as well as those where we want to gain an in-depth perspective on people within the contexts and environments in which these events occur. It is exceptionally useful when it is applied to the study of processes, interrelationships among people and their situations, and events that happen over time and the patterns that have developed, as well as the social and cultural contexts in which human experiences occurred (Jorgensen, 1989).

Participant observation allows for the collection of data about phenomena that are not obvious from the viewpoint of the nonparticipant. It provides an opportunity to achieve a comprehensive understanding of human situations, and richly textured perspectives. Furthermore, when conducted in natural settings, it has the potential to elucidate certain nuances of attitude or behaviors that may not be included when data are gathered using other data-collection methods.

Participant observation is often helpful in identifying problem areas that can be the topics for subsequent studies that use other data-collection methodologies. We

can then *triangulate*, or compare and contrast, the data gathered via these different methods in order to enhance our study's credibility. We may initially select a role as a volunteer in a women's emergency shelter, for example, find that we would like to learn more about the conditions that led women to the shelter, and subsequently gain permission to both review intake records and conduct structured interviews with a sample of women who enter the shelter. Participant observation is especially appropriate for scholarly problems in the following circumstances (Jorgensen, 1989):

* Little is known about a situation or event (e.g., job satisfaction among workers at a women's emergency shelter).
* There are important differences between the views of one group and those of another (e.g., perspectives on domestic violence among police and medical service professionals versus perspectives of social workers inside a women's emergency shelter).
* The phenomenon is obscured in some way from those outside a setting (e.g., spouse battering within a community of immigrants who do not commonly interact with social service agencies and who do not speak English).
* The phenomenon is hidden from society in general (e.g., drug abuse treatment for those in higher socioeconomic statuses).

While participant observation is appropriate for gathering data for almost any aspect of human existence, it is not suited to every scholarly research enquiry that involves humans and their interactions with one another. It is particularly applicable to exploratory and descriptive studies out of which theoretical interpretations and hypotheses emerge. Its primary contribution allows for the creation of in-depth understandings of situations in an effort to support the development of different theoretical view points.

Minimal Conditions for Participant Observation

In using participant observation as a data-collection method, there are minimal conditions that must be present (Jorgensen, 1989):

- The research question is concerned with human meanings and interactions viewed from the insider's perspective.
- The phenomenon is observable within an everyday life setting or situation.
- Gaining access to an appropriate setting is not a problem.
- The phenomenon is sufficiently limited in size and location to be studied as a case.
- The research question is appropriate for a case study.
- The research question can be addressed by qualitative data gathered by direct observation and other means pertinent to the field setting.

Getting Involved and Observing

Participant observation involves a dual purpose: *getting involved* in activities appropriate to the situation and *observing* people, the physical site, and the events happening in a particular context or setting. While a regular member experiences events in a direct and personal manner, the participant observer experiences being both an insider (with a "subjective" viewpoint) and an outsider (with a more "objective" viewpoint). Thus, it requires personal preparation and ongoing mindfulness to maintain an objective perspective even while one is involved in a field setting as a participant. It means being explicitly aware of one's values and assumptions while holding one's judgments in abeyance. This is often challenging and proves to be a very intensive experience for the participant observer.

There is little question that the participant observer's involvement in a setting can have an emotional impact of varying degrees. As Neuman (1994) notes:

Field research can be fun and exciting, but it can also disrupt one's personal life, physical security, or mental well being. More than other types of

social research, it reshapes friendships, family life, self identity, or personal values. (335)

Since the researcher is the primary instruments through which data are gathered and interpreted, he or she may have a potential influence on the study. This is why it is crucial to prepare oneself as much as possible in advance for this experience, maintain a separate log of personal notes and reflections, and make arrangements for regular advisory and debriefing sessions.

It is also important to note that some of us may be very well suited to use participant observation as a data-collection method, while others may be advised to use other data-collection methodologies. Thus, a team approach is often appropriate, with one person doing participant observation and another conducting structured interviews and examining existing documentation, for example.

ROLES

This section provides an overview of the various roles for those involved in a participant observation study and describes the tasks associated with each role. Being a *participant observer* in a field setting is quite different from being a *regular participant* in a field setting. Researchers who use participant observation as a data-collection method often assume a variety of roles. These roles can be placed on a continuum and are classified into four categories as presented in Figure 15.1: (1) complete participant, (2) observer-participant, (3) participant-observer, and (4) complete observer.

We can sit in on staff meetings, for example, and view other operational activities as a *complete observer* to gather data on how the agency staff function in an office setting; or, with varying degrees of involvement as a *participant observer* or *observer participant*, we can be volunteers who come in to help with some aspect of the

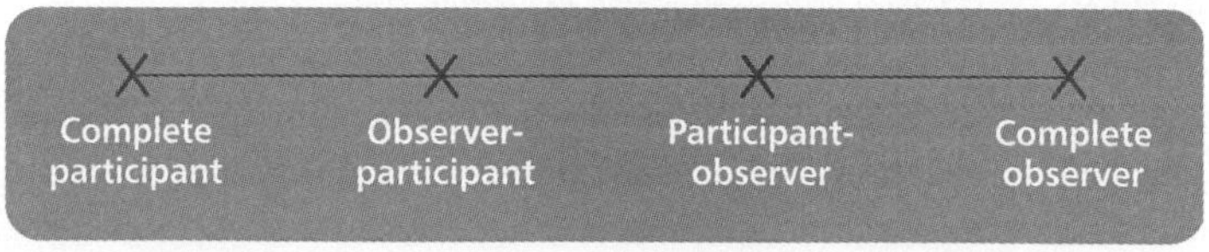

X — Complete participant   X — Observer-participant   X — Participant-observer   X — Complete observer

Figure 15.1
Continuum of Participant Observation

agency's operation on a regular basis to gather data on how a particular program works; or, as a *complete participant*, we can, at the other end of the continuum, be one of the permanent staff in an agency who also happens to be doing a research study on the day-to-day activities within the program.

Balancing the Roles

In assuming any one of the four roles in doing a participant observation study, we need to be acutely aware of the need to maintain a balance between our participation and our ability to be objective. There may be so many temptations to become totally involved that we can easily lose this balanced perspective. This is often a particular challenge when we are *complete participants* as compared to *complete observers*. Some aids to maintaining this balance include reflective journal writing and regular debriefing sessions with other professionals who are not familiar with our field setting.

When we take on different roles, however, these roles can be overtly revealed, or in some cases they can be undertaken on a covert basis and not revealed. We strongly recommend, whenever possible, that any role played be on an overt or openly explained basis. This helps us with ethical considerations and is in keeping with the way in which participant observation has evolved in relation to social work settings.

If we are going to be studying a women's emergency shelter, with all the appropriate advance clearances for access to that setting, for example, and if we assume a role as a children's playroom assistant so that we can observe the interaction of the children with their mothers and with the shelter's staff, it is absolutely mandatory that we let the parents, the shelter's staff, and the children know why we are there (our dual role) and what we will be doing with the data collected. These need not be lengthy explanations initially, but they set the stage for trust and acceptance. We should be ready to answer questions as they surface. On the other hand, sharing of the initial analyses of our raw observational data or of our personal recorded reflections is not appropriate. Yet, it is quite reasonable to provide a summary (or a full copy) of our final research report to interested participants.

In assuming roles in a field setting, we should be aware that the social and physical locations are very important influences on the type of data we will be able to collect. As we note *what* occurs at different points in time and space, we may begin to recognize that *when* something occurs is often important. In a women's emergency shelter, for example, the physical locations at which we observe could include the children's playroom, the outside playground, and the dining room. The different roles we could take—such as a social worker or a children's playroom aide—affect our interactions with those at the shelter and, in turn, provide us with a rich variety of different perspectives. In some cases, it might be difficult to operate in these different roles in one field setting, so we might choose to select one or two roles at one women's shelter and take on others at another shelter.

NEEDED STRATEGIES AND SKILLS

As previously mentioned, the participant observation experience is intense and demanding. Participant observation is both an art and a science, calling on many aspects of our capabilities. In order to deal with the many situations that come up in a field setting, we can use a few strategies to minimize difficulties and stresses for all those involved, as well as to ensure that a high-quality research study takes place.

- We need to practice observing and making notes that are as detail-rich as possible and that are based on our recall of events (e.g., we might observe people interacting in a busy city recreation center).
- We need to keep a daily personal journal that includes our reflections on events that are occurring in our life; this will help with both the discipline of writing field notes and with enhancing our self-knowledge.
- We need to get help from a knowledgeable adviser in designing, planning, and implementing our research study, as well as in setting up a regular schedule of debriefing and advisory sessions throughout the study.
- We need to tap into supporting systems and

services to help us maintain our physical, emotional, and spiritual well-being.

- We need to develop a working knowledge of our topic area by reading the literature and by talking with people who have done research studies in our particular research area.
- We need to identify, record, and, if possible, let go of our assumptions or preconceptions that might influence the study.

The specific skills needed for using participant observation as a data-collection method are:

- The skills of careful looking and listening—paying attention to all possible details
- The skills of remembering things—including verbatim comments, nonverbal cues, and "climatic" conditions
- The skills of disciplined, regular writing—describing events and exchanges as well as personal reactions and reflections
- The skills of tuning into oneself—knowing our vulnerabilities, values, and views and owning our thoughts and feelings, assumptions, and biases

STEPS IN DOING PARTICIPANT OBSERVATION

Our direct participation in, and observation of, events as they occur in their natural field settings is the cornerstone of participant observation as a data-collection method. Thus, it is essential that we be well organized and prepared, but also flexible and adaptable enough to change with the circumstances. The specific steps of using participant observation as a data-collection method cannot be entirely predetermined; however, they can serve as a guide to the overall process. We need to recognize and seize opportunities and rapidly adjust to these new situations as they occur in the field. In the beginning of our study, we can expect to have little control over our data and not much focus. Once we are socialized into our field setting, however, we can focus our inquiry and gain some control over the data we finally end up gathering.

Notwithstanding that participant observation is characterized by a back-and-forth, nonlinear process,

there are six fundamental steps that serve as a guide. These steps are (1) gaining access and entry to a study site, (2) engaging and forming relationships, (3) gathering the data, (4) recording the data, (5) making sense of the data, and (6) reporting the findings.

Step 1: Gaining Access and Entry to a Study Site

A site is the context in which our study occurs, and it need not be a fixed geographic location. A particular group of research participants, for example, may interact across several sites. In addition, our own characteristics may limit access to a site. A white single male, for example, may have a difficult time gaining access to a group of single-parent women of color. Physical access can also be an issue; we may find that we are not allowed on a site(s) or that there are legal or political barriers to access, such as in public schools, hospitals, and prisons.

Access to such settings depends on *gatekeepers*—those with formal or informal authority to control access to sites. Permission is usually required from a gatekeeper and involves bargaining and negotiating. In some cases, permission from gatekeepers may inhibit the cooperation of people whom we want to study. Juvenile offenders, for example, may not want to participate in a study if they know that the Director of Secure Treatment has authorized us to be there. Gaining access and entering a site depends on our personal attributes, prior connections, and social skills.

Entry and access is more analogous to peeling away the layers of an onion than it is to opening a door. We begin at the outermost layer where access is easy. At this stage, as outsiders, we are most likely looking for data more or less in the public domain. The next layer requires an increased degree of access as we become more of a passive, unquestioning observer of events as they occur in the field setting. Over time, and as trust develops, we peel off another layer and observe more sensitive interactions or activities and ask for clarification of our personal observations. At yet a deeper layer, we can shape or influence the interaction so that particular data or certain behaviors are revealed. This layer is also necessary in order to access highly sensitive material that requires a deep level of trust.

Step 2: Engaging and Forming Relationships

The process of engaging and developing relationships with our research participants requires sensitivity and well-developed communication and interpersonal skills. We must be prepared to explain what we are doing and why, repeatedly, with each research participant. We should be ready to deal with a degree of hostility, rejection, and resistance. These reactions will be more or less intense depending on who we are and the population we are studying. Gaining entry and access to women with breast cancer, for example, may pose fewer obstacles if the researcher is a woman who has had breast cancer than if the researcher is a white woman who is trying to enter a poor Hispanic neighborhood but is seen as part of the "white establishment."

The participant observer must establish rapport and build relationships. This is not always easy, as field settings can be very uncomfortable and individuals in these settings can behave in frightening ways. Building trust is a complex matter: It develops over time and requires continual reaffirmation. We need to learn the language and the meanings constructed by the research participants we are studying—how to think and act from the perspective of the *insiders*. In short, we need to empathize and understand their experiences. Thus, it is crucial to monitor how our actions and appearances affect the members so that the data we gather are as rich and reflective as possible. This requires a degree of sharing and disclosure on our part; we cannot remain neutral or distant and expect to be a participant observer.

Our relationships must be characterized by dialogue and partnership, mutual interest and reciprocity, and trust and cooperation, while remaining within the parameters of professional ethics. This means that we must be alert to the dimensions of cultural, ethnic, and other differences, while being sensitive to the dynamics of power and privilege in the relationships we are building. The longer (or more often) we are in a field setting, the more we will be regarded as nonthreatening and our presence taken for granted.

As our relationships evolve and deepen over time, we must be careful about not slipping into roles that may be an aside to being a researcher, which would breach the agreement we made with our research participants. In some circumstances, it may be easier to become a therapist, change agent, advocate, or active member (full participant) than it is to remain a participant observer. Should we undertake such roles, however, we will change the nature of our relationships, which will impact and likely thwart the original purpose of our research study.

Some of the first questions that research participants ask are "Why should I cooperate with your research study?," "What's in it for me/us?," and "What's in it for you?" Our direct and candid answers to these questions are important. Research participants need to know that we seek to understand and describe their reality from their point of view and that ultimately there is value in having their stories told. But they also need to know that we expect to gain such things as publications, expertise, or an academic degree from the study. The data collected will, we hope, contribute to the knowledge base and may lead to solutions to their problems. Participants also need to know, however, that there are no absolute guarantees; nor is it the intent that our study will change their lives in any meaningful way.

Engaging and forming relationships that are sustained over time with insiders in a field setting is imperative to gathering meaningful, valid, and reliable data. Building these relationships is like being socialized into a way of life. We need to "be there," to "hang out," to "watch, listen, and learn the norms, language, and patterns of interaction." The same skills used to make friends are used to connect with the insiders, our research participants, in a field setting so that we have the ability to gather meaningful data that will be used to answer our research question.

Step 3: Gathering the Data

Participant observation data are usually gathered in four nonmutually exclusive ways: (1) observing, (2) interviewing, (3) using existing documents and other materials, and (4) reflecting upon our personal experiences.

Observing

Good observers need to use all of their senses to notice what they see, hear, touch, smell, and taste. Start with the physical surroundings of the settings, for example, and pay particular attention to the details that influence human behavior, such as lighting, temperature, colors, odors, and available space.

The next level is to observe people and their actions. Begin by noting observable physical characteristics of individuals and the composition of the group in such areas as gender, ethnicity, age, shape/size, and appearance. Notice what people do in relation to each other, such as who talks, who listens, and who sits or stands next to whom. As our observations become more focused, we pay more attention to such issues as the nature of the gathering and discern whether this is typical or unusual. At this stage, our observations serve the purpose of familiarizing ourselves with the field setting, helping us to get a "feel for the people and the place." These observations allow the widest possible field of vision. We are, however, limited to learning by looking and listening and will soon need to more sharply focus our attention and move away from passive observation to being a more active participant by asking questions through interviewing.

Interviewing

The data collected at the beginning of a participant observation study are in the form of words, including direct quotes and thick descriptions of particular events. There are general guidelines for asking good questions, but the type and style depend on the purpose and nature of the specific research study.

Questions that ask *what, when, where,* and *how* provide good descriptive data. Questions that ask *why* pressure people, put them on the defensive, and should therefore be used selectively. *Compare-and-contrast* questions constitute another type of inquiry. By asking how things are similar to and different from one another, we can discern what is included or excluded, what is part of or outside the phenomenon, and thus we can start to grasp the multiple meanings and layers involved in understanding the phenomenon we are studying.

Data gathering by engaging in dialogue and asking questions may be undertaken in a variety of situations ranging from casual conversations to formal interviews. Structured interview schedules used in formal inter-

views, where specific questions are asked in exactly the same way of each research participant, have the advantage of producing a uniform set of data.

On the other hand, as we know from the previous chapter, unstructured interviews have the advantage of producing richly qualitative data at a more in-depth level of disclosure. Both structured and unstructured interviewing contribute useful and meaningful data. Gayla Rogers and Elaine Bouey (1996) present a clear description of how to collect interview data in qualitatively oriented research studies. Figure 15.2 provides a summary of the main differences between survey and participant observation interviewing (Neuman, 2003).

Using Existing Documents and Other Materials

In the course of a participant observation study, it is not unusual to come across existing documents such as files, records, articles, pamphlets, and other materials, such as objects, artwork, videos, and clothing. These data sources are extremely useful in providing support for the findings we derived from our observing and interviewing. They provide a background, in addition to offering alternative points of view or explanations. The use of existing documents is an unobtrusive data-collection method that collect data that already exist (see Chapters 18–21).

Reflecting upon Our Personal Experiences

Our feelings, insights, and perceptions are other sources of data and should be treated as just that—duly documented and reported, however. By participating in the world of those we are studying, we generate the experiences of an insider. Reflecting upon our personal experiences in our field setting gives us access to the standpoint of the insider. It provides us with insights and new understandings of particular ways of life. These data can be used as a source of further questions to be asked of our research participants in order to check out our inner responses, hypotheses, and assumptions.

Through these various methods, high-quality data are gathered. This means that our data are richly varied, detailed descriptions that emerge from our observations and experiences.

Survey Interview	Participant Observation Interview
1. It has a clear beginning and conclusion.	1. The beginning and end are not clearly defined. The interview can be picked up later.
2. The same standard questions are asked of all research participants in the same order.	2. The questions and the order in which they are asked are tailored to certain people and situations.
3. The interviewer remains neutral at all times.	3. The interviewer shows interest in responses, encourages elaboration.
4. The interviewer asks questions, and the interviewee answers.	4. It is like a friendly conversational exchange, but with more interview-like questions.
5. It is almost always with a single research participant.	5. It can occur in a group setting or with others in the area, but varies.
6. The researcher maintains a professional tone and businesslike focus. Diversions are ignored.	6. It is interspersed with jokes, asides, stories, diversions, and anecdotes, which are recorded.
7. Closed-ended questions are common, with rare probes.	7. Open-ended questions are common, and probes are frequent.
8. The interviewer alone controls the speed and direction of the interview.	8. The interviewer and insider jointly influence the pace and direction of the interview.
9. The social context in which the interview takes place is not considered and is assumed to make little difference.	9. The social context of the interview is noted and seen as essential for interpreting the meaning of responses.
10. The interviewer attempts to shape the communication pattern into a standard framework.	10. The interviewer adjusts to the insider's norms and language usage, following his or her lead.

Figure 15.2   Survey Research Interviews Versus Participant Observation Interviews

Step 4: Recording the Data

Regardless of the type of data collected, their purpose is lost if we fail to adequately record our observations, impressions, and actual words. In addition to our notes, tapes, and transcriptions, we can use visual aids, such as diagrams, flowcharts, eco-maps and genograms, and photographs. Their type, form, and content depend on a number of factors: the field setting, the available and suitable technologies, the purpose of our study, and our personal preferences.

There is a great temptation to postpone systematically recording the gathered data. This is a mistake, as data that are not carefully organized and stored after they have been recorded create many challenges in the data analysis stage. Researchers are strongly encouraged to develop the habit of regularly recording what they see, hear, and experience.

There are many ways to record data when using participant observation as a data-collection method. Three of the more common ones are: (1) using field notes, (2) using taping devices, and (3) using visual aids.

Using Field Notes

The majority of gathered data are in the form of field notes. Writing field notes requires self-discipline and the allocation of time for the task. We will save a lot of backtracking (not to mention aggravation) if we organize our notes into categories at the outset of the study. Visualize creating separate containers to hold different types of notes. Factual observations, for example, are noted separately from personal feelings, impressions, or speculations; notes about our reactions to an interview or extraneous factors affecting the interview are kept separate from transcriptions or direct quotes from an interview. It may be hard to decide, particularly during the initial stages, what constitutes something worth noting. It may also worry us at later stages that, having made all these notes, we have so much data that it seems impossible to decipher any of them. These concerns can be addressed by following the recommendations for making field notes (Neuman, 2003):

- Make notes as soon as possible after each period in the field.
- Begin a record of each field visit with a new page, and note the date and time.
- Use jotted notes only as a temporary memory aid—use key words or terms, or note the first and last things said.
- Use wide margins and double-space everything to make it easy to add to notes at any time. Add to the notes if you remember something later.
- Type notes and store them on disks in separate files so that it will be easy to go back to them later.
- Record events in the order in which they occur, and note how long they last (e.g., a 15-minute wait, a one-hour ride).
- Make notes as concrete, specific, complete, and comprehensible as possible.
- Use frequent paragraphs and quotation marks. Exact recall of phrases is best, with double quotes; use single quotes for paraphrasing.
- Record small talk or routines that do not appear to be significant at the time; they may become important later.
- "Let your feelings flow," and write quickly without worrying about spelling or "wild ideas." Assume that no one else will see the notes, but use pseudonyms as a precaution to maintain confidentiality.
- Never substitute tape recordings completely for field notes.
- Include diagrams or maps of the setting, and note your own movements and those of others during the period of observation.
- Include your own words and behavior in the notes. Also record emotional feelings and private thoughts in a separate section.
- Avoid evaluative summarizing words. Use non-judgmental, descriptive words. Instead of "The sink looked disgusting," say, "The sink was rust-stained and looked as if it had not been cleaned in a long time. Pieces of food and dirty dishes that looked several days old were piled into it."
- Reread notes periodically, and record ideas triggered by the rereading.
- Organize materials neatly into types or methods of data collected so that they can be easily accessed.
- Always make one or more backup copies, keep them in a locked location, and store the copies in different places in case of fire.

There are many different types of field notes. We have chosen to describe four that represent different levels of data: (1) direct observation notes, (2) interpretive notes, (3) thematic notes, and (4) personal journal notes.

Using Direct Observation Notes.   The first level of field notes, *direct observation notes*, is usually organized chronologically and contains a detailed description of what was seen and heard. At this level, the notes report the facts—who, what, when, and where—and include verbatim statements, paraphrases, and nonverbal communications. These also include summary notes made after an interview.

Using Interpretive Notes.   The next level of field notes is *interpretive notes*. Our interpretations of events are kept separate from the record of the facts noted as direct observations but should be written in a column adjacent to the direct observations. These notes include our interpretation of the meanings implied by the words and gestures we observed. We can speculate about the social relationships, the emotions, and the influence of culture and context on what actually took place. By keeping our interpretations separate, we leave room for multiple interpretations (or different interpretations) to arise as our knowledge and experience increase. If we are not vigilant, however, it is quite easy to combine the facts with our interpretation of them, and we run the risk later on of viewing our interpretations as fact, which in turn might narrow our ability to see other versions or meanings as they emerge.

Using Thematic Notes.   The third level of field notes is *thematic notes*. These provide a place to record our emerging ideas, hypotheses, theories, and conjectures. This is the place to speculate and identify themes, make linkages between ideas and events, and articulate our thoughts as they emerge while we are still in the field setting. In these notes, we might expand on some of the ideas that have occurred to us, and develop our theories as we go or as we reread our direct observation notes and interpretive notes. This is the place to describe the thoughts that emerge in the middle of the night or to elaborate on any "Aha!" connections. It is critical to have a separate container for thoughts at this level, even if they are speculative and in the early stages of development, because we might lose an important seed for later analysis if they are not recorded.

Using Personal Journal Notes.   A journal of *personal notes* provides an outlet for our feelings and emotional reactions, as well as for the personal experiences of being the researcher or the participant observer. These reactions are a rich source of data. They give voice to our journey over time and provide a place to consider such things as what is going on at any given time during our involvement in the field. A running record of personal life events, feelings, physical well-being, and our moods, particularly as they relate to events in the field, will facilitate our data analysis. In this way, we can capture any particular intrapersonal or interpersonal experiences that might affect the way we make sense of the data. The process has an effect upon the quality of

the content gathered, our interpretation of the content, and what steps we decide to take next. Identifying these effects as they are revealed also facilitates our interpretation and reporting of them later.

The four different levels of field notes are shown below using an example of recording a period of observation in a field setting with a woman named Kay (Neuman, 2003):

> Direct Observation. *Sunday, October 4, 2005: Kay's Cafe 3:00 P.M. Large white male in mid-40s, overweight, enters. He wears worn brown suit. He is alone sits at booth #2. Kay comes by, asks, "What'll it be?" Man says, "Coffee, black for now." She leaves and he lights cigarette and reads menu. 3:15 P.M. Kay turns on radio.*
> Interpretive. *Kay seems friendly today, humming. She becomes solemn and watchful. I think she puts on the radio when nervous.*
> Thematic. *Women are afraid of men who come in alone since the robbery.*
> Personal Journal. *It is raining. I am feeling comfortable with Kay but am distracted today by a headache.*

Using Taping Devices

As we participate more actively and purposefully in the field setting and as our interactions with our research participants become less casual and more planned, we conduct interviews that are recorded and later transcribed. There are three typical approaches to recording the data gathered in qualitative research interviews: (1) taping the interview (either audio or video); (2) taking notes during the interview; and (3) recording notes immediately following the interview.

Taping the Interview.   There are both advantages and disadvantages to *tape-recording* interviews. The presence of a recorder can be intrusive and a barrier to full disclosure; however, it may be the only way to capture the richness and subtleties of speech. Video recording is the only way to capture the nonverbal language used by our research participants or to accurately identify each speaker in a group situation. Recording devices may also be a means of self-monitoring and self-improvement for the interviewer. Using a tape recorder may provide us with the confidence to focus all our attention on the person being interviewed, knowing that we do not have to worry about remembering all of the details or writing notes. At the same time, however, knowing the tape will record everything that is said, we might be tempted to let our minds wander.

Ultimately, the decision about whether to tape depends on what we want to do with the data gathered. If we want to include many direct quotations, for example, then it is useful to have the verbatim account, which can be transcribed and subjected to editing at a later date. If capturing the exact phrasing of all interview responses is not critical to the study, then note-taking may suffice. If time and money are not an issue, it is clearly best to fully transcribe all interviews from the tape. On the other hand, if time and money are limited, we might listen to the tape and use our notes to help decide what parts to transcribe and paraphrase.

Taking Notes During the Interview.   Many interviewers advocate *taking notes during the interview* as well as tape-recording them. The notes serve as a backup or safeguard against mechanical difficulties. They also serve as guides to the tape in helping decide what to transcribe and what to leave out. In some cases, where tape recording is not possible, brief notes may be the only way of recording the data. In this case we would try to write down some exact quotations and brief comments, supplemented by notes recorded after the interview.

Recording Notes Immediately Following the Interview. The third approach to recording interview data is to *make a record of the interview soon after it occurs.* This can be done in a variety of ways, but it is important to allow sufficient time for this. One hour of interviewing may require four hours later spent developing the notes, particularly if they will be the only record of the interview. Writing a process recording of the interview as soon as possible after the interview helps. The same four levels used in making field notes can be used in writing up research interviews—that is, to use a four-column

format. In the first column we write as close to a verbatim account of the interview as we can recall. This column includes our questions, probes, and statements, as well as the interviewee's responses.

We use the next column to note our interpretations of the meanings, emotions, and relationships inferred from the words and gestures. In the third column, any insights or themes that occur are noted. The fourth column is for reflections on what we were thinking or feeling at the time and for recording other things that were occurring that may have caused interference (e.g., the room was too warm or too noisy).

Using Visual Aids

Visual aids record data in a way that supplements and supports our field notes and tapes. Diagrams show how ideas are related, and flow charts outline sequences, processes, and events. Eco-maps and genograms present relationships and their various dimensions. Photographs capture the field setting or environment. All of these visual aids contain a great deal of data and depict our specific field setting and the people within it in a manner that written words simply cannot convey as effectively or as economically. Visual aids add an additional dimension in combination with other data-collection methods.

Step 5: Making Sense of the Data

Methods for analyzing qualitative data are presented in depth in Chapter 26. It is important to keep in mind at this point, however, that we need to make some sense of our experiences as participant observers. This involves analyzing the data collected. At some point, notwithstanding some initial prior reviews of the data as they are being gathered and organized, there comes a time when a full-scale intensive analysis occurs as the next step in the research process.

This step is marked by a critical shift in how we have been working so far, and it requires the use of a different set of skills and abilities. It also comes at a time when we are overwhelmed by the prospect of wading through masses of data and making sense of them. It may be a particular challenge to move into this step, particularly if our forte has been the developing of social relationships, taking on various participant observer roles, and being flexible and resourcefully adaptable in our field setting in an effort to ensure that we have good data to analyze.

The analysis step allows our data to be coded, sifted, sorted, and categorized so that themes, theories, and generalizations can be constructed and generated. In this way, meaning can be made of our research endeavor, and our results can be reported.

Step 6: Reporting the Findings

As should be evident by now, participant observation studies allow for the creation of a rich source of data about a situation or phenomenon that involves people. The raw data include such items as our written observation notes and correspondence, audiotapes, videotapes, and personal journals with reflections, as well as notes made after debriefing and consultation sessions with research advisers. A final report of our study includes an overview of our research question and the methods and techniques used in the study, detailed descriptions of the people and related phenomena, themes or hypotheses that have emerged from all the different data sources, information about our personal process, biases, and assumptions, and recommendations based upon our findings.

Normally, once the data are gathered and analyzed, they are written up as a case study, with quite detailed descriptions about the events or situation being studied. The final report includes themes and theoretical interpretations (or hypotheses) that have emerged from the data. It also includes recommendations for further study or action.

The intended audience of the report affects what and how it is written. The general public requires a different level of explanation from an academic audience. The use of jargon is avoided unless the audience comprises others who work in similar or related areas. Other possible audiences include other researchers or professional practitioners and government departments or agencies. Given the newly emerging view of research participants as having a vital partnership role in the research process, all those who have had a part in our study should have access to, or otherwise be provided with, a summary or a full copy of the final report.

Writing is facilitated by having blocks of uninterrupted time and perseverance. It involves drafting and editing and often includes showing early drafts to some or all of the insiders and consulting with research advisors. Eventually, a unique document is produced that is appropriate for the study undertaken and its intended audience.

Chapter 27 presents a very clear description of exactly how to write up a qualitatively oriented final report.

ETHICAL CONSIDERATIONS

As we know from Chapter 3, ethical considerations must be taken into account for any research situation. There are additional ethical issues that must be addressed in doing participant observation because of the close and sustained relationships between the researcher and the research participants and the fact that the balance of research activities occurs in a field setting where many other influences may surface and need to be dealt with as the study proceeds. Thus, through proper sponsorship and approvals, plus the informed consent of all those involved, it is crucial to attend to what is required to prevent adverse consequences.

Beyond this, there is the issue of the level of information we provide our research participants in reference to the roles we assumed during the study and the degree to which we disclosed personal information. While there are different views on this, we advise that, wherever possible, research participants be included as copartners in the research study in as open and as equal a way as possible. We have to decide how much to reveal about ourselves and the research project itself. Disclosure ranges on a continuum from fully covert (no one in the field setting is aware of the study) to fully disclosed (everyone knows the specifics of the study).

It is unlikely, however, that a social work research project would get approval from an ethics board either in an academic or in a social-work–related setting unless it was near the fully disclosed end of the spectrum, where research participants give their informed consent and know how the data will be stored and used. Covert research studies are simply not ethical.

SUMMARY

This chapter presented an overview of participant observation as an obtrusive data-collection method. It described its unique characteristics, such as issues of gaining access and entry into a field setting, forming and sustaining relationships (which includes the continuum of roles adopted by the researcher), and data gathering involving the use of relatively unstructured data-gathering approaches.

We included strategies for recording the data and attempted to create an awareness of the fine and delicate balance that exists between the participant-observer and the research participants and of the importance of the researcher's being attuned to this and making the necessary adjustments as the study unfolds to ensure that the perspective of the research participants comes through clearly, accurately, and in considerable detail.

As we know, using participant observation as a form of data collection is obtrusive; that is, the researcher intrudes into the research participants' lives in some form or another. The following chapter continues our discussion of obtrusive data-collection methods by presenting how interviews can be used to collect data for a research study.

Interviewing

16

Harvey L. Gochros

· ·

Interviewing is at the core of social work practice and is the most consistently and frequently employed social work technique. Social work education emphasizes the skills and purposes of the interview; therefore, it is not surprising that social workers are most comfortable with interviewing as a method of collecting data for research studies. Indeed, the goal of much of the interviewing social work researchers do is to gather data about clients and their situations or data on which program evaluations can be based. Familiarity with the purposes and techniques of interviewing, therefore, is a necessity in conducting research studies that depend on data elicited from interviews.

The two major sources of self-reported data in research studies are material presented by individuals in written form through questionnaires and data elicited from interviewees through research interviews. This chapter describes the uses of research interviews in the social work researcher's problem-solving process, suggests some procedures for conducting effective research interviews, and considers the advantages and disadvantages of interviews for collecting research data.

ADVANTAGES OF RESEARCH INTERVIEWING

The advantages of interviewing as a data-collection method are related primarily to naturalness and spontaneity, flexibility, and control of the environment. Combined with a high response rate, they provide a good argument for the use of this method when compared to mailed survey questionnaires, which are discussed in the following chapter.

Naturalness and Spontaneity

Interviews usually create a natural situation in which individuals can present information. For most people, it is easier and more natural to respond to questions orally than in writing, and a casual, relaxed setting leads to more spontaneous answers. What people say "off the top of their heads" may be free of the self-censorship often encountered in written responses. Also, it is more difficult in an interview than in a mailed survey questionnaire to "erase" an answer and replace it with a more "appropriate" and perhaps less valid answer.

High Response Rate

As we will see in the following chapter, research participants may leave out answers in mailed survey questionnaires because they lack reading or language skills, do not understand the questions, are unmotivated to answer the instrument, or simply overlook some items. In a research interview, the interviewer is there to see that each item is answered, and the interviewer can interpret or reword the item if necessary without distorting it. Many people not only are more comfortable expressing their ideas in speech than in writing; they may even enjoy talking to an interviewer, whereas they would consider filling out a survey questionnaire a nuisance and toss the form in a wastebasket.

Interviewers also are much harder to avoid than survey questionnaires, particularly survey questionnaires that arrive in the mail. The presence of a trained interviewer allows for a far more detailed and complex set of questions than is possible in a mailed questionnaire. The interviewer can slowly and carefully go over intricate items and make sure every question is covered.

Flexibility

Interviews permit far more flexibility than survey questionnaires. In talking with an interviewee, areas that might be difficult to frame in specific questions can be explored, and probing questions can be used to give responses greater depth. The interviewer can also adapt the sequence and timing of questions, change the way items are phrased, and even decide which questions can be eliminated, according to the characteristics of a particular interviewee (such as age, ethnic group, intelligence, or experience).

In past studies of sexual behavior, for example, researchers soon learned that the areas with which people are most uncomfortable tend to vary with their socioeconomic levels. Thus, the interviewers were instructed to ask people from lower socioeconomic levels about premarital intercourse (a behavior they tended to be comfortable about) early in the interview, while items about masturbation (a behavior they tended to be more uncomfortable about) were to be asked later. The reverse order was used with interviewees of higher socioeconomic levels because of their different relative ease with these two behaviors.

Access to Serendipitous Information

Since interviewers are present, they can make use of any unanticipated data interviewees offer. Content thus "stumbled on" can provide useful data for the study and, perhaps, subsequent investigations. The concept of unexpected events was expanded upon in Chapters 14 and 15, on participant observation.

For example, in the pretest of a study conducted on postplacement adoption services by Gochros (1970), an adoptive parent mentioned quite casually the extent to which she and her husband had lied to their social worker during their adoptive study. Her degree of comfort in sharing this information impressed the interviewer, and in subsequent interviews a question about parents' misinforming and withholding information from the social workers was added.

Nonverbal Responses

Skilled social workers are sensitive to their clients' nonverbal responses, which also can supply significant data in research interviews. The tone of the interviewee's voice, an interruption of eye contact, an unexplained smile or frown can all reflect on the verbal response they accompany and can lead the interviewer to probe for explanations.

Observation of and Control over the Environment

In mailed survey questionnaires, investigators have little or no control over when, where, or how the measuring instruments are answered, or even who answers them. The interviewer can both observe and, to some extent, control these factors. For example, with group-administered survey questionnaires (see Chapter 17), research participants may have little control over who

is looking over their shoulders. Indeed, they may choose to have others in their environment help them with their answers. The interviewer can see to it that research participants answer the questions in private and without the prompting or influence of others. Thus, the answers are clearly the interviewees' own answers.

DISADVANTAGES OF RESEARCH INTERVIEWING

There are problems and limitations in any data-collection method that depends on research participants' self-reports, whether the data come from a survey questionnaire or an interview. According to Bailey (1994), there are four major sources of research participant errors and biases in self-reported data. Research participants may:

1. Deliberately lie because they do not know an answer.
2. Make mistakes without realizing it (often because they are not able to admit socially undesirable feelings, attitudes, or traits, even to themselves).
3. Give inaccurate answers by accident simply because they misunderstand or misinterpret the question.
4. Be unable to remember, despite their best efforts. Research participants may even blend truth with fiction to cover up their memory gaps.

In addition to these problems, which are endemic to self-report studies, there are other problems that particularly affect research based on the interview method in comparison to survey research. These are principally related to time and cost constraints, the reactions of research participants and possible interviewer influence or distortion.

Time and Expense

Perhaps the most obvious limitation of interview research is its high cost and the considerable amount of time involved. The postage involved in mailing questionnaires in surveys is far less expensive than hiring, training, and supervising interviewing staff, let alone paying for the long hours of the interviews, as well as the time and expense involved in getting to and from them. Further, translating data from interview notes and completed instruments adds an extra, often expensive, step in the research process that may not be necessary with the relatively simpler survey questionnaire forms.

Unless an extravagantly large interviewing team is accessible—and affordable—interview research is a slow process. Especially in situations in which it is necessary to go to the interviewees (which is often the case), the number of interviews anyone interviewer can cover in a day is quite limited. In contrast, large numbers of mailed survey questionnaires can be accumulated and coded in a relatively short time. There are also problems in coding responses that are associated with interviewers' having worded items differently. The time problems are aggravated when research participants are hard to reach, fail to keep appointments, or do not complete interviews because of outside distractions. These are old stories to social workers who are experienced with home visits with clients, but the motivation for being a research participant is usually weaker than that for receiving social work services. The number of interviews that may be needed to accumulate a large enough sample for many research studies adds to the difficulty of conducting these interview-based research projects.

Interview Intensity

While many people enjoy the attention and stimulation of being interviewed, others may consider it a nuisance, particularly if the interview comes at a time when they are tired, preoccupied, or uncomfortable. With mailed surveys, research participants can determine when and where they will answer the questionnaire; they may even choose to answer it in dribs and drabs. When interviewers are seated opposite research participants, urging them on, they have little choice but to stay with the interview until the end, and the resulting fatigue, discomfort, and even anger may well influence their responses. Research participants may provide poor answers in an interview situation merely because the interviewer arrives when the baby is crying, the dog is barking, dinner is burning, or they need to go to the bathroom.

Inaccessibility of Potential Interviewees

An obvious limitation of research interviews is that the investigators may have a hard time getting to the interviewees. Sampling procedures may suggest a group of research participants who are geographically widely distributed or located in areas that are hard to reach, such as the hollows of West Virginia or distant military bases.

Loss of Anonymity

Mailed survey questionnaires, especially those that for little identifying data, can provide anonymity for research participants, who can feel relatively sure their participation will have no negative effects. Responding to a research interview can pose greater anticipated and perhaps real threats to interviewees, despite reassurances of confidentiality. The interviewer not only sees the interviewee in person but, if the interview is in the home, may come to know the interviewee's address and observe her home as well as her family, neighbors, and friends. Some people could consider such "observations" embarrassing or even incriminating. For example, in the postplacement adoption study referred to earlier, interviewees may well have feared the interviewer's impressions of their handling of their adopted children. Furthermore, interviewers may be seen by neighbors and others as they enter or leave research participants' homes, with possibly uncomfortable implications.

Interviewer Distortion

The research interviewer adds a link in the chain from the research participants' responses to the data that does not exist in mailed survey questionnaires (see Chapter 17). In mailed questionnaires, research participants read the questions and place their answers directly on the instrument. In interview research, the interviewer asks items in what may or may not be a standardized format, listens to the answers, and then summarizes or attempts to put the full response into notes that may be later rewritten or reformulated and then put into the data bank.

While the presence of the interviewer can facilitate the gathering of more meaningful data, for reasons stated earlier, there are risks of interviewer distortion or error at several points in the process. Interviewers may misread or badly phrase a question, or they may interpret or hear an interviewee's answer incorrectly. It is also possible for the interviewer to check an answer on the wrong line or in other ways fail to record responses accurately. Further distortion may occur later if the interviewer misreads or cannot understand the notes taken during interviews.

In general, there are four common interviewer distortions based on various types of errors:

1. *Asking errors.* Interviewers may change the wording of questions or even fail to ask a particular item.
2. *Probing errors.* Interviewers may negatively affect their interviewees' answers by asking follow-up questions or probes that are unnecessarily challenging, hostile, biased, or irrelevant.
3. *Recording errors.* Unless interviewers use tape recorders or have excellent memories, they must record their interviewees' answers by either the cumbersome and time-consuming process of writing exactly what their interviewees have said or by summarizing their responses. Such processes have a high potential for error.
4. *Cheating.* Interviewers are subject to the same temptations as any other employed mortal. Whatever the motivation, an interviewer may deliberately fill in gaps in interviews or even record a response for an item that was never asked.

Interviewer Influence

Interviewers can influence their interviewees not only by the phrasing of questions and tone of voice but by their own apparent comfort or discomfort with a particular question. This can be demonstrated, for example, by a change in eye contact or in the rapidity with which a question is asked.

Even the words that are emphasized in an item can influence the response. Consider the different implications of these two questions:

Did you *ever* feel like hurting your children?
Did you ever feel like *hurting* your children?

Other characteristics of the interviewer, in addition to specific behaviors in the interview, may have an effect, for better or worse, on the reliability of the data gathered from a research interview. Such variables as the interviewer's age, gender, physical appearance, racial or ethnic group, or language and accent, can affect the quality of the interviewees' responses. Moreover, these same variables and other characteristics of the interviewees (such as "apparent intelligence") may well elicit diverse patterns of behavior from interviewers, and this can affect the way they carry out the interviews, which in turn affects the data gathered.

CONSIDERATIONS IN RESEARCH INTERVIEWS

Once an area of study that lends itself to self-reports elicited through research interviews has been selected and the necessary resources for conducting such interviews have been assembled, the researcher is concerned with how to prepare for, conduct, and record the data from such a study. The remainder of this chapter discusses some of the points to consider in going through these stages in research interviewing. The procedures include determining the degree of structure in content, developing the interviewing schedule, determining the format of interview items, selecting interviewers, gaining access to interviewees, deciding where to conduct the interviews, checking the interviewers' appearance, developing the interviewer-interviewee relationship, formulating and asking questions, and recording the data.

DEGREE OF STRUCTURE

The preparation of the interview instrument or schedule (a written instrument that sets out the overall plan for the interviews and determines the structure, sequence, and content of the specific items to be asked) is crucial to the outcome of the study. Many of the considerations in the development of the instrument, as well as the overall plan for research conducted through interviews, are somewhat similar if not identical to those associated with mailed survey questionnaire construction (Chapter 10) and group-administered survey research (Chapter 17).

An important variable in planning research interviews, however, is the degree to which the interview is to be structured. Structure refers to the extent to which the interview schedule or instrument includes predetermined, specific items. There are three options for structure in research interviews: (1) structured; (2) semistructured, or focused; and (3) unstructured. Each has particular purposes, advantages, and disadvantages.

Structured Interviews

In a structured interview, the instrument prescribes exactly what items will be asked, their sequence, and even their specific wording. Both open- and closed-ended items may be used. This is the easiest type of interview to code, since all interviewees are asked exactly the same items in the same order. Predetermining the exact wording of the items reduces the risk that interviewers may introduce their biases by the way they word questions. Structured interviews also provide consistency in the nature of the data collected from interview to interview. The investigator can use interviewers with relatively little training, since individual decisions are kept at a minimum and the interviewers need only follow specific instructions.

Structured interviews have a number of limitations, however. Interviewers have little freedom to draw fully on their interviewees' knowledge of the research question or to explore respondents' answers or encourage them to expand on answers by the use of probing questions. They may not even seek clarification of ambiguous or vague answers. Thus, structured interviews provide few of the advantages of interviews over mailed survey questionnaires, yet they are more expensive and time-consuming.

Semistructured, or Focused Interviews

The semistructured interview schedule may include some specific items, but considerable latitude is given to interviewers to explore in their own way matters pertaining to the research question being studied. A form

of the semistructured interview called the focused interview centers on selected topics and hypotheses, but the specific items used are not entirely predetermined. Usually this form of interview is used for research participants who have shared a common experience, such as having received a particular type of social work service, been the victim of a particular crime, or suffered a certain illness.

The semistructured interview requires a more skilled and better trained interviewer than does the structured form. Interviewers must learn as much as possible about the particular attribute or experience the interviewees have shared. On the basis of this knowledge, they decide before the interviews what aspects of the interviewees' experience are to be explored, and they may develop hypotheses about these experiences to be tested in the interviews. Thus the general areas to be explored are determined before the interviews, although few, if any, of the questions may be formulated in advance. The process was described many years ago by Merton, Fiske, and Kendall (1956) as follows:

First of all, the persons interviewed are known to have been involved in a particular situation: they have seen a film, heard a radio program, read a pamphlet, article or book, taken part in a psychological experiment or in an uncontrolled, but observed, social situation (for example, a political rally, a ritual, or a riot). Secondly, the hypothetically significant elements, patterns, processes and total structure of this situation have been provisionally analyzed by the social scientist. Through this content or situational analysis, he has arrived at a set of hypotheses concerning the consequences of determinate aspects of the situation for those involved in it. On the basis of this analysis, he takes the third step of developing an interview guide, setting forth the major areas of inquiry and the hypotheses which provide criteria of relevance for the data to be obtained in the interview. Fourth and finally, the interview is focused on the subjective experiences of persons exposed to the pre-analyzed situation in an effort to ascertain their definitions of the situation. The array of reported unanticipated responses gives rise to fresh hypotheses for more systematic and rigorous investigation.

Since the hypotheses may be formulated before a semistructured interview, the interviewer must avoid biasing the items to confirm the hypotheses. Moreover, although research participants have a right to be informed about the general purposes of a study in which they are participating, it may not be advisable to inform them of the specific hypothesis being tested, because knowing this might bias their responses.

Semistructured interviews allow for the introduction of unanticipated answers from interviewees. For example, Gochros had not anticipated before the pretest for the study of postplacement adoption services mentioned earlier that adoptive parents would volunteer that they had misled their adoption study workers and that they were concerned that their postplacement workers would discover their deceptions. As a result, probes in this area were later introduced.

Such exploration in semistructured interviews often is accomplished with "funneling" techniques, in which a general item is followed up with more specific probing questions. An example of this procedure was used in an interview study of 300 mothers whose children had been placed in foster care. The interviewers were all trained social workers who visited the mothers in their homes. After explaining the purposes of the study and obtaining the mothers' agreement to explore their experiences with foster care, the researchers recorded the responses as accurately as possible following a very detailed semistructured instrument, the opening segment of which is shown in Figure 16.1. The full interview instrument covered 34 pages and required an interview approximately two hours long. It included open- and closed-ended questions, checklists, and scales. This obviously long and complicated instrument was necessitated by the quantity and complexity of the data the researchers hoped to gather.

Semistructured and focused interviews allow for considerable latitude in the length and detail of the instrument. If only one or two researchers who are intimately familiar with the phenomenon being studied and the goals of the study will be conducting the interviews, the instrument can be comparatively shorter and less

detailed. In Gochros's study of postplacement adoption services, for example, he was the sole interviewer. While there may be a considerable hazard of interviewer bias when the researcher is both the hypothesis formulator and the interviewer, such economy of personnel does allow for a much simpler measuring instrument. The instrument used for the interviews with each of the 114 adoptive parent research participants (and a similar one used with their 18 postplacement social workers) was less than two pages in length. This interview schedule is shown in Figure 16.2.

The brevity of the instrument in Figure 16.2 leads to less disconcerting paper-shuffling during the interview and fuller attention to the folks being interviewed. Extensive use of abbreviations (e.g., AP = adoptive parent, CW = caseworker, SP = supervisory or postplacement period) allows the instrument to be further condensed. The interview schedule (the measuring instrument, if you will) does not need to conform to the strict design and construction methods as presented in Chapter 10 because only the interviewer sees it. The person being interviewed does not see the interview schedule.

To determine the degree of detail that will be necessary in the instrument for the semistructured or focused interview, the researcher must answer three questions:

1. What is it that is to be learned, and how much is already known about it?
2. To what extent are the interviewers trained, prepared, and able to elicit data on their own from their research participants (the interviewees)?
3. To what extent is the simplicity of coding responses (with its implications for validity) to be a determining factor?

Unstructured Interviews

In unstructured interviews, only the general problem area to be studied is determined in advance of the interviews. The interviewers choose the timing, structure, and content of items to be asked, not unlike the procedures used in worker-client fact-gathering interviews.

The major advantage of unstructured interviews is that the interviewer has almost unlimited freedom to ask

A. MAIN QUESTION: Respondent's Statement of Problem

1. First of all, would you tell me in your own words what brought about the placement of _____ away from home in foster care?

    (Probe if not spontaneously answered)

1a. Who first had the idea to place_____ _ ?

    Did anyone oppose it or disagree with it? If yes:
    a. Who?
    b. Why?

1b. Were any attempts made to make other arrangements for_____ other than placement? If yes:
    a. What
    b. Who did this?
    c. Why didn't it work out?

1c. Was there anyone whom you usually depend on who couldn't or didn't help out? If yes:
    a. Who? (relationship)
    b. Why not?

1d. Did all your children who were in your home go into placement at that time? If no:
    a. Which children were not placed at that time (name, age, etc.)?
    b. Why weren't they placed?

1e. Who was caring for _____ just before he/she was placed? If other than natural mother:
    a. For how long had she been caring for_____?
    b. Why was she caring for the child (rather than the child's mother)?

(If sample child two years or older, ask if)

1f. Was _____told that he/she was going into placement? If yes:
    a. By whom? What was he/she told?
    If no:
    b. What was the reason for that?

1g. Was _____prepared for placement in any (other) way? If yes:
    a. By whom? In what way(s)?
    If no:
    b. What was the reason for that?

1h. Did anyone help you get ready for _____going into placement away from home? If yes:
    a. Who?
    b. In what way(s)?

1i. Who actually took _____to the agency the day he/she went into placement?

2. From all you have told me, what would you say was the one main reason for _____going into foster care?

2a. When would you say this problem first started?

3. And what would you say was the next most important reason for _____going into foster care?

3a. When would you say this problem first started?

Figure 16.1 Opening Segment of a Semistructured Interview Instrument

1. What were you told about the purposes and content of the SP?
   By whom:
2. What did you expect the visits to be like?
3. How were they different from what you expected?
4. Why do you think there is a SP?
5 How many SP visits were there?
6. Average length?
7. How many AP initiated? Why?
8. How many unexpected? Opinion
9. How many were you present:
10. Ever feel left out?
11. What did you talk about?
12. What do you think CW wanted you to bring up or discuss in SP visits?
13. Subsequent contacts.
14. What sort of problems did you run into during the SP?
   Freedom
   Rel: Husband-Wife
   Rel: Parent-Child
   Depressed
   Neglected
15. Books recommended? Why? Read?　Useful?
16. Did you think of CW more as a friend or caseworker?
17. What did you like most about CW?
18. What did you like least about CW?
19. Did CW create the kind of atmosphere where you felt free to talk over your real feelings about things?
20. Did you ever withhold any information or feelings from CW?
21. How much do you think CW knew about child care and development?
22. What did you think about when you knew a visit was scheduled?
23. What did you think about just after the visit was over?
24. Did your feelings change about the visits during the SP?
25. What did you find the most helpful result of the visits?
26. What did you find to be the least helpful or most unpleasant aspect of the visits?
27. Any way agency could have been more helpful during the SP?
28. How helpful was the SP to you, overall?
29. Can you think of any way that the visits may be helpful to you in the future?
30. How did you feel when the decree was finally granted?
31. Do you think there should be a waiting period?
32. If yes, how long?
33. Should there be CW visits? Why?
34. Compulsory? Why?
35. If they had been voluntary, would you have requested any?
36. If adopt again and if voluntary, would you have requested any?
37. Groups for parents of 5-year-olds, interested?
38. Groups for parents of adolescents, interested?
39. If ran into a problem with a child, contact worker?
40. Second child: planning, applied, placed, not planning
41. If worker was different from study, was transition difficult?
42. Comments:

Figure 16.2　Interview Schedule with Adoptive Parents

interviewees wide-ranging items, to seek in-depth clarification of their answers, and to explore any possibly profitable avenues which may emerge in the interview. The interviewee is clearly at the center of this form of interview. Responses are often elicited from neutral probes provided by the interviewer. This form of research interview is derived from the field of psychotherapy. It often seeks to probe the interviewees' deepest feelings and experiences and may well uncover emotions, attitudes, and beliefs the interviewee was not even aware of prior to the interview.

This type of research interviewing depends heavily on the competence and self-awareness of the interviewer. It requires well-trained interviewers who are skilled in techniques for developing working relationships and eliciting data from research participants. They must be able to make quick decisions about what to ask and when and how to ask productive questions. They must also be knowledgeable about the general subject they are exploring. Further, they must be fully aware of the dangers of leading or biasing interviewees, which are greater because of the nature of the unstructured give-and-take.

One of the most significant limitations of this type of interview is the problems it creates in coding. However, if little is known about the research question being studied or if the question is a sensitive one, unstructured interviews may lead to the acquisition of useful data for more structured future inquiries. Indeed, unstructured interviews are generally not as useful for testing out hypotheses or for deriving accurate measurements of specific phenomena as they are for developing preliminary data in relatively uncharted areas that may lead to the formulation of hypotheses later down the line. Such research studies usually require very small samples.

For example, Gochros (1978) contacted only six former male clients who were homosexually oriented and heterosexually married. He interviewed them by focusing on their hopes and expectations from treatment and their reactions to it, as well as their subsequent experiences. While the general purposes of his interviews were clear to both the interviewer and interviewees (i.e., what they wanted and what they got from their social work contact), the interviews were entirely unstructured. The report of the study included hypotheses about counseling gay husbands derived from the interviews, illustrated with extensive direct quotations from his former clients. Such an exploratory study can provide a stepping stone to larger, more detailed descriptive and explanatory studies.

DEVELOPING THE INTERVIEW SCHEDULE

As noted in Chapter 10, there is no "right" way to construct a measuring instrument, despite advances in research methods and techniques—many of which are reported in this book. Decisions on how to structure and design an instrument must generally be based on informed hunches that are pretested before being used with the actual sample or population. One of the few generalities that can be drawn from the experience of social work researchers is that usually far more data are elicited from the interviews than will subsequently be used in the research analysis and report. The social work researcher, having the typical limitations of time and money, may be well advised to be parsimonious in deciding what will be covered in a measuring instrument.

In deciding what is to be covered and how the items can best elicit these data, a number of questions must first be answered:

1. What do we want to know that we don't know already?
2. Who can tell us what we don't know and what we want to know?
3. How can we formulate and ask questions that will increase the probability that the interviewees will tell us what we want to know?
4. What would keep the interviewees from telling us what we want to know or would lead them to deceive us or present us with incomplete data?
5. How can we override these sources of withholding and distortion?

The answers to the first three questions have been presented in Parts I–III of this text. To answer the remaining two questions, it is necessary to consider some successful strategies that have been developed to elicit desired data through research interviews.

Sequencing of Questions

Generally, the funneling techniques referred to earlier have been found to be useful in gaining honest and complete answers from research participants. This involves starting the interview with broad, general questions and then moving on to narrower, more specific, and perhaps more difficult and sensitive questions as the interview progresses. The advantage of this approach is that rapport can be established early in the interview with questions that do not make the interviewee particularly uncomfortable. As the folks being interviewed establish more trust and confidence in their interviewers, more challenging questions can be asked.

Bailey (1994) has suggested six guidelines for establishing an order for questions in interviews. These suggestions are the basis for the discussion in this section.

First, open-ended questions, and those that are likely to be sensitive or difficult to answer, should be placed late in the interview. If difficult items come early, the interviewee may become resentful or immobilized and may refuse to continue. What is sensitive to one interviewee, however, may not be sensitive to another. For example, Pomeroy's finding that research participants of low socioeconomic standing tended to be uncomfortable with questions about masturbation but were relatively comfortable with items about premarital sex was noted earlier. The degree of sensitivity was generally reversed among research participants who were at the higher socioeconomic levels.

Thus, interviewers may need some flexibility in the order in which they ask such items. Even if open-ended questions are not sensitive, they should generally be placed last, because answers to this type of question take more time and energy. For example, in studying reactions to group therapy, it may be easier for interviewees to answer such items as "How often did you meet?" and "Was the group therapist always there?" than a question like "How did you feel when other group members were confronting you?"

Second, easy-to-answer items should be asked first in the interview. Such questions usually ask for facts, rather than feelings, beliefs, or opinions. Thus, interviews usually start with questions about such demographic variables as age, gender, home address, marital status, occupation, and place of employment. (In survey research, demographic variables are asked last; see Chapters 10 and 17.) Although even such seemingly innocuous items can cause discomfort, they are usually at least clear and nonthreatening (demographic variables about race, income, and religion are more likely to be discomforting). Whenever possible, opening questions should also be interesting and perhaps mildly provocative so as to gain the interviewees' interest and clarify the subject matter of the interview.

Third, answers should be obtained early in the interview to items that may be necessary to guide the remainder. For example, getting the names, gender, and ages of siblings and determining whether they are still living would be a logical, early step in studies of family relationships.

Fourth, items should be asked in a logical order. This provides a flow to the interview that facilitates moving easily from item to item. The most obvious and frequently used organizing theme is time sequence. In describing children, for example, it seems most logical to ask about them in order of birth. Indeed, that is the sequence in which most people usually present these data. The frame of reference of the interview should also be clear and orderly. Each segment should be covered completely before you move on to the next. It is both awkward and confusing to the interviewee to move back and forth between topics.

For example, in Gochros's study of adoptive parents' experiences with postplacement services, the unstructured interview (see Figure 16.2) was constructed in the following sequence:

1. How parents were prepared by the agency for postplacement services (Item 1)
2. What they expected postplacement services to be like (Items 2 through 4)
3. What the postplacement services were like (specific facts, such as number of visits, followed by more difficult questions, including reactions) (Items 5 through 15)
4. Evaluation of the social workers and the usefulness of their services (Items 16 through 28)

5. Suggestions for how services could be improved (Item 29)

6. Reactions to the postplacement period itself (Items 30 through 35)

7. Anticipation of any future problems and whether agency services might be used in the future (Items 36 through 41).

8. Any other comments (Item 42).

Fifth, the creation of a "response set" should be avoided. The suggestion that there should be a logical sequence of questions and the interviewer should avoid skipping around from topic to topic should not be regarded as a rigid requirement. Indeed, if the researcher senses that asking items in a particular order will lead an interviewee to answer in a particular way, that order should probably be changed. This avoids what is called a response set, whereby the interviewers cause their interviewees to reply in ways that do not reflect the questions' content or the interviewees' accurate answers.

As we know from Chapter 8, one of the most common response sets is a function of social desirability, or the tendency to reply to items in a way the research participants perceive as conforming to social norms. The order of items may well encourage such a response set. An exaggerated example would be asking an item such as "Do you think most people love their mothers?" followed by another item such as "Do you love your mother?" When research participants are asked to give their salaries in a succession of jobs, they may well have a response set to report increased salaries from job to job, whether or not such a pattern really existed.

The probability of response sets can be reduced by changing the order of questions or the answer format. This has the disadvantage of possibly confusing the interviewee, but if it is done with moderation, such a procedure may also lessen the boredom of a long series of items. In the postplacement adoption study, for example, items about parents' perceptions of the social worker's activities were interspersed with an activity in which research participants were presented with a deck of index cards on which various worker activities were written and asked to rearrange them in order of what they believed their social workers were trying to do—from "most trying to do" to "least trying to do."

Sixth, reliability-question pairs should be asked at various points in the interview. In this procedure, two questions, one phrased negatively and the other phrased positively, are asked to check the reliability of the research participants' answers. For example, at one point in an interview, the interviewer may ask, "Did you think your social worker generally understood what you were up against?" and at another, "Did you get the feeling that your social worker didn't understand the problems you were facing?" Such a procedure can be used to double-check the reliability of particularly strategic items for either a particular research participant or for an entire sample. Where there is a disparity in the responses, the interviewer can ask probing items in order to amplify or clarify the interviewees' ideas. This procedure should be used cautiously for a variety of reasons, most conspicuously because the interviewees may perceive the device—accurately—as a trick.

DETERMINING THE FORMAT OF INTERVIEW ITEMS

It is often desirable to vary the format of items in an interview schedule. For example, the interviewee may be asked to read a statement, then be asked some questions about it. The length and type of answers expected can also be varied; at various times, facts, beliefs, opinions, or experiences can be requested. In addition to adding variety to an interview and thus avoiding response sets and maintaining interest in the interview, the use of different types of items can achieve different purposes. The relative merits of the two primary forms of items, open- and closed-ended questions, were discussed in Chapters 8–10, and we need only summarize some of their advantages and disadvantages in research interviews.

Utilizing Open- and Closed-Ended Questions

In closed-ended questions, the interviewee has a limited, predetermined range of answers, such as "yes–no," and "male–female." With open-ended questions, research participants can give any answer they choose, rather than selecting from a range of options. For example, "Do you get along with your children?" is a closed-ended question that invites a yes or no response, while "How do you get along with your children?" is an open-ended question that allows for a wide range of answers.

Open-ended questions are relatively easy to formulate and to ask, but the answers are difficult to code and categorize. For example, the item "If you had three wishes, what would they be?" can produce data that may be a practitioner's dream but a researcher's nightmare. However, for the price of agonizing over more complex response categories, the interviewer may gain a greater range of responses, many of which may not have been anticipated.

It may seem logical that open-ended questions would elicit answers reflecting greater depth and feelings from research participants, but this is not necessarily the case. There is no evidence that open-ended questions produce answers of greater depth or validity than closed-ended questions do. Indeed, with situations in which research participants are considered resistant, the closed-ended, "objective" questions often provide more valid results. Additionally, closed-ended questions are most useful when specific categories are available against which the interviewees' replies can be measured and when a clear conceptual framework exists in which the interviewees' replies will logically fit.

Using Probes

Perhaps the most useful type of item in semistructured interviews is the probe, or follow-up question. The intent of such items is to seek greater depth or clarity about answers the interviewee has already given. Often, vague or general replies will be given to open-ended items because the research participants have not completely thought through their replies or are not sure how to answer. They may also be holding back from giving a complete answer for fear of appearing sick, bad, stupid, or worthless. This is when a probe is called for. The intent of such questions is to help interviewees provide more complete and accurate data.

Probes may also be used to increase the probability that all areas of interest to the interviewer have been explored. For this purpose, the need for probes may be anticipated and included in the interview schedule, on the basis of the interviewer's experience with responses

to particular areas of questioning in the pretest. These predetermined probes can then be used as "contingency questions" the interviewer can draw upon if the interviewee answers—or fails to answer—questions in certain anticipated ways.

There are a variety of interviewing techniques that can be used as probes to encourage interviewees to amplify, expand, or clarify responses. These probes need not be included in the interview schedule but should become part of the interviewer's standard repertoire, to be called upon when the interviewees' answers suggest their use. Bailey (1994) has described the procedures investigators can use in probing for responses. They are:

1. *Repeating the question.* This is done whenever the interviewee hesitates or appears not to understand the question.
2. *Repeating the answer.* This type of neutral probe can be used by an interviewer who is not certain about understanding the interviewee's answer correctly. Repetition of the answer can correct errors and assure both interviewee and interviewer that the answer is recorded carefully. Repetition also gives the interviewee an opportunity to think about elaborating it further.
3. *Indicating understanding and interest.* The interviewer indicates that the answer has been heard and approved of, thus stimulating the interviewee to continue.
4. *Pausing.* The interviewer pauses and says nothing if the response is obviously incomplete. This indicates that the interviewer knows the interviewee has begun to answer and is waiting for the rest of the reply.
5. *Using a neutral question or comment.* "How do you mean that?" or "Tell me more" indicates to the interviewee that an answer is on the right track but that more data are desired.

SELECTING INTERVIEWERS

It would appear logical for social workers to do their own research interviewing, since their training and experience should have made them knowledgeable about human behavior and social problems. This background would seem to equip them for interviewing in sensitive areas. However, there are a number of significant differences between social work practice interviewing and research interviewing. As a result, years of service-oriented practice may, paradoxically, be both a limitation and an asset for the social worker as research interviewer. Moreover, trained social work researchers are expensive to employ and may be hard to recruit for research interviewing positions.

The choice of the particular level of training required for a research interviewing assignment should be determined by a review of the population to be interviewed, the content of the interview, and the availability of supervisory staff and other resources for the study. Interviewers who lack social work training, such as indigenous community residents, graduate students, paraprofessionals, and social work moonlighters, have been used effectively in a wide range of social work research efforts.

Indeed, such classifications of researchers are used more often than full-time trained social workers. Since there is some evidence that the personality of interviewers is more predictive of effectiveness than is education or social status, there is good reason to at least consider alternatives to social work staff. Nevertheless, as Jenkins (1975) suggests, "Where feasible and appropriate filling the role of research interviewer is one way for the practitioner to contribute to social work research." Indeed, doing so may provide social workers with new and useful perspectives on their practice and is one way to introduce them to the practitioner/researcher concept. Matching other characteristics of the interviewee and interviewer may be more significant for the quality of the data derived from research interviews than the formal, professional training of the interviewer.

Matching Interviewer and Interviewee Characteristics

Social work researchers usually have limited financial resources and thus have little control over which interviewers will interview which research participants, regardless of similar or different characteristics. However, the differences or similarities of interviewers and interviewees can have considerable influence on the usefulness of the data acquired. Thus, if the luxury of choice is available, deliberately matching interviewers to interviewees may be desirable. But what should be matched to what? Generally, interviewees and interviewers seem to do best when they can identify with each other. However, the means to achieve such empathy is not always simple or clear. This section briefly reviews the effects of a number of physical and social characteristics of interviewers on the answers their interviewees provide. These variables are (1) gender, (2) age, (3) language, (4) socioeconomic level, and (5) race or ethnicity.

Gender

Since rapport is usually (but not always) better when interviewer and interviewee have somewhat similar characteristics, it would seem likely that interviewers who are of the same gender as their interviewees would get better results. Such would certainly seem to be the case in such situations as research studies on rape. Gender-linked patterns of relating may also affect perceptions of interviewers. Mark Benney and his colleagues (1956) asked male and female interviewers who had surveyed political attitudes to rate each of their interviewees in terms of their honesty. The male interviewers rated 68 percent of their male interviewees and 56 percent of their female interviewees as "completely frank and honest," while the female interviewers rated 79 percent of *both* their male and female interviewees this way. Another study found that both men and women responded to questions about whether they would like to see a particular movie in a way that they thought would please their interviewers on the basis of the interviewer's gender, especially if the interviewer was of the other gender.

Age

Considerable disparity in age between interviewers and interviewees may also contribute to the biases of either. One study, for example, examined the effect of age differences with the hypothesis that the closer in age interviewees and interviewers were, the more rapport there would be. Although the results of the study were inconclusive, interviewers who were considerably older or younger than their interviewees often rated the respondents as being equally or more frank and honest than did interviewers who were in the same age group as their interviewees. However, when both age and gender were considered together, it was found that young female interviewers rated young male interviewees significantly higher for honesty than they did older males. Older interviewers did not display such a disparity.

Language

Matching interviewer and interviewee in language and accent has been found to be of considerable importance. If interviewees are more comfortable in a language other than English, it would, of course, be desirable to use bilingual interviewers. Obviously, also, translations of items originally composed in English must not distort the meaning of the original item. This might best be accomplished by having a professional with competence in both languages develop the items to be used.

Word use also is important in interviewing research participants who use a particular argot or slang words peculiar to their particular situation. Populations such as drug users, prostitutes, homosexually oriented individuals, and ethnic minorities often develop a unique vocabulary to describe concepts important to them. Terms such as "cracker," "closet queen," or "angel dust," which are a part of some group's everyday vocabulary, may be incomprehensible to the uninitiated.

Interviewers with life situations similar to those of their research participants may be more comfortable and conversant with this language than those who have merely been tutored in the argot. Professionals studying former drug users have successfully involved them in developing the interview schedule and doing the actual interviewing, thus permitting the meaningful, unstilted, and appropriate use of the vernacular of addicts. Indeed, interviewers who ask questions in simple language compatible with the everyday speech of those who are being interviewed tend to get better results. One study examined low-income families and found that abstract and complex items elicited far fewer responses than items that were simply phrased.

Socioeconomic Level

It is sometimes difficult to separate socioeconomic differences from racial disparity in matching interviewers to potential interviewees. They are often interrelated; one research study, for example, found an inverse relationship between biased data and the social distance between interviewees and interviewers. In the case of white interviewers, there was a stronger bias against lower-socioeconomic-level black interviewees than against those who were in a higher socioeconomic level. Dohrenwend and her colleagues (1968) asked white interviewers what variables (e.g., gender, age, race, and economic level) they preferred in the interviewees they interviewed. She found that those interviewers who preferred not to interview older people also rejected poor people and blacks in general.

In a discussion of social work interviewing, Kadushin and Kadushin (1997) introduced the concept of *homophily,* the idea that social workers and clients from similar cultural backgrounds will be more comfortable with each other and thus will work together more effectively. However, it may be dangerous to translate this observation from social work practice to research interviewing. Overidentification, lack of control of bias, and confusion of roles are possible consequences of overemphasis on matching. As an example, in a study of welfare mothers in which both interviewers and interviewees were black, the social distance between the interviewers and interviewees was examined in relation to their rapport and to the validity of the study. Surprisingly, the results indicated that it was similarity in background, rather than difference, that was associated with interviewer bias. Furthermore, the interviewers who had the greatest rapport with their interviewees were the most biased.

There is evidence that interviewers who are socially too close to their interviewees may become too involved with them, rather than relating to the task of the study. It may be that either too little or too much social distance between interviewer and interviewee can create biases that reduce the value of a study.

In the past, most research interviewers in studies of interest to social workers were from the middle socioeconomic levels, white, and well educated, while most of the interviewees were less educated, from a lower socioe-conomic level, and often nonwhite. In a classic study on interview bias in polls, Daniel Katz (1942) demonstrated a lack of rapport between interviewers and lower-socioe-conomic-level interviewees that led to a clear bias in the research participants' answers on matters of concern to them. Socioeconomic disparity between interviewees and interviewers continues to be a problem in social work research.

Race or Ethnicity

The effects of racial differences and similarities between interviewers and interviewees are longstand-ing social research topics. A study conducted during World War II found that blacks interviewed by black interviewers gave significantly more responses indicat-ing the existence of racial protest and discrimination in the army than those interviewed by whites. For another study in Memphis, Tennessee (a southern city during a period of considerable racial tension), 1,000 black research participants were randomly assigned to black and white interviewers, and there were significant differences in the responses to the interviews of the two groups (Hyman, 1954). Black social aspirations and problems were presented in a more passive way to white interviewers than to black interviewers. Further, the white interviewers obtained significantly higher pro-portions of what might be called "proper" or "accept-able" answers.

Much has changed, of course, in black-white rela-tions today, but differences in blacks' responses to black interviewers and to white ones still are apparent. One research study reported that this difference showed up most clearly when questions were directed at race rela-tion issues and were less significant in questions related to family patterns and other aspects of daily living (Schuman & Converse, 1970). In terms of social work services, both black and white research interviewers asked blacks' preferences for black or white workers. The study found that blacks preferred receiving their social services from blacks, assuming equal competence for black and white workers, and this preference was expressed more strongly to black interviewers than to whites (Brieland, 1969).

Racial and ethnic bias is not limited to black-white differences. In a study of the effects of Gentile research participants interviewed by Gentile and Jewish inter-viewers in New York City, for example, research partici-pants were asked whether they believed Jewish people had too much influence, not enough influence, or about the amount of influence they should have in the business world (Hyman, 1954). When the interviewer was also a Gentile, one-half of the interviewees reported that they believed Jewish people had too much influence. However, only 22 percent stated that they thought Jewish people had too much influence when they were asked the ques-tion by a Jewish interviewer.

Many of these studies concerning the impact of eth-nic and racial differences between interviewers and their interviewees were conducted when racial, religious, and ethnic biases were socially more acceptable than they are today (Robinson & Rhodes, 1946). There is little doubt, however, that such biases still exist and may be a factor in both interviewee and interviewer behavior. Indeed, growing minority assertiveness among such racial and social groups as women, gays, Latinos, and blacks may maintain biases that can well affect interview behaviors on both sides of the notepad.

In any case, matching interviewers and their inter-viewees can enhance the value of social work research. The biases of both interviewers and interviewees deriv-ing from gender, race, and social distance must be con-sidered. However, it is important to recognize that women interviewers *can* be sexists, older people *can* be ageists, gays *can* be homophobic, and blacks *can* be racists. These biases can be minimized by careful selec-tion of interviewers, open exploration of biases, and con-sideration of how to minimize the impact of any residual biases on the interview process.

GAINING ACCESS TO INTERVIEWEES

As we have seen in Chapter 3, it is often necessary to get permission to approach potential research participants. When an organization is involved, this may entail going through a chain of command. For example, in order to interview prisoners, the investigator may have to ask not only the prisoners but also the warden, who might in turn have to seek permission from the commissioner of corrections, who might have to check with the governor. For most populations or samples social workers study, such official permission will be necessary, and it is not always easy to obtain. Some communities, such as Beverly Hills, California, require a city permit before some forms of interview research can be undertaken.

Governmental and organizational regulations pertaining to access to samples should be examined to determine to what extent the population has already been studied. Many social work studies call for interviews of lower-income groups, ethnic minorities, or other populations that already consider themselves "overstudied." Their resentment and feelings of being used as guinea pigs for more affluent, mainstream investigators may impair the formal or informal group acceptance of the study. Many African Americans, for example, have suggested that what needs to be studied is white racism, not black family dynamics. Similarly, some gays feel that research studies should explore the homophobia of non-homosexuals, and some women feel that male investigators should study their own sexism.

Obtaining Organizational Consent

As we have seen in Chapter 3, many procedures have been adopted in recent years to protect people who are asked to participate in research studies. Studies supported by federal or other institutional funds or conducted under university auspices generally must be subjected to review by research committees, which must be satisfied that no harm will be done to the study's research participants. The National Institutes of Health requires that statements to that effect be filed for the studies it funds. Such reviews usually cover the measurement instruments to be used and the methods to be undertaken to safeguard the confidentiality of the research participants. The risks to research participants, as well as the benefits anticipated from the study, must be specified.

It is appropriate that social work researchers protect the rights of research participants as carefully as social work ethics and social service program policies protect the rights of clients. The ethics involved in social work research are discussed in Chapter 3.

Obtaining Potential Research Participant's Cooperation

Once organizational consent has been obtained, the researcher must secure evidence of the potential research participants' willingness to be interviewed. If the sample refuses, the result is nothing but a list of nonrespondents. The two most important elements in achieving a research participant's cooperation are (1) convincing the potential interviewees that their participation is important and that the study is legitimate, and (2) appealing to the potential interviewees' self-interest by showing how the results of their participation will be worthwhile to them.

Demonstrating the Importance and Legitimacy of the Study

Prospective interviewees will be more likely to participate if they are made aware that the proposed study is sponsored, approved by, or conducted under the auspices of a prestigious organization, social service program, or philanthropic association. This information is especially valuable if they are familiar with the organization and have positive experiences and feelings for it.

The endorsement of the organization can be demonstrated in a cover letter written under the organization's letterhead endorsing the project and encouraging the interviewees' cooperation. Such a letter should spell out the purposes of the study and reassure the potential research participant of the legitimacy of the project and the "safety" of their participation. The letter can also prepare the potential interviewees for a direct contact from the interviewer.

In the study of adoption postplacement services, letters to adoptive parents were sent to the sample selected for the study from the social service programs that had placed babies with the parents. The request letter attempted to communicate the following five points to the sample:

1. The program considered research important for improving services, and parents' participation in the present study would be helpful in accomplishing this.

2. The project had been legitimized by the involvement of both the adoption agency and the state division of child welfare.

3. There were reasons why the particular parents had been chosen to participate.

4. The parents were guaranteed confidentiality, and there were ways to safeguard this confidentiality.

5. The interviewer, identified by name, would contact them soon.

Appeal to Research Participants' Self-Interests

The cover letter presented in Figure 16.3 also appealed to the adoptive parents' self-interest. Many parents wished to show their appreciation to the program for having had a baby placed with them, and participating in the study afforded this opportunity. Many also wanted to help in any way they could to improve the quality of the programs' services, in view of their hopes of adopting more children. Others wanted a chance to express dissatisfaction with the services they had received.

There are also more general ways in which partici-

pating in interviews may appeal to research participants' self-interest. Being "selected" for a study in itself may be valued by those who enjoy the prospect of the attention they will receive. Participating in social work studies may appeal to the altruism of research participants and provide a chance to contribute to the common good, while demanding relatively little. The purposes of a study can often be phrased in a way that conveys the idea that the findings will help improve life, create a better society, aid individuals, or in some other fashion be beneficial to people or organizations.

Other techniques can enhance potential research participants' belief that they will get some benefit from being interviewed. When they are contacted to get their agreement to participate and to arrange for an appointment, for example, they should be told the limits of time and data to be required. The idea that the interview should be interesting—perhaps even fun—can be conveyed, and the interviewees can be offered a summary of the research findings if they request it.

For example, one research study found that when unmarried couples were approached to be interviewed

---

[Agency Letterhead]

Dear _____:

    Our agency recognizes research as a basic method for evaluating old ways and developing new ways of providing more effective services for couples adopting children. The State Division of Child Welfare, in cooperation with this and other Twin City adoption agencies, is currently conducting a study of the supervisory period in adoption.

    Because you have recently adopted a child through this agency, your experi ences and opinions would be of much value. We are therefore asking your cooperation in this study. Your participation will involve an interview between each of you and a researcher from the State Division of Child Welfare.

    We wish to emphatically assure you that the information requested in your interview will be treated confidentially by the researcher. Your observations and comments will in no way be identified with your name to this agency. Your information will be known only to the researcher who is conducting this study and will be incorporated anonymously, with that of many other adoptive parents, into the final research report.

    Within the next few weeks you will be called by Mr. Smith to arrange an appointment with you. We hope you will be able to participate in this most important study. Thank you for your anticipated cooperation.

Sincerely,

Executive Director

Figure 16.3
Example of a Simple Cover Letter Requesting a Research Interview

for a student research project that was to study the patterns and problems encountered in such relationships, a number expressed considerable interest in receiving the results of the study. They wanted to be able to compare their relationships to those of other couples who were studied. As perhaps a final resort, research participants may be paid a fee for participating in a research study. Such a procedure has been used in a study of delinquents and their rehabilitation, for example.

Of course, any promises, offers, and incentives given by the interviewer must be honored. Generally, prospective research participants will make themselves available if they feel a study is legitimate, will not demand excessive time, will respect their limits on what they choose to disclose, will protect their confidentiality, and will in some way be advantageous to them.

Another approach to encourage potential interviewee cooperation is to involve representatives, especially acknowledged leaders, of the population to be studied in the development of the research procedures and measurement instruments. This gives such populations greater commitment to the study, since it is not only *about* them but *for* them, and, at least partially, *by* them, as well. The involvement of representatives of the sample also provides useful inputs on such matters as areas to explore, access to the sample or population, and the language and phrasing of items.

DECIDING WHERE TO CONDUCT THE INTERVIEWS

Several locations may be available for conducting the interview: (1) the researchers' offices, (2) the interviewees' homes, or (3) "neutral" settings. The determination of which option to select may boil down to what is available, or where the interviewee is willing to be interviewed. However, if the interviewer has a choice, the advantages and disadvantages of the most common settings should be considered.

Offices

Conducting interviews in the offices of the sponsoring organization (assuming that space is available) is certainly the most economical arrangement in terms of money and time. Furthermore, it provides the researcher with the most control over environmental conditions, such as privacy, temperature, lighting, and seating arrangements. However, if research participants have to come to the site of the interviews, they are more vulnerable to the vagaries of motivation—they simply may not show up. The formality of the office setting may be intimidating to some research participants, who may make their discomfort evident by withholding or distorting responses.

This distortion is most likely if the office represents an organization whose services the interviewees are evaluating. They may be understandably cautious about giving honest feedback regarding services from a social service program in whose offices they are sitting. Such an arrangement could well call into question any promises of confidentiality.

Interviewees' Homes

Conducting the interview in the interviewee's home poses a number of problems. It takes time and money to get to and from interviewees' homes, and they may not even be there when the interviewer arrives, regardless of previous arrangements. Privacy may be limited if children and other family members and neighbors wander in and out. The physical surroundings (e.g., furniture arrangement) also may not be conducive to interviewing.

The home interview also offers a number of advantages, however. In the postplacement adoption services study, all parents were interviewed in their homes, and the social workers were interviewed in their offices. It was anticipated that the adoptive parents would be more relaxed and would behave and respond more naturally on their own turf. They would be less inhibited at home about evaluating the services they had received than they would have been in a social service program's office. Furthermore, the interviewer would have the opportunity to observe interactions between parents and their children in their natural settings.

A special problem with this setting was that both parents were to be interviewed separately, using the same instrument, and it was preferable that neither parent be biased by hearing the responses of the other. This would have been comparatively easy to arrange in an office by having one parent wait outside while the other was being interviewed. It was possible, however, to arrange for nearly the same privacy in the parents' home by starting the interview with both parents present and then instructing one parent to fill out some written checklists in another room while the other was being interviewed. Since there was nothing particularly confidential in the interviews, the fact that one parent would occasionally overhear the other was not considered a drawback to the use of the home as the site for the interviews.

Neutral Places

Some research interviews are best conducted on neutral territory—neither the interviewer's office nor the interviewee's home. With such research participants as teenagers or people with deviant lifestyles (e.g., prostitutes), a public setting may be the most acceptable setting for an interview. Although such settings may not be very private in terms of the proximity of strangers, they may be preferable to some interviewees because of the absence of family and acquaintances.

CHECKING THE INTERVIEWERS' APPEARANCE

Most research interviewers spend considerably less time with their research participants than social workers do with their clients. Because rapport must be established relatively quickly, the physical appearance of the interviewer is important.

Few studies have reported the effects of grooming and clothing on interviewers' effectiveness, but, as with other social work roles, an unobtrusive, neat, and conservative appearance that is compatible with the interviewees' standards of proper dress for someone in a researcher's role seems advisable. Interviewers should dress in a fashion fairly similar to that of the people they will be interviewing. A too well-dressed interviewer will probably not get good cooperation and responses from disadvantaged research participants, and a poorly dressed interviewer will have similar difficulties with others.

Too much jewelry, sexually provocative clothes, unorthodox hairstyles, or excessive makeup can all be distracting to those who are being interviewed. In brief contacts such as occur in research interviews, first appearances, including clothing and grooming, are cues that can profoundly affect the way people subsequently relate to each other.

Interviewers must create a climate in which their interviewees will be able and willing to provide clear and complete answers. Therefore, they should appear the way they anticipate the interviewees will expect them to appear.

The University of Michigan Survey Research Center employs interviewers throughout the United States to carry out studies on a wide variety of topics. The center's *Interviewer's Manual* instructs its interviewers to:

> Aim for simplicity and comfort: a simple suit or dress is best. Avoid identification with groups or orders (pins or rings, for instance, of clubs or fraternal orders). The respondent should be led to concentrate on you as a person and the interview you want to take, and not the way you are dressed.

The manual goes on to recommend that the interviewer always carry the "official blue folder." Interviewers may or may not have an official folder to carry with them, but a neat binder carried in a clean, untattered briefcase can enhance the image of a purposeful, well-organized interviewer, while a pile of dogeared papers balanced precariously could shatter it.

DEVELOPING THE INTERVIEWER-INTERVIEWEE RELATIONSHIP

There are both similarities and differences between worker-client and research interviewer-interviewee relationships. Ideally, both are purposeful, goal-directed relationships. Both are, or should be, guided by basic social work values and ethics regarding clients and research participants, such as respect for personal dignity, protection of confidentiality, and acceptance of the right to self-determination, including the right of the interviewee to refuse to answer any question. In both situations, the social worker and the researcher try to create a climate in which the client or the research participant will be able to provide honest and complete data.

But there are differences between the worker-client relationship and the researcher interviewer-interviewee relationship that some social workers may have difficulty adjusting to. The social worker who either conducts or supervises research interviews must understand these differences and accommodate them. The social work practice interview is generally focused on establishing a helping relationship and eliciting data in order to provide services to clients. In the research interview, however, acquiring data is an end in itself, although the long-range effect of the study may be beneficial to the interviewees.

Again, since the time for research interviews is limited and the parameters for the data to be obtained are predetermined (as opposed to the generally more open-ended goals of social work treatment interviews), research interviews tend to be much more focused. Social work relationships are often ongoing; research relationships are almost always relatively brief. The goal of social work *practice* interviews is to help a particular client system. The goal of *research* interviews is to obtain data about and from a particular population. The social worker represents help to be offered to the client; the research interviewer cannot make promises or commitments.

These differences in purpose account for the differences between worker-client and research interviewer-interviewee relationships. In the research interview, the interviewer takes the major (if not entire) responsibility for the direction of the interview, including the topics covered and the sequence of questions asked. In a social work interview, it is often preferable to follow the client's lead. The social work *practice* interview is for the *client*; the social work *research* interview is for the *interviewer*.

There is considerable evidence in research of clinical relationships that the therapists' communication of warmth, empathy, and genuineness to clients is positively associated with effective treatment. Whether similar communication by the research interviewer would enhance research interviews has not been determined; no studies are yet available that compare the effectiveness of research interviewers who have high ratings on any or all of these dimensions with the effectiveness of those who do not.

We could hypothesize that since these attributes in an interviewer seem to be effective because they allow interviewees to be truly themselves, to trust the interviewer, and to explore their feelings and experience more easily, they would be equally useful in enabling the research participant to provide more valid and reliable data. However, a number of the factors that differentiate research from treatment interviewing raise questions about just how much, and what kind of, warmth, empathy, and genuineness should be communicated in research interviews.

While research interviewers who communicate empathy may indeed be brought closer to their interviewees, at the same time this could make them "anticipate" or even prejudice their interviewees' answers. The interviewers might project themselves into their interviewees' feeling and beliefs, rather than objectively eliciting and recording their answers.

The warmth emanating from the interviewer also could delay or inhibit their interviewees from sharing personal data. It is sometimes easier to convey sensitive information to a neutral stranger than to a friend; witness the ease with which people reveal personal details to fellow passengers on an airplane. Objectivity and even professional detachment on the part of the interviewer may be more effective in obtaining valid and reliable answers.

It is neither fair to the interviewee nor an effective use of research time to involve interviewees in a pseudotherapeutic relationship, which the active communication of warmth and empathy may do. If interviewees reveal problems amenable to professional treatment intervention during the course of research interviews and indicate a desire to seek help, it would certainly be appropriate for interviewers to refer them to appropriate resources. But offering professional social work services is not the intent of research interviews.

Since there have been few studies to guide investigation of the interviewer-interviewee relationship, and since worker-client relationship research may be of limited applicability, we can only suggest some attributes of interviewers which may guide research interview relationships. Interviewers should:

1. Clearly communicate to the interviewees the purposes and limits of the interviewer's contact.
2. Be trustworthy, friendly, courteous, and kind to interviewees, yet focus clearly on the goals of the study.
3. Communicate to the interviewees that the interviewer's only interest in their answers is for the purposes of the study and that the interviewer has no personal interest in the responses. In conducting the sexual behavior interviews in Pomeroy's study cited at the beginning of this chapter, for example, the interviewers communicated to their research participants that, personally, they didn't care what sexual behaviors their interviewees reported, other than for the contribution a response could make to the study.

Certainly research interviewers, as social workers and human beings, care about any pain or suffering they may be told about, and they may well communicate this caring to their research participants who are being interviewed. However, the research process calls for the interviewer to omit neutral reactions to any data provided within the research interviews.

FORMULATING AND ASKING QUESTIONS

Most of the guidelines for formulating and asking questions in interviews are similar to those that have already been suggested for survey measuring instruments (see Chapters 10 and 17). Some of the basic guidelines that are especially applicable to asking questions in interviews are described in this section.

Keeping the Language Simple

The wording of questions should generally be simple, clear, and unobtrusive. Words from the average person's vocabulary, rather than the jargon of graduate social workers, should be used. "Meaningful others" is meaningless to most research participants. Generally, "angry" is better than "hostile," "sad" is better than "depressed," and certainly "brothers and sisters" is better than "siblings." It has been suggested that the interviewer should use the type of vocabulary usually found in most newspapers and popular magazines (*not* in professional journals). Further, the use of slang expressions such as "getting stoned," "giving head," or "being ripped off" may be unclear to research participants and may also "turn them off" to the interviewer.

Avoiding Double-Barreled Questions

The interviewee should be asked for only one reply at a time. There are three ways in which double-barreled questions can confuse research participants, thereby leaving the interviewer unsure about the intent of their answers. The first is that some double-barreled questions essentially ask two questions at once. For example, medical students on psychiatric rotation were given an interviewing schedule prepared by the staff psychiatrists to be used in obtaining a brief sexual history. One of the items was clearly double-barreled: "Have you ever masturbated *or* participated in a homosexual activity?" Of course, most patients hurriedly answered "no" (much to the relief of the medical students). What they were saying no to remained obscure.

A second type of double-barreled question starts with a statement of alleged fact that is the premise on which the question is based. For example, parents could be asked: "Of course, you wanted your daughter to finish high school. How did you go about keeping her going?" Such a question has a built-in bias that may or may not reflect the thinking or feelings of the interviewee.

The third type of double-barreled question is built on a hidden premise, such as the classic "When did you stop beating your child?" Some assumptions may be useful in facilitating questioning, but these must be used cautiously. It's best to assume very little. Assumptions often lead the interviewee to offer socially desirable but inaccurate answers.

Avoiding Double-Negative Questions

Double negatives imply a positive, and such questions can be confusing: "Do you feel that most married women would really prefer not to work if they were not under financial stress?" might better be phrased, "Do you feel most married women prefer to work only if they are under financial stress?"

Discouraging Biased Responses

Questions should be asked in such a way that the interviewee will not feel constrained to give only those answers that they perceive would fit generally accepted social norms. Research participants often choose to provide answers that sound good—whether they're true or not. For example, pupils in a third-grade class were asked to tell the teacher their greatest wish. Most of the children replied with such answers as "to go to Disneyland" or "to get a bicycle," but one boy said "to have peace on earth." The teacher was impressed and sent home a laudatory note to his parents. The student confided a few years later that he knew that answer would get him "strokes" from the teacher and that what he really wanted to answer was "to be able to fly!"

It will help those being interviewed to be more open about sensitive areas if such items are phrased in a way to convey the idea that the interviewer knows there is a wide range of human behaviors, most people have problems, and there is nothing (well, almost nothing) that will shock the interviewer.

One of the most effective ways to encourage research participants to answer questions truthfully, even if the answers might be embarrassing or violate social norms, is the "many people" technique. This approach enabled Pomeroy's investigators to uncover data about sexual behavior that might otherwise have been impossible to obtain.

For example, rather than asking a married adult "Do you masturbate?," which might prompt an immediate and defensive "no," the interviewer might say, "Many married men and women find that stimulating themselves to orgasm is a satisfying supplement to other sexual experiences" and then ask, "Have you found this to be true for you?" It is unlikely that such a question would lead people to answer "yes" if they did not masturbate at least occasionally, but it does provide support for a yes answer if that is the case. It also could pave the way to subsequent, more detailed items. Note that in the rephrased question the emotionally laden "masturbation" was replaced with the more cumbersome but less emotionally charged euphemism "stimulating yourself to orgasm." As long as a concept is clear in meaning, it is best to use the least emotionally charged word or phrase—even a euphemism—that describes it.

For example, it might be better to ask "How often is your behavior altered by drinking alcoholic beverages?" than "How often do you get drunk?" Similarly, "How often has an employer let you go?" may be a less threatening question than "How often have you been fired?"

Investigators also found that presenting a wide range of options for answers in random order enables research participants to avoid biasing their answers according to what might be expected of them. Thus, after asking the questions "How often do you and your husband have sexual intercourse?," the interviewers would add, "Once a month? Twice a day? Less than once a year? Four times a week? Every six months?" This provides interviewees with considerable latitude in answering what might otherwise be an embarrassing item.

It is often difficult for research participants to give negative evaluations of social service programs and the experiences they have had with these programs. A technique that can help them overcome this resistance is to ask paired questions that make it possible to offer both praise and criticism, ideally in that order. For example, "What did you like most about your social worker?" can be followed with "What did you like least about your social worker?" The overall effect of such pairs of questions is to elicit a balanced evaluation that can justify the expression of negative opinions or observations.

Avoiding Interviewer Bias

Research participants may feel, or be made to feel, that the research interview is essentially an examination or trial and that they must somehow please or satisfy the interviewer. Often, therefore, they will try to get the interviewer's opinions or experiences on particular questions before they respond.

Interviewers may bias answers by the way they phrase questions or by the expressions on their faces. They can also bias subsequent answers by their verbal and nonverbal reactions to responses. Asking the questions as consistently as possible, and reviewing tape recordings of interviewer-interviewee interchanges, can reduce this bias.

Reinforcing Interviewees' Answers

Research interviewees, like everyone else, respond to reinforcement. If interviewers demonstrate that they appreciate and value their interviewees' answers, the quality of subsequent answers will generally be enhanced. A previous study on the effects of experimental interviewing techniques used in health interview studies demonstrated that verbal reinforcement by the interviewer increased both the amount and the quality of research participants' recall in interviews. Without overdoing it, the interviewer can follow interviewees' answers with reactions ranging from a simple head nod and "uh-huh" to "Thanks for giving me such a detailed answer." Comments that do not evaluate the content of the response but do reinforce its completeness need not bias the interviewee.

RECORDING THE DATA

The final consideration in research interviewing is how best to record the interviewees' answers. The conversion of these answers to a pool of valid, useful data challenges the interviewer's skill in avoiding distortion or omission of data.

Generally, the recording procedure chosen should meet the following three criteria:

1. It should accurately record the manifest intent if not the exact wording of the interviewees' answers.
2. It should be as unobtrusive as possible so that it does not inhibit the flow of the interview or distract the interviewee from giving complete, candid answers.
3. It should facilitate transmittal of the data from the recording instrument to the data bank.

Interviews that rely on closed-ended questions are the easiest to record and run the least risk of recording distortion and bias. All the interviewer has to do is check, underline, or circle the appropriate answer on the interview schedule. At most, it is necessary to record a few words per answer.

Semistructured and unstructured interviews pose greater problems in recording. Two alternative methods of recording are available to interviewers: (1) handwritten and (2) mechanical.

Using Handwritten Recording

In the unlikely event that interviewers were skilled at taking shorthand, they would still have difficulty taking down their interviewees' answers verbatim. And, even if that were possible, excessive note taking can be distracting not only to those who are being interviewed but to the interviewers, as well. Furthermore, verbatim responses are rarely necessary for recording useful data. The interviewer may choose to wait until the interview is over and then try to recall and record answers as completely and accurately as possible. However, this procedure is risky. The interviewer may forget significant answers and nuances. Furthermore, if the researcher has interviewed a number of research participants in a relatively short amount of time, one respondent's answers may blur with another's, seriously distorting the data.

A safer procedure is for the interviewer to record summaries of responses from time to time throughout the interview, supplemented with direct quotations for illustrative purposes. If necessary, the interviewer may interrupt or slow down the interviewee with such comments as "Wait a second, that was an interesting point, I want to get it down in my notes." Again, the social work research interview is different from a social work practice interview. The purpose of research interviews is clearly defined as data gathering, not service delivery. Therefore, while note taking may be distracting and even inappropriate in a treatment interview, it can be an acceptable and integral part of the research interview.

However, the recording procedures used by research interviewers should be as brief and uncomplicated as possible. This can be achieved by developing a coding procedure and other shortcuts to recording data—as long as the interviewer can remember what the notes and codes mean. Pomeroy's sexual behavior investigators, for example, developed a code by which they could record extensive, detailed sexual life histories on a single index card.

Using Mechanical Recording

The development of compact, reliable cassette recorders makes it possible to record exactly what is said by the interviewees. Furthermore, once the recorder is turned on, it provides none of the distractions that handwritten recording can. Clients generally have no objection to being recorded. A research participant should, of course, be informed that an interview is being recorded. However, no extensive discussion of its use is necessary unless the interviewee initiates such a discussion.

Although there are obvious advantages to the absolute accuracy that mechanical recording can provide, tape-recorded data has their limitations. Machines can break down, tapes can break, and microphones can pick up background noises that obscure the comments of the interviewee. Occasionally, research participants will object to having their comments recorded. The greatest limitation, however, is the considerable time and expense of either transcribing the recording or listening to the entire recording for research analysis. In some ways, this is a duplication of energy, since the interviewees' answers have already been heard by the interviewer while the interview was being taped. It is possible, however, that after the taped interviews have been analyzed, the researcher will choose additional variables to study and return to the original tapes for reanalysis. Thus, taped interviews provide more comprehensive and flexible data.

SUMMARY

This overview of interviewing in social work research began with a consideration of the advantages of research interviewing over questionnaires in self-report surveys and of some of the limitations of interviews in research. The tasks in planning and organizing interview-based research were then discussed: determining the content of interviews and developing the interview schedule, phrasing the questions, selecting the interviewers, gaining access to the research participants, deciding where to conduct the interviews, deciding how interviewers should be groomed and dressed, and being aware of the nature of effective interviewer-interviewee relationships. Finally, the manner in which questions should be asked in the interview and procedures for recording answers were explored.

Throughout this discussion, differences and similarities between treatment and research interviews have been described. While there are numerous differences, the significance of social work skills, knowledge, and values for research interviewing must be stressed.

As we know, using interviewing as a form of data collection is obtrusive; that is, the researcher intrudes into the research participants' lives in some form or another. The following chapter continues our discussion of obtrusive data collection methods by presenting how a social work research study can use another obtrusive data collection method, known as surveys.

Surveys

17

Steven L. McMurtry

· · · · · · · · · · · · · · · · · · · ·

Almost everyone has been asked to take part in a survey of some form or another—a curbside interview, an exit poll after voting, a mass-mailed marketing survey, a seemingly random telephone opinion poll. To some extent, every research study that uses a survey as the data collection method can be called "survey research."

These studies can be designed to achieve a variety of ends, but they all seek to collect data from many individuals in order to understand something about them as a whole. It is essential, therefore, that survey research procedures produce data that are accurate, reliable, and representative so that findings can be generalized from a sample to the larger population or to different research situations. Survey research thus is a systematic way of collecting data by obtaining opinions or answers from selected research participants who represent the population of interest, or, occasionally, from an entire population.

The major steps in survey research are outlined on the left side of Figure 17.1, and the tasks to be completed in each step are listed on the right side.

Development and application of the sampling plan are essential to ensure the representativeness of the data collected (see Chapter 11). In most surveys, random sampling procedures are used to increase the probability that every person in the population has an equal opportunity of being selected for the sample. Probability sampling makes it possible to calculate the degree to which the sample is representative of the population from which it was drawn.

The steps in the research process that are unique to the survey method of data collection correspond to the measurement process that is at the center of any research effort. These steps include the construction of the survey questionnaire, the collection of the data, and to some extent, the coding and analysis of the data.

Survey research was introduced in Chapter 10 as an example for the discussion of the design and construction of measuring instruments. Surveys can be used to collect data on facts about individuals separately and in organizations and communities, as well as data on their behaviors and on unobservable variables such as attitudes, beliefs, feelings, and ethical standards.

SURVEY RESEARCH DESIGNS

Because survey research studies social phenomena by collecting data on numerous individuals in order to understand the group or population they represent, the research designs used usually follow the principles of group designs discussed in Chapter 13.

Knowledge Level

As can be seen in Figure 1.5, the knowledge levels at which research studies are conducted are arranged on a three-point continuum from exploratory at the lowest level, to descriptive, to explanatory at the highest level, where "ideal" experiments can be conducted. Data can be collected with surveys at all three levels of design.

In exploratory designs, data are collected in order to form general ideas and tentative theories about the research question. In descriptive designs, the collection of data should result in more specific descriptions of the variables of interest; surveys are used as the data collection method in most descriptive studies to gather data on a sample or population in order to characterize it in terms of the variables under study.

A survey design that serves a descriptive purpose can also be exploratory if the collection of data allows the formulation of hypotheses that can be submitted to further study. One way this can be accomplished is with the use of open-ended questions in the survey instrument.

Explanatory research designs are concerned with developing an understanding of social phenomena on the basis of the relationships among the variables of interest. Surveys are less commonly thought of as tools for explanatory studies, but they can be used effectively in these situations. Consider an executive director in a social work agency who is trying to determine whether the agency should adopt a new technique for counseling victims of violent crime. For a number of reasons, it is decided that an experimental study (in which clients would be randomly assigned to the old or new method) is just not feasible. The director, however, reasons that another way to assess the quality of the new counseling approach would be to ask clients how satisfied they were with the outcomes it produced. This is a very simple

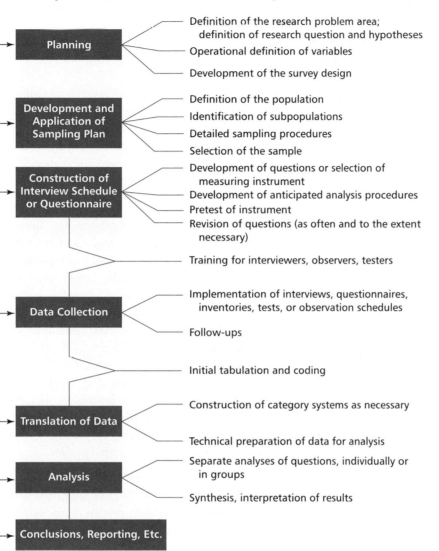

Steps in
Survey Research   Major Tasks

Figure 17.1 Steps and Tasks in the Survey Research Process

Planning — Definition of the research problem area; definition of research question and hypotheses
— Operational definition of variables
— Development of the survey design

Development and Application of Sampling Plan — Definition of the population
— Identification of subpopulations
— Detailed sampling procedures
— Selection of the sample

Construction of Interview Schedule or Questionnaire — Development of questions or selection of measuring instrument
— Development of anticipated analysis procedures
— Pretest of instrument
— Revision of questions (as often and to the extent necessary)

— Training for interviewers, observers, testers

Data Collection — Implementation of interviews, questionnaires, inventories, tests, or observation schedules
— Follow-ups

— Initial tabulation and coding

Translation of Data — Construction of category systems as necessary
— Technical preparation of data for analysis

Analysis — Separate analyses of questions, individually or in groups
— Synthesis, interpretation of results

Conclusions, Reporting, Etc.

explanatory research problem, but in this case the only way to address it would be with survey methods, such as mailing self-administered questionnaires to former clients of the agency.

The Dimension of Time

The dimension of time also must be taken into account in deciding on a survey research design. Most phenom-ena are subject to change over time, and many variables that are of interest in social work research, such as atti-tudes, emotional states, and social service utilization, can change rapidly. The two basic types of survey research designs are defined in terms of whether the variable is to be measured once, with a cross-sectional design, or over time, with a longitudinal design. Examples of these two types of survey designs are discussed in Chapter 13—the cross-sectional survey and the longitudinal survey.

To find out how satisfied an agency's clients are with the quality of services they have received, for example, the simplest and most direct approach would be to survey a sample of former clients about their attitudes toward services at the time they terminated. Even though a few weeks might be needed to survey enough clients to secure a sample of reasonable size, all data would be collected within a narrow time interval to provide data on clients' attitudes toward services at the time of termination. Cross-sectional designs use a "snapshot" method of data collection to provide data that are specific to a particular point in time.

If only the most satisfied clients actually complete the program, however, and many others who are dissatisfied drop out before completion, surveying only those who completed the program could provide a distorted picture of the true level of client satisfaction with the program. To control for this threat to internal validity, a sample of clients might be followed from the start of services until they have all either dropped out or completed them. During this time, regular measurements would be taken of the clients' satisfaction with their services, and the variation of these measurements across time would be evaluated. Longitudinal designs use this method of data collection to monitor changes in variables of interest over an extended period of time.

Cross-Sectional Designs

Studies based on cross-sectional designs are usually associated with exploratory and descriptive research designs because they do a good job of providing data on the characteristics of a sample or population. A cross-sectional survey can be used to determine whether a particular problem exists within a group of clients and what the level of the problem is. Needs assessments, used by community development workers to identify neighborhood problems and service gaps, are an example. The principal advantage of this approach to survey research is that the necessary data can be collected quickly and inexpensively.

Cross-sectional studies are also used in explanatory designs to test relationships among characteristics of members of a sample or population. The main problem

with these studies is that, because of their one-shot nature, they cannot clearly establish the time order of variables (see Chapter 12).

Longitudinal Designs

In longitudinal studies, data on the characteristics of a sample or population are collected over two or more time periods, which allows consideration of how the sample's characteristics have changed. The three types of longitudinal studies—trend, cohort, and panel studies—all use this repeated-measures approach to data collection.

Trend Studies. Trend studies utilize data from surveys carried out at periodic intervals on samples drawn from a particular population. The U.S. Department of Labor, under contract with the Census Bureau, for example, conducts the Current Population Survey (CPS) every March. Though a new sample is drawn each year, the population of interest remains the same. The data collected by the CPS are used primarily to gauge annual trends in unemployment and labor-force participation, but they also provide valuable data on other changes in the characteristics of the U.S. population. The accuracy of the assessments of trends revealed by these types of surveys depends on their regular use over a considerable period of time.

Cohort Studies. Cohort studies focus on specific groups of people who share certain characteristics. A cohort can be defined as a set of individuals who undergo a particular experience at a certain time, such as all high school graduates who enter college in a certain year. Successive random samples are drawn from this group to monitor how the characteristics of members change over time. The baby boom generation is an example of a birth cohort—in this case, all persons born in the period from approximately 1946 to 1962. Studies of random samples of its members have been used to identify trends in American life, from fashion to family structure to political preferences.

A foster care administrator might use a cohort study to evaluate services to children who entered foster homes during a particular year. In each subsequent year, a random sample would be drawn from among members of the cohort who remained in care, and data from these samples could be used to distinguish children who had exited quickly from the program from those who had experienced long or repeated stays in out-of-home care.

Panel Studies.   Both trend studies and cohort studies monitor changes in a population through the use of a series of random samples of the members of the group, with each sample comprising a different group of individuals. In contrast, a panel study is designed to follow the same set of individuals over time and to collect data on a regular basis.

Some of the best-known research studies on the effects of public assistance programs have come from the Panel Study on Income Dynamics (PSID), conducted by researchers at the University of Michigan's Survey Research Center. The project began with 5,000 families in 1968 and included more than 20,000 families some 20 years later. The longitudinal nature of this study has enabled researchers to examine transitions into and out of poverty and to study events associated with these transitions through related studies that have produced important results. Mary Jo Bane (1986), for example, studied episodes of poverty among children in the sample, recognizing that most poor children are not always poor but instead live in families that move into and out of poverty as their circumstances change. Her findings showed that many white children made the transition into poverty as a result of becoming part of a female-headed household; for African American children, in contrast, poverty more often resulted from being born into a poor family.

Social workers have begun to recognize the advantages offered by longitudinal studies over the cross-sectional approach. The opportunity to monitor the service histories of clients or groups over time is often more valuable than simply determining their average condition at a particular point in time. Still, longitudinal designs are more costly, time-consuming, and complex than cross-sectional studies. In addition, the successful use of longitudinal designs requires careful planning and an orientation toward long-term rather than short-term research goals.

GROUP-ADMINISTERED SURVEYS

As we have seen in Chapter 16, the critical barrier to the use of face-to-face interviews is the expense involved in hiring, training, and transporting interviewers. The obvious solution to this problem is to devise means whereby research participants can complete the survey instrument by themselves without the necessity of having an interviewer present.

Group-administered questionnaires are used in situations where research participants can be brought together for the purpose of completing a survey instrument. The questionnaire is distributed to a group of research participants who complete it individually, though a member of the research team is usually present to assist. A cover letter to explain the project and obtain the research participants' consent should be handed out with the questionnaire (see Figure 16.3). A more detailed discussion of cover letters for use with self-administered questionnaires is given in the section on mail surveys.

To assess client satisfaction with agency services, for example, we might begin by sampling clients by community areas and making arrangements for those living in each area to gather at a central location. The cost of securing a meeting place and transporting clients to and from the site is likely to be much less than the cost of sending interviewers to many locales to meet with individual research participants.

The arrangements for group administration are outlined in Figure 17.2. In addition, a checklist for introducing group-administered questionnaires to potential research participants is displayed in Figure 17.3.

Group administration is also used with groups that meet on a regular basis. An agency administrator examining social workers' reactions to revised state guidelines for assistance to low-income people could use this approach, for example. At a regular meeting of workers for case staffings and training, questionnaires could be distributed to solicit workers' anonymous opinions on the change and their experiences in acquainting clients with the new regulations.

Group administration is less expensive than face-to-face interviews (see Chapter 16), and it usually yields a much higher response rate than mail surveys. Never-

	Yes	No
1. Are there enough questionnaires?	____	____
2. Have plans been developed for persons unable to attend the questionnaire completion session to complete and return the instrument at another time?	____	____
3. Have all staff been notified in writing and verbally at a staff meeting about the date and time of the group administration?	____	____
4. Has the physical environment been checked in advance to make sure there will be sufficient space and adequate lighting for writing?	____	____
5. Have efforts been made to anticipate and eliminate possible sources of noise or distraction during the questionnaire completion session?	____	____
6. Are there plans to read aloud the instructions on the face sheet at the questionnaire completion session?	____	____
7. Will specific instructions be given on how to mark the questionnaire or answer sheet?	____	____
8. Is sufficient time allowed for questions from respondents before beginning to complete the questionnaire?	____	____
9. Will clarification announcements based on respondents' questions about an item on the questionnaire be made slowly, in a clear voice that is loud enough for all to hear?	____	____
10. Are all questionnaires to be collected immediately after completion and checked for completed identification information and consent form signature?	____	____
11. Have all respondents been informed of a sign-up roster to receive copies of the results of the study?	____	____
12. Will each respondent be personally thanked when the questionnaire is returned?	____	____
13. Are follow-up letters to be sent to agency administrators and key staff members who facilitate the implementation of the group-administered questionnaire?	____	____

Figure 17.2   Checklist for Administration of Group-Administered Questionnaires

	Yes	No
1. Does the face sheet of the questionnaire include general information about the purpose of the study?	_____	_____
2. Is there an indication of how much time it should take to complete the questionnaire?	_____	_____
3. Is a separate consent form attached to the questionnaire for the respondent to sign?	_____	_____
4. Does the face sheet include all necessary instructions for completing all items (e.g., "Don't skip around," "Answer all items to the best of your ability")?	_____	_____

Figure 17.3 Checklist for Introducing Group-Administered Questionnaires

theless, for numerous other reasons, mailed questionnaires are the type of self-administered survey that is used most frequently.

MAIL SURVEYS

Until recently, when telephone surveys became commonplace, mail questionnaires were the method of data collection most commonly associated with survey research. In the United States, the most familiar example of a mail survey is the national population census conducted every 10 years by the Bureau of the Census, most recently in March 2000. Though the census still makes some use of face-to-face interviews, most of the data are collected from mail questionnaires.

Indeed, with a survey that attempts to collect data on the entire population of a country with some 290 million people, no other method of data collection currently used would be economically feasible. The U.S. census is unusual because it attempts to cover an entire population rather than a sample of its members, but it demonstrates the importance of mail surveys in allowing us to study a much larger number of research participants than would otherwise be possible.

By far the most important advantage of mail surveys is their low unit cost. These savings are possible because recipients themselves complete the questionnaire, so there is no cost for interviewers' time, and the survey instrument is both delivered and returned by mail, which is substantially less expensive than transporting interviewers to and from research participants' locations. Mail surveys also usually are less expensive than telephone interviews, particularly where research participants are widely distributed geographically. The cost of mailing a questionnaire is the same whether it is mailed across town or across the country.

The fact that the questionnaire is self-administered, so that no contact with another person is required, can be a disadvantage. Research participants who do not understand a question cannot readily obtain clarification, and more detailed verbal responses cannot be recorded. At the same time, there are no problems with interviewer error or bias, either in asking for data or in recording the research participant's responses.

Reliance on written instruments can also be a liability. It is virtually impossible to write a questionnaire that does not contain at least a few potentially confusing questions. In the absence of an interviewer who can explain the questions, research participants must interpret each one as best they can, which increases the possibility of error in the data. Moreover, written questionnaires are useful only with research participants who have the reading comprehension, sight, and other physical capacities necessary to complete the forms. Surveys of populations that include illiterate or visually or physically disabled persons cannot make use of these instruments unless personnel are assigned to assist research participants who are unable to complete the questionnaires on their own.

Nevertheless, the ability of mail surveys to present questions in written form can greatly enhance both the clarity of the questions and the types of data that can be gathered. Interview schedules, for example, have a restricted range of response categories for a given question because research participants can keep only a limited number of options in mind. Written questionnaires can list a wide range of options for review and reference as necessary.

Graphic illustrations of response categories also can be provided to enhance research participants' understanding. A study that would focus on children, for example, could use pictorial scales, including one that offered response categories in the form of simple drawings of faces with expressions ranging from happy to sad. Children who might not comprehend the numerical gradations on a typical rating scale could then use this type of visual representation to express variations in their feelings.

Overcoming the Disadvantage of Low Response Rates

The primary disadvantage of a mail survey is its low response rate. A person who receives a questionnaire in the mail usually can opt not to participate by passive means such as setting it aside and forgetting it, deciding not to fill it out, or throwing it away. Choosing not to participate in other types of surveys usually involves a more direct (and therefore more difficult) refusal.

Without careful efforts to increase returns, it is not uncommon for mail surveys to yield response rates of only 10 to 20 percent. Rates this low call into question the external validity of the data, which has its basis in the assumption that those who did return the questionnaire constitute a sample that is representative of the larger population. The measurement validity of a survey design, or the assumption that the survey measures what it is supposed to measure and does so accurately, also can be jeopardized by a low response rate.

To ensure the most accurate count in the 1990 national census of the U.S. population, massive information programs preceded the mailing of official survey forms to residential addresses, follow-ups were sent requesting compliance with instructions to complete the forms, and face-to-face interviews were conducted among the homeless, immigrants, and others who might be missed. Nevertheless, after a follow-up survey, including a random sample of racial, ethnic, and other groups, the Census Bureau reported in June 1991

that the 1990 census had missed 2.1 percent of the U.S. population overall and that 4.8 percent of African Americans and 5.2 percent of Hispanics had not been counted. By the revised figures, the U.S. population was 253.9 million in 1990, 5.3 million people more than had originally been counted, and the percentages of African Americans and Hispanics missed were more than double the average.

There are no absolute standards for response rates in mail surveys used by social workers, and the question of what constitutes a minimally acceptable response rate can be a difficult one. Earl R. Babbie (2004) offers a rough guide of 50 percent as an "adequate" response rate, 60 percent as a "good" rate, and 70 percent as "very good." This is consistent with the views of most social work researchers, but the question still remains about what to do with studies that yield lower response rates.

This question is gaining greater immediacy as mail survey research becomes harder to carry out effectively. The proliferation of pseudosurveys, such as sales promotions or political tracts disguised as questionnaires, along with surveys that are poorly designed or executed, make the public less willing to participate. Because of this, those of us who conduct legitimate, good-quality studies are struggling to obtain adequate response rates.

When initial response rates are low, we must be willing to make a dispassionate and open-minded assessment of whether our study is worth pursuing further. Among the questions to be considered in such an assessment are these:

- Have procedures for maximizing response rates been fully employed (see discussion in this chapter), and is it clear that further follow-up efforts would not be helpful?
- What are the potential sources of bias in the responses received (e.g., is it likely that certain types of sample members responded while others did not)? What effect might these biases have had, and how substantial is that effect?
- Did the original sample include extra cases (an oversample) in anticipation of survey nonresponse? If so, was the number of extra cases appropriate to the actual number of nonresponses?

- What is the purpose of the study? Will the benefits of providing data on a previously little-studied topic outweigh the risks of reporting results that may be inaccurate due to low response rates? What data will be provided to readers to allow them to make their own judgments about this issue?

As these questions suggest, determination of what constitutes a satisfactory response rate is more often a matter of reasoned judgment than of the application of absolute standards. In general, the best way to deal with the problem is to minimize it through vigorous efforts to reduce nonresponses. The following sections of this chapter offer ways in which response rates can be optimized without sacrificing the cost-effectiveness and other advantages of mail surveys.

Use a Good Cover Letter

A straightforward, easy-to-read cover letter may improve return rates and response accuracy more than any other single factor, while a vague or highly technical letter can have the opposite effect. A good cover letter for a mail survey should perform the following functions:

- Give the exact date of the mailing of the questionnaire
- Identify the researcher and institutional affiliation, preferably on official, printed stationery that is unique to the project or organization
- Explain the research project sufficiently to allow the research participant to understand its general purpose, but not in such detail as to be confusing or discouraging
- Explain the significance of the study in terms of its potential benefit to policy or practice
- Convey to the research participant the importance of participation in the study
- Estimate how long the questionnaire will take to complete
- Explain how the responses are to be used and how confidentiality will be maintained
- Instruct the research participant how to return the completed form
- Identify the person to contact with questions or concerns about the survey

Some cover letters contain basic instructions on how to complete a questionnaire, but detailed directions should usually be reserved for the survey instrument. Some also specify a date by which the questionnaire is to be returned. This gives research participants a greater sense of urgency about the project, but the message must be carefully worded so that they do not feel they are being pressured.

Before word processors made it easy to personalize letters, generic cover letters that were not addressed to any particular individual were used, or stick-on labels identical to those used to address the envelopes were added to the letters. Now most word processing and data management software programs for desktop computers can create individual labels and merge the names into the text of the letter. Personalized cover letters, which improve the likelihood of a response, then can be generated quickly and easily. The computerized label file also can produce address labels for the mailing envelopes, or, with some computer printers, envelopes can be fed in and addressed directly from the file. See Figure 17.4 for a brief checklist for developing cover letters.

Reduce Mailing Costs

Preparing a survey mailing becomes a balancing act between minimizing mailing costs and maximizing the appearance and readability of the questionnaire and the likelihood that it will be completed and returned. In an era of scarce funding for social programs in general and research projects in particular, the ability to cut costs is a critical factor in the successful completion of a study.

One problem is how to minimize the weight of the questionnaire in order to reduce the cost of both the initial mailing and the return postage. A comparatively easy option is to use both sides of the paper when printing the instrument, but this does not work when single sheets are stapled together.

The cover letter may appear on the front page of the booklet, with the questionnaire beginning on the first inside or first right-hand page. Using double-sided printing can cut as much as half the weight of the questionnaire. With lengthy instruments, it also reduces bulkiness, making them appear less formidable to research participants.

	Yes	No
1. Does the letter communicate the appeal to respondents?	___	___
2. Does it include a reasonable explanation of the study by anticipating and countering respondents' questions?	___	___
3. Does it set forth the benefits of the study?	___	___
4. Does it describe the importance of the respondent to the study and indicate that no one else can be substituted?	___	___
5. Does it exceed the maximum of one page?	___	___
6. Does it appear under an appropriate letterhead?	___	___
7. Do the individualized name and address and the date appear on the letter?	___	___
8. Is the investigator's individually applied signature included?	___	___
9. Does the letter include a confidentiality statement and explanation of the coding procedures?	___	___
10. Does the attachment to the cover letter include a stamped, self-addressed questionnaire reply envelope?	___	___
11. Does the letter indicate how results will be shared with respondents?	___	___
12. Are there instructions for indicating that a copy of the results is wanted (e.g., placing name and address on back of return envelope)?	___	___
13. Is the letter reproduced on a word processor?	___	___

Figure 17.4 Checklist for Developing a Cover Letter

Other savings can be obtained in mailing survey instruments by using bulk mail rates or special discounts for nonprofit organizations. Bulk mail rates are based on volume—the larger the number of mailings, the cheaper the rate. The discount is higher still for nonprofit agencies.

Using bulk mail rates does have certain drawbacks. One is that the U.S. Postal Service requires all such mailings to be sorted by zip code before being delivered to the post office. This regulation can involve substantial expense in studies with a large number of mailings, and it has prompted many researchers to organize lists of survey recipients by zip code rather than in alphabetical order. Another drawback is that bulk mail receives the lowest priority for handling, and slow delivery can cause problems if a timely response is needed.

Moreover, letters sent by bulk mail to incorrect or nonexistent addresses are usually discarded by the Postal Service, rather than returned to the sender, and this makes the survey's nonresponse rate seem higher than it actually is. A comparatively new drawback of bulk mailings is their effect on recipients as mass mailings have proliferated. Many recipients have become skilled in spotting "junk" mail, usually by looking for the bulk mail classification on the postage stamp or meter mark, and envelopes bearing such marks are often discarded without being opened.

For any of these reasons, when a high return rate is important, we may choose to bear the added expense of first-class (or sometimes even special delivery) mail rates in order to improve the chances that the mail will be delivered on time, opened, and examined.

Enclose Suitable Return Envelopes

Another consideration in preparing mailings is to make it easy for research participants to return the completed questionnaire. Usually, a return envelope is enclosed in the initial mailing, in most cases with return postage attached. The return envelope must fit easily inside the outgoing envelope but be large enough to accommodate the completed questionnaire.

Too little postage on the return envelope will cause the questionnaire to be sent back to the research participant, so the questionnaire should be weighed with the return envelope to determine the exact amount of postage needed. In the United States, an alternative is to use business reply envelopes. Users of such envelopes are billed only for questionnaires that are returned, but business reply mail is billed at a higher rate than regular postage, so it might not be cost-effective when high return rates are expected. Because bulk mail rates cannot be used on return envelopes, it is not unusual for the cost of returns to exceed that of outgoing mailings. A checklist for survey mailing procedures can be found in Figure 17.5.

Ensure the Confidentiality of Research Participants

Including some sort of identification of research participants on survey instruments is helpful in keeping track of those who have completed and returned them, so that the number of follow-ups necessary is reduced. However, the use of any type of identifier (such as a number) can jeopardize the principle of confidentiality of participants. One way to deal with this is to inform research participants that identifying information included on the questionnaires in the form of a numerical code can be interpreted only from a master list retained by those administering the survey. Research participants also should be apprised of the measures that will be taken to maintain the security of this list and assured that it will be destroyed once the study has been completed.

Instead of identifying information on the questionnaire, each initial mailing could include a self-addressed, stamped postcard with coded information identifying the research participant. When research participants return these postcards separately at the same time they put the completed questionnaires in the mail, we can identify those who have returned the survey without being able to link them to a particular completed form. Follow-ups then need to be sent only to

	Yes	No
1. Is the envelope an unusual size, shape, or color to attract attention, along with embellishments such as "Immediate reply requested"?	___	___
2. Has the size of the questionnaire and envelope been determined in relationship to using first-class postage and minimizing the appearance of bulky contents?	___	___
3. Has a mailing list been developed that includes the number of the questionnaire beside the name of the respondent?	___	___
4. Are the envelope contents folded together when inserted so that respondents will find all relevant materials on opening the envelope?	___	___
5. Is the mailing planned for early in the week in anticipation of time needed to forward mail to new addresses?	___	___
6. Will the mailing avoid a holiday period when respondents are likely to be away from home, and will it avoid December and the crush of holiday mail?	___	___

Figure 17.5 Checklist for Survey Mailing Procedures

those who did not return the postcards and the completed questionnaires.

Follow Up on the Mailing

Procedures for following an initial mailing with subsequent reminders are often crucial to attaining a satisfactory return rate. The two major considerations in planning follow-ups are timing, or the intervals at which follow-ups should be sent, and format, or the types of follow-ups to be sent. Generally, for any survey there should be at least two follow-ups at roughly three-week intervals.

These intervals can be reduced if initial returns are slow, but postponing follow-ups for more than three weeks risks losing the impact of the mailings. More than two follow-ups also may be appropriate, particularly if each is successful in bringing in a new wave of returns.

A variety of formats may be used for follow-ups, including postcards, letters, additional copies of the questionnaire, telephone calls, and face-to-face contacts. Donald A. Dillman (1999) argues for the use of a variety of these methods, with certain types of follow-ups occurring at specific intervals after the initial mailing. A postcard reminder is sent one week after the initial mailing;

a follow-up letter, with an additional copy of the questionnaire and return envelope, two weeks later; and a final letter and another questionnaire copy and return envelope by certified mail on the seventh week following the initial mailing.

Some of us have added telephone contacts to this sequence. These can be extremely effective, because they convey our desire to obtain a response much more personally and directly than is possible in a letter, and they can produce immediate responses. A checklist for survey follow-up procedures is found in Figure 17.6.

TELEPHONE SURVEYS

Indeed, telephone surveys have become something of a modern phenomenon, assuming a place in the mind of the public that was once occupied by person-on-the-street interviewers or door-to-door census takers. These developments have been both favorable and unfavorable for surveys, as is shown in this section.

One reason for the growth of telephone surveys is that they offer many of the merits of face-to-face interviews and mail survey techniques, without some of their drawbacks. Telephone interviews are relatively inexpen-

	Yes	No
1. Is there a preprinted follow-up postcard for mailing one week after mailing of cover letter?	_____	_____
2. Does the postcard include the respondent's name and address and the investigator's signature?	_____	_____
3. Does it thank the respondent if the questionnaire has already been returned?	_____	_____
4. Is a second follow-up letter ready for sending three weeks after mailing of the cover letter, with a replacement questionnaire and return envelope?	_____	_____
5. Is a third follow-up letter ready for certified mailing to remaining nonrespondents seven weeks after original mailing, with a replacement questionnaire and return envelope?	_____	_____

Figure 17.6   Checklist for Survey Follow-Up Procedures

sive, particularly compared to face-to-face interviews, because there are no transportation costs for either the interviewers or the research participants.

Moreover, local telephone calls are often cheaper than first-class postage, and even if long-distance calls are necessary, WATS lines and other discounts for high-volume calling can keep unit costs comparatively low. Printing expenses also are generally lower for telephone surveys because interviewers need only one copy of an interview schedule. Nevertheless, telephone surveys are more expensive than mailings, falling about midway between mail surveys and face-to-face interviews.

Another reason telephone interviews are popular is that studies that employ this technique can be completed much faster than those that use other methods. Survey findings based on a representative sample of the U.S. population can be obtained by telephone interviewers in less than 24 hours, provided that a large and well-trained staff of interviewers, ample access to direct-dial long-distance telephone lines, and a prepared and tested interview schedule are all available.

Political pollsters and other public opinion research firms now employ telephone methods almost exclusively, for example. Opinion poll results and survey ratings of winners and losers in political debates can be announced quickly, because interviewers can enter responses directly into a computer file that can be analyzed immediately once the data collection has been completed.

As with face-to-face interviews, in telephone interviews an interviewer is present to offer assistance to research participants who need it. Thus, it is possible to directly explain instructions, clarify questions, and deal with any other concern a research participant may have.

Limitations

The interaction of an interviewer with research participants is not always an advantage in telephone surveys. It can be a drawback, because it introduces opportunities for interviewer bias in data collection and coding. This source of error must be controlled for through the careful selection and training of the interviewers. At the same time, because telephone interviews do not allow visual contact between the interviewer and research

participant, establishing rapport with research participants and gaining their trust and cooperation is more difficult. In addition, there is no opportunity to observe or record nonverbal communication.

Because the time research participants are willing to talk with an interviewer is usually much shorter on the telephone than in person, both the length of the survey instrument and the scope of research participants' answers are restricted. Telephone interview schedules also must be kept simple and direct because research participants cannot refer to written versions of the questions. To allow more latitude, a cover letter and questionnaire may be sent by mail in advance for research participants to use as a reference during the telephone interview. Of course, this appreciably increases costs.

Despite the fact that the great majority of households now have telephones, a disproportionate number of poor people are among those who do not. This is important for social work researchers because low-income families make up a sizable share of social service clients, and underrepresentation of these individuals can lead to measurement error in survey results. Accordingly, telephone surveys are inappropriate for use with rural populations or in geographic areas that are known to have a large number of low-income residents.

Sampling Approaches for Telephone Surveys

Most sampling approaches used with face-to-face interviews or mail surveys can also be used in telephone surveys. It can be more difficult to obtain telephone numbers than addresses of potential research participants, however. Even if most people have telephones, some will have unlisted numbers, which are not available to researchers. In some parts of the country (California, for example), the proportion of households with unlisted numbers is almost one-half. Since such households may differ in some systematic way from those with listed numbers, a sample that excludes them can threaten the external validity of the data for making inferences about the population of interest.

One way to address this problem is with random-digit dialing (RDD), in which numbers that have been generated at random are dialed. In fact, RDD is not entirely random, since most research projects are targeted toward a particular geographic location, and telephone companies generally assign seven-digit numbers with different three-digit prefixes for various localities. Thus, a researcher interested in households in a particular neighborhood who knows that all residents of that area have telephone numbers that begin with 256, 257, 292, or 294 can restrict the selection of random numbers to the range of possible telephone numbers that begin with these four prefixes.

As a rule, the best use of RDD is for studies in which results from a sample will be generalized to the entire population of interest. The selection of potential sample members cannot be narrowed by any other criteria than three-digit prefixes or area codes that encompass an entire city or metropolitan area. In public opinion polls or practice applications such as needs assessments, this is not a major drawback. RDD, however, would clearly be inappropriate in cases such as an agency study to evaluate former clients' satisfaction with services. A telephone survey could be used, but it would be necessary to work from a list of former clients in order to identify the sample of potential research participants. If the list has a high percentage of missing, incorrect, or unlisted telephone numbers, the likelihood of obtaining a representative sample of former clients would be small.

A new type of telephone poll, promoted by newspapers, television stations, and special-interest groups, asks people to call a particular number to record their opinion about some topic or issue. Often a 900 area-code number is used and a charge is added to the caller's phone bill. Such polls do not constitute telephone survey research, because the sampling techniques do not produce generalizable data. The people who call in to register their opinions have strong feelings on the subject (especially if they are willing to pay the fee), and those who do not feel so strongly are not represented in the survey. As a consequence, the results of such surveys cannot be generalized to any larger population.

Telephone Interviewing Skills

The skills and attributes necessary for effective telephone interviewers vary in some respects from those required for face-to-face interviewers. The need to match charac-

teristics of interviewers and research participants is not so great in telephone surveys, because personal differences are less apparent over the telephone. Other considerations such as voice quality, telephone manner, and ability to cope with the sometimes tedious aspects of telephone interviewing have a greater priority.

Of greatest importance in telephone surveys are the interviewer's verbal skills and familiarity with telephone etiquette—the conventions for considerate, polite behavior in telephone communications. A courteous attitude must be maintained, even if telephone customers decline to participate in ways that are not socially acceptable. Some may agree to complete the survey but change their minds or become uncooperative midway through the interview. In such situations, the interviewer must be able to avoid losing composure, be able to reassure research participants and encourage them to continue, and know when and how to end a session.

Since telephone interviews are rarely preceded by cover letters, interviewers must be able to establish their own legitimacy and that of the study to the satisfaction of the research participant. An interviewer's legitimacy can be undermined by unclear speech, a flippant or disinterested attitude, exaggerated mannerisms, or poor grammar. Sometimes it is best for the interviewer to strictly follow the text of the interview schedule, though this can create other problems, such as reading in a dull or halting manner.

Interviewers must also know how to mediate between the goals of the study and the needs of the research participant. While some contacts refuse to participate, others provide far more data than the interviewer can handle or indulge in conversation that has nothing to do with the study. The interviewer must be able to weigh the benefits of completing such an interview against the costs of taking too long to do so. If research participants are uncommunicative, the interviewer must know how to probe for additional information without seeming to be too inquisitive or aggressive. If research participants have difficulty understanding or keeping track of questions, the interviewer must be prepared to repeat or clarify.

Perhaps the best way to develop the skills needed by telephone interviewers is through techniques such as role-playing, in which prospective interviewers take the roles of interviewers and research participants in hypothetical telephone surveys in a controlled setting. By participating in problematic situations, they learn how to deal with them and can practice appropriate responses until they become confident. Another training technique is to allow prospective interviewers to listen in on a second phone to interviews conducted by more experienced staff. Or the researcher or a supervisor might listen in on an interviewer's first few calls to prospective research participants and offer feedback on the exchange and suggestions for improvement. Calls also can be monitored throughout the data collection to ensure that the interviews are being conducted properly.

COMPUTERIZED DATA COLLECTION IN SURVEYS

Computers have become a basic tool in surveys, particularly for recording and analyzing data. In many cases, however, the process of translating data from research participants onto a form that can be read by a computer (called coding) still requires a number of laborious steps. In self-administered surveys, for example, responses to a questionnaire are usually reviewed and translated into numerical codes by a reader who writes them out in rows of numbers on a coding form. Data from these forms are then transferred by entering them into a computer file, using a keyboard and video display screen. Some of us have begun coding data from survey instruments onto optical scanning forms similar to those used with standardized tests. These forms can be read by a scanner, which then transfers the data to a computer, thus saving a step in the coding process.

The greater the number of steps between getting an answer from a research participant and recording it in a computer, the greater the number of coding errors the data are likely to contain. With telephone surveys, interviewers can enter data on responses directly into a computer. This process is known by the acronym CATI, for computer-assisted telephone interviewing. It is not possible with self-administered questionnaires, except in rare cases where skilled research participants

can sit at a computer to answer questions. It also has not been feasible in face-to-face interviews, though the growing use of laptop computers is creating new possibilities.

CATI allows the elimination not only of coding forms but also of written interview schedules. Questions to be asked of research participants are displayed on the computer screen, along with prompts for recording the answer, gathering supplementary data, or proceeding to another part of the instrument.

Figure 17.7 provides an example of a computerized interview schedule in the form of a series of computer screens developed for a telephone interview. An interviewer sitting in front of the computer would see only one screen at a time. As each question is read and the required data are entered, the program automatically proceeds to the next screen. In cases where one type of response leads to a certain question and a different response leads to another, the program automatically takes the interviewer to the appropriate screen.

In Screen 1, for example, when the interviewer enters a 9, indicating that the research participant has refused to participate, the program skips to a screen that provides a message for the interviewer to read, expressing regrets that the person has chosen not to participate. If the research participant agrees to complete the survey, the program skips to Screen 2, where the interviewer is instructed to enter the person's identifier, and so on.

With this approach, the interviewer is unlikely to lose the place or skip questions. The computer can be programmed to signal when invalid values are entered, thus reducing coding errors. Data entered on each screen are automatically entered in the computer in a form that can be directly extracted and analyzed. CATI systems require a personal computer for each interviewer or a network of keyboards and display screens linked to a single computer.

Some types of telephones are better than others; a headset with earphones and microphone that fits into a standard-sized jack can be purchased or rented for moderate cost. Using a headset frees up the interviewer's hands to dial the telephone and record data. With personal computers, the interviewer's headset can be connected to a

———————————— SCREEN 1 ————————————

question 0a   column(s) —
        The ASU Center for Business Research is sponsoring a survey about when and why people move into and out of Arizona. This information is important for the economy of the state.
        In order for men and women to have an equal chance of being interviewed, I need to talk to the head of the household or the spouse of the head of the household. Which one had the most recent birthday?

        1. *GIVES NAME* - type in at next question
        9. *REFUSED* (skip to q 998c)

———————————— SCREEN 2 ————————————

question 0b   column(s) — 1-3
[Type in RESPONDENT'S NAME OR IDENTIFIER C- husband, wife, son, father, etc.]
        (If informant is respondent, Type in ID)

———————————— SCREEN 3 ————————————

question 0c   column(s) — 4
[REPEAT intro if necessary]
        (The ASU Center for Business Research is sponsoring a survey about when and why people move into and out of Arizona. This information is important for the economy of the state.)
        Before I start, I would like to assure you that this interview is completely confidential, voluntary, and will only take five minutes.

        (Press RETURN to continue)

———————————— SCREEN 4 ————————————

question 1a   column(s) — 5
        I am going to begin with some questions about how long you have been in Arizona and how much time you spend here.
        Do you usually spend more than thirty days in a row per year outside of Arizona?

        1. *YES*
        2. *NO* (skip to q 5)
        9. *DON'T KNOW* (skip to q 5)

———————————— SCREEN 5 ————————————

question 2   column(s) — 6-7
        How many months per year do you spend outside of Arizona?
        (Type in NUMBER)

Figure 17.7   Example of a Computerized Telephone Interview Schedule

telephone modem in the computer, and the machine will automatically dial each number. Beyond a basic knowledge of the use of personal computers, special expertise is not required to create and use computerized interview schedules. With commercial software packages, users can devise their own CATI and other computer systems for recording and analyzing survey data.

EMERGING DATA COLLECTION APPROACHES

Approaches to data collection in survey research are tied to the means by which information may be exchanged; thus, new modes of communication bring about fresh possibilities for conducting surveys. Face-to-face communication, for example, is as old as the human race, but reliable mail service has been around for a few hundred years at best, and the telephone came into wide use only in the twentieth century. Now, the pace of advancement in technology may soon bring about a variety of new methods of conducting surveys.

One example is email, in which people communicate through computers. Many American households now have at least one computer, however, and the presence of both computers and online capabilities continues to grow rapidly. Also, virtually all American households have television sets, and the technology of interactive cable television is another source of two-way communication that will gradually become widespread.

Still, many barriers need to be overcome before these technologies become broadly useful for survey research in social work. One problem is that computers, modems, and interactive cable links are expensive; thus, there is a wide disparity in access to them between wealthy and poor families. Ownership is also distributed unequally across ethnic and racial groups, with more white families owning computers than black or Hispanic families.

Finally, as noted earlier in the chapter, the proliferation of junk mail, telephone solicitations, and sales pitches disguised as surveys has made legitimate survey research much harder to conduct. The same is likely to be true of surveys that use newer technologies, the difficulty increasing almost simultaneously with the growth of new communication technologies.

SUMMARY

As one of the most common forms of data collection methods, survey research is often chosen as the means for studying groups and social phenomena by collecting data on individuals, organizations, and communities. As with other types of data collection methods, the genesis of survey research is in the formulation of the research question; only by clearly defining what it is we wish to know can the means for obtaining an answer be selected.

If our research question can be addressed by survey methods, the choice is between cross-sectional designs, which gather data on a particular population at a given moment in time, and longitudinal designs, which examine changes in the population over time. The two main methods of data collection in surveys are mail and telephone.

The following chapter continues our discussion of data collection by describing secondary analysis. Unlike surveys, which collect original data to address research questions, secondary analyses draw on data that already exist.

PART VI

Collecting Existing Data

· ·

HISTORICAL

The first four chapters in Part VI discuss the four

main data collection methods that collect existing

and unobtrusive data for social work research

studies. Unlike the data collection methods

discussed in Part V, these methods require no

involvement of the research participant, and they

collect data that already exist. The final chapter,

Chapter 22, presents a model for selecting the best

data collection method to answer a research

question.

Judy L. Krysik

Secondary
Analysis

18

The practice of analyzing an existing data set for a purpose other than the purpose for which it was originally collected is referred to as a *secondary analysis*—an unobtrusive data collection method. Thus, secondary analysis is any further analysis of an existing data set that presents interpretations, conclusions, or knowledge additional to, or different from, those presented in prior analyses of the same data set.

SECONDARY ANALYSIS: PAST AND PRESENT

Although it has gained in popularity, the use of secondary data sets is not new. One of the earliest examples of a secondary analysis of existing data sets is Emile Durkheim's 1897 study on suicide. Durkheim and his associates collected data from existing hospital death records to understand the social factors associated with suicide (Pope, 1976). Thus, Durkheim used existing data for a purpose not intended by those who originally collected them. As should be very evident by now, analyzing existing data sets is an unobtrusive data collection strategy in that it does not collect original data from research participants.

Advanced computer technology and the widespread implementation of management information systems (MIS) have made the task of accessing and analyzing secondary data sets much easier than in Durkheim's era. In fact, a plethora of data sets are available on individuals, families, organizations, communities, and countries. The current state of secondary analyses was perhaps best captured by Hyman (1987) who stated, "Now, late in the twentieth century, social scientists can also be described as standing atop of a giant mountain of data, from which they might see farther back into the past, away into remoter regions of the world, and over a larger vista of problems than ever before."

Upon identifying a research problem area appropriate for a secondary analysis, we need to choose from a variety of data sets. Most of these secondary data sets can be accessed in a matter of a week or two, in computer-readable form, ready for analysis. Along with the data set we can expect to receive information on: (1) the name and affiliation of the data collector, (2) the data collection period, (3) the type of sampling method used, (4) the size of the sample, (5) the data collection method, including the survey instrument or interview schedule, (6) the data source, (7) notes on data coding procedures, and (8) suggestions for analyses. Most data sets are available at a fraction of what they cost to produce.

TYPES OF SECONDARY DATA

There are three principal types of secondary data that are available. They are (1) micro-level data, (2) aggregate-level data, and (3) qualitative-level data.

Micro-Level Data

The term *micro-level data* is used to describe data derived from individual units of analysis, whether these data sources are persons, households, or organizations. Number of children, for example, is a micro-level variable. For the past two centuries, the federal government has been the most important source of micro-level data by providing large national surveys of households through means such as the population census (Oyen, 1990).

Aggregate-Level Data

Aggregate-level data consist of statistics and/or tables derived from quantitative micro-level data, in which the characteristics of individual units of analysis are no longer identifiable. Unemployment rate, for example, is an aggregate-level variable. The calculation of an unemployment rate requires a number of individuals to respond to a question asking whether or not they are gainfully employed. The micro-level data from individual respondents are then aggregated to produce an aggregate measure of unemployment. Chapter 23 describes in detail how to use aggregate-level data to answer research questions or test hypotheses.

Qualitative-Level Data

Qualitative-level data are any kind of nonquantitative data. Secondary data sets that are qualitative in nature include descriptive narratives and records of personal communication such as diaries and letters. Understanding soldiers' experiences of war by examining letters they sent home would be an example of a secondary analysis using qualitative-level data. Chapter 26 describes in detail how to analyze qualitative data.

Combining Types of Data for a Particular Analysis

As stressed throughout this book, most research problems are best understood and answered through the use of both qualitative-level data and quantitative data. Secondary analysis provides a means to this end by blending both research approaches. Although many studies using secondary data are based on only one type of data (i.e., micro-, aggregate-, or qualitative-level), some studies combine all three types.

LOCATING SECONDARY DATA SETS

A major challenge in collecting primary data for a given research study is to locate and secure the participation of research participants. In contrast, for the secondary analyst, the challenge is to locate an appropriate existing data set. Thus, we need to be aware of the many published guides, directories, and other resources available for identifying existing data sets. However, although books and articles that list existing data sets are available, such resources can become quickly obsolete (e.g., Dale, Arber, & Proctor, 1988; Kiecolt & Nathan, 1985).

Increased computer technology has prompted the development of numerous data archives throughout Europe and North America. They primarily hold micro-level data and have become an important source in secondary data analyses. The largest data archive in the world is the Inter-University Consortium for Political and Social Research (ICPSR). Currently, the ICPSR has more than 17,000 files of computer-readable data that span two centuries and more than 130 countries. The ICPSR, as do many data archives, has a system of university member affiliates that entitles faculty and students to use the data sets at a minimal cost (if any). Most data archives publish catalogues on an annual basis to inform the public of their holdings.

Other less formal sources of micro-level data exist, however, such as government departments, social service agencies, private foundations, charitable organizations, and private industry, and usually require more effort to locate.

Aggregate data are available in standardized and unstandardized formats. The Congressional Information Services (CIS) publishes an index to the statistical publications of international, intergovernmental organizations on an annual basis. It is not the intent of CIS, however, to present data in a standardized format. As an alternative, the Organization for European Cooperation and Development (OECD), the International Labor Office (ILO), and the Euro-monitor are three sources that publish data using standardized operational definitions of certain variables.

Data from publications that attempt standardization of variables are superior for secondary analyses. For instance, in Durkheim's era, official suicide rates varied by region according to whether secular or religious officials were responsible for recording the cause of death. We could argue, therefore, that the lack of a standardized operational definition of suicide was a limitation in Durkheim's study.

Secondary data sets are not always in the form of surveys and official records, however. Qualitative-level data may be gathered from a variety of sources such as books, unpublished manuscripts, articles, monographs, personal communication, and even audiotape and videotape recordings. Locating the best source (or sources) of data for a particular research study is often a trial-and-error process. Contacting a reference librarian at a university library for assistance is an excellent way to start.

EXAMPLE: THE WELFARE STATE AND WOMEN'S EMPLOYMENT

To demonstrate how a secondary analysis is done, an example is used throughout this chapter that involves the use of several existing data sets archived in the Luxembourg Income Study (LIS). The LIS is an international data cooperative that has available family and household micro-level data for over 21 countries from the late 1960s to early 1990s. The data sets for LIS are national income surveys administered by each member country. The U.S. Current Population Survey and the Canadian Survey of Consumer Finances are included in the LIS database.

Even though women in North America have entered the labor force in large numbers, they remain disadvantaged. This disadvantage has multiple forms—for instance, low employment participation rates, low pay, a predominance of part-time labor, and occupational segregation. For women, full integration into paid labor has implications that extend far beyond economic well-being. Employment may impact women's physical and emotional well-being, for example, as well as their participation in cultural, political, and social life.

Although women are increasingly involved in employment, they still carry the majority of responsibility for family care. The interface between employment and family creates significant tensions that may present barriers to women's participation in paid labor. Women's opportunities to enhance their employment careers rest on their access to income-generating work and on support for domestic responsibilities. For many women, such access may be reflected in welfare state policies and programs that address issues such as employment equity, parental leave, and child care.

Thus, to the extent that the modern welfare state intervenes to address tensions between employment and family and thereby attempts to influence gender equity, it would be expected that the welfare state would be more or less successful in decreasing women's labor force disadvantage. Examining the relationship between the welfare state and women's employment falls clearly in the domain of our profession.

STEPS IN SECONDARY ANALYSES

At a basic level, a secondary analysis follows seven steps: (1) selecting a problem area, (2) formulating a research question or hypothesis, (3) formulating a research design, (4) evaluating the data set, (5) constructing operational definitions, (6) analyzing the data, and (7) writing the research report.

Step 1: Selecting a Problem Area

The first task in conducting any research study is to decide on a problem area. It is important that we devote as much time and effort defining the research problem in a secondary analysis as we would in conducting a primary research study that requires original data. As can be expected, there is some temptation with a secondary analysis to formulate the research problem based on whatever data are available. This approach, however, will seldom lead to good results.

With regard to our example, a review of the literature indicated that the welfare state has been a major contributor in reducing poverty among demographic groups such as the elderly and the disabled. When observed cross-nationally, however, a great deal of variation in the redistributive capacities of various welfare states has been noted. In Scandinavian countries, for example, the redistributive effects of the welfare state are substantial, whereas the United States is often characterized as a welfare state laggard. This variation in welfare state performance has been explained in a typology of welfare state regimes (Esping-Andersen, 1990).

The research problem in our example is, "How might Esping-Andersen's typology of welfare state regimes apply to women's employment outcomes?" If three different types of welfare state regimes do exist, then it could be expected that women's employment outcomes would vary across countries according to the type of welfare state regime each has. Thus, if policy makers could identify countries based on their achievement of positive outcomes, then they could consider the transferability of the welfare state strategies employed in these countries.

Step 2: Formulating a Research Question or Hypothesis

In order for a problem area to be studied it must be formulated into more manageable questions or hypotheses. A review of the literature on women's employment suggested that inequities resulting from macroeconomic conditions such as unemployment, as well as social differences such as marital status, education, and number of children, could be reduced by policies and programs introduced by the welfare state.

Based on Esping-Andersen's typology of welfare state regimes we were able to hypothesize what employment outcomes each type of welfare state regime would produce. For instance, countries with social democratic welfare state regimes, because of their commitment to full employment and gender equity, should be characterized by high levels of female participation in employment, a predominance of full-time labor at relatively high wages, and low gender segregation within occupations.

The conservative welfare state regime, in contrast, supports the traditional roles of wife and mother. Women's employment participation in the conservative welfare state regime was therefore predicted to be low and characterized by part-time status in female-dominated occupations. Because the state monetarily supports non-employment, the demand for labor in the conservative welfare state regime would be low.

Given that some participation in paid labor among women is necessary to meet the demands of capitalism, wages must be high enough to make women's employment worthwhile, and low enough to keep demand and supply in equilibrium, resulting in moderate wage rates. In the liberal welfare state, the inability to earn income outside of the market system will force women to accept whatever labor is available. Because women need paid labor to survive, the supply of female laborers will exceed the demand for labor, increasing competition and forcing wages downward. A lack of support for family responsibilities will constrain women's availability, leading to moderate rates of labor force participation and a predominance of part-time, gender-segregated labor.

Finally, if women's employment is systematically influenced by the welfare state, employment outcomes should be different across the various regime types and similar within each regime. Without a thorough understanding of the problem area, we might not have considered the multifaceted nature of employment inequity. For instance, we may have dealt only with women's employment participation, ignoring hours employed, pay, and occupational segregation.

Two research questions (derived from the research problem) were formulated to represent our study's general problem area: (1) What are the differences in women's labor force participation outcomes across western industrialized countries? and (2) Are differences in

women's labor force participation outcomes related to the nature of the welfare state? At times, the only way to answer a certain research question is through a secondary analysis. Imagine, for a moment, that we were interested in women's employment and attempted to collect nationally representative, original data from several countries. The scope of the data required and cost would be prohibitive, not to mention language barriers and time.

Step 3: Formulating a Research Design

Secondary analyses are extremely versatile in the sense that they can be used to examine the present or the past, understand change over time, examine phenomena comparatively, and replicate or expand on prior research studies. Each of these uses requires a different research design, developed according to the requirements of the research question or hypothesis. Three of the most common research designs that are easily facilitated through a secondary analysis are (1) comparative research designs, (2) temporal research designs, and (3) cross-sectional research designs.

Comparative Research Designs

The study of more than one group, event, or society to isolate factors that explain patterns is called *comparative research*. Designs that facilitate comparative studies can be divided into two basic strategies: (1) the study of elements that differ in many ways but that have some major factor in common, or (2) the study of elements that are highly similar but that differ in some important respect (Vogt, 1993).

Following the first strategy, if we were interested in gender we could examine the distribution of unpaid labor and educational attainment across many countries to explain the universal nature of women's disadvantaged economic status. To ascertain the impact of the welfare state on women's employment, however, we choose to study only western industrialized countries. Holding constant key variables that could influence employment, such as democratic political institutions, market economies, and cultural and religious traditions, was important to do in order to isolate their effects on the welfare state.

Temporal Research Designs

All temporal research designs include time as a major variable. Their purpose is to investigate change in the distribution of a variable (or in relationships among variables) for entire populations or subgroups. They investigate characteristics of groups that have experienced some major life event, such as entry into the labor force at a particular interval. A temporal study, for example, might compare the employment profiles of women born in three different decades: pre-World War II, baby boomers, and Generation X.

Temporal studies also can use data to study the same persons or entities over time. We could, for example, analyze data to understand how employment careers change before, during, and after childbearing years. These studies require data to be collected more than once from the same individuals.

Temporal studies can also be used to look at change, but not require data from the same persons or entities. A temporal study, for example, might look at attitudes toward women's employment over three different time periods, such as the 1930s, the 1970s, and the 1990s.

Cross-Sectional Research Designs

Cross-sectional designs examine a phenomenon at one point in time and can be used to address a wide range of research questions. Our study on women's employment, for example, was interested in only one period of data collection. We chose data from the mid-1980s because this period was characterized by slow economic growth, high unemployment rates, and rising deficits in social service budgets among all western nations. Thus, the period was considered appropriate for assessing welfare state performance under adverse economic conditions.

Step 4: Evaluating the Data Set

Not all secondary data sets are equally valid or reliable. We need to answer four questions prior to engaging in analyzing an existing data set.

Question 1: What Was the Original Purpose of the Data Set?

Data are not collected without a purpose. At times, they may be collected to support a particular point of view or to test a particular research hypothesis. If this is the case, the data set may be limited in scope and may not lend itself to testing an alternative explanatory model.

The degree of precision in data collection, the variable categories used, and the method of data collection are all influenced by the primary researcher's intent. Understanding the original purpose of the study, therefore, is mandatory.

Question 2: How Credible Are the Data Source and Data Set?

Credibility refers not only to potential biases the original researcher might have had, but to his or her knowledge of research methodology and level of access to physical and financial resources. Official surveys tend to have greater financial sponsorship, which generally results in larger samples and higher response rates than those obtained by nonofficial surveys. Sample size and representation have implications for those of us who are interested in studying small subgroups within a population.

Another advantage of using data from official sources is that the limitations of standard operational definitions are well documented by both the provider of the data set and by others who have used it. This provides some preliminary guidance for those of us who are embarking on a statistical analysis of the data.

Question 3: Are the Data Representative of the Population?

Knowledge of the sampling frame used provides an indication of the extent to which the study's sample is likely to correspond to the true population from which it was drawn. For instance, our interpretation of a finding that 80 percent of survey respondents did not support affirmative action might be very different if we were to learn that the sample was drawn from a list of

Republicans in California. Knowledge of the sampling frame, rates of nonresponse, and the amount of missing data are important points to consider if generalizations from the data set's sample to the population are to be supported. If rates of nonresponse and/or missing data are high, we may want to obtain additional information from other sources and data sets to evaluate the extent of misrepresentation. The sampling method used also has implications for the kinds of statistical analyses that are appropriate.

Question 4: Are Weighting Procedures Needed?

When subgroups in the data set are over- or underrepresented in comparison with their actual distribution within the population, we may need to employ a weighting procedure. Adjusting data to reflect differences in the number of population units that each case represents is referred to as *weighting*.

Some data sets, the LIS data in particular, provide the option of using weighted or nonweighted data. It is also possible to pool data from two or more data sets to create a larger data set that will facilitate the examination of underrepresented groups. This procedure is particularly helpful for studying ethnic minorities and never-married mothers, for example.

Step 5: Constructing Operational Definitions

As we know, operationalization is the process of defining variables so they can be measured. In primary research studies, a considerable amount of effort is invested in operationalizing variables before the data are actually collected. On the other hand, in secondary analyses, we create operational definitions after the data are in hand, making the most of whatever is available within the data set. A distinctive feature of a secondary analysis, therefore, is the creation of new variables by combining a number of variables or by recoding existing ones.

In our study, for example, the LIS data sets did not include a variable to indicate whether or not women were employed. The absence of a variable to indicate employment participation prompted us to construct a new oper-

ational definition. In our new operational definition, women were considered to be employed if their income from annual wages (or salaries) was greater than zero. If income from annual wages or salary was equal to zero, a woman was classified as nonemployed. We made a decision to exclude "self-employed income" from the calculation of income because the LIS data sets did not differentiate between income from labor and income from capital, such as rental property. This process of redefining one variable, such as income, into a second variable, such as employment participation, is accomplished through recoding.

At times we may want to create an index as an alternative to using a single indicator variable. An index is nothing more than a composite measure of a general concept that is constructed from multiple variables to produce a single variable (Vogt, 1993). Jodi Jacobson (1992), for instance, developed a single index of "human development" that included three variables: (1) the degree to which people have the option to lead a long and healthy life, (2) the degree to which people have the option to be become knowledgeable, and (3) the degree to which people have the option to find access to the assets, employment, and income needed for a decent standard of living.

It is our task when doing a secondary analysis to create operational definitions that are meaningful, valid, and reliable. If this is not possible given the existing data set, an alternative data set may have to be accessed or the objectives of our research study revised. If a secondary analysis will not permit us to adequately measure the variables required, it may not be the appropriate data collection method to use.

Step 6: Analyzing the Data

The statistical methods used to analyze secondary data sets are the same as those used to analyze original data sets. A common characteristic of secondary data sets, however, is the generally large number of cases and variables they contain. Thus, the statistical techniques employed often require advanced knowledge of statistical methods and competency in computer use. There is no single computerized statistical software program that is most appropriate for statistical analyses. Many are available, and the final choice is dictated by the requirements of the analysis, availability, familiarity, and personal preference.

The data sets used in our example present an anomaly. Whereas most secondary analysts access data sets from a computer-readable data tape that can be copied onto a personal or mainframe computer, direct access to our LIS data sets was not permitted. Researchers access the LIS data sets by electronic mail. Computerized statistical programs were developed in SPSS (Statistical Package for the Social Sciences) language and were sent to the Government of Luxembourg mainframe computer where the data sets are stored. Statistical results were returned by electronic mail. The rationale for limiting access to the LIS data sets is to protect the privacy and confidentiality of survey respondents.

We should always begin the statistical analysis of secondary data by investing time in becoming familiar with the data set. This means generating basic descriptive statistics for key variables and comparing them with existing sources to check for compatibility. When the data are congruent across multiple independent sources, we can have more confidence in our analysis.

When disagreement results, it may be necessary to identify potential reasons for such differences and to determine which data source is the more credible. When differences occur, however, we should be skeptical of the data. Some data sources provide basic descriptive statistics on key variables to facilitate comparison. Besides basic descriptive statistics, those people judged to be specialists in a particular area can assist in evaluating the validity of the results.

Step 7: Writing the Research Report

Research reports based on the analysis of a secondary data set are not readily distinguishable from those based on an original data set. The author may refer the reader to the original research report for details of the methodology used. Moreover, it is contingent upon the author to document the limitations of the data set being used. In addition, some suppliers of data sets have certain requirements regarding their use. The source for the LIS data sets, for example, requires that any paper published using the LIS data sets must be included in the

Luxembourg Income Study Working Paper Series. Chapters 24 and 27 discuss in detail how to write quantitative and qualitative research reports, respectively.

ADVANTAGES AND DISADVANTAGES

Weighing the advantages of a secondary analysis against its limitations can help one decide when to use a secondary data set versus gathering original data.

Advantages

Five of the most salient advantages of secondary data analyses are: (1) maximizing resources, (2) increasing accessibility, (3) avoiding intrusiveness, (4) developing knowledge, and (5) facilitating replication.

Maximizing Resources

One of the most important ways to maximize limited resources is to build on the work already done by others. The cost of conducting original research studies includes the development of survey instruments and interview schedules, and the hiring and training of data collectors, data coders, and data-entry personnel. By using secondary data, savings are incurred in money, time, and personnel. Often it is the only feasible means of obtaining representative data. Conducting a secondary data analysis is not, however, cost free. The cost of conducting a secondary analysis can vary depending on the cost of the data set(s) and the requirements of its use. Some data archives offer workshops to those interested in a secondary analysis. With research dollars becoming increasingly scarce, it is important that resources be saved by using secondary data wherever possible so that money can be diverted to studies requiring original data.

Increasing Accessibility

The current state of secondary analyses means that the opportunity of conducting research studies is no longer in the hands of a privileged few. Affordable computer technology has made secondary data sets broadly accessible to the point that even a social work student can conduct a large-scale research project. The development of numerous data archives has both increased the likelihood that data will be discovered and facilitated their use.

Avoiding Intrusiveness

As we know from Chapter 17, studies have shown that survey response rates are declining in general (Groves & Cialdini, 1992). This decrease has been attributed in part to the large number of surveys that are now being conducted. The use of secondary data sets limits the reporting burden placed on the public. Also, there are occasions when the introduction of a survey would create tensions or intensify negative emotions. In these circumstances, secondary data can be particularly beneficial.

Developing Knowledge

Secondary data analyses are used to create knowledge at all three levels. At the exploratory level, secondary data are used to generate relevant research questions and tentative hypotheses. They are used at the descriptive level by describing a phenomenon or the characteristics of a population. Many descriptive demographic research studies are based on the analysis of secondary data. Secondary analysis is also useful in explanatory studies. By comparing Esping-Andersen's three theoretical welfare state regimes with actual situations, for example, knowledge development moves from comparative descriptions to explanatory statements.

Facilitating Replication

Because secondary data sets exist in the public domain, further research studies are easily replicable. Replication is a powerful tool for making research findings less vulnerable to error, as well as protecting them from the transient circumstances of respondents. Also, the same data set can be analyzed from different perspectives and theoretical frameworks, producing a more holistic understanding of the phenomena under study (Dale, Arber, & Procter, 1988).

Disadvantages

As a secondary data analysis is not without limitations, before embarking on one we should avoid potential difficulties by becoming aware of the more common ones. Four of these are: (1) lack of standardization, (2) omission of relevant variables, (3) overabundance of data, and (4) complicated statistical analyses.

Lack of Standardization

Secondary data sets are commonly confronted with a lack of standardized operational definitions of their variables. In the LIS data sets used in our example, the education variable was coded as "years of schooling" in the United States and as "education level" in Canada, Australia, Germany, and the Netherlands. This required recoding of the education variable into the two dichotomous categories of high and low, where "high" represented some postsecondary education, and "low" represented no postsecondary education. The process of dichotomizing the variable was necessary to include "education" in the statistical analysis of more than one country, but it resulted in decreased measurement precision. The lack of fit between concepts and the variables they contain is always a problem in analyzing secondary data sets.

Despite recoding, some variables are not sufficiently comparable to allow for their inclusion in a data analysis. In the LIS data, for example, the categories for the ethnicity variable were not comparable across country data sets. The United States differentiated ethnicity by the categories: white, black, Spanish origin, and other races. In Australia, ethnicity was defined by country of birth and included Australia, the United Kingdom, Italy, Other Europe, Asia, North/South America, Africa, and Oceania. In Canada, ethnicity was defined as Canadian born or immigrant. In Germany, ethnicity was recorded as German, Turkish, Yugoslav, Greek, Italian, Spanish, or other nationality.

The data set for the Netherlands did not contain any information on ethnicity, and, surprisingly, aboriginal status was not recognized in any of the U.S., Australian, and Canadian data sets. Because of the variability in definition and the lack of validity in variable categories, ethnicity is not a valid variable to include in cross-national research studies using the LIS data sets. In our study on women's employment, the inability to include ethnicity may have masked important differences in employment participation and pay across all countries included in our study.

Omission of Relevant Variables

The omission of relevant variables in secondary data sets can also be a problem. Studies focusing on gender may be particularly difficult because many national census and surveys have not included social indicators meaningful to the experiences of women (Norris, 1987). Data on unpaid domestic labor, for instance, are not collected despite its impact on paid labor. In our example on women's employment, social characteristics such as the number of children, age of the youngest child, and marital status were used as proxies for domestic responsibility. A proxy is an indirect measure of a variable.

The use of proxies to represent domestic responsibility is somewhat problematic in that domestic responsibility associated with marriage and children is likely to be inversely related to class status. Households with higher overall income, for example, are more apt to purchase domestic services such as ready-made foods, child care, laundry, and cleaning, than are low-income households. The extent that women and men conform to traditional gender roles will also influence women's domestic responsibilities. The lack of a better measure of domestic responsibility contained in the LIS data sets represents a threat to the validity of our study's findings and implications.

Overabundance of Data

For many secondary data sets, the abundance of variables is so great that it sometimes gets difficult to decide which variables to include and which to exclude from any given data analysis. The decision on which variables to include is made easier when our study is guided by a thorough literature review. Without such advance preparation, we can be adrift in a sea of computer printouts, searching aimlessly for statistically significant results that will invariably occur but which are unlikely

to have any substantive meaning. An overabundance of data is best confronted by having a thorough understanding of the research problem, and a well-designed and well-documented plan of data analysis.

Complicated Statistical Analyses

The degree of difficulty involved in analyzing secondary data sets depends to a large extent on the number of data sources required for a particular analysis. In general, the greater the number of sources, the more complex the data analysis. This is especially true if different units of analysis, (e.g., individual, family, community) must be considered. In the example we have been using on women's employment, one of the research questions we were interested in answering was: Are differences in women's employment participation rates affected by the welfare state, controlling for macroeconomic and social factors? Ideally, to answer this question, we should have included in our statistical analysis variables from each of the welfare states, macroeconomic, and social subsets.

Examining a small number of countries, however, limits the ways in which aggregate-level and micro-level data can be combined. Five countries are too few to represent sufficient variation on aggregate-level variables such as unemployment rate. When aggregate-level data are merged with micro-level data, each case in a specific country is assigned the category, or value, for unemployment rate. Unemployment rates for the five countries included in our study on women's employment ranged from a low of 6.9 percent to a high of 9.6 percent, a mere 2.7 percentage points' difference. A lack of variability in the range of responses on this variable severely limited its utility to our research study.

SUMMARY

Secondary analyses in social work research are increasing. Much of this increase can be easily attributed to advanced computer technology that has made the analysis of secondary data sets more accessible and affordable. There are many data archives available, and the search for the most appropriate one is a process of trial and error.

There are many benefits in analyzing secondary data sets. They include savings in time, money, and personnel; increased access to research opportunities; decreased intrusiveness; and ease of replication. Certain limitations are also present, however. Data available through secondary sources are often not exactly what is desired. The lack of standardized operational definitions among variables and the omission of relevant variables within various existing data sets are common problems. We must be prepared to do the best we can with what is available. This may mean recoding variable values, using proxy variables, and developing indexes. If the data are not sufficient to represent the study's important concepts, using more than one data set may be necessary.

It is particularly important that we become fully aware of the nature of the data set to be used, its method of data collection, and any limitations that this imposes on our study's findings and implications. Prerequisite skills that the secondary analyst should have are a good knowledge of research designs, statistical techniques, and facility with computers.

As we know, using a content analysis as a form of data collection is unobtrusive, that is, we do not intrude into our research participants' lives in any way. The following chapter continues our discussion of unobtrusive data collection methods by presenting how a social work research study can use another unobtrusive data collection method, known as content analysis.

Rodney Stark

Lynne Roberts

Content
Analysis

19

secondary and

christianizing data

The natural sciences have an advantage over the social sciences because bacteria and molecules don't blush. As we know from Chapter 14, because human beings often do blush as a result of being observed, those conducting surveys, field studies, and experiments must take care to ensure that the act of observation does not alter the behavior of those being studied. But there are many opportunities to measure social scientific concepts that run no risk of influencing behavior because they do not involve direct observation. In fact, such measurements typically take place after the behavior has occurred (sometimes centuries later), and those whose behavior was measured didn't know they would be studied and perhaps never did find out. Such measurement is referred to as *unobtrusive* (Webb, Campbell, Schwartz, and Sechrest, 1981).

UNOBTRUSIVE MEASUREMENT

An unobtrusive measure is one that has no effect on the objects being studied—it is a measurement that does not intrude. Such measures sometimes are referred to as *nonreactive measures*—ones that produce no reaction.

Unobtrusive measurements are possible because humans typically leave traces of their behavior. During the past several decades, archaeologists have reconstructed an exquisitely detailed portrait of the Maya civilization, which flourished from 200 B.C. through A.D. 900 in Central America (Schele & Freidel, 1990). But these scholars have never met an ancient Mayan. What they have observed are the Mayans' buildings (including their magnificent temples), their sculpture, and their graves. The final breakthrough came when an international group of scholars succeeded in deciphering Mayan writing (Coe, 1992). This immense body of scholarship is based entirely on these cultural artifacts.

Cultural Artifacts

An artifact is any object made by human work, and a cultural artifact is any such object that informs us about the physical and/or mental life of some set of human beings.

The word *object* is interpreted very broadly to include written, filmed, and recorded material.

Fortunately for social scientists, humans leave an immense wake of cultural artifacts. For example, the museums of Europe are crowded with suits of armor worn by medieval knights. An enterprising scholar was able to calculate that the average European knight was only about 5 feet tall by measuring several thousand of these suits of armor. Scholars have reconstructed General George Custer's "Last Stand" at Little Big Horn by using metal detectors to locate cartridge casings; these enabled them to chart each successive firing line as Custer's troops withdrew toward a hilltop.

It will be useful to consider several examples in greater detail.

Example: Turning Wine Into Communicants

For many years there has been a debate about how religious Europeans were a few centuries ago. Some argue that, once upon a time, people in Europe were very active church members, far more active than today. Others disagree, arguing that Europeans never were very involved in church and that the so-called Age of Faith is a nostalgic myth. Then a French sociologist discovered very appropriate, unobtrusive data on religious practice in France centuries ago.

For at least 50 years, Catholic sociologists in Europe, especially in France and Belgium, have devoted themselves to parish studies—to exploring the dynamics of religious life at the very local level. Eventually, some of them began to explore the history of various parishes, using the elaborate records that have been kept by parish priests for many centuries. One day, Jacques Toussaert (see Delumeau, 1977) discovered solid data on religious practice hidden in these documents: receipts for the purchase of communion wine. Until recently, to remain in good standing, all Roman Catholics were required to attend a communion service at least once a year, Easter being the preferred time to do so. A communion service briefly reenacts the Last Supper during which Jesus shared bread and wine with his disciples. Hence, groups of parishioners come to the front of the church where the priest gives each a sip of wine and a wafer of unleavened bread.

There are many grumbles in surviving letters, documents, and official reports from medieval and early modern times that only a small number of persons in any French community met this obligation, despite the fact that "everyone" was ostensibly a Catholic. But Toussaert now had a basis for estimating the actual attendance at communion services. That is, knowing the amount of wine purchased for the occasion, and having established amount per sip, he could simply divide to obtain the maximum number of people who attended. Dividing this number by the number of those eligible to attend, yields a rate of attendance. If we suppose that the priest drank some of the wine, or that some was left over, or that some people gulped rather than sipped, then attendance was lower than Toussaert's figures show. But, even assuming that every drop was sipped by communicants, Toussaert ended up finding low levels of attendance. At least in terms of taking communion, the Age of Faith did not exist in medieval France.

Example: Exploring Occult America

Suppose you wished to study the popularity of occult (nonstandard) religious, mystical, and magical beliefs and practices in the United States and Canada. The occult would include such beliefs and practices as psychic readings, astrology, fortune-telling, meditation, and the like. You could do a survey asking questions, such as this one included in the 1994 General Social Survey of the United States:

Astrology—the study of star signs—has some scientific truth.

Definitely true	9%
Probably true	38%
Can't say	10%
Probably not true	24%
Definitely not true	19%

Another approach would be to examine cultural artifacts. The *Yellow Pages* of the telephone books are a very good source. The complete *Yellow Pages* for the United States and Canada now are available on CD-ROM from several different companies. The software included

with these databases allows a user to search for listings under a variety of headings and to search for listings containing various key words. Using the 1994 edition, we searched for all listings under each of these headings: Aquarian, Aquarius, Astrology, Astrologer, Aura, Card Reading, Card Reader, Color Therapy, Crystals, ESP, Fortune, Fortune Teller, Horoscope, Madame, Meditate, Meditation, Mediator, Metaphysical, Mind Reader, Mystic, Mystical, New Age, Occult, Palmist, Palmistry, Palm Reading, Parapsychology, Parapsychologist, Psychic, Psychics, Reader, Readings, Seer, Tarot, Telepath, Telepathic, Yoga, Zen, and Zodiac.

The software creates complete lists for each subject heading, including the full name for the listing (such as Mildred's Astrology Center), the city and state in which the listing is located, and the phone number. Many listings came up under more than one heading. We eliminated all duplicates from the combined list. Some listings were irrelevant—an immense number of conventional businesses in Mystic, Connecticut, were included in the list for *mystic*, for example. These also were eliminated (when in doubt, we simply called the number).

At that point, we began counting the total number of listings for each city and each state. Then we divided by the total population to create a rate of occult listings per million population. Following are the total listings and the rates for two U.S. states and two Canadian provinces.

Washington

Business Name	City
Akasha Metaphysical Bookstore	Bellingham
Astrological Therapies	Mercer Island
Astrology Club	Malaga
Astrology Et AI Metaphysical	Seattle
Astrology Transformational	Seattle
Aum-Nee Crystals and Books	Tacoma
BJ International Psychic	Clinton
Barbara, Palm Reader	Blaine
Betty Atwater Astrology	Gig Harbor
CDM Psychic Institute	Seattle
CDM Psychic Institute	Spokane
CDM Psychic Institute	Tacoma
CDM Psychic Institute and School	Everett

Business Name	City
Crystal Wizard Metaphysical Bookstore	Lynnwood
Egyptian Mysteries Astrology	Tacoma
Inner Sound Metaphysical Bookstore	Goldendale
Joshua-Astrologer	Tacoma
Marie's New Age Books	Leavenworth
Meditation Station	Bellevue
Metaphysical Counseling Service	Seattle
Metaphysical Institute	Seattle
Mystic Way	Seattle
Mystical General Store	Vashon Island
Mystic Power Psychic Treatment	Yakima
Northwest Center-Tarot and Arts	Seattle
Open Door Metaphysical Bookstore	Spokane
Osho Meditation Retreat	Redmond
Psychic Reader	Bellevue
Ruth, Psychic Reader	Seattle
Siddha Yoga Meditation Center	Seattle
Transcendental Meditation	Bremerton
Transcendental Meditation	Silverdale
Transcendental Meditation	Spokane
Unity Metaphysical Bookstore	Port Angeles

Rate per million population = 6.8

Minnesota

Business Name	City
Astrology by Moonrabbit	Minneapolis
Circle of Light Psychic Reader	St. Louis Park
Dial-A-Meditation	Edina
Fatima Psychic	St. Paul
Meditation Center	Minneapolis
Mikal and Associates Psychic Readings	Minneapolis
Minnesota Zen Meditation Center	Minneapolis
New Age Bookstore	Winona
New Age Stones	Plymouth
Psychic Reading Shop	Forest Lake
Shannon's Psychic Shop and Tarot	Minneapolis
Shirley Strasburg—Astrologer	Minneapolis
Siddha Meditation Center	St. Paul
Tarot by Marlene DeLott	Minneapolis
Transcendental Meditation Program	St. Paul
Uptown Psychic Studio	Minneapolis
West Suburban Meditation	Hopkins
Yoga Meditation Center	Hopkins

Rate per million population = 4.1

British Columbia

Business Name	City
Aster Metaphysical Counselling	Chemainus Avalon
Metaphysical Center	Victoria
Dennis A Readings, Inc.	Nanaimo
Dial-A-Meditation	Victoria
Fortune Teller and Associate	Richmond
Hermaglo Psychic International	Vancouver
International Meditation Society	Victoria
Joseph Ip Astrology Consultant	Vancouver
New Age Holistic Health Center	Prince Rupert
Nirvana Modern Metaphysics	Terrace
Phoenix Metaphysical Books	Surrey
Sara, Psychic Reader	Vancouver
Transcendental Meditation Center	Vancouver
Transcendental Meditation Center	Victoria
Vancouver Psychic Society	Vancouver

Rate per million population = 4.6

Quebec

Business Name	City
Centre Astrology du Quebec	Granby
Centre Astrology M Perras	St. Jean-Sur-Richel
Centre de Meditation Transcendantale	Montreal
Madame Simone	Montreal
Madame Jennie	St. Basile-ie-Grand
Meditation Transcendantale	Hull
Meditation Transcendantale	Doliard-de-Ormeau
Meditation Transcendantale	Sherbrooke
Meditation Transcendantale	Trois-Rivières
Mireille Tarot	Sherbrooke
Palmistry Centre	Westmount
Transcendental Meditation Centre	Doliard-de-Ormeau

Rate per million population = 1.8

These data from the *Yellow Pages* show that occult activities are more prevalent in Washington than in Minnesota and that British Columbia's rate is higher than Minnesota's, lower than nearby Washington's, but much higher than Quebec's. When occult practitioners obtained business telephones, they would not have been wondering if we were watching them. This measure was entirely unobtrusive.

Many studies based on cultural artifacts involve nothing more elaborate than counting and comparing—although, as in this example, comparisons often will require that the totals be converted into rates. However, such studies sometimes involve very detailed and elaborate coding schemes. This approach is known as content analysis.

CONTENT ANALYSIS

Over the past few years, there has been increasing concern about violence in the media—not only on television and in the movies, but in song lyrics, comic books, magazines, and even newspapers. This concern prompts many possible questions:

- Is this movie more violent than that one?
- Are the movies produced by one studio more violent than those from another?
- Has the amount of violence shown on TV been increasing?
- Is there more violence in the lyrics of rap music than in the lyrics of heavy metal?
- Have comics become more violent?

Many answers have been offered to questions such as these. Often, these answers are simply unsupported judgments, regarded as self-evident: "To watch network television these days is to be subjected to unending violence." Other answers recite many examples of the violence found in a particular set of communications to demonstrate its prevalence. But there is no way to tell whether these examples are typical or even frequent—perhaps they are the only examples. The questions listed above and others like them can be answered only by proportional facts, not subjective impressions, guesses, or examples. Thus, finding answers to such questions requires that we obtain accurate and systematic data. But how can we obtain "data" by watching television, reading comic books, or listening to music?

A *content analysis* systematically transforms non-quantified verbal, visual, or textual material into quan-

titative data to which standard statistical analysis techniques may be applied such as those presented in Chapter 23.

Put another way, a content analysis involves transforming qualitative material into data, in accord with Stephan Thernstrom's witticism that "facts are not born but made." However, while survey researchers, field researchers, and experimentalists take an active approach to eliciting the data they use, content analysts specialize in *coding* data they played no part in eliciting—data created by others for reasons having nothing to do with the research study at hand. For example, content analysts don't write or produce movies. Nor do they ask movie directors or producers about their movies. Instead, they watch the movies and systematically note (observe—see Chapter 14) certain specific aspects. For example, they might record each instance of violence, thus making it possible to compare movies in terms of the number of such instances. They also might categorize each instance of violence by type: torture, maiming, death, and so on. Or they might rank the instances on the basis of explicitness or of severity. The same thing could be done with TV shows, comics, novels, or song lyrics.

What content analysts create is a *set of codes* based on concepts and *rules for applying these codes*. Analysis consists of seeking correlations (or contrasts) among the measures produced by applying the codes: Is the size of the production budget correlated with the amount or severity of violent content—do movies tend to be more violent when they are more expensive? Does the sex ratio of the cast correlate with the amount of violence—the higher the percentage of male roles, the more violent the film?

RELIABILITY

Content analysis depends on materials that were not created for the purposes to which we wish to put them. Those who gave speeches, wrote letters, produced movies, composed lyrics, edited magazines, painted portraits, or otherwise created the materials used in a content analysis were entirely unaware of the categories and coding rules that subsequently were used to quantify their efforts. These categories and codes are *imposed* on the content of these materials, and it is always possible, therefore, that the categories distort the true meaning of the material.

Although a content analysis is an entirely *unobtrusive measure,* this does not mean that the material was created without self-consciousness on the part of its creators—most of this material was created for specific audiences and with specific intentions as to its effect on those audiences. To whom this material was addressed often is of primary interest to content analysts.

Manifest and Latent Content

In addition to imposing categories on materials, a content analysis often can attempt to quantify subjective judgments. For example, was a particular remark meant to be taken as sarcasm? Such judgments often are rather subtle and depend on the *latent* rather than the *manifest* content of the material.

- *Manifest content* refers to the explicit, clear, and perhaps superficial meaning of verbal, visual, or textual materials.
- *Latent content* refers to "deeper" or implicit meanings.

When someone writes or says, "I'd love that," the manifest content is that the person welcomes whatever "that" refers to. But facial expression and/or tone of voice may suggest that the person really means, "I'd dislike that a lot"—the latent content of the material. Coders often must make very subjective judgments to distinguish latent content from manifest content.

These aspects of content analysis make reliability a significant problem. There are two primary sources of unreliability in content analysis, unreliable codes and unreliable coders.

Reliable Codes

All of the principles applied to survey questions in Chapters 10 and 17 also apply to content analysis coding. If the codes are too subjective or too vague, if the categories overlap or are not exhaustive, if the categories do not provide sufficient scope for variation, or if the codes are biased, then the results may be unreliable because no one can apply them consistently or correctly.

Reliable Coding

Given a reliable coding scheme, a primary source of unreliability involves coder errors or inconsistencies. The coder misperceives or misunderstands the material to be coded and miscodes it. The coder mistakenly scores a case as 2 on a variable when the coder meant to score it as a 1—perhaps the coder is careless or working too fast. The coder applies rules inconsistently so that an incident involving only verbal abuse is sometimes scored as violent and sometimes not. The problem may be an inattentive coder or even a biased coder. For example, a coder might code an incident differently depending on whether it involved a man shouting at a woman or a woman shouting at a man.

The solution to these problems is to use several coders, each of whom codes the same material. Then their coding is compared. Each disagreement is carefully checked and the appropriate code assigned, if possible. In all instances of which we are aware, comparisons across coders have revealed disagreements. Consequently, a content analysis should never be considered as a data collection method unless multiple coders are used and a complete report is made available on interrater reliability (see Chapter 14).

VALIDITY

It is far easier to achieve reliable data from a content analysis than it is to ensure that the data are valid. Here, concern centers on biases in the material itself as well as on the extent to which we may draw inferences about more general matters from the materials. The following example will clarify these concerns.

Suppose we wish to explore the extent to which people in Colonial New England (before the American Revolution) did or did not openly express their sexual feelings and interests. We are in possession of a large number of love letters as well as many diaries written in this era. We also can examine novels written by New England authors at that time.

So we create a set of codes to classify these materials. Upon examination of the coding scheme, it is clear that the variables measuring the expression of sexual feelings and interests have compelling face validity. When a letter writer expresses admiration for his or her correspondent's sexual organs, for example, this is not a case of latent content. So, satisfied that our coding will be valid, we employ multiple coders so that it also will be reliable.

That takes care of validity, right? Hardly. Our data could be extremely biased and, therefore, could yield an entirely invalid portrait of sexual expression in New England.

Deposit Bias

The first major source of bias has to do with selection. Who wrote these letters, diaries, and novels? Whoever they were, they were not a random sample drawn from the population.

Deposit bias refers to circumstances in which only some portion of the pertinent material was originally included in the set of materials to be coded.

Illiterates do not write letters, diaries, or novels. In fact, most people in most eras do not. Consequently, our set of materials is far more limited in scope than the question we wish to answer. As the social historian Edward Shorter (1975) noted,

> What kind of people, after all, tended to burst forth in love letters, write novels, or compose memoirs other than a tiny elite at the pinnacle of the social order. [Such written materials] represent the experience of perhaps 5 percent of the population.
>
> The vast bulk of writing about intimate experience comes from people who had very little in common with the classes in which we are interested, the other 95 percent of the population.... The gulf between upper middle-class life and the experience of the lower orders was enormous in times past. And the accounts of the one are not acceptable substitutes for descriptions of the other. (9–10)

Deposit bias extends far beyond the realm of historical materials. Suppose you wished to compare the religiousness of communities based on the amount of church advertising in local newspapers. Other things being equal, we might conclude that communities having more column inches of church advertising (proportionate to their population) were more religious than communities with fewer inches. But other things probably are not equal, and many factors could greatly bias how many church ads are purchased. The papers in some communities may give churches a substantial discount, thus increasing both the number and the size of the ads.

There may be marked denominational differences in attitudes toward church ads—some denominations may regard advertising as tacky. Because communities also differ greatly in their denominational profiles, this might be the primary cause of observed differences. Or it may be that churches tend to advertise only when they aren't attracting enough people, hence a lot of church advertising reflects a lower level of community religiousness. These are biases that would occur in the deposit of the materials.

Survival Bias

Survival bias refers to circumstances in which only some portion of the pertinent phenomena was *retained* in the set of materials to be coded.

During the 1960s, an incredible number of small newspapers sprang up to report on the local counterculture. They differed from the "straight" press in their advocacy of drug use, opposition to the draft, and interest in new rock bands. But, like the hippie counterculture they represented, their days were numbered. By the mid-1970s, most of these papers were long gone and generally forgotten.

Suppose someone today wanted to base a study of this period on the contents of the counterculture press. It would be hard to find copies of many of these papers. And it would be very hard to know whether the copies that still survive are representative of the whole. In fact, they probably are not as it seems reasonable to suppose that the more successful papers—the ones that had larger circulations and survived for a longer period—would differ significantly from the less successful ones and would be far more likely to be available still.

In assessing the validity of content analysis data, it is vital to consider the impact of both deposit and survival biases. What's missing from the collection and why? However, the major source of invalidity in the use of content analysis has to do with attempting to generalize findings based on verbal, visual, or textual materials to human populations. To be more specific, a magazine article is text, not flesh and blood.

Invalid Generalizations

The questions posed earlier about media violence are entirely appropriate for a content analysis. Each is a question about verbal, visual, or textual materials—about movies, TV, comic books, and the like. In each instance, it is relatively clear what materials ought to be coded and how to draw valid conclusions from such data.

However, social scientists frequently must rely on content analyses when what they really want to know about is people. In the hypothetical example about sexual expression in New England, the real research question was about how Puritans behaved, not about what letters or diaries contained. The hope was that these textual materials would offer a valid portrait of real life. Sometimes such generalizations are valid. Sometimes they aren't. As an instructive example, let's pause and examine a classic study, long offered as a model of a well-done content analysis.

Leo Lowenthal (1944) believed there had been a major shift in cultural values in the United States during the first half of the 20th century. He thought that, at the beginning of the century, people greatly admired what he called "idols of production": founders of large corporations (such as Henry Ford) or people who had invented the items such corporations produced (such as Thomas Edison).

But then, Lowenthal hypothesized, public preferences began to shift so that the most admired people were "idols of consumption"—movie and sports stars, for example. To test this hypothesis, Lowenthal coded biographies that appeared in popular magazines between 1901 and 1941. The results gave very strong support to his hypothesis (Lowenthal, 1944). Idols of production dominated magazine biographies prior to World War I.

But, by the late 1920s, the pattern had shifted, and biographies of idols of consumption (such as Babe Ruth, Clark Gable, and Clara Bow) far outnumbered those of business leaders.

Lowenthal's findings were widely publicized and sustained an immense number of critiques of popular culture. In fact, his study had considerable impact on the most influential book of the time, *The Lonely Crowd: A Study of the Changing American Character* (Riesman, Glazer, & Denney, 1950). Although Lowenthal's data showed only what magazine editors chose to print, it seemed entirely valid to assume that their choices reflected popular taste. But it wasn't so.

More than a decade later, Fred I. Greenstein (1968) discovered a series of neglected surveys of elementary and high school students, each of which asked students whom they would "most like to resemble." The studies were done as dissertation projects by people doing graduate work in education departments. The oldest dated from 1902 and included 2,333 students. Others were conducted in 1910, 1928, 1944, and 1958.

What these data showed is that few kids *ever* wanted to be like idols of production; rather, they overwhelmingly named idols of consumption—Babe Ruth beat out Henry Ford many times over. Magazines had changed. Kids hadn't. Those who wished to claim a shift in the American character "are able to do so only by idealizing the American past" (Greenstein, 1968).

SELECTING UNITS AND CASES

The conflicting results of studies have been due to the use of different units of analysis. Lowenthal's units were biographical stories in popular magazines. Greenstein's units were students. As we know from Chapter 11, it is always problematic to generalize results based on one kind of unit of analysis to another variety—from aggregates to individuals, for example. This problem is especially acute in a content analysis because so often it is used as a substitute for data on individuals.

Lowenthal didn't really care about shifts in popular biographies—he wanted to demonstrate changes in the preferences of people. When the real focus is on people, folks doing content analyses should proceed at their own peril and always be very aware of the risk that their results will not generalize to people.

Appropriate Units

It is far better when a content analysis is used to test hypotheses concerning the units of analysis used in the research study. As noted, a content analysis of movies can answer questions such as "Are movies more violent today?" Thus, the selection of units of analysis generally should be determined by the research question. Suppose you had the hypothesis that American business communication has become less formal. Business letters would seem to be an appropriate set of units, and each letter would be a case. The hypothesis that retailers have reduced their emphasis on price and now stress quality could be tested with advertisements in catalogues, in newspapers, or on television—each ad would be a case.

Sample versus Census

The decision to sample or to examine all available cases depends on how many cases there are. If you have decided to limit the cases to one newspaper, for example, it might be possible to code all advertisement of a particular kind for a period of years. However, no one could code all such ads for all American papers even for the past year, let alone all ads for many years. Thus, it usually is necessary to select a sample of cases. The principles of sampling presented in Chapter 11 apply to *any* units of analysis, not just to people. First, it is necessary to define the population or universe of cases to be sampled. Then, random procedures must be followed in selecting cases.

Suppose you wished to analyze data based on personal ads in newspapers in which people solicited introductions to members of the opposite sex. First, you would need to identify the universe—perhaps all American daily newspapers that have a special section devoted to such ads. Next, you would need to draw a sample of papers (perhaps weighting them according to their circulation). Then, you would need to draw a sample of issues. At that point, you could either include all ads published on those dates by each paper in the sample or select a sample from each paper. You would then have a stratified random sample of personal ads. The next step would be to begin coding.

CONSTRUCTING CODING SCHEMES

A content analysis coding scheme is, in an important sense, a questionnaire that coders fill out on behalf of each case. As such, it must adhere to the fundamental principles of question construction presented in Chapter 10. As with survey interview schedules or questionnaires, pretesting is vital. So, after you have a draft of your coding scheme, try it out on a few cases. You undoubtedly will discover many things that need to be changed. Fortunately, coding and recoding a case does not make it unfit for inclusion in the final study. Pretest survey respondents may be so sufficiently changed by having been interviewed that it is unwise to include them in the final sample, but a letter, advertisement, or movie is a fixed communication.

In creating and refining a coding scheme, remember that the important issue is what you are going to do with the data after they are coded. What are your hypotheses? What data will you need to test them—are you leaving out something important? If you hypothesize that men who run ads seeking to meet women will be more apt to mention appearance when describing their preferences in women, whereas women will be more apt to stress long-term relationships in their ads, you will need to remember to code gender. Although that may seem like absurdly obvious advice, you would be shocked at how often even very experienced researchers omit something really vital when collecting data.

Asking what you will do with the data also will help you recognize the inclusion of superfluous material. It is typical for preliminary coding schemes to include too many variables and for many to be dropped during pretesting.

The need to use multiple coders has been discussed. It also is best if the coders do not know the hypotheses to be tested. For example, if they know that the investigator thinks that, compared with women, men will emphasize looks in their personal ads, many coders will tend to shade their judgments in that direction. Therefore, although coders will need training to apply the codes accurately, this training must not tip off the researcher's expectations about findings.

STUDYING CHANGE

Content analysis often examines social change because cultural artifacts tend to be deposited over time. Magazines and newspapers, for example, invite the search for trends—thus, Lowenthal measured changes in the biographies published in popular magazines. The study of American occultism could be transformed into a study of change merely by coding *Yellow Page* listings from past years. Many studies have examined shifts in the proportion of nonwhites in advertisements and in television shows. Others have charted the rapid increase in the percentage of book sales made up by romance novels.

Studies of change based on verbal, visual, or textual materials must, of course, ensure that biases are constant over the period being studied. If materials were more or less likely to be deposited at various periods, the observed changes might not have taken place—the same applies to differential probabilities of survival. In general, however, no special methods beyond those used to analyze data from one period in time are required to study change.

A series of studies based on content analyses have assessed the hypothesis that the American news media are becoming increasingly judgmental and biased in their coverage of presidential election campaigns. Kiku Adatto (1990) coded television network news coverage of the 1968 and 1988 campaigns. In 1968, when presidential candidates were shown on the screen, the spoken words accompanying the image were the candidates' own words 84 percent of the time. Moreover, the average "sound bite" of uninterrupted speech by a candidate on television news lasted 42 seconds. But, during the 1988 election, the average uninterrupted sound bite was only 10 seconds long, and the candidate's actual words were seldom heard. For every minute a presidential candidate was allowed to speak on the news, the reporter covering him was broadcast for 6 minutes. Replication research found the 1988 pattern held in 1992 (Patterson, 1994).

The hypothesis was about what was shown on television, not about how people may have responded to it—hence, television news tapes were the appropriate units of analysis. Timing sound bites and reporters' comments does not present problems of validity. The generalization from these data seems clear: television no longer *covers* the campaign as candidates actually conduct it, instead it *interprets* the campaign.

These results were confirmed by Thomas E. Patterson (1994), who found that presidential candidates' words are also being squeezed out of the print media. Patterson coded all front-page presidential election campaign stories that appeared in the *New York Times* from the 1960 election (Kennedy/Nixon) through 1992 (Clinton/Bush/Perot). In 1960, the average quote of a candidate's words was 14 lines. In 1992, it was 6 lines. In 1960, most campaign statements by candidates were interpreted as representing their policies. In 1992, more than 80 percent of the time campaign statements were interpreted on the basis of strategy—the *Times* writers interpreted campaigns as games to be won or lost, not as reflections of political philosophies.

In addition, Patterson coded 4,264 paragraphs randomly selected from stories about major party presidential nominees, as published in *Time* and *Newsweek* magazines during the 1960–1992 period. Among his coding categories were whether the paragraph contained evaluative references and, if so, whether these were favorable or unfavorable to the candidate. In 1960, of all evaluative references to John F. Kennedy and Richard M. Nixon, 75 percent were positive. In 1992, only 40 percent of reporters' evaluative references to Bill Clinton and to George Bush were favorable. Patterson also coded the covers of both magazines. In 1960, neither magazine printed a negative campaign cover. For example, when *Time* ran a cover story on Kennedy, the cover merely said, "Candidate Kennedy," and the Nixon cover said, "Candidate Nixon." In 1992, *Time* covers included "Why Voters Don't Trust Clinton" and "Is Bill Clinton for Real?"

Here, too, the selection of units of analysis was appropriate and the coding categories clear. Consequently, Patterson is justified in concluding that leading print publications have shifted from reporting what the candidates say to featuring partisan interpretations of what's "really" going on.

ETHICAL CONCERNS

Typically, unobtrusive methods have no capacity to harm. The material reported is public and does not relate to specific individuals. Of course, if you steal private letters or company documents to code, you are committing ethical as well as legal violations. However, there exist borderline cases in which care must be taken to protect the confidentiality of transactions and the privacy of individuals. For example, studies often are based on coding medical records. The confidentiality of doctor-patient relationships must be preserved, and it must never be possible for any individual case to be identified. The same principles apply to research studies based on other sorts of individual records: arrest records, credit histories, academic transcripts, or personnel files.

SUMMARY

Of all the data collection methods presented in this book, content analysis is the cheapest. Most studies are conducted in the library, using published documents. All that is required is a worthwhile research question and some effort. For example, the study of occult America discussed early in the chapter required only the purchase of an inexpensive CD-ROM (about $150). The rest was nothing more than clerical work. It seems surprising that professional journals aren't bursting with content analyses, but it remains the least utilized method of data collection. Perhaps that is because social work researchers tend to focus on individuals, and content analyses are better suited to studies of aggregate units or of cultural artifacts.

As we know, using a content analysis as a form of data collection is unobtrusive; that is, we do not intrude into our research participants' lives in any way. The following chapter continues our discussion of unobtrusive data collection methods by presenting how a social work research study can use another unobtrusive data collection method—using existing statistics—for doing a research study.

Jackie D. Sieppert

Steven L. McMurtry

Robert W. McClelland

Utilizing Existing Statistics

20

The previous chapter presented how a content analysis is used as an unobtrusive data collection method. This chapter continues our discussion of using existing data by concentrating on the use of aggregate-level data within a secondary analysis, as presented in Chapter 18. In a nutshell, analyzing existing statistics is nothing more than performing a secondary analysis of aggregate-level data.

This unobtrusive data collection method requires our *utilizing existing statistics,* the title of this chapter. Like the other data collection methods contained in Part VI, this unobtrusive data collection method does not collect primary, or firsthand, data. Rather, we turn to existing statistical records as our data sources.

As we know by now, an unobtrusive data collection method uses existing data sources located within government, private, and collaborative international organizations. It is technically correct to assume, however, that the "real data sources" are not those organizations that have the existing data, but are the individual units of analyses on which the statistics are based.

As we know from the chapters in Part V of this book, obtrusive data collection methods (i.e., observations, participant observation, interviewing, surveys) collect firsthand data directly, in one way or another, from the research participants themselves (individual units of analyses). When using these obtrusive data collection methods, we are totally responsible for our study's internal and external validities, from selecting our research question to disseminating our results. This is not true when using existing statistics as a data collection method because we have no control over how the statistics were derived; they have been computed by other researchers.

Thus, research studies that use existing statistical records focus not on reexamining the *data* collected by others, but rather on examining the *data analyses* previously generated by others. Aggregated summaries and reports, not micro-level data, are the fuel that drive research studies using existing statistical records. This point represents a subtle but important difference that makes research studies using existing aggregated statistics sufficiently unique to warrant a closer examination. We will now turn our attention to locating these existing aggregated statistics.

LOCATING SOURCES OF EXISTING STATISTICS

The range of research topics that can be studied using existing statistical data is matched by the wide variety of organizations and groups that collect such data. Aggregated statistics are reported on almost all aspects of our personal and professional lives—by governments, by employers, by private marketing firms, by professional associations, and so on. For this reason, finding the right sources of existing statistics to answer a particular research question can be a huge task.

The single most important piece of advice that can be given to a person using existing statistics as a data collection method is to seek help from information specialists found in local college and university libraries. These people are often very familiar with major sources of existing statistical data and are knowledgeable about the types of data (unit of analysis) contained in each source. If they do not know of a particular existing source appropriate to answer a specific research question, they have the knowledge and skills to track down sources that otherwise might never be discovered. Thus, we usually begin a search for an existing statistical data source at the local college or university library.

As we have said, sources of statistical data are generally classified into three broad categories: (1) government and other public agencies, (2) private or proprietary organizations, and (3) collaborative, international organizations. Each offers aggregated-level data, in the form of statistics, suitable for answering different types of research questions. Thus, with relevant research questions and variables in mind, we can locate an appropriate source(s) of statistical data and then examine it to answer our research question. Let us now turn our attention to the first source of existing statistics—government and other public agencies.

Government and Other Public Agencies

Federal, state, and municipal governments are the most accessible and largest sources of existing statistics. Departments and agencies at most levels produce numerous books, reports, and computerized compilations of data acquired through various sources. The U.S. Bureau of the Census annually publishes a book called the *Statistical Abstract of the United States,* for example, which is a collection of statistics gathered from over 200 government and private agencies. Presented in a wide variety of statistical lists, charts, figures, and tables, the *Statistical Abstract of the United States* contains data about many of the topics relevant to our profession. It contains, for example, statistics about death rates within states, the percentage of families with children who live in poverty, spending on law enforcement and rehabilitation, changes in divorce rates, number of physicians by region of the country, trends in the population of elderly Americans, and hundreds of other topics relevant to social work.

In fact, the only way to grasp the scope and magnitude of the *Statistical Abstract* is to obtain a copy and explore its contents. Best of all, the book is available free of charge at most public libraries. Computerized versions are being developed for easy access through large-scale data networks such as the Internet. Also, most university and college libraries and larger municipal libraries have separate sections for government documents such as the *Statistical Abstract.*

Many other forms of federal, state, and municipal statistics also exist. Answers to research questions can be found in existing statistics published by public agencies such as the National Center for Health Statistics, the Department of Labor, and the Federal Bureau of Investigation. State agencies (such as each state's department of social services) provide statistics about social workers' caseloads in public social service agencies, changes in reporting of alleged child sexual abuse cases, recidivism rates among young offenders, patterns of physical and mental health care usage, and so on.

Municipal departments are obviously more limited in scope and resources, but they too compile statistics relevant to our profession. We must never overlook any of these public departments and organizations, as they are often a good starting point for any piece of social work research that uses existing statistics as a data collection method. Government agencies can be found in local telephone books (many of which have a "blue pages" section for governmental listings). We need to look through these listings and make note of those agencies that appear to be related to our research question. We can then call these

agencies to find out whether they publish annual reports on our topic.

Private or Proprietary Organizations

A second source of existing statistical data is the myriad of nonprofit or proprietary agencies and organizations. Statistics collected and/or reported by private sources are often harder to locate than those provided by governmental sources. They may be more expensive to access as well. However, such sources provide statistical data that may be unavailable in any other form. If we wanted to conduct a research study on attitudes about abortion in a particular state, for example, the best source of data might be existing statistics that were generated by a commercial polling firm in the region. Or to find data about changes in housing availability and construction in a particular geographical area, we might turn to the local Chamber of Commerce.

Even private social service agencies increasingly collect and report statistical data as part of their emphasis on accountability. Finally, "watchdog" organizations and various advocacy groups make disseminating statistics a particular part of their work. Together, these can provide data to examine an agency's effectiveness and efficiency, for example.

There are other nongovernmental organizations that can also provide useful statistics. Two private sources of existing statistical data most relevant to our profession are the National Association of Social Workers (NASW) and the Council on Social Work Education (CSWE). Like other professional accrediting organizations, they keep records regarding the characteristics and activities of their members. Both organizations produce numerous statistical reports about issues of interest to their members. We could turn to the NASW for data about the number of Americans with no or inadequate health insurance coverage, for example. The CSWE regularly publishes statistics on faculty and students within all accredited schools and departments of social work in the United States.

What about organizations that focus on specific substantive issues? In child welfare, for example, there are organizations such as the Child Welfare League of America, the American Association for Protecting

Children, the American Public Welfare Association, and the Children's Defense Fund. Other fields have similar organizations and serve the same purpose as those in social work.

Collaborative International Organizations

The third, and final, source of existing statistical data is collaborative international organizations. These organizations operate on a cooperative basis to collect and distribute statistical data that allow for cross-cultural comparisons on issues of direct relevance to social policy. The United Nations, for example, publishes the *Demographic Yearbook* and the *United Nations Statistical Yearbook*. These two publications supply data from many countries regarding birth rates, death rates, literacy rates, the proportion of people living in urban areas, and numerous other variables.

With the rapid evolution of computers, and thus information technology, international compilations of existing statistics are increasing in both their scope and quality. Statistical databases are becoming more comprehensive, more timely, and more easily accessed. A good illustration of this is the Luxembourg Income Study (LIS), mentioned in Chapter 18. The LIS is a financially independent division of the Center for the Study of Population, Poverty, and Public Policy/International Networks for Studies in Technology, Environment, Alternatives, and Development (CEPS/INSTEAD). This lengthy acronym just means that the Luxembourg Government has created an independent organization whose mandate is to foster international comparative research on income and well-being.

The LIS organization maintains over 40 data sets that contain comprehensive measures of income and well-being for over 17 modern industrialized welfare states. Each country contributes a wide range of statistical data, such as population demographics, family structure, levels of income, and changes in industrial or agricultural output. Use of these statistical summaries is restricted to social science research purposes, however, and no private or commercial use is permitted. The LIS is one example of a source for comparative and policy research in applied economics, sociology, and public policy. Existing statistical data sets on other topics are increasingly becoming available through improved computer technology.

Whether we turn to governmental agencies, private and proprietary channels, or international organizations, it is clear that existing statistical data *are* available to answer many research questions. Once we know what we want to study and go to the library to talk with an information specialist, we will soon be immersed in statistical data that we might never have dreamed existed.

Let us take a simple example to illustrate how the forgoing data sources can be used to examine a simple research problem—the overrepresentation of ethnic minorities in foster care services. How might the named organizations, the data sources, be helpful in studying this issue? The example in Box 20.1 shows how we could turn to private and governmental child welfare organizations as a way of gathering data on this issue.

ADVANTAGES AND DISADVANTAGES

Like all data collection methods, analyzing existing statistics has its advantages and disadvantages.

Advantages

Analyzing existing statistics has many benefits. Among these are that existing statistics: (1) provide historical and conceptual contexts to a research study that uses primary, or firsthand, data; (2) can be the only data collection method available; (3) save time, money, and labor; (4) facilitate the development and refinement of the research question; and (5) facilitate theory development.

Provides Historical and Conceptual Contexts

Utilizing existing statistics provides a historical or conceptual context to a research study that uses primary, or firsthand, data. If we wanted to study the effects of poverty among single-parent families, for example, we might first want to determine the nature of poverty in our society. Existing statistics are ideal for this purpose. Through official governmental reports we could determine overall poverty rates, poverty rates for different

BOX 20.1

Using Governmental and Private-Agency Statistics

Fran is clinical director of a private, nonprofit agency that provides foster care, group-home care, and residential treatment for children in a small city in Arizona. She has noticed that there is a higher number of ethnic minority children in her agency's caseload than would be expected based on the proportion of ethnic minority children in the general population. She decides to do a study of this issue using existing statistics already gathered by various sources as her data collection method.

Fran first talks with the information specialist at the local library, asking for help to conduct a computer search through the library's existing data bases. The search reveals a series of reports, titled *Characteristics of Children in Substitute and Adoptive Care,* that were sponsored by the American Public Welfare Association and that provide several years of data reported by states on their populations of children in various kinds of foster and adoptive care. She also locates an annual publication produced by the Children's Defense Fund, and this provides a variety of background data on the well-being of children in the United States. Next, Fran checks in the library's government documents section. She locates recent census data on the distribution of persons under the age of 18 across different ethnic groups in her county.

Fran now turns to state-level resources, where a quick check of government listings in the telephone book reveals two agencies that appear likely to have relevant data. One is the Foster Care Review Board, which is comprised of citizen volunteers who assist juvenile courts by reviewing the progress of children in foster care statewide.

A quick call to the Board reveals that they produce an annual report that lists a variety of statistics. These include the number of foster children in the state, where they are placed, and how long they have been in care,

and descriptive data such as their ethnicity, race, gender, age and so on.

Fran also learns that the Board's annual reports from previous years contain similar data, thus a visit to the Board's office provides her with the historical data needed to identify trends in the statistics she is using. Finally, she discovers that two years earlier the Board produced a special issue of its annual report that was dedicated to the topic of ethnic minority children in foster care, and this issue offers additional statistics not normally recorded in most annual reports.

Another state agency is the Administration for Children, Youth, and Families, a division of the state's social services department. A call to the division connects her with a staff member who informs her that a special review of foster children was conducted by the agency only a few months before. Data from this review confirm her perception that minority children are overrepresented in foster care in the state, and it provides a range of other data that may be helpful in determining the causes of this problem.

From these sources Fran now has the data she needs to paint a detailed picture of minority foster children at the national and state levels. She also has the ability to examine the problem in terms of both point-in-time circumstances and longitudinal trends, and the latter suggests that the problem of overrepresentation has grown worse. There is also evidence to indicate that the problem is more severe in her state than nationally. Finally, corollary data on related variables, together with the more intensive work done in the special studies by the Foster Care Review Board and the Administration for Children, Youth, and Families, gives Fran a basis for beginning to understand the causes of the problem and the type of research study that must be done to investigate solutions.

types of families, long-term changes in family incomes, and so on. We might even be able to tell what percentage of families live under the poverty line in a particular geographical region, and how many of these are single-parent families. These data alone would allow us to do a better job in conceptualizing and operationalizing our study.

Can Be the Only Data Collection Method Available

Existing statistical records are extremely useful in situations where our research questions are unanswerable by other data collection methods. Take, for example, the concepts of crime rates, health indicators, prevalence of child abuse, death rates, affirmative action, immigration trends, and changes in unemployment. We cannot directly observe these concepts, and primary, firsthand, obtrusive data collection methods such as surveys are usually far beyond the resources available. However, the data (the statistics) we need may already exist; we just have to find them and make them work for us to answer our research question.

Much of what we know about our past, the current structures in society, and societal change is a direct product of analyzing existing statistics gathered by others. It is best, therefore, not to view the use of existing statistics as a limited, rarely employed data collection method. Instead, our ability to answer many important research questions may be limited only by our own research skills and the quality of available statistical data sources.

Saves Time, Money, and Labor

On a practical level, we can save a considerable investment in time, money, and labor by using existing statistics (Singleton, Straits, & Miller-Straits, 1993). These savings are realized because the cost of developing data collection instruments and the effort of actually collecting the data have already been borne by others. We do not have to find resources to design questionnaires or interview schedules, train interviewers, devise sampling strategies, or place telephone calls to research participants.

Similarly, the process of collecting, aggregating, and reporting the statistics has been done for us. This obviously saves time and money. Even when a fee is charged for using an existing statistical data set, the true cost of conducting the original study is almost always substantially higher than the fee. In a nutshell, using existing statistical data often allows us to answer research questions that we could not possibly answer on our own limited research budgets.

Facilitates the Development and Refinement of the Research Question

In addition to making a large-scale research study more feasible, existing statistics also facilitate the development and refinement of our research question. By first exploring statistical records, for example, we can often

test the potential of future research efforts. This is usually accomplished by testing our preliminary hypothesis using existing statistics. If our hypothesis is not supported, we can rethink the theoretical foundations underlying the hypothesis, reshape the conceptual and operational definitions of the concepts within it, or consider alternative measurement instruments.

Facilitates Theory Development

Using existing statistical records as a data collection method contributes to theory development. Most social work research studies, for example, are based on small sample sizes and often lack longitudinal time frames. This obviously limits their generalizability and thus their contributions to our profession's knowledge base. Statistical data are often compiled (via aggregation) from large, randomly selected samples. The statistics provided by the U.S. Census Bureau, for example, are based on a wide range of data collection methods and data sources. They incorporate data about diverse respondents and social problems.

The unique nature of statistical data contributes to theory development in one more way. Many organizations that distribute statistical data have been collecting the same data for decades. This enables us to compare statistical data across different time periods in an attempt to understand social and cultural change. We can use statistics from the U.S. Census Bureau, for example, to trace changes in family structures in America, the aging of our population, the impact of Generation X on the labor force, and so on. The contribution of existing statistical records to this type of theory development cannot be overemphasized. Research studies using existing statistics as a data collection method is one of the few ways we can effectively conduct long-term longitudinal studies.

Disadvantages

Existing statistical records are usually intended to serve administrative and public policy uses. This creates a number of methodological concerns when they are employed for research purposes. In general, there are four broad concerns that apply to any given statistical record. They include: (1) the "ecological fallacy" issue, (2) reliability, (3) validity, and (4) missing data.

The "Ecological Fallacy"

We frequently want to learn something about single individuals (units of analysis). What do we know about individuals who live below the poverty line in a particular city or town, for example? What is their life like, and what problems do they face in trying to make a living? Existing statistics often cannot provide data that easily answer these questions. As we know, existing statistics are published in the form of aggregate-level data. They summarize and describe the characteristics of larger groups, but tell us nothing about individuals, or micro-level data. This represents a critical distinction in terms of our unit of analysis.

Published statistics provide estimates of how many people live below the poverty line in the whole nation, or in a particular state, for example. They may even provide the sources of income the poor rely on, what their average income is, or how that income is spent. All of these aggregated statistical estimates, though, tell us only about "groups" of the poor. We cannot make any inferences about the characteristics or experiences of any individual person from the aggregated statistics. To do so would be to commit an *ecological fallacy*, which is a serious threat in research studies using existing statistical records. An ecological fallacy occurs when the characteristics or properties of a group are used to draw conclusions about an individual.

Using our example, we might be tempted to make inferences about the poor who rely on a local food bank for assistance. Based on *group* data, or aggregated-level data, it would be all too easy to conclude that these people are mother-only families, work in unpaid or low-wage jobs, or have limited educational attainment. In reality, though, some individuals who visit the food bank may be very different than the aggregated-level data suggest. Some people may be comparatively well educated and members of intact family units who were unexpectedly caught in the decline of a vital local industry.

The lesson to be drawn from these examples is that, when using existing statistical records for any research study, we must first identify our unit of analysis. It is then necessary to examine our data source to ensure that the data relate to the unit we wish to describe.

Assessing Reliability

As we know, reliability is essentially a matter of consistency. The reliability of existing statistical records refers to the same thing. That is, do the records reliably report the variables they claim to report? There are two common reliability problems that appear when using existing statistical records: (1) changes over time in how variables are conceptually and operationally defined, and (2) alternate definitions of those variables across multiple data sources.

Changes in Conceptual and Operational Definitions. The first reliability issue—changes in conceptual and operational definitions over time—is one that affects most existing statistical records. Changes occur in the official definitions of many variables targeted by social work researchers. The operational definitions of variables measuring poverty, unemployment, types of crime, child abuse, and so on often change as our own perspectives about the problem change. Child abuse is a good example. Thirty or 40 years ago, views about what constitutes child abuse were very different than those now espoused by our society. A slight spanking was considered by many to be a routine part of parenting. Now, this once-sanctioned act might often be considered a form of child abuse. Thus, the findings from a longitudinal study on the rates of child abuse, using existing statistics, may be inconsistent and thus not reliable. The operational definition of the variable being measured has simply changed over time.

Temporal changes affect more than operational definitions, however. They also have subsequent impacts on the way the data are collected. Let us look again at child abuse as an illustration of this point. Twenty years ago, all recording of alleged child abuse perpetrators was done on paper files. Today, most of our child welfare agencies rely on computerized management information systems. These changes allow for more timely and accurate record keeping regarding alleged perpetrators. In other words, computerized management information systems may have indirectly helped to increase the apparent rates of child abuse. Also, public awareness of child abuse may have made it much more likely to be reported, though the actual incidence may not have changed.

Alternate Operational Definitions of Variables. The second major issue surrounding reliability of existing statistics relates to the equivalence of the statistics across multiple data sources. There is always more than one way to measure any variable, and many are open to a variety of operational definitions. A good example of this can be found in crime statistics.

Most police departments maintain records about the incidence of domestic violence in their particular communities. Keeping statistics about domestic violence would appear to be a relatively routine and straightforward matter. The operational definition of domestic violence, however, more often than not differs from one department to another. In reports of domestic violence, some departments might include incidents of verbal abuse, or cases where official charges were not filed against the alleged offender.

On the other hand, other departments might record only those incidents in which official criminal charges were filed or some severe form of violence occurred. This makes discrepancies between police department records not only possible, but very likely. *Reported* incidence of domestic violence, therefore, may often be very different than the *actual* incidence of domestic violence in any particular geographical area. It would be high if a department chose to have a very loose and global operational definition of domestic violence, and it would be low if a department chose to have a narrow and strict operational definition of domestic violence.

The reliability of existing domestic violence statistics depends on more than operational definitions alone, however. Let us say that police statistics report the incidence of domestic violence to be much higher in California than in other states. Even if we have ruled out differences in operational definitions, there are other factors that could produce this result. The state's apparently higher incidence of domestic violence might simply reflect the results of a crackdown on domestic violence, which served to increases domestic violence arrest rates. The results might also reflect a broader societal awareness of domestic violence, or increased media coverage

of the problem (such as during the O.J. Simpson trial in California). In any case, the reliability of these data would have to be examined closely.

Another reliability problem is that changes occur over time in both *how* statistics are reported and *which* statistics get reported. Suppose we are tracking physical and mental health records that report the incidence of alcoholism by age groups. For several years, data may be reported on age groups 15 to 25, 26 to 35, 36 to 45, and over 45. Suddenly, however, the age groups are changed to 10 to 20, 21 to 30, and 31 to 40. Comparisons of alcoholism in age groups across time would thus be difficult to analyze because of the inconsistency in the way age groups were aggregated.

Changes in which statistics are reported are also problematic. We may be interested in tracking trends in binge drinking as one particular form of alcoholism, for example. Current statistical reports available from one key source may provide these data, breaking down alcoholism into statistics on binge drinking and other forms. We may find, however, that earlier reports from the same source do not separate various types of alcoholism in this way. Thus, we could be thwarted in our efforts to make comparisons over time, because we would have no reliable way of determining how many alcoholics were binge drinkers at the earlier date.

Assessing Validity

Some of the major benefits offered by existing statistical records can also lead to validity problems. As we know from Chapter 8, validity has to do with whether the variable we are measuring is being measured accurately. Problems can occur because we trade savings in time, money, and labor for our direct control over the entire research study. Such control is always maintained by the organization that originally collected and aggregated the data. This means that our research question, conceptual and operational definitions, research methods and procedures, and statistical reports were all previously chosen by the organization supplying the statistics. Any errors in these areas represent errors in measurement, and hence validity problems.

There are a few methods we can use to ensure that conceptual or data collection errors have been avoided in any given existing statistical data source. Most important of these is that we must carefully and critically examine how the data were collected in the first place, with an eye toward the study's "scientific rigor." Were understandable questions asked, and could they in fact be answered? Were respondents selected using appropriate random sampling techniques? Were data collection procedures rigorous, and were they closely followed? Were the variables measured correctly? Answering such questions provides a solid foundation from which to judge the validity of an existing statistical data record.

Deductive Versus Inductive Reasoning.   Even if a critical review of the statistical data is positive, however, problems of validity still arise. One of the most common validity problems revolves around the issue of using existing data in an inductive research study. A research study using existing statistics as a data collection method can indeed be a deductive one, however. That is, a deductive study starts with a theoretical framework and has a hypothesis derived from the framework. The hypothesis is operationally defined, research measuring instruments are selected, and data collection is implemented. The data are analyzed, and based upon the data analysis, the hypothesis is rejected or accepted. As can be seen in Figure 1.4, our study is conducted in a deductive manner, progressing from an abstract way of thinking to a concrete way of thinking.

As noted above, however, research studies using existing statistics as a data collection method do not have to rely on a deductive process. Instead, they can also use inductive processes where we move from a concrete way of thinking to an abstract way of thinking. Our inquiry begins not with a well-defined theoretical framework, as in deductive studies, but with micro-level data aggregated in a statistical report(s). These inductive studies start out by examining the existing statistics in relation to the general research questions.

From this point, we focus on detecting patterns within the statistics themselves. Are there, for instance, employment, educational, and family characteristics that are typical of poor families in a particular state? If such patterns are found, our next step is to develop hypotheses and theories that might explain the findings. Over time these hypotheses might be supported by detecting

the same patterns in other existing statistical records, thereby building upon or altering an existing theory.

There are two major ways that the inductive research process generates validity problems: (1) the lack of an original theoretical framework for collecting the data, and (2) the need to construct indirect measures of variables.

1. Lack of an Original Theoretical Framework.   The theoretical framework used to guide the original data collection strategy is often not made clear in subsequent statistical reports. This means that the rationale underlying such steps as the selection of and the operationalization of variables is unknown. Just as frequently, our own conceptualizations can differ from those of the persons who collected the original data. In either case, a common theoretical framework is lacking, meaning that the variables found in the existing statistical records may not be a valid measure of the concept we are trying to assess in our study.

Consider the work that women do in our society as an example. In studying the contributions made by women to the workforce, official government agencies tend to define women's labor only in terms of paid employment, and they tend to ignore work that does not earn cash for the family (Jacobson, 1992). When studying the same topic, using the statistics provided by those same government agencies, we would likely want to expand our operational definition of "work."

Along with paid labor, our new operational definition of work might include meal preparation, child care, and general housework. This new operational definition would not be measured by official statistics, however. It might be argued that our definition of "work" is more valid than that used in the government statistics. The problem is that by expanding our operational definition of work we might begin to address an entirely different concept than the one measured by the "official statistics." By relying on existing statistical records, therefore, we are constrained by the initial measures used in compiling the statistics, and our own study may be limited by the degree of validity of those initial measurements.

2. Indirect Measurement of Variables.   The second validity issue directly relates to the first. It occurs when the variables of interest are not measured directly within the existing statistical records. This situation is common in social science research. Even though social service programs collect statistics on many aspects of their operations, few directly measure the achievement of their objectives, client change, or worker effectiveness.

In such situations, we are forced to construct proxy variables from the available statistics. In other words, we need to create an indirect measure of the concept we are studying. Unfortunately, the validity of this indirect measure or proxy variable is hard to establish.

A good example of constructing indirect measures is found in assessments of physical and mental health in the elderly. The U.S. Census Bureau might ask elderly citizens a series of questions about their physical and mental health. These questions might ask them to compare how "healthy" they are relative to others their age, whether they are physically active, whether they have had a major physical or mental problem over the last year, whether they received medical assistance over the last year, and whether they suffered an accidental injury over the last year.

Now, suppose we want to use these existing statistics to conduct a study of the elderly, and we need a measure of their *current* physical and mental health status. None of these variables directly measure what we want. However, we could construct a proxy variable—an index that uses all of these variables—to identify those seniors who are most likely to enjoy good health right now. If the seniors are physically active, feel healthy, and have been both accident and illness free for the last year, we could conclude that they are probably healthy right now. There are, however, no guarantees that such responses to these questions ensure current good health. Our proxy variable, physical and mental health, would have an unknown degree of error, or uncertain measurement validity.

Assessing the Extent of Missing Data

We all know some people who refuse to answer certain questions on any survey. It might be a question about their income, their age, or any other topic they might consider sensitive. Whenever an individual refuses to answer such questions, it creates gaps in the subsequent data set and any statistics computed from it. Such refusals are common in most studies. We are rarely able

to ensure that all respondents answer every question asked of them. This means that missing data are inevitably an issue in any research study using existing statistical records.

Missing data cannot be blamed on respondents alone, however. Many other factors play a role in contributing to missing data. The original research team, for example, may have inadvertently neglected to interview all respondents from a preselected neighborhood. Or perhaps social workers delegated to collect data on particular variables found it very difficult to do so and thus did not provide data on those variables for many of their cases. One example is data on household income which, for a variety of reasons, is often very difficult to collect accurately.

Still other reasons for missing data include failure by the administrator, or researcher, to provide clear instructions on how line-level staff should record the data. A common example is written forms or computerized information systems that are sometimes so difficult to understand that data are frequently omitted. Finally, we may find that data are missing from statistical records simply because those who originally collected the data did not share our ideas about what was important and thus did not gather data on one or more variables we see as being critical.

Next to respondent refusals, the most common reason for missing data in existing statistical data sets is probably societal change itself. As society changes, questions that are deemed important also change. Statistics regarding liquor prohibition do not mean much in today's society, for example. Nor were questions about the growth of HIV/AIDS even known in past decades. As a reflection of these changes, organizations that collect data regularly start or stop gathering certain types of data. This practice inevitably generates missing data in statistical records.

Random and Systematic Errors.   Regardless of the reason for missing data, it is a very serious issue. The occurrence of missing data introduces error into the statistics. As we know from Chapters 8 and 11, this error has two forms, random error and systematic error. Random error occurs when, for no particular reason, data are lacking on some cases in the data set from which the statistics were compiled. Because there is no pattern as to which cases are missing data and which cases are not, it is also unlikely that the presence of random error will bias the statistics in any particular direction.

Of greater concern is systematic error. This occurs when data are missing on specific types of cases from which statistics were compiled. For example, suppose statistics were gathered on employment in a particular region, but the people on which the statistics were based included only those with known residences. This would mean that homeless people would not be among those included in the statistics. Because homeless people have a much higher rate of joblessness, the effect of their omission would be to cause the statistics to underestimate the level of joblessness in the region, and this, in turn, would drastically limit the overall value of the data.

The only solution is to exercise caution when using statistical records. Before we commit to conducting a research study using a particular statistical record, we need to ensure that the data set is not missing an inordinate amount of data. In addition, we need to spend some time exploring the statistics provided. Not only should the data be generally complete, but the people who collected the original data should have reported the steps that were taken to minimize missing data.

STEPS IN ANALYZING EXISTING STATISTICS

We recently completed a study that used existing statistical records as a data collection method. We will use it as an example here because of our familiarity with how the study was conducted and because it addresses an issue of interest to social work students—faculty/student ratios within graduate schools of social work (McMurtry & McClelland, 1995). This section address four basic steps when using existing statistics as a data collection method: (1) formulating the research question, (2) finding existing statistical records, (3) assessing validity and reliability, and (4) analyzing the data.

Step 1: Formulating the Research Question

Our study began with personal experiences that suggested that the number of undergraduate and graduate

social work students was increasing, but few corresponding increases were occurring in the number of social work faculty available to teach them. This raised a concern that there may be too few qualified faculty to meet the needs of social work students. From this assumption, two research questions were generated: (1) What are the trends in social work student enrollments, staffing patterns, and faculty/student ratios in schools and departments of social work in recent years? and (2) How do these trends compare with those in related disciplines?

Step 2: Finding Existing Statistical Records

As mentioned earlier, after developing the initial research questions, our next step in using existing statistical records as a data collection method was to identify an appropriate data source. In our case, we were aware that the accrediting body for social work programs in the United States, CSWE, publishes an annual report on accredited schools and departments. This report is titled *Statistics on Social Work Education in the United States*. Its primary unit of analysis is the social work programs themselves. These data are collected via cross-sectional surveys mailed to each social work program each year.

Schools and departments are asked to provide data on their students, their faculty, and other aspects of their program as of November 1 of the year being studied. Five standardized, self-administered survey instruments are used to collect data on faculty, bachelor's programs, master's programs, doctoral programs, and programs in candidacy. Each school or department receives only the instrument(s) that apply to its specific programs.

Our study's original intent was to examine faculty/student ratios in social work programs at all three degree levels. Standards recommended by the CSWE are for a 1:12 ratio of faculty to students at the master's level and a 1:25 ratio at the bachelor's level (no specific standard is suggested for doctoral programs). As can be all too common when doing a research study using statistical records, we found we had to narrow our study's focus because of the lack of data in the CSWE's published statistics.

Specifically, the CSWE annual statistics did not record data on faculty/student ratios at the bachelor's level, and it was impossible to compute these ratios retroactively from the data available. General data on faculty/student ratios were available for doctoral programs, but other data (such as the number of faculty specifically assigned to doctoral education in each school or department) were not present, so our study had to be narrowed to master's programs alone, where a full range of necessary data were readily available.

Step 3: Assessing Validity and Reliability

Our next consideration was the validity and reliability of the statistics in the CSWE annual reports, our data sources. Copies of these reports were obtained for the years 1977 to 1993, which allowed us to review trends over the 17-year period. To do this reliably, however, data on key variables such as student enrollment and faculty numbers would have to have been collected in a consistent way over that entire 17-year period. Fortunately, we found that, in gathering data from member schools and departments, the CSWE has used the same operational definition over time for each variable used in computing faculty/student ratios in schools and departments of social work. All part-time students, for example, are assigned a value of one-half, and full-time students a value of one.

Faculty numbers are differentiated by whether they hold tenured or nontenured positions and by the amount of time they spend teaching students at the bachelor's, master's, and doctoral levels. Also, data in the annual report show that response rates for the survey have remained high over the years. For master's programs, nonresponse rates averaged between 1 and 3 percent per year, meaning that missing data were not sufficiently frequent to cast doubt on the consistency of the data over time.

Although these factors suggest that the CSWE data were reliable, determining validity is an equally important but often more difficult task. Low reliability is often a sign that validity is also low, but high reliability is not a guarantee of high validity. This is because the measure in question may be reliably measuring the wrong variable. In our study, for example, the reliability of the CSWE data appeared to be high, so our task in assessing the validity of these data was to examine whether ambiguity existed

in the operational definitions of the variables that could lead to their being misunderstood and thus mismeasured. Fortunately, the CSWE data had four important strengths that, when combined, suggested that the validity of the statistics they presented was high. First, the variables being measured—student enrollments and faculty numbers—are relatively straightforward and unambiguous variables.

Second, these variables (and others, such as full-time-equivalency of faculty and students, and distinctions between degree-seeking and nondegree-seeking students) are based on established measurement practices in higher education and are thus familiar to most respondents. Third, these variables were clearly explained and operationalized in the data collection instruments. Finally, the instruments used in the CSWE's data collection process remained similar and predictable over time, and response rates remained high over the 17-year period assessed in our study.

One issue regarding validity did arise, however. Despite ongoing high response rates to the CSWE surveys, there were usually some missing data. In a few cases all the data for a particular variable were missing; in other cases some but not all of the data for a variable were provided. No patterns in the missing data were evident, and the amount of missing data was small (seldom exceeding 1 to 2 percent of all cases). Still, as in other research studies using existing statistics as a data collection method, the issue of missing data should be considered a caution against overgeneralizing a study's findings.

To discover how trends in social work education compared with those in related disciplines, we then had to find the accrediting organization for each of those disciplines and determine whether the organization published data similar to that in the CSWE annual statistics.

An information specialist at our university library helped us find a publication titled *Accredited Institutions of Post Secondary Education,* which is published by the American Council on Education. This book lists all the accredited programs in various disciplines at U.S. universities and colleges, and it also lists the name, address, and telephone number of each accrediting organization. From this list, we identified 13 related disciplines with which social work might appropriately be compared.

Each organization was contacted by phone, given a description of the CSWE annual statistics, and asked whether it published a similar report. Unfortunately, only four disciplines—communication sciences and disorders, law, public affairs and administration, and psychology—were found to publish comparable statistics. Copies of relevant reports were obtained either directly from the accrediting bodies for these disciplines or, when available, in our university library. Data from these reports became the basis for comparing these fields with social work.

Step 4: Analyzing the Data

This brings us to the question of what our study found. After producing numerous statistics and graphs, we found that faculty/student ratios rose steadily, from a median of 1 faculty member to 9.9 students in 1981 to a median of 1 faculty member to 13.4 students in 1993. Remembering the 1 to 12 ratio recommended by CSWE, it is evident that faculty/student ratios have been higher than desirable since 1988, with the current ratio now being almost 12 percent above the maximum ratio set by the CSWE.

In 1981, for example, most schools had a faculty/student ratio in the range of eight to nine students per faculty member, and only about 10 percent of them reported faculty/student ratios over 1 to 14. In contrast, by 1993 the most frequently occurring level of faculty/student ratios was over 15 students per faculty member. Almost 40 percent of the schools and departments had faculty/student ratios at or above the level of 1 to 14.

The CSWE statistics were also used to examine other aspects of the issue of faculty/student ratios. We looked at trends in student enrollment for Master of Social Work programs, for example. Results showed that MSW enrollment has grown markedly in recent years. Though the number of full-time MSW students declined during the early and middle 1980s, since 1986 enrollments have increased by 50 percent. As of late 1993, more than 21,000 full-time MSW students were enrolled in accredited U.S. schools and departments of social work, a higher number than ever before.

Growth has also occurred in the number of part-time MSW students. The CSWE statistics show that enrollment of part-time MSW students has increased steadily, almost tripling since 1977 to a total of more than 11,000. Together, part-time and full-time MSW students numbered more than 32,000 in late 1993.

We also found that the number of full-time, tenure-track faculty members in the CSWE-accredited schools and departments was about the same in 1993 as in 1977, with the 1993 number actually being slightly lower. This contrasts sharply with the high growth in student (undergraduate and graduate) enrollment of more than 50 percent over that same period. Clearly, schools and departments of social work in the United States have taken in many additional students without commensurately increasing tenure-track faculty.

With regard to whether similar trends have occurred in related disciplines, we were able to obtain suitable comparative data from the four fields noted earlier (communication sciences and disorders, law, public affairs and administration, and psychology). In the process, though, we also encountered one of the major difficulties of using existing statistical records. This is, the CSWE statistics and those of the other four accrediting organizations were collected at different times, for different periods, and in different ways. Thus, we had to report separately the data gathered from each discipline, and it also made the process of comparing across disciplines more difficult.

Our research study could not have been done without the use of statistical records. With them, we were able to show some important changes that have affected how graduate social work education is provided. These changes are meaningful for social work graduate students because they imply that each student now has a one-third smaller share of any faculty member's time than a decade ago. Moreover, the faculty members whose time students now seek are more likely to be part-time instructors and other non-tenure-track faculty than they are to be full-time faculty. Because part-time faculty usually do not remain on site, students are probably even more isolated from faculty than the overall faculty/student ratios suggest.

Of course, many part-time and non-tenure-track faculty are very capable instructors, and some are better than many tenure-track faculty. Still, data from the CSWE statistics show that, as of 1993, full-time tenure-track faculty were four times more likely to have a doctoral degree than full-time non-tenure-track faculty or part-time faculty. Assuming that doctoral-level training has value for social work educators, there are clearly qualitative issues raised by these trends.

One implication is that graduate social work education may be making a de facto return to a kind of apprentice model, where experienced practitioners (part-time faculty hired from field settings) teach those in the next generation. Meanwhile, workloads for full-time faculty may continue to increase as their numbers relative to part-time faculty drop and student enrollments rise. It should be no surprise to learn that full-time faculty report feeling less productive, while graduate students struggle to gain access to their professors.

SUMMARY

The process of using existing statistical records as a data collection method is relatively straightforward and quite simple. We begin with a general research question or a specific hypothesis. A statistical data record that might answer our question or hypothesis is then identified, often with the assistance of an information specialist located at a local library. Existing statistics are obtained and their quality is assessed by examining factors such as the conceptual framework used to shape the data collection process, the scientific rigor of data collection procedures, and the appropriateness of measures used to collect the data. If the reported statistics indeed seem to be empirically sound, we then conduct a quantitative data analysis of the statistics to answer our research question or to test our hypothesis.

As we know, using existing statistics as a form of data collection is unobtrusive, that is, we do not intrude into our research participants' lives in any way. The following chapter continues our discussion of unobtrusive data collection methods by presenting how a social work research study can use another unobtrusive data collection method, known as historical analysis, for doing a research study.

Paul H. Stuart

Historical
Research

21

The word *history* has three distinguishable meanings. In everyday speech, it refers to events that have occurred in the past, a living reality that is not accessible in the present. Second, it refers to the writings that attempt to describe and explain that past reality—history as a written product. Finally, there is "doing history," the process by which written history is produced, as we construct a report from the evidence left from the past (Hexter, 1971).

This chapter focuses on historical research in our profession in the third sense: the process by which we study the past. It is the fourth and last unobtrusive data collection method that is presented in this book. It should be noted, however, that a historical research study can indeed become an obtrusive data collection method if people are interviewed as data sources. As with the eight data collection methods described in Parts V and VI, historical analysis, sometimes referred to as historical research, can also be viewed as a research approach.

THE PURPOSE OF HISTORICAL RESEARCH

There are potentially as many reasons for doing a historical research study as there are people. Some of us simply find the past interesting, sometimes because we are disaffected with the present and wish to return to a presumably simpler time. On the other hand, others may find in the past heroes and heroines whose exemplary behavior provides a model for the present. Some historians view history as a story of progress: They seek the origins of modern practices and institutions in the past. Others see history as a story of decline; they look for the seeds of decay (D.H. Fischer, 1970).

Ideally, we should always attempt to understand the past on its own terms. Real historical understanding is not achieved by the subordination of the past to the present, but rather by making the past our present and attempting to see life with the eyes of another century than our own (Butterfield, 1931). Such a goal implies that we attempt to achieve objectivity in our description of a past empirical reality.

A *biography* tells the story of one individual's life, often suggesting what the person's importance was for social, political, or intellectual developments of the times.

Much historical writing in social work is biographical. There are book-length biographies that focus on prominent individuals as well as collections of brief biographical sketches of important social workers and social reformers (e.g., Seidl, 1995; Trattner, 1987).

Collective biographies are studies of the characteristics of groups of people who lived during a past period and who had a common trait. These biographies make it possible to concentrate on ordinary individuals. A study of people who worked for the Philadelphia Society for Organizing Charity in 1880, for example, provides a useful check on generalizations derived from biographies of individuals who were prominent in the charity organization movement (Rauch, 1975). An examination of early settlement house leaders enabled a researcher to explore the forces that led to a long-term commitment to activism (Kalberg, 1975).

Much historical research in our profession is generated by general theoretical questions. Studies of the development of social work, for example, may be informed by general theories about how professions develop. In addition, theories of organizational change have led to studies of agency development. Many of the hypotheses derived from social science theory can be investigated only by using historical research methodology. The nature of the ideas underlying social work at various points in time has stimulated many historical research studies. Often, a historical report on a specialized topic suggests new research areas.

What these efforts have in common is that they attempt to describe a past reality. Because the past is inaccessible to direct observation, historical research methods rely on analyzing existing documents, physical remains, and memories left over from the past. Social workers doing a historical research study are seldom present at the events they are studying; thus, they must rely on unobtrusive measures that yield data not obtained directly by personal interviews or survey questionnaires.

We frequently use in our historical studies the *findings* from past personal interviews and surveys, however. Unobtrusive measures have the advantage of being nonreactive; that is, the people being studied are not aware that they are being observed. Thus, they do not alter their "normal" responses for the benefit of the researcher. We have the additional advantage of knowing the outcomes of the events—a knowledge that was obviously denied to the participants.

Explaining the Past

Written history is based on an analysis of the remains left over from the past. These remains are both abundant and incomplete, and we must assess them for accuracy and significance before we can synthesize them into written history. Such remains are generally documents produced by people with a personal stake in the events being studied. Thus, it is important for us to understand these people and the social contexts in which they lived. It is this appreciation of the context of events that provides the greatest utility of historical research because it requires us to enter into the life of another era. We must have empathy as well as an objective understanding of the social forces that influenced the past events.

There is a large range of material that we must take into account when doing a historical research study. Some have argued that we need to make more use of social science concepts and methods. Each topic presented in this book is potentially useful to those of us who wish to carry out a historical research study. As we know, the research question we are trying to answer determines which data collection method and analysis are used in any given research study.

STEPS IN DOING HISTORICAL RESEARCH

Social workers who are doing a historical research study attempt to explain the past based on surviving remains. These remains can be documents, artifacts, and sometimes people's memories, if the participants in the events we are studying are still alive or if their recollections have been preserved in interviews or recorded by some other means. As we have previously mentioned, our temporal distance from the events we are studying makes direct observation impossible, but in another way a temporal distance might be to our advantage. We may be able to be more objective and to take a "broader view."

The difficulties we face when doing a historical research study have to do with focusing on a specific researchable topic, assembling the sources of data necessary to provide objective data, arriving at an understanding of the topic, and constructing a narrative that describes and explains what happened.

We can list these four steps as follows: (1) choosing a research question, (2) gathering evidence that bears on the research questions, (3) determining what the evidence means (synthesis), and (4) writing the report. Together, these four steps provide us with a framework for doing a historical research study.

Step 1: Choosing a Research Question

In choosing a research question, the most important consideration is the extent of our personal interest in the topic, although we must also know something about the period we choose. We may be interested in a specialization within the field of social work, such as school social work; or in an early use of a particular social work method, such as behavior modification; or in services to a racial or ethnic group, such as day care services; or in the development of an agency or organization, such as the United Way. The ideas about poverty and deviance that people had in the past might also be of interest to us. As in every other kind of research endeavor, it is important to know what others have written on our topic.

It has been said that historians write for today, for their own times. The history we write is influenced by the times in which we live. New times yield new ideas and thus new ways of understanding our past. Also, new problems in the present may cause us to search the past for analogs. Thus, publications on the major topics in American history appear every generation, offering different explanations and interpretations of the past.

Presentism

There is a danger in selecting research questions solely on the basis of their importance for the present. We may emphasize "modern" elements that occurred in the past to the extent that certain other important elements that have no analog in the present are excluded from our study. This error is called *presentism*. Some social workers in the 1920s, for example, were interested in psychoanalytic thought. Later, social work historians who were conscious of the significance of psychoanalysis for casework practice in their own times wrote about a "psychiatric deluge" as characterizing the period (Borenzweig, 1971). These writers implied that most social workers became Freudians after World War I.

A reexamination of the casework literature of the period, however, produced little evidence for this interpretation (Alexander, 1972). A subsequent investigation of casework practice in one Illinois social work agency led to the conclusion that psychoanalytic theory had very little impact on actual casework practice in that agency until after World War II (Field, 1980). Because most social workers doing historical research are highly aware of today's social problems, presentism is a problem to which they are unusually prone. This underscores the importance of choosing the best evidence (or data) and assessing it carefully.

Antiquarianism

The reverse of presentism is *antiquarianism,* which is an interest in past events without reference to their importance or significance. A fascination with the past as the past may lead us to distort our understanding of it by focusing only on those elements that made the past different from the present. It is analogous to the fascination with the exotic that characterizes some students of other cultures, who emphasize differences between groups and ignore commonalties.

Antiquarianism is perhaps rare in social work history. It is most likely to be a problem characteristic of those of us who detest the present or those who seek too rigidly to avoid presentism. These people may be tempted to cut themselves off from the present, but, in doing so, they may also cut themselves off from new methods of understanding the past. In short, we need a *balance* between present-mindedness and total isolation from the present when we do a historical research study.

Step 2: Gathering Evidence

Once we have selected a specific research question, our next task is to locate sufficient data to describe and explain what happened. Our goal is to write a report about the past—a report that is accurate and relatively complete, which provides an explanation for past events and which will be meaningful for today's practitioners. To write such a report, it is necessary to rely on the work of other historians and the best data available from the past.

The primary materials that we use are the documents and other remains left over from the past. More often than not, we find that these materials are, paradoxically, both abundant and scarce. An imposing amount of material remains, although materials that bear on our research question may be incomplete and fragmentary. We must be skilled in selecting particular materials from the many that are available. We must be skilled, too, in dealing with fragmentary and incomplete sources.

Types of Source Materials

We can use virtually any surviving document, artifact, or person's memory in doing a historical research study. Often these materials, particularly those that have been published, can be found in libraries. Many libraries have interlibrary loan services to exchange scarce materials.

Unpublished materials, such as letters, reports, and memoranda, are held by specialized libraries and archives. The most important archive for social workers is the Social Welfare History Archives Center at the University of Minnesota, at Minneapolis. Klaassen (1995) discusses the holdings of the Center, as well as major holdings in other depositories. Individuals associated with many important social welfare activities may still be alive and may respond to requests for interviews or correspondence. Some social welfare leaders have consented to be interviewed for oral history collections. Prucha (1994, Chapter 12) describes the major aids that help us to locate oral history materials.

Social service agencies also produce a variety of printed and nonprinted materials, including annual reports, manuals of procedures, employee and client records, and interoffice memoranda. Some of these materials have been placed in libraries or archives; others may be held by the originating agency. Romanofsky (1978) provides essays on the major national voluntary social service agencies, together with a discussion of the secondary literature and information on the location of the records of each agency. Foundations were important funders of social work, particularly in the decades before the Great Depression; Keele and Kiger (1984) provide similar essays on the major foundations.

Newspapers provide a record of social and political developments, including the activities of social service agencies. Files of back issues are held by newspapers and libraries; their availability is improved if they have been microfilmed. Many newspapers, as well as transcripts of some oral history interviews, have been microfilmed by the Microfilming Corporation of America (P.O. Box 10, Sanford, North Carolina 27330).

Locating these printed and unprinted documents is made easier by the finding aids available in college and university libraries. Prucha (1994) provides a guide to these finding aids as well as other reference works found in academic libraries. General and specialized bibliographies are a good place for us to start in the search for secondary sources. Freidel (1974) provides a useful general bibliography of American history, subdivided by topical, chronological, and geographical categories. It also lists the major archives and serials. Trattner and Achenbaum (1983) have compiled the best available published bibliography of social welfare history. It may be supplemented by the work of Chambers (1995), who provides annotations of writings published between 1982 and 1990. *The Newsletter of the Social Welfare History Group* (1956–present) provides an annual bibliography of writings in social welfare history.

Printed documents issued by state and federal governments are primary sources for many topics. Government documents include reports of legislative committee hearings and investigations, studies commissioned by legislative commissions and executive agencies, statistical compilations such as the census, the regular and special reports of executive agencies, and much more. Major federal agencies are described in Whitnah's (1983) *Government Agencies*. The laws of the state and federal governments form a specialized group of government documents. M.R. Lewis (1976) provides a useful guide to compilations of state and federal laws and other legal documents.

Most academic libraries have librarians who specialize in government publications or reference. They can help users locate needed government publications. Because of the large volume of U.S. government docu-

ments, specialized finding aids have been published to help us in the identification of the documents important to our research question. Schmeckebier and Eastin (1969) provide a good introduction to government documents. It may be supplemented by Prucha (1994, Chapter 13). Depository libraries of U.S. government documents are available; these are libraries that have agreed to receive selected government publications and make them available to the public. Many academic libraries are depository libraries for U.S. government documents. Most urban areas have several depository libraries.

State documents may be found in state libraries and archives and sometimes in academic and large public libraries. The availability of many specific documents and records can be established only by inquiry.

Unpublished records of federal, state, and local governments provide a rich primary source for social welfare history. Agencies that are part of the local, state, or federal government are governed by general policies regarding the disposition, accessibility, and retention of records. Many governments have archives that preserve the more important records of their agencies. Federal records are held by the National Archives and Records Service. This agency maintains central facilities in Washington, D.C., and College Park, Maryland, as well as 12 Regional Archives and 10 presidential libraries. Some of the unprinted documents in the National Archives have been microfilmed and are available for purchase; they are also available through interlibrary loan services.

Selection of Sources

Once we have identified a group of sources like those mentioned above, our next question is which source(s) to use. In general, our guiding criteria will involve the closeness of the source to the event described. If we are going to use a document as a source, for example, we must first determine whether the writer was present when the event took place. If the writer was not present, we must find out how the writer learned of the event. If the writer read of the event in a newspaper, for example, the newspaper account would be a better source to use because it is "closer" to the event that was described.

The best historical research study, therefore, is based on the exploration of primary sources. A *primary* source provides the words of the witnesses or first recorders of an event. *Secondary sources* are accounts, including books and articles, that are based on the analyses of primary sources. Although secondary sources are important for framing questions and getting a context for an investigation, with few exceptions historical reports based only on secondary sources add little that is new to our knowledge of the past. In addition, using secondary sources exclusively may perpetuate the errors made by earlier writers.

Primary sources include a broad range of materials: diaries, letters, and other documents produced by the participants in an event; laws, regulations, and records produced by organizations; and many others. Obviously, these are not of equal value for any given study. We must always assess the value of the primary sources before we decide which ones to use. Primary sources may be assessed by asking whether the author of the document had the opportunity to observe what was recorded, whether he or she was an objective witness, and whether the author was honest and unbiased. In addition, when the document was written may be important. Was it completed soon enough after the event described so that problems of faulty memory need not be of concern?

Some historians have emphasized that those doing historical research should assess the source's internal and external validity. Internal validity involves asking whether the document is internally consistent. External validity is a measure of the degree to which information in the document is consistent with what is already known about the period or event in question.

The transcripts of oral history interviews as well as autobiographies present additional problems. If a central person or an autobiography can be located, we must ask how much time has elapsed between the event being described and the person's recollection of the event. In general, the shorter the time between observation and recording, the better the evidence may be. A second question involves the bias of the source. The production of most documentary evidence is subjective: the author may have an interest in the event that biases the account. That is, people may recall or record events in such a way as to magnify their role in them or to make them conform to their own ideological beliefs. Such a problem may be par-

ticularly acute in oral history interviews where the individuals know that they are "speaking for the record."

Few sources are completely acceptable on all counts. If the authors of primary sources were able to observe the events they described, they probably had a vested interest in them. We must also recognize the fact that the observers may have been limited in their ability to observe because of their preconceptions or ignorance. Consequently, it is important to use as many relevant sources as possible in writing a historical report. We must always know our sources well. Did the writers have a vested interest in the outcome of an event? Were their beliefs involved in the event? In what ways do their accounts of the event differ from those of other participants?

Special Problems With Sources.   We may find that particular sources present special problems. Some sources may be systematically selective in the information they provide. Newspapers that slanted the news in accordance with a particular political point of view provide a familiar example. We can attempt to neutralize such selectivity by using a second source that corrects for the bias of the first one. Other sources that we find may be "unslanted" but may provide us with a very incomplete picture of what happened.

The laws passed by a legislature, for example, tell us little about how or whether the laws were enforced. One historical researcher dismissed a series of books on colonial public welfare programs written in the 1930s because they often provided "a sterile and unimaginative survey of the laws, without attention to colonial society" (Rothman, 1971). We should never neglect an available source that may bear on our research question. If we rely on a single source alone, our account may lack vitality because of the restricted information on which the narrative rests.

A recent novel makes this point well. The narrator described an account of a riot in an African country in the 1930s. Although many of the participants in the riot must still have been alive, the author of the account chose to rely on local newspapers alone, and the newspapers of colonial Africa printed only a portion of the truth. The resulting account was obviously biased. It reduced a complex human event to a recitation of dry half-truths, all properly footnoted (Naipaul, 1979).

Those of us who use existing statistical data, such as census reports, agency reports of caseloads and expenditures, and enrollment figures for schools of social work, face an analogous problem (see Chapter 20). Data are only as good as the procedures used to gather them. Quite frequently, the data collection methods have been less than desirable. A notorious example is the reporting of American Indian reservation populations by American Indian agents in the late 19th century. Some agents reported more American Indians than were actually present as a means of increasing the supplies allocated to the reservations by the United States Office of Indian Affairs. Consequently, the population figures for tribes reported by the Indian Office can be accepted only with caution.

It must not be assumed that only 19th century data are questionable. Reports of local governments on how they spent federal revenue-sharing funds in the 1970s were often inaccurate, to say the least (Magill, 1977). For some widely used statistical data, such as the United States decennial census reports, the problems of accuracy have been well-documented. For less frequently used data, we must evaluate the accuracy of the data for ourselves. An understanding of the accepted techniques of survey research, as presented in Chapter 17, can help to assess the strengths and weaknesses of statistical data.

Agency and other organizational records can provide information regarding how these data were collected. The completed questionnaires, interview schedules, or forms, if they are available, may suggest how much care was taken in compiling the data. Our knowledge of agency interests may provide us with clues for investigating probable data collection problems. As we have seen in Chapter 18, we can reanalyze the data if the questionnaires and unanalyzed responses are available.

An excellent example of a reevaluation of a source on which many earlier historians had relied involved an 1834 British government report. The report, which was based on a questionnaire distributed to English poor-law officials, resulted in the enactment of the restrictive Poor Law Amendment Act of 1834. Over 100 years later, an investigation of the original questionnaires revealed examples of faulty data analysis. Reanalysis of the data supported the conclusion that the providing of relief to large families was the *result* of low wages in the agricul-

tural parishes of England, not the *cause*, as the Poor Law Commission had concluded (Blaug, 1963, 1964).

Fragmentary Evidence

Gaps usually remain even when we have assembled all of the sources bearing on our research problem. Remains from the past are subject to attrition for a variety of reasons. Documents may be destroyed or lost, memories may be faulty, and individuals may not have had access to paper and pencil until long after the event. As the research questions that interest us may not have interested the participants in a past event, the sources may not speak to the questions we wish to study. For this reason, many of our historical research studies involve filling in the gaps in the historical record. For some of us, the gaps alone are the primary reasons for conducting a historical research study. The fact that the record is always incomplete is what makes history possible.

Gaps in the documentation may be welcomed as providing the incentive to do a historical research study. The "leaps" we make when writing our report, however, must always be consistent with the known facts. Our leaps must also be plausible, given our understanding of the period. We need to understand individual psychology, culture, and social systems theory in order to avoid making implausible connections across the gaps. Social science theory may provide useful hypotheses to bridge the gaps.

Gaps in statistical data present a special problem. Most standard computer packages have subroutines for handling missing observations, based on the assumption that the missing observations are randomly distributed. This assumption is untenable for many of the statistical data with which we work. Limiting the analysis to the surviving complete observations may be worse than assuming that individual missing observations are distributed randomly; the sample may be severely biased as a result.

In some cases, it may be possible to estimate the values of the missing observations using statistical techniques. In other cases, we may simply present our fragmentary data with a full account of their shortcomings. Often, in historical research, we either use incomplete data and learn something, however inadequate, or reject such data and learn nothing.

Step 3: Determining What the Evidence Means (Synthesis)

After we have selected our research question and have extracted as much data as possible that bear on the research question, our real work begins. We will seldom find that the evidence speaks for itself. The heart of a historical research study involves asking certain questions about the data we have gathered. It is somewhat artificial, therefore, to discuss synthesis in isolation from the selection of the research question and data gathering. The search for meaning in our sources is an activity to be engaged in at every step of the research process. The manner in which we write a historical research report must reflect this process.

In framing the research question, we are usually guided by a theoretical framework, or a set of statements about how the world works, which guides our research study. Sometimes this is left unstated, as an implicit theoretical framework, but it is always better to make the framework explicit. Specifying our theoretical framework and assumptions clarifies our written report because our assumptions determine the way in which our evidence is used and identify what evidence we consider to be important (Fogel, 1970).

Social workers doing a historical research study enjoy an interactive relationship with their sources. The work consists of presenting a number of hypotheses to the sources that they have found. A hypothesis that can be ruled out may advance the progress of a piece of historical research as much as a hypothesis that can be confirmed. Usually, in asking questions we will be led to search for other sources of information. It is helpful to use an explicit organizing framework to guide the investigator in the acceptance or rejection of the hypotheses. The research methods should always be appropriate for the research question being studied (P. Stuart, 1981).

Synthesis involves determining how the facts established from the evidence fit together. Written history fills in the gaps in our understanding of the past by providing an interpretation that is plausible and consistent with available evidence. Most historical writing can be distinguished from writings in other social sciences by its primary purpose, which is to describe a past reality rather than to search for general laws of human behavior (Berkhofer, 1969).

In attempting to describe a past reality, we strive to present an interpretation of a whole—whether the unit is a person, a group, a social service agency, a social welfare system, or a society. This understanding is based on an implicit or explicit set of propositions about human behavior that provide a way for us to structure the facts derived from our evidence. The propositions we use should be made explicit because these are an essential part of the historical research process. In many recent historical research studies, the propositions were derived from the social sciences.

As an example, consider the synthesis presented in an administrative history of the United States Office of Indian Affairs between 1865 and 1900 (Stuart, 1979). The major "facts" that were derived from the evidence included the following: during the late 19th century, the Indian Office changed the way it selected employees, the way it monitored the behavior of employees, the number of employees in various categories, and the purposes for which it spent money. The tendencies increasingly were for the employees to be appointed by the Commissioner of Indian Affairs, for their behavior to be circumscribed by rules and monitored by inspectors rather than supervisors, and for staff and funds to be channeled into the organization's educational subdivisions.

Without a theoretical framework, these might seem to be a set of unrelated facts, of little interest in themselves except to antiquarians interested in western lore. But when viewed in the light of institutionalization, a shorthand term for a set of propositions about organizational behavior, these isolated "facts" seem to take on new meaning. Organizations that institutionalize tend to become more centralized, to become better bounded, to develop automatic, objective criteria for making decisions, and to develop clearer goals and objectives (Selznick, 1957). Changes in personnel selection and the monitoring of employee behavior in the Indian Office increased centralization and boundedness.

The proliferation of rules further increased centralization and made the criteria for decision making explicit. The increasing emphasis on education in the organization's budget and deployment of staff reflected the development of a set of goals for American Indians that guided organizational effort. The Indian Office thus became an institution in the late 19th century, and the concept of institutionalization tells us something more about the organization than we had known previously.

The task of synthesis, then, is to determine what the facts derived from the evidence mean when they are put together. In putting the facts together, we are always guided by implicit or explicit propositions about individual or collective behavior. As stated previously, these propositions must be made explicit because they are an essential part of the historical research process. The underlying propositions, the steps in gathering the evidence, the assessment of the quality of the evidence, and the facts and syntheses derived from the evidence must be clearly stated in written history that is produced.

Step 4: Writing the Report

The purpose of writing a historical research report is twofold—to describe a past reality and to describe the methods we used to investigate it. Consequently, the organization of our report must reflect our methods of investigation, as well as the answer to our research question. In addition, our writing should be clear and simple, without jargon or clichés. As we know, the purpose of any report is to communicate with, not to impress or overwhelm, the reader.

It is helpful to begin our report with a statement of our research question. As suggested above, if our topic can be put in the form of a question, the specific steps we take to answer the research question become more clear, and the reader can better understand where our report is going. We may also state our research question in the form of a hypothesis, which is derived from existing theory and specifies the conditions under which it can be confirmed.

The introduction of our report discusses the assumptions and propositions that guided the entire research study. In addition, the secondary sources (other histories) that speak to our research question are discussed in the introduction. Primary sources that presented unusual or special problems are also discussed. Technical discussions regarding evidence are presented in appendixes.

Our introduction may be a few paragraphs in a short report or one or more chapters in a longer one. Its purpose is to introduce the reader to our research question, the various data sources we used, and our assumptions and guiding propositions that informed the entire research process. Consequently, its form and content will be determined by the topic being investigated.

Just as an introduction is needed, so is a conclusion. The introduction tells the readers where they are going; the conclusion reviews where they have been. The major conclusions may be summarized, and directions for further study also may be suggested. The importance of the synthesis presented must be made clear. The book on the late 19th century Indian Office, discussed previously, ends with a chapter that pulls together the evidence for institutionalization presented in earlier chapters. It also relates this synthesis to developments in other parts of the federal government in the late 19th century and suggests how the institutionalization of the Indian Office may help to explain what happened to the organization in the 20th century (Stuart, 1979).

Between the introduction and the conclusion lies the body of the report. It can be organized in a variety of ways, always keeping in mind the question being studied and the techniques employed in answering it. Some historical research reports are organized chronologically, others topically, and still others by a combination of the two methods. A rigid adherence to chronology may distort the reader's understanding of important events. The occurrence and magnitude of change should be built into the structure of the report (Berkhofer, 1969).

Most reports are organized on principles somewhere between strictly chronological and strictly thematic. The specific organization used depends on the topic and the nature of the research question being examined.

THE PROMISE OF HISTORICAL RESEARCH

Although many social workers like to describe our profession as a young one, it nevertheless has had a long history. It was founded at the turn of the century, and its roots go back a century or more. Social welfare (organized social provision for human needs) has an even longer history. There is little that is new in social work. Most of the problems our profession faces today have analogs in the past; continuity, rather than revolutionary change, characterizes much of our profession's development. Social workers study the past for many reasons: to learn how our profession faced problems similar to those it faces today, to understand the origins of modern social policies and social problems, and to add to knowledge of how organizations grow and change.

Recent historical writings have examined the social work profession's "abandonment of the poor" (Specht & Courtney, 1994), the failure of the settlement house movement to address the problems of African Americans (Lasch-Quinn, 1993), the functions of orphanages in early 20th century Baltimore (Zmora, 1994), the changing treatment of unmarried mothers (Kunzel, 1993), the origins of Aid for Families with Dependent Children (AFDC) (Gordon, 1994), and the evolution of the American social security system (Berkowitz, 1991). These problems are important to social work today; studying how people addressed them in the past may help us to better understand present-day social problems and the social service programs created to address them. We may also gain a better idea about where we have been as a profession and where we are going.

The value of historical research for our profession depends on how well it is conducted. Some of the past historical writings are of limited value because secondary sources were used to the exclusion of primary ones; questions and assumptions that underlay the research question were not stated explicitly; or the reports were written in too rigid a chronological format. Better history will tell us where we have been. These writings may also help us to understand where we are now and suggest hypotheses regarding the future of our profession.

SUMMARY

Social workers study the past to learn how our profession faced problems similar to those it faces today, to understand the origins of modern social policies and social problems, or to add to the knowledge of how organizations grow and change, among other reasons. What these efforts have in common is that they all attempt to describe a past reality. Because the past is inaccessible to direct observation, we must rely on secondary analyses of existing documents, physical remains, and memories left over from the past. As in any research study, we must inquire into the validity and reliability—that is, the significance and accuracy—of the sources used before we attempt to synthesize them into a written history.

No research study can be attempted without a theoretical framework or paradigm. A general framework for doing a historical research study includes choosing a research problem, gathering evidence that bears on the research problem, determining what the evidence means, and writing the report. Discussing these steps in isolation from one another is somewhat artificial. To a certain extent, as with any problem-solving paradigm, all the steps are conducted simultaneously.

To choose a topic intelligently, we must know the previously published literature and how it relates to the research problem we are trying to study. This knowledge enhances our understanding of the gaps that demand historical explanation and the questions about which historians disagree. It is also helpful for us to know something of the primary sources that bear on the research problem. Thus, the first requirement in doing a historical research study is to read widely, paying careful attention to the footnotes. What sources did the authors use? Do the same sources lead different people to different conclusions?

The library is the place to begin a historical research study. General histories of social work and social welfare provide the broad outlines of development. Collections of documents make it possible to follow these developments as they were described by contemporaries. More narrow topics in the history of social work and social welfare are explored in monographs and journals.

Reading secondary sources may lead to questions about an author's contentions or curiosity about some area that is not treated fully. This curiosity and questioning are often the source of the ideas that guide a study. Once the primary sources that bear on the area under investigation have been located—in archives, libraries, or in the possession of individuals or social agencies—we can be well on the way to producing our own history.

Yvonne A. Unrau

Selecting a Data Collection Method and Data Source

. . . .

22

As we know, Chapters 14 through 17 presented four ways to collect original data (obtrusive techniques) for a research study, and Chapters 18 through 21 discussed four ways to collect existing data (unobtrusive techniques). This chapter examines the data collection process from the vantage point of choosing the most appropriate data collection method and data source for any given research study.

Data collection is the heartbeat of a research project. The goal is to have a steady flow of data collected systematically and with the least amount of bias. When the flow of data becomes erratic or stops prematurely, a research study is in grave danger. When data collection goes well, it is characterized by an even pulse and is rather uneventful.

DATA COLLECTION METHODS AND DATA SOURCES

There is a critical distinction between a data collection method and a data source, which must be clearly understood before developing a viable data collection plan. A data collection method consists of a detailed plan of procedures that aims to gather data for a specific purpose—that is, to answer a research question or to test a hypothesis. As we know, the previous seven chapters in this book presented seven different data collection methods. Each one can be used with a variety of data sources, which are defined by who (or what) supplies the data. Data can be provided by a multitude of sources such as people, existing records, and existing databases.

When data are collected directly from people, data may be firsthand or secondhand. Firsthand data are obtained from people who are closest to the problem we are studying. Male inmates participating in an anger management group, for example, can provide firsthand data about their satisfaction with the program's treatment approach. Secondhand data may come from other people who are indirectly connected to our primary problem area. The anger management group facilitator or the prison social work director, for example, may be asked for a personal opinion about how satisfied inmates are with treatment. In other instances, secondhand data can be gained from existing reports written about

inmates or inmate records that monitor their behavior or other important events.

DATA COLLECTION AND THE RESEARCH PROCESS

Data collection is a critical step in the research process because it is the link between theory and practice. Our research study always begins with an idea that is molded by a conceptual framework, which uses preexisting knowledge about our study's problem area. Once our research problem and question have been refined to a researchable level, data are sought from a selected source and gathered using a systematic collection method. The data collected are then used to support or supplant our original study's conceptions about our research problem under investigation. The role of data collection in connecting theory and practice is understood when looking at the entire research process.

As we have seen throughout this book, choosing a data collection method and data source follows the selection of a problem area, selecting a research question, and developing a sampling plan. It comes before the data analysis phase and writing the research report phase. Although data collection is presented in this text as a distinct phase of the research process, it cannot be tackled separately or in isolation. All phases of the research process must be considered if we hope to come up with the best strategy to gather the most relevant, reliable, and valid data to answer a research question or to test a hypothesis. This section discusses the role of data collection in relation to four steps of the research process: (1) selecting a problem area and research question, (2) formulating a research design, (3) analyzing the data, and (4) writing the report.

Selecting a Problem Area and Research Question

The specific research question identifies the general problem area and the population to be studied. It tells us what we want to collect data about and alerts us to potential data sources. It does not necessarily specify the exact manner in which our data will be gathered, however. Suppose, for example, a school social worker proposes the following research question: How effective is our Students Against Violence Program (SAVP) within the Forest Lawn High School? One of the many objectives of our program is "To increase student's feelings of safety at school." This simple evaluative research question identifies our problem area of interest (school violence) and our population of focus (students). It does not state how the question will be answered.

Despite the apparent clarity of our research question, it could in fact be answered in numerous ways. One factor that affects how this question is answered depends on how its variables are conceptualized and operationalized. Students' feelings of safety, for example, could be measured in a variety of ways. Another factor that affects how a research question is answered (or a hypothesis is tested) is the source of data—that is, who or what is providing the data. If we want to get firsthand data about the student's school safety, for example, we could target the students as a potential data source.

If such firsthand data sources were not a viable option, secondhand data sources could be sought. Students' parents, for example, can be asked to speculate on whether their children feel safe at school. In other instances, secondhand data can be gained from existing reports written about students (or student records) that monitor any critical danger or safety incidents.

By listing all possible data collection methods and data sources that could provide sound data to answer a research question, we develop a fuller understanding of our initial research problem. It also encourages us to think about our research problem from different perspectives, via the data sources. Because social work problems are complex, data collection is strengthened when two or more data sources are used. If the students, teachers, and parents rate students' feelings of safety as similar, then we can be more confident that the data (from all these sources) accurately reflect the problem being investigated. Reliability of data can be assessed, or estimated, when collected from multiple sources.

The exercise of generating a list of possible data collection methods and sources can be overwhelming. With reasonably little effort, however, we can develop a long list of possibilities. We may also end up seeing the problem in a different light than what we had thought of previously. By considering parents as a source of secondhand

data, for example, we open up a new dimension of the problem being studied. Suddenly family support factors may seem critical to how safe students feel at school.

We may then want to collect data about the family. This possibility should be considered within the context of our study's conceptual framework. Once we have exhausted all the different ways to collect data for any given study, we need to revisit our original research question. In doing so, we can refocus it by remembering the original purpose of the study.

Formulating a Research Design

As we know, the research design flows from the research question, which flows from the problem area. A research design organizes our research question into a framework that sets the parameters and conditions of the study. As mentioned, the research question directs *what* data are collected and *who* data could be collected from. The research design refines the *what* question by operationalizing variables and the *who* question by developing a sampling strategy. In addition, the research design also dictates *when, where,* and *how* data will be collected.

The research design states how many data collection points our study will have and specifies the data sources. Each discrete data gathering activity constitutes a data collection point and defines *when* data are to be collected. Thus, using an exploratory one-group, posttest-only design, we will collect data only once from a single group of research participants. On the other hand, if a classical experimental design is used, data will be collected at two separate times with two different groups of research participants—for a total of four discrete data collection points.

The number of times a research participant must be available for data collection is an important consideration when choosing a data collection method. The gathering of useful, valid, and reliable data is enhanced when the data collection activities do not occur too frequently and are straightforward and brief. Consider the high school students targeted by our SAVP. Already, many of the students live with the fear of avoiding confrontations with hostile peers and wonder whether they should tell someone about being threatened or harmed.

Asking students about their feelings of safety too often may inadvertently make them feel less safe; alternatively, they may tire of the whole process of inquiry and refuse to participate in our study.

Where the data are collected is also important to consider. If our research question is too narrow and begs for a broader issue that encompasses individuals living in various geographic locations, then mailed surveys would be more feasible than interviews. If our research question focuses on a specific population where all research participants live in the same geographic location, however, it may be possible to use direct observations or individual or group interviews.

Because most social work studies are applied, the setting of our study usually involves clients in their natural environments where there is little control over extraneous variables. If we want to measure the students' feelings toward school safety, for example, do we observe students as they walk the school halls, observe how they interact with their peer groups, or have them complete a survey form of some kind? In short, we must always consider which method of data collection will lead to the most valid and reliable data to answer a specific research question or to test a specific hypothesis.

The combination of potential data collection methods and potential data sources is another important consideration. A research study can have one data collection source and still use multiple data collection methods. High school students (one data source) in our study, for example, can fill out a standardized questionnaire that measures their feelings of safety (first data collection method) in addition to participating in face-to-face interviews (second data collection method).

In the same vein, another study can have multiple data sources and one data collection method. In this case, we can collect data about how safe a student feels through observation recordings by the students' parents, teachers, or social workers. The combination of data collection methods should not be too taxing on any research participant or any system, such as the school itself. That is, data collection should try not to interfere with the day-to-day activities of the persons providing (or responsible for collecting) the data.

In some studies, there is no research design per se. Instead we can use existing data to answer the research question. Such is the case when a secondary analysis is used. Content analysis may also be used on existing data, as when we gather data from existing client records. When the data already exist, we must then organize them using the best-case scenario, given the data at hand and the details of how they were originally gathered and recorded. In these situations, we give more consideration to the analysis of the data.

Analyzing the Data

Collecting data is a resource-intensive endeavor that can be expensive and time consuming. The truth of this statement is realized in the data analysis phase of our research study. Unless a great deal of forethought is given to what data to collect, data may be thrown out because they cannot be organized or analyzed in any meaningful way. In short, data analyses should always be considered when choosing a data collection method and data source because the analysis phase must summarize, synthesize, and ultimately organize the data in an effort to have as clear-cut an answer as possible to our research question. When too much (or too little) data have been collected, we can easily become bogged down or stalled by difficult decisions that could have been avoided with a little forethought.

After we have thought through our research problem and research question and have arrived at a few possible data collection methods and data sources, it is worthwhile to list out the details of how the dependent and independent variables will be measured by each data collection method and each data source. We must think about how they will be used in our data analysis. This exercise provides a clearer idea of the type of results we can expect.

One of the dependent variables in our example is the students' feelings of safety. Suppose the school social worker decides to collect data about this variable by giving students (data source) a brief standardized questionnaire (data collection method) about their feelings of safety. Many standardized questionnaires contain several subscales that, when combined, give a quantitative measure of a larger concept. A questionnaire measuring the concept of feelings of safety, for example, might include three subscales: problem awareness, assertiveness, and self-confidence. We need to decide if each subscale will be defined as three separate subvariables, or if only the total combined scale score will be used.

Alternatively, if data about feelings of safety were to be collected using two different data sources such as parent (source 1) and teacher (source 2) observations, we must think about how the two data types "fit" together. That is, will data from the two sources be treated as two separate variables? If so, will one variable be weighted more heavily in our analysis than the other? Thinking about how the data will be summarized helps us to expose any frivolous data—that is, data that are not suitable to answer our research question.

It is also important to be clear on how our independent variable(s) will be measured and what data collection method would be most appropriate. In our example, we want to know whether our SAVP is effective for helping students feel more safe in the school environment. Because a social service program is being evaluated, it is essential to know what specific intervention approach(es), procedures, and techniques are used within the program. What specific intervention activities are used? Is student participation in our SAVP voluntary? How often do our SAVP's intervention activities occur in the school? Anticipating the type of data analysis that will be used helps to determine which data collection method and data source provide the most meaningful and accurate data to gather.

Besides collecting data about the independent and dependent variables, we must also develop a strategy to collect demographic data about the people who participated in our study. Typical demographic variables include age, gender, education level, and family income. These data are not necessarily used in the analysis of the research question. Rather, they provide a descriptive context for our study. Some data collection methods, such as standardized questionnaires, include these types of data. Often, however, we are responsible for obtaining them as part of the data collection process.

Writing the Report

It is useful to think about our final research report when choosing a data collection method and data source as it forces us to visualize how our study's findings will ulti-

mately be presented. It identifies both who the audience of the study will be and what people will be interested in our findings. Knowing who will read our research report and how it will be disseminated helps us to take more of an objective stance toward our study.

In short, we can take a third-person look at what our study will finally look like. Such objectivity helps us to think about our data collection method and data source with a critical eye. Will consumers of our research study agree that the students in fact were the best data collection source? Were the data collection method and analysis sound? These are some of the practical questions that bring scrutiny to the data collection process.

CRITERIA FOR SELECTING A DATA COLLECTION METHOD

Thinking through the research process from the vantage point of collecting data permits us to refine the conceptualization of our study and the place of data collection within it. It also sets the context within which our data will be gathered. At this point, we should have a sense of what the ideal data collection method and data source would be. Clearly, there are many viable data collection methods and data sources that can be used to answer any research question. Nevertheless, there are many practical criteria that ultimately refine the final data collection method (and sources) to fit the conditions of any given research study. These criteria are: (1) size, (2) scope, (3) program participation, (4) worker cooperation, (5) intrusion into the lives of research participants, (6) resources, (7) time, and (8) previous research findings. They all interact with one another, but for the sake of clarity each one is presented separately.

Size

The size of our study reflects just how many people, places, or systems are represented in it. As with any planning activity, the more people involved, the more complicated the process and the more difficult it is to arrive at a mutual agreement. Decisions about which data collection method and which data source to use can be stalled when several people, levels, or systems are consulted. This is simply because individuals have different interests and opinions. Administrators, for example, may address issues such as accountability more than do line-level social workers.

Imagine if the effectiveness of our SAVP were examined on a larger scale such that all high schools in the city were included. Our study's complexity is dramatically increased because of such factors as the increased number of students, parents, school principals, teachers, and social workers involved. Individual biases will make it much more difficult to agree upon the best data collection method and data source for our study.

Our study's sample size is also a consideration. The goal of any research study is to have a meaningful sample of the population of interest. With respect to sample size, this means that we should strive for a reasonable representation of the sampling frame. When small-scale studies are conducted, such as a program evaluation in one school, the total sampling frame may be in the hundreds or fewer. Thus, dealing with the random selection of research participants poses no particular problem.

On the other hand, when large-scale studies are conducted, such as when the federal government chooses to examine a social service program that involves hundreds of thousands of people, dealing with a sample is more problematic. If our sample is in the thousands, it is unlikely that we would be able to successfully *observe* all participants in a particular setting. Rather, a more efficient data collection method—say a mailed *survey*—may be more appropriate.

Scope

The scope of our research study is another matter to consider. Scope refers to how much of our problem area will be covered. In our SAVP, if we are interested in gathering data about students' academic standings, family supports, and peer relations, then three different aspects of our problem area will be covered. In short, we need to consider whether one method of data collection and one data source can be used to collect all the data. It could be that school records are used to collect data about students' academic achievements, interviews with students are conducted to collect data about

students' family supports, and observation methods are used to gather data about students' peer relationships.

Program Participation

Many social work research efforts are conducted in actual real-life program settings. Thus, it is essential that we gain the support of program personnel to conduct our study. Program factors that can impact the choice of our data collection methods and data sources include variables such as the program's clarity in its mandate to serve clients, its philosophical stance toward clients, and its flexibility in client record keeping.

First, if a program is not able to clearly articulate a client service delivery plan, it will be difficult to separate out clinical activity from research activity, or to determine when the two overlap.

Second, agencies tend to base themselves on strong beliefs about a client population, which affect who can have access to their clients and in what manner. A child sexual abuse investigation program, for example, may be designed specifically to avoid the problem of using multiple interviewers and multiple interviews of children in the investigation of an allegation of sexual abuse. As a result, the program would hesitate to permit us to conduct interviews with the children to gather data for "research purposes."

Third, to save time and energy there is often considerable overlap between program client records and research data collection. The degree of willingness of a program to change or adapt to new record-keeping techniques will affect how we might go about collecting certain types of data.

Worker Cooperation

On a general level, programs have few resources and an overabundance of clients. Such conditions naturally lead their administrators and social workers to regard clinical activity as a top priority. When our research study requires social workers to collect data as a part of their day-to-day client service delivery, it is highly likely that they will view it as additional work. In short, they may not be likely to view these new data collection activities as a means to expedite their work, at least not in the short term.

Getting cooperation of social workers within a program is a priority in any research study that relies directly or indirectly on their meaningful participation. They will be affected by our study whether they are involved in the data collection process or not. Workers may be asked to schedule additional interviews with families or adjust their intervention plans to ensure that data collection occurs at the optimal time. Given the fiscal constraints faced by programs, the workers themselves often participate as data collectors. They may end up using new client recording forms or administer questionnaires. Whatever the level of their participation, it is important for us to strive to achieve a maximum level of their cooperation.

There are three factors to consider when trying to achieve maximum cooperation from workers. First, we should make every effort to work effectively and efficiently with the program's staff. Cooperation is more likely to be achieved when they participate in the development of our study plan from the beginning. Thus, it is worthwhile to take time to explain the purpose of our study and its intended outcomes at an early stage. Furthermore, administrators and front-line workers can provide valuable information about what data collection method(s) may work best.

Second, we must be sensitive to the workloads of the program's staff. Data collection methods and sources should be designed to enhance the work of professionals. Client recording forms, for example, can be designed to provide focus for supervision meetings as well as summarize facts and worker impressions about a case.

Third, a mechanism should be set up by which workers receive feedback based on the data they have collected. When data are reported back to the program's staff before the completion of our study, we must ensure that the data will not bias later measurements (if any).

Intrusion Into the Lives of Research Participants

When clients are used as a data source, client self-determination takes precedence over research activity. As we know, clients have every right to refuse participation in a research study and cannot be denied services because they are unwilling to participate. For example, it is unethical to use participant observation (Chapter 15) as a data collection method in a group-based treatment intervention when one member of the group has not consented to participate in the study. This is unethical because the nonconsenting group member ends up being observed as part of the group dynamic in the data collection process. The data collection method(s) we finally select must be flexible enough to allow our study to continue even when some clients will not participate.

Cultural consideration must also be given to the type of data collection method used. One-to-one interviewing with Cambodian refugees, for example, may be extremely terrifying for them, given its resemblance to the interrogation they may have experienced in their own country. If direct observational strategies are used in studies in which we are from a different cultural background than our research participants, it is important to ensure that interpretation of their behaviors, events, or expressions is accurate from their perspectives.

We must also recognize the cultural biases of standardized measuring instruments because most are based on testing with Caucasian groups. The problems here are twofold. First, we cannot be sure if the concept that the instrument is measuring is expressed the same way in different cultures. For instance, a standardized self-report instrument that measures family functioning may include an item such as, "We have flexible rules in our household that account for individual differences," which would likely be viewed positively by North American cultures but negatively by many Asian cultures. Second, because standardized measuring instruments are written in English, research participants must have a good grasp of English to ensure that the data collected from them are valid and reliable.

Another consideration comes into play when particular populations have been the subject of a considerable amount of research studies already. Many aboriginal people living on reservations, for example, have been subjected to government surveys, task force inquiries, independent research projects, and perhaps even to the curiosity of social work students learning in a practicum setting. When a population has been extensively researched, it is even more important that we consider how the data collection method will affect those people participating in the study. Has the data collection method been used previously? If so, what was the nature of the data collected? Could the data be collected in other ways, using less obtrusive measures?

Resources

There are various costs associated with collecting data in any given research study. Materials and supplies, equipment rental, transportation costs, and training for data collectors are just a few things to consider when choosing a data collection method. In addition, once the data are collected, additional expenses can arise when they need to be entered into a computer or transcribed.

An effective and efficient data collection method is one that collects the most valid and reliable data to answer a research question or test a hypothesis while requiring the least amount of time and money. In our example, to ask students about their feelings of safety via an open-ended interview may offer rich data, but we take the risk that students will not fully answer our questions in the time allotted for the interview. On the other hand, having them complete a self-report questionnaire on feelings of safety is a quicker and less costly way to collect data, but it gives little sense about how well the students understood the questions being asked of them or whether the data obtained reflect their true feelings.

Time

Time is a consideration when our study has a fixed completion date. Time constraints may be self-imposed or externally imposed. Self-imposed time constraints are personal matters we need to consider. Is our research project a part of a thesis or dissertation? What are our personal time commitments?

Externally imposed time restrictions are set by someone other than the one doing the study. For instance, our SAVP study is limited by the school year. Other external pressures may be political, such as an administrator who wants research results for a funding proposal or annual report.

Previous Research Studies

Having reviewed the professional literature on our problem, we need to be well aware of other data collection methods that have been used in similar studies. We can evaluate earlier studies for the strengths and weaknesses of their data collection methods and thereby make a more informed decision as to the best data collection strategy to use in our specific situation. Further, we need to look for diversity when evaluating other data collection approaches. That is, we can triangulate results from separate studies that used different data collection methods and data sources to answer a research question or test a hypothesis.

SELECTION OF A DATA COLLECTION METHOD

As should be evident by now, choosing a data collection method and data source for a research study is not a simple task. There are numerous conceptual and practical factors that must be thought through if we hope to arrive at the best possible approach to gathering data. How do we appraise all the factors to be considered in picking the best approach? The previous seven chapters in this book present seven different non-mutually exclusive data collection methods. Theoretically, all of them could be used to evaluate the effectiveness of our SAVP. Each one would offer a different perspective to our research question and would consider different data sources.

Table 22.1 is an example of a grid that can be used to assist us in making an informed decision about which data collection method is best. The grid includes both general and specific considerations for our study question. The first section of the grid highlights the eight criteria for selecting a data collection method discussed earlier. The bottom section of the grid identifies five additional considerations that are specific to our SAVP.

The grid can be used as a decision-making tool by subjectively rating how well each data collection method measures up to the criteria listed in the left column of Table 22.1. We mark a "+" if the data collection method has a favorable rating and a "−" if it has an unfavorable one.

TABLE 22.1

Decision-Making Grid for Choosing a Data Collection Method

	Data Collection Methods				
	Survey Research (*Chapter 17*)	Observation (*Chapter 14*)	Secondary Analysis (*Chapter 18*)	Content Analysis (*Chapter 19*)	Existing Statistics (*Chapter 20*)
General Criteria					
1. Size	+	0	+	+	+
2. Scope	+	–	–	–	–
3. Program participation	+	0	+	+	+
4. Worker cooperation	+	–	+	+	+
5. Intrustion to clients	–	–	+	+	+
6. Resources	+	–	+	+	+
7. Time	+	–	+	+	+
8. Previous research	+	0	–	–	–
Specific Criteria					
1. Student availability	+	+	0	0	0
2. Student reading level	+	0	0	0	0
3. School preference	+	–	–	–	–
4. School year end	–	–	+	+	+
5. Access to existing records	0	0	+	+	+
Totals	8	–6	5	5	5

When a particular criterion is neutral, in which case it has no positive or negative effect, then a zero is indicated.

Once each data collection method has been assessed on all eight criteria, we can simply add the number of pluses and minuses to arrive at a plus or minus total for each method. This information can be used to help us make an informed decision about the best data collection method, given all the issues raised. Based on Table 22.1, where only five of the eight data collection methods are illustrated, the survey research method is most appealing for our study if a single method of data collection is used.

TRYING OUT THE SELECTED DATA COLLECTION METHOD

Data collection is a particularly vulnerable time for a research study because it is the point where "talk" turns to "action." So far, all the considerations that have been weighed in the selection of a data collection method

have been in theory. All people involved in our research endeavor have cast their suggestions and doubts on the entire process. Once general agreement has been reached about which data collection method and data source to use, it is time to test the waters.

Trying out a data collection method can occur informally by simply testing it out with available, willing research participants or, at the very least, with anyone who has not been involved with the planning of the study. The purpose of this trial run is to ensure that those who are going to provide data understand the questions and procedures in the way that they were intended. Data collection methods might also be tested more formally, such as when a pilot study is conducted.

A pilot study involves carrying out all aspects of the data collection plan on a miniscale. That is, a small portion of our study's actual sample is selected and run through all steps of the data collection process. In a pilot study, we are interested in the process of the data collection as well as the content. In short, we what to know whether our chosen data collection method produces the expected data. Are there any unanticipated barriers to gathering the desired data? How do research participants (data source) respond to our data collection procedures? Is there enough variability in research participants' responses?

IMPLEMENTATION AND EVALUATION

The data collection phase of a research study can go smoothly if we are proactive. That is, we should guide and monitor the entire data collection process according to the procedures and steps that were set out in the study's planning stage and were tested in the pilot study.

Implementation

The main guiding principle to implementing the selected data collection method is that a systematic approach to data collection must be used. This means that the steps to gathering data should be methodically detailed so that there is no question about the tasks of the person or people collecting the data—the data collectors. This is true whether we are using a quantitative or qualitative research approach. As we know from Chapters 5 and 6, the difference between these two research approaches is that the structure of the data collection process within a qualitative research study is often documented as the study progresses. On the other hand, in a quantitative research study the data collection process is decided at the study's outset and provides much less flexibility after the study is under way.

It must be very clear from the beginning who is responsible for collecting the data. When we take on the task, there is reasonable assurance that the data collection will remain objective and be guided by our research interests. Data collection left to only one person may be a formidable task. We must determine the amount of resources available to decide what data collection method is most realistic. Regardless of the study size, we must attempt to establish clear roles with those involved in the data collection process.

The clearer our research study is articulated, the less difficulty there will be in moving through all the phases of the study. In particular, it is critical to identify who will and will not be involved in the data collection process. To further avoid mix-ups and complications, specific tasks must be spelled out for all persons involved in our study. Where will the data collection forms be stored? Who will administer them? How will their completion be monitored?

In many social work research studies, front-line social workers are involved in data collection activities as part of their day-to-day activities. They typically gather intake and referral data, write assessment notes, and even use standardized questionnaires as part of their assessments. Data collection in programs can easily be designed to serve the dual purposes of research *and* service delivery. Thus, it is important to establish data collection protocols to avoid problems of biased data. As mentioned, everyone in a research study must agree *when* data will be collected, *where,* and in *what* manner. Agreement is more likely to occur when we have fully informed and involved everyone participating in our study.

Evaluation

The process of selecting a chosen data collection method is not complete without evaluating it. Evaluation occurs at two levels. First, the strengths and weakness of a data collection method and data source are evaluated, given the research context in which our study takes place. If, for example, data are gathered about clients' presenting problems by a referring social worker, it must be acknowledged that the obtained data offer a limited (or restricted) point of view about the clients' problems. The strength of this approach may be that it was the only means for collecting the data. Such strengths and weakness are summarized in the decision-making grid presented in Table 22.1.

A second level of evaluation is monitoring the implementation of the data collection process itself. When data are gathered using several methods (or from several sources), it is beneficial to develop a checklist of what data have been collected for each research participant. Developing a strategy for monitoring the data collection process is especially important when the data must be collected in a timely fashion. If pretest data are needed before a client enters a treatment program, for example, the data collection must be complete before admission occurs. Once the client has entered the program, the opportunity to collect pretest data is lost forever.

Another strategy for monitoring evaluation is to keep a journal of the data collection process. The journal records any questions or queries that arise in the data-gathering phase. We may find, for example, that several research participants completing a questionnaire have difficulty understanding one particular question. In addition, sometimes research participants have poor reading skills and require assistance with completion of some self-report standardized questionnaires. Documenting these idiosyncratic incidents accumulates important information that can be used to comment on our data's validity and reliability.

SUMMARY

There are many possible data collection methods and data sources that can be used in any given research situation. We must weigh the pros and cons of both within the context of a particular research study to arrive at the best data collection method and data source. This process involves both conceptual and practical considerations. On a conceptual level, we review the phases of the research process through a "data collection and data source lens." We think about how various data collection methods and data sources fit with each phase of the research process. At the same time, considering the different data collection methods and data sources helps us to gain a fuller understanding of our problem area and research question.

There are many considerations that need to be addressed when deciding on the best data collection method(s) and data source(s) for a particular study. Factors such as worker cooperation, available resources, and consequences for the clients all influence our final choices. We can map out such decision-making criteria by using a grid system on which all criteria to be considered are listed and evaluated for each potential data collection method and data source.

PART VII

Quantitative Data Analysis, Proposals, and Reports

The three chapters contained in Part VII are

specifically geared to the quantitative research

approach. More specifically, Chapter 23 discusses

how to analyze quantitative data, and Chapter 24

presents how to write quantitative proposals and

reports. The remaining chapter, Chapter 25,

discusses how to evaluate published quantitative

reports.

Analyzing Quantitative Data

Margaret Williams

Leslie Tutty

Richard M. Grinnell, Jr.

23

After quantitative data are collected they need to be analyzed—the topic of this chapter. To be honest, a thorough understanding of quantitative statistical methods is far beyond the scope of this book. Such comprehension necessitates more in-depth study, through taking one or more statistics courses. Instead, we briefly describe a select group of basic statistical analytical methods that are used frequently in many quantitative *and* qualitative social work research studies. Our emphasis is not on providing and calculating formulas, but rather on helping the reader to understand the underlying rationale for their use.

We present two basic groups of statistical procedures. The first group is called *descriptive statistics,* which simply describe and summarize one or more variables for a sample or population. They provide information about only the group included in the study. The second group of statistical procedures is called *inferential statistics,* which determine if we can generalize findings derived from a sample to the population from which the sample was drawn. In other words, knowing what we know about a particular sample, can we infer that the rest of the population is similar to the sample that we have studied? Before we can answer this question, however, we need to know the level of measurement for each variable being analyzed. Let us now turn to a brief discussion of the four different levels of measurement that a variable can take.

LEVELS OF MEASUREMENT

The specific statistics used to analyze the data collected are dependent on the type of data that are gathered. The characteristics or qualities that describe a variable are known as its *attributes.* The variable *gender,* for example, has only two characteristics or attributes—*male* and *female*—because gender in humans is limited to male and female, and there are no other possible categories or ways of describing gender. The variable *ethnicity* has a number of possible categories: *African American, Native American, Asian, Hispanic American,* and *Caucasian* are just five examples of the many attributes of the variable ethnicity. A point to note here is that the attributes of gender differ in kind from one

another—male is different from female—and, in the same way, the attributes of ethnicity are also different from one another.

Now consider the variable *income.* Income can only be described in terms of amounts of money: $15,000 per year, $288.46 per week, and so forth. In whatever terms a person's income is actually described, it still comes down to a number. Because every number has its own category, as we mentioned before, the variable income can generate as many categories as there are numbers, up to the number covering the research participant who earns the most. These numbers are all attributes of income and they are all different, but they are not different in *kind,* as male and female are, or Native American and Hispanic; they are only different in *quantity.*

In other words, the attributes of income differ in that they represent more or less of the same thing, whereas the attributes of gender differ in that they represent different kinds of things. Income will, therefore, be measured in a different way from gender. When we come to measure income, we will be looking for categories that are lower or higher than each other; when we come to measure gender, we will be looking for categories that are different in kind from each other.

Mathematically, there is not much we can do with categories that are different in kind. We cannot subtract Hispanics from Caucasians, for example, whereas we can quite easily subtract one person's annual income from another and come up with a meaningful difference. As far as mathematical computations are concerned, we are obliged to work at a lower level of complexity when we measure variables like ethnicity than when we measure variables like income. Depending on the nature of their attributes, all variables can be measured at one (or more) of four measurement levels: (1) nominal, (2) ordinal, (3) interval, or (4) ratio.

Nominal Measurement

Nominal measurement is the lowest level of measurement and is used to measure variables whose attributes are different in kind. As we have seen, gender is one variable measured at a nominal level, and ethnicity is another. *Place of birth* is a third, because "born in California," for example, is different from "born in

Chicago," and we cannot add "born in California" to "born in Chicago," or subtract them or divide them, or do anything statistically interesting with them at all.

Ordinal Measurement

Ordinal measurement is a higher level of measurement than nominal and is used to measure those variables whose attributes can be rank ordered: for example, socioeconomic status, sexism, racism, client satisfaction, and the like. If we intend to measure *client satisfaction,* we must first develop a list of all the possible attributes of client satisfaction: that is, we must think of all the possible categories into which answers about client satisfaction might be placed. Some clients will be *very satisfied*—one category, at the high end of the satisfaction continuum; some will be *not at all satisfied*— a separate category, at the low end of the continuum; and others will be *generally satisfied, moderately satisfied,* or *somewhat satisfied*—three more categories, at differing points on the continuum, as illustrated in Figure 23.1.

Figure 23.1 is a 5-point scale, anchored at all 5 points with a brief description of the degree of satisfaction represented by the point. Of course, we may choose to express the anchors in different words, substituting *extremely satisfied* for *very satisfied,* or *fairly satisfied* for *generally satisfied.* We may select a 3-point scale instead, limiting the choices to *very satisfied, moderately satisfied,* and *not at all satisfied;* or we may even use a 10-point scale if we believe that our respondents will be able to rate their satisfaction with that degree of accuracy.

Whichever particular method is selected, some sort of scale is the only measurement option available because there is no other way to categorize client satisfaction except in terms of more satisfaction or less satisfaction. As we did with nominal measurement, we might assign numbers to each of the points on the scale. If we used the 5-point scale in Figure 23.1, we might assign a 5 to *very satisfied,* a 4 to *generally satisfied,* a 3 to *moderately satisfied,* a 2 to *somewhat satisfied,* and a 1 to *not at all satisfied.*

Here, the numbers do have some mathematical meaning. Five (*very satisfied*) is in fact better than 4 (*generally satisfied*), 4 is better than 3, 3 is better than 2, and 2 is better than 1. The numbers, however, say nothing about *how much better* any category is than any other. We cannot assume that the difference in satisfaction between *very* and *generally* is the same as the difference between *generally* and *moderately.* In short, we cannot assume that the intervals between the anchored points on the scale are all the same length. Most definitely, we cannot assume that a client who rates a service at 4 (*generally satisfied*) is twice as satisfied as a client who rates the service at 2 (*somewhat satisfied*).

In fact, we cannot attempt any mathematical manipulation at all. We cannot add the numbers 1, 2, 3, 4, and 5, nor can we subtract, multiply, or divide them. As its name might suggest, all we can know from ordinal measurement is the order of the categories.

Interval Measurement

Some variables, such as client satisfaction, have attributes that can be rank-ordered—from *very satisfied* to *not at all satisfied,* as we have just discussed. As we saw, however, these attributes cannot be assumed to be the same distance apart if they are placed on a scale; and, in any case, the distance they are apart has no real meaning. No one can measure the distance between *very satisfied* and *moderately satisfied;* we only know that the one is better than the other.

Conversely, for some variables, the distance, or interval, separating their attributes *does* have meaning, and these variables can be measured at the interval level. An example in physical science is the Fahrenheit or Celsius temperature scales. The difference between 80 degrees and 90 degrees is the same as the difference between 40

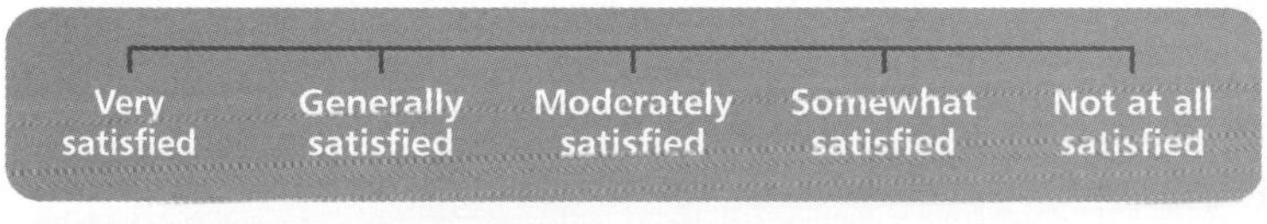

Figure 23.1
Scale to Measure Client Satisfaction

and 50 degrees. Eighty degrees is not twice as hot as 40 degrees, nor does zero degrees mean no heat at all.

In social work, interval measures are most commonly used in connection with standardized measuring instruments, as presented in Chapter 9. When we look at a standardized intelligence test, for example, we can say that the difference between IQ scores of 100 and 110 is the same as the difference between IQ scores of 95 and 105, based on the scores obtained by the many thousands of people who have taken the test over the years. As with the temperature scales mentioned above, a person with an IQ score of 120 is not twice as intelligent as a person with a score of 60, nor does a score of 0 mean no intelligence at all.

Ratio Measurement

The highest level of measurement, ratio measurement, is used to measure variables whose attributes are based on a true 0 point. It may not be possible to have zero intelligence, but it is certainly possible to have zero children or zero money. Whenever a question about a particular variable might elicit the answer "none" or "never," that variable can be measured at the ratio level. The question "How many times have you seen your social worker?" might be answered "Never." Other variables commonly measured at the ratio level include length of residence in a given place, age, number of times married, number of organizations belonged to, number of antisocial behaviors, number of case reviews, number of training sessions, and number of supervisory meetings.

With a ratio level of measurement we can meaningfully interpret the comparison between two scores. A person who is 40 years of age, for example, is twice as old as a person who is 20 and half as old as a person who is 80. Children aged 2 and 5, respectively, are the same distance apart as children aged 6 and 9. Data resulting from ratio measurement can be added, subtracted, multiplied, and divided. Averages can be calculated and other statistical analyses can be performed.

It is useful to note that, although some variables *can* be measured at a higher level, they may not need to be. The variable *income*, for example, can be measured at a ratio level because it is possible to have a zero income;

however, for the purposes of a particular study, we may not need to know the actual incomes of our research participants, only the range within which their incomes fall. A person who is asked how much he or she earns may be reluctant to give a figure ("mind your own business" is a perfectly legitimate response) but may not object to checking one of a number of income categories, choosing, for example, between:

1. less than $5,000 per year
2. $5,001 to $15,000 per year
3. $15,001 to $25,000 per year
4. $25,001 to $35,000 per year
5. more than $35,000 per year

Categorizing income in this way reduces the measurement from the ratio level to the ordinal level. It will now be possible to know only that a person checking Category 1 earns less than a person checking Category 2, and so on. Although we will not know *how much* less or more one person earns than another and we will not be able to perform statistical tasks such as calculating average incomes, we will be able to say, for example, that 50 percent of our sample falls into Category 1, 30 percent into Category 2, 15 percent into Category 3, and 5 percent into Category 4. If we are conducting a study to see how many people fall in each income range, this may be all we need to know.

In the same way, we might not want to know the actual ages of our sample, only the range in which they fall. For some studies, it might be enough to measure age at a nominal level—to inquire, for example, whether people were born during the depression, or whether they were born before or after 1990. In short, when studying variables that can be measured at any level, the measurement level chosen depends on what kind of data are needed, and this in turn is determined by why the data are needed, which in turn is determined by our research question.

COMPUTER APPLICATIONS

The use of computers has revolutionized the analysis of quantitative and qualitative data. Where previous generations of researchers had to rely on hand-cranked adding machines to calculate every small step in a data analysis, today we can enter raw scores into a personal computer, and, with few complications, direct the computer program to execute just about any statistical test imaginable. Seconds later, the results are available. Although the process is truly miraculous, the risk is that, even though we have conducted the correct statistical analysis, we may not understand what the results mean, a factor that will almost certainly affect how we interpret the data.

We can code data from all four levels of measurement into a computer for any given data analysis. The coding of nominal data is perhaps the most complex because we have to create categories that correspond with certain possible responses for a variable. One type of nominal level data that is often gathered from research participants is *place of birth*. If, for the purposes of our study, we are interested in whether our research participants were born in either the United States or Canada, we would assign only three categories to *place of birth*:

1. United States
2. Canada
9. Other

The *other* category appears routinely at the end of lists of categories and acts as a catch-all, to cover any category that may have been omitted.

When entering nominal level data into a computer, because we do not want to enter *Canada* every time the response on the questionnaire is Canada, we may assign it the code number 1 so that all we have to enter is 1. Similarly, the United States may be assigned the number 2, and "other" may be assigned the number 9. These numbers have no mathematical meaning: We are not saying that Canada is better than the United States because it comes first, or that the United States is twice as good as Canada because the number assigned to it is twice as high. We are merely using numbers as a shorthand device to record *qualitative* differences: differences in *kind*, not in amount.

Most coding for ordinal, interval, and ratio level data is simply a matter of entering the final score, or number, from the measuring instrument that was used to measure the variable directly into the computer. If a person scored a 45 on a standardized measuring instru-

ment, for example, the number 45 would be entered into the computer.

Although almost all data entered into computers are in the form of numbers, we need to know at what level of measurement the data exist so that we can choose the appropriate statistic(s) to describe and compare the variables. Now that we know how to measure variables at four different measurement levels, let us turn to the first group of statistics that can be helpful for the analyses of data—descriptive statistics.

DESCRIPTIVE STATISTICS

Descriptive statistics are commonly used in most quantitative and qualitative research studies. They describe and summarize a variable(s) of interest and portray how that particular variable is distributed in the sample, or population. Before looking at descriptive statistics, however, let us examine a social work research example that will be used throughout this chapter.

Thea Black is a social worker who works in a treatment foster care program. Her program focuses on children who have behavioral problems who are placed with "treatment" foster care parents. These parents are supposed to have parenting skills that will help them provide for the children with special needs who are placed with them. Thus, Thea's program also teaches parenting skills to these treatment foster care parents. She assumes that newly recruited foster parents are not likely to know much about parenting children who have behavioral problems. Therefore, she believes that they would benefit from a training program that teaches these skills to help them deal effectively with the special needs of these children who will soon be living with them.

Thea hopes that her parenting skills training program will increase the knowledge about parental management skills for the parents who attend. She assumes that, with such training, the foster parents would be in a better position to support and provide clear limits for their foster children.

After offering the training program for several months, Thea became curious about whether the foster care providers who attended the program were, indeed, lacking in knowledge of parental management skills as she first believed (her tentative hypothesis). She was fortunate to find a valid and reliable standardized instrument that measures the knowledge of such parenting skills, the Parenting Skills Scale (PSS). Thea decided to find out for herself how much the newly recruited parents knew about parenting skills—clearly a descriptive research question.

At the beginning of one of her training sessions (before they were exposed to her skills training program), she handed out the PSS, asking the 20 individuals in attendance to complete it and also to include data about their gender, years of education, and whether they had ever participated in a parenting skills training program before. All of these three variables could be potentially extraneous ones that might influence the level of knowledge of parenting skills of the 20 participants.

For each foster care parent, Thea calculated the PSS score, called a *raw score* because it has not been sorted or analyzed in any way. The total score possible on the PSS is 100, with higher scores indicating greater knowledge

of parenting skills. The scores for the PSS scale, as well as the other data collected from the 20 parents, are listed in Table 23.1.

At this point, Thea stopped to consider how she could best use the data that she had collected. She had data at three different levels of measurement. At the nominal level, Thea had collected data on gender (third column) and whether the parents had any previous parenting skills training (fourth column). Each of these variables can be categorized into two responses.

The scores on the PSS (second column) are ordinal because, although the data are sequenced from highest to lowest, the differences between units cannot be placed on an equally spaced continuum. Nevertheless, many measures in the social sciences are treated as if they are at an interval level, even though equal distances between scale points cannot be proved. This assumption is important because it allows for the use of inferential statistics on such data.

Finally, the data on years of formal education (fifth column) that were collected by Thea are clearly at the

---

TABLE 23.1

Data Collection for Four Variables from Foster Care Providers

Number	PSS Score	Gender	Previous Training	Years of Education
01	95	male	no	12
02	93	female	yes	15
03	93	male	no	08
04	93	female	no	12
05	90	male	yes	12
06	90	female	no	12
07	84	male	no	14
08	84	female	no	18
09	82	male	no	10
10	82	female	no	12
11	80	male	no	12
12	80	female	no	11
13	79	male	no	12
14	79	female	yes	12
15	79	female	no	16
16	79	male	no	12
17	79	female	no	11
18	72	female	no	14
19	71	male	no	15
20	55	female	yes	12

Note: PSS = Parenting Skills Scale.

ratio level of measurement, because there are equally distributed points and the scale has an absolute zero.

In sum, it seemed to Thea that the data could be used in at least two ways. First, the data collected about each variable could be described to provide a picture of the characteristics of the group of foster care parents. This would call for descriptive statistics. Secondly, she might look for relationships between some of the variables about which she had collected data, procedures that would use inferential statistics. For now let us begin by looking at how the first type of descriptive statistic can be used with Thea's data set.

Frequency Distributions

One of the simplest procedures that Thea can employ is to develop a frequency distribution of her data. Constructing a frequency distribution involves counting the occurrences of each value, or category, of the variable and ordering them in some fashion. This *absolute* or *simple frequency distribution* allows us to see quickly how certain values of a variable are distributed in our sample or population.

The *mode,* or the most commonly occurring score, can be easily spotted in a simple frequency distribution (Table 23.2). In this example, the mode is 79, a score obtained by five parents on the PSS scale. The highest and the lowest score are also quickly identifiable. The top score was 95, and the foster care parent who performed the least well on the PSS scored 55.

There are several other ways to present frequency data. A commonly used method that can be easily integrated into a simple frequency distribution table is the *cumulative frequency distribution,* shown in Table 23.3.

In Thea's data set, the highest PSS score, 95, was obtained by only one individual. The group of individuals who scored 93 or above on the PSS measure includes four foster care parents. If we want to know how many scored 80 or above, if we look at the number across from 80 in the cumulative frequency column, we can quickly see that 12 of the parents scored 80 or better.

Other tables use percentages rather than frequencies, sometimes referred to as *percentage distributions,* shown in the far right column in Table 23.3. Each of these numbers represents the percentage of participants who obtained each PSS value. Five individuals, for example, scored 79 on the PSS. Because there was a total of 20 foster care parents, 5 out of the 20, or one-quarter of the total, obtained a score of 79. This corresponds to 25 percent of the participants.

Finally, *grouped frequency distributions* are used to simplify a table by grouping the variable into equal-sized ranges, as is shown in Table 23.4. Both absolute and cumulative frequencies and percentages can also be displayed using this format. Each is calculated in the same way that was previously described for nongrouped data, and the interpretation is identical.

TABLE 23.2

Frequency Distribution of Parental Skill Scores

PSS Score	Absolute Frequency
95	1
93	3
90	2
84	2
82	2
80	2
79	5
72	1
71	1
55	1

Note: PSS = Parenting Skills Scale.

TABLE 23.3

Cumulative Frequency and Percentage Distribution of Parental Skill Scores

PSS Score	Absolute Frequency	Cumulative Frequency	Percentage Distribution
95	1	1	5
93	3	4	15
90	2	6	10
84	2	8	10
82	2	10	10
80	2	12	10
79	5	17	25
72	1	18	5
71	1	19	5
55	1	20	5
Total	**20**		**100**

Note: PSS = Parenting Skills Scale.

TABLE 23.4			
Grouped Frequency Distribution of Parental Skill Scores			
PSS Scores	Absolute Frequency	Cumulative Frequency	Absolute Percentage
90 –100	6	6	30
80 – 89	6	12	30
70 – 79	7	19	35
60 – 69	0	19	0
50 – 59	1	20	5

Note: PSS = Parenting Skills Scale.

Looking at the absolute frequency column, for example, we can quickly identify that seven of the foster care parents scored in the 70 to 79 range on the PSS. By looking at the cumulative frequency column, we can see that 12 of 20 parents scored 80 or better on the PSS. Further, from the absolute percentage column, it is clear that 30 percent of the foster parents scored in the 80 to 89 range on the knowledge of parenting skills scale. Only one parent, or 5 percent of the group, had significant problems with the PSS, scoring in the 50 to 59 range.

Note that each of the other variables in Thea's data set could also be displayed in frequency distributions. Displaying years of education in a frequency distribution, for example, would provide a snapshot of how this variable is distributed in Thea's sample of foster care parents. With two category nominal variables, such as gender (male, female) and previous parent skills training (yes, no), however, cumulative frequencies become less meaningful and the data are better described as percentages. Thea noted that 55 percent of the foster care parents who attended the training workshop were women (obviously the other 45 percent were men) and that 20 percent of the parents had already received some form of parenting skills training (while a further 80 percent had not been trained).

Measures of Central Tendency

We can also display the values obtained on the PSS in the form of a graph. A *frequency polygon* is one of the simplest ways of charting frequencies. The graph in Figure 23.2 displays the data that we had previously put in Table 23.2. The PSS score is plotted in terms of how many of the foster care parents obtained each score.

As can be seen from Table 23.2 and Figure 23.2, most of the scores fall between 79 and 93. The one extremely low score of 55 is also quickly noticeable in such a graph because it is so far removed from the rest of the values.

A frequency polygon allows us to make a quick analysis of how closely the distribution fits the shape of a normal curve. A *normal curve,* also known as a *bell-shaped distribution* or a *normal distribution,* is a frequency polygon in which the greatest number of responses fall in the middle of the distribution and fewer scores appear at the extremes of either very high or very low scores (Figure 23.3).

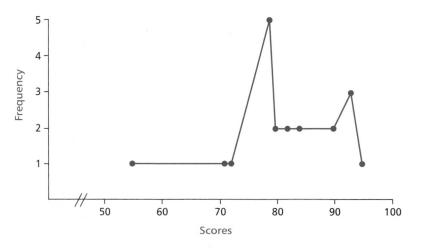

Figure 23.2
Frequency Polygon of Parental Skill Scores (from Table 23.2)

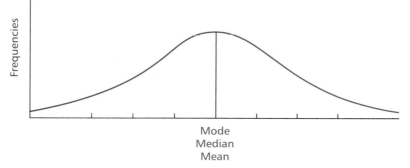

Figure 23.3
The Normal Distribution

Many variables in the social sciences are assumed to be distributed in the shape of a normal curve. Low intelligence, for example, is thought to be relatively rare when compared with the number of individuals with average intelligence. On the other end of the continuum, extremely gifted individuals are also relatively uncommon.

Of course, not all variables are distributed in the shape of a normal curve. Some are such that a large number of people do very well (as Thea found in her sample of foster care parents and their parenting skill levels). Other variables, such as juggling ability, for example, would be charted showing a fairly substantial number of people performing poorly. Frequency distributions of still other variables would show that some people do well, and some people do poorly, but not many fall in between. What is important to remember about distributions is that, although all different sorts are possible, most statistical procedures assume that there is a normal distribution of the variable in question in the population.

When looking at how variables are distributed in samples and populations, it is common to use measures of *central tendency,* such as the mode, median, and mean, which help us to identify where the typical or the average score can be found. These measures are used so often because, not only do they provide a useful summary of the data, they also provide a common denominator for comparing groups with each other.

Mode

As mentioned earlier, the mode is the score, or value, that occurs the most often—the value with the highest frequency. In Thea's data set of parental skills scores the mode is 79, with five foster care parents obtaining this value. The mode is particularly useful for nominal level data. Knowing what score occurred the most often, however, provides little information about the other scores and how they are distributed in the sample or population. Because the mode is the least precise of all the measures of central tendency, the median and the mean are better descriptors of ordinal level data and above. We now turn our attention to the second measure of central tendency, the median.

Median

The median is the score that divides a distribution into two equal parts or portions. To do this, we must rank-order the scores, so at least an ordinal level of measurement is required. In Thea's sample of 20 PSS scores, the median would be the score above which the top 10 scores lie and below which the bottom 10 fall. As can be seen in Table 23.2, the top 10 scores finish at 82, and the bottom 10 scores start at 80. In this example, the median is 81 because it falls between 82 and 80.

Mean

The mean is the most sophisticated measure of central tendency and is useful for interval or ratio levels of measurement. It is also one of the most commonly used statistics. A mean is calculated by summing the individual values and dividing by the total number of values. The mean of Thea's sample is 95 + 93 + 93 + 93 + 90 + 90 + ...72 + 71 + 55/20 = 81.95. In this example, the obtained mean of 82 (we rounded off for the sake of clarity) is larger than the mode of 79 or the median of 81.

The mean is one of the previously mentioned statistical procedures that assumes that a variable will be distributed normally throughout a population. If this is not an accurate assumption, then the median might be a better descriptor. The mean is also best used with relatively large sample sizes where extreme scores (such as the lowest score of 55 in Thea's sample) have less influence.

Measures of Variability

Measures of central tendency provide valuable information about a set of scores, but we are also interested in knowing how the scores scatter themselves around the center. A mean does not give a sense of how widely distributed the scores may be. This is provided by measures of variability such as the range and the standard deviation.

Range

The range is simply the distance between the minimum and the maximum score. The larger the range, the greater the amount of variation of scores in the distribution. The range is calculated by subtracting the lowest score from the highest. In Thea's sample, the range is 40 (95 to 55).

The range does not necessarily assume equal intervals, so it can be used with ordinal, interval, or ratio level data. It is, like the mean, sensitive to deviant values because it depends on only the two extreme scores. We could have a group of four scores ranging from 10 to 20: 10, 14, 19, and 20, for example. The range of this sample would be 10 (20 to 10). If one additional score that was substantially different from the first set of four scores was included, this would change the range dramatically. In this example, if a fifth score of 45 was added, the range of the sample would become 35 (45 to 10), a number that would suggest quite a different picture of the variability of the scores.

Standard Deviation

The standard deviation is the most well-used indicator of dispersion. It provides a picture of how the scores distribute themselves around the mean. Used in com-

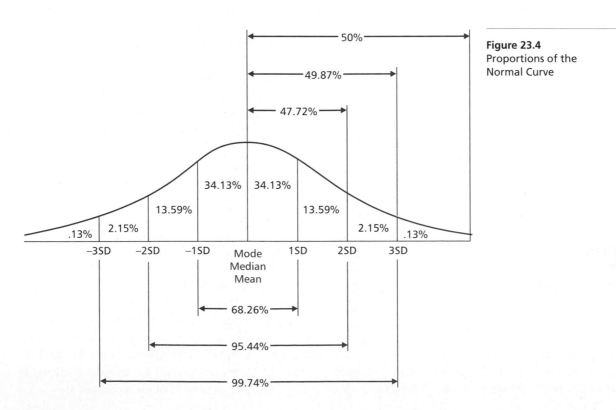

Figure 23.4
Proportions of the Normal Curve

bination with the mean, the standard deviation provides a great deal of information about the sample or population, without our ever needing to see the raw scores. In a normal distribution of scores, described previously, there are 6 standard deviations: 3 below the mean and 3 above, as is shown in Figure 23.4.

In this perfect model, we always know that 34.13 percent of the scores of the sample fall within 1 standard deviation above the mean, and another 34.13 percent fall within 1 standard deviation below the mean. Thus, a total of 68.26 percent, or about two-thirds of the scores, is between +1 standard deviation and −1 standard deviation from the mean. This leaves almost one-third of the scores to fall farther away from the mean, with 15.87 percent (50% to 34.13%) above +1 standard deviation, and 15.87 percent (50% to 34.13%) below −1 standard deviation. In total, when looking at the proportion of scores that fall between +2 and −2 standard deviations, 95.44 percent of scores can be expected to be found within these parameters. Furthermore, 99.74 percent of the scores fall between +3 standard deviations and −3 standard deviations about the mean. Thus, finding scores that fall beyond 3 standard deviations above and below the mean should be a rare occurrence.

The standard deviation has the advantage, like the mean, of taking all values into consideration in its computation. Also similar to the mean, it is used with interval or ratio levels of measurement and assumes a normal distribution of scores.

Several different samples of scores could have the same mean, but the variation around the mean, as provided by the standard deviation, could be quite different, as is shown in Figure 23.5a. Two different distributions could have unequal means and equal standard deviations, as in Figure 23.5b, or unequal means and unequal standard deviations, as in Figure 23.5c.

The standard deviation of the scores of Thea's foster care parents was calculated to be 10. Again, assuming that the variable of knowledge about parenting skills is normally distributed in the population of foster care parents, the results of the PSS scores from the sample of parents about whom we are making inferences can be shown in a distribution like Figure 23.6.

As can also be seen in Figure 23.6, the score that would include 2 standard deviations, 102, is beyond the

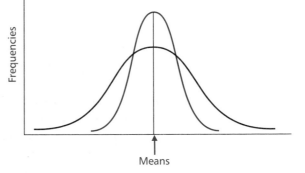

Frequencies

Means

(a) Equal means, unequal standard deviations

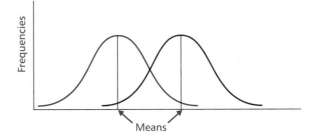

Frequencies

Means

(b) Unequal means, equal standard deviations

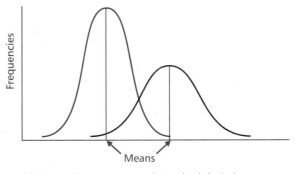

Frequencies

Means

(c) Unequal means, unequal standard deviations

Figure 23.5 Variations in Normal Distributions

total possible score of 100 on the test. This is because the distribution of the scores in Thea's sample of parents does not entirely fit a normal distribution. The one extremely low score of 55 (see Table 23.1) obtained by one foster care parent would have affected the mean, as well as the standard deviation.

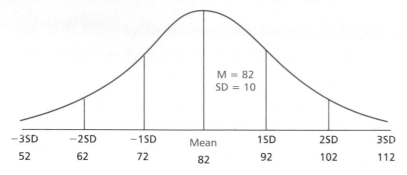

Figure 23.6
Distribution of Parental Skill Scores

INFERENTIAL STATISTICS

The goal of inferential statistical tests is to rule out chance as the explanation for finding either associations between variables or differences between variables in our samples. Because we are rarely able to study an entire population, we are almost always dealing with samples drawn from that population. The danger is that we might make conclusions about a particular population based on a sample that is uncharacteristic of the population it is supposed to represent.

For example, perhaps the group of foster parents in Thea's training session happened to have an unusually high level of knowledge of parenting skills. If she assumed that all the rest of the foster parents that she might train in the future were as knowledgeable, she would be overestimating their knowledge, a factor that could have a negative impact on the way she conducts her training program.

To counteract the possibility that the sample is uncharacteristic of the general population, statistical tests take a conservative position as to whether we can conclude that there are relationships among the variables within our sample. The guidelines to indicate the likelihood that we have, indeed, found a relationship or difference that fits the population of interest are called *probability levels*.

The convention in most social science research is that variables are significantly associated or groups are significantly different if we are relatively certain that in 19 samples out of 20 (or 95 times out of 100) from a particular population we would find the same relationship. This corresponds to a probability level of .05, written as

(p <.05). Probability levels are usually provided along with the results of the statistical test to demonstrate how confident we are that the results actually indicate statistically significant differences. If a probability level is greater than .05 (e.g., .06, .10), this indicates that we did not find a statistically significant difference.

Statistics That Determine Associations

There are many statistics that can determine if there is an association between two variables. We will briefly discuss two: chi-square and correlation.

Chi-Square

The *chi-square test* requires measurements of variables at only the nominal or ordinal level. Thus, it is very useful because much data in social work are gathered at these two levels of measurement. In general, the chi-square test looks at whether specific values of one variable tend to be associated with specific values of another. In short, we use it to determine if two variables are related. It cannot be used to determine if one variable *caused* another, however.

In thinking about the foster care parents who were in her training program, Thea was aware that women are more typically responsible for caring for their own children than men. Even if they are not mothers themselves, they are often in professions such as teaching and social work where they are caretakers. Thus, she wondered whether there might be a relationship between having had previous training in parenting skills and gender, such that women were less likely to have taken such training because they already felt confident in their knowledge of parenting skills. As a result, her one-tailed hypothesis was that fewer women than men would have previously taken parenting skills training courses. Thea could examine this possibility with her 20 foster care parents using a chi-square test.

In terms of gender, Thea had data from the nine (45%) men and 11 (55%) women. Of the total group, four (20%) had previous training in foster care training, and 16 (80%) had not. As shown in Table 23.5, the first task was for Thea to count the number of men and women who had had previous training and the number of men and women who had not had previous training. She put these data in one of the four categories in Table 23.5. The actual numbers are called *observed frequencies*. It is helpful to transform these raw data into percentages, making comparisons between categories much easier.

We can, however, still not tell simply by looking at the observed frequencies whether there is a statistically significant relationship between gender (male or female) and previous training (yes or no). To do this, the next step is to look at how much the observed frequencies differ from what we would expect to see if, in fact, if there was no relationship. These are called *expected frequencies*. Without going through all the calculations, the chi-square table would now look like Table 23.6 for Thea's data set.

Because the probability level of the obtained chi-square value in Table 23.6 is greater than .05, Thea did not find any statistical relationship between gender and previous training in parenting skills. Thus, statistically speaking, men were no more likely than women to have received previous training in parenting skills; her research hypothesis was not supported by the data.

TABLE 23.5

Frequencies (and Percentages) of Gender by Previous Training (From Table 23.1)

Gender	Previous Training		Total
	Yes	No	
Male	1 (11)	8 (89)	9
Female	3 (27)	8 (73)	11
Total	**4 (20)**	**16 (80)**	**20**

TABLE 23.6

Chi-Square Table for Gender by Previous Training (From Table 23.5)

Gender	Previous Training	No Previous Training
Male	$O = 1.0$	$O = 8.0$
	$E = 1.8$	$E = 7.2$
Female	$O = 3.0$	$O = 8.0$
	$E = 2.2$	$E = 8.8$

$\chi^2 = .8$, $df = 1$, $p > .05$.
O = observed frequencies (from Table 23.5).
E = expected frequencies.

Correlation

Tests of correlation investigate the strength of the relationship between two variables. As with the chi-square test, correlation cannot be used to imply causation, only association. Correlation is applicable to data at the interval and ratio levels of measurement. Correlational values are always decimalized numbers, never exceeding ±1.00.

The size of the obtained correlation value indicates the strength of the association, or relationship, between the two variables. The closer a correlation is to zero, the less likely it is that a relationship exists between the two variables. The plus and minus signs indicate the direction of the relationship. Both high positive (close to +1.00) or high negative numbers (close to −1.00) signify strong relationships.

In positive correlations, though, the scores vary similarly, either increasing or decreasing. Thus, as parenting skills increase, so does self-esteem, for example. A negative correlation, in contrast, simply means that as one variable increases the other decreases. An example would be that, as parenting skills increase, the stresses experienced by foster parents decrease.

Thea may wonder whether there is a relationship between the foster parents' years of education and score on the PSS knowledge test. She might reason that the more years of education completed, the more likely the parents would have greater knowledge about parenting skills. To investigate the one-tailed hypothesis that years of education are positively related to knowledge of parenting skills, Thea can correlate the PSS scores with each person's number of years of formal education using one of the most common correlational tests, Pearson's *r*.

The obtained correlation between PSS score and years of education in this example is $r = -.10$ ($p > .05$). It was in the opposite direction of what she predicted. This negative correlation is close to zero, and its probability level is greater than .05. Thus, in Thea's sample, the parents' PSS scores are not related to their educational levels. If the resulting correlation coefficient (*r*) had been positive and statistically significant ($p < .05$), it would have indicated that as the knowledge levels of the parents increased so would their years of formal education. If the correlation coefficient had been statistically significant but negative, this would be interpreted as showing that, as years of formal education increased, knowledge scores decreased.

If a correlational analysis is misinterpreted, it is likely to be the case that the researcher implied causation rather than simply identifying an association between the two variables. If Thea were to have found a statistically significant positive correlation between knowledge and education levels and had explained this to mean than the high knowledge scores were a result of higher education levels, she would have interpreted the statistic incorrectly.

Statistics That Determine Differences

Two commonly used statistical procedures, *t* tests and analysis of variance (ANOVA), examine the means and variances of two or more separate groups of scores to determine if they are statistically different from one another. A *t* test is used with only two groups of scores, whereas ANOVA is used when there are more than two groups. Both are characterized by having a dependent variable at the interval or ratio level of measurement, and an independent, or grouping, variable at either the nominal or ordinal level of measurement. Several assumptions underlie the use of both *t* tests and ANOVA.

First, it is assumed that the dependent variable is normally distributed in the population from which the samples were drawn. Second, it is assumed that the variance of the scores of the dependent variable in the different groups is roughly the same. This assumption is called *homogeneity of variance*. Third, it is assumed that the samples are randomly drawn from the population.

Nevertheless, as mentioned in Chapter 13 on group research designs, it is a common occurrence in social work that we can neither randomly select nor randomly assign individuals to either the experimental or the control group. In many cases this is because we are dealing with already preformed groups, such as Thea's foster care parents.

Breaking the assumption of randomization, however, presents a serious drawback to the interpretation of the research findings, which must be noted in the limitations and the interpretations section of the final research report. One possible difficulty that might result from nonrandomization is that the sample may be uncharacteristic of the larger population in some manner. It is important, therefore, that the results not be used inferentially; that is, the findings must not be generalized to the general population. The design of the research study is, thus, reduced to an exploratory or descriptive level, being relevant to only those individuals included in the sample.

Dependent t Test

Dependent *t* tests are used to compare two groups of scores from the same individuals. The most frequent example in social work research is looking at how a group of individuals changes from before they receive a social work intervention (pre) to afterward (post). Thea may have decided that, while knowing the knowledge levels of the foster care parents before receiving training was interesting, it did not give her any idea whether her program helped the parents to improve their skill levels. In other words her research question became: "After being involved in the program, did parents know more about parenting skills than before they started?" Her hypothesis was that knowledge of parenting skills would improve after participation in her training program.

Thea managed to contact all of the foster care parents in the original group (Group A) one week after they had graduated from the program and asked them to fill out the PSS knowledge questionnaire once again. Because it was the same group of people who were responding

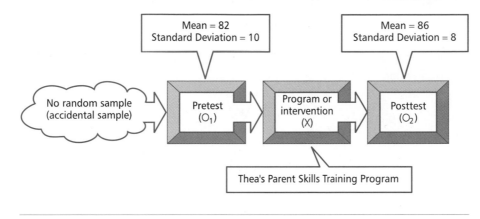

Figure 23.7   One-Group Pretest-Posttest Design Utilized in Thea's Study

twice to the same questionnaire, the dependent *t* test was appropriate. The research design is the one-group prettest-posttest design (Figure 23.7).

Using the same set of scores collected by Thea previously as the pretest, the mean PSS was 82, with a standard deviation of 10. The mean score of the foster care parents after they completed the program was calculated as 86, with a standard deviation of 8.

A *t* value of 3.9 was obtained, statistically significant at the .05 level, indicating that the levels of parenting skills significantly increased after the foster care parents participated in the skills training program.

The results suggest that the average parenting skills of this particular group of foster care parents significantly improved (from 82 to 86) after they had participated in Thea's program.

Independent t Test

Independent *t* tests are used for two groups of scores that have no relationship to each other. If Thea had PSS scores from one group of foster care parents and then collected more PSS scores from a second group of foster care parents, for example, these two groups would be considered independent, and the independent *t* test would be the appropriate statistical analysis to determine if there was a statistically significant difference between the means of the two groups' PSS scores.

Thea decided to compare the average PSS score for the first group of foster care parents (Group A) with the average PSS score of parents in her next training program (Group B). This would allow her to see if the first group (Group A) had been unusually talented, or conversely, were less well-versed in parenting skills than the second group (Group B). Her hypothesis was that there would be no differences in the levels of knowledge of parenting skills between the two groups.

Because Thea had PSS scores from two different groups of participants (Groups A and B), the correct statistical test to identify if there are any statistical differences between the means of the two groups is the independent *t* test. Let us use the same set of numbers that we previously used in the example of the dependent *t* test in this analysis, this time considering the posttest PSS scores as the scores of the second group of foster care parents. As can be seen from Figure 23.8, the mean PSS of Group A was 82 and the standard deviation was 10. Group B scored an average of 86 on the PSS, with a standard deviation of 8. Although the means of the two groups are 4 points apart, the standard deviations in the distribution of each are fairly large, so there is considerable overlap between the two groups. This would suggest that statistically significant differences will not be found.

The obtained *t* value to establish whether this 4-point difference (86 to 82) between the means for two groups was statistically significant was calculated to be $t = 1.6$ with a $p > .05$. The two groups were, thus, not statistically different from one another, and Thea's hypothesis was supported. Note, however, that Thea's

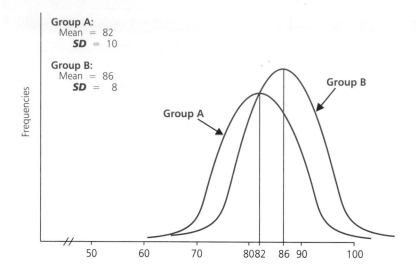

Group A:
Mean = 82
SD = 10

Group B:
Mean = 86
SD = 8

Group B

Group A

Frequencies

50   60   70   8082 86 90   100

Figure 23.8   Frequency Distributions of PSS Scores from Two Groups of Foster Care Providers

foster care parents were not randomly assigned to each group, thus breaking one of the assumptions of the *t* test. As discussed earlier, this is a serious limitation to the interpretation of the study's results. We must be especially careful not to generalize the findings beyond the groups included in the study.

Note that, in the previous example, when using the same set of numbers but a dependent *t* test, we found a statistically significant difference. This is because the dependent *t* test analysis is more robust than the independent *t* test, because having the same participant fill out the questionnaire twice, under two different conditions, controls for many extraneous variables, such as individual differences, that could negatively influence an analysis of independent samples.

One-Way Analysis of Variance

A one-way ANOVA is the extension of an independent *t* test that uses three or more groups. Each set of scores is from a different group of participants. For example, Thea might use the scores on the PSS test from the first group of foster care parents from whom she collected data before they participated in her program, but she might also collect data from a second and a third group of parents before they received the training. The test for significance of an ANOVA is called an *F* test. We could actually use an ANOVA procedure on only two groups,

and the result would be identical to the *t* test. Unlike the *t* test, however, obtaining a significant *F* value in a one-way ANOVA does not complete the analysis. Because ANOVA looks at differences between three or more groups, a significant *F* value only tells us that there is a statistically significant difference among the groups— it does not tell us between which ones.

To identify the groups, we need to do a *post hoc* test. A variety are available, such as Duncan's multiple range, Tukey's honestly significant difference test, and Newman—Keuls, and these are provided automatically by most computer statistical programs. But one caution applies: A post hoc test should be used *only after finding a significant F value*, because some of the post hoc tests are more sensitive than the *F* test and so might find significance when the *F* test does not. Generally, we should use the most conservative test first, in this case the *F* test.

In the example of Thea's program, let us say that she collected data on a total of three different groups of foster care parents. The first group of foster care parents scored an average of 82 on the PSS (standard deviation 10). The second group scored an average of 86 (standard deviation 8), while the mean score of the third group was 88 with a standard deviation of 7.

The obtained *F* value for the one-way ANOVA is 2.63, with a $p > .05$. Thus, we must conclude that there are no statistically significant differences between the means of the groups (i.e., 82, 86, 88). Because the F value was not significant, we would not conduct any post hoc tests. This finding would be interesting to Thea, because it suggests that all three groups of foster care parents started out with approximately the same knowledge levels, on the average, before receiving training.

SUMMARY

This chapter provided a beginning look at the rationale behind some of the most commonly used statistical procedures, both those that describe samples and those that analyze data from a sample in order to make inferences about the larger population.

The level of measurement of the data is key to the kind of statistical procedures that can be used. Descriptive statistics are used with data from all levels of measurement. The mode is the most appropriate measure of central tendency for measurements of this level. It is only when we have data from interval and ratio levels that we can use inferential statistics—those that extend the statistical conclusions made about a sample by applying them to the larger population.

Descriptive measures of central tendency, such as the mode, median, and mean of a sample or population, all provide different kinds of information, each of which is applicable only to some levels of measurement. In addition to knowing the middle or average of a distribution of scores as provided by measures of central tendency, it is useful to know the value of the standard deviation that shows us how far away from the mean the scores are distributed. It is assumed that many variables studied in social work can be found in a normal distribution in the total population. Consequently, many descriptive and inferential statistics assume such a distribution for their tests to be valid.

Chi-square and correlation are both statistical tests that determine whether variables are associated, although they do not show causation. In contrast, t tests and analysis of variance (ANOVA) are statistical procedures for determining whether the mean and variance in one group (often a treatment group) is significantly different from those in another (often a comparison or control group).

Writing
Quantitative
Proposals
and Reports

Margaret Williams

Leslie Tutty

Richard M. Grinnell, Jr.

· ·

24

In this chapter, we discuss both how to write a quantitative research proposal, which is done *before* the study begins, and how to write a quantitative research report, which is done *after* the study is completed. They will be presented together because a quantitative research proposal describes what is *proposed* to be done, whereas a research report describes what *has been* done. As will be emphasized throughout the chapter, there is so much overlap between the two that a majority of the material written for a quantitative research proposal can be used in writing the final research report.

This chapter will incorporate most of the contents of the preceding ones, so it is really a summary of the entire quantitative research process (and this book) up to report writing. We will use an example of Lula Wilson, a social work practitioner who wants to do a quantitative research study on children who come to her women's emergency shelter with their mothers. She has been working at the shelter for the past 2 years. The shelter is located in a large urban city.

WRITING QUANTITATIVE RESEARCH PROPOSALS

When writing any research proposal, we must always keep in mind the purposes for its development and be aware of politically sensitive research topics. These are, primarily, to get permission to do the study and, second, perhaps to obtain some funds with which to do it.

There is a third purpose—to persuade the people who will review the proposal that its author, Lula, is competent to carry out the intended study. Finally, the fourth purpose of a proposal is to force Lula to write down exactly *what* is going to be studied, *why* it is going to studied, and *how* it is going to studied. In doing this, she may think of aspects of the study that had not occurred to her before. For example, she may look at the first draft of her proposal and realize that some essential detail was forgotten—for instance, that the research participants (in her case, children) who are going to fill out self-report standardized measuring instruments must be able to read.

The intended readers of the proposal determine how it will be written. It is important to remember that the reviewers will probably have many proposals to evaluate at once. Some proposals will need to be turned down because there will not be sufficient funds, space, or staff time to accept all of them. Thus, proposal reviewers are faced with some difficult decisions on which studies to accept and which ones to reject. People who review research proposals often do so on a voluntary basis.

With the above in mind, the proposal should be written so that it is easy to read, easy to follow, easy to understand, clearly organized, and brief. It must not ramble or go off into anecdotes about how Lula became interested in the subject in the first place. Rather, Lula's proposal must describe her proposed research study simply, clearly, and concisely.

Now that we know the underlying rationale for the proposal, the next step is to consider what content it should include. This depends to some extent on who will be reviewing it. If the proposal is submitted to an academic committee, for example, it will often include a more extensive literature review and more details of the study's research design than if it were submitted to a funding organization. Some funding bodies specify exactly what they want included and in what order; others leave it to the author's discretion.

The simplest and most logical way to write the proposal is in the same order that a quantitative research study is conducted. For example, when a quantitative research study is done, a general topic area is decided on as presented in Chapter 5. This is followed by a literature review (Chapter 4) in an attempt to narrow the broad research area into more specific research questions or hypotheses. We will now go back and look at how each step of a quantitative research study leads to the writing of a parallel section in a research proposal. Let us turn to the first task of proposal writing, specifying the research topic.

Part 1: Research Topic

The first step in beginning any research study is to decide what the study will be about. The first procedure in writing a proposal, therefore, is to describe in general terms what it is that is going to be studied. Lula may describe, for example, her proposed study's general problem area as:

> General Problem Area:
> Problems experienced by children who witness the husband physically abusing his partner.

The first task is to convince the proposal reviewers that the general problem area is a good one to study. This task is accomplished by outlining the significance of Lula's proposed study in three specific social work areas: its practical significance, its theoretical significance, and its social policy significance.

Depending on to whom the proposal is submitted, Lula may go into detail about these three areas or describe them briefly. It may be known, for example, that the funding organization that will review the proposal is mostly interested in improving the effectiveness of individual social workers in their day-to-day practice activities. If this is the case, the reviewers will more likely be interested in the practical significance of Lula's proposed study than its theoretical and/or policy significance.

Therefore, Lula's proposal would neither go into detail about how her study might generate new social work theory, nor elaborate on the changes in social policy that might follow directly from the study's results. Because Lula is going to submit the proposal to the women's emergency shelter where she works, she would be smart in obtaining informal input from the agency's executive director at this stage in writing the proposal. Informal advice at an early stage is astronomically important to proposal writers. In sum, Part 1 of the proposal describes *what* is going to be studied and *why* it should be studied.

Part 2: Literature Review

The second part of a proposal contains the literature review. This is not simply a list of all the books and journal articles that vaguely touch on the general problem area mentioned in Part 1. When a quantitative research study is done, it is basically trying to add another piece to a jigsaw puzzle already begun by other researchers. The purpose of a literature review, then, is to show how *Lula's* study fits into the whole.

The trouble is that it might be a very big whole. There may be literally hundreds of articles and books filled with previous research studies on the study's general topic area. If Lula tries to list every one of these, the reviewers of the proposal—probably her colleagues who work with her at the shelter—will lose interest and patience somewhere in the middle of Part 2. The literature review has to be selective—listing enough material to show that Lula is thoroughly familiar with her topic area, but not enough to induce stupor in the reviewers. This is a delicate and sensitive balance. She should include findings from recent research studies along with any classic ones.

On the other side of the coin, another possibility is that previous research studies on Lula's general topic area may be limited. In this case, all available material is included. However, her proposal can also branch out into material that is partially related or describes a parallel topic area. Lula might find a research article, for example, that claims that children whose parents are contemplating divorce have low social interaction skills. This does not bear directly on the matter of problems children have who witnessed domestic violence (the general problem area mentioned above). However, because marital separation can be a result of domestic violence, it might be indirectly relevant.

A literature review serves a number of purposes. First, it shows the reviewers that Lula understands the most current and central issues related to the general topic area that she proposes to study. Second, it points out in what ways her proposed study is the same as, or different from, other similar studies. Third, it describes how the results of her proposed study will contribute to solving the puzzle. Fourth, it introduces and conceptually defines all the variables that will be examined throughout the study.

At this stage, Lula does not operationally define her study's variables—that is, in such a way that allows their measurement. They are only abstractly defined. For example, if Lula is going to study the social interaction skills of children who witness domestic violence, her proposal so far introduces only the concepts of children, domestic violence, children witnessing domestic violence, and children's social interaction skills.

Part 3: Conceptual Framework

A conceptual framework takes the variables that have been mentioned in Part 2, illustrates their possible relationship to one another, and discusses why the relationship exists the way it is proposed and not in some other, equally possible way. The author's suppositions might be based on past professional experience. For example, Lula has observed numerous children who accompanied their mothers to women's emergency shelters. She has made subjective observations of these children over the past 2 years and finally wishes to test out two hunches objectively.

First, Lula believes that children who have witnessed domestic violence *seem* to have lower social interaction skills than children who have not witnessed domestic violence. Second, Lula believes that of the children who have been a witness to domestic violence, boys *seem* to have lower social interaction skills than girls. However, these two hunches are based on only 2-year subjective observations, which need to be objectively tested—the purpose of her quantitative study.

As we know, ideally, Lula's hunches should be integrated with existing theory or findings derived from previous research studies. In any case, Lula should discuss these assumptions and the reasons for believing them as the basis for the variables that are included in her proposed study.

In sum, Lula wants to see if children who have witnessed domestic violence have lower social interaction skills than do children who have not witnessed it. And of the children who have witnessed domestic violence, she wants to determine whether boys have lower social interaction skills than girls. It must be remembered that the two areas her study proposes to explore have been delineated out of her past experiences and have not been formulated based on existing theory or previous research findings.

Part 4: Questions and Hypotheses

As previously discussed at the beginning of this book, when little is known about a topic, only general research questions are asked. Many general research questions relating to Lula's general problem area can be asked. One of the many could be:

> **General Research Question:**
> Is there a relationship between children witnessing domestic violence and their social interaction skills?

On the other hand, when a lot of previous research studies have been done, a specific hypothesis can be formulated. A specific hypothesis derived from the above general research question might be:

> **Specific Research Hypothesis:**
> Children who have witnessed domestic violence will have lower social interaction skills than children who have not witnessed such abuse.

Part 5: Operational Definitions

As already mentioned, variables are abstractly and conceptually defined in the conceptual framework part of the proposal (Part 3). Part 5 provides operational definitions of them; that is, they must be defined in ways in which they can become measurable.

Let us take Lula's simple research hypothesis as previously mentioned. In this hypothesis there are four main variables that must be operationalized before Lula's study can begin: children, domestic violence, children witnessing domestic violence, and children's social interaction skills. Each must be described in such a way that there is no ambiguity as to what they mean.

Variable 1: Children

For example, what constitutes a child? How old must the child be? Does the child have to be in a certain age range, for example, between the ages of 5 and 10? Does the child have to be a biological product of either the mother or the father? Can the child be a stepchild? Can the child be adopted? Does the child have to live full time at home?

Because Lula's study is at the descriptive level, she may wish to define a child operationally in such a way that permits the largest number of children to be included in the study. She would, however, go to the literature and find out how other researchers have operationally defined "children," and she would use this operational definition if it made sense to her.

However, in a simple study such as this one, a child could be operationally defined as "any person who is considered to be a child as determined by the mother." This is a very vague operational definition at best, but it is more practical than constructing one such as "a person between the ages of 5 and 17 who has resided full time with the biological mother for the last 12-month period."

If such a complex operational definition was used, Lula would have to provide answers to questions as: Why the ages of 5 and 17, why not 4 and 18? What is the specific reason for this age range? Why must the child live at home full time, why not part time? Why must the mother be the biological mother, why not a nonbiological mother? What about biological fathers? Why must the child have had to live at home for the past 12 months, why not 2 years, 4 years? In short, Lula's operational definition of a child must make sense and be based on a rational or theoretical basis. For now, Lula is going to make matters simple: A child in her study will be operationally defined as any child whose mother validates their relationship. This simple operational definition makes the most practical sense to Lula.

Variable 2: Domestic Violence

Let us now turn to Lula's second variable—domestic violence. What is it? Does the male partner have to shove, push, or threaten his partner? How would a child, as operationally defined above, know when it occurs? Does a husband yelling at his partner imply domestic violence? If so, does it have to last a long time? If it does, what is a long time? Is Lula interested in the frequency,

duration, or magnitude of yelling—or all three? A specific operational definition of domestic violence has to be established in order for the study to be of any value.

Like most variables, there are as many operational definitions of domestic violence as there are people willing to define it. For now, Lula is going to continue to make her descriptive study simple by operationally defining domestic violence as: "women who say they have been physically abused by their partners." Lula can simply ask each woman who enters the shelter if she believes she has been physically abused by her partner. The data provided by the women will be "yes" or "no." Lula could have looked at the frequency, duration, or magnitude of such abuse, but for this study, the variable is a dichotomous one: Either domestic violence occurred, or it did not occur—as reported by the women. Questions regarding its frequency (how many times it occurred), its duration (how long each episode lasted), and its magnitude (the intensity of each episode) are not asked.

Variable 3: Children Witnessing Domestic Violence

The third variable in Lula's hypothesis is the child (or children) who witness domestic violence. Now that operational definitions of a "child" and "domestic violence" have been formulated, how will she know that a child has witnessed such an abuse? Each child could be asked directly, or a standardized checklist of possible verbal and physical abuses that a child might have witnessed can be given to the child, who is then asked how many times such abuse has been observed.

Obviously, the child would have to know what constitutes domestic violence to recognize it. In addition, the child would have to be old enough to respond to such requests, and the operational definition that is used for domestic violence must be consistent with the age of the child. For example, the child must be able to communicate to someone that domestic violence has in fact occurred—not to mention the question of whether the child could recognize it in the first place.

In Lula's continuing struggle to keep her study as simple as possible, she operationally defines "a child witnessing domestic violence" by asking the mothers who come to the women's emergency shelter if their child or children witnessed the physical abuse. She is interested only in the women who come to the shelter as a result of being physically abused by their partners. Women who come to the shelter for other reasons are not included in her study. It must be kept in mind that Lula's study is focusing only on physical abuse and not emotional or mental abuse.

So far, Lula's study is rather simple in terms of operational definitions. Up to this point she is studying mothers who bring their child or children with them to one women's emergency shelter. She simply asks the mother if each of the people with her is her child, which operationally defines "child." The mother is asked if she believes her partner physically abused her, which defines 'domestic violence." The mother is also asked if any of the children who are accompanying her to the shelter saw the physical abuse occur, which operationally defines "children witnessing domestic violence."

Variable 4: Children's Social Interaction Skills

Let us now turn to Lula's fourth and final variable in her hypothesis—the children's social interaction skills. How will they be measured? What constitutes the social skills of a child? They could be measured in a variety of ways through direct observations of parents, social work practitioners, social work researchers, social work practicum students, teachers, neighbors, or even members from the children's peer group. They could also be measured by a standardized measuring instrument such as the ones discussed in Chapters 8 and 9. Lula decides to use one of the many standardized measuring instruments that measure social interaction skills of children, namely, the Social Interaction Skills of Children Assessment Instrument (SISOCAI).

All in all, Part 5 of a proposal provides operational definitions of all important variables that were abstractly defined in Part 3. It should be noted that the four variables that have been operationally defined should be defined from the available literature, if appropriate. (This procedure makes a study's results generalizable from one research situation to another.) However, there may be

times when this is not possible. The proposal must specify what data gathering instruments are going to be used, including their validity and reliability, as presented in Chapters 8 and 9.

In summary, let us review how Lula intends to operationally define her four key variables: child, domestic violence, child witnessing domestic violence, and children's social interaction skills:

1. *Child.* Any person who the mother claims is her child.
2. *Domestic Violence.* Asking the mother if her partner physically abused her.
3. *Child Witnessing Domestic Violence.* Asking the mother if the child(ren) who accompanied her to the shelter witnessed the abuse.
4. *Children's Social Interaction Skills.* The SISOCAI score for each child in the study.

The first three operational definitions are rather rudimentary, at best. There are many more sophisticated ways of operationally defining them. However, alternative definitions will not be explored, because Lula wants to keep her quantitative research proposal as uncomplicated as possible as she knows that the shelter does not want a study that would intrude too heavily into its day-to-day operations. On a very general level, the more complex the operational definitions of variables used in a quantitative research study, the more the study will intrude on the research participants' lives and on the agency's day-to-day operations.

Part 6: Research Design

This part of a quantitative research proposal presents the study's research design. Suppose Lula formulated two related research hypotheses from her general problem area mentioned above:

> Research Hypothesis 1:
> Children who have witnessed domestic violence will have lower social interaction skills than children who have not witnessed such abuse.

Research Hypothesis 2:
Of those children who have witnessed domestic violence, boys will have lower social interaction skills than girls.

In relation to Research Hypothesis 1, Lula's study would use the children who accompanied their mothers to the women's emergency shelter. These children would then be broken down into two groups, (1) those children who witnessed domestic violence, and (2) those children who did not witness it (as determined by the mother).

As presented in Chapter 13, a very simple two-group research design could be used to test Research Hypothesis 1. The average social interaction skill score, via the SISO-CAI, between the two groups can then be compared.

In relation to Research Hypothesis 2, within the group of children who have witnessed domestic violence, the children's social interaction skills, via the SISOCAI, between the boys and girls can be compared. This simple procedure would test Research Hypothesis 2. Once again, as presented in Chapter 13, a simple two-group research design could be used to test Research Hypothesis 2.

In Lula's study, there are two separate mini-research studies running at the same time—Research Hypotheses 1 and 2. All Lula wants to do is to see if there is an association between the social interaction skills of children who have and have not witnessed domestic violence (Research Hypothesis 1). In addition, for those children who have witnessed domestic violence, she wants to see if boys have lower social interaction skills than girls (Research Hypothesis 2).

In Part 6 of a quantitative research proposal, information should be included about *what* data will be collected, *how* these data will be collected, and *who* will be the research participants.

Next, Lula must now describe *when* the data are to be collected. She will have her research assistant complete the SISOCAI for each child during a half-hour interview. Finally, the *conditions* under which the data will be gathered are discussed; that is, the research assistant will complete the SISOCAI for each selected child one day after the mother has entered the shelter.

Of necessity, recording all of this will involve some repetition. For example, in the discussion of operational

definitions in Part 5, we looked at what data would be collected and how. Part 7, the next part, will discuss the study's population and sample (i.e., who will be studied) in much more detail. It has been repeated in Part 6, both to give an overview of the whole positivist research process, and to form links between Parts 5 and 7 so that the entire proposal flows smoothly.

Part 7: Population and Sample

This part of the proposal presents a detailed description of who will be studied. Lula's quantitative research study will use the children who accompanied their mothers to one women's emergency shelter who wish to voluntarily participate, and whose mothers agree that they can be included in the study. The children will then each go into one of two distinct groups: those who have witnessed domestic violence, and those who have not (according to the mothers, that is). Lula's study could have used a comparison group of children from the same local community who have never witnessed domestic violence and have never been to a women's emergency shelter. However, Lula chose to use only those children who accompanied their mothers to the shelter where she works.

There is no question of random selection from some population, and it is not possible to generalize the study's findings to any general population of children who have and have not witnessed domestic violence. The results of Lula's study will apply only to the children who participated in it.

Part 8: Data Collection

This part of a quantitative research proposal presents a detailed account of how the data are going to be collected—that is, the specific data collection method(s) that will be used. As we know, data can be collected using interviews (individual or group), surveys (mail or telephone), direct observations, participant observations, secondary analyses, and content analyses. Lula is going to collect data on the dependent variable by having her research assistant complete the SISOCAI for each identified child during a half-hour interview one day after the mother has entered the shelter with her child or children. Those mothers who do not bring their children with them will not be included in Lula's study.

In addition to the children, their mothers are also going to be interviewed to some small degree. Each mother will be asked by Lula if she believes her partner physically assaulted her. These responses will then be used to operationally define "domestic violence." Each mother will also provide data on whether her children who accompanied her to the shelter saw the abuse occur. The mothers' responses will then operationally define whether the children witnessed domestic violence.

Finally, this section should discuss ethical issues involved in data collection. Chapters 14 to 22 in this book present various data collection methods that can be used in research studies. These chapters should be reread thoroughly before writing Part 8 of a quantitative research proposal.

Part 9: Data Analysis

This part of a quantitative research proposal describes the way the data will be analyzed, including the statistical procedures to be used, if any. Having clearly specified the research design in Part 6, this part specifies exactly what statistical tests will be used to answer the research questions or hypotheses. Most of the more common statistical procedures were presented in Chapter 23.

The SISOCAI produces interval-level data, and a child's social interaction skill score on this particular instrument can range from 0 to 100, where higher scores mean higher (better) social skills than lower scores. Because there are two groups of children who are being used to test both research hypotheses, and the dependent variable (SISOCAI) is at the interval-level of measurement, an independent t test would be used to test both research hypotheses.

Part 10: Limitations

There are limitations in every quantitative research study, often due to problems that cannot be eliminated entirely, even though steps can be taken to reduce them. Lula's study is certainly no exception. Limitations inher-

ent in a study might relate to the validity and reliability of the measuring instruments, or to the generalizability of the study's results. Sometimes the data that were needed could not be collected for some reason. In addition, this part should mention all extraneous variables that have not been controlled for.

For example, Lula may not have been able to control for all the factors that affect the children's social interaction skills. Although she believes that having witnessed domestic violence leads to lower social skills for boys as compared with girls, it may not be possible to collect reliable and valid data about whether the children saw or did not see an abuse occur. In Lula's study, she is going to simply ask the mothers, so in this case, she has to take the mothers' word for it.

She could ask the children, however. This would produce another set of limitations in and of itself. For example, it would be difficult for Lula to ascertain whether a child did or did not see a form of domestic violence as perceived by the child. It may be hard for a child to tell what type of abuse occurred. Also the frequency, duration, and magnitude of a particular form of domestic violence may be hard for the child to recall. All of these limitations, and a host of others, must be delineated in this part of the proposal. In addition, asking a child if he or she saw the abuse occur might in itself prove to be a traumatic experience for the child.

Some limitations will not be discovered until the study is well underway. However, many problems can be anticipated and these should be included in the proposal, together with the specific steps that are intended to minimize them.

Part 11: Administration

The final part of a quantitative research proposal contains the organization and resources necessary to carry out the study. First, Lula has to find a base of operations (e.g., a desk and telephone). She has to think about who is going to take on the overall administrative responsibility for the study. What staff will be involved? How many individuals will be needed? What should their qualifications be? What will be their responsibilities? To whom are they responsible? What is the chain of command? Finally, Lula has to think about things such as a computer, stationery, telephone, travel, and parking expenses.

When all of the details have been put together, an organizational chart can be produced that shows what will be done, by whom, where, and in what order. The next step is to develop a time frame. By what date should each anticipated step be completed? Optimism about completion dates should be avoided, particularly when it comes to allowing time to analyze the data and writing the final report (to be discussed shortly). Both of these activities always take far longer than anticipated, and it is important that they be properly done—which takes more time than originally planned.

When the organizational chart and time frame have been established, the final step is to prepare a budget. Lula has to figure out how much each aspect of the study— such as office space, the research assistant's time, staff time, and participants' time, if any—will cost.

We have now examined 11 parts that should be included when writing a quantitative research proposal. Not all proposals are organized in precisely this way; sometimes different headings are used or information is put in a different part of the proposal. For example, in some proposals, previous studies are discussed in the conceptual framework section rather than in the literature review. Much depends on for whom the proposal is being written and on the author's personal writing style.

Much of the content that has been used to write the 11 parts of a quantitative research proposal can be used to write the final research report. Let us now turn to that discussion.

WRITING QUANTITATIVE RESEARCH REPORTS

A quantitative research report is a way of describing the completed study to other people. The findings can be reported by way of an oral presentation, a book, or a published paper. The report may be addressed solely to colleagues at work or to a worldwide audience. It may be written simply so that everyone can understand it, or it may be so highly technical that it can only be understood by a few.

The most common way of sharing a study's findings with other professionals is to publish a report in a pro-

fessional journal. Most journal reports run about 25 double-spaced, typewritten pages, including figures, tables, and references.

As we know, quantitative proposals are written with the proposal's reviewers in mind. Similarly, a research report is written with its readers in mind. However, some of the readers who read research reports will want to know the technical details of how the study's results were achieved, others will only want to know how the study's results are relevant to social work practice, without the inclusion of the technical details.

There are a number of ways to deal with this situation. First, a technical report can be written for those who can understand it, without worrying too much about those who cannot. In addition, a second report can be written that skims over the technical aspects of the study and concentrates mostly on the practical application of the study's findings. Thus, two versions of the same study can be written; a technical one and a nontechnical one.

The thought of writing two reports where one would suffice will not appeal to very many of us, however. Usually, we try to compensate for this by including those technical aspects of the study that are necessary to an understanding of the study's findings. This is essential because readers will not be able to evaluate the study's findings without knowing how they were arrived at.

However, life can be made easier for nontechnical audiences by including some explanation of the technical aspects and, in addition, paying close attention to the practical application of the study's results. In this way, we will probably succeed in addressing the needs of both audiences—those who want all the technical details and those who want none.

A quantitative report can be organized in many different ways depending on the intended audience and the author's personal style. Often, however, the same commonsense sequence is followed when the basic problem-solving method was discussed at the beginning of this book. In order to solve a problem, the problem must be specified, ways of solving it must be explored, a solution to solve the problem must be tried, and an evaluation must take place to see if the solution worked.

In general, this is the way to solve practice and research problems. It is also the order in which a quantitative research report is written. First, a research problem is defined. Then, the method used to solve it is discussed. Next, the findings are presented. Finally, the significance of the findings to the social work profession is discussed.

Part 1: Problem

Probably the best way to begin a quantitative research report is to explain simply what the research problem is. Lula might say, for example, that the study's purpose was to ascertain whether children who have witnessed domestic violence have lower social interaction skills than children who have not witnessed such abuse. In addition, the study wanted to find out, of those children who have witnessed domestic violence, whether boys have lower social interaction skills than girls.

But why would anyone want to know about that? How would the knowledge derived from Lula's study help social workers? Thinking back to Part 1 of her proposal, this question was asked and answered once before. In the first part of her proposal, when the research topic was set out, the significance of the study was discussed in the areas of practice, theory, and social policy. This material can be used, suitably paraphrased, in Part 1 of the final report.

One thing that should be remembered, though, is that a quantitative research report written for a journal is not, relatively speaking, very long. A lot of information must be included in less than 25 pages, and the author cannot afford to use too much space explaining to readers why this particular study was chosen. Sometimes, the significance of the study will be apparent, and there is no room to belabor what is already obvious.

In Part 2 of the proposal, a literature review was done in which Lula's proposed study was compared with other similar studies, highlighting the similarities and differences. Also, key variables were conceptually defined. In her final report, she can use both the literature review and her conceptually defined variables that she presented in her proposal. The literature review might have to be cut back if space is at a premium, but the abstract and conceptual definitions of all key variables must be included.

In Part 3 of her proposal, she presented a conceptual framework. This can be used in Part 1 of the final report, where Lula must state the relationships between the variables she is studying.

In Part 4 of the quantitative research proposal, a research question or hypothesis to be answered or tested was stated. In the final report, we started out with that, so now we have come full circle. By using the first four parts of the proposal for the first part of the research report, we have managed to considerably cut down writing time. In fact, Part 1 of a quantitative research report is nothing more than a cut-and-paste job of the first four parts of the research proposal. Actually, if the first four parts of the quantitative research proposal were done correctly, there should be very little original writing within Part 1 of a research report.

One of the most important things to remember when writing Part 1 of a quantitative report is that the study's findings have to have some form of utilization potential for social workers, or the report would not be worth writing in the first place. More specifically, the report must have some practical, theoretical, or policy significance. Part 1 of a quantitative research report tells why the study's findings would be useful to the social work profession. This is mentioned briefly but is picked up later in Part 4.

Part 2: Method

Part 2 of a quantitative research report contains the method used to answer the research problem. This section usually includes descriptions of the study's research design, a description of the research participants who were a part of the study (the study's sample), and a detailed description of the data gathering procedures (who, what, when, and how), and presents the operational definition of all variables.

Once again, sections of the original quantitative research proposal can be used. For example, in Part 5 of the proposal, key variables were operationally defined; that is, they were defined in a way that would allow them to be measured. When and how the measurements would occur were also presented. This material can be used again in the final report.

Part 6 of the proposal described the study's research design. This section of the proposal was used—about halfway through—to link the parts of the study together into a whole. Because a research design encompasses the entire quantitative research process from conceptualizing the problem to disseminating the findings, Lula could take this opportunity to give a brief picture of the entire process. This part presents *who* would be studied (the research participants, or sample), *what* data would be gathered, *how* the data would be gathered, *when* the data would be gathered, and *what* would be done with the data once obtained (analysis).

In the final report, there is not a lot of space to provide this information in detail. Instead, a clear description of how the data were obtained from the measuring instruments must be presented. For example, Lula could state in this part of the report, that "a research assistant rated each child on the SISOCAI during a one-half-hour interview one day after the mother had entered the shelter."

Part 3: Findings

Part 3 of a report presents the study's findings. Unfortunately, Lula's original proposal will not be of much help here because she did not know what she would find when it was written—only what she hoped to find.

One way to begin Part 3 of a report is to prepare whatever figures, tables, or other data displays that are going to be used. For now, let us take Lula's Research Hypothesis 1 as an example of how to write up a study's findings. Suppose that there were 80 children who accompanied their mothers to the shelter. All of the mothers claimed they were physically abused by their partners. Lula's research assistant rated the 80 children's social skills, via the SISOCAI, one day after they accompanied their mothers to the shelter. Thus, there are 80 SISOCAI scores. What is she going to do with all those data?

The goal of tables and figures is to organize the data in such a way that the reader takes them in at a glance and says, "Ah! Well, it's obvious that the children who witnessed domestic violence had lower SISOCAI scores than the children who did not see such abuse."

As can be seen from Table 24.1, the average SISO-CAI score for all of the 80 children is 60. These 80 children would then be broken down into two subgroups: those who witnessed their mother's abuse, and those who did not—according to their mothers, that is. For

the sake of simplicity, let us say there were 40 children in each subgroup. In the first subgroup, the average SISOCAI score for the 40 children is 45; in the second subgroup, the average SISOCAI score for the 40 children is 75.

Table 24.1 allows the reader to quickly compare the average SISOCAI score for each subgroup. The reader can see, at a glance, that there is a 30-point difference between the two average SISOCAI scores ($75 - 45 = 30$). The children who witnessed domestic violence scored 30 points lower, on the average, on the SISOCAI than those children who had not witnessed domestic violence. Thus, by glancing at Table 24.1, Lula's Research Hypothesis 1 is supported in that children who had witnessed domestic violence had lower social interaction skills than children who had not witnessed it.

However, it is still not known from Table 24.1 whether the 30-point difference between the two average *SISOCAI* scores is large enough to be statistically significant. The appropriate statistical procedure for this design is the independent *t* test, as described in Chapter 23. The results of the *t* test could also be included under Table 24.1, or they could be described in the findings section:

> The result of an independent *t* test between the SISOCAI scores of children who had witnessed domestic violence as compared with those children who had not witnessed it was statistically significant ($t = 3.56$, $df = 78$, $p < .05$). Thus, children who had witnessed domestic violence had statistically significant lower social interaction skills, on the average, than children who had not witnessed such abuse.

TABLE 24.1

Mean and Standard Deviation of Social Interaction Skills of Children Who Did and Did Not Witness Mother's Abuse

Witness?	Mean	Standard Deviation	n
Yes	45	11	40
No	75	9	40
Average	**60**	**10**	

TABLE 24.2

Mean and Standard Deviation of Social Interaction Skills of Boys and Grils Who Witnessed Mother's Abuse (From Table 24.1)

Gender	Mean	Standard Deviation	n
Boys	35	12	20
Girls	55	10	20
Average	**45**	**11**	

Table 24.2 presents the study's findings for Lula's second research hypothesis. This table uses the data from the 40 children who had witnessed domestic violence (from Table 24.1). As can be seen from Tables 24.1 and 24.2, the average social skill score for the 40 children who had witnessed domestic violence is 45. Table 24.2 further breaks down these 40 children into two subgroups: boys and girls. Out of the 40 children who had witnessed domestic violence, 20 were boys and 20 were girls. As can be seen from Table 24.2, boys had an average social skill score of 35 as compared with the average score for girls of 55. Thus, the boys scored, on the average, 20 points lower than the girls. So far, Lula's second research hypothesis is supported.

However, it is still not known from Table 24.2 whether the 20-point difference between the two average SISOCAI scores is large enough to be statistically significant. The appropriate statistical procedure for this design is the independent t test, as described in Chapter 23. The results of the t test could be included under Table 24.2, or they could be described in the findings section as follows:

> The result of an independent t test between the SISOCAI scores for boys and girls who had witnessed domestic violence was statistically significant ($t = 2.56$, $df = 38$, $p < .05$). Thus, boys had statistically significant lower social interaction skills, on the average, than girls.

Once a table (or figure) is constructed, the next thing that has to be done is to describe in words what it means. Data displays should be self-explanatory if done correctly. It is a waste of precious space to repeat in the text something that is perfectly apparent from a table or figure.

At this point, Lula has to decide whether she is going to go into a lengthy discussion of her findings in this part of the report or whether she is going to reserve the discussion for the next part. Which option is chosen often depends on what there is to discuss. Sometimes it is more sensible to combine the findings with the discussion, pointing out the significance of what has been found as she goes along.

Part 4: Discussion

The final part of a quantitative research report presents a discussion of the study's findings. Care should be taken not to merely repeat the study's findings that were already presented in Part 3. It can be tempting to repeat one finding to remind the reader about it as a preliminary to a discussion, and then another finding, and then a third . . . and, before we know it, we have written the whole of the findings section all over again and called it a discussion. What is needed here is control and judgment—a delicate balance between not reminding the reader at all and saying everything twice.

On the other hand, Lula might be tempted to ignore her findings altogether, particularly if she did not find what she expected. If the findings did not support her hypothesis, she may have a strong urge to express her viewpoint anyway, using persuasive prose to make up for the lack of quantitative objective evidence. This temptation must be resisted at all costs. The term "discussion" relates to what she found, not to what she thinks she ought to have found or to what she might have found under slightly different circumstances.

Perhaps she did manage to find a relationship between the variables in both of her hypotheses. However, to her dismay, the relationship was the opposite of what she had predicted. For example, suppose her data indicated that children who had not witnessed domestic violence had lower social interaction skills than children who had witnessed it (this is the opposite of what she predicted). This unexpected result must be discussed, shedding whatever light on the surprising finding. Any relationship between two variables is worthy of discussion, particularly if they seem atypical or if they are not quite what was anticipated.

A common limitation in social work research has to do with not being able to randomly sample research participants from a population. Whenever we cannot randomly select or assign research participants to two or more groups, the sample cannot be considered to be truly representative of the population in question, and we cannot generalize the study's results back to the population of children who witnessed or did not witness domestic violence in the community. The simplest way to deal with this limitation is to state it directly.

Another major limitation in this study is that we will never know the social skills of children who did not accompany their mothers to the shelter. The social skills of children who stay home may somehow be quite different from those children who accompanied their mothers. In fact, there are a host of other limitations in this simple study, including the simple fact that, in reference to Research Hypothesis 2, boys who did not see domestic violence may also have lower social interaction skills than girls—this was never tested in Lula's study. Nevertheless, we should also bear in mind that few social work studies are based on truly representative random samples. In Lula's study, however, she still managed to collect some interesting data.

All social work researchers would like to be able to generalize their findings beyond the specific research setting and sample. From a quantitative research perspective (not a practice perspective), Lula is not really interested in the specific children in this particular study. She is more interested in children who witness domestic violence in general. Technically, the results of her study cannot be generalized to other populations of children who witness domestic violence, but she can suggest that she might find similar results with other children who accompany their mothers to similar women's shelters. She can imply and can recommend further research studies into the topic area.

Sometimes we can find support for our suggestions in the results of previous studies that were not conclusive either, but that also managed to produce recommendations. It might even be a good idea to extract these studies from the literature review section in Part 1 of the report and resurrect them in the discussion section.

On occasion, the results of a study will not agree with the results of previous studies. In this case, we should give whatever explanations seem reasonable for the disagreement and make some suggestions whereby the discrepancy can be resolved. Perhaps another research study should be undertaken that would examine the same or different variables. Perhaps, next time, a different research design should be used or the research hypothesis should be reformulated. Perhaps other operational definitions could be used. Suggestions for future studies should always be specific, not just a vague statement to the effect that more research studies need to be done in this area.

In some cases, recommendations can be made for changes in social work programs, interventions, or policies based on the results of a study. These recommendations are usually contained in reports addressed to people who have the power to make the suggested changes. When changes are suggested, the author has to display some knowledge about the policy or program and the possible consequences of implementing the suggested changes.

Finally, a report is concluded with a summary of the study's findings. This is particularly important in longer reports or when a study's findings and discussion sections are lengthy or complex. Sometimes it is indeed true that people read only the summary and a few sections of the study that interest them when the report is long.

SUMMARY

The purpose of writing a quantitative research proposal is fourfold. A research proposal is necessary, first, to obtain permission to carry out the study and, second, to secure the funds with which to do it. Third, the researcher needs to convince the proposal reviewers that he or she is competent enough to do the study. Fourth, we need to think over precisely what we want to study, why we want to study it, what methods we should use, and what difficulties we are likely to encounter.

A quantitative proposal should be well organized and easy to read so that reviewers have a clear picture of each step of the study. The information included in most proposals can be set out under 11 general headings or parts: research topic, literature review, conceptual framework, questions and hypotheses, operational definitions, research design, population and sample, data collection, data analysis, limitations, and administration.

Using the majority of the material from the quantitative research proposal, a report is written that can be broken down into four general headings or parts: problem, method, findings, and discussion. The four parts of a quantitative research report parallel the 11 parts of the research proposal. This is not surprising because both the report and the proposal are describing the same study.

Now that we know how to write quantitative research proposals and reports, the next chapter presents how to evaluate the final research report.

Joel Fischer

Evaluating Quantitative Research Reports

25

This chapter has two basic functions. It provides a framework for evaluating published quantitative research reports. It also undertakes to integrate and synthesize the content of the preceding chapters in this book as it pertains to the evaluation of such studies.

Quantitative research reports are published articles based on studies designed to contribute to the social work knowledge base through rigorous, replicable, and empirical methods. This definition is based on the belief that the systematic, orderly procedures of social work research provide a productive means to organize, understand, test, and develop social work knowledge. Moreover, research studies should be applicable in social work practice situations, and the field of social work should not be dichotomized into separate practice and research orientations. The capacity to perform competently in the social work profession, therefore, is based in part on the ability to analyze and utilize the results of social work research studies.

Social work practice must be guided as much as possible by empirically validated principles and techniques. However, few, if any, quantitative studies of social work research are without limitations. Thus, social workers must be able to analyze research findings from reports and make judgments as to their applicability to practice. Otherwise, even minimal effectiveness in applications of the results is unlikely, and the contributions of research studies to the knowledge base may go unrecognized or unused.

THE FRAMEWORK FOR EVALUATION

The framework presented in this chapter defines the key criteria for the evaluation of quantitative research reports in the field of social work. It should help social workers develop the basic skills for analyzing reports and evaluating research studies and alert them to how these skills can be applied in conducting and writing up their own studies. The key evaluative criteria suggested for each category of the analysis can be applied on a point-by-point basis in the evaluation of a single study or in comparing several studies.

The framework for evaluation given in Figures 25.1 through 25.5 is built around the four parts of a research report identified in Chapter 24—problem, method, findings, and discussion—with the addition of a separate section for conclusions as to utilization. Together, the criteria in these categories constitute a crude measurement instrument for rating quantitative research reports and the studies they represent. Each criterion is to some extent distinct, although there is a clear overlap among them. The criteria are to be rated on a 4-point scale, with a rating of 1 meaning low, unclear, poor, or not addressed by the study, and a rating of 4 meaning high, clear, excellent, or well covered.

Analyzing a report criterion by criterion makes it easier to draw accurate conclusions about the study. The criteria listed are related to various dimensions of the social work research process, but they apply after the fact to the completed study, as reported in the publication. The criteria therefore ask for ratings of various components of the report according to such qualities as clarity, adequacy, and reasonableness. Thus, in using the framework, the content of the research report is what is being evaluated, but the analysis can also be a vehicle for evaluating the research study reported. The final category of the analysis, conclusions, goes beyond the research study to evaluate how its findings can be applied in social work practice.

The framework was developed by abstracting and synthesizing criteria for analysis from a number of different sources, both from within the field of social work and outside it. The criteria in each category are described in the following sections.

PROBLEM CRITERIA

The problem category of the framework for evaluation is concerned with the problem area under investigation, out of which the research question or hypothesis is formulated for a study. It deals with the researcher's conceptualization of the phenomenon to be tested and can be used as an aid in understanding and evaluating the overall background and aims of the study. The criteria cover such components of the research process as formulation of the research question or hypothesis, operational definition of the independent and dependent variables, and statement of rival hypotheses. The

	Low			High
1. Adequacy of the literature review	1	2	3	4
2. Clarity of the problem area and research question under investigation	1	2	3	4
3. Clarity of the statement of the hypothesis	1	2	3	4
4. Clarity of the specification of the independent variable	1	2	3	4
5. Clarity of the specification of the dependent variable	1	2	3	4
6. Clarity of the definitions for major concepts	1	2	3	4
7. Clarity of the operational definitions	1	2	3	4
8. Reasonableness of assumption of relationship between the independent and dependent variables	1	2	3	4
9. Number of independent variables tested	1	2	3	4
10. Specification of independent variables in rival hypotheses	1	2	3	4
11. Adequacy in the control of independent variables in rival hypotheses	1	2	3	4
12. Clarity of the researcher's orientation	1	2	3	4
13. Clarity of the study's purpose	1	2	3	4
14. Clarity of the study's auspices	1	2	3	4
15. Reasonableness of the author's assumptions	1	2	3	4

Figure 25.1   Criteria for Assessing the "Problem Category" of a Research Report that Utilizes the Positivist Research Approach to Knowledge Building

15 criteria to be ranked in evaluating the problem category of a research report are shown in Figure 25.1.

The Literature Review

Most social work research studies are based on previous research studies or established theoretical concepts. The report of a study must demonstrate an adequate knowledge of the relevant literature in the problem area under investigation and should include references citing existing studies of similar phenomena.

The evaluation of the author's use of the literature should examine how the study is related to the existing literature, conceptually and methodologically. It should also assess how the research question derived from the problem area is related to the literature. This facilitates comparison of similarities between the study and others that address the same research problem area.

The Research Hypothesis

The research hypothesis should clearly formulate a proposed answer to the research question in the form of a prediction. For example, a hypothesis derived from the research question "Are the social work services in a given agency effective?" might be restated as "Professional social work services in a given agency will produce significantly more positive changes in clients' self-images than will services provided by other professionals."

The hypothesis should serve as a guide for the design of the study and the selection of the methods for data collection and analysis. In the evaluation of the study report, it is the basis for rating many other criteria. The analyses of the next three framework categories (method, findings, and discussion) rest on the study's purpose, as indicated by the research hypothesis.

The Independent and Dependent Variables

As we have seen from Chapter 5, a hypothesis is stated in terms of a predicted effect of the independent variable on the dependent variable. Thus, a testable hypothesis requires a clear definition of these variables. The independent variable is the assumed or predicted causal variable, and the dependent variable is the outcome variable, or the one that the independent variable is assumed to affect.

The independent and dependent variables comprise the major concepts of the study. Because concepts are abstractions of ideas, the variables must have nominal definitions, or be defined in terms of the general meaning they are intended to convey. These concepts should also have operational definitions, that is, be defined in quantitative, concrete terms with regard to the procedures used to measure or observe the variables. The greater the extent to which the variables are operationalized, the better. A study that simply suggests that "casework services" affect clients' self-esteem provides much less information than one that defines the exact techniques comprising the casework services. Unless the variables are clearly operationalized, they cannot be measured, and application of the results to social work practice is difficult.

A study should be rated higher if it tests more than one kind of independent variable. This rating criterion (Number 9 in Figure 25.1) can be explained in terms of the type and amount of information that can be generated from studies that test one independent variable, as compared with studies that test more than one. For example, comparisons between several interventions can be made. Studies that have examined one social work intervention technique provide valuable information, but the information is increased tremendously if the effectiveness of the technique in interaction with other variables (such as the practitioner's level of interpersonal skills) can be simultaneously evaluated.

Evaluation of the report in terms of the independent and dependent variables therefore should address several issues. Is there a clear specification of these variables? Is the anticipated cause-effect relationship stated clearly in the hypothesis? Are the assumptions of the relationships between the two variables reasonable (i.e., is it reasonable to believe that the independent variable can affect the dependent variable)? Is more than one independent variable tested?

In addition to the independent and dependent variables in the research hypothesis, the independent variables in the rival hypotheses that the researcher has designated as possible explanations of the research question should be identified. These variables have the potential to qualify, modify, or explain any obtained relationship between the independent and dependent variables. Attempts to control for the possible effects of rival hypotheses through the study's design should be examined in the evaluation. If they are not controlled for, a variety of other variables, rather than those in the research hypothesis, may be the true cause of change in the dependent variable.

The Researcher's Orientation

The next part of the evaluation of the problem seeks to identify any biases of the researcher. What is the orientation (theoretical and otherwise) of the researcher? What is the stated purpose or goal of the study? Why was it undertaken? How is the researcher's conceptualization of the research question or hypothesis under investigation different from those in similar studies? What information was sought? How are the findings to be used, and who is to use them? The study's auspices should also be clarified. Who sponsored the study? Where was it conducted?

These questions are important in the identification of possible biasing effects. For example, an administrator may want (or need) to prove that a particular social service program is effective, or a researcher may hope to prove that a particular social work intervention is worthwhile. If either the administrator or the researcher becomes directly involved in the research process, intentionally or unintentionally, the supervision of the intervention or the collection of the data could influence or alter the study's results. Their presence in the intervention would emerge as a potential bias that would affect the independent-dependent variable relationship.

In addition, the reasonableness of the researcher's assumptions about the study—both methodological and conceptual—should be assessed. These assumptions are propositions that are taken for granted ("given") in a study and usually are not subject to investigation in that study. They can be evaluated by reviewing other knowledge concerning the study's problem area. An example is a study in which it was assumed that group therapy is a universal phenomenon, independent of profession, style of group therapist, and so on; thus group therapy was "whatever group therapists do." The reasonableness of this assumption is open to question on the basis of information provided in the report regarding the differential effects of the therapists' personality conditions.

The problem area thus should be evaluated in terms of the researcher's conceptualization of the study and possible biases. A study may be conceptualized very thoroughly and still be subject to question on theoretical or ideological grounds; in addition, researcher bias may help to explain or define methodological weaknesses or strengths of the methods.

METHOD CRITERIA

The method category of the framework for evaluation is concerned with the methodology of the study—the research design and data collection techniques that are at the heart of any study. The criteria in this category concern such research concepts as outcome measures, random assignment, and internal and external validity. The 35 criteria to be rated in evaluating the method category of a research report are given in Figure 25.2.

The Outcome Measures

Examination of the type of outcome (or criterion) measures adopted to indicate change in the dependent variable is one of the most important steps in the evaluation of the data collection techniques for a study. Statement of the research question and adoption of a research design should reflect the kind of change that has been hypothesized, or, at least, the kind of changes or outcomes to be examined. In the specification of the outcome measures, the conceptual or empirical basis for selecting the desired types of change should be identified.

For example, if a study of casework intervention focuses on positive changes in family functioning, this section of the research report should clarify how these changes are to be identified; that is, the outcome measures used should be specified. The evaluation is concerned with whether the outcome measures selected are clearly defined and described in regard to how they are to be applied and their potential limitations.

In addition, the measures (or measuring instruments) selected by the researcher should be appropriate to the study's purpose (see Part III). In a study to examine the effects of casework intervention on family interaction, for example, individual psychological

tests might not be appropriate outcome measures. To verify the appropriateness of the measures, the validity and reliability for each outcome measure used should be clearly stated.

Measurement reliability has been defined in this text as the degree of consistency provided by the measuring instrument. Sufficient reliability must be established so the results of the study can be generalized from the sample to the population or to another research situation. The methods for establishing reliability described in Chapter 8 are the test-retest, alternate-forms, and split-half methods including coefficient alpha. The higher the reliability, the greater is the confidence that can be placed in the reliability of the measure. Measurement validity has been defined as the extent to which a measuring instrument actually measures what it is supposed to measure and does so accurately. The three major types of validity described in Chapter 8—content, criterion, and construct—are related to the purposes of measures.

Use of a variety of outcome measures is preferable because change tends to be multidimensional. Extensive examples in the literature examining the effects of social work interventions show that client change may surface in numerous, often unrelated, areas. A major client change demonstrated in a projective test, for example, may not be reflected in actual behavioral change, and clients' subjective self-reports of improvement frequently are not reflected in other, more objective measures. Outcome measures therefore should involve both objective measures, such as behavior ratings or physiological indicators, and subjective measures, such as self-report questionnaires, whenever possible.

The Data Collection

In reporting the data collection procedures for the study, it should be made clear who collects the data, how and when they are collected, and how errors are avoided (see Parts V and VI). Analysis of this aspect of the study's method is primarily directed toward author objectivity and data reliability. Specifically, the controls for interviewer, test, and judgment biases in data collection should be examined. In a study to assess

	Low			High
1. Clarity of the specification of the kinds of changes desired	1	2	3	4
2. Appropriateness of the outcome measures in relation to the purpose of the study	1	2	3	4
3. Degree of validity of the outcome measures	1	2	3	4
4. Degree of reliability of the outcome measures	1	2	3	4
5. Degree of use of a variety of outcome measures (e.g., subjective and objective)	1	2	3	4
6. Clarity about how data were collected	1	2	3	4
7. Clarity about who collects data	1	2	3	4
8. Degree of avoidance of error in process of data collection	1	2	3	4
9. Clarity of the statement of the research design	1	2	3	4
10. Adequacy of the research design (re: purpose)	1	2	3	4
11. Clarity and adequacy of time between pretest and posttest	1	2	3	4
12. Appropriateness in the use of control group(s)	1	2	3	4
13. Appropriateness in the use of random assignment procedures	1	2	3	4
14. Appropriateness in the use of matching procedures	1	2	3	4
15. Experimental and control group equivalency at pretest	1	2	3	4
16. Degree of control for effects of history	1	2	3	4
17. Degree of control for effects of maturation	1	2	3	4
18. Degree of control for effects of testing	1	2	3	4
19. Degree of control for effects of instrumentation	1	2	3	4
20. Degree of control for statistical regression	1	2	3	4
21. Degree of control for differential selection of clients	1	2	3	4
22. Degree of control for differential mortality	1	2	3	4
23. Degree of control for temporal bias	1	2	3	4
24. Degree of control for integrity of treatment	1	2	3	4
25. Ability to distinguish causal variable	1	2	3	4
26. Degree of control for interaction effects	1	2	3	4
27. Overall degree of success in maximizing internal validity (16-26)	1	2	3	4
28. Adequacy of sample size	1	2	3	4
29. Degree of accuracy in defining the population	1	2	3	4
30. Degree of adequacy in the representativeness of the sample	1	2	3	4
31. Degree of control for reactive effects of testing (interaction with independent variable)	1	2	3	4
32. Degree of control for interaction between selection and experimental variable	1	2	3	4
33. Degree of control for special effects of experimental arrangements	1	2	3	4
34. Degree of control for multiple-treatment interference	1	2	3	4
35. Overall degree of success in maximizing external validity	1	2	3	4

Figure 25.2   Criteria for Assessing the "Method Category" of a Research Report that Utilizes the Positivist Research Approach to Knowledge Building

casework effectiveness, for example, social workers were requested to provide basic data on their clients' progress in the experimental group, while a group of "trained researchers" provided data on the control group. Such differential procedures present an obvious source of potential bias.

The Research Design

The method for collecting and analyzing data is usually specified in the research design. The design used, the methodological issues involved in using the design, and the methods specified for handling data collection and analysis should be clearly stated in the report. The general adequacy of the research design with regard to the purpose of the study should also be evaluated. If, for example, the purpose of the study is to evaluate the effectiveness of a specific casework technique, an exploratory research design would be inappropriate.

If the research design involves multiple measurements of the dependent variable, the adequacy of the time provided between the pretest and posttest should be examined. The question is whether the desired changes could logically be expected to have taken place over the length of time allowed. If the period is fairly brief, a judgment must be made of the likelihood that the posttest results were affected by the pretest. Participants may remember the answers from the pretest and answer the posttest accordingly, or they may be less interested, less motivated, or less anxious during the second testing.

The Use of Control Groups and Group Assignment

Another consideration in analyzing a research design is whether control or comparison groups are used. If one or more control groups is used, the author should identify the type of control. Types of control groups include untreated groups, waiting lists, terminations, attention/placebo groups, and groups receiving other treatment. Probably the most desirable control group situation represents some combination, such as an untreated group whose characteristics are comparable with those of the experimental group, plus a group that receives another form of social work treatment, plus an attention/placebo group. The strengths and weaknesses of the types of control groups selected must also be considered.

Because control or comparison groups are desirable in most social work studies to rule out the alternative explanations for the independent variables, it is important to evaluate how the members of the experimental and control groups are assigned (see Chapter 13). Group assignment is sometimes done on a haphazard, arbitrary, or post hoc basis, but methods such as random assignment or matching can be used to avoid sampling error.

Random assignment is the preferred method of group assignment. It should ensure that every individual has the same chance of being assigned to either group. Ideally and theoretically, the experimental and control groups should consist of individuals who differ only with regard to the group assignment; that is, some are assigned to the experimental group and others are assigned to the control group. In this sense, the term "random" is not synonymous with arbitrary. Rather, it refers to strict scientific procedures for the assignment of individuals to two or more groups.

In matching, group assignment is made on the basis of similarities among individuals on certain meaningful variables, particularly client characteristics that may be expected to affect the outcome of the study in some way. Matching may be done on the basis of pretest scores, age, gender, type of client problem, and so on. Matching is also initiated to ensure an equal distribution of any given variable in both groups, as opposed to a priori, individual-by-individual matching. The main problem with matching is that it does not control for differences between the groups on any other variables that could affect the outcome (i.e., that are not matched).

Another form of group assignment combines matching and randomization procedures. For example, individuals can be screened in advance and matched according to meaningful variables, and then randomly assigned to either the experimental or control group. This allows for equivalency between groups at the pretest occasion, although each individual still has an equal chance of being assigned to either the experimental or control group.

With any method of group assignment, it is important to determine whether the two groups are equivalent at the beginning of the study. Differences between the groups existing at the beginning could be responsible for differences in the results at the end. Within a certain probability level, pretest equivalence can be achieved through randomization and matching as presented in Figure 13.2.

Internal Validity of the Research Design

Random assignment and the appropriate use of control groups is the best method for handling problems of internal validity. Evaluation of the control of extraneous variables allows for conclusions that the introduction of the independent variable alone can be identified as the cause of change in the dependent variable.

Extraneous variables that must be controlled for are called threats to internal validity. Those discussed in Chapter 13 include the effects of history, maturation, testing, instrumentation, statistical regression, differential selection, mortality, and interaction effects. Others are temporal bias, integrity of treatment, and ability to distinguish the causal variable. A review of these threats is useful in evaluating the report's research methodology.

The effects of history occur when anything happening outside the study produces changes in the dependent variable. These effects are due to changes in the environment, such as a client getting a job or resolving family problems, that produce changes in the dependent variable that cannot be attributed to the introduction of the independent variable. They are the most plausible rival hypotheses for explaining changes when appropriate controls are not (or cannot be) used. A similar variable is the effects of maturation, which include physiological or psychological processes that may occur in individuals with the passage of time. For example, maturation occurs as clients grow older or go through different developmental stages.

The pretest can contribute to poor internal validity by influencing scores on the posttest. These are the effects of testing. Testing can be controlled to some extent under one or both of the following conditions:

1. The time between the two tests is long enough to reduce memory of the first test.
2. Both experimental and control groups are subject to the same testing conditions.

Closely related to testing biases are the effects of instrumentation, or instrument error or decay. Instrument decay is due to a change in either the measuring instrument or the users of the instrument (e.g., observers may become more sensitive).

A particularly important threat to internal validity to control for is statistical regression, or regression to the mean. Especially within groups selected on the basis of their extreme high or low scores, the scores tend to change over time by moving toward the mean. Change

of this type is predictable and is more likely to be due to statistical regression than to the independent variable. Statistical regression is controlled for by random assignment to control groups. For example, groups of clients who score poorly on certain psychological tests are often provided with treatment, but they tend to change whether or not they receive treatment. If there is no control group for comparison purposes, it is tempting to conclude that such groups receive treatment and then show improvement as a result.

Another threat to internal validity is differential selection, or bias in the selection of members of experimental and control groups so the potential for change differs. The principles of randomization aid in preventing this threat. A related threat is differential mortality, which occurs when one group loses more members than the other group during the study. For example, in a study that compared the effectiveness of groups of professional and nonprofessional practitioners, the author concluded that the nonprofessionals were favored on the outcome measures at the end of the treatment. But though the groups started with similar sample sizes, by the end of the study the nonprofessionals had lost 21 percent of their clients and the professionals had lost only 3.4 percent, so the groups were no longer comparable. Perhaps the only conclusion that could be drawn was that the professionals maintained a lower client dropout rate than the nonprofessionals.

To control for temporal bias, all groups involved in the study should be measured at precisely the same time. If, as in the example above, two groups of practitioners are being compared, the frequency and length of contacts with their respective clients also should be similar.

Integrity of treatment is a threat that could operate in several ways. Social workers may not use the treatment techniques they have agreed to provide for the study, for example, or they may vary their treatments from client to client, such as using behavior therapy with one client or insight therapy with another. This would make it difficult to conclude why any observed improvements took place.

Inability to distinguish the experimental or causal variable is a threat because even in a study with random assignment and a control group, it is not always possible to rule out a range of possible alternative explanations in addition to the standard threats to internal validity. Observed differences between groups may be due to attention; heightened expectations; the treatment itself; the practitioner's style, enthusiasm, or interpersonal skills; a placebo effect; and so on. Such alternative explanations can be addressed by adding additional groups to the study (e.g., an attention/placebo group, or alternative treatments), by using factorial designs that control for interpersonal skill differences, or by logical analysis by both the author and the evaluator as to the plausibility of explanations of observed changes.

A final threat to internal validity is a result of interaction between any of the other threats. This occurs, for example, when the selection of the experimental and control groups is not equivalent in terms of other possible threats such as maturation or regression. An example would be comparing "normal" with distressed clients, or clients with extremely negative pretest scores to clients in another group with far more positive pretest scores. Independent of the treatment, the group with more negative scores ("distressed") would be expected to change far more than the other group ("normal").

Once the study has been evaluated by these criteria, a summary judgment as to the overall success in maximizing internal validity is required.

External Validity of the Research Design

Another key concern in evaluating a study has to do with its external validity. This refers to limitations on the extent to which findings can be generalized to individuals, agencies, environmental conditions, or measures other than those involved in the study being evaluated. The main considerations in assessing external validity are the representativeness of the sample, internal validity of the design (without good internal validity, it would be unclear what could be generalized), and replication.

Sampling Considerations

In assessing generalizability, sampling plans and procedures (see Chapter 11) must be taken into account. The adequacy of the study's sample size is related to the description of the exact population for the study, an

entire set or universe of all individuals or elements (objects or events) that conform to some designated set of specifications. The sample consists of elements or members drawn from the population in order to find out something about the population in general. If the study uses an extremely small sample as representative of a large population, for example, the grounds for selecting such a sample should be clearly stated and justifiable. Few social work research studies can claim a representative random sample drawn from either clients or social workers, the principal populations used, because they usually are too large and complex. Nevertheless, every study must be evaluated in terms of the ways in which the author attempts to deal with sample selection.

The essence of external validity is the degree to which the sample is representative of the population from which it was drawn. The most obvious approach lies with the sampling procedure. The relevant populations to which the generalizations are to be made must be clearly defined, and, in the optimal study, samples must be randomly drawn from them. Usually this is very difficult, but without random selection, generalizability cannot be ensured.

Other limitations might be placed on the sample. For example, a study might have a limited sample in regard to size, time, place, type of problem, demographics, and so on. Such limitations must be reported so that the adequacy of the sampling procedures can be evaluated. There may be genuine attempts to obtain representative samples of some client groups, for example, but attempts to obtain representative samples of practitioners are rare. A study may focus on social workers selected from a single agency, or graduate social work students may be used as substitutes for experienced social workers. Generalizations from such studies are constrained by failure to obtain a representative sample of practicing social workers.

Representativeness can also be addressed by testing or comparing the sample with other known samples from the same population or with data from the population as a whole. Tests or inventories may be administered to the sample group, or demographic data can be used. These data can then be compared with the known facts about the population of concern. For example, the age, gender, and socioeconomic status of social workers studied can be compared with the demographic characteristics of other social workers at one or more agencies or with social workers nationally, using NASW data. Or social workers might complete inventories of therapeutic attitudes and preferences, which could then be compared with similar inventories completed by other workers.

Threats to External Validity

The threats to external validity described in Chapter 13 include pretest-treatment interaction, selection-treatment interaction, specificity of variables, reactive effects, multiple-treatment interference, and researcher bias. These threats are discussed here in terms of perhaps the most common research situation in social work, where the independent variable is the treatment or intervention provided to clients, and the dependent variable is the client's outcome.

The threat of pretest-treatment interaction has to do with the possibility of reactive or interactive effects between the testing and the independent or experimental variable. The pretest may have made clients more sensitized to the treatment so that changes in treatment effectiveness occur. This may mean that results would be generalizable only to clients who had been pretested and thereby sensitized. The best method to control for such effects is to choose outcome measures that are not specifically related to the treatment, such as everyday performance or a behavioral criterion like the frequency of marital arguments during the month prior to treatment.

The threats of selection-treatment interaction and specificity of variables involve a possible interaction between selection of the sample (clients) and the independent experimental variable (treatment). In these circumstances, special characteristics of the sample selected for treatment could interact with the treatment and change its effects. For example, if a study shows that middle-class children respond well to verbal therapy, it cannot be assumed that all children, or children from low-income groups, will also respond well to this type of treatment. Rather, special characteristics of the sample such as socioeconomic status (rather than verbal therapy) could have produced the results. Generalizability would therefore be limited to groups similar to those in the study being evaluated.

The possibility of reactive effects due to experimental arrangements refers to the fact that knowledge of being in a study may have special meaning to some research participants, and their performance or reactions therefore may be atypical. An example would be an experimental group that becomes more productive as a result of knowing they were taking part in a study. Another example would be changes due to clients' expectations. The fact that the clients had sought and obtained services could lead to a change in the outcome, which would be independent of (or sometimes prior to) treatment.

Reactive effects can also be due to the perhaps unintentional communication of the researcher's orientation. This results in researcher bias, another threat based on the tendency of researchers to find the results they expect or want to find. The researcher's knowledge of which clients are in the experimental group and which clients are in the control group may be enough to alter the study's results.

With all of these effects, limits are placed on generalizability unless the groups to which the findings are to be generalized also are exposed to such effects. Thus, reactions to experimental arrangements could preclude generalizations regarding the effects of the intervention to any client who was not exposed to the treatment in experimental situations.

Lack of control for multiple-treatment interference requires caution in making generalizations in order to avoid commingling results of successive treatments. Multiple-treatment interference occurs, for example, when clients in all groups receive other interventions, such as medication or an institutional regimen, in addition to the experimental intervention. The effects of the additional treatment may either not be erasable or may have some sort of enhancing or depressing effect on the intervention. Generalizations therefore would pertain only to those groups who receive all the same treatments.

Once the analysis of all these criteria has been completed, a judgment as to the overall degree of control for external validity can be made. At the least, both the independent and dependent variables should be described clearly enough to allow for replication.

FINDINGS CRITERIA

The findings section of the framework for evaluation concentrates on assessing the ways in which the data collected for a study are analyzed and conclusions are derived. The appropriateness of the statistical procedures and tests used is an important consideration in this category. Figure 25.3 summarizes the six criteria to be evaluated in assessing the findings category of a research report.

The first task in this evaluation is to determine whether manipulation of the independent variable was adequate to influence the dependent variable (see Chapter 13). In a sense, this is assessing the strength of the independent variable. It can be accomplished by examining the intensity of the independent variable, duration of time over which the variable was presented, frequency of treatment sessions, and so forth.

Related to this factor is the persistence of the outcome, or change, over time. Evaluation of appropriateness of the outcome measures (the second criterion for evaluating method) might include the suitability of the length of time chosen for the follow-up. This should be based, at least in part, on the rationale for this decision presented in the study.

Data Collection and Statistical Procedures

Overall, the data collected must be adequate to provide evidence for the testing of the hypothesis. They also should be of sufficient quantity and quality, in both the experimental and control groups, to allow further evaluation. Basic judgments about the statistics used in the

study include the clarity of presentation of the statistics or statistical tests used and the appropriateness of the statistical controls. As noted in Chapter 13, statistical procedures are often used to control for the intervening variables in alternative hypotheses. For example, if it is not possible to match the experimental and control groups on potentially meaningful variables, they should be controlled by statistical means, using procedures such as analysis of covariance.

The Statistical Analysis

An evaluation of the appropriateness of the statistics used in the study reported depends on the type of data collected and the type of conclusions derived from the data. This analysis requires a greater knowledge of statistics than can be provided in this text, though some general concepts have been discussed. The statistical concepts and tests referred to in this section are introduced to give an idea of the possible content of this part of the study report. The five topics (i.e., 6a–6e in Figure 25.3) included in this criterion cover different aspects of the statistical analysis.

Every statistic assumes a particular level of measurement; for example, interval and ratio measurement are necessary for the use of parametric tests such as analysis of variance. Information on the level of measurement should be the first step in determining whether the statistics used are appropriate for the conditions of the study.

Analysis of the use of between-groups procedures involves consideration of the type of conclusions the

	Low			High
1. Adequacy of the manipulation of the independent variable	1	2	3	4
2. Appropriateness in the use of follow-up measures	1	2	3	4
3. Adequacy of data to provide evidence for testing of hypotheses	1	2	3	4
4. Clarity in reporting statistics	1	2	3	4
5. Appropriateness in the use of statistical controls	1	2	3	4
6. Appropriateness of statistics utilized				
a. Statistics appropriate to level of measurement	1	2	3	4
b. Use of between-groups procedures	1	2	3	4
c. Multivariate statistics used appropriately	1	2	3	4
d. Post hoc tests used appropriately	1	2	3	4
e. Overall appropriateness of statistics	1	2	3	4

Figure 25.3 Criteria for Assessing the "Findings Category" of a Research Report that Utilizes the Positivist Research Approach to Knowledge Building

author attempts to draw from the data. If the conclusions are regarding cause and effect, a between-groups statistic designed to test hypotheses in which the independent variable is introduced to the experimental group and not to the comparison or control group should be used. The statistic should indicate a probability or significance level, which allows for a conclusion regarding whether or not observed differences between the groups are due to chance and are likely to reflect true differences in the populations from which the groups, or samples, were drawn. Statistically significant results provide a basis for drawing inferences about causality.

In an explanatory study, for example, a t test between the groups or analysis of variance should be used rather than a correlational statistic such as Pearson's r, the correlation coefficient, because these statistical techniques provide information that allows an inference regarding cause and effect. However, use of a statistic provided by a particular test or procedure in itself cannot generate causal conclusions, because the nature of the design and the research question being studied are the critical factors in making this judgment.

Between-group measures are also needed for statistics used in inferring cause-effect relationships between or among variables. One of the most common statistical errors is to compute two separate correlated t tests for the differences between pretest and posttest scores within the experimental group and within the control group. If the differences are statistically significant for the experimental group but not for the control group, the researcher might conclude that the independent variable has had an effect, though no direct statistical comparison between the two groups was calculated. A hypothetical study of social workers can demonstrate this effect. In a comparison of three groups to assess the effects of different methods of training, two groups may show statistically significant pretest-to-posttest mean changes within the groups on two different outcome variables. An overall analysis of variance between the groups, however, may fail to show statistically significant differences among the three groups.

Analysis of the use of multivariate statistics involves an understanding of the number of outcome measures in the study. For a variety of reasons, when more than one outcome measure is involved in a study, and espe-cially when those measures are correlated, repeated use of standard univariate statistics—such as t tests, analyses of variance or covariance, and nonparametric statistics—are inappropriate.

Essentially, these statistics are likely to produce Type I errors (finding "statistically significant" results that actually are due to chance) or Type II errors (not finding statistical significance when, in fact, it is present). In such cases, more sophisticated multivariate statistics should be used. These include Hotelling's T^2 for two groups and multivariate analysis of variance and covariance for two or more groups.

The choice of univariate or multivariate statistics is complicated to assess. Multivariate statistics require a substantially larger sample than univariate statistics, if they are to be used with any degree of reliability. Both the use of univariate statistics with more than one outcome measure and the use of multivariate statistics with a small sample can be reasons for lack of confidence in the obtained results.

Another aspect of the statistical analysis is the appropriate use of post hoc tests. Whenever three or more groups are involved in one of the independent variables and a significant effect is found on the primary test (such as a statistically significant F test), specialized post hoc, follow-up, or multiple-comparison tests must be used to determine which group is significantly different from which other groups. The use of standard t tests to examine these differences is inappropriate and likely to result in Type I error. Several post hoc tests are available for this task, including Fisher's least significant difference (LSD), Duncan's new multiple-range test, Newman—Keuls test, Tukey's honestly significant difference (HSD), and Scheffei's test.

Once these four subcriteria have been evaluated, a judgment can be made as to the fifth criterion—overall appropriateness of the statistics used.

DISCUSSION CRITERIA

The discussion category of a study report gives the researcher's ideas about the meaning and implications of the findings. Among the 14 criteria to be evaluated in this category (see Figure 25.4), the first is the extent to which

	Low		High	
1. Degree to which data support the hypothesis	1	2	3	4
2. Extent to which the researcher's conclusions are consistent with data	1	2	3	4
3. Degree of uniformity between tables and text	1	2	3	4
4. Degree of researcher bias	1	2	3	4
5. Clarity as to cause of changes in dependent variable	1	2	3	4
6. Degree to which rival hypotheses were avoided in the design	1	2	3	4
7. Degree to which potential rival hypotheses were dealt with in discussion	1	2	3	4
8. Degree of control for threats to internal validity	1	2	3	4
9. Reasonableness of opinions about implications	1	2	3	4
10. Clarity as to meaning of change(s)	1	2	3	4
11. Adequacy in relating findings to previous literature	1	2	3	4
12. Adequacy of conclusions for generalizing beyond data	1	2	3	4
13. Extent to which the research design accomplishes the purpose of the study	1	2	3	4
14. Appropriateness in the handling of unexpected consequences	1	2	3	4

Figure 25.4   Criteria for Assessing the "Discussion Category" of a Research Report that Utilizes the Positivist Research Approach to Knowledge Building

the data support the research hypothesis and the kinds of qualifications stated in the report. For example, it may be suggested that when additional variables were introduced (e.g., age, gender), the strength of the findings was diminished. In fact, the findings may have been weakened when such variables were introduced, or they may have been applicable in only certain select circumstances.

Consistency in using the data should also be assessed. The conclusions should be consistent with the data, and there should be uniformity in the data presented in the tables and in the text. This calls for a careful review of the description of the data in the report. Researcher bias, a threat to external validity described in the method section, may show up in the design or data analyses, or in inadequate or erroneous interpretations or conclusions drawn from the data. Results that do not support the hypothesis also should be dealt with to ensure that such data are not simply ignored.

Conclusions about the Study

The other criteria in the discussion category address the results and implications of the study, in terms of both the researcher's conclusions and the evaluator's judgments. First to be assessed is the evidence presented regarding the degree to which change in the dependent variable is actually a function of the independent variable. A main consideration is the researcher's success in controlling threats to internal validity. If the threats to internal validity have not been successfully controlled and it still is argued that a cause-effect relationship exists, the basis and soundness of these judgments must be evaluated.

The reasonableness of the opinions stated about the implications of the study and judgments regarding the meaning of the changes found should also be assessed. The author should be clear as to the social, psychological, and professional meaning of the findings. The findings should be discussed in terms of existing norms or standards, cost effectiveness, efforts to obtain results, efficacy of the methods, and so on.

The findings and conclusions should be related to the literature, and changes in theory or methodology suggested by the results should be proposed. The adequacy of the conclusions regarding the generalizability of the findings should then be evaluated in terms of applicability of the data to different samples or populations.

Finally, the extent to which the study accomplishes its purpose as developed in the formulation of the research question or hypothesis should be evaluated. If there were unexpected consequences, the researcher should address these and attempt to determine whether they were produced by some aspect of the research design or by the research methods or treatment used.

UTILIZATION CONCLUSIONS CRITERIA

The final part of the evaluation of a quantitative research report consists of eight criteria for conclusions as to the utilization of knowledge gained from the study (see Figure 25.5). This calls for making judgments and decisions regarding the possible ways in which knowledge derived from the study can be applied in social work research or practice. Utilization is concerned with the relevance or meaningfulness of the study to the social work profession and the development of practical applications of the knowledge derived.

In a sense, this conclusions section of the analysis is a general summary of all the 70 previous criteria presented in the framework. Decisions regarding utilization are based on the information gathered from analyzing the problem, method, and findings, and the discussion is drawn from these analyses.

The meaningfulness of the study's findings for social work practice can be determined by assessing its major implications in terms of the dimensions of social work it addresses. These dimensions include clients, service delivery systems, methods and techniques of intervention, and qualities of social workers. Of course, a study need not be specifically conducted on social workers or their clients to be relevant to social work. Social work knowledge can be derived from numerous related fields such as anthropology, political science, clinical psychology, and sociology.

The next two criteria are concerned with the internal and external validity of the study's design and results. An overall evaluation of the soundness of the study is a summary judgment based on preceding sections of the framework. For the sake of convenience, this judgment can be based on the extent to which threats to internal validity have been avoided. It should consider the extent to which the independent variable clearly leads to the changes observed and whether it is specified clearly enough for replication. The generalizability of the study's findings, or the extent to which threats to external validity are avoided, must also be evaluated. Can similar methods be applied for different goals or purposes or with different individuals, groups, or problems? Is it reasonable to expect that positive results would ensue? The greater the internal and external validity (soundness and generalizability) of the study, the greater value it will have.

There are several additional criteria for assessing the potential utilization of reported research findings. One is the extent to which the independent variables in the study are actually accessible to control by social workers. They should be clearly identifiable (observable) and easy to manipulate (able to be affected by the social worker). If need be, as with reports of new techniques, they should also be teachable.

	Low			High
1. Degree of relevance to social work practice	1	2	3	4
2. Overall soundness of the study (internal validity)	1	2	3	4
3. Degree of generalizability of the study's findings (external validity)	1	2	3	4
4. Degree to which the independent variables are accessible to control by social workers	1	2	3	4
5. Extent to which a meaningful difference would occur if the independent variable were utilized in actual social work practice situations	1	2	3	4
6. Degree of economic feasibility of the independent variable if utilized in actual social work practice situations	1	2	3	4
7. Degree of ethical suitability of the manipulation of the independent variable	1	2	3	4
8. Extent to which the research question has been addressed	1	2	3	4

Figure 25.5 Criteria for Assessing the "Utilization and Conclusions Category" of a Research Report That Utilizes the Positivist Research Approach to Knowledge Building

The difference a particular independent variable would make in social work practice if it were actually utilized also should be assessed. For example, a study might show that the use of an intervention technique successfully decreases the number of clients' eye blinks per minute. Could this technique be evaluated as involving an important goal for professional social work practice? Could the use of such a technique reasonably be expected to produce other more pervasive or more meaningful changes?

The economics of utilizing the independent variable must always be considered. Another criterion is whether it is ethically suitable to manipulate the independent variable. For example, as we have seen in Chapter 3, changes can be demonstrated under laboratory conditions that would be entirely unethical in practice with clients. An intervention technique may also appear unethical, either professionally or personally, to other social workers.

The final criterion is the extent to which the primary research question has been answered. In other words, in the typical social work research study, what kinds of social workers, working with what kinds of clients, with what kind of client problems, in what practice situations, using what techniques, derived from what theory, produced what kinds of results?

RATING THE CRITERIA

The framework for the evaluation of quantitative research reports presented in Figures 25.1 through 25.5 includes a total of 78 criteria. Some are obviously far more important than others, and there is considerable overlap among them. Some criteria are actually subtopics, such as the various threats to internal and external validity listed in Figure 25.2 for the method category.

In social work as in other fields of knowledge, ideal research conditions are rarely possible, due to any number of economic, personal, political, or organizational constraints. Most researchers are forced to compromise on some of these conditions. Therefore, in the conclusions category, the overall impact of a study's deficiencies should be taken into account in judging the applicability of the knowledge derived from the study to social work research or practice. By themselves, low ratings on a few criteria would not necessarily invalidate a study. No matter how inappropriate the statistics or how serious the design flaws, for example, the results of a study may still be useful enough to be applied. Serious flaws, however, do diminish the confidence with which such results can be viewed.

The rating of the criteria on a scale from 1 to 4 calls for careful observation and personal judgment. In some instances, the report indicates that the study either meets a criterion or it does not. For example, on Criterion 12 in Figure 25.2, a study that uses some type of control group would be rated with a 3 or 4; a study that does not would be rated with a 1 or 2. In other situations, it is necessary to decide whether or not the study "adequately" meets a given criterion. An example is deciding whether there is a sufficiently clear specification of the independent variable (Criterion 4 in Figure 25.1). In other circumstances, the relative rating will be less evaluative. For example, a study using three independent criterion measures would be rated higher on Criterion 5 in Figure 25.2 than a study using only one.

Because there are clear differences in the importance of the various criteria, the overall rating given a study may be less important than ensuring that certain criteria have been met. With an experimental or explanatory study, for example, it is more important to demonstrate appropriate use of a control group than to specify the theoretical orientation of the researcher. The implications for social work of research that meets the various criteria must always be considered.

In using this framework, one standard to consider is that, if a study's results cannot be readily incorporated into the knowledge base of the social work profession, it is, for all intents and purposes, practically useless. A study may be designed and executed perfectly yet have only limited value to the profession because it does not address a meaningful problem area and the results cannot be put into practice by social workers. Utilization of results is the ultimate outcome in social work research and evaluation.

SUMMARY

In presenting a framework for the evaluation of quantitative research reports, this chapter has demonstrated how the same criteria can be used to evaluate the research studies on which the reports are based. It also has served as a summary of the main topics of the preceding chapters in the text.

The framework for evaluation is built around the four parts of a quantitative research report discussed in Chapter 24—problem, method, findings, and discussion. An additional category on conclusions reflects a concern with the utilization of the knowledge derived from the study in social work practice. Criteria for evaluating each of these categories are presented in figures representing rating scales.

Qualitative Data Analysis, Proposals, and Reports

Part VIII follows the exact format as Part VII. It

pertains to the qualitative research approach.

More specifically, Chapter 26 discusses how to

analyze qualitative data, and Chapter 27 presents

how to write qualitative proposals and reports.

Chapter 28, the remaining chapter, discusses how

to evaluate published qualitative studies.

Heather Coleman

Yvonne A. Unrau

Analyzing Qualitative Data

26

qualitative

analysis

So far, this book has discussed the initial phases in designing and organizing a qualitative research study. The next important phase is to analyze the data you have collected—the topic of this chapter.

By now it should be apparent that qualitative data are typically in the form of words. According to Matthew B. Miles and Michael A. Huberman (1994), words contain both rich descriptions of situations and an understanding of their underlying meaning. Words are "fatter" than numbers and have multiple meanings, making the analysis of qualitative data quite a challenge.

We will detail the steps that one uses when doing a qualitative data analysis by referring to Leslie Tutty's (1993) qualitative research study on why women leave abusive relationships after they leave a shelter. We will use her study to illustrate how to do a qualitative data analysis in a straightforward, step-by-step process.

In contrast to quantitative studies, in which you collect your data and then analyze them using an appropriate statistical procedure, in qualitative studies it is not uncommon to conduct further and/or new interviews after you have analyzed the data collected from your previous research participants. Furthermore, the analysis is not a one-step process, but involves considering the fit of each piece of data in relationship to all the other pieces.

Thus, you must continually move back and forth between initial and later interviews, identifying units of meaning, coding, and interpreting the data as you go along. Such a blending of data collection and data analysis permits you to continue interviewing people for as long as is necessary until you truly grasp the meaning of your study's findings.

There are several ways to approach the task of analyzing interview data. One way to analyze interview data is to look for the major themes and patterns in the data, and then to break these down into subthemes and categories as such distinctions become important. In essence, you start out with a broad look at the data and then break them into smaller issues.

This chapter, in contrast, suggests that you start your analysis by looking at the smaller units. Later, you will identify similarities and differences between these to formulate how they fit together as themes and patterns. With this approach, then, you begin with the smaller issues but ultimately identify the broad themes.

Both forms of analysis are appropriate, and the two can converge to yield a similar interpretation of the data. We decided to present a systematic analysis of small units in this chapter for one reason only: we believe that this approach is more likely to allow the results to emerge from the data. The process of systematically comparing and contrasting the small segments of interviews will keep you thinking about what each individual is saying. There is a greater risk when you start with the broad perspective that once having identified important themes, you will apply these to segments with less attention to what is actually being said.

Nevertheless, you have the capacity to consider both broad themes and small meaning units almost simultaneously. The main point is, experiment with the best method for you, and do not be disconcerted by the existence of different approaches.

THE PURPOSE OF DATA ANALYSIS

The central purpose of analysis in qualitative studies is to sift, sort, and organize the masses of data acquired during data collection in such a way that the themes and interpretations that emerge from the process address the original research problem(s) that you have previously identified. The strength of the conclusions drawn from your study ultimately rests with the plan for *data analysis*. If you develop a research project without a systematic plan to guide the data analysis you are likely to produce biased results.

Nevertheless, as with the use of an unstructured interview where the questions unfold throughout the process instead of being fixed at the outset, the data analysis will develop differently from study to study, depending on what your research participants reveal. Rather than present a set of concrete rules and procedures about how to analyze qualitative data, we will describe the general process of such an analysis. The interaction between data collection and data analysis will allow you greater flexibility in interpreting your data and will permit greater adaptability when you draw your conclusions.

There are assumptions underlying the qualitative research approach that we discussed earlier and that are directly relevant to the analysis phase. A very brief reminder of those assumptions is therefore in order:

- The goal of your research study (and thus of the analysis) is to understand the personal realities of research participants in depth, including aspects of their experience that may be unique to them.
- You should strive to understand human experience in as much complexity as possible. This means aiming for a deep understanding of the experience and the meanings attached to it, but also of the context within which the experience is reported. The context includes the research study itself—for example, your relationship with the research participants is part of what needs to be understood when your findings are analyzed.
- Given the complexity of social behavior, there are many topics in social work that are difficult to measure in the way that you would in a quantitative study. For example, in Tutty's study, one woman was beaten to the point of needing medical treatment and another's life was threatened regularly with a gun. It would be a questionable goal to attempt to establish which woman experienced more fear. With such research topics, quantification reduces the data to trivial levels. In contrast, in a qualitative study we could describe the experience of each woman in a meaningful way. In the data analysis phase, you should organize the data in such a manner that the words, thoughts, and experiences of the research participants can be clearly communicated.
- The extent to which previous research studies and theory should influence your study is a contentious issue, and one about which you will have to exercise your own best judgment. The arguments for and against familiarity with the literature do not need repetition here, but we do need to note that the issues remain relevant. For example, you may find a literature search is relevant in the middle of the data analysis. As you are analyzing your transcripts, the concepts and relationships between the concepts that you identify may suggest more reading to discover what others have thought of similar ideas.

- In Tutty's qualitative research study, the extent to which the women expressed difficulties about going to court over custody, access to children, and divorce issues prompted her to search for literature identifying this as a problem. Similarly, when you approach the end of your analysis, a literature search comparing your conclusions with the findings of other studies is often advisable.

ESTABLISHING AN INITIAL FRAMEWORK

There are two major steps involved in establishing an initial framework for data analysis. First, you must prepare your data in transcript form, and second, you should develop a preliminary plan for proceeding with your data analysis.

Step 1: Preparing Your Data in Transcript Form

A transcript is the written record of your interviews and any other written material that you may have gathered. As the core of your analysis, it will consist of more than merely the words spoken by each person during the interview. In addition, you will include comments that reflect nonverbal interactions such as pauses, laughing, and crying.

Preparing transcripts involves five basic tasks: (1) choosing a method of analysis, (2) determining who should transcribe the data, (3) considering ethical implications in the data analysis, (4) transcribing raw data, and (5) formatting the transcript for analysis.

Task 1a: Choosing a Method of Analysis

As you know by now, the qualitative research process usually results in masses of data. A tape-recorded interview lasting an hour may result in a typed transcript of 20 to 50 pages. Interview data can be collected using a variety of aids, such as tape recordings, videotapes, and your field notes. You may gather additional data from preexisting documents, such as newspaper clippings, abstracts, diaries, and letters. Throughout data collection, you will actively examine any relevant written materials and take copious notes on your reactions and ideas.

Word-processing programs have made the task of transcribing large amounts of data much simpler. Besides presenting the data in a uniform way, such programs allow you to make changes to the interviews quickly and easily, producing a clean copy of the data to analyze. Nevertheless, it is important to remember that, after being transcribed, the original sources of data must be safely stored away in case you wish to use these sources again.

Part of the reason that a qualitative analysis is considered to be a massive responsibility is that you ultimately end up comparing and sorting multiple segments from the large amount of information that you collected previously. Several methods of analysis are possible, and this choice will affect the manner in which you transcribe your data. The first option is to analyze your data using the traditional "cut-and-paste" method, whereby you use scissors to cut the typed transcript into the categories you have decided on, and to sort these into relevant groupings. Some qualitative researchers still prefer this method, remaining skeptical about the use of computers.

A second option is to use a regular word-processing program in the analysis. Even with limited knowledge of word processing, you are likely to be familiar with enough commands to sort your data into the appropriate categories for your analysis.

The third option is to use a computer program that has been developed specifically to assist in the qualitative data analysis process. Programs such as *The Ethnograph, AskSam,* NUD*IST, and ATLIS.ti are only four of the more familiar names. The software market changes so quickly that we encourage you to consult with other qualitative researchers or computer companies about what programs they recommend. Although no one has yet found a way to replace the thinking that is the critical determinant of whether an analysis truly reflects the material, a qualitative analysis has become simpler with the introduction of computer programs that are able to sort and organize segments of the text with relative ease. Computers can also assist in mechanical tasks, such as recording, editing, and formatting, leaving the analytical work to you.

One rationale for using computers in a qualitative analysis is to free up your time so you can concentrate on interpreting the meaning of the data. It is doubtful that any computer program will ever replace your role in analysis because you need to be intensely involved in the reading of the data in order to understand them. Please note that the analysis of qualitative data consequently draws heavily on *your own* personal skills and resources.

Most computer programs that aid in the analysis of qualitative data require you to first enter the interview data into a word processor. There are dozens of word-processing software packages available on the market. However, it is necessary to select a package that can download the text into an ASCII format, because a number of the qualitative data analysis programs require that the data be in ASCII.

ASCII stands for American Standard Code for Information Interchange, the basic computer language for all IBM-compatible hardware. ASCII files are stripped of special formatting commands, such as tabs and special fonts. Converting a file to ASCII is quite simple.

Task 1b: Determining Who Should Transcribe the Data

The scope of a study determines the number of resources needed to complete each step and task. In smaller studies, you are likely to have the sole responsibility for all phases, steps, and tasks from beginning to end. Although the data analysis phase may sound like a lot of work, there is a considerable benefit to you in transcribing the interviews yourself. You will become thoroughly acquainted with the content of the interviews, a critical aspect for the process of analysis, and transcribing provides an additional opportunity to review and connect with your data.

In large studies, you may have secretarial support or a research assistant to help with transcribing your data. When you are fortunate enough to have the assistance of others, it is essential that all persons working on your project operate according to the same principles and procedures. It is up to you to provide some form of systematic training for them so that all data are treated according to the same decision-making rules. In this case, you might transcribe some of the interviews yourself at the beginning so that you can be clear with your assistants about what you want. Also, all transcribers should be informed about the importance of including nonverbal communication, such as laughs or pauses in conversation, in the data text. Despite the advantages of having additional assistance in transcribing, many qualitative researchers prefer to transcribe their own data if at all possible.

Task 1c: Considering Ethical Issues

As discussed in previous chapters in this book, ethics is a critical consideration throughout the research process. In the data analysis phase, confidentiality is a central ethical issue, especially when tapes and transcripts are given to research assistants or to secretaries. To safeguard the interviewee's confidentiality, no identifying information should be included on this material. Instead, you might assign a code name or number to identify the research participant at the beginning of the tape and then use only first names throughout the transcript. Do not use recognizable information such as birth date, social security number, or address in your code names. In addition, you must make adequate provision to protect the privacy of your research participants by ensuring that details that might identify them are concealed. For example, if you include excerpts of interviews in your final report (see Chapter 27), a reader could potentially identify a person on the basis of his or her professional status, the names, ages, and gender of children, and the details of the unique experience. Such recognizable information should be masked in any examples.

In the study we are reporting in this chapter, the researcher had to be particularly careful to disguise identifying features because of the intensely personal nature of the situations that the women were describing. In one case, a woman's husband was being investigated as a suspect in the sexual abuse and abduction of her 10-year-old daughter. With the widespread newspaper coverage of the event, she was extremely cautious—not only did she transcribe the tape herself, but no details of the family's situation were typed into the transcript or her final report.

Task 1d: Transcribing Raw Data

Transcribing data from audiotapes or videotapes is a long and arduous process, requiring careful attention and precise transcription. In most cases, transcripts should be produced *verbatim* to allow the context of the conversation to provide as much meaning as possible. Editing and censoring during transcription can easily wipe out the context of the data and, in the process, conceal the meaning of the text.

Interviews provide context of the conversation and give flavor and texture to the data. Most importantly, it allows you to become completely involved in the data and to view it holistically. It is, therefore, critical for you to record nonverbal interview events such as pauses, laughs, nervous moments, and excitement. You may also choose to insert notes based on your impressions or guesses about the context of the verbal comments, such as "seems reluctant to talk about what her parents thought about her going to a shelter."

Below is part of an interview from Tutty's study that includes the interviewer's notes about nonverbal communication in parentheses:

Interviewer: Now that we've got the ethics forms completed, I'd like to tell you how much I appreciate you taking this time to talk about your experience after leaving Transition House.

Joy: (enthusiastically) I have only good things to say about that place. It was so peaceful being there, you know, you don't have to worry, you don't have to be concerned. You know your children are safe and everything (pause) and you're safe. The counselors were really helpful, too. No, I really liked that place. That was my second time there (pause). Silly me (in an embarrassed tone, shifting in seat, sounds uncomfortable) I've got involved in the same relationship twice. (Sounding more solid) I decided to give it another chance because of the baby. Yeah, no . . . I liked that place a lot, it was just excellent.

Task 1e: Formatting the Transcript for Analysis

The format of the transcripts should facilitate very easy reading and allow sufficient space for writing comments. We recommend using standard-size paper and leaving the right margin as wide as 2 to 4 inches. In this way, the transcripts are structured so that you can easily write notes, codes, and line numbering alongside the corresponding text.

Numbering each line of the transcripts helps to organize data; some word-processing or computer programs that assist qualitative data analysis, such as *The Ethnograph,* will do this for you. With such numbering you can easily identify specific sections and determine where a particular word, sentence, or paragraph begins and ends, as illustrated:

1. **Joy:** (sadly) The booze was just too much. He destroyed our house
2. and two apartments—things broken everywhere, holes in the wall,
3. doors torn off hinges, all kinds of stuff. (pause) Yeah,
4. after the last time at Transition House my initial thought
5. was to leave him and not go back, pregnant or not. And then we
6. got talking. (sighs) I didn't phone him for a long time
7. but he kept phoning me at work, trying to see me at work, you
8. know, saying, "I want to work this through." That was great,
9. I believed him, I trusted him, and then when I finally said,
10. "Okay, I'll come back," (pause) he kept to it for a little while.
11. And then he just started breaking his promises again.
12. And then he started sneaking drinks. It kept on increasing . . .
13. problems, fights kept on intensifying and that was all I could take.
14. The final blow was down at the fairgrounds because he wanted a
15. gun, a little carved gun that shoots elastics . . .
16.
17. **Interviewer:** You're kidding!

Step 2: Establishing a Plan for Data Analysis

Having spent a great deal of time in the initial phases of your qualitative study, you may now be feeling anxious to get the data analysis out of the way quickly. Unfortunately, given the many steps and tasks and the complex thinking involved in a qualitative analysis, you can expect to expend considerably more time and patience in processing all of the data you have collected.

One advantage of a qualitative analysis is that it is not subject to the same methodological rigor as a quantitative analysis. The researcher has more freedom to consider the unique qualities of the data set, rather than being limited to how people do "on the average." This does not mean, however, that a qualitative analysis is not systematic. It is essential that you document the rules and procedures used in your analysis in enough detail that the analytic procedures can be repeated and applied to each unit of data in the analysis.

Although a qualitative analysis is both purposeful and systematic, in the initial stages it will be guided only by *general* rules. You will develop these rules to guide you in deciding what bodies of data fit together in a meaningful way and how these should be coded, processes that we will discuss in more detail shortly. In subsequent stages of the analysis, you will clarify and refine the rules through reflection on and critical analysis of the situations in which each should be applied. By the end of the study, you must consistently apply the rules to all units of data.

Developing a preliminary plan for a data analysis involves two general tasks: (1) previewing the data, and (2) planning what to record in your journal.

Task 2a: Previewing the Data

Although in some cases, you will transcribe and analyze your interviews as you collect them, in others you will start your analysis only after you have completed interviewing. Before you launch into the steps and tasks of coding and interpreting your data, it is important to become familiar with the entire data set by reading all of the available interviews. At this point, it is important not to impose a framework or categories on the data. As mentioned previously, when you first become familiar with your qualitative data, you may be tempted to begin classifying it into meaning units (or categories) from your first glance.

You might also apply theories with which you are familiar, or create hypotheses. Doing so, however, may create a funnel effect by which you screen out important information that is recorded in the latter parts of the data set. The meaning of the data in a qualitative analysis should emerge from the data. Thus, if categories are prematurely imposed, the interpretation of data could be colored by preconceived notions or your own particular viewpoint.

There are several strategies that will help you to avoid becoming focused too quickly. First, if the transcripts are extensive, do not attempt to read them all at once. When your mind starts to wander or you become impatient or start feeling uninterested, it is time to pause. Remember that a qualitative analysis takes time. If you want to produce a quality product, you must respect the process. To a large extent, the process cannot be forced.

Second, refrain from always reading notes and transcripts from the beginning of a document. When you begin reading, you are usually in peak form. If you always confine this energy to the first section of your data, you are more likely to exclude or overlook valuable data from later sections. Reading the last third of the interview before the first portion is one technique that may help you to shed new light on each interview.

Task 2b: Using a Journal During Data Analysis

We recommend that you use a journal to record the process of the qualitative research study and your reactions to the emerging issues in your analysis. Yvonna Lincoln and Egon Guba (1985) suggest that a qualitative journal should include two key components: (1) notes on the method used in your study, and (2) notes on issues of credibility and audit trail notes (to be described later). Each component should include a section on what decisions were made during the analysis and the rationale for these.

The category scheme that you will develop will be a critical segment of the methodology section of your journal. When you unitize and initially categorize (code) your data, you will come up with numerous questions and ideas about the data. Making notes in your journal about these questions or comments with respect to identifying meaning units and categories is referred to as writing "analytical memos." It is a useful strategy for organizing your thoughts. Although the format used for analytical memos tends to reflect the individual style of the researcher, Anselm Strauss and Juliet Corbin (1998) offer some hints about how to make useful analytical memos:

- Record the date of the memo.
- Include any references or important sources.
- Label memos with headings that describe the primary category or concept being earmarked.
- Identify the particular code(s) to which the theoretical note pertains.
- Use diagrams in memos to explain ideas.
- Keep multiple copies of all memos.
- Do not restrict the content of memos; allow for a flow of ideas.
- Note when you think that a category has been sufficiently defined.
- Keep analytical memos about your own thinking process to assist you in moving the analysis from description to interpretation.

In part, the process of writing analytical memos is what some authors refer to as leaving an "audit trail." An audit trail is used when an outside person is called in to review what you have done, to ensure that there were no serious flaws in the conduct of your study. This individual may retrace your steps starting from collection of the raw data, carefully examining every decision you have made in the study. Because the work you do should be open to scrutiny by others, precise journal notes about your methodology are crucial.

Your journal will also help to ensure that the rules guiding the definition of categories and the assignment of units of data to those categories become universal and are consistently applied. Keeping notes about the coding process will ensure greater consistency of coding to protect rules from any whims or impulsive decisions. You will also record the code acronym (the shortened version of the category name) that is assigned to each category, as well as the characteristics of the meaning unit that qualify it to be categorized in that particular way. Later, you may want to revise the category scheme, a point at which you again clearly record the reasons for your decision and how the characteristics of the data have changed. This process, then, will track the developmental history of your data analysis.

As presented in Chapters 15 and 16, we recommend using a journal to record your notes about what transpired in your interviews and how you obtained your research participants. You were asked to take special note of your honest reactions to the people that you interviewed, as these comments will eventually be used to assess the credibility of the research participants in your study. If, for example, you have overrelied on one informant or developed a bias against one subset of interviewees, then your conclusions will be one-sided. Such biases will, hopefully, become more evident as you read your journal entries.

It is also essential to record other attempts at establishing the credibility of your study, such as asking others to unitize and categorize your data to provide evidence that your categorization scheme is useful and appropriate. This process, called "triangulation of analysts," will be described in more detail later. Finally, your journal should contain a section that covers your personal reactions to your study, not unlike a personal diary. Following is an example of a comment from Tutty's journal that she used in her qualitative research study. The example shows an analytical memo that speaks to issues of both credibility and reactions to the study as a whole:

> *May 16, 2005.* I can't help but feel that the interview with Joy went extremely well. She was surprisingly open about her story and seemed very concerned that other women who might be living with men such as her ex-partner know what options they have. She is really quite remarkable to have set up a new home with two small children, and so little income. I think her narrative really adds to the interviews we've conducted so far because she is doing so well under difficult circumstances.

FIRST- AND SECOND-LEVEL CODING

The previous two steps deal with establishing an initial framework for doing a qualitative data analysis. Steps 3 and 4 deal with first- and second-level coding.

Step 3: First-Level Coding

Once you have transcribed your data, and reviewed it in a preliminary way, you can launch into first-level coding: a combination of identifying meaning units, fitting them into categories, and assigning codes to the categories. In this section we will describe each of these tasks individually, but, once again, in practice you may find that they overlap. For example, you may be thinking about how to categorize certain meaning units as you are identifying these units in the transcripts (and will use analytical memos to make sure that you do not forget these initial ideas).

Coding begins at the point when you first notice similarities and differences between data segments or meaning units. You may also see patterns in the data that you will mentally label. As you read new data and reread old data, you will conceptually connect similar meaning units together as categories. You will use a procedure called the constant comparison method: meaning units of data with the same characteristics are considered as fitting within the same category and are given the same code; meaning units that are different in important ways are put into a different category and given another code.

Coding proceeds in stages, and there are several steps involved in coding at various stages of the analysis. First-level coding is predominantly concrete, and involves identifying properties of data that are clearly evident in the text. Such content is found without combing the data for underlying meaning. Second-level coding (Step 4) is more abstract and involves interpreting the meaning underlying the more obvious ideas portrayed in the data.

By the end of the analysis phase, you will have worked with both concrete and abstract content. You will start with concrete coding at the beginning of the analysis, but work toward understanding the deeper, abstract content in the final stages of analysis. Remember, qualitative research is more than description—it takes a natural interest in the meaning underlying the words.

In summary, the primary task of coding is to identify and label relevant categories of data, first concretely (in first-level coding) and then abstractly (in second-level coding). First-level coding is a lengthy and detailed process that involves five tasks: (1) identifying meaning units, (2) assigning category names to groups of similar meaning units, (3) assigning codes to categories, (4) refining and reorganizing codings, and (5) deciding when to stop. Once again, the tasks sometimes overlap one another and they should be viewed as absolutely essential in the first-level coding process.

Task 3a: Identifying Meaning Units

Once you have previewed the data they need to be organized into a manageable format. To do this, you first identify the important experiences or ideas in your data. This is the process of classifying and collapsing the data into "meaning units." You make decisions about what pieces of data fit together; ultimately, these are the segments that will be categorized, coded, sorted, and then form the patterns that will be used to summarize your interpretation of the data.

Units are the segments (or chunks) of information that are the building blocks of a classification scheme. A unit can consist of a single word, a partial or complete sentence, a paragraph, or more. It is a piece of the transcript that you consider to be meaningful by itself. At this point you are not analyzing what the data mean, you are simply identifying the important bits of what the research participants are saying.

What constitutes a meaning unit may be clear to outside readers, but this will not necessarily be the case. The developers of *The Ethnograph* computer program, for example, studied how a group of students analyzed an identical data file. While some students identified very small meaning units of 5 to 50 lines of transcript, others identified larger units, analyzing segments of between 50 and 200 lines. Further, the category labels that the students attached to the meaning units varied considerably. Some students labeled categories in a concrete and detailed manner, but others were more impressionistic and abstract. Some students identified categories similar to those of other students, but still others identified categories that were unique. This example simply illustrates the fact that different individuals will identify and label the same meaning units differently within the same data set. The lesson is that there is no inherent "right" or "wrong" way to organize

qualitative data. How one chooses to reduce data into a manageable form is an individual endeavor.

In the segment of the data set previously presented, the following meaning units were identified (the first underlined, the next in italics) early in the first-level coding process:

1. **Joy:** (sadly) <u>The booze was just too much.</u> *He destroyed our house*
2. *and two apartments—things broken everywhere, holes in the wall,*
3. *doors torn off hinges, all kinds of stuff.* (pause) <u>Yeah,</u>
4. <u>after the last time at Transition House my initial thought</u>
5. <u>was to leave him and not go back,</u> <u>pregnant or not.</u> <u>And then we</u>
6. <u>got talking.</u> (sighs) <u>I didn't phone him for a long time</u>
7. <u>but he kept phoning me at work,</u> <u>trying to see me at work,</u> <u>you</u>
8. <u>know,</u> <u>saying "I want to work this through."</u> <u>That was great,</u>
9. <u>I believed him,</u> <u>I trusted him,</u> <u>and then when I finally said,</u>
10. <u>"Okay, I'll come back,"</u> (pause) <u>he kept to it for a little while.</u>
11. *And then he just started breaking his promises again.*
12. *And then he started sneaking drinks. It kept on increasing . . .*
13. *problems, fights kept on intensifying and that was all I could take.*
14. *The final blow was down at the fairgrounds because he wanted a*
15. *gun, a little carved gun that shoots elastics . . .*
16.
17. **Interviewer:** You're kidding!

In the journal, the researcher recorded that the first meaning unit related to her ex-partner's drinking (line 1), and the second is about his past destructive behavior (lines 1–3).

The third meaning unit (lines 3–10) is rather long and may need to be broken down into more than one category later on. It describes the process of reuniting with a partner after a previous shelter stay. The final meaning unit (lines 11–15) documents the experience that prompted the final shelter stay. The topics in the meaning units may become categories if the content is repeated later on in this interview or if other interviewees identify similar issues.

The first run-through to identify meaning units will always be somewhat tentative and subject to change. If you are not sure whether to break a large meaning unit into smaller ones, it may be preferable to leave it as a whole. You can always break down meaning units more finely later on in your study. This process is somewhat easier than combining units later, especially once second-level coding (Step 4) begins.

Task 3b: Identifying Categories

Once you have identified the meaning units in the transcripts, your next task is to consider which of them fit together into categories. Especially in first-level coding, the categories you identify should logically and simply relate to the data they represent. The categories may emerge from the questions you ask, or they may simply reflect the critical events that you identify in your research participants' stories. As mentioned previously, though, while the rationale behind the categories does not have to be explained at the beginning, you must clearly explain your grounds as the data analysis proceeds and becomes more complex. The categories and their respective codes must all be defined by the end of the study.

Earlier, we introduced the method of constant comparison, which is the major technique guiding the categorization process. Constant comparison begins after the complete set of data has been examined and meaning units have been identified. Each unit is classified as either similar or different from the others. If the first two meaning units possess somewhat similar qualities, they are tentatively placed in the same category and classified by the same code created for that category.

Remember to make notes about the characteristics of the meaning units that make them similar, and record these observations in your journal. If the first two meaning units are not similar in these identified qualities, a

separate category and a new code are produced for the second one. Again, the information about what defines the second category should be recorded because the process will solidify the rules governing when to include specific meaning units in that category.

You simply repeat these steps to examine the remaining meaning units. For example, the third meaning unit is examined for similarities and differences with the first and the second category. If it differs, a third category and code are created. Constant comparison continues until all meaning units are classified into either previously described or new categories.

To illustrate how to create categories from meaning units, we will use the previous excerpt. The first meaning unit identified, "the booze was just too much" (line 1), fit with a number of Joy's other comments, as well as comments from other research participants relating to their ex-partner's abuse of substances. The category was hence labeled "Partner's Substance Abuse." The rule was that past and present substance abuse issues of the ex-partner would be included under this category.

However, issues related to any substance abuse by the interviewee herself were placed in a different category: "Research Participant's Substance Abuse." Thus, each meaning unit is considered in comparison to other similar meaning units, and the category is a way of identifying important similarities within and across individuals.

The number of categories will expand every time you identify meaning units that are dissimilar in important ways from those you have already categorized. However, you also need to attempt to keep the number of categories within manageable limits. At the beginning of constant comparison, new categories will be created quickly, and then more slowly after you have analyzed between four and five dozen data segments. Sometimes, meaning units cannot be clearly placed into any of the categories developed in the analysis and fall into the category of "miscellaneous." These misfits should be set aside in a separate "pile" with other units that are difficult to classify. Make special note of why they do not fit. At some point, such unclassifiable meaning units may begin to resemble one another and can be placed in a category of their own. After reviewing all the categories, inspect the miscellaneous pile to decide what units might fit together in a new category or a new set of categories.

If you find that you are throwing data into the miscellaneous pile too often, you may be fatigued. This would be a good time to pause and return to the analysis when you are refreshed. The use of a miscellaneous pile will prevent you from throwing out what seem to be irrelevant meaning units. Such tossing is a risky move, because in some situations you may decide that your categorization scheme needs massive revision and that you must start the whole process again from scratch. We recommend that miscellaneous units make up less than 10 percent of the total data set. More than that suggests that you have a problem with your original categorization scheme.

Occasionally, you will need to stop and reaffirm the rules that qualify the meaning units to be placed within each category. These decisions need to be justified, a factor that will later serve as the basis for tests of whether others who use your rules identify similar meaning units and categories.

The categories for your study will develop and change over time. It is natural for some categories to change or to become irrelevant (decay) in the later stages of analysis. In such instances, new categories can be created and old categories can be either revised, merged with others, or eliminated completely.

The number of categories in a study depends on the breadth and the depth you seek in your analysis of the data. Some topics require very detailed and precise analyses, with nearly every line of the transcript coded into different categories. For less detailed work, it is possible to code larger segments, for example, every 50 or even every 200 lines.

The complexity of the categorization also needs to be considered. One meaning unit may, in fact, fit into more than one category. It is also possible to code meaning units that overlap with one another. In another case called a nested code, smaller categories fit within larger, more inclusive ones. Furthermore, there can also be a complex combination of multiple, nested, and overlapping categories.

For example, in the interview with Joy, the large meaning unit talking about the couple's reconciliation (lines 3–10) could also be considered as fitting into two smaller categories, one labeled "Partner's Past Reconciliation Attempts" (lines 5–10) and another called "Reasons for Past Breakdown of Reconciliation" (lines 11–13). These may overlap with the category "Partner's Substance Abuse," (lines 1 and 12) so that substance abuse issues will sometimes be coded into the category of "Reasons for Past Breakdown of Reconciliation."

The categories must be clear enough to simplify the data and prevent the generation of unnecessary backtracking and recoding. The category labels must also reflect the substance of the meaning units. For example, in Tutty's study, many women reported having low self-esteem, which they found interfered in their ability to feel successful or to live independently from their abusive partner. In the first round of categorization, meaning units reflecting the self-esteem issue were categorized as "Self-concept: Valueless." These words did not adequately reflect the meaning of the segments in the interviews, as not one interviewee reported that she was valueless, but many noted that they had low self-esteem. The relabeled category "Low Self-esteem" more accurately reflected what the data meant.

Task 3c: Assigning Codes to Categories

Codes are simply a form of the category name that becomes a shorthand method of identifying the categories. Codes typically take the form of strings of letters and/or symbols. The form of the code used in *The Ethnograph,* for example, can assume up to 10 letters and can also include symbols. Codes are usually displayed in the margins (often the right margin) of the transcribed text.

As you can see, some distinctions that should be included in part of the code have already been made. One obvious issue is that some comments are about the woman herself, some about her partner, and some about her children. Thus, *W* was used as the first letter of the code name if related to the woman, *P* if related to her partner, and *C* if related to her children. A second important distinction was whether issues were past (*P*), current (*C*), or anticipated in the future (*F*). Finally, in a list of categories about the problems encountered, the substance abuse category was labeled *SA*. Thus, the code that was written in the margin next to the meaning unit "The booze was just too much" was *P-P-SA,* standing for the partner's past substance abuse. As the data analysis becomes more complex, the codes become longer.

In the initial stages of second-level coding, the codes in the margins will be used to collect together all the meaning units from all of the interviews that fit within a particular category.

Task 3d: Refining and Reorganizing Coding

Before moving on from first-level coding, we suggest that you make a final sweep through the data to ensure that your analysis reflects what your research participants have said. Pause and reflect upon your analysis thus far, considering the logic of the ideas that form the basis of the rules for each category. Rather than discovering at the end of your analysis that you have made an error in judgment, now is the most appropriate time to reexamine your thinking.

You may, for example, be confused about why you created some categories, or feel uncertain about the rules of categorization for others. You may find that some categories are too complex and may be effectively split into several new categories. This is the time to clarify and confirm what qualifies each meaning unit to fit within a particular category.

You should review all the categories to see how the units "fit" with each. You can now tighten your rules to ensure that there is no vagueness about how any meaning unit is categorized. If you have conceptualized the meaning units accurately, the categories will "hang together" internally and be easily distinguished from other categories.

You might find that some categories are not completely developed or are only partially defined. Similarly, you might discover that categories that you had originally thought would emerge from the data are completely missing. You are most likely to discover missing categories while you are thinking about the underlying logic of your categorization scheme. In such a case, make a note of the missing categories, as well as of incomplete or otherwise unsatisfactory categories. You may, in fact, wish to conduct additional interviews to address any of these gaps.

This would be a good time to ask a colleague to code one or two of your interviews using the rules that you have devised. This process is a check to ensure that the categories and the rules that define them make sense. If your colleague codes meaning units in a significantly different way than yours, your categorization scheme may need to be substantially revised.

Task 3e: Deciding When to Stop

What are the indicators that signal that this may be an appropriate time to stop first-level coding? The most common indicator is that when you interview new research participants the meaning units fit easily into your current categorization scheme and no new categories emerge. This process is called "category saturation." In essence, the data become repetitive and further analysis only confirms the ground that you have already covered. This is a good point in time to perform one final review of all the categories to ensure the thoroughness of your analysis. We will now turn our attention away from first-level coding and address the next step in the data analysis process—second-level coding.

Step 4: Second-Level Coding

When completed thoroughly, the tasks of initial coding (Step 3) produce a solid foundation from which to further refine the data analysis process. By this point, your data have been reduced and transformed in several ways. Sections from the transcribed interviews have been selected and identified as meaning units. The units have been subsequently classified as fitting into categories, with an identifying code attached. You have read through your entire set of transcripts, coding the appropriate meaning units with the category code name. As a part of this process you have also reviewed the rules that you have developed to ensure that you can clearly explain what types of information are included in each category.

As noted earlier, second-level coding is more abstract, and involves interpreting what the first-level categories mean. Reporting on abstract content demands that you produce detailed examples of the transcript to back up each interpretation. Bruce L. Berg (2004) suggests that you need at least three independent examples to support each of these interpretations. In second-level coding, you will pull together or "retrieve" the meaning units that fit within each category, either by computer or by cutting and pasting. This process allows you to examine the units in the categories away from any association with the person who originally stated the idea. The focus of the analysis thus shifts from the context of the interviewee to the context of the categories. In so doing, the analysis has become one level more abstract, because it is one step further removed from the original interviews.

The major task in second-level coding is to identify similarities and differences between the categories in an attempt to detect relationships. In sum, the next step of coding involves two tasks: (1) retrieving meaning units into categories, and (2) comparing categories.

Task 4a: Retrieving Meaning Units into Categories

Earlier you identified distinct units of data and grouped and coded these based on similarities and differences. During second level coding, you will retrieve the coded units of each category, either by cutting and pasting the typed manuscript or by using a computer program. Via this process, all the meaning units that fit within the first category are grouped together, as are the units that fit within category two, and so on. Remember that the meaning units have been collected from a number of different interviewees. Thus, this process pulls each unit away from the context of the individual's story. A drawback of the process, then, is that you might lose or misinterpret a meaning unit once it is separated from the context of each research participant's experience. The advantage is that you can consider the information in each category in a different way, across individuals. You can thus see how important it is that your rules for placing a meaning unit into a particular category were clarified during the initial coding process (Task 4a).

Task 4b: Comparing Categories

Whereas previously you looked for similarities and differences between meaning units to separate them into distinct categories, the next step is to compare and contrast the categories themselves in order to discover the relationships between them. At this point in the analysis, your goal is to integrate the categories into themes and subthemes based on their properties. Finding themes involves locating patterns that repeatedly appear in your data set. Once a theme is identified, you will develop a code for it in the same manner as you coded categories. The themes will, in most cases, form the basis of the major conclusions emerging from your analysis.

What possible types of relationships among categories might you find?

- There might be a temporal relationship, in which one category always precedes another. In cases such as this you may be able to identify a process that has some importance to the issue at hand. For example, Tutty found that, although children often initially react positively to living away from their abusive father, later they are likely to push for a reconciliation.
- There may be a causal relationship, in which one category is the cause of another. For example, Tutty found that the women who had no further contact with their assaultive partners after leaving the shelter seemed generally able to function better. Note, though, that it is risky to assume that one category caused another when, in fact, the opposite may be true. In this example, perhaps it is the fact that the women were functioning well that led them to cease contact with their ex-partners.
- One category may be contained within another category or may be another type of the first category. In Tutty's study, she originally saw the category wherein the men beseeched and even bribed the women to return to the relationship as different from the category of threatening the women with, for example, further abuse or no support payments if they did not return. However, in this phase of analysis she shifted to seeing the "loving" pleas as related to the threats. The new theme combining these was called "Partner's Strategies to Reunite."

Obviously, you may find other types of relationships between categories, but the previous examples are commonly found. Some categories may contain enough information to be considered themes in and of themselves.

As another example of combining categories into themes, consider the study on abused women. The three categories of "Custody Issues Regarding Children," "Separation or Divorce Proceedings," and "Obtaining Restraining Orders" all involve relationships with various aspects of the legal system, including the police, lawyers, and judges. The substance of the three categories was similar in that the women were more likely than not to have had difficulty in adequately dealing with these systems. Furthermore, the experience was likely to reignite marital issues, putting the women at risk of further abuse. The theme "Difficulties with the Legal System" was, therefore, created by combining the three categories.

LOOKING FOR MEANING AND RELATIONSHIPS

In addition to organizing the data, coding also brings meaning to the information being examined. However, once you move to the "formal" step of interpreting the data, coding at both levels is considered complete. Two important steps are involved in looking for meaning and relationships in your data. First, you will have to develop an interpretation of your data. Interpretations are sometimes descriptive, but may also suggest causal explanations of important events. Second, the research process and the conclusions must be assessed for credibility and dependability.

Step 5: Interpreting Data and Theory Building

Drawing meaning from your data is perhaps the most rewarding step of a qualitative data analysis. It involves two important tasks: (1) developing conceptual classifications systems, and (2) presenting themes or theory.

Task 5a: Developing Conceptual Classification Systems

The ultimate goal of a qualitative research is to identify any relationships between the major themes that emerge from the data set. To do this you must develop logical interpretations of the themes that remain consistent with your earlier categorization schemes and

meaning units. One idea that may help you to get a sense of the relationships between the themes and the overall nature of the data is to visually display themes and categories in a diagram. The visual representation of your themes may help you to organize the write-up of your conclusions. It may also help you to clearly identify the interconnections between themes and categories or to identify missing categories among the data set. Matthew B. Miles and Michael A. Huberman (1994) suggest several strategies for extracting meaning from a data set.

- Draw a Cluster Diagram: This form of diagram helps you to think about how themes and categories may or may not be related to each other. Draw and label circles for each theme and arrange them in relation to each other. Some of the circles will overlap, others will stand alone. The circles of the themes of more importance will be larger, in comparison to themes and categories that are not as relevant to your conclusions. The process of thinking about what weight to give the themes, how they interact, and how important they will be in your final scheme will be valuable in helping you to think about the meaning of your research study.

- Make a Matrix: Matrix displays may be helpful for noting relations between categories or themes. Designing a matrix involves writing a list of categories along the side of a piece of paper and then another list of categories or themes across the top. In each cell you will document how the two categories fit or do not fit together. For example, along the side you could write categories that reflect the theme "Partner's Strategies to Reunite." Across the top you could write categories from the theme of "Women's Beliefs about Leaving Their Abusive Partner." Where two categories intersect on the matrix you could note with a plus sign (+) beliefs that fit with the ex-partner's desire to live together once more, and mark with a minus sign (−) those at odds with each other. Such a matrix will give you a sense of the balance of the push to leave the abusive relationship and the pull to return.

- Count the Number of Times a Meaning Unit or Category Appears: Although numbers are typically associated with quantitative studies, it is acceptable to use numbers in qualitative ones to document how many of the participants expressed a particular theme. You might, for example, be interested in finding out how many of your interviewees experienced different problems after separating from their abusive partners. You would write the code names for the women down the left side of a piece of paper and the list of problems across the top. To fill in the chart, you would simply place a check mark beside each woman's name if she experienced that particular problem.

  Numbers will help to protect your analysis against bias that occurs when particularly poignant but rare examples of themes are presented. For example, in Tutty's qualitative study, one woman described the death of her daughter at the hands of her ex-partner, an event that immediately preceded their separation. Although an emotionally laden event, it was certainly not typical of the experience of most of the other women. A majority of the women, however, did express concerns about past abuse of their children by their ex-partners. Although the researcher did not discount the experience of the woman whose daughter died, that event could be better discussed in the context of the range of severity of abuse of the children.

- Create a Metaphor: Developing metaphors that convey the essence of your findings is another mechanism for extracting meaning. For example, in her qualitative study of battered women who remain with their partners, Lenore Walker (1979) identified a cycle that commonly occurs whereby tension builds between a couple until the husband beats his wife. This abusive incident is followed by a calm, loving phase until the tension starts to build once again. Walker's name for this process, "the cycle of violence," is an example of a metaphor that so effectively describes this pattern that the metaphor has been extensively adopted.

- Look for Missing Links: If two categories or themes seem to be related, but not directly so, it

may be that a third variable connects the two.

- Note Contradictory Evidence: Remember that contradictory evidence must be accounted for. The chain of evidence must be thorough so that any connections between categories and themes are accounted for. Although we traditionally focus on looking for evidence to support our ideas, we must also identify themes and categories that raise questions about our conclusions. Such evidence can ultimately be very useful in providing exceptions to the process that you have described.

Task 5b: Presenting Themes or Theory

Although many qualitative researchers conclude their studies by presenting descriptions of the major themes that emerged from their data, others use the themes and their interpretations to create hypotheses or theory. In Tutty's study, for example, she simply presented the major themes that emerged from the data without any attempt to formulate these into a theory. Even so, the themes could have been reworded as questions that could then become hypotheses in future research efforts. For example, one core theme was that the ex-partner's access to children created a situation wherein women were placed at risk of continued abuse. As a hypothesis, this could be reworded as "Women whose abusive partners visit with their children after a marital separation are more likely to experience continued abuse than women who do not see their partner under such circumstances."

In contrast, theories answer questions such as "Why does a phenomenon occur?" or "How are these two concepts related?" If theory does develop from the study, it will not be apparent at the beginning, but will grow out of the process of analysis. This is most likely to occur during the stage of classifying the categories into themes and looking for relationships between those themes.

An example of a theory that emerged from a different qualitative study of battered women is Lenore Walker's (1979) "cycle of violence," mentioned previously as an example of a metaphor. The development of theories such as Walker's involves a shift from looking at specific instances to examining general patterns. With each step of data analysis, your thinking becomes more abstract; in other words, you become further removed from the concrete examples on the original transcript. By using the constant comparison method, you arrive at an understanding of basic patterns or ideas that connect the categories and themes developed earlier.

Step 6: Assessing the Trustworthiness of Your Results

Although developing interpretations and theory can be an exciting step in a qualitative analysis, throughout the research process you must act responsibly to ensure the trustworthiness of the conclusions that you finally draw. Qualitative researchers have identified a number of issues to think about to enhance the believability of your research findings. Approaches and emphases vary (as does the depth of detail in discussions of techniques that can be employed). These issues will be revisited again in the following chapter, because they are relevant to report writing. At this point, we will discuss the challenges that are important to address during the analysis. The three tasks include: (1) establishing your own credibility, (2) documenting what you have done to ensure consistency, and (3) documenting what you have done to control biases and preconception.

Task 6a: Establishing Your Own Credibility

Because a qualitative study depends so much on the human judgment and discipline of the researcher, it is necessary for you to indicate why you should be believed. This is partly a matter of indicating your relevant training and experience and partly a matter of recording, in your journal, the procedures you followed, the decisions you made (with the rationale for them), and the thought processes that led you to your conclusions. Meticulous records of this sort will do much to convince those who must assess your work that they can believe in it.

Task 6b: Document What You Have Done to Ensure Consistency

Consistency (which is sometimes called dependability) is another key to establishing the believability of your

study. Qualitative work is influenced by the unique events and relationships that unfold in the course of the study, but a reasonable degree of consistency is still desirable. Hopefully, you have been rigorous in your interviewing and in developing the rules for coding, and have written detailed records of your decision making. If this is the case, another researcher should be able to follow your process and arrive at similar decisions. Also, if you yourself redo parts of the analysis at a later date, the outcome should be closely similar to that produced in your original analysis. Specific issues and procedures that you may need to address to ensure consistency include:

- Specifing the Context of the Interviews and How You Incorporated This in Your Analysis. Some data collection circumstances yield more credible information than others, and you may thus choose to weight your interviews accordingly. For example, some authors claim that data collected later in the study may be more relevant than those gathered in the beginning, likely because your interviewing style will be more relaxed and less intrusive. In addition, data obtained firsthand is considered stronger than that reported by a third person. Data provided voluntarily can be assumed to be more trustworthy, as are data collected when the research participant is alone with you.
- Triangulation. This is a common method to establish the trustworthiness of qualitative data. There are several different kinds of triangulation, but the essence of the term is that multiple perspectives are compared. This might involve having a colleague use your data collection rules to see if he or she makes the same decisions about meaning units, categories, and themes; or it may consist of collecting multiple sources of data in addition to your interviews. The hope is that the different perspectives will confirm each other, adding weight to the credibility of your analysis.
- Member Checking. Obtaining feedback from your research participants is an essential credibility technique that is unique to qualitative methods. Although feedback from research participants should be part of the ongoing process of the

qualitative research study, it is particularly useful when your analysis and interpretations have been made and conclusions drawn. In other words, you go back to your research participants asking them to confirm or refute your interpretations.

Note that research participants may not always agree with the data, with each other, or with your interpretations. In such cases you need to decide whether to exclude the data to which the research participants object, or to record the dissenting opinion in some way and indicate your position in relation to it.

Task 6c: Document What You Have Done to Control Biases and Preconceptions

When you report your findings, it is useful to include a careful inventory of your biases and preconceptions. Cataloguing these will remind you to keep checking to ensure that your conclusions are dictated by the data rather than by your established beliefs. A list of this sort is also useful to readers, who will want to assess how successful you have been in keeping your biases under control during data collection and analysis.

Your journal recording analytical memos and a record of your decision-making process will also be valuable for this purpose. Someone who wishes to scrutinize your work especially closely will be interested in the evidence these offer regarding your attempts to be open to what your research participants had to say. Below are a few threats to the credibility of qualitative research studies, which are relevant to the question of bias, and which you may wish to think about (and address in your journal):

- Your personal bias and life view may affect your interpretation of the data. Bias is a natural human quality, and as we move from the particular to the general there is a tendency to manipulate data to fit with what we already believe.
- You may draw conclusions before the data are analyzed or before you have decided about the trustworthiness of the data collected.
- You might censor, ignore, or dismiss data as irrelevant. This may occur as a result of data overload

or because the data contradict an already established mainstream way of thinking.
- You may make unwarranted or unsupported causal statements based on your impressions rather than on solid analysis.
- You may be too opinionated and reduce your conclusions to a limited number of choices or alternatives.

Matthew B. Miles and Michael A. Huberman (1994) have suggested strategies to deal with the above risks:

- Member checking has already been described in the above task, but is noted again here for its utility as a way of guarding against your own biases dictating your conclusions.
- In your analysis, it is easy to unthinkingly give certain events and people more credibility than others. However, this prevents you from making accurate interpretations of your data, because the people and the events selected are not sufficiently representative. You may come to the conclusion that you relied upon data that were too easily accessible or that you weighted your results toward people you liked. To compensate for such possibilities, you can deliberately search for events and people that differ markedly from those you have already interviewed, to help balance the perspective of the data that you have collected. If you detect such a bias, you can interview more people, looking especially for atypical research participants and events.
- Assess your interaction with the research participants: another source of bias is the effect that you may have on your interviewees as well as the effect that they may have on you. Such effects are particularly powerful in qualitative methods, where data collection may involve your spending long periods of time with your interviewees. It is not uncommon for the interviewer to become personally responsive to interviewees, especially when they are revealing intimate details of their experience. We we are not suggesting that you remain aloof, but if you are too responsive your interviewees may become misleading in an effort

to please you.

- Looking for negative evidence resembles constant comparison, looking for outliers and using extreme cases. Negative evidence should be actively sought at the time when preliminary conclusions are made, to see if any data contradict or are inconsistent with your conclusion. The researcher must actively hunt for contradictory data in case it counters the preliminary conclusion and what the researcher believes.

SUMMARY

This chapter presented a systematic and purposeful approach to data analysis in qualitative research studies. The predominant steps of data analysis include transcript preparation (Step 1), establishing a preliminary plan for data analysis (Step 2), first-level coding (Step 3), second-level coding (Step 4), data interpretation and theory building (Step 5), and assessing the trustworthiness of your results (Step 6). Although these steps are presented in a linear fashion, the data analysis process is not that simple, as you can see from Figure 6.1. You must be flexible and move back and forth between and among the steps and tasks to produce rich and meaningful findings.

Now that you have analyzed and interpreted your data, the next phase of the qualitative research process is to write up your results so that other interested social work practitioners, policy makers, educators, and researchers have access to them. How to disseminate your findings so that they will be read is the topic of the following chapter.

Writing Qualitative Proposals and Reports

Margaret Williams

Yvonne A. Unrau

Richard M. Grinnell, Jr.

27

qualitative

Like quantitative research proposals and reports as presented in Chapter 24, qualitative research proposals and their corresponding reports are also similar to one another. If we explain clearly what we intend to do when we write our proposal and we actually carry out our study as we originally planned, then writing our research report is largely a matter of changing "we will do" (as in the proposal) to "we did" (as in the report). This is true for everything but describing our study's findings in the research report.

As we will see, there is a good deal of similarity between quantitative and qualitative research proposals and reports. After all, the research process follows a logical progression whether it is quantitative or qualitative. We need to know from the beginning of our research study what we want to study, why we want to study it, what methods we will use to study it, how long our research study will take, and how much it will cost. In addition, we need to know what data will be collected, from whom, in what way, and how they will be analyzed.

For the sake of continuity, this chapter—on qualitative proposals and reports—will use the same headings and subheadings that were used in Chapter 24 that described quantitative proposals and reports. We will also uses the same example: Lula Wilson, a social work practitioner who wants to do a qualitative research study on children and their mothers in the women's emergency shelter where she works.

WRITING PROPOSALS

Before we begin to write the very first word of a research proposal—whether quantitative or qualitative—we need to know why we want to write it and who will read it. Knowing the purpose and our intended audience helps us to make important decisions about what we should include, in what order, and what writing style should be used.

Purpose of Writing a Proposal

There are three general purposes for writing a research proposal, no matter whether the study being proposed is quantitative or qualitative:

1. We need to obtain permission to do the study.
2. We need to obtain funding for the study.
3. We need to write down exactly what we intend to study, why, and how.

As we know by now, obtaining permission to do our study is often a matter of resolving ethical and informed consent issues to the satisfaction of various ethics committees. Most universities and colleges have ethics committees, which decide whether our proposed study is designed in such a way that the interests of its research participants are ethically addressed. Many social services agencies have their own ethics committees, which vet all proposed research endeavors that involve their clients and staff.

If Lula were associated in any way with a university, for example, and if her women's emergency shelter had its own ethics committee, she would have to obtain permission from both ethics committees before she could begin her study. Even if no ethics committees are involved, Lula would have to discuss her proposed study with her supervisor, who would probably have to obtain official permission from the shelter's board of directors.

All research studies require some level of funding. Even if Lula is prepared to do all the work on her own time using her own clients, there will still be direct and indirect costs such as photocopying, travel, phone, fax, and postage. If Lula wants her shelter to cover these costs, she must include a budget in her proposal and get the budget approved before she begins her study. If it is a larger study, necessitating money from a funding body, then Lula must tailor her research proposal to meet the requirements of the particular funding body to which she is applying.

Most funding bodies have application forms that ask the applicant to supply the study's details under specific headings. Usually, funding bodies also want to know how qualified the particular applicant is to undertake the proposed study. In other words, Lula will have to convince the funding body that she, personally, has the experience and educational qualifications necessary to obtain meaningful and trustworthy results from her proposed study.

After permission and funding, the third purpose of writing a proposal is to force Lula to clarify her thoughts a bit more. In the process of describing her proposed study in sufficient detail in an attempt to convince others of its importance, Lula may think of aspects of her study that she has not thought of before. She may realize, for example, that she has little experience with interviewing children, and someone who has more experience with interviewing children may be in a better position to interview them.

Intended Audience

Most research proposals are reviewed by busy people who have a great deal of other work and probably a number of proposals to review. Lula's proposal, therefore, should be as short as she can possibly make it. It should concisely describe her proposed study, its budget, and its time frame in a way that is easy to read, follow, and understand. Many proposals have to be rejected because there is insufficient funding or facilities to support them all, and those that are rejected are not necessarily the least worthy in terms of their importance. They are, however, often the least worthy in terms of how well they were organized and written. Lula will therefore be well advised to keep her proposal simple, clear, and brief.

Content and Writing Style

A proposal's content and writing style will largely depend on who is going to review it. As already noted, some funding bodies stipulate on their application forms what, and how much, they want included, and in what format and order. If there is no such stipulation, it is simplest and most logical to write the research proposal in the order that the study will be conducted— that is, the order followed in this chapter. How much to include under what heading depends on the intended audience: A research proposal submitted to an academic committee, for example, often requires a more extensive literature review than a proposal submitted to a funding organization.

Style similarly depends on the recipient. In most cases, it is safest to write formally, using the third person. As we know, however, qualitative research studies are often more subjective than quantitative ones: their terminology is different, their underlying assumptions are different, and the researcher's own thoughts and feelings

are an important component. It may therefore be appropriate to acknowledge the qualitative nature of the study by using a more personal writing style. As will be the case in writing the final research report, the style used depends on the proposal's intended audience and the author's personal judgment.

Organizing the Proposal

As previously noted, if the proposal's recipients have provided no guidance as to how its contents should be organized, it is simplest to present the proposed study in the order in which it would be conducted. That is the order that follows.

Part 1: Research Topic

This first section of a research proposal does nothing more than introduce the study to its readers. It examines the nature of the research question being explored and its significance, both to social work in general and to the recipient of the proposal in particular. As with quantitative studies, a qualitative study should have practical significance, theoretical significance, or significance with respect to social policy; or it may touch on all three areas. The author's task is to explain what research question is being asked and why the answer to this question will be of benefit, paying particular attention to the interests of the proposal's reviewers. Lula may write, for example, about the general topic area in her study as follows:

> **General Topic Area:**
> The problems experienced by children who witness their mothers being physically abused by their fathers.

The results of such a study—knowing what these problems are—might generate new social work theory or it might lead to changes in social policy. If Lula is going to submit her proposal to the women's emergency shelter where she works, however, her fellow social workers are more likely to be interested in how an understanding of the children's problems might help them to address the children's needs on a very practical level. Lula will therefore emphasize the practical significance of her study in the first part of her proposal.

Part 2: Literature Review

As with quantitative research studies, there are four purposes in carrying out a literature review for qualitative studies:

1. *To assure the reviewers that Lula understands the current issues related to her research topic.*
2. *To point out ways in which her study is similar to, or different from, other studies that have been previously conducted.* As many qualitative studies deal with topics about which little is known, Lula may find very few studies that have explored children's experiences with respect to their witnessing partner abuse. Such a paucity of information will support Lula's contention that her study needs to be conducted.
3. *To fit Lula's study into the jigsaw puzzle of present knowledge.* Even if there is little knowledge in the area, there will still be some, and Lula's task is to explain how her study will fit with what is known already and will help to fill the knowledge gaps.
4. *To introduce and conceptualize the variables that will be used throughout the study.* Lulu's proposal, for example, will include such concepts as children, domestic violence (or marital, partner, or wife abuse, whichever term is preferred) and children witnessing the abuse.

Part 3: Conceptual Framework

As we know, in quantitative research studies, the conceptual framework identifies the possible relationships between and among concepts. Identifying the ways that concepts might be connected lays the groundwork for developing a research question or research hypothesis. In Chapter 24, for example, Lula formulated the research hypothesis as follows:

> **Quantitative Research Hypothesis:**
> Children who have witnessed domestic violence will have lower social interaction skills than children who have not witnessed such abuse.

That is, her conceptual framework included the idea that a particular concept—children's social interaction skills—was directly related to another concept—whether the children witnessed the abuse or not.

In qualitative studies, the level of knowledge in the topic area will probably be too low to allow such possible connections between and among concepts to be envisaged. Children's poor social interaction skills may indeed be one of the problems experienced by children who witness their mothers being physically abused by their fathers, but Lula does not know that yet. Her simple research question at this stage is simply, "What problems do these children experience?"

Relationships between and among concepts can still be hypothesized, however, even at an exploratory level, even if the hypothesized relationships will not be tested during the course of the study. People reading a qualitative study, for example, are usually more interested in where the study took place and whether the influence of the clinical setting (i.e., the shelter) was appropriately acknowledged in the data analysis.

Lula must therefore take into account the possibility that the problems experienced by the children in her study may have been due to the study's setting (i.e., the shelter) and not so much from their witnessing the abuse. If she conceptualizes this possibility early, she may decide to interview the children's mothers, asking them not only to identify their children's problems, but to describe each problem before and after coming into the shelter. Similarly, she may want to explore the possibility that the children's problems may have been related to the children being abused themselves and not just to their witnessing their mothers being physically abused by their fathers.

Part 4: Questions and Hypotheses

A qualitative research study rarely tests a research hypothesis. It is very important, however, that the questions to be answered during the course of a qualitative study be clearly formulated before it begins. Lula could formulate quite specific research questions, such as:

Specific Qualitative Research Questions:
- What types of emotional problems are experienced by children who have witnessed domestic violence?
- Does the type of abuse witnessed (e.g., hitting, yelling) affect the type of problems experienced by the children?
- Does the intensity of the abuse—as witnessed by the children—affect the problems they experience?
- Does the frequency (e.g., daily, weekly) of the abuse—as witnessed by the children—affect the problems they experience?
- Does the duration (e.g., over months, years) of the abuse—as witnessed by the children—affect the problems they experience?
- Does the child's gender affect the types of problems he or she experiences?
- Does the child's age affect the types of problems he or she experiences?
- Do the child's problems—as perceived by the mother—affect the mother's decision to leave the abusive relationship?
- Do the child's problems—as perceived by the mother—affect the mother's decision about whether to return to the abusive relationship?

If Lula is going to formulate specific research questions, she will probably need to use a fairly structured interview schedule when she collects interview data from the mothers and their children. On the other hand, she may prefer to formulate just a few, more general research questions, such as:

General Qualitative Research Questions:
- What types of problems are experienced by children who have witnessed domestic violence?
- What effects do these problems have on the children and their mothers?

In this case, she would use an unstructured interview schedule, which would allow the mothers and children to guide the interviews themselves, relating what is important to them in their own way.

Lula's decision about whether to formulate specific or general research questions depends on the level of knowledge about the study's topic area. If enough knowledge is available to enable her to formulate specific research questions, she will probably do that. If not, one of the purposes of her study would be to gain enough knowledge to allow specific research questions to be formulated in the future.

Part 5: Operational Definitions

As we know, operationally defining a variable in a quantitative research study means defining the variables in ways that they can be measured. In Chapter 24, Lula operationally defined the level of a child's social interaction skills in terms of the child's score derived from a standardized measuring instrument, the Social Interaction Skills of Children Assessment Instrument (SISOCAI). The idea behind operationally defining a variable in this way is that both its definition and its measurement are consistent and objective. Lula did not define "children's social interaction skills" herself (except insofar as she selected the measuring instrument) and she did not ask the children or their mothers what they perceived "children's social interaction skills" to be. Similarly, the measured result for each child (a numerical score) did not depend on anyone's personal perception on how well, or how badly, the child interacted socially with others.

Conversely, in qualitative studies, we are not as interested in objectively defining or measuring our concepts as we are when doing quantitative studies. Indeed, we actively encourage our research participants to provide us with their own, subjective definitions, because we are trying to understand their problems as they perceive them to be. Similarly, we measure the extent, or effect, of a problem in terms of the research participants' subjective viewpoints.

Hence, Lula will not have to worry about how to operationally define "a child" or "a child's problem," and she will not have to decide whether "a child witnessing domestic violence" means seeing it, or hearing it, or merely being aware that it is occurring. Lula might want to collect data about the ages of the children in her study, whether they are the biological children of their mothers, and whether they live full time at home, but none of these data will be used to exclude any child from the study on the grounds that the child is too old or too young, or otherwise does not fit Lula's operational definition of "a child."

Lula does not have her own preset specific operational definition of a child. In her study, "a child" is operationally defined as "any person whom the mother considers to be her child." Similarly, "a problem" is whatever the mother and/or child considers to be problematic. "Domestic violence" is defined as whatever the research participants think it is; and children have "witnessed domestic violence" if they and/or their mothers believe that they have.

It might be as well here to put in a word about measurement. The word "measurement" is often associated with numbers, and hence with quantitative studies. To "measure" something, however, only means to describe it as accurately and completely as possible. If we cannot describe it with numbers, we may still be able to describe it with words, and this qualitative type of measurement is just as valid as a quantitative numerical measurement. Hence, Lula is "measuring" the problems experienced by children when she encourages the mothers and their children to describe those problems as accurately and completely as they can.

In quantitative studies, efforts are made to mitigate the effects of researcher bias through objective measurement. In qualitative studies, however, the use of measurement is to capture the subjective experiences of the research participants. Thus, it is vital for Lula to be aware of the effects of her own feelings upon the research participants she will be interviewing. Any prior assumptions she has made, and any position she might hold, must be clearly outlined at the beginning of her study so that the reader of her proposal can evaluate the degree to which her study's potential findings would reflect the research participants' opinions rather than Lula's opinions.

Similarly, it is important to record the interests and possible biases of the organization who is funding the study in addition to the agency where the study actually takes place. Would certain findings be more welcome to the funding body or the agency than other findings? Is the researcher under any pressure to emphasize certain aspects of the study's results to the detriment of other aspects? Again, the reader of a research proposal must be able to evaluate the degree to which the proposed study's auspices would potentially affect the study's findings.

A clear statement of the study's purpose might deflect critics who argue that the proposed study did not fulfill other purposes that the critics themselves may perceive as more important. Lula's research study might have a practical purpose, for example, where it would be in tune with staff interests who work within the women's emergency shelter that would provide both funding for the study and access to its clients.

Lula simply wants to know what the children's problems are so that the shelter can better meet the needs of the children and their mothers. She is not overly interested in adding to social work theory or changing social policy, although her study's results may indeed have implications in both of these areas. She is less likely to be criticized for not placing sufficient emphasis on theory and policy in her discussion if she has clearly stated from the beginning that her proposed study's purpose is to inform day-to-day practice activities within her specific shelter.

Part 6: Research Design

We come now to the *how* of the study. This section includes information about what data will be collected, in what way and from whom, and how they will be analyzed.

While writing about these matters, she will have to address issues related to her study's *trustworthiness*. Evidence of a study's trustworthiness is provided by paying attention to four major concerns:

- Credibility, or truth value
- Transferability, or applicability
- Dependability, or consistency
- Confirmability, or neutrality

The above are roughly equivalent to the quantitative concepts of internal validity, external validity or generalizability, reliability, and objectivity. The first issue related to trustworthiness, credibility (akin to internal validity), is particularly important and is built on the following aspects of a qualitative research study:

- *Triangulation of data sources*—collecting data about the same thing from a number of different data sources; also engagement with research participants over a long period of time.
- *Consulting with colleagues*—consulting with them about ethical and legal matters, and about the methods chosen to select the sample of research participants and to collect and analyze the data.
- *Negative case analysis*—ensuring that information from all data sources is included in the data analysis, even when information from one data source seems to contradict themes or conclusions common to other data sources.
- *Referential adequacy*—keeping a complete and accurate record of all personal interviews and observations, such as videotapes, audiotapes, case notes, and transcriptions.
- *Member checks*—asking research participants to provide feedback on the information collected from the researcher and the conclusions drawn by the researcher.

Transferability (akin to external validity, or generalizability), the second issue related to trustworthiness, is addressed through a rich description of the study's clinical setting and research participants. Findings from a qualitative research study are usually not generalized beyond the setting in which the study took place. The findings may be applicable, however, to other similar client populations such as women and children in similar women's emergency shelters elsewhere. Readers can only judge to what degree a study's findings may be applicable to their own clientele if the researcher provides a detailed description of the study's research participants in addition to their special needs and circumstances.

The third issue, dependability (akin to reliability), relates to efforts to maintain consistency throughout the study. Were all interviews conducted in the same setting, according to the same format, and recorded in the same way? Were all research participants asked to provide feedback on the data collected, or only some of them? During data analysis, were rules concerning categorization and coding consistently applied? Aspects of the study related to credibility, as already described, may be used to demonstrate dependability as well, such as ensuring referential adequacy, providing evidence of consistent interviewing procedures, and providing evidence that all research participants were asked for their feedback.

The last issue, confirmability (akin to objectivity), has to do with Lula's awareness of her own role in influencing the data provided by the research participants and the conclusions she drew from the data. All qualitative researchers should keep journals in which they record their own thoughts and feelings about the study's research participants and about their interviews and observations. Lula should note in her journal why she made the decisions she did about methodological matters such as sampling procedures, and data collection and analysis techniques. While conducting the data analysis, she will record decisions and concerns about organizing and interpreting the data she collected.

These journal entries disclose the degree of impartiality she brought to the entire research process; and, where she was not impartial, it discloses her awareness, or lack thereof, about her own assumptions and biases. With respect to dependability (as previously discussed), it provides a record of how consistent her decision making was and how consistently she conducted her interviews and analyzed her data.

Part 7: Population and Sample

In this part of the proposal, Lula provides only a general description of who her research participants will be, together with a rationale for selecting these and not others. In qualitative studies, there is no attempt to select a random sample. Indeed, the sample often consists of all those persons available to be studied who fit broad criteria. Lula could draw her sample of research participants, for example, from all those women who are residents in her women's emergency shelter at a specific time.

Because Lula's study involves the effects on children who have witnessed domestic violence, she will need to exclude from her sample all women who do not have children *and* all women who say that their children did not witness the abuse. Lula may personally believe that no child whose mother is being abused can remain unaware of that abuse, and the definition of "witnessing" for her may include a child's awareness, as well as seeing or hearing.

In addition, it would be interesting to explore the conflicting perceptions of the mothers and their children when the children believe that they have witnessed their mothers being abused but their mothers believe that they have not. Lula is unlikely, however, to elicit information about the effects of witnessing domestic violence from women who do not believe that their children witnessed it; nor are these women likely to give Lula permission to interview their children on the subject.

Lula may decide to include women who do not have their children with them at the shelter. Whether she does so or not will depend on a number of factors. First, how many women can she interview, given her own and the women's time constraints? This will depend on how long she expects each interview to take, which, in turn, depends on such factors as the structure and depth of the interview. In addition, she must consider the time involved in transcribing and analyzing each interview in its entirety. If the number of women who have their children at the shelter is equal to, or larger than, the number of women Lula can reasonably interview, then she will exclude women whose children are not present.

If the number is smaller, she may consider including these women, but that decision as well will depend on a number of factors. Uppermost in the mind of any qualitative researcher is the notion of the study's trustworthiness. As discussed earlier, one way of establishing the trustworthiness of data is to collect data about the same thing from a number of different data sources.

As presented in Chapter 22, data on the problems experienced by children, for example, may be collected from at least three data sources: (1) the children themselves, (2) their mothers, and (3) shelter staff who have observed the children. Such a triangulation of data sources allows assessment of the trustworthiness of the data obtained from any one given source. If children are not present at the shelter, then data on their problems can be obtained only from their mothers and there will be no way to check on the accuracy of the data they provide.

Another way to establish trustworthiness is to ask each research participant to comment on the data gath-

ered and the conclusions that the researcher drew from the data. Lula might want to submit the transcript of each interview to the research participant concerned to make sure that she has adequately captured what the participant was trying to say. Then she might want to discuss her findings with the other research participants to see if they believe that she has interpreted what they said correctly and has drawn conclusions that seem reasonable to them as well.

None of this will be possible if the research participants have left the emergency shelter and disappeared before Lula has transcribed and analyzed her data. She might, therefore, want to restrict her sample of women to those who are likely to remain in her shelter for a number of weeks or who will go on to a halfway house or some other traceable address. Of course, if she does this, she will lose data from women whose very transience might affect their children's problems and the way those problems are perceived.

Lula must also consider whether to interview the children and, if so, children in what age groups. She may not be skilled in interviewing young children and may feel that children under school age cannot be meaningfully interviewed at all. If there are enough women in the shelter who have older children present, she may consider restricting her sample of research participants to women whose children are, say, 10 years old or older. She will have to justify selecting age 10 instead of 8 or 12, and she will lose data pertaining to the problems experienced by the younger children.

With this in mind, she may consider enlisting the assistance of a colleague who is more skilled at eliciting information from younger children—through data collection methods such as drama, art, or play—than she is. But now she has to think about how such interview data would be analyzed and how she would integrate them with the data collected through her own personal interviews with the mothers.

The child's gender may be another consideration. Perhaps Lula has an idea that girls tend to display more internalizing problem behaviors—such as withdrawal and depression—than boys. And she may believe that boys tend to display more externalizing behaviors—such as hostility and aggression—than girls. She might therefore want to ensure that her study contains approximately equal numbers of girls and boys. If she purposefully drew her sample of research participants in this way, she would have to explain that she expected to find more internalizing behaviors in girls and more externalizing behaviors in boys. This would constitute a research hypothesis, which would need to be included in the Questions and Hypotheses section and justified through the literature review. Or perhaps Lula would phrase it as a research question, simply asking whether the gender of the child was related to the type of problem behavior he or she exhibited.

Similarly, Lula might have an idea that the types of problem behaviors exhibited by children depend on their ethnic background. If she were able to conduct only a small number of interviews, for example, she might purposefully select women and children from different ethnic backgrounds to make up her sample of research participants (called *purposive sampling;* see Chapter 11). Here again, she would have to justify her choice, including a relevant research question or research hypothesis and addressing the matter in the literature review.

Lula thus has a number of factors to consider in deciding whom to include as research participants in her study. The main consideration, however, is always the willingness of the research participant to take part in the study. Like most social work populations, women in emergency shelters are an extremely vulnerable group, and it is vital to ensure that they feel freely able to refuse to participate in the study, knowing that their refusal will in no way affect the quality of the services they receive.

Similarly, the social workers within Lula's women's emergency shelter must also feel able to refuse, knowing that their refusal will not affect the terms of their employment. It is quite likely that Lula will not have the luxury of selecting her research participants in terms of the age, gender, or ethnic background of the children. More probably, Lula will just interview those women who agree to be interviewed and who also give permission for her or a colleague to interview their children as well. The children will not be in a position to sign an informed consent form, as their mothers and the social workers will do, but it is still extremely important to ensure that they understand their rights with

respect to refusing to take part in the study or withdrawing from it at any time.

Part 8: Data Collection

This part of the qualitative research proposal provides a detailed account of how the data are going to be collected, together with a justification for using the data collection method selected rather than some other method. Lula could use focus groups, for example, rather than unstructured interviews to collect data from the women. She could decide not to interview children but instead to observe the children's behaviors herself, without involving a colleague or other social workers. If she does involve the shelter's social workers, she might decide just to interview them and ask how they define the children's problem behaviors and what problem behaviors they have observed in the children under study.

On the other hand, she might ask them first to define children's problem behaviors, then to purposefully observe certain children with respect to these behaviors, and finally to report their observations back to her. She might even ask them to use structured methods of observation, such as frequency, magnitude, or duration recording instruments.

Whatever she decides, she must first justify her decisions and then clearly describe the methods to be used. She should state, for example, that the abused women, the shelter's social workers, and the children aged 10 or over will be interviewed by herself, if that is what she has decided to do.

She should also specify where these interviews will take place, how long approximately each is expected to last, and to what degree the content will be guided by an interview schedule. She should also specify the time frame within which all the interviews will be completed and how the interviews will be recorded. Videotaping, audiotaping, and taking notes during the interview all have their advantages and disadvantages, which need to be discussed.

If a colleague is to work with the younger children, for example, details of the methods used to elicit interview data from these children must be given. In addition, the colleague's credentials must be included at the beginning of the proposal, as this colleague is now a co-researcher and her experience and qualifications will affect the trustworthiness of the study's findings.

Ethical considerations that were not covered in the discussion about selecting research participants should also be addressed in this section. Should Lula obtain informed consent from the mothers and their children, for example, before she asks the shelter's social workers to observe the children or to discuss their behaviors with her? Should she share the social worker's comments with the mothers and their children concerned and tell the social workers beforehand that this is to be done? Should she share data obtained from the children with their mothers, or make it clear that such data will not be shared? Social workers might not be so honest in their comments if they know that the data will be shared, and neither might the children.

In addition, children who know they are being observed might not behave as they otherwise would. These are old dilemmas that always affect data collection methods, and Lula must specify what dilemmas she may encounter and how she plans to resolve them. It is as well to state how the mothers, children, and social workers are to be approached, and precisely what they are going to be told about her study and their own part in it. Samples of informed consent forms should be included as an appendix at the end of the proposal.

Lula's journal is also a form of data. Although it will include little in the way of data collected from her study's research participants, it will include Lula's reactions to these data and a chronology of her study's process. Lula might therefore want to state in her proposal that she will keep a journal, recording notes on the decisions she is going to make during every stage of her study, with particular reference to the study's trustworthiness.

Part 9: Data Analysis

This part of the research proposal describes the way the data will be analyzed. There are usually no statistical procedures to be discussed, as there may be in a quantitative study, but there are a number of other matters. As presented in Chapter 26, a decision must be made about whether to use a software computer program to aid in the data analysis and, if so, which one. Then Lula must decide who will transcribe the interviews and how the transcripts should be formatted. She must establish a plan for her data analysis, including some plan for making journal entries. She might want to add in her proposal that, after she has analyzed the data, using first-level and second-level coding methods, and after she has drawn conclusions, she will assess the trustworthiness of her study's findings. She will do this by documenting what she is going to do to establish credibility, transferability, dependability (consistency), and confirmability (control of biases and preconceptions).

Part 10: Limitations

All research studies have limitations. It might even be suggested that one of the main limitations of a qualitative study is that it is not a quantitative one. This is simply not true. Every study is judged on how well it fulfills its own purpose; and one of the purposes of a qualitative study is usually to understand the experiences of the research participants in depth, including experiences that are unique to them. The purpose of Lula's study is to gain a better understanding of the problems experienced by children who have witnessed domestic violence, from the different perspectives of the mothers, their children, and the shelter's social workers, so that the needs of these children can be better identified and met.

A discussion of a study's limitations should include only factors that impede the fulfillment of this purpose. Lula's study, for example, is not limited because she did not operationally define the concepts "domestic violence" and "children witnessing domestic violence." Part of her study's purpose is to find out how the mothers and their children, themselves, define "domestic violence"— that is, to find out what it was that the children in her study actually witnessed, and what they and their mothers think that "witnessing" includes.

From an ideal standpoint, Lula's study is limited with respect to its transferability (generalizability, in quantitative terms). It would have been ideal if she could have constructed a sampling frame of all the children in the world who had witnessed domestic violence, taken a random sample, and interviewed all these children and their mothers in depth.

A quantitative researcher restricts the study to a manageable population of research participants and then generalizes from the sample to the population from which it was drawn. It is a limitation if the sample did not adequately represent its population, thus restricting the ability to generalize; but it is not considered a limitation that the study did not use a larger population in the first place. Similarly, Lula does not need to apologize for having chosen to work only with those women and their children who were residents in her particular women's emergency shelter at the time she wanted to conduct her study. On the other hand, some of these women whose children had witnessed domestic violence may have refused to participate, and that would be a limitation to Lula's study because those women may have felt particularly traumatized by their children's involvement to the point where they felt unable to discuss it. By losing them, Lula would lose a different and valuable perspective.

Another limitation to Lula's study is that many of the children who have witnessed domestic violence may have been abused themselves. It may be impossible for the mothers and/or children to distinguish between the effects of being abused themselves and the effects of witnessing the abuse. The only way Lula could deal with this is to divide her population of children who have witnessed abuse into two groups: those who have been abused, according to their mothers, and those who have not. Of course, it might be argued that witnessing domestic violence constitutes emotional abuse. If Lula subscribes to this view, she might wish to ask the mothers specifically if their children have been physically or sexually abused, because all the children in her sample will have been emotionally abused according to her own definition.

Nevertheless, in practical terms, Lula can form her two groups of children merely by including a question about physical or sexual abuse during her interviews with them and with their mothers. If Lula identifies this limitation early on while she is conceptualizing her study, she can include the two groups in her study's research design, mentioning the question about domestic violence in the data collection section, and noting, in the data analysis section, that she will accord each group a separate category. Thus, her study's limitation will have ceased to be a limitation and will have become an integral part of her study. This is one of the purposes of a research design, of course: to identify and address a study's potential limitations so that they can be eliminated, or at least alleviated, to the greatest possible extent.

Essentially, what Lula has done in thinking about children who have been abused themselves is to identify a confounding or intervening variable that might interfere with the relationship between their witnessing domestic violence and their experiencing problems, if any, due to witnessing it. Inevitably, there will be a host of other confounding variables as no one can tell for certain whether children's particular problematic behaviors are due to witnessing domestic violence or to some other factor(s). Without random assignment to a control group, which is not possible in this study, Lula will be able to conclude only that children who witnessed the abuse experienced certain problems, not that the problems were caused by witnessing the abuse in the first place.

Failure to establish causality, however, is only a limitation if the establishment of causality was one of the purposes of the study. In this case, it was not; indeed, the kind of rigorous research design needed to establish causality is usually inappropriate in a qualitative study.

Lula may find that her sample of children is not diverse enough in terms of age, gender, or ethnic background to allow her to draw conclusions about the effects of these variables on their problem behaviors. Again, this is a study limitation only if she has stated her intention to draw such a conclusion. The major limitation that Lula is likely to encounter in her study is related to the issue of credibility or truth value (internal validity, in quantitative terms). How will she know whether the mothers and their children were truthful in relating their experiences or whether their remarks were geared more toward pleasing her or making themselves appear more socially desirable? And, if their remarks were based on memories of previous abusive behaviors, how far were those memories reliable?

These are common dilemmas in both research and clinical interviews. One way to handle them is through triangulation: obtaining data on the same issue from more than one data source. Another way is to constantly reflect on the quality of the data being obtained throughout the interview process and to record the results of these reflections in the study's journal. The following are examples of the kinds of questions Lula might ask herself while she is pursuing her reflections:

- Is the interviewee withholding something—and what should I do about it?
- What impact might my race, age, social status, gender, or beliefs have on my interviewee?
- What difference might it make that I work at the women's emergency shelter?
- Did what the interviewee said ring true—or did she want to please me, or look good, or protect someone else, or save herself embarrassment?
- Why am I feeling so stressed after this interview?
- Am I getting the kinds of data that are relevant for my study?

These questions might improve the quality of the data obtained by making Lula more aware of possible sources of error. Even if they do not, Lula will have shown that she has recognized her study's limitations and will take the necessary steps to deal with each limitation.

Part 11: Administration

The final part of a research proposal deals with the organization and resources necessary to carry out the proposed study. Lula might want to separate her role as a researcher from her role as one of the shelter's social workers, for example, by equipping herself with a desk and computer in a room other than that which she usually uses. If "researcher space" is not a problem, Lula will still need to think about where she should base her operations: where she will write up her notes, analyze her data, and keep the records of her interviews. Then, she has to think about administrative responsibilities. Will she take on the overall responsibility for her study herself or will that fall to her supervisor? What will be the responsibilities of her colleague and the shelter's social workers? To whom will they report? What is the chain of command?

When Lula has put together the details of who does what, in what order, and who is responsible to whom, she will be in a position to consider a time frame. How long will each task take and by what date ought it to be completed? It is very easy to underestimate the amount of time needed to analyze qualitative data and to feed the information back to the research participants for their comments. It is also easy to underestimate the time needed to write the final report. Neither of these tasks should be skimped, and it is very important to allow adequate time to complete them thoroughly—more time, that is, than the researcher believes will be necessary at the beginning of the qualitative study.

Finally, Lula must consider a budget. If she has to purchase a software computer program to help her analyze her interview data, who will pay for it? Who will cover the costs related to transcribing the data and preparing and disseminating the final report? How much money should she allocate to each of these areas? How much should she ask for overall?

When she has decided on all this, Lula will have completed her research proposal. As discussed, not all proposals are organized in this way, but all essentially contain the information that has been discussed in the preceding sections.

This same information can be used to write the final research report, and it is to this that we now turn our attention.

WRITING REPORTS

As with a quantitative research report, a qualitative report is a way of describing the research study to other people. How it is written and, to some degree, what it will contain depend on the audience it is written for. Lula may want to present her study's findings, for example, only to the board of directors and staff of the women's emergency shelter where she works. In this case, it will be unnecessary to describe the clinical setting (i.e., the shelter) in detail because the audience is already familiar with it. This very familiarity will also mean that Lula must take extra care to protect the identities of her research participants because personal knowledge of the women and children concerned will make it easier for her audience to identify them. Lula will probably want to submit a written report—particularly if her shelter funded her study—but she may also want to give an oral presentation.

As she imagines herself speaking the words she has written, she may find that she wants to organize the material differently or use a different style than she would if she were preparing a written report. Perhaps she will use less formal language, or include more detail about her own thoughts and feelings, or shorten the direct quotes made by the research participants.

Other possible outlets for her work include books, book chapters, journal articles, and presentations at conferences. Again, depending on the audience, she might write quite simply or she might include a wealth of technical detail, perhaps describing at length the methods she used to categorize and code her interview data. To avoid writing a number of reports on the same study aimed at different audiences, she might choose to include in the main body of the report just sufficient technical detail to establish the study's trustworthiness, while putting additional technical material in an appendix for those readers who are interested. Whatever approach she chooses, it is important to remember that qualitative research studies are based on a different set of assumptions than quantitative ones.

As we know by now, the goal of a qualitative study is to understand the experiences of the study's research participants in depth, and the personal feelings of the researcher cannot be divorced from this understanding. It is therefore often appropriate to report a qualitative study using a more personal style, including both quotes from interviews with the research participants and the researcher's own reflections on the material. The aim is to produce a credible and compelling account that will be taken seriously by the reader.

The material itself can be organized in a number of ways, depending on whether it is to be presented in book form or more concisely in the form of a journal article. An article usually contains six parts: (1) an abstract, (2) an introduction, (3) a discussion of methodology, (4) a presentation of the analysis and findings, (5) a conclusion or discussion of the significance of the study's findings, and (6) a list of references.

Abstract

An abstract is a short statement—often about 200 words—that summarizes the purpose of the study, its methodology, its findings, and its conclusions. Journal readers often decide on the basis of the abstract whether they are sufficiently interested in the topic to want to read further. Thus, the abstract must provide just enough information to enable readers to assess the relevance of the study to their own work. A statement of the study's research question, with enough context to make it meaningful, is usually followed by a brief description of the study's methodology that was used to answer the research question.

Lula might say, for example, that she interviewed eight women and 11 children who were residents in a women's emergency shelter in a small town in Alberta, Canada, plus three of the shelter's social workers. She might go on to identify the problems experienced by the children who had witnessed domestic violence, stating that these problems were derived from analyses of interview data. Finally, she would outline the practical implications from the study for social work practice resulting from a greater understanding of the children's problems.

Introduction

The main body of the report begins with the introduction. It describes the *what* and *why* components of the study, which Lula has already written about in the first five parts of her research proposal. If she goes back to what she wrote before, she will see that she has already identified her research question and put it into the context of previous work through a literature review.

She has discussed why she thinks this question needs to be answered, clarified her own orientation and assumptions, and commented on the interests of the women's emergency shelter or other funding organizations. In addition, she has identified the variables relevant to her study and placed them within an appropriate framework. In short, she has already gathered the material needed for her introduction, and all that remains is to ensure that it is written in an appropriate style.

Methods

After the *what* and *why* components of the study comes the *how*. In the methods section, Lula describes how she selected her sample of research participants and how she collected her data. She would provide a justification for why she chose to use the particular sampling and data collection methods. Again, if she looks back at her research proposal, she will see that she has already written about this in Parts 6, 7, and 8: research design, population and sample, and data collection, respectively. As before, she can use this same material, merely ensuring that it is written in a coherent and appropriate style.

Analysis and Findings

Materials on data analysis and findings are often presented together. Descriptive profiles of research participants and their direct quotes from interviews are used to answer the research question being explored. In her proposal, Lula has already written the part on data analysis in her research proposal, which stated the computer program she was going to use (if any) and the use of first-level and second-level coding methods. In her research report, however, she would want to identify and provide examples of the meaning units she derived from the first-level coding process. One segment from one of her interviews might have gone as follows:

1. **Pam** (sounding upset): The poor kid was never the same after that. **The**
2. **first time, you know, it was just a slap on the butt that she might even**
3. **have mistaken for affection, but that second time he slammed me right**
4. **against the wall and he was still hitting my face after I landed.** (pause) No
5. mistaking that one, is there, even for a 4-year old? (longer pause) No, well,
6. I guess I'm kidding myself about that first time. She knew all right. *She was*
7. *an outgoing sort of kid before, always out in the yard with friends,* but then
8. she stopped going out, and she'd follow me around, kind of, as if she was
9. afraid to let me out of her sight.

Lula may have identified three meaning units in this data segment. The first (in **bold**, lines 1 to 4) relates to what might and might not constitute domestic violence in the mind of a 4-year-old child. The second (in *italics,* lines 6 and 7) relates to the child's behavior prior to witnessing the abuse; and the third (underlined, lines 7 to 9)

relates to the child's behavior after witnessing the abuse. In her report, Lula might want to identify and briefly describe the meaning units she derived from all her interviews, occasionally illustrating a unit with a direct quote to provide context and meaning.

As discussed in Chapter 26, Lula's next task in the analysis is to identify categories, assign each meaning unit to a category, and assign codes to the categories. A description of these categories will also come next in her report. She may have found, for example, that a number of mothers interpreted their child's behavior after witnessing abuse as indicative of fear for the mother's safety. Instead of one large category "child's behavior after witnessing domestic violence."

Lula may have chosen instead to create a number of smaller categories reflecting distinct types of behavior. One of these was "after witnessing domestic violence, child demonstrates fear for mother's safety," and Lula coded it as *CAWFMSAF,* where *C* stands for "the child," *AW* stands for "after witnessing abuse," and *FMSAF* stands for "fear for mother's safety."

Depending on the number and depth of the interviews conducted, Lula may have a very large number of meaning units, and may have gone through an intricate process of refining and reorganizing to come up with appropriate categories. In a book, there will be room to describe all this, together with Lula's own reflections on the process; but in a journal article, running to perhaps 25 pages overall, Lula will have to be selective about what parts of the process she describes and how much detail she provides.

Although meaning units and categories are certainly a major part of Lula's findings, the majority of readers will be more interested in the next part of the analysis: comparing and contrasting the categories to discover the relationships between and among them to develop tentative themes or theories. By doing this, Lula may have been able to finally identify the problems most commonly experienced by children who have witnessed domestic violence.

She may even have been able to put the children's problems in an order of importance as perceived by the mothers and their children. In addition, she may have been able to add depth by describing the emotions related to the children's problems: perhaps guilt, on the mother's part, or anger toward the father, or a growing determination not to return to the abusive relationship. These themes will constitute the larger part of Lula's analysis and findings section, and it is to these themes that she will return in her discussion.

Discussion

This part of the research report presents a discussion of the study's findings. Here, Lula will point out the significance of her study's findings as they relate to the original purpose. If the purpose of her study was to inform practice by enabling the shelter's social workers to better understand the needs of children who have witnessed domestic violence, then Lula must provide a link between the children's problems and their needs resulting from those problems. She must also point out exactly how the shelter's social workers' practice might be informed. If she has found from her study, for example, that children who witnessed the abuse tend to experience more fear for their mothers' safety than children who had not witnessed the abuse, then a related need might be to keep the mother always within sight.

Social workers within the shelter who understand this need might be more willing to tolerate children underfoot in the shelter's kitchen, for example, and might be less likely to tell Mary to "give Mom a moment's peace and go and play with Sue." These kinds of connections should be made for each theme that Lula identified in her study.

The final part of a research report often has to do with suggestions for future research studies. During the process of filling knowledge gaps by summarizing the study's findings, Lula will doubtless find other knowledge gaps that she believes ought to be filled. She might frame new research questions relating to these gaps; or she might even feel that she has sufficient knowledge to enable her to formulate research hypotheses for testing in future research studies.

References

Finally, both quantitative and qualitative researchers are expected to provide a list of references that will enable the reader to locate the materials used for documentation within the report. If the manuscript is accepted for publication, the journal will certainly ask for any revisions it considers appropriate with regard to its style. It is important to note that quotes from a study's research participants do not have to be referenced, and adequate steps should always be taken to conceal their identities.

SUMMARY

The purposes of writing a research proposal are threefold: to obtain permission to do the study, to obtain funding for the study, and to encourage the author to think carefully through what he or she wants to study and what difficulties are likely to be encountered.

The proposal itself should be clear, brief, and easy to read. Although proposals may be differently organized depending on who is to receive them, the information included in most proposals may be logically set out under general headings identified in this chapter.

The information contained under all these headings—except for limitations and administration—also can be used to write the research report. Because the proposal outlines *what will be done* and the research report describes *what was done*, the proposal and the report should parallel each other closely, unless the implementation of the study differed widely from what was planned.

A research report is often written under four general headings: introduction, method, analysis and findings, and discussion.

Reliability and Validity in Qualitative Research

Cynthia Franklin

Michelle Ballan

28

qualitative

analysis

It is important for qualitative studies to emulate the scientific method in striving for empirical groundedness, generalizability, and minimization of bias (Hammersly, 1992). Reliability and validity depend on the skills of the researcher. Questions concerning reliability and validity are associated with how reliable and valid the researcher's data collection and analysis are. Using research methods that ensure that the data recording is accurate and the interpretations of data are empirical and logical is important to increasing reliability and validity in qualitative studies.

This chapter defines reliability and validity in the context of qualitative research. Methods are suggested for helping researchers to increase the reliability and validity of qualitative studies. A case example is presented illustrating how one social work researcher combined methods to increase reliability and validity in a qualitative research study.

RELIABILITY

In science, reliability is concerned with the replicability and consistency of findings (Kirk & Miller, 1986; Rafuls & Moon, 1996). LeCompte and Goetz (1982) define *reliability* in qualitative research as the extent to which the set of meanings derived from several interpreters are sufficiently congruent. Reliability refers to the degree to which other researchers performing similar observations in the field, and analysis such as reading field notes transcribed from narrative data, would generate similar interpretations and results. From this viewpoint, reliability is the extent to which a data collection procedure and analysis yield the same answer for multiple participants in the research process (Kirk & Miller, 1986).

Intersubjective agreement, consensus between two or more observers, is necessary for establishing reliability in any scientific study. Confirmation checks by more than one observer also are important for establishing reliability in qualitative studies. The cross-checking process is the reliability check of choice for most researchers (Brink, 1989, as cited in Newfield, Sells, Smith, Newfield, & Newfield, 1996). Although some qualitative researchers do calculate interrater reliability, most do not. Instead, qualitative researchers use differ-

ent observers to check interpretations and to help them question differing observations, with a goal of achieving a higher continuity and dependability of observations across different settings and time periods.

For this reason, in qualitative research, reliability also is called dependability. Dependability involves researchers' attempts to account for changing conditions in their observations as well as changes in the design that may occur once they are collecting data in the field (Marshall & Rossman, 1995). Qualitative research designs often evolve once researchers begin collecting data. It is important for researchers to carefully document how their design decisions are made and how their methods and interpretations evolved. As we know from the last two chapters, this type of documentation is called an audit trail and provides a basis for checking the researchers' methods and interpretations to see whether they are dependable from the perspective of other collaborators or independent researchers. The audit trail is discussed in more detail later.

Synchronic reliability refers to the similarity of observations within the same time period. Synchronic reliability is most useful to qualitative researchers when it fails to yield similar results because a disconfirmation of synchronic reliability forces researchers to imagine how multiple, but somehow different, observations might simultaneously be true (Kirk & Miller, 1986). Therefore, it promotes both critical and creative thinking aimed at reaching resolutions to the differences in observations. Such resolutions require researchers to find empirical answers that include or exclude the differing interpretations based on various evidence that is compiled.

Internal and External Reliability

Reliability depends on the resolution of both internal and external research design issues (Hansen, 1979, as cited in LeCompte & Goetz, 1982). Internal reliability refers to the degree to which other researchers given a set of previously generated constructs would match them with data in the same way as did the original researcher (LeCompte & Goetz, 1982). External reliability addresses the issue of whether independent researchers would discover the same truth or generate the same constructs in the same or similar setting.

Threats to internal and external reliability can be circumvented by providing the reader with explicit details regarding researchers' theoretical perspective and the research design being used. Explication of data collection may include selection criteria of participants, interview guide questions, description of researchers' roles, and the methods of analysis (e.g., explaining coding procedures, development of categories and hypotheses) (Rafuls & Moon, 1996).

Criteria for Assessing Reliability

To assess reliability in qualitative research, Miles and Huberman (1994) suggest asking the following questions:

1. Are the research questions clear, and are the features of the study design congruent with them?
2. Are the researcher's role and status within the site explicitly described?
3. Do findings show meaningful parallelism across data sources?
4. Are basic paradigms and analytic constructs clearly specified?
5. Were data collected across the full range of appropriate settings, times, respondents, and so on suggested by research questions?
6. If multiple field-workers are involved, do they have comparable data collection protocols?
7. Were coding checks made, and did they show adequate agreement?
8. Were data quality checks made?
9. Do multiple observers' accounts converge in instances, settings, or times when they might be expected to?
10. Were any forms of peer or colleague review in place?

Methods for Increasing Reliability

Examining Informant Responses Across Alternate-Form Questions

Equivalence of responses to various forms of the same question provides a useful reliability check. Using a questioning process that requires informants to provide in-depth explorations of their perspectives guards against a socially desirable response set because informants must expand on their responses to questions in ways that help researchers to examine the internal consistency. When informants are interviewed only once, identical and alternate form questions within that interview may be used to test informants' reliability (Brink, 1989, as cited in Newfield et al., 1996).

Establishing Recording Procedures for Field Notes

When completing field notes, greater reliability can be established if researchers keep four separate types of field notes: (1) a condensed (verbatim) account that serves as an immediate recording of what happened; (2) an expanded account that serves as a log of events and should be recorded as soon as possible after each field session; (3) a "fieldwork journal" that contains more reflective experiences such as ideas, emotions, mistakes, and concerns that may be noted as memos to oneself about the fieldwork process; and (4) a running record of the analysis and interpretations that researchers perform while in the fieldwork process (Kirk & Miller, 1986, p. 55).

Procedures must be documented with meticulous detail and behavioral descriptions so that all the internal workings of research projects are made apparent to those examining the findings. Researchers should take thorough notes and keep logs and journals that record each design decision and the rationale behind it to allow others to inspect their procedures, protocols, and decisions. Researchers can improve reliability by keeping all collected data in a well-organized and retrievable format that makes it easy for other researchers to retrieve and reanalyze (Marshall & Rossman, 1995). The maintenance of a research database is highly recommended. A database can be established using qualitative software, database systems, or even old-fashioned notebooks and files. We discuss qualitative data analysis software later.

Some data collection circumstances yield more dependable information than do others, so researchers may choose to rank their interviews and observation time points according to how closely their codebooks and procedures were followed in different situations. Data collected later in the study might be more relevant than data collected early in the study because the procedures will have been worked out to be more uniform across informants. Also, data provided voluntarily might be more consistent across accounts than data collected from individuals whose participation was mandatory. Lying and falsifying information is an ongoing issue that must be evaluated during researchers' interactions with participants in fieldwork.

Cross-Checking

Qualitative researchers use multiple team members and research participants to confirm their observations in the field, their interpretations, and their transcriptions. Cross-checking of coding and findings usually is built into qualitative studies to improve reliability because humans are subject to numerous judgment errors (Franklin & Jordan, 1997). Some research teams use second-coding of the data. Second-coding data means that two researchers working independently of one another code the data. This method allows researchers to develop an interobserver reliability coefficient for the data in the same manner as in a quantitative study. Miles and Huberman (1994) suggest that 70 percent is an acceptable level of agreement for qualitative data. In addition, it is possible for researchers to calculate an agreement rate between the sources of data and to use multiple researchers in the field so that their observations can be confirmed. Some researchers even have all the data coded by one or more independent coders who are not involved with the research process. These coders serve like copy editors who can check the logic and assignment of meanings to the text (Hill, Thompson, & Williams, 1997). Other researchers use members of their teams to confirm part of their coding or to check their observations in the field.

Most qualitative researchers do not calculate reliability statistics for second-coding but do use this procedure to improve the consistency of their data analyses. For example, these researchers would note every discrepancy between coders and use team meetings to discuss these discrepancies and to make decisions about which way the data should be coded. Through this process, researchers hope to improve the consistency of the coding; if this is the case, then there likely will be fewer discrepancies over time. Researchers also vary on how much of the data should be second-coded. Some settle for portions of the data, whereas others insist on most or all of the data being second-coded.

Staying Close to the Empirical Data

Qualitative researchers often speak of staying close to their data. What is meant by this statement varies across researchers, but in general, researchers mean staying close to the descriptive verbatim accounts and subjective meanings of the research participants. Researchers do not move to a higher level of inference without first thoroughly testing those assumptions against the descriptive data and the interpretations of the participants. In qualitative research, problems with internal reliability are resolved by providing the verbatim accounts of participants. For example, descriptions phrased precisely and with good definitions of constructs under study help to improve interrater reliability and yield consistent coding (Rafuls & Moon, 1996).

To stay close to the empirical data, qualitative researchers usually support their inferential statements about the data with exact quotes from research participants. They also establish a chain of evidence that is linked with different data sources and might even be represented pictorially as one would do in a path analysis diagram. Another method used to establish internal reliability of narrative data is to calculate the number of statements made across cases that support the inferential conclusion. This simple descriptive statistical account keeps researchers from making too much out of one compelling statement. Grigsby, Thyer, Waller, and Johnston (1999), for example, used this method when verifying the statements from medical patients who were found to have a culturally bound syndrome of chalk eating.

Using Homogeneous Samples

As one makes samples more homogeneous, the reduced variability generally tends to increase reliability (Zyzanski, McWhinney, Blake, Crabtree, & Miller, 1992). Hill, Thompson, and Williams (1997) recommend randomly selecting the small samples used in qualitative research based on homogeneous characteristics as a first method for sample selection. In general, qualitative researchers do not use random selection because they use purposive samples as exemplars that illustrate their points.

Hill and colleagues, however, believe that by using some random selection within homogeneous samples, researchers can increase consistency and transferability of their findings. For example, Hill, Gelso, Mohr, Rochlen, and Zack (1997, cited in Hill, Thompson, & Williams, 1997), in a study investigating the resolution of transference in psychotherapy, randomly selected their sample from a professional directory of therapists who self-identified themselves as being psychoanalytic and proceeded to further screen and include only those therapists who met all the criteria they had set for the study.

Hill et al. (1997) also believe that it is important to sample enough cases to allow across-case comparisons and a thorough testing of one's findings. They recommend 8 to 15 cases for establishing consistency in findings and providing examples to initially hypothesize about the limits of those findings.

Developing an Audit Trail

According to Tutty, Rothery, and Grinnell (1996), a process audit conducted by a researcher's peers may provide additional evidence of an effort to maintain consistency throughout one's study. The researcher should develop an audit trail in the form of documentation and a running account of the process throughout the study. After the study is completed, the researcher can arrange for an external auditor or researcher to examine the audit trail and to verify whether procedures were followed and interpretations were reasonable (Guba, 1981).

Applying a Consistent Analytic Method

An analytical approach is a set of methods that researchers use to interpret and make sense of the data. Analytical approaches for a qualitative data analysis consist of a theoretical framework and a set of methods for gathering and interpreting data. The grounded theory method of data analysis provides an approach that is helpful for understanding the essence of structured

qualitative data analysis (Glaser & Strauss, 1967; Strauss & Corbin, 1999). Grounded theory is an approach to qualitative research that emphasizes discovering theories, concepts, propositions, and new hypotheses from the data sources collected in the field instead of relying on already existing theories.

Using Computer Software

Qualitative researchers use multiple methods for data management, ranging from color coding schemes, folders, and word processing programs to computer data analysis programs developed especially for managing this type of narrative data. The computer approaches are highlighted here because they have potential for helping researchers to develop a consistent method for handling their data. Computer programs such as Ethnograph, Hyperqual, ATLAS.ti, NUD*IST, and NVIVO make the coding and data analysis process easier to manage. Computer programs can: (1) serve as a database for researchers' mountains of narrative data, (2) allow researchers to code the data in a computer program, (3) sort the narrative data by codes and categories for researchers' viewing, (4) give researchers frequency counts of codes, (5) test hypotheses using different systems of logic, (6) provide technical aids to help in theorizing and concept building, and (7) provide graphic representations of data that build schematics demonstrating how researchers' variables or ideas are connected (these schematics look like path models or structural equation diagrams). Programs are available for both IBM-compatible and Macintosh computer systems (Fielding & Lee, 1991; Miles & Huberman, 1994; Miles & Weitzman, 1999; Richards & Richards, 1992; Tesch, 1990).

All data management and analysis software programs have strengths and weaknesses. For a recent comprehensive review of the specific features of qualitative data analysis software, see Miles and Weitzman (1999).

VALIDITY

In science, "validity is concerned with the accuracy of findings" (Rafuls & Moon, 1996, p. 77). Reliability is a precondition for validity (Guba, 1981). For example, in quantitative studies, it is easy to show that the validity of a measurement cannot exceed the square root of its reliability (Gulliksen, 1950). In other words, if observations are not consistent and dependable, then they are not likely to be accurate. Validity in qualitative research addresses whether researchers see what they think they see (Kirk & Miller, 1986). Validity in qualitative research also is referred to as credibility (Guba, 1981). Credibility involves the "truthfulness" of study findings, and it is a researcher's responsibility to provide chains of evidence and sets of narrative accounts that are plausible and credible (Hammersly, 1992).

Qualitative researchers are most concerned with testing the credibility of their findings and interpretations with the various sources (audiences or groups) from which data were collected (Guba, 1981). According to Padgett (1998), most threats to validity fall under one of three broad headings: reactivity, researcher biases, or respondent biases. Reactivity refers to the potentially distorting effects of qualitative researchers' presence in the field. Researchers' biases may distort the findings. For example, according to Schacter (1999), numerous studies demonstrate that bias is one of the major attributes of human cognition and memory.

Memory, encoding, and retrieval of memories are highly contingent on preexisting beliefs and knowledge. For this reason, it is easy for researchers to ignore information that does not support their conclusions. Humans also experience consistency bias, which is a tendency for people to recall and report past events in the same way as they feel in the present instead of in the manner in which they experienced them in the past. This type of bias makes it especially important to use various sources of information instead of relying exclusively on the subjective accounts of participants.

There is an equal threat due to respondents' biases. Respondents may withhold information or present facts differently from how other observers may perceive them. In addition, respondents may forget, experience recall or temporary amnesia, or consider it necessary to present themselves in a positive manner to enhance their self-portraits. Researchers always should assess the rewards for giving differing answers as well as the threat of socially desirable responses. Lying or malin-

gering also might come into play in some qualitative studies, and researchers may guard against fraudulent data by including diverse data sources and increasing their sample sizes.

There are a number of threats to the credibility and trustworthiness of qualitative research. Similar to the issues covered in reliability, qualitative researchers have to be concerned with both internal and external validity in their research designs.

Internal and External Validity

Internal validity refers to the extent to which researchers' observations and measurements are accurate representations of some reality. Are researchers actually observing or measuring what they think they are observing or measuring? (LeCompte & Goetz, 1982). To achieve internal validity using narrative data, researchers must demonstrate that data collection was conducted in such a manner as to ensure that the subjects under study were identified and described accurately. In other words, the observations and interpretations must be "credible" to the participants as well as to those who are involved in reading and checking the study results (Marshall & Rossman, 1995).

External validity, or transferability, depends on the degrees of similarity (match) between one sample and its setting events (Guba, 1981). Most qualitative researchers follow in the scientific tradition of Cronbach (1975), who explains that multiple contingencies and historical constraints limit generalizations. Cronbach argues that all generalizations "decay" like radioactive substances with half-lives so that, after a time, every generalization is "more history than science."

Qualitative researchers rely on analytic generalization (which focuses on the generalizability of findings from one case to the next) rather than on probabilistic generalization used in quantitative studies (which focuses on generalizing findings from a sample to a population). Researchers are responsible for the provision of sufficiently descriptive data that will enable the reader to assess the validity of these analyses and the transferability to his or her own situation (Firestone, 1993). Therefore, qualitative researchers do not attempt to form generalizations that will hold at all times and in all places; rather, they try to form working hypotheses that may be transferred from one context to another depending on the degree of match between the contexts (Guba, 1981).

Criteria for Assessing Validity

Eisner (1979, as cited in Phillips, 1987, p. 18) provides three criteria for assessing the validity of qualitative research: (1) structural corroboration, (2) referential adequacy, and (3) multiplicative replication. Structural corroboration is the process by which various parts of the account, description, or explanation give each other mutual support. It is a process of "gathering data or information and using it to establish links that eventually create a whole that is supported by the bits of evidence that constitute it" (p. 18). According to Eisner (1979, as cited in Phillips, 1987), a work has referential adequacy when it enables us to see features that it refers to but that we might not ourselves have noticed.

Relevant questions that help researchers to assess internal validity in qualitative studies include the following (Miles & Huberman, 1994, p. 279):

1. How context rich and meaningful ("thick") are the descriptions (Denzin, 1989; Geertz, 1973)?
2. Does the account "ring true," seem convincing, make sense, or enable a "vicarious presence" for the reader?
3. Did triangulation among complementary methods and data sources produce generally converging conclusions?
4. Are the presented data well linked to the categories of prior or emerging theory?
5. Are the findings internally coherent (Eisner, 1991)?
6. Are areas of uncertainty identified?
7. Was negative evidence sought?
8. Have rival explanations been actively considered?
9. Have findings been replicated in different parts of the database?
10. Were the conclusions considered to be accurate by original informants?
11. Were any predictions made in the study, and how accurate were they?

Relevant questions pertaining to external validity include the following (Miles & Huberman, 1994):

1. Are the characteristics of the original sample of persons, settings, processes, and the like fully described to permit adequate comparisons with other samples?
2. Does the report examine possible threats to generalizability?
3. Is the sampling theoretically diverse enough to encourage broader applicability?
4. Does the researcher define the scope and the boundaries of reasonable generalization from the study (McGrath & Brinberg, 1983)?
5. Do the findings include enough thick description for the reader to assess the potential transferability, or appropriateness, for his or her own setting?
6. Do a range of readers report the findings to be consistent with their experiences?
7. Are the findings congruent with, connected to, or confirmatory of prior theory?
8. Are the processes and outcomes described in conclusions generic enough to be applicable in other settings, even those of a different nature?
9. Have narrative sequences been preserved unobscured?
10. Does the report suggest settings in which the findings could be fruitfully tested further?
11. Have the findings been replicated in other studies to assess their robustness?

Methods for Increasing Validity

Using Prolonged Engagement

To increase the likelihood of attaining credibility, qualitative researchers should use prolonged engagement at a site or a field setting so that distortions produced by their presence can be overcome. Prolonged engagement also provides researchers with the opportunity to test their own biases and perceptions as well as those of their respondents (Guba, 1981). Extended time is used to reflect on journals and field notes and to test how their perceptions changed over the extended time frame. Researchers need to be able to show that sufficient time was spent in the field setting to justify their characterization of it, whereas their journals will reflect their questioning of their interpretations and findings (Guba, 1981).

Purposive Sampling

Qualitative researchers should demonstrate how the samples they selected are governed by emergent insights about what is important and relevant to the research questions and emerging findings. Being able to demonstrate emergent findings and important insights sometimes is called "catalytic validity" (Reason & Rowan, 1981). Interest in a specific question and the need for across-case analysis to test findings is the basis for most purposive sampling techniques. This means that researchers must intentionally select a few cases and proceed to select additional cases so that they can test the findings of the cases they have analyzed. Researchers also may first select similar cases and then proceed to collect divergent cases to further test the limits of their findings. For example, if transferability depends on a match of characteristics, then it is incumbent on researchers to provide the information necessary to test the degree of match between cases.

Purposive sampling also can mean that successive interview respondents were selected by asking each respondent to suggest someone whose point of view is as different as possible from his or her own so as to test findings (Guba, 1981). Purposive sampling guides researchers to think in terms of replicating their findings. If a researcher can reproduce his or her findings in a new context or in another case, then the hypothesis gains more credibility. If someone else can reproduce the findings, then the hypothesis becomes even more persuasive. Researchers should be replicating findings as they collect data from new participants, settings, and events. "Doing replication at the very end of the fieldwork, during final analysis and write-ups, is very difficult and less credible" (Miles & Huberman, 1994).

Using Triangulation

Triangulation can be used for the purpose of achieving confirmation of constructs using multiple measurement methods (Campbell, 1956) or as a method to gain comprehensive information about a phenomenon (N. Fielding & J. Fielding, 1986; Jick, 1983). Qualitative researchers seek trustworthiness in data collection by using multiple methods and divergent data sources. Through cross-checking observations among divergent data sources, apparent differences eventually may resolve themselves, and a favored interpretation may be constructed that coheres with all of the divergent data sources and that itself accounts for the differences observed earlier (Brody, 1992).

Denzin (1994, pp. 97–98, as cited in Padgett, 1998) identifies four types of triangulation relevant to a qualitative study.

1. Theory Triangulation: the use of multiple theories or perspectives to interpret a single set of data. The goal is not to corroborate study findings, but to analyze them in different ways and through different theoretical lenses.

2. Methodological Triangulation: the use of multiple methods to study a single topic, for example, combining quantitative and qualitative methods in a single study. Methodological triangulation can also be accomplished by using the methods of different disciplines.

3. Observer Triangulation: the use of more than one observer in a single study to achieve intersubjective agreement. Qualitative researchers may use multiple observers in the field during data collection (see Snow and Anderson's 1991 study of the urban homeless) or may use multiple coders (analytic triangulation) to ensure that the categories and themes that emerge are confirmed by intercoder consensus.

4. Data Triangulation: the use of more than one data source (interviews, archival materials, observational data, etc.). This refers to the use of different types of data as a means of corroboration. When data from field notes, interviews, and archival materials are convergent and support each other, we can be more confident of our observations and study conclusions. Triangulation helps to counter all threats to trustworthiness (reactivity, researcher bias, and respondent bias). When there is disagreement among data sources, researchers are faced with a decision about which version to rely on or might

view the discrepancies as an opportunity to explore new insights.

Using Measurement Instruments to Corroborate Findings

In verifying constructs in a qualitative study, some researchers recommend using standardized measurement instruments to test the observations of the researcher or as a method of triangulation (Hill, Thompson, & Williams, 1997). This method is similar to the way in which a clinician might use a psychosocial measure to assess a client on characteristics that the clinician has observed, thus allowing for a corroboration of one's perceptions.

Using Structured Codebooks

Qualitative data analysis requires the categorization of narrative data into themes. Qualitative researchers use codebooks not only to sort and organize the data but also as a means of developing useful schemata for understanding the data. Codebooks allow data to be sorted into meaningful codes (descriptive narrative labels) and linked in categories (conceptual narrative labels) so that researchers can begin to make sense of the data. Using a codebook serves a function similar to the statistical techniques (e.g., cluster analysis, factor analysis) used in quantitative research.

A codebook can be constructed prior to data collection (a priori codebook) or in the process of data analysis and interpretation (priori codebook). If researchers begin with a codebook, then they are more likely to achieve greater construct validity. But if they wait and develop the codebook in the field, then they may gain more representativeness. Some researchers use both approaches, starting with a codebook but also modifying it while in the field. This might be the best approach for achieving internal and external validity.

The validity of the coding process is important to qualitative research designs, and some cognitive researchers have tried to determine the best and worst cognitive strategies used by studying coding using experimental research methods (Chwalisz, Wiersma, & Stark-Wroblewski, 1996). Findings suggest that, in the best cognitive strategies, data are grouped together into coherent and consistent categories of meaning and then are further linked into higher order inferences that explain different clusters. Findings also suggest that familiarity with the data is important and that there is no advantage to using simple descriptive units, pointing to the necessity of being able to see the larger connecting themes.

Peer Debriefing

Peer debriefing serves a function similar to that of peer supervision in clinical practice. It provides researchers with the opportunity to test their growing insights and to expose themselves to critical questions and feedback (Guba, 1981). Researchers select one or more peers to serve as guides and discuss interpretations and concerns with those colleagues. Researchers should regularly detach themselves from the field and seek out the counsel of other professionals who are willing and able to perform the debriefing function. Researchers' journals and field activities need to indicate that they acted on critical reflections and timely redirection by the peer debriefers and to show that their analyses changed due to the critiques obtained during the debriefings (Guba, 1981).

Using Negative Case Analysis

To increase the likelihood of attaining credibility, researchers should use negative case analysis, which involves "revising your analysis until it accounts for all the findings of all of your cases" (Tutty, Rothery, & Grinnell, 1996, p. 126). To perform negative case analyses, researchers must look for contrasting cases and be able to increase the number of cases if needed to resolve questions. Stratification and randomization methods used by experimental researchers also may enhance internal validity in negative case analysis. Qualitative researchers use experimental methods as verification devices to guard against sampling and measurement error (Miles & Huberman, 1994).

Using a Guiding Theory to Verify Findings

To counter challenges to transferability and construct validity in qualitative research studies, researchers can refer back to the original theoretical framework to show how data collection and analysis are guided by concepts and models (Marshall & Rossman, 1995). For example, individuals who design research studies within the same parameters of another study can determine whether the cases described can be transferred to other settings, and the reader can see from the findings how the research ties into the development of a theory or other empirical findings.

Leaving an Audit Trail

Audit trails, or meticulous logs and records concerning one's research methods and decisions, ensure that every aspect of the data collection and analysis can be traced and verified by others. Audits were discussed earlier in relationship to reliability, but they also are an important method for validity. Chwalisz et al. (1996) suggest that qualitative researchers consider combining "think aloud" techniques with keeping journals during their analyses, thus producing a protocol of cognitive strategies for analysis that other researchers could examine subsequently. Thus, the spirit of the audit trail is captured in this method. An audit trail allows research teams and outside researchers to reconstruct the work of the original researcher. This method may be used to critically investigate or cross-check the data collection and analysis.

Using Reflexivity

Reflexivity is the "ability to examine one's self" (Padgett, 1998). To ensure reflexivity, open disclosures of preconceptions and assumptions that might have influenced data gathering and processing become an important part of the research method (Brody, 1992). Franklin (1996) provides an example of how reflexivity was used by a doctoral student whom she was supervising during a qualitative study. The student, a feminist activist, was doing a study on the effects of taking a polygraph test on female rape victims. The person conducting the research had a strong bias and set of theoretical assumptions that assumed that being exposed to the polygraph test was disempowering to women. However, the interview data she collected did not support this conclusion; instead, the researcher found that the women felt vindicated by the positive results of the test. It was an emotional struggle for the researcher to give up her biases in favor of the empirical data from the women. But through careful examination of her beliefs and biases, she finally was able to do so.

Using Member Checks

Obtaining feedback from research participants is an essential credibility technique that is unique to qualitative methods. Although feedback from research participants should be part of the ongoing process of the qualitative research study, it is particularly useful when the analysis and interpretations have been made and conclusions have been drawn (Tutty, Rothery, & Grinnell, 1996). Researchers should work out a method for documenting member checks as well as the interpretations that were changed as a result of the member feedback (Guba, 1981).

Establishing Structural Corroboration and Referential Adequacy

Establishing structural corroboration, or coherence, is essential to hermeneutics and other forms of narrative analysis. This method involves testing every data source and interpretation against all others to be certain that there are no internal conflicts or contradictions (Guba, 1981). Interpretations also should take into account possible rival explanations and negative or deviant cases (Patton, 1980). Establishing referential adequacy also involves testing analyses and interpretations made after completion of the field study against other research, theories, and data sources (Guba, 1981).

Establishing Causal Network

Miles and Huberman (1994) invented an approach for testing the validity of findings by predicting what will happen in the case after a period of 6 months or 1 year has elapsed. The basic idea for establishing the causal network involves obtaining feedback from informants to verify the causal explanations that researchers conclude. The result is the qualitative researchers' version of predictive validity, where researchers can verify that their predictions hold true based on future sets of evidence. For example, will it hold true that grades predict later job success (Miles & Huberman, 1994)?

Checking the Meaning of Outliers

Researchers should take a good look at the exceptions, or the ends of a distribution, because they can test and strengthen the basic findings. Researchers need to find the outliers and then verify whether what is present in them is absent or different in other, more mainstream examples. Extreme cases can be useful in verifying and confirming conclusions. When researchers take the time and do the critical thinking necessary to rule out spurious relations between variables, many outliers are explained. A spurious relation exists when two variables appear to be correlated, especially when the researcher thinks that they are causally associated, but they are not. Usually, a third variable of interest can explain the differences (Miles & Huberman, 1994).

Making "If-Then" Tests

Using basic algebraic logic can help us to test our notions. The use of the conditional future tense in "if-then" statements helps to remind us that we have to look to see whether the "then" happened. If-then statements are a way in which to formalize "propositions" for testing causal statements that imply that explanations are different (Miles & Huberman, 1994). Computer programs mentioned previously (e.g., Nudist) provide software functions for testing these hypotheses in the data and may aid analysis of causal explanations.

Using Thick Descriptions in Write-Up

After their studies are completed, qualitative researchers can develop thick descriptions of the content. This helps the reader to make judgments about how transferable the findings are from one case to next. Researchers should make available appendixes to their studies providing full descriptions of all contextual factors impinging on the studies (Guba, 1981). The typi-

cal final qualitative research report, as Carney (1990) notes, normally will contain a mixture of full-scale narrative text where thoroughly thick description is needed, displays, and associated analytic text. As Krathwohl (1991) suggests, the reader can "reconstruct how an analysis developed, check the translation fidelity of constructs, and [check] the logical validity of conclusions" (p. 243).

QUALITATIVE CASE EXAMPLE

Beeman (1995) conducted a qualitative study to better understand the concept of social support as it relates to parenting and child neglect. Based on gaps in previous research, Beeman identified a clear need for research that: (1) differentiated among social relationships, social interaction, and social support; (2) identified the characteristics and dimensions of social relationships and social interactions that the individual himself or herself perceived as "supportive"; and (3) compared and contrasted these characteristics for parents who have neglected their children and for parents who have not.

According to Beeman (1995), there were several qualitative methods used that enhanced validity and reliability in the study. First, a guiding theoretical concept of the social network and social network analysis was used to operationalize the distinctions among social relationships, social interaction, and social support as well as to explore the importance of characteristics of social relationships as described in the social network literature. Second, a type of comparative analysis was used to compare social network characteristics of a group of mothers who had neglected their children with those of a group of sociodemographically similar mothers who were identified as key community contacts successfully raising their children in a high-risk environment—in this case, low-income, single, African American mothers living in the same inner-city neighborhood.

Thus, Beeman's (1995) study allowed for excellent across-case comparisons and for the testing of divergent cases. Finally, qualitative data collection and data analysis methods were used, and these allowed for the discovery of important aspects of social relationships and social interaction from the respondents' perspectives using member checks as a method of increasing validity of the researcher's interpretations.

The main method of data collection chosen for the Beeman (1995) study was repeated, semi-structured interviewing. An interview guide consisting of open-ended questions was developed with input from other researchers who were experienced in interviewing mothers living in high-risk environments and with extensive piloting and pretesting with representatives of both groups of mothers. Therefore, the qualitative researcher maximized the internal validity of the study by using a structured interview guide developed from theory and advisement of participants. The interview guide was based on past theory and research and, therefore, made use of sensitizing concepts.

Repeated interviews contributed to the building of rapport between the interviewer and research participants, and the prolonged engagement in the field. Data collection and data analysis ran concurrently. During the interview process, the researcher recorded emerging insights, data themes, and patterns in a field journal. The emerging insights and themes, along with portions of the transcripts that represented those themes, were discussed at regular meetings with the external case reviewers. This helped to improve reliability of coding (Beeman, 1995).

Data credibility and accountability, characteristics that were guided by past research and theory and thus anticipated in advance, were systematically recorded on data matrices during the interview process. These data matrices served as a structured method for coding that aided the analysis of the data. After the interview tapes were transcribed, data on the matrices were rechecked against the transcripts for verification (Beeman, 1995).

The second part of data analysis took an inductive approach to understanding the data and involved the following five stages. First, the raw field material was prepared for content analysis. Interview tapes were transcribed verbatim. Second, a general scheme for categorizing field data was developed. Thus, the researcher made use of an a priori codebook. At this step, open coding is used involving the identification of themes or categories in the data and placing a preliminary label on them. Themes are identified through a process in which the analyst alternates between asking questions about the data and returning to the data to verify and compare (Beeman, 1995).

Third, the researcher also made use of multiple case and across-case analyses, first analyzing a subset of four cases. Two cases were chosen from the sample of neglecting mothers and two from the sample of non-neglecting mothers on which to focus the initial comparative analysis. Homogeneity was a principle guiding case analysis in that cases were chosen that did not seem atypical of other cases in their group and for which a large amount of data were available to maximize the possibility of discovering important differences. Fourth, grouping by similar characteristics helped the researcher to compare the subsets and to preliminarily identify dimensions of similarity and differences (Beeman, 1995).

During the process and summarizing of the four cases, key areas of differences were noted in a summary form and disseminated in a memo to two external advisers and reviewers. This memo served as a record of the process of analysis and provided a means by which external reviewers could review case material and provide feedback on the credibility and interpretation. Memos, the reduction forms, data matrices, and the field journal provided a chronology of the identification and evolution of data collection themes, and they served as documentation of the process of data collection and data analysis. Fifth, working the existing set of themes and codes, the researcher proceeded to add the remaining cases into the analysis. To increase the consistency and validity of the coding, a computer software program (Ethnograph) was used to analyze the data (Beeman, 1995).

According to Beeman (1995), the study example involves a process of research that left "footprints" (thus maximizing accountability) at the same time that it enabled the researcher to discover and identify meaning from the respondents' perspectives (thus maximizing credibility). The process of data analysis also used methods of documentation and external reviews of case materials to maximize intersubjectivity and accountability.

SUMMARY

This chapter defined reliability and validity in the context of the qualitative research process. Several steps were discussed that can help the social work researcher increase the reliability and validity of qualitative studies. Although it is not possible for the researcher to include every method discussed in this chapter, it is important to combine as many diverse methods as is feasible. By doing so, researchers will increase the reliability and validity of their studies. The chapter ended by presenting a case example illustrating one qualitative research study in which a social work researcher combined different methods to increase reliability and validity of the study.

From Research to Evaluation

29
Program Evaluation

Part IX contains one chapter on program evaluation. As you will know by now, "program evaluation" overlaps heavily with "social work research." Because most of the research techniques contained in this book are used in program evaluations in some form or another, Chapter 29 deals less with the methods of program evaluation—methods contained in the previous 28 chapters of this book—and focuses more on five simple ways a social service program can be evaluated.

Program Evaluation

Yvonne A. Unrau

Peter A. Gabor

Richard M. Grinnell, Jr.

29

With the contents of the previous chapters in mind, this chapter examines the types of program-level evaluations that can be done within social service programs. Generally speaking, there are five different types of program-level evaluations.

- Needs Assessment: Determines the nature, scope, and locale of a social problem (if one exists) *and* proposes feasible, useful, and relevant solution(s) to the problem(s).

- Evaluability Assessment: Determines a program's "readiness" for evaluation.

- Process Evaluation: Describes the nature (e.g., type, frequency, duration) of *actual* program operations and client service activities.

- Outcome Evaluation: Determines the amount and direction of change experienced by clients during or after a program's services.

- Cost-Benefit Evaluation: Demonstrates fiscal accountability and raises awareness of costs associated with studying and providing services to specific populations.

We present each type of evaluation in what we consider to be the ideal order for starting a new social service program. First, a needs assessment verifies that a need exists and offers possible program solutions. Second, evaluability assessment assesses the conceptual and operational logic of the program, which in turn is monitored through a process evaluation. After establishing that the program is being implemented as designed, we then assess its impact on client change using an outcome evaluation. Efficiency of client change, or the cost of outcomes, is then assessed using cost-benefit evaluation.

Each type of evaluation is presented separately in this chapter; however, most real-life evaluations mix-and-match strategies from many types of evaluation, thus using a multimodal evaluation plan. Moreover, as presented in past chapters, the various forms of evaluation use similar tools such as sampling (Chapter 11) and data collection methods (Chapters 14 through 22), measurement techniques (Chapters 8 through 10), and evaluation designs (Chapters 12 and 13).

NEEDS ASSESSMENT

The evaluation of need, more commonly called "needs assessment," is a type of evaluation that aims to establish the degree to which a social need (e.g., day care facilities) actually exists (Do we really need day care facilities?), as well as corresponding solutions (e.g., programs and policies). Thus, and under ideal conditions, a needs assessment should take place *before* a program (or a new program component) is conceptualized, funded, staffed, and implemented.

Needs assessments are born out of gaps in (or absence of) existing social services. Community leaders in response to public unrest, landmark cases, fluctuations in political and economic conditions, and changes in basic demographic trends often request needs assessments. A director of a family social service agency, for example, may notice low attendance at parent support groups and may request a needs assessment to determine if the agency's group intervention is outdated or, perhaps, targeting the wrong needs. Or a child is abducted from a public school ground during the lunch hour and an inquiry is undertaken to explore the general safety of children and supervision practices at all public schools. A third scenario could be that the number of street panhandlers is observed to be growing, so a municipal task force is formed to learn more about "the problem" and to decide what action, if any, the city should take.

When conducting needs assessments, it is not enough to establish that social problems exist (e.g., child prostitution, drug abuse, discrimination), it is also extremely important to identify possible strategies to address them.

Visibility of Social Problems

Some social problems present a visible threat to how society is organized and to what people believe is necessary for a basic level of well-being. Domestic violence, juvenile crime, child abuse, unemployment, racism, poverty, and suicide are examples of problems that threaten social stability in local and national communities, and as such generally have been given a great deal of attention in popular media. These visible problems have been the traditional focus of our profession since its inception. They are the social problems for which our society has drawn a minimum line of acceptability. Once the line is crossed—a child is physically abused, a teenager is caught selling drugs—there is some societal action that takes place to "solve" the problem. Generally, the more visible the social problem, the more aware people are of it, and the more response it gets.

Other less-visible problems are regularly addressed by social workers but are not as prominent for the general public. These problems do not have a definite "bottom-line" to indicate when and what action ought to take place. Children with behavior problems, individuals with low self-esteem, marital dissatisfaction, and unfair employment policies are only a few examples of problems that might be considered part and parcel of daily life. Further, these problems are less likely to receive the attention of public money unless they are paired with one or more visible needs, as described above. In short, needs assessments are extremely useful in that they help us to learn more about seen and unseen problems in our society.

Wants, Demands, and Needs

In developing a definition of need, it is helpful to distinguish among the terms *wants*, *demands*, and *needs*. A want is something people are willing to pay for and a demand is something people are willing to march for. These two definitions differentiate wants and demands by people's actions—that is, what people are willing to do for a particular situation or cause. These two definitions help define a "need," which is a basic requirement necessary to sustain the human condition, to which people have a right.

Clearly, how one defines wants, demands, or needs is open to considerable debate and depends on personal views and beliefs. Prison inmates, for example, may protest the removal of televisions from their cells, thereby *demanding* that televisions are a necessary part of their recreational outlets. The public, on the other hand, may not see a *need* for televisions in prison and feel that inmates' basic recreational outlets are met through educational magazines and radio programming.

Perceived and Expressed Needs

When considering any social problem, we must differentiate between perceived needs and expressed (or felt) needs. Perceived needs are the opinions and views of people who are not directly experiencing the problem of interest. Perceived needs are typically shaped by consulting experts in the field, research or published reports, or people who are experiencing the problem. Perceived needs are commonly held by politicians, funders, agency directors, and helping professionals.

Expressed needs (or felt needs), on the other hand, are made known when the people experiencing them talk about how the problem impacts them personally and, perhaps, what they feel should be done about it. In short, the users of social services have expressed needs. For example, inner-city parents who have teenage runaways have expressed needs, as do the teenagers who are running away. Unless the city's mayor also has a teenager on the run, the mayor has only perceived needs about this problem. Because one individual can have two perspectives, we must be clear about which perspective we are interested in.

Identifying who is defining a need helps us to become aware of what perspective is being represented. It is always preferable, if possible, to include both perspectives (perceived and expressed) in a single needs assessment. If the two different perspectives agree, then we obviously have stronger support for the social needs that we determine to exist. On the other hand, when perceived needs and expressed needs differ to some extent, it is usually necessary to include an educational component as part of our proposed solution. The educational intervention may target people with perceived needs, people with expressed needs, or both.

Social workers at an AIDS clinic, for example, may have concerns about an increasing number of sexually active youth who are not practicing "safe sex" (perceived need). Although adolescents may admit to being sexually active, they may not express any concerns about sexually transmitted diseases, pregnancy, or AIDS (expressed need). A reasonable solution to this mismatch of perceptions is to educate the youths in the community about the risks of unprotected sex and how to practice safe sex.

So how do we come up with a definition of need? The most important thing to remember when answering this question is to include input from the various people who have a stake in the social problem being investigated. We might solicit the views of professionals, researchers, clients, and so on. It is a big mistake to develop a definition of need in isolation from other people. Because a needs assessment is usually conducted within a specific community (geographic or population), we must include as many divergent perspectives as possible.

Needs Assessment Questions

Questions asked in needs assessments are usually exploratory in nature. Open-ended questions are used to produce a wide array of possible answers. At the core of needs assessment questions is an effort to better understand a social need. In addition, they seek innovative strategies to respond to the problems identified. Of course, it is always possible for needs assessments to reveal that a particular need or problem does not exist, or does not exist in the way that we had thought. A simple mail survey to local residents of a particular community, for example, can easily obtain useful needs assessment data.

How we frame needs assessment questions influences the kinds of data (answers) we receive. Consider the following two questions.

- What are the most pressing social problem(s) (or issues) affecting residents of your nearest inner-city neighborhood (e.g., Figure 9.4)?
- What additional social services do residents of your nearest inner-city neighborhood need?

The first question directs us to better understand the current state of affairs for inner-city residents and poises us to learn more about their *needs*. In turn, we can then devise new solutions or modify existing services based on our understanding of residents' most salient needs. In contrast, the second question steers us away from efforts to further understand current problems in our inner-city neighborhood and directs us toward adding *solutions*. If the latter question alone were the main focus of our needs assessment, we would risk recommending more of the same social services without considering other problems or solutions for the community.

Suppose, for example, that the adolescent runaway shelters in our inner city report that they are filled to capacity and are turning *away* teen runaways daily. It is tempting and easy to conclude that more shelter space is needed to accommodate teens who are being turned away. Is the problem fixed? Not necessarily. Foisting a "space" solution on the community without any data to help us better understand the current state of the problem at best only provides a bandage solution to a difficult problem. As social workers, we want to develop and implement effective and lasting solutions, which means that we must fully assess problems before intervening. For example, we could ask the following questions to learn more about the inner-city teen runaway problem:

- Who are the teens using the shelter?
- What reasons are given to explain why the teens are running away?
- Where are the teens running away from?

The answers to these questions may lead us to arrive at a different solution than proposing more shelter space. A crisis-counseling program could be added to the shelter, for example, to help teens negotiate with their parents or caregivers to return home, or to stay with friends or relatives. It may also be that a large percentage of teens using the shelters are actually homeless, in which case we might propose a different program altogether.

There are many examples of how needs assessments can help us in our professional practice (see Box 29.1). The questions they can answer can be classified under five general categories.

- Demographics: What is the demographic profile of the community, or the people experiencing the need? For example, what is the average age, socioeconomic level, family constellation, and so on?
- Timeliness: Are existing services outdated? If so, in what ways? What are the *current* needs of the community? What are the most pressing needs within the community?
- History: Have needs changed over time? What

conditions have changed in the community in the past 5 years? What types of solutions have worked in the past?

- Demand: Are existing program services meeting the needs of the people being served? What are the gaps in existing services? Are there specific groups asking for services but not receiving any?
- Strengths: What are the positives in the community? What are the signs of resiliency in the community?

EVALUABILITY ASSESSMENT

Evaluability assessment is simply assessing a program's readiness for evaluation. Ideally, it occurs *after* a needs assessment and *before* a process, an outcome, or a cost—

benefit evaluation. How do we get a program ready for an evaluation? By creating program models—a program plan or design that describes a program's approach to resolving the social problem being targeted for an identified population.

Strange as it may seem, many social service programs do not have a clearly documented program model or an accepted client service delivery system. In these cases, an evaluability assessment can expose areas of the program's conceptualization and/or organization that interfere both with the delivery of its services and with the program evaluation effort itself.

Indeed, many social service programs are not "evaluateable" in their current states. Many do not have a program goal or program objectives written. These programs are not necessary ineffective or inefficient. They just have a great degree of difficulty proving otherwise.

BOX 29.1

Published Examples of Needs Assessments

Substantive areas are in **bold**.

Berkman, B., Chauncey, S., Holmes, W., Daniels, A., Bonander, E., Sampson, S., & Robinson, M. (1999). Standardized screening of **elderly patients'** needs for social work assessment in primary care. *Health and Social Work, 24,* 9–16.

Chen, H., & Marks, M. (1998). Assessing the needs of **inner city youth**: beyond needs identification and prioritization. *Children and Youth Services Review, 20,* 819–838.

Davidson, B. (1997). Service needs of **relative caregivers**: A qualitative analysis. *Families in Society, 78,* 502–510.

Ford, W.E. (1997). Perspective on the integration of **substance user** needs assessment and treatment planning. *Substance Use and Misuse, 32,* 343–349.

Gillman, R.R., & Newman, B.S. (1996). Psychosocial concerns and strengths of **women with HIV infection**: An empirical study. *Families in Society, 77,* 131–141.

Hall, M., Amodeo, M., Shaffer, H., Bilt, J. (2000). **Social workers** employed in substance abuse treatment agencies: A training needs assessment. *Social Work, 45,* 141–154.

Herdt, G., Beeler, J., & Rawls, T. (1997). Life course diversity among **older lesbians and gay men**: A study in Chicago. *Journal of Gay, Lesbian, and Bisexual Identity, 2,* 231–246.

Palmeri, D., Auld, G., Taylor, T., Kendall, P., & Anderson, A. (1998). Multiple perspectives on nutrition education needs of **low-income Hispanics**. *Journal of Community Health, 23,* 301–316.

Pisarski, A., & Gallois, C. (1996). A needs analysis of Brisbane **lesbians**: Implications for the lesbian community. *Journal of Homosexuality, 30,* 79–95.

Safyer, A.W., Litchfield, L.C., & Leahy, B.H. (1996). **Employees with teens**: The role of EAP needs assessments. *Employee Assistance Quarterly, 11,* 47–66.

Shields, G., & Adams, J. (1996). **HIV/AIDS** among **youth**: A community needs assessment study. *Child and Adolescent Social Work Journal, 12,* 361–380.

Weaver, H.N. (1997). The challenges of research in **Native American communities**: incorporating principles of cultural competence. *Journal of Social Service Research, 23,* 1–15.

Weiner, A. (1996). Understanding the social needs of **streetwalking prostitutes**. *Social Work, 41,* 97–105.

Zahnd, E., Klein, D., & Needell, B. (1997). **Substance use** and issues of violence among **low-income, pregnant women**: The California perinatal needs assessment. *Journal of Drug Issues, 27,* 563–584.

Program Development

Social service programs are dynamic organizations that exist in a context of political, economic, and social flux. Whether new or old, programs must be responsive to their surroundings and be continually evolving into more efficient and effective service delivery systems. In short, social service programs are in a constant state of program development, and evaluability assessment gives direction and structure to this growth.

Evaluability assessment usually takes place after programs have been established and have been in operation for some time. The excitement of building a program logic model is somewhat dampened in existing programs because old practices come under close scrutiny and change is inevitable. Moreover, many social service programs drift from their original mandate over time. Evaluability assessment can assist the workers and staff in regaining focus and taking charge of program development.

A 10-year-old afterschool program for children from urban low-income families, for example, was originally established with a program objective to increase children's involvement in positive recreational activities during afterschool hours. Program activities included organized sports, crafts, one-to-one coaching, positive reinforcement for group participation, sticker charts for displaying friendship skills, and so on. A favorite activity of program staff and children alike was an annual ski trip—an opportunity that children could access only through the program because their parents could not afford such extravagant recreational outlets. For most children, the program ski trip was the one and only time that they would experience skiing.

In the early years of the program, the ski trip was just that—one activity of many that was popular with the children. Without the benefit of a program logic model, however, program staff focused on this one activity and over time began adjusting program activities accordingly. In short, the program began to drift. For example, rather than playing organized sports after school, children were instead engaging in fundraising activities that were necessary to fund the ski trip.

As part of an evaluability assessment, program staff examined the ski trip in light of the program's original objective—*to increase children's involvement in positive recreational activities during after-school hours*. The result was the realization that the ski trip had taken program resources and staff attention away from the program's original objective. In particular, planning for the ski trip meant that other positive and more accessible recreational activities (e.g., sports, reading storybooks, and crafts) were done away with.

By developing a program logic model for the afterschool program, staff were able to revisit their program goal, objectives, and activities giving a renewed direction for planning program development. The ski trip was reconceptualized as only one of many positive recreational activities, and staff turned their program development energy to efforts at coming up with various other activities to increase children's involvement in positive recreational activities during afterschool hours.

Teamwork

Development of a program logic model is best accomplished through teamwork. Ideally, a "team" involves representatives from different stakeholder groups such as funders, administrators, practitioners, and clients. It is more typical, however, for program administrators and practitioners to assume major responsibility for this task, particularly since monitoring a program model is an ongoing effort.

The importance of teamwork is that all levels of program staff participate in the creating, implementing, and evaluating the program model. With participation comes a professionalism that promotes an atmosphere of quality service and change for the better. The benefits of working as a team toward a common purpose (i.e., goal) is that staff morale is higher, turnover is lessened, service delivery is superior, and knowledge generated by the program has more meaning.

Evaluability Assessment Questions

Evaluability assessment questions are subject to the same political and personal influences as needs assessment questions. The nature of evaluability assessment questions, however, is different and falls into four categories.

- Program Design: Is the program model logically organized? Does it easily communicate the program's intent to stakeholders? Is the program goal clear and concise, identifying the target population, social problem, direction of change, and means of achieving the desired change?
- Coverage: Do program objectives appropriately target knowledge-based, affective-based, and behaviorally based change?
- Feasibility: Given the scope (e.g., size, duration, and innovativeness) of the program, can its objectives be reasonably accomplished? Are program objectives meaningful, specific, measurable, and directional?
- Integrity: Do program staff accept the program model as a desirable approach to practice? How much involvement do staff have in modifying the program? Were research and theory considered in the development of the program model?

PROCESS EVALUATION

A process evaluation focuses on the program's approach to client service delivery, as well as on how the program manages its day-to-day operations. It is not interested in the end result of a program. In short, a process evaluation examines how a program's services are delivered to clients and what administrative mechanisms exist within the program to support these services.

Ideally, a process evaluation occurs before, or at the same time, as an outcome evaluation. It clearly makes sense to check whether a program is implemented in the way it was intended before evaluating its outcomes. This is particularly the case because it is our assumption (or hope) that the program's services will produce the desired client change as articulated by the program's objectives.

In the language of our program logic model, program processes refer specifically to the activities and characteristics that describe how a program operates. In general, there are two major categories of processes—the client service delivery system within the program and the program's administrative support systems that sustain client service delivery. Client service delivery is composed of what workers do (e.g., interventions, activities) and what clients bring to the program (e.g., client characteristics). On the other hand, administrative support systems comprise the organizational activities that exist to support the program's client service delivery system (e.g., supervision, support staff, emergency petty cash funds, evaluation activities).

Process evaluation, therefore, involves monitoring and measuring things such as communication flow, decision-making protocols, staff workload, client record-keeping, program supports, staff training, and worker-client activities. Indeed, the entire sequence of activities that a program undertakes to achieve its objectives or outcomes is open to evaluation.

An evaluation of process might include the sequence of events throughout the entire program or it might focus on a particular program component such as assessment, treatment, or follow-up. A careful examination of *how* something is done may help us to understand *why* or *how* it is more or less effective or efficient. Ultimately, we undertake process evaluations to improve services for clients. Thus, even when evaluating internal mechanisms of a program such as staff communication between departments, we want to do so not just for the results of increasing staff morale but because we believe that higher-quality staff communication will lead to better services for clients.

Formative and Summative Evaluations

A process evaluation is sometimes referred to as a *formative evaluation*: the gathering of relevant data for the continuous ongoing feedback and improvement of the client-related services a program offers. Although formative evaluations generally include measures of client outcome, their purpose is to fine-tune services that the programs deliver to their clients. In this spirit, a process evaluation is a critical component of delivering quality social services. By monitoring their interventions and activities, workers can assess whether they are helping their clients in the best way possible. Similarly, administrators are responsible for maintaining a healthy, supportive, and progressive work environment.

The opposite of formative evaluations are *summative evaluations*. Summative evaluations gather relevant data for the conclusive determination of a program's success or failure in affecting their target population. As such, they necessarily pair program processes with program outcomes. Summative evaluations are most likely to be carried out using a project approach to evaluation, while formative evaluations use a monitoring approach.

Given that process evaluations play a critical role in shaping how a program develops over time, we recommend that they begin by focusing on improving client service delivery systems. After a well-conceptualized program is established (a procedure that can take up to 2 years), a process evaluation can shift its emphasis to the program's administrative operations. The reason for beginning with direct client service delivery is that all worker supervision, training, and other administrative support ultimately exists to support direct services that workers provide to their clients. Unless we are clear about what the nature of the program's client service delivery approach is, our beginning attempts to design and implement supporting systems to help workers may be misdirected.

Client Path Flow Charts

A useful tool for describing client service delivery systems within a program is a *client path flow chart.* An example of one is contained in Figure 29.1, which illustrates how adolescent clients move through the Adolescent Program (AP). The chart displays the general sequence of events that clients will experience from first contact with the program to termination. Additionally, the chart shows critical decision-making points where agreements to provide AP services to clients are either made (e.g., referral and assessment) or renewed (e.g., contracting and reassessment).

By mapping out program processes, we gain a better understanding of what types of interventions (and associated activities) lead to what type of client outcomes (positive and negative). These data are a first step to uncovering the mystery of the "black box" of intervention that, as we will see, is ignored in outcome evaluations.

Process Evaluation Questions

There are many examples of how process evaluations can help us in our professional practice (see Box 29.2).

The questions they can answer can be classified under six general categories.

- Program Structures: What is the program's organizational structure? What is the flow of communication? How are decisions made? What are the minimum qualifications for staff hiring?
- Program Supports: What program supports exist to help workers do their jobs? How much and what type of staff training and supervision is available?
- Client Service Delivery: What is the nature of worker activity? What do workers do? How often? At what level?
- Decision Making: How are practice decisions made? How are worker activities and decision making documented?
- Program Integrity: Is the program being implemented in the way that it was designed? If not, how does the program deviate from the original program blueprint?
- Compliance: Is the program meeting standards set by funders, accrediting bodies, or governmental agencies?

OUTCOME EVALUATION

The fourth type of evaluation focuses on program outcomes. Outcome evaluation aims to demonstrate the degree and nature of change, if any, for clients after they have received program services—that is, after they have left the program. Outcome evaluation is the most popular of the five evaluation types that we discuss.

The essence of an outcome evaluation is captured by the familiar phrase "begin with the end in mind." Outcome evaluations serve as a conceptual program map because they tell us where program staff and clients are headed as they work together. This focus helps to keep program administrators and workers in sync with the program's mandate (which is reflected in the program's goal).

Outcome evaluations primarily stem from an interest in knowing whether social programs benefit the clients they serve. Funders and policy-makers are the major stakeholder groups that apply external pressure on

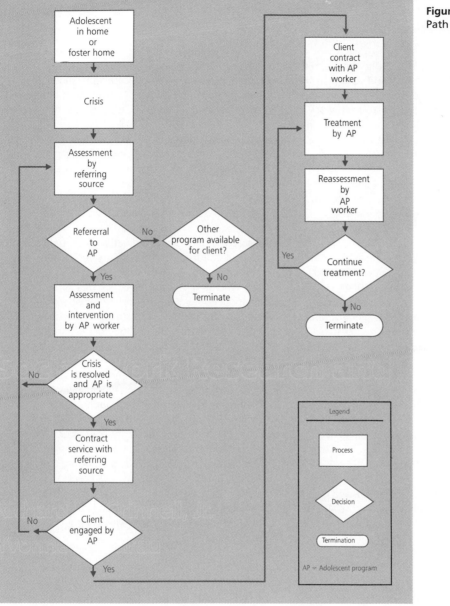

Figure 29.1   Example of a Client Path Flow

programs to produce outcome data. Enforcing accreditation standards, legislating record-keeping protocols, and setting guidelines for annual program reports apply such pressures. Administrators, in turn, are charged with the responsibility of ensuring that outcome evaluations occur in their programs. Finally, practitioners are given the task of collecting outcome data from clients. This task can provide practitioners with meaningful data and insight into how program services are impacting

clients—a result that is of interest to all stakeholder groups.

Outcome evaluations are always designed for a specific social service program. Their results tell us about specific program objectives and not general social indicators. For example, a four-week unemployment program showing that 75 percent of its clients found employment after being taught how to search for jobs cannot make any claims about impacting the general unemployment rate.

BOX 29.2

Published Examples of Process Evaluations

Substantive areas are in **bold**.

Allen, J., Philliber, S., & Hoggson, N. (1990). School-based prevention of **teen-age pregnancy and school dropout**: Process evaluation of the National Replication of the Teen Outreach Program. *American Journal of Community Psychology, 18,* 505–524.

Andersson, L. (1984). Intervention against loneliness in a group of **elderly women**: A process evaluation. *Human Relations, 37,* 295–310.

Bazemore, G., & Cruise, P. (1993). Resident adaptations in an Alcoholics Anonymous based residential program for the **urban homeless**. *Social Service Review, 67,* 599–616.

Bentelspacher, C., DeSilva, E, Goh, T., & LaRowe, K. (1996). A process evaluation of the cultural compatibility of psychoeducational family group treatment with **ethnic Asian** clients. *Social Work with Groups, 19,* 41–55.

Berkowitz, G., Halfon, N., & Klee, L. (1992). Improving access to health care: Case management for **vulnerable children**. *Social Work in Health Care, 17,* 101–123.

Blaze Temple, D., & Honig, F. (1997). Process evaluation of an Australian EAP. *Employee Assistance Quarterly, 12,* 15–35.

Cheung, K., & Canda, E. (1992). Training **Southeast Asian refugees** as social workers: Single-subject evaluation. *Social Development Issues, 14,* 88–99.

Deacon, S., & Piercy, F. (2000). Qualitative evaluation of **family therapy** programs: A participatory approach. *Journal of Marital and Family Therapy, 26,* 39–45.

Dehar, M., Casswell, S., & Duignan, P. (1993). Formative and process evaluation of health promotion and disease prevention programs. *Evaluation Review, 17,* 204–220.

Devaney, B., & Rossi, P. (1997). Thinking through evalua-

tion design options. *Children and Youth Services Review, 19,* 587–606.

Jackson, J. (1991). The use of psychoeducational evaluations in the clinical process: **Therapists** as sympathetic advocates. *Child and Adolescent Social Work Journal, 8,* 473–487.

Jones, L., & Strandness, D. (1991). Integrating research activities, practice changes, and monitoring and evaluation: A model for academic health centers. *Quality Review Bulletin, 17,* 229–235.

Lusk, M. (1983). The psychosocial evaluation of the **hospice patient**. *Health and Social Work, 8,* 210–218.

Miller, T., Veltkamp, L., & Janson, D. (1988). Projective measures in the clinical evaluation of **sexually abused children**. *Child Psychiatry and Human Development. 18,* 47–57.

Pithers, W. (1994). Process evaluation of a group therapy component designed to enhance sex offenders' empathy for **sexual abuse survivors**. *Behavior Research and Therapy, 32,* 565–570.

Pithers, W. (1999). Empathy definition, enhancement, and relevance to the treatment of **sexual abusers**. *Journal of Interpersonal Violence, 14,* 257–284.

Rotheram, M. (1987). Evaluation of imminent danger for **suicide among youth**. *American Journal of Orthopsychiatry, 57,* 102–110.

Sieppert, J.D., Hudson, J., & Unrau, Y.A. (2000). **Family group conferencing** in child welfare: Lessons from a demonstration project. *Families in Society, 81,* 382–391.

Smith, M., Knickman, J., & Oppenheimer, L. (1992). Connecting the disconnected adult day care for **people with AIDS** in New York City. *Health and Social Work, 17,* 273–281.

The results are *specific* to one *specific* group of clients, experiencing the *specific* conditions of one *specific* program over a *specific* time frame at a *specific* time.

Outcome evaluations tell us *whether* programs are working, but they are silent about *why* programs are working (or failing to work). For this reason they are often dubbed the "black box" evaluation. Nor is there any mention of the costs associated with of client success. After all, if a program achieves what it is supposed to achieve, via the attainment of its program objectives, what does it matter how it achieves it? If the program is to be replicated or even improved, it does matter; nev-

ertheless, client outcome alone is the focus of many evaluations.

Outcomes and Outputs

Outcomes are sometimes confused with outputs. Outputs are completed products or amount of work done resulting from internal program activities. For example, the number of clients served, the total hours of counseling services provided, and the number of crisis calls received. The pressure to collect data on program outputs typically comes from program funders.

While *outputs* focus on the results of program operations, *outcomes* focus on the results of client change. Programs declare their targeted outcomes by articulating and documenting program objectives.

The distinction between outcomes and outputs is important to understand because high outputs are not always associated with positive outcomes, and vice versa. For example, a program that aims to reduce the number of high school dropouts among Native American youth may report high outputs (e.g., an average of 10 counseling hours per week to all 12 Native American youth in a school for the three-month period of the program) but poor outcomes (e.g., half of the 12 youth drop out of high school by the end of the three-month period).

When outcomes are defined in terms of counting events or occurrences, they can be measured with little effort. It is relatively easy to tally the number of kids who stay in school, or how many welfare recipients find full-time work, or the number of completed adoptions in a given year. Outcome evaluations of social service programs, however, are not simple counting exercises because the targeted events or occurrences are often beyond the scope of the programs. For example, a school year may be 9 months long but the drop-out prevention program only lasts for three months. Additionally, outcomes sometimes identify difficult-to-measure concepts—such as family functioning and acceptance of diversity.

As discussed in Chapter 2, social service programs are often faced with limited resources (e.g., not enough staff, time, or money), as well as a limited knowledge base. In the face of these limitations, social workers define program objectives or outcomes in terms of smaller client changes that, if accomplished, will eventually lead to positive outcomes. The program to prevent Native American youth from dropping out of high school may pare down its objectives to increase youths' self-esteem or to improve students' literacy skills, for example. These program objectives are targeted because workers believe that increased self-esteem and improved literacy skills will keep Native American youth in school.

Benchmarking

A challenge of selecting outcomes (or objectives) for a specific social service program is setting sites for desired change high enough to produce a meaningful amount of client change but not so high that the program will never successfully achieve its objectives. We have already addressed this challenge to some degree by paying attention to how we phrase program objectives. Instead of claiming to eradicate domestic violence, for example, program objectives are more likely to claim "reducing" domestic violence. Rather than expunge social problems, programs aim to restore positive conditions or diminish negative ones.

How much change programs can reasonably expect to achieve can be thought out through benchmarking, which is a strategy that flags expected rates of change. Examples of benchmarking program outcomes include: 95 percent of clients will secure full-time employment within six months of completing the program, 70 percent of adolescents will show a minimum increase of 10 self-esteem points (as measured on a self-esteem scale) by the end of the program. In short, benchmarking concretizes the program's objectives by setting numerical markers of change. Of course, benchmarking can also be applied to program outputs.

How does one decide a benchmark value? Is it likely that 95 percent of clients will secure full-time employment within six months of a program, or is 55 percent a more realistic figure? Most social service programs address chronic social problems that are unlikely to disappear with one dose of a single program. One way to establish benchmark values is to examine outcome rates of other similar programs. Evaluation and research studies of family preservation programs, for example, typically report that 80 percent or more families are preserved (i.e., a child that was at-risk for out-of-home placement remained in the home) after about three months of intensive in-home intervention. New family preservation programs, therefore, can safely choose to benchmark their preservation rate at 80 percent, or perhaps 70 percent to give leniency to program start-up pains.

When programs address social problems where repeat offenses are high (e.g., perpetrators of child sexual abuse and drug addictions) or problems are chronic (e.g., developmental disabilities or mental illness), the benchmark value for change may be low, say 10 percent improvement. To set a program's sites unrealistically high is to set up false hopes and unrealistic expectations for program workers and clients alike.

The most important feature of benchmarking is selecting a known value. If a benchmark value cannot be discerned from existing research or evaluation reports, then programs can determine their own rates by establishing a baseline measure. This is simply achieved by avoiding benchmarks altogether for the first year of the program. At the year's end, the program can calculate the average amount of change by clients using data collected to measure program objectives. This figure then can be used or adjusted (higher or lower) as the benchmark for the following year.

Consumer Satisfaction

Consumer satisfaction is an elusive concept for social service programs. As social workers, we want our clients to feel content with their experiences in our programs. Yet for many social service clients a move to positive change involves periods of considerable personal discomfort and distress. A battered woman must often be confronted with the realities of risk to her (and her children's) physical safety, for example, before she will choose to leave an abusive partner. Moreover, many clients do not end up reaching the expected outcomes pledged by the programs they receive services from. Nevertheless, measuring satisfaction of social service program is a concern of all stakeholder groups.

Satisfaction measures can yield fertile data for programs that serve hard-to-reach or diverse client groups. Program services must be marketed, offered, implemented, and evaluated in diversity-sensitive ways. When serving diverse populations (e.g., gay and lesbian, racial and ethnic minorities, women, the elderly), satisfaction measures can gauge whether the program is neglecting or offending important values of particular groups.

Policymakers, administrators, funders, and practitioners want reassurance that clients and the general public are satisfied with the services they receive from social programs. Because clients are direct users of the social services, it is they who are most often asked about their satisfaction with program services, as well as about any results they experienced.

In a nutshell, satisfaction, as an outcome, measures clients' contentment or approval with a program. As it is, most clients who respond to satisfaction surveys do so favorably; that is, programs can expect that the majority of their clients will report being reasonably satisfied with program services. Programs with less than 75 percent of clients expressing satisfaction are atypical. As such, most programs that choose to benchmark client satisfaction can safely aim for 75 percent satisfaction from their clients.

Staff in programs with less than 75 percent of clients expressing satisfaction with services may well want to reflect on their program operations and client service delivery system in light of the complaints received. Client satisfaction is almost never the central focus of outcome evaluation because such measures show little variation. Additionally, satisfaction is rarely the only measurement in an outcome evaluation.

Outcome Questions

There are many examples of how outcome evaluations can help us in our professional practice (see Box 29.3). The questions they can answer can be classified under five general categories.

- Program Integrity: Is the program achieving the desired client change? To what degree is the program accomplishing its program objectives? Is the program achieving predetermined minimum standards of achievement (benchmarks)?
- Program Effects: Are people who have been through the program better for it? Are they better off than others who went through similar programs? How long do client improvements last?
- Differential Effects: Given the demographics of clients served, are there subgroups of clients who experience more success than others?
- Causality: Is there any evidence that the program can claim responsibility for positive changes in clients?
- Satisfaction: Are stakeholders satisfied with program services?

COST-BENEFIT EVALUATION

Administrators of social service programs are concerned with the costs associated in producing their pro-

BOX 29.3

Published Examples of Outcome Evaluations

Substantive areas are in **bold**.

Auslander, W., Haire-Joshu, D., Houston, C., Williams, J.H., & Krebill, H. (2000). The short-term impact of a health promotion program for **low-income African American women**. *Research on Social Work Practice, 10*, 78–97.

Bacha, T., Pomeroy, E.C., & Gilbert, D. (1999). A psychoeducational group intervention for **HIV-positive children**: A pilot study. *Health and Social Work, 24*, 303–306.

Bagley, C., & Young, L. (1998). Long-term evaluation of group counseling of **women with a history of child sexual abuse**: Focus on depression, self-esteem, suicidal behaviors, and social support. *Social Work with Groups, 21*, 63–73.

Barber, J., & Gilbertson, R. (1998). Evaluation of a self-help manual for the **female partners of heavy drinkers**. *Research on Social Work Practice, 8*, 141–151.

Barker, S.B., Knisely, J.S., & Dawson, K. (1999). The evaluation of a consultation service for delivery of **substance abuse services** in a hospital setting. *Journal of Addictive Diseases, 18*, 73–82.

Burry, C.L. (1999). Evaluation of a training program for **foster parents** of infants with prenatal substance effects. *Child Welfare, 78*, 197–214.

Collins, M.E., Mowbray, C.T., & Bybee, D. (1999). Measuring coping strategies in an educational intervention for **individuals with psychiatric disabilities**. *Health and Social Work, 24*, 279–290.

Comer, E., & Fraser, M. (1998). Evaluation of six **family-support programs**: Are they effective? *Families in Society, 79*, 134–148.

Conboy, A., Auerbach, C., Schnall, D., & LaPorte, H. (2000). **MSW student** satisfaction with using single-system design computer software to evaluate social work practice. *Research on Social Work Practice, 10*, 127–138.

Deacon, S.A., & Piercy, F.P. (2000). Qualitative evaluation of **family** therapy programs: A participatory approach. *Journal of Marital and Family Therapy, 26*, 39–45.

de Anda, D. (1999). Project Peace: The evaluation of a skill-based violence prevention program for **high school adolescents**. *Social Work in Education. 21*, 137–149.

Deschenes, E., & Greenwood, P. (1998). Alternative placements for **juvenile offenders**: Results from the evaluation of the Nokomis challenge program. *Journal of Research in Crime and Delinquency, 35*, 267–294.

Ford, C.A., & Okojie, F.A. (1999). A multi-dimensional approach to evaluating **family preservation programs**. *Family Preservation Journal, 4*, 31–62.

Harrison, R.S., Boyle, S.W., Farley, W. (1999). Evaluating the outcomes of family-based intervention for **troubled children**: A pretest-posttest study. *Research on Social Work Practice, 9*, 640–655.

Hughes, R.H., & Kirby, J. (2000). Strengthening evaluation strategies for **divorcing family support services**: Perspectives of parent educators, mediators, attorneys, and judges. *Family Relations, 49*, 53–61.

Jenson, J.M., Jacobson, M., Unrau, Y.A., & Robinson, R.L. (1996). Intervention for victims of child sexual abuse: An evaluation of the children's advocacy model. *Child and Adolescent Social Work Journal, 13*, 139–156.

Jinich, S., & Litrownik, A. (1999). Coping with **sexual abuse**: Development and evaluation of a videotape intervention for nonoffending parents. *Child Abuse and Neglect, 23*, 175–190.

Mecca, W.F., Rivera, A., & Esposito, A.J. (2000). Instituting an outcomes assessment effort: Lessons from the field. *Families in Society, 81*, 85–89.

Myers, L., & Rittner, B. (1999). Family functioning and satisfaction of **former residents of a non-therapeutic residential care facility**: An exploratory study. *Journal of Family Social Work, 3*, 54–68.

Nicholson, B.C., Brenner, V., & Fox, R.A. (1999). A community-based parenting program with **low-income mothers of young children**. *Families in Society, 80*, 247–253.

Prior, V., Lynch, M.A., & Glaser, D. (1999). Responding to **child sexual abuse**: an evaluation of social work by children and their carers. *Child and Family Social Work, 4*, 131–143.

Raschick, M., & Critchley, R. (1998). Guidelines for conducting site-based evaluations of intensive **family preservation programs**. *Child Welfare, 77*, 643–660.

Salzer, M.S., Rappaport, J., & Segre, L. (1999). Professional appraisal of professionally led and **self-help groups**. *American Journal of Orthopsychiatry, 69*, 530–540.

Scriven, M. (1999). The fine line between evaluation and explanation. *Research on Social Work Practice, 9*, 521–524.

Secret, M., Jordan, A., & Ford, J. (1999). Empowerment evaluation as a social work strategy. *Health and Social Work, 24*, 120–127.

Shifflett, K., & Cummings, E.M. (1999). A program for educating parents about the effects of **divorce and conflict on children**: An initial evaluation. *Family Relations, 48*, 79–89.

(continued)

BOX 29.3

(continued)

Short, J.L. (1998). Evaluation of a substance abuse prevention and mental health promotion program for **children of divorce**. *Journal of Divorce and Remarriage, 28*, 139–155.

Smith, L., Riley, E., Beilenson., P., Vlahov, D., & Junge, B. (1998). A focus group evaluation of drop boxes for safe **syringe disposal**. *Journal of Drug Issues, 28*, 905–920.

Stone, G., McKenry, P., & Clark, K. (1999). Fathers' participation in a **divorce education program**: A qualitative evaluation. *Journal of Divorce and Remarriage, 30*, 99–113.

Welsh, W., Jenkins, P., & Harris, P. (1999). Reducing **minority** over-representation in juvenile justice: Results of community-based delinquency prevention in Harrisburg. *Journal of Research in Crime and Delinquency, 36*, 87–110.

grams' objectives, which leads us to a fifth type of evaluation, cost-benefit evaluation. Improving human lives and social conditions is a priority of all social service programs, but we are expected to accomplish a program's objectives in an efficient and cost-effective manner. A program is considered cost-efficient when it is able to achieve its program objectives at lower cost compared with another program striving for the same program objectives.

A "probation program," for example, costs less than a "jail program" simply because the probation program is not required to have 24-hour supervision, an institutional facility, and so on. If the probation program is successful in preventing future criminal behavior, the savings are even greater. Costs associated with prevention, however, are difficult to estimate because we cannot know for certain whether the absence of the problem was a result of the program.

Cost-benefit evaluations alone provide us with data and information associated with program expenses. When combined with process and outcome evaluation, data from cost-benefit evaluations can give us valuable insight as to how program resources are best allocated. Because cost-benefit evaluations produce dollar figures for program processes and outcomes, they have utility only when we know precisely what the program is doing (process evaluation) and precisely how much client change is produced (outcome evaluation).

Figuring Costs

A simple way to calculate general costs of a program is to first determine the total amount of money spent on program operations. These expenditures include costs associated with personnel (e.g., salaries, benefits, training), facilities (e.g., office space, computers, telephone, photocopying), clients (e.g., petty cash, special services, food), and other needs of the program. Once the overall costs have been determined, we can divide this amount by the total number of clients served for that fiscal period. The result will be an "outside estimate" of how much the program spent per client. For more detailed information on program effectiveness, we need to pay attention to program structure and process, something we do through process evaluation. The figures at the end of our calculations fluctuate, depending on what we have included in program costs and how we have counted clients.

Neither of these tasks is as straightforward as it may seem. Do we include overtime, secretarial support, and advertising in our program costs, for example? In the case of counting clients, do we include repeat clients, or clients who drop out of the program after the first day? Do we factor in clients who call the program for information but never actually participate? The way a social service program is conceptualized has a considerable influence on the way data are collected and analyzed, as well as how costs are calculated.

Valuing Human Experiences

Cost-benefit evaluations in social services are necessary for fiscal accountability but are not sufficient for understanding the nature of human conditions or how social programs endeavor to improve them. It is difficult, if not impossible, to place a dollar amount on people's experience with social problems. How much does it cost to stop child abuse, for example? How much should society spend to bring discrimination of the elderly to an end? Such questions cannot be addressed in program-level evaluations.

Cost-benefit evaluations are particularly difficult to carry out in social work because so many of our client outcomes cannot be realistically (socially and professionally) measured in terms of dollars. In fact, it would be unthinkable to measure some client outcomes in terms of efficiency—such as counseling terminally ill cancer patients. Efficiency in terms of what?

The benefits of a job-training program that removes its clients from welfare rolls can be more easily quantified in terms of efficiency (cost savings) than a program that is designed to reduce the feeling of hopelessness in terminal cancer patients. Nevertheless, there is only so much money available for social service programs, and decisions regarding which ones to fund, no matter how difficult, have to be made—especially if funding deci-

---

BOX 29.4

Published Examples of Cost-Benefit Evaluations

Substantive areas are in **bold**.

Beshai, N.N. (1991). Providing cost efficient detoxification services to **alcoholic patients**. *Public Health Reports, 105*, 475–481.

Egger, G.M., Friedman, B., & Zimmer, J.G. (1990). Models of **intensive case management**. *Journal of Gerontological Social Work, 15*, 75–101.

Ell, K. (1996). Social work and **health care practice** and policy: A psychosocial research agenda. *Social Work, 41*, 583–592.

Essock, S.M., Frisman, L.K., & Kontos, N.J. (1998). Cost-effectiveness of assertive **community treatment teams**. *American Journal of Orthopsychiatry, 68*, 179–190.

Fahs, M.C., & Wade, K. (1996). An economic analysis of two models of hospital care for **AIDS patients**: Implications for hospital discharge planning. *Social Work in Health Care, 22*, 21–34.

Greene, V.L., Lovely, M.E., & Ondrich, J.I. (1993). The cost-effectiveness of community services in a **frail elderly population**. *The Gerontologist, 33*, 177–189.

Holosko, M.J., Dobrowolsky, J., & Feit, M.D. (1990). A proposed cost effectiveness method for use in policy formulation in **human service organizations**. *Journal of Health and Social Policy, 1*, 55–71.

Holtgrave, D.R., & Kelly, J.A. (1998). Cost-effectiveness of an **HIV/AIDS prevention intervention for gay men**. *AIDS, and Behavior, 1*, 173–180.

Hughes, W.C. (1999). Managed care meets community support: Ten reasons to include **direct support services** in every behavioral health plan. *Health and Social Work, 4*, 103–111.

Jackson, N., Olsen, L., & Schafer, C. (1986). Evaluating the treatment of **emotionally disturbed adolescents**. *Social Work, 31*, 182–185.

Keigher, S.M. (1997). What role for social work in the new **health care practice** paradigm? *Health and Social Work, 22*, 149–155.

Knapp, M. (1988). Searching for efficiency in long-term care: De-Institutionalisation and privatisation. *The British Journal of Social Work, 18*, 149–171.

Levy, R.L., & Bavendam, T.G. (1995). Promoting **women's urologic self-care**: Five single-case replications. *Research on Social Work Practice, 5*, 430–441.

Pike, C.L., & Piercy, F.P. (1991). Cost effectiveness research in **family therapy**. *Journal of Marital and Family Therapy, 16*, 375–388.

Pinkerton, S.D., & Holtgrave, D.R. (1998). A method for evaluating the economic efficiency of **HIV behavioral risk reduction interventions**. *AIDS, and Behavior, 2*, 189–201.

Prentky, R., & Burgess, A.W. (1990). Rehabilitation of **child molesters**: A cost-benefit analysis. *American Journal of Orthopsychiatry, 60*, 108–117.

Robertson, E., & Knapp, M. (1988). Promoting **intermediate treatment**: A problem of excess demand or excess supply? *The British Journal of Social Work, 8*, 131–147.

Segal, E.A., & Gustavsson, N.S. (1990). The high cost of neglecting **children**: The need for a preventive policy agenda. *Child and Adolescent Social Work Journal, 7*, 475–485.

Winegar, N., Bistline, J.L., & Sheridan, S. (1992). Implementing a **group therapy program** in a managed-care setting: Combining cost effectiveness and quality care. *Families in Society, 73*, 56–58.

sions are made on efficiency criteria. We do not need to put a price on program results in order to use costs in decision making, but it is necessary to be able to describe in detail what results have been achieved via the expenditure of what resources.

The role of cost-benefit evaluation for social service programs is not to attempt placing a value on human lives or experiences. Rather, it provides social workers a means to demonstrate responsible use of public funds. In so doing, we report not only the outputs and outcomes accomplished with support of program funds but also significant developments in our program's processes. Highlighting program developments along with program outcomes can show how we, as a profession, contribute to the understanding the complexities of the populations and problems targeted.

Another role of cost-benefit evaluation is to bring to light the real costs associated with studying and resolving social problems in society. Moreover, such evaluations can provide data that not only support future program funding requests but also allocate money to pay for associated evaluation efforts.

Cost-Benefit Questions

There are many examples of how cost-benefit evaluations can help us in our professional practice (see Box 29.4). The questions they can answer can be classified under three general categories.

- Unit Costs: What is the average cost per client? What is the average cost per unit of service (e.g., intake, assessment, intervention, follow-up)?
- Cost Distribution: What percentage of costs goes to direct client services, administrative activities, and program development? What services were not provided because of lack of funds?
- Cost Reduction/Recovery: Is there any way in which cost could be reduced without loss of effectiveness, perhaps by offering group therapy instead of individual therapy? Are strategies for cost recovery possible?

SUMMARY

This chapter briefly presented five types of evaluations. It stressed that each one has its separate purpose and each one answers a different type of evaluation question. It should be noted that program evaluations use many the research techniques that are contained in this book. Thus, a through understanding of this book's contents in very important before one does a program evaluation.

Glossary

Yvonne A. Unrau

Judy L. Krysik

Richard M. Grinnell, Jr.

Abstracting indexing services Providers of specialized reference tools that make it possible to find information quickly and easily, usually through subject headings and/or author approaches.

Abstracts Reference materials consisting of citations and brief descriptive summaries from positivist and interpretive research studies.

Accountability A system of responsibility in which program administrators account for all program activities by answering to the demands of a program's stakeholders and by justifying the program's expenditures to the satisfaction of its stakeholders.

Aggregated case-level evaluation designs The collection of a number of case-level evaluations to determine the degree to which a program objective has been met.

Aggregate-level data Derived from micro-level data, aggregate-level data are grouped so that the characteristics of individual units of analysis are no longer identifiable; for example, the variable "gross national income" is an aggregation of data about individual incomes.

Alternate-forms method A method for establishing reliability of a measuring instrument by administering, in succession, equivalent forms of the same instrument to the same group of research participants.

Alternative hypothesis See *Rival hypothesis.*

Analytical memos Notes made by the researcher in reference to interpretive data that raise questions or make comments about meaning units and categories identified in a transcript.

Analytic generalization The type of generalizability associated with case studies; the research findings of case studies are not assumed to fit another case no matter how apparently similar; rather, research findings are tested to see if they do in fact fit; used as working hypotheses to test practice principles.

Annual report A detailed account or statement describing a program's processes and results over a given year, usually produced at the end of a fiscal year.

Antecedent variable A variable that precedes the introduction of one or more dependent variables.

Antiquarianism An interest in past events without reference to their importance or significance for the present; the reverse of presentism.

A Phase In case-level evaluation designs, a phase (*A Phase*) in which the baseline measurement of the target problem is established before the intervention (*B Phase*) is implemented.

Applied research approach A search for practical and applied research results that can be used in actual social work practice situations; complementary to the pure research approach.

Area probability sampling A form of cluster sampling that uses a three-stage process to provide the means to carry out a research study when no comprehensive list of the population can be compiled.

Assessment-related case study A type of case study that generates knowledge about specific clients and their situations; focuses on the perspectives of the study's participants.

Audit trail The documentation of critical steps in an interpretive research study that allows for an independent reviewer to examine and verify the steps in the research process and the conclusions of the research study.

Authority The reliance on authority figures to tell us what is true; one of the six ways of knowing.

Availability sampling See *Convenience sampling.*

Axes Straight horizontal and vertical lines in a graph upon which values of a measurement, or the corresponding frequencies, are plotted.

Back-translation The process of translating an original document into a second language, then having an independent translator conduct a subsequent translation of the first translation back into the language of origin; the second translation is then compared with the original document for equivalency.

Baseline A period of time, usually three or four data collection periods, in which the level of the client's target problem is measured while no intervention is carried out; designated as the *A* Phase in single-system designs (case-level designs).

Between research methods approach Triangulation by using different research methods available in *both* the interpretive and the positivist research approaches in a single research study.

Bias Not neutral; an inclination to some form of prejudice or preconceived position.

Biased sample A sample unintentionally selected in such a way that some members of the population are more likely than others to be picked for sample membership.

Binomial effect size display (BESD) A technique for interpreting the *r* value in a meta-analysis by converting it into a 2 × 2 table displaying magnitude of effect.

Biography Tells the story of one individual's life, often suggesting what the person's influence was on social, political, or intellectual developments of the times.

B Phase In case-level evaluation designs, the intervention phase, which may, or may not, include simultaneous measurements.

Case The basic unit of social work practice, whether it be an individual, a couple, a family, an agency, a community, a county, a state, or a country.

Case-level evaluation designs Designs in which data are collected about a single-client system—an individual, group, or community—in order to evaluate the outcome of an intervention for the client system; a form of appraisal that monitors change for individual clients; designs in which data are collected about a single-client system—an individual, group, or community—in order to evaluate the outcome of an intervention for the client system; also called single-system research designs.

Case study Using research approaches to investigate a research question or hypothesis relating to a specific case; used to develop theory and test hypotheses; an in-depth form of research in which data are gathered and analyzed about an individual unit of analysis, person, city, event, or society. It allows more intensive analysis of specific details; the disadvantage is that it is hard to use the results to generalize to other cases.

Categories Groupings of related meaning units that are given one name; used to organize, summarize, and interpret qualitative data. Categories in an interpretive study can change throughout the data analysis process, and the number of categories in a given study depends upon the breadth and depth the researcher aims for in the analysis.

Category In an interpretive data analysis, an aggregate of meaning units that share a common feature.

Category saturation The point in a qualitative data analysis when all identified meaning units fit easily into the existing categorization scheme and no new categories emerge; the point at which first-level coding ends.

Causality A relationship of cause and effect; the effect will invariably occur when the cause is present.

Causal relationship A relationship between two variables for which we can state that the presence of, or absence of, one variable determines the presence of, or absence of, the other variable.

CD-ROM sources Computerized retrieval systems that allow searching for indexes and abstracts stored on compact computer discs (CDs).

Census data Data from the survey of an entire population in contrast to a survey of a sample.

Citation A brief identification of a reference that includes name of author(s), title, source, page numbers, and year of publication.

Classic experimental design An explanatory research design with randomly assigned experimental and control groups in which the dependent variable is measured before and after the treatment (the independent variable) for both groups, but only the experimental group receives the treatment (the dependent variable).

Client system *An* individual client, *a* couple, *a* family, *a* group, *an* organization, or *a* community that can be studied with case- and program-level evaluation designs and with positivist and interpretive research approaches.

Closed-ended questions Items in a measuring instrument that require respondents to select one of several response categories provided; also known as fixed-alternative questions.

Cluster diagram An illustration of a conceptual classification scheme in which the researcher draws and labels circles for each theme that emerges from the data; the circles are organized in a way to depict the relationships between themes.

Cluster sampling A multistage probability sampling procedure in which the population is divided into groups (or clusters); the groups, rather than the individuals, are selected for inclusion in the sample.

Code The label assigned to a category or theme in a qualitative data analysis; shortened versions of the actual category or theme label; used as markers in a qualitative data analysis;

usually no longer than eight characters in length and can use a combination of letters, symbols, and numbers.

Codebook A device used to organize qualitative data by applying labels and descriptions that draw distinctions between different parts of the data that have been collected.

Coding (1) In data analysis, translating data from respondents onto a form that can be read by a computer; (2) In interpretive research, marking the text with codes for content categories.

Coding frame A specific framework that delineates what data are to be coded and how they are to be coded in order to prepare them for analyses.

Coding sheets In a literature review, a sheet used to record for each research study the complete reference, research design, measuring instrument(s), population and sample, outcomes, and other significant features of the study.

Cohort study A longitudinal survey design that uses successive random samples to monitor how the characteristics of a specific group of people, who share certain characteristics or experiences (cohorts), change over time.

Collaterals Professionals or staff members who serve as indigenous observers in the data collection process.

Collective biographies Studies of the characteristics of groups of people who lived during a past period and had some major factor in common.

Collectivist culture Societies that stress interdependence and seek the welfare and survival of the group above that of the individual; collectivist cultures are characterized by a readiness to be influenced by others, preference for conformity, and cooperation in relationships.

Comparative rating scale A rating scale in which respondents are asked to compare an individual person, concept, or situation with others.

Comparative research design The study of more than one event, group, or society to isolate explanatory factors; there are two basic strategies in comparative research: (1) the study of elements that differ in many ways but that have some major factor in common, and (2) the study of elements that are highly similar but different in some important aspect, such as modern industrialized nations that have different health insurance systems.

Comparison group A nonexperimental group to which research participants have not been randomly assigned for purposes of comparison with the experimental group. Not to be confused with control group.

Comparison group posttest-only design A descriptive research design with two groups, experimental and comparison, in which the dependent variable is measured once for both groups, and only the experimental group receives the treatment (the independent variable).

Comparison group pretest-posttest design A descriptive research design with two groups, experimental and comparison, in which the dependent variable is measured before and after the treatment for both groups, but only the experimental group receives the treatment.

Compensation Attempts by researchers to compensate for the lack of treatment for control group members by administering it to them; a threat to internal validity.

Compensatory rivalry Motivation of control group members to compete with experimental group members; a threat to internal validity.

Completeness One of the four criteria for evaluating research hypotheses.

Complete observer A term describing one of four possible research roles on a continuum of participant observation research; the complete observer acts simply as an observer and does not participate in the events at hand.

Complete participant The complete participant is at the far end of the continuum from the complete observer in participant observation research; this research role is characterized by total involvement.

Comprehensive qualitative review A nonstatistical synthesis of representative research studies relevant to a research problem, question, or hypothesis.

Computerized retrieval systems Systems in which abstracts, indexes, and subject bibliographies are incorporated in computerized databases to facilitate information retrieval.

Concept An understanding, an idea, or a mental image; a way of viewing and categorizing objects, processes, relations, and events.

Conceptual classification system The strategy for conceiving how units of qualitative data relate to each other; the method used to depict patterns that emerge from the various coding levels in qualitative data.

Conceptual framework A frame of reference that serves to guide a research study and is developed from theories, findings from a variety of other research studies, and the author's personal experiences and values.

Conceptualization The process of selecting the specific concepts to include in positivist and interpretive research studies.

Conceptual validity See *Construct validity*.

Concurrent validity A form of criterion validity that is concerned with the ability of a measuring instrument to predict accurately an individual's status by comparing concurrent ratings (or scores) on one or more measuring instruments.

Confidentiality An ethical consideration in research whereby anonymity of research participants is safeguarded by ensuring that raw data are not seen by anyone other than the research team and that data presented have no identifying marks.

Confounding variable A variable operating in a specific situation in such a way that its effects cannot be separated; the effects of an extraneous variable thus confound the interpretation of a research study's findings.

Consistency Holding steadfast to the same principles and procedures in the qualitative data analysis process.

Constant A concept that does not vary and does not change; a characteristic that has the same value for all research participants or events in a research study.

Constant comparison A technique used to categorize qualitative data; it begins after the complete set of data has been examined and meaning units identified; each unit is classified as similar or different from the others; similar meaning units are lumped into the same category and classified by the same code.

Constant error Systematic error in measurement; error due to factors that consistently or systematically affect the variable being measured and that are concerned with the relatively stable qualities of respondents to a measuring instrument.

Construct See *Concept*.

Construct validity The degree to which a measuring instrument successfully measures a theoretical construct; the degree to which explanatory concepts account for variance in the scores of an instrument; also referred to as conceptual validity in meta-analyses.

Content analysis A data collection method in which communications are analyzed in a systematic, objective, and quantitative manner to produce new data.

Content validity The extent to which the content of a measuring instrument reflects the concept that is being measured and in fact measures that concept and not another.

Contextual detail The particulars of the environment in which the case (or unit of analysis) is embedded; provides a basis for understanding and interpreting case study data and results.

Contradictory evidence Identifying themes and categories that raise questions about the conclusions reached at the end of qualitative data analysis; outliers or extreme cases that are inconsistent or contradict the conclusions drawn from qualitative data; also called negative evidence.

Contributing partner A social work role in which the social worker joins forces with others who perform different roles in positivist and interpretive research studies.

Control group A group of randomly assigned research participants in a research study who do not receive the experimental treatment and are used for comparison purposes. Not to be confused with comparison group.

Control variable A variable, other than the independent variable(s) of primary interest, whose effects we can determine; an intervening variable that has been controlled for in the study's research design.

Convenience sampling A nonprobability sampling procedure that relies on the closest and most available research participants to constitute a sample.

Convergent validity The degree to which different measures of a construct yield similar results, or converge.

Correlated variables Variables whose values are associated; values of one variable tend to be associated in a systematic way with values in the others.

Cost-benefit analysis An analytical procedure that not only determines the costs of the program itself but also considers the monetary benefits of the program's effects.

Cost-effectiveness analysis An analytical procedure that assesses the costs of the program itself; the monetary benefits of the program's effects are not assessed.

Cover letter A letter to respondents or research participants that is written under the official letterhead of the sponsoring organization and describes the research study and its purpose.

Credibility The trustworthiness of both the steps taken in qualitative data analysis and the conclusions reached.

Criterion validity The degree to which the scores obtained on a measuring instrument are comparable with scores from an external criterion believed to measure the same concept.

Criterion variable The variable whose values are predicted from measurements of the predictor variable.

Cross-cultural comparisons Research studies that include culture as a major variable; studies that compare two or more diverse cultural groups.

Cross-sectional research design A survey research design in which data are collected to indicate characteristics of a sample or population at a particular moment in time.

Cross-tabulation table A simple table showing the joint frequency distribution of two or more nominal level variables.

Cultural encapsulation The assumption that differences between groups represent some deficit or pathology.

Culturally equivalent Similarity in the meaning of a construct between two cultures.

Cultural relativity The belief that human thought and action can be judged only from the perspective of the culture out of which they have grown.

Cut-and-paste method A method of analyzing qualitative data whereby the researcher cuts segments of the typed transcript and sorts these cuttings into relevant groupings; it can be done manually or with computer assistance.

Data The numbers, words, or scores, generated by positivist and interpretive research studies. The word *data* is plural.

Data analyses The process of turning data into information; the process of reviewing, summarizing, and organizing isolated facts (data) such that they formulate a meaningful response to a research question.

Data archive A place where many data sets are stored and from which data can be accessed.

Data coding Translating data from one language or format into another, usually to make it readable for a computer.

Data collection method Procedures specifying techniques to be employed, measuring instruments to be used, and activities to be conducted in implementing a positivist or interpretive research study.

Data set A collection of related data items, such as the answers given by respondents to all the questions in a survey.

Data source The provider of the data, whether it be primary—the original source—or secondary—an intermediary between the research participant and the researcher analyzing the data.

Datum Singular of *data*.

Decision-making rule A statement that we use (in testing a hypothesis) to choose between the null hypothesis; indicates the range(s) of values of the observed statistic that leads to the rejection of the null hypothesis.

Deduction A conclusion about a specific case(s) based on the assumption that it shares a characteristic with an entire class of similar cases.

Deductive reasoning Forming a theory, making a deduction from the theory, and testing this deduction, or hypothesis, against reality; in research, applied to theory in order to arrive at a hypothesis that can be tested; a method of reasoning whereby a conclusion about specific cases is reached based on the assumption that they share characteristics with an entire class of similar cases.

Demand needs When needs are defined by only those individuals who indicate that they feel or perceive the need themselves.

Demographic data Vital and social facts that describe a sample or a population.

Demoralization Feelings of deprivation among control group members that may cause them to drop out of a research study; a threat to internal validity.

Dependability The soundness of both the steps taken in a qualitative data analysis and the conclusions reached.

Dependent events Events that influence the probability of occurrence of each other.

Dependent variable A variable that is dependent on, or caused by, another variable; an outcome variable, which is not manipulated directly but is measured to determine if the independent variable has had an effect.

Derived scores Raw scores of research participants, or groups, converted in such a way that meaningful comparisons with other individuals, or groups, are possible.

Descriptive research Research studies undertaken to increase precision in the definition of knowledge in a problem area where less is known than at the explanatory level; situated in the middle of the knowledge continuum.

Descriptive statistics Methods used for summarizing and describing data in a clear and precise manner.

Design bias Any effect that systematically distorts the outcome of a research study so that the study's results are not representative of the phenomenon under investigation.

Determinism A contention in positivist research studies that only an event that is true over time and place and that will occur independent of beliefs about it (a predetermined event) permits the generalization of a study's findings; one of the four main limitations of the positivist research approach.

Deterministic causation When a particular effect appears, the associated cause is always present; no other variables influence the relationship between cause and effect; the link between an independent variable that brings about the occurrence of the dependent variable every time.

Dichotomous variable A variable that can take on only one of two values.

Differential scale A questionnaire-type scale in which respondents are asked to consider questions representing different positions along a continuum and to select those with which they agree.

Differential selection A potential lack of equivalency among preformed groups of research participants; a threat to internal validity.

Diffusion of treatments Problems that may occur when experimental and control group members talk to each other about a research study; a threat to internal validity.

d index A measure of effect size in a meta-analysis.

Directional hypothesis See *One-tailed hypotheses.*

Directional test See *One-tailed hypotheses.*

Direct observation An obtrusive data collection method in which the focus is entirely on the behaviors of a group, or persons, being observed.

Direct observation notes These are the first level of field notes, usually chronologically organized, and they contain a detailed description of what was seen and heard; they may also include summary notes made after an interview.

Direct relationship A relationship between two variables such that high values of one variable are found with high values of the second variable, and vice versa.

Discriminant validity The degree to which a construct can be empirically differentiated, or discriminated from other constructs.

Divergent validity The extent to which a measuring instrument differs from other instruments that measure unrelated constructs.

Double-barreled question A question in a measuring instrument that contains two questions in one, usually joined by an *and* or an *or.*

Duration recording A method of data collection that includes direct observation of the target problem and recording of the length of time each occurrence lasts within a specified observation period.

Ecological fallacy An error of reasoning committed by coming to conclusions about individuals based only on data about groups.

Edge coding Adding a series of blank lines on the right side of the response category in a measuring instrument to aid in processing the data.

Effect size In meta-analysis, the most widely used measure of the dependent variable; the effect size statistic provides a measure of the magnitude of the relationship found between the variables of interest and allows for the computation of summary statistics that apply to the analysis of all the studies considered as a whole.

Empirical Knowledge derived from the six ways of knowing.

Error of central tendency A measurement error due to the tendency of observers to rate respondents in the middle of a variable's value range, rather than consistently too high or too low.

Error of measurement See *Measurement error.*

Ethical research project The systematic inquiry into a problem area in an effort to discover new knowledge or test existing ideas; the research study is conducted in accordance with professional standards.

Ethics in research Positivist and interpretive data that are collected and analyzed with careful attention to their accuracy, fidelity to logic, and respect for the feelings and rights of research participants; one of the four criteria for evaluating research problem areas *and* formulating research questions out of the problem areas.

Ethnicity A term that implies a common ancestry and cultural heritage and encompasses customs, values, beliefs, and behaviors.

Ethnocentricity Assumptions about normal behavior that are based on one's own cultural framework without taking cultural relativity into account; the failure to acknowledge alternative worldviews.

Ethnograph A computer software program that is designed for qualitative data analyses.

Ethnographic A form of content analysis used to document and explain the communication of meaning, as well as to verify theoretical relationships; any of several methods of describing social or cultural life based on direct, systematic observation, such as becoming a participant in a social system.

Ethnography The systematic study of human cultures and the similarities and dissimilarities between them.

Ethnomethodology Pioneered by Harold Garfinkel, this method of research focuses on the commonsense understanding of social life held by ordinary people (the ethos), usually as discovered through participant observation; often the observer's own methods of making sense of the situation become the object of investigation.

Evaluation A form of appraisal using valid and reliable research methods; there are numerous types of evaluations geared to produce data that in turn produce information that helps in the decision-making process; data from evaluations are used to develop quality programs and services.

Evaluative research designs Case- and program-level research designs that apply various research designs and data collection methods to find out if an intervention (or treatment) worked at the case level and if the social work program worked at the program level.

Existing documents Physical records left over from the past.

Existing statistics Previously calculated numerical summaries of data that exist in the public domain.

Experience and intuition Learning what is true through personal past experiences and intuition; two of the six ways of knowing.

Experiment A research study in which we have control over the levels of the independent variable and over the assignment of research participants, or objects, to different experimental conditions.

Experimental designs (1) Explanatory research designs or "ideal experiments"; (2) Case-level research designs that examine the question, "Did the client system improve because of social work intervention?"

Experimental group In an experimental research design, the group of research participants exposed to the manipulation of the independent variable; also referred to as a treatment group.

Explanatory research "Ideal" research studies undertaken to infer cause—effect and directional relationships in areas where a number of substantial research findings are already in place; situated at the top end of the knowledge continuum.

Exploratory research Research studies undertaken to gather data in areas of inquiry where very little is already known; situated at the lowest end of the knowledge continuum. See *Nonexperimental design.*

External evaluation An evaluation that is conducted by someone who does not have any connection with the program; usually an evaluation that is requested by the agency's funding sources; this type of evaluation complements an in-house evaluation.

External validity The extent to which the findings of a research study can be generalized outside the specific research situation.

Extraneous variables See *Rival hypothesis.*

Face validity The degree to which a measurement has self-evident meaning and measures what it appears to measure.

Feasibility One of the four criteria for evaluating research problem areas *and* formulating research questions out of the problem areas.

Feedback When data and information are returned to the persons who originally provided or collected them; used for informed decision making at the case and program levels; a basic principle underlying the design of evaluations.

Field notes A record, usually written, of events observed by a researcher. The notes are taken as the study proceeds, and later they are used for analyses.

Field research Research conducted in a real-life setting, not in a laboratory. The researcher neither creates nor manipulates anything within the study, but observes it.

Field-tested The pilot of an instrument or research method in conditions equivalent to those that will be encountered in the research study.

File drawer problem (1) In literature searches or reviews, the difficulty in locating studies that have not been published or are not easily retrievable; (2) In meta-analyses, errors in effect size due to reliance on published articles showing statistical significance.

Firsthand data Data obtained from people who directly experience the problem being studied.

First-level coding A process of identifying meaning units in a transcript, organizing the meaning units into categories, and assigning names to the categories.

Flexibility The degree to which the design and procedures of a research study can be changed to adapt to contextual demands of the research setting.

Focus group interview A group of people brought together to talk about their lives and experiences in free-flowing, open-ended discussions that usually focus on a single topic.

Formative evaluation A type of evaluation that focuses on obtaining data that are helpful in planning the program and in improving its implementation and performance.

Frequency recording A method of data collection by direct observations in which each occurrence of the target problem is recorded during a specified observation period.

Fugitive data Informal information found outside regular publishing channels.

Gaining access A term used in interpretive research to describe the process of engagement and relationship development between the researcher and the research participants.

Generalizable explanation evaluation model An evaluation model whose proponents believe that many solutions are possible for any one social problem and that the effects of programs will differ under different conditions.

Generalizing results Extending or applying the findings of a research study to individuals or situations not directly involved in the original research study; the ability to extend or apply the findings of a research study to subjects or situations that were not directly investigated.

Goal Attainment Scale (GAS) A modified measurement scale used to evaluate case or program outcomes.

Government documents Printed documents issued by local, state, and federal governments; such documents include reports of legislative committee hearings and investigations, studies commissioned by legislative commissions and executive agencies, statistical compilations such as the census, the regular and special reports of executive agencies, and much more.

Grand tour questions Queries in which research participants are asked to provide wide-ranging background information; mainly used in interpretive research studies.

Graphic rating scale A rating scale that describes an attribute on a continuum from one extreme to the other, with points of the continuum ordered in equal intervals and then assigned values.

Grounded theory A final outcome of the interpretive research process that is reached when the insights are grounded on observations and the conclusions seem to be firm.

Group evaluation designs Evaluation designs that are conducted with groups of cases for the purpose of assessing to what degree program objectives have been achieved.

Group research designs Research designs conducted with two or more groups of cases, or research participants, for the purpose of answering research questions or testing hypotheses.

Halo effect A measurement error due to the tendency of an observer to be influenced by a favorable trait(s) of a research participant(s).

Hawthorne effect Effects on research participants' behaviors or attitudes attributable to their knowledge that they are taking part in a research study; a reactive effect; a threat to external validity.

Heterogeneity of respondents The extent to which a research participant differs from other research participants.

Heuristic A theory used to stimulate creative thought and scientific activity.

Historical research The process by which we study the past; a method of inquiry that attempts to explain past events based on surviving artifacts.

History in research design The possibility that events not accounted for in a research design may alter the second and subsequent measurements of the dependent variable; a threat to internal validity.

Homogeneity of respondents The extent to which a research participant is similar to other research participants.

Hypothesis A theory-based prediction of the expected results of a research study; a tentative explanation that a relationship between or among variables exists.

Hypothetico-deductive method A hypothesis-testing approach that a hypothesis is derived on the deductions based from a theory.

Ideographic research Research studies that focus on unique individuals or situations.

Implementation of a program The action of carrying out a program in the way that it was designed.

Independent variable A variable that is not dependent on another variable but is believed to cause or determine changes in the dependent variable; an antecedent variable that is directly manipulated to assess its effect on the dependent variable.

Index A group of individual measures that, when combined, are meant to indicate some more general characteristic.

Indigenous observers People who are naturally a part of the research participants' environment and who perform the data collection function; includes relevant others (e.g., family members, peers) and collaterals (e.g., social workers, staff members).

Indirect measures A substitute variable, or a collection of representative variables, used when there is no direct measurement of the variable of interest; also called a proxy variable.

Individualism A way of living that stresses independence, personal rather than group objectives, competition, and power in relationships; achievement measured through success of the individual as opposed to the group.

Individual synthesis Analysis of published studies related to the subject under study.

Inductive reasoning Building on specific observations of events, things, or processes to make inferences or more general statements; in research studies, applied to data collection and research results to make generalizations to see if they fit a theory; a method of reasoning whereby a conclusion is reached by building on specific observations of events, things, or processes to make inferences or more general statements.

Inferential statistics Statistical methods that make it possible to draw tentative conclusions about the population based on observations of a sample selected from that population and, furthermore, to make a probability statement about those conclusions to aid in their evaluation.

Information anxiety A feeling attributable to a lack of understanding of information, being overwhelmed by the amount of information to be accessed and understood, or not knowing if certain information exists.

Informed consent Signed statements obtained from research participants prior to the initiation of the research study to inform them what their participation entails and that they are free to decline participation.

In-house evaluation An evaluation that is conducted by someone who works within a program; usually an evaluation for the purpose of promoting better client services; also known as an internal evaluation. This type of evaluation complements an external evaluation.

Institutional review boards (IRBs) Boards set up by institutions to protect research participants and to ensure that ethical issues are recognized and responded to in the a study's research design.

Instrumentation Weaknesses of a measuring instrument, such as invalidity, unreliability, improper administrations, or mechanical breakdowns; a threat to internal validity.

Integration Combining evaluation and day-to-day practice activities to develop a complete approach to client service delivery; a basic principle underlying the design of evaluations.

Interaction effects Effects produced by the combination of two or more threats to internal validity.

Internal consistency The extent to which the scores on two comparable halves of the same measuring instrument are similar; inter-item consistency.

Internal validity The extent to which it can be demonstrated that the independent variable within a research study is the only cause of change in the dependent variable; overall soundness of the experimental procedures and measuring instruments.

Interpretive research approach Research studies that focus on the facts of nature as they occur under natural conditions and emphasize qualitative description and generalization; a process of discovery sensitive to holistic and ecological issues; a research approach that is complementary to the positivist research approach.

Interobserver reliability The stability or consistency of observations made by two or more observers at one point in time.

Interpretive notes Notes on the researcher's interpretations of events that are kept separate from the record of the facts noted as direct observations.

Interquartile range A number that measures the variability of a data set; the distance between the 75th and 25th percentiles.

Interrater reliability The degree to which two or more independent observers, coders, or judges produce consistent results.

Interrupted time-series design An explanatory research design in which there is only one group of research participants and the dependent variable is measured repeatedly before and after treatment; used in case- and program-evaluation designs.

Interval level of measurement The level of measurement with an arbitrarily chosen zero point that classifies its values on an equally spaced continuum.

Interval recording A method of data collection that involves a continuous direct observation of an individual during specified observation periods divided into equal time intervals.

Intervening variable See *Rival hypothesis*.

Interview data Isolated facts that are gathered when research participants respond to carefully constructed research questions; data in the form of words, recorded by transcription.

Interviewing A conversation with a purpose.

Interview schedule A measuring instrument used to collect data in face-to-face and telephone interviews.

Intraobserver reliability The stability of observations made by a single observer at several points in time.

Intrusion into lives of research participants The understanding that specific data collection methods can have negative consequences for research participants; a criterion for selecting a data collection method.

Itemized rating scales A measuring instrument that presents a series of statements that respondents or observers rank in different positions on a specific attribute.

Journal A written record of the process of an interpretive research study. Journal entries are made on an ongoing basis throughout the study and include study procedures as well as the researcher's reactions to emerging issues and concerns during the data analysis process.

Key informants A subpopulation of research participants who seem to know much more about "the situation" than other research participants.

Knowledge base A body of knowledge and skills specific to a certain discipline.

Knowledge creator and disseminator A social work role in which the social worker actually carries out and disseminates the results of a positivist and/or interpretive research study to generate knowledge for our profession.

Knowledge level continuum The range of knowledge levels, from exploratory to descriptive to explanatory, at which research studies can be conducted.

Latent content In a content analysis, the true meaning, depth, or intensity of a variable, or concept, under study.

Levels of measurement The degree to which characteristics of a data set can be modeled mathematically; the higher the level of measurement, the more statistical methods that are applicable.

Limited review An existing literature synthesis that summarizes in narrative form the findings and implications of a few research studies.

Literature review See *Literature search* and *Review of the literature*.

Literature search In a meta-analysis, scanning books and journals for basic, up-to-date research articles on studies relevant to a research question or hypothesis; sufficiently thorough to maximize the chance of including all relevant sources. See *Review of the literature*.

Logical consistency The requirement that all the steps within a positivist research study must be logically related to one another.

Logical positivism A philosophy of science holding that the scientific method of inquiry is the only source of certain knowledge; in research, focuses on testing hypotheses deduced from theory.

Logistics In evaluation, refers to getting research participants to do what they are supposed to do, getting research instruments distributed and returned; in general, the activities that ensure that procedural tasks of a research or evaluation study are carried out.

Longitudinal case study An exploratory research design in which there is only one group of research participants and the dependent variable is measured more than once.

Longitudinal design A survey research design in which a measuring instrument(s) is administered to a sample of research participants repeatedly over time; used to detect dynamic processes such as opinion change.

Magnitude recording A direct-observation method of soliciting and recording data on amount, level, or degree of the target problem during each occurrence.

Management information system (MIS) System in which computer technology is used to process, store, retrieve, and analyze data collected routinely in such processes as social service delivery.

Manifest content Content of a communication that is obvious and clearly evident.

Manipulable solution evaluation model An evaluation model whose proponents believe that the greatest priority is to serve the public interest, not the interests of stakeholders, who have vested interests in the program being evaluated; closely resembles an outcome evaluation.

Matching A random assignment technique that assigns research participants to two or more groups so that the experimental and control groups are approximately equivalent in pretest scores or other characteristics, or so that all differences except the experimental condition are eliminated.

Maturation Unplanned change in research participants due to mental, physical, or other processes operating over time; a threat to internal validity.

Meaning units In a qualitative data analysis, a discrete segment of a transcript that can stand alone as a single idea; can consist of a single word, a partial or complete sentence, a paragraph, or more; used as the basic building blocks for developing categories.

Measurement The assignment of labels or numerals to the properties or attributes of observations, events, or objects according to specific rules.

Measurement error Any variation in measurement that cannot be attributed to the variable being measured; variability in responses produced by individual differences and other extraneous variables.

Measuring instrument Any instrument used to measure a variable(s).

Media myths The content of television shows, movies, and newspaper and magazine articles; one of the six ways of knowing.

Member checking A process of obtaining feedback and comments from research participants on interpretations and conclusions made from the qualitative data they provided; asking research participants to confirm or refute the conclusions made.

Meta-analysis A research method in which mathematical procedures are applied to the positivist findings of studies located in a literature search to produce new summary statistics and to describe the findings for a meta-analysis.

Methodology The procedures and rules that detail how a single research study is conducted.

Micro-level data Data derived from individual units of analysis, whether these data sources are individuals, families, corporations, etc.; for example, age and years of formal schooling are two variables requiring micro-level data.

Missing data Data not available for a research participant about whom other data are available, such as when a respondent fails to answer one of the questions in a survey.

Missing links When two categories or themes seem to be related, but not directly so, it may be that a third variable connects the two.

Mixed research model A model combining aspects of interpretive and positivist research approaches within all (or many) of the methodological steps contained within a single research study.

Monitoring approach to evaluation Evaluation that aims to provide ongoing feedback so that a program can be improved while it is still underway; it contributes to the continuous development and improvement of a human service program; this approach complements the project approach to evaluation.

Mortality Loss of research participants through normal attrition over time in an experimental design that requires retesting; a threat to internal validity.

Multicultural research Representation of diverse cultural factors in the subjects of study; such diversity variables may include religion, race, ethnicity, language preference, gender, etc.

Multigroup posttest-only design An exploratory research design in which there is more than one group of research participants and the dependent variable is measured only once for each group.

Multiple-baseline design A case-level evaluation design with more than one baseline period and intervention phase, which allows the causal inferences regarding the relationship between a treatment intervention and its effect on clients' target problems and which helps control for extraneous variables. See *Interrupted time-series design*.

Multiple-group design An experimental research design with one control group and several experimental groups.

Multiple-treatment interference Effects of the results of a first treatment on the results of second and subsequent treatments; a threat to external validity.

Multistage probability sampling Probability sampling procedures used when a comprehensive list of the population does not exist and it is not possible to construct one.

Multivariate (1) A relationship involving two or more variables; (2) A hypothesis stating an assertion about two or more variables and how they relate to one another.

Multivariate analysis A statistical analysis of the relationship among three or more variables.

Narrowband measuring instrument Measuring instruments that focus on a single, or a few, variables.

Nationality A term that refers to country of origin.

Naturalist A person who studies the facts of nature as they occur under natural conditions.

Needs assessment Program-level evaluation activities that aim to assess the feasibility for establishing or continuing a particular social service program; an evaluation that aims to assess the need for a human service by verifying that a social problem exists within a specific client population to an extent that warrants services.

Negative case sampling Purposefully selecting research participants based on the fact that they have different characteristics than previous cases.

Nominal level of measurement The level of measurement that classifies variables by assigning names or categories that are mutually exclusive and exhaustive.

Nondirectional test See *Two-tailed hypotheses*.

Nonexperimental design A research design at the exploratory, or lowest, level of the knowledge continuum; also called preexperimental.

Nonoccurrence data In the structured-observation method of data collection, a recording of only those time intervals in which the target problem did not occur.

Nonparametric tests Refers to statistical tests of hypotheses about population probability distributions, but not about specific parameters of the distributions.

Nonprobability sampling Sampling procedures in which all of the persons, events, or objects in the sampling frame have an unknown, and usually different, probability of being included in a sample.

Nonreactive Methods of research that do not allow the research participants to know that they are being studied; thus, they do not alter their responses for the benefit of the researcher.

Nonresponse The rate of nonresponse in survey research is calculated by dividing the total number of respondents by the total number in the sample, minus any units verified as ineligible.

Nonsampling errors Errors in a research study's results that are not due to the sampling procedures.

Norm In measurement, an average or set group standard of achievement that can be used to interpret individual scores; normative data describing statistical properties of a measuring instrument such as means and standard deviations.

Normalization group The population sample to which a measuring instrument under development is administered to establish norms; also called the norm group.

Normative needs When needs are defined by comparing the objective living conditions of a target population with what society—or, at least, that segment of society concerned with helping the target population—deems acceptable or desirable from a humanitarian standpoint.

Null hypothesis A statement concerning one or more parameters that is subjected to a statistical test; a statement that there is no relationship between the two variables of interest.

Numbers The basic data unit of analysis used in positivist research studies.

Objectivity A research stance in which a study is carried out and its data are examined and interpreted without distortion by personal feelings or biases.

Observer One of four roles on a continuum of participation in participant observation research; the level of involvement of the observer participant is lower than of the complete participant and higher than of the participant observer.

Obtrusive data collection methods Direct data collection methods that can influence the variables under study or the responses of research participants; data collection methods that produce reactive effects.

Occurrence data In the structured-observation method of data collection, a recording of the first occurrence of the target problem during each time interval.

One-group posttest-only design An exploratory research design in which the dependent variable is measured only once.

One-group pretest-posttest design A descriptive research design in which the dependent variable is measured twice—before and after treatment.

One-stage probability sampling Probability sampling procedures in which the selection of a sample that is drawn from a specific population is completed in a single process.

One-tailed hypotheses Statements that predict specific relationships between independent and dependent variables.

On-line sources Computerized literary retrieval systems that provide printouts of indexes and abstracts.

Open-ended questions Unstructured questions in which the response categories are not specified or detailed.

Operational definition Explicit specification of a variable in such a way that its measurement is possible.

Operationalization The process of developing operational definitions of the variables that are contained within the concepts of a positivist and/or interpretive research study.

Ordinal level of measurement The level of measurement that classifies variables by rank-ordering them from high to low or from most to least.

Outcome The effect of the manipulation of the independent variable on the dependent variable; the end product of a treatment intervention.

Outcome measure The criterion or basis for measuring effects of the independent variable or change in the dependent variable.

Outcome-oriented case study A type of case study that investigates whether client outcomes were in fact achieved.

Outside observers Trained observers who are not a part of the research participants' environment and who are brought in to record data.

Paired observations An observation on two variables, where the intent is to examine the relationship between them.

Panel research study A longitudinal survey design in which the same group of research participants (the panel) is followed over time by surveying them on successive occasions.

Parametric tests Statistical methods for estimating parameters or testing hypotheses about population parameters.

Participant observation An obtrusive data collection method in which the researcher, or the observer, participates in the life of those being observed; both an obtrusive data collection method and a research approach, this method is characterized by the one doing the study undertaking roles that involve establishing and maintaining ongoing relationships with research participants who are often in the field settings, and observing and participating with the research participants over time.

Participant observer The participant observer is one of four roles on a continuum of participation in participant observation research; the level of involvement of the participant observer is higher than of the complete observer and lower than of the observer participant.

Permanent product recording A method of data collection in which the occurrence of the target problem is determined by observing the permanent product or record of the target problem.

Pilot study See *Pretest* (2).

Population An entire set, or universe, of people, objects, or events of concern to a research study, from which a sample is drawn.

Positivism See *Positivist research approach*.

Positivist research approach A research approach to discover relationships and facts that are generalizable; research that is "independent" of subjective beliefs, feelings, wishes, and values; a research approach that is complementary to the interpretive research approach.

Posttest Measurement of the dependent variable after the introduction of the independent variable.

Potential for testing One of the four criteria for evaluating research hypotheses.

Practitioner/researcher A social worker who guides practice through the use of research findings; collects data throughout an intervention using research methods, skills, and tools; disseminates practice findings.

Pragmatists Researchers who believe that both interpretive and positivist research approaches can be integrated in a single research study.

Predictive validity A form of criterion validity that is concerned with the ability of a measuring instrument to predict future performance or status on the basis of present performance or status.

Predictor variable The variable that, it is believed, allows us to improve our ability to predict values of the criterion variable.

Preexposure Tasks to be carried out in advance of a research study to sensitize the researcher to the culture of interest; these tasks may include participation in cultural experiences, intercultural sharing, case studies, ethnic literature reviews, value statement exercises, etc.

Preliminary plan for data analysis A strategy for analyzing qualitative data that is outlined in the beginning stages of an interpretive research study; the plan has two general steps: (1) previewing the data, and (2) outlining what to record in the researcher's journal.

Presentism Applying current thinking and concepts to interpretations of past events or intentions.

Pretest (1) Measurement of the dependent variable prior to the introduction of the independent variable; (2) Administration of a measuring instrument to a group of people who will not be included in the study to determine difficulties the research participants may have in answering questions and the general impression given by the instrument; also called a pilot study.

Pretest-treatment interaction Effects that a pretest has on the responses of research participants to the introduction of the independent variable or the experimental treatment; a threat to external validity.

Previous research Research studies that have already been completed and published, which provide information about data collection methods used to investigate research questions that are similar to our own; a criterion for selecting a data collection method.

Primary data Data in its original form, as collected from the research participants. A primary data source is one that puts as few intermediaries as possible between the production and the study of the data.

Primary language The preferred language of the research participants.

Primary reference source A report of a research study by the person who conducted the study, usually an article in a professional journal.

Probability sampling Sampling procedures in which every member of the designated population has a known probability of being selected for the sample.

Problem area In social work research, a general expressed difficulty about which something researchable is unknown; not to be confused with research question.

Problem-solving process A generic method with specified phases for solving problems; also described as the scientific method.

Process-oriented case study A type of case study that illuminates the micro-steps of intervention that lead to client outcomes; describes how programs and interventions work and gives insight into the "black box" of intervention.

Professional standards Rules for making judgments about evaluation activity that are established by a group of persons who have advanced education and usually have the same occupation.

Program An organized set of political, administrative, and clinical activities that function to fulfill some social purpose.

Program development The constant effort to improve program services to better achieve outcomes; a basic principle underlying the design of evaluations.

Program efficiency Assessment of a program's outcome in relation to the costs of obtaining the outcome.

Program evaluation A form of appraisal, using valid and reliable research methods, that examines the processes or outcomes of an organization that exists to fulfill some social purpose.

Program goal A statement defining the intent of a program that cannot be directly evaluated; it can, however, be evaluated indirectly by the program's objectives, which are derived from the program goal; not to be confused with program objectives.

Program-level evaluation A form of appraisal that monitors change for groups of clients and organizational performance.

Program objectives A statement that clearly and exactly specifies the expected change, or intended result, for individuals receiving program services; qualities of well-chosen objectives are meaningfulness, specificity, measurability, and directionality; not to be confused with program goal.

Program participation The philosophy and structure of a program that will support or supplant the successful implementation of a research study within an existing social service program; a criterion for selecting a data collection method.

Program process   The coordination of administrative and clinical activities that are designed to achieve a program's goal.

Program results   A report on how effective a program is at meeting its stated objectives.

Project approach to evaluation   Evaluation that aims to assess a completed or finished program. This approach complements the monitoring approach.

Proxy   An indirect measure of a variable that a researcher wants to study; often used when the variable of inquiry is difficult to measure or observe directly.

Pure research approach   A search for theoretical results that can be used to develop theory and expand our profession's knowledge bases; complementary to the applied research approach.

Purists   Researchers who believe that interpretive and positivist research approaches should never be mixed.

Purpose statement   A declaration of words that clearly describes a research study's intent.

Purposive sampling   A nonprobability sampling procedure in which research participants with particular characteristics are purposely selected for inclusion in a research sample; also known as judgmental or theoretical sampling.

Qualitative data   Data that measure a quality or kind. When referring to variables, qualitative is another term for categorical or nominal variable values; when speaking of kinds of research, qualitative refers to studies of subjects that are hard to quantify. Interpretive research produces descriptive data based on spoken or written words and observable behaviors.

Quantification   In measurement, the reduction of data to numerical form in order to analyze them by way of mathematical or statistical techniques.

Quantitative data   Data that measure a quantity or amount.

Quasi-experiment   A research design at the descriptive level of the knowledge continuum that resembles an "ideal" experiment but does not allow for random selection or assignment of research participants to groups and often does not control for rival hypotheses.

Questionnaire-type scale   A type of measuring instrument in which multiple responses are usually combined to form a single overall score for a respondent.

Quota sampling   A nonprobability sampling procedure in which the relevant characteristics of the sample are identified, the proportion of these characteristics in the population is determined, and research participants are

selected from each category until the predetermined proportion (quota) has been achieved.

Race   A variable based on physical attributes that can be subdivided into the Caucasoid, Negroid, and Mongoloid races.

Random assignment   The process of assigning individuals to experimental or control groups so that the groups are equivalent; also referred to as randomization.

Random error   Variable error in measurement; error due to unknown or uncontrolled factors that affect the variable being measured and the process of measurement in an inconsistent fashion.

Randomized cross-sectional survey design   A descriptive research design in which there is only one group, the dependent variable is measured only once, the research participants are randomly selected from the population, and there is no independent variable.

Randomized longitudinal survey design   A descriptive research design in which there is only one group, the dependent variable is measured more than once, and research participants are randomly selected from the population before each treatment.

Randomized one-group posttest-only design   A descriptive research design in which there is only one group, the dependent variable is measured only once, and research participants are randomly selected from the population.

Randomized posttest-only control group design   An explanatory research design in which there are two or more randomly assigned groups, the control group does not receive treatment, and the experimental groups receive different treatments.

Random numbers table   A computer-generated or published table of numbers in which each number has an equal chance of appearing in each position in the table.

Random sampling   An unbiased selection process conducted so that all members of a population have an equal chance of being selected to participate in a research study.

Rank-order scale   A comparative rating scale in which the rater is asked to rank specific individuals in relation to one another on some characteristic.

Rating scale   A type of measuring instrument in which responses are rated on a continuum or in an ordered set of categories, with numerical values assigned to each point or category.

Ratio level of measurement   The level of measurement that has a nonarbitrary, fixed zero point and classifies the values of a variable on an equally spaced continuum.

Raw scores Scores derived from administration of a measuring instrument to research participants or groups.

Reactive effect (1) An effect on outcome measures due to the research participants' awareness that they are being observed or interviewed; a threat to external and internal validity; (2) Alteration of the variables being measured or the respondents' performance on the measuring instrument due to administration of the instrument.

Reactivity The belief that things being observed or measured are affected by the fact that they are being observed or measured; one of the four main limitations of the positivist research approach.

Reassessment A step in a qualitative data analysis in which the researcher interrupts the data analysis process to reaffirm the rules used to decide which meaning units are placed within different categories.

Recoding Developing and applying new variable value labels to a variable that has previously been coded. Usually, recoding is done to make variables from one or more data sets comparable.

Reductionism In the positivist research approach, the operationalization of concepts by reducing them to common measurable variables; one of the four main limitations of the positivist research approach.

Relevancy One of the four criteria for evaluating research problem areas *and* formulating research questions out of the problem areas.

Reliability (1) The degree of accuracy, precision, or consistency in results of a measuring instrument, including the ability to produce the same results when the same variable is measured more than once or repeated applications of the same test on the same individual produce the same measurement; (2) The degree to which individual differences on scores or in data are due either to true differences or to errors in measurement.

Replication Repetition of the same research procedures by a second researcher for the purpose of determining if earlier results can be confirmed.

Researchability The extent to which a research problem is in fact researchable and the problem can be resolved through the consideration of data derived from a research study; one of the four criteria for evaluating research problem areas *and* formulating research questions out of the problem areas.

Research attitude A way that we view the world. It is an attitude that highly values craftsmanship, with pride in creativity, high-quality standards, and hard work.

Research consumer A social work role reflecting the ethical obligation to base interventions on the most up-to-date research knowledge available.

Research design The entire plan of a positivist and/or interpretive research study from problem conceptualization to the dissemination of findings.

Researcher bias The tendency of researchers to find results they expect to find; a threat to external validity.

Research hypothesis A statement about a study's research question that predicts the existence of a particular relationship between the independent and dependent variables; can be used in both the positivist and interpretive approaches to research.

Research method The use of positivist and interpretive research approaches to find out what is true; one of the ways of knowing.

Research participants People utilized in research studies; also called subjects or cases.

Research question A specific research question that is formulated directly out of the general research problem area; answered by the interpretive and/or positivist research approach; not to be confused with problem area.

Resources The costs associated with collecting data in any given research study; includes materials and supplies, equipment rental, transportation, training staff, and staff time; a criterion for selecting a data collection method.

Response categories Possible responses assigned to each question in a standardized measuring instrument, with a lower value generally indicating a low level of the variable being measured and a larger value indicating a higher level.

Response rate The total number of responses obtained from potential research participants to a measuring instrument divided by the total number of responses requested, usually expressed in the form of a percentage.

Response set Personal style; the tendency of research participants to respond to a measuring instrument in a particular way, regardless of the questions asked, or the tendency of observers or interviewers to react in certain ways; a source of constant error.

Review of the literature (1) A search of the professional literature to provide background knowledge of what has already been examined or tested in a specific problem area; (2) Use of any information source, such as a computerized database, to locate existing data or information on a research problem, question, or hypothesis.

Rival hypothesis A hypothesis that is a plausible alternative to the research hypothesis and might explain the results as well or better; a hypothesis involving extraneous or intervening variables other than the independent variable in the research hypothesis; also referred to as an alternative hypothesis.

Rules of correspondence A characteristic of measurement stipulating that numerals or symbols are assigned to properties of individuals, objects, or events according to specified rules.

Sample A subset of a population of individuals, objects, or events chosen to participate in or to be considered in a research study.

Sampling error (1) The degree of difference that can be expected between the sample and the population from which it was drawn; (2) A mistake in a research study's results that is due to sampling procedures.

Sampling frame A listing of units (people, objects, or events) in a population from which a sample is drawn.

Sampling plan A method of selecting members of a population for inclusion in a research study, using procedures that make it possible to draw inferences about the population from the sample statistics.

Sampling theory The logic of using methods to ensure that a sample and a population are similar in all relevant characteristics.

Scale A measuring instrument composed of several items that are logically or empirically structured to measure a construct.

Scattergram A graphic representation of the relationship between two interval- or ratio-level variables.

Science Knowledge that has been obtained and tested through use of positivist and interpretive research studies.

Scientific community A group that shares the same general norms for both research activity and acceptance of scientific findings and explanations.

Scientific determinism See *Determinism*.

Scientific method A generic method with specified steps for solving problems; the principles and procedures used in the systematic pursuit of knowledge.

Scope of a study The extent to which a problem area is covered in a single research study; a criterion for selecting a data collection method.

Score A numerical value assigned to an observation; also called data.

Search statement A preliminary search statement developed by the researcher prior to a literature search and which contains terms that can be combined to elicit specific data.

Secondary analysis An unobtrusive data collection method in which available data that predate the formulation of a research study are used to answer the research question or test the hypothesis.

Secondary data Data that predate the formulation of the research study and that are used to answer the research question or test the hypothesis.

Secondary data sources A data source that provides nonoriginal, secondhand data.

Secondary reference source A source related to a primary source or sources, such as a critique of a particular source item or a literature review, bibliography, or commentary on several items.

Secondhand data Data obtained from people who are indirectly connected to the problem being studied.

Selection-treatment interaction The relationship between the manner of selecting research participants and their response to the independent variable; a threat to external validity.

Self-anchored scales A rating scale in which research participants rate themselves on a continuum of values, according to their own referents for each point.

Self-disclosure Shared communication about oneself, including one's behaviors, beliefs, and attitudes.

Semantic differential scale A modified measurement scale in which research participants rate their perceptions of the variable under study along three dimensions—evaluation, potency, and activity.

Sequential triangulation When two distinct and separate phases of a research study are conducted and the results of the first phase are considered essential for planning the second phase; research questions in Phase 1 are answered before research questions in Phase 2 are formulated.

Service recipients People who use human services—individuals, couples, families, groups, organizations, and communities; also known as clients or consumers; a stakeholder group in evaluation.

Simple random sampling A one-stage probability sampling procedure in which members of a population are selected one at a time, without a chance of being selected again, until the desired sample size is obtained.

Simultaneous triangulation When the results of a positivist and interpretive research question are answered at the same time; results to the interpretive research questions, for example, are reported separately and do not necessarily relate to, or confirm, the results from the positivist phase.

Situationalists Researchers who assert that certain research approaches (interpretive or positivist) are appropriate for specific situations.

Situation-specific variable A variable that may be observable only in certain environments and under certain circumstances, or with particular people.

Size of a study The number of people, places, or systems that are included in a single research study; a criterion for selecting a data collection method.

Snowball sampling A nonprobability sampling procedure in which individuals selected for inclusion in a sample are asked to identify other individuals from the population who might be included; useful to locate people with divergent points of view.

Social desirability (1) A response set in which research participants tend to answer questions in a way that they perceive as giving favorable impressions of themselves; (2) The inclination of data providers to report data that present a socially desirable impression of themselves or their reference groups; also referred to as impression management.

Socially acceptable response Bias in an answer that comes from research participants trying to answer questions as they think a "good" person should, rather than in a way that reveals what they actually believe or feel.

Social work research Scientific inquiry in which interpretive and positivist research approaches are used to answer research questions and create new, generally applicable knowledge in the field of social work.

Socioeconomic variables Any one of several measures of social rank, usually including income, education, and occupational prestige; abbreviated "SES."

Solomon four-group design An explanatory research design with four randomly assigned groups, two experimental and two control; the dependent variable is measured before and after treatment for one experimental and one control group, but only after treatment for the other two groups, and only experimental groups receive the treatment.

Specificity One of the four criteria for evaluating research hypotheses.

Split-half method A method for establishing the reliability of a measuring instrument by dividing it into comparable halves and comparing the scores between the two halves.

Spot-check recording A method of data collection that involves direct observation of the target problem at specified intervals rather than on a continuous basis.

Stakeholder A person or group of people having a direct or indirect interest in the results of an evaluation.

Stakeholder service evaluation model Proponents of this evaluation model believe that program evaluations will be more likely to be utilized, and thus have a greater impact on social problems, when they are tailored to the needs of stakeholders; in this model, the purpose of program evaluation is not to generalize findings to other sites, but rather to restrict the evaluation effort to a particular program.

Standardized measuring instrument A professionally developed measuring instrument that provides for uniform administration and scoring and generates normative data against which later results can be evaluated.

Statistics The branch of mathematics concerned with the collection and analysis of data using statistical techniques.

Stratified random sampling A one-stage probability sampling procedure in which a population is divided into two or more strata to be sampled separately, using simple random or systematic random sampling techniques.

Structured interview schedule A complete list of questions to be asked and spaces for recording the answers; the interview schedule is used by interviewers when questioning respondents.

Structured observation A data collection method in which people are observed in their natural environments using specified methods and measurement procedures. See *Direct observation.*

Subscale A component of a scale that measures some part or aspect of a major construct; also composed of several items that are logically or empirically structured.

Summated scale A questionnaire-type scale in which research participants are asked to indicate the degree of their agreement or disagreement with a series of questions.

Summative evaluation A type of evaluation that examines the ultimate success of a program and assists with decisions about whether a program should be continued or chosen in the first place among alternative program options.

Survey research A data collection method that uses survey-type data collection measuring instruments to obtain opinions or answers from a population or sample of research participants in order to describe or study them as a group.

Synthesis Undertaking the search for meaning in our sources of information at every step of the research process; combining parts such as data, concepts, and theories to arrive at a higher level of understanding.

Systematic To arrange the steps of a research study in a methodical way.

Systematic random sampling A one-stage probability sampling procedure in which every person at a designated interval in a specific population is selected to be included in a research study's sample.

Systematic error Measurement error that is consistent, not random.

Target population The group about which a researcher wants to draw conclusions; another term for a population about which one aims to make inferences.

Target problem (1) In case-level evaluation designs, the problems social workers seek to solve for their clients; (2) A measurable behavior, feeling, or cognition that is either a problem in itself or symptomatic of some other problem.

Temporal research design A research study that includes time as a major variable; the purpose of this design is to investigate change in the distribution of a variable or in relationships among variables over time; there are three types of temporal research designs: cohort, panel, and trend.

Temporal stability Consistency of responses to a measuring instrument over time; reliability of an instrument across forms and across administrations.

Testing effect The effect that taking a pretest might have on posttest scores; a threat to internal validity.

Test-retest reliability Reliability of a measuring instrument established through repeated administration to the same group of individuals.

Thematic notes In observational research, thematic notes are a record of emerging ideas, hypotheses, theories, and conjectures; thematic notes provide a place for the researcher to speculate and identify themes, make linkages between ideas and events, and articulate thoughts as they emerge in the field setting.

Theme In a qualitative data analysis, a concept or idea that describes a single category or a grouping of categories; an abstract interpretation of qualitative data.

Theoretical framework A frame of reference that serves to guide a research study and is developed from theories, findings from a variety of other studies, and the researcher's personal experiences.

Theoretical sampling See *Purposive sampling.*

Theory A reasoned set of propositions, derived from and supported by established data, which serves to explain a group of phenomena; a conjectural explanation that may, or may not, be supported by data generated from interpretive and positivist research studies.

Time orientation An important cultural factor that considers whether one is future-, present-, or past-oriented; for

instance, individuals who are "present-oriented" would not be as preoccupied with advance planning as those who are "future-oriented."

Time-series design See *Interrupted time-series design.*

Tradition Traditional cultural beliefs that we accept "without question" as true; one of the ways of knowing.

Transcript A written, printed, or typed copy of interview data or any other written material that have been gathered for an interpretive research study.

Transition statements Sentences used to indicate a change in direction or focus of questions in a measuring instrument.

Treatment group See *Experimental group.*

Trend study A longitudinal study design in which data from surveys carried out at periodic intervals on samples drawn from a particular population are used to reveal trends over time.

Triangulation The idea of combining different research methods in all steps associated with a single research study; assumes that any bias inherent in one particular method will be neutralized when used in conjunction with other research methods; seeks convergence of a study's results; using more than one research method and source of data to study the same phenomena and to enhance validity. There are several types of triangulation, but the essence of the term is that multiple perspectives are compared. It can involve multiple data sources or multiple data analyzers; the hope is that the different perspectives will confirm each other, adding weight to the credibility and dependability of qualitative data analysis.

Triangulation of analysts Using multiple data analyzers to code a single segment of transcript and comparing the amount of agreement between analyzers; a method used to verify coding of qualitative data.

Two-phase research model A model combining interpretive and positivist research approaches in a single study where each approach is conducted as a separate and distinct phase of the study.

Two-tailed hypotheses Statements that *do not* predict specific relationships between independent and dependent variables.

Unit of analysis A specific research participant (person, object, or event) or the sample or population relevant to the research question; the persons or things being studied. Units of analysis in research are often persons, but may be groups, political parties, newspaper editorials, unions, hospitals, schools, etc. A particular unit of analysis from which data are gathered is called a case.

Univariate A hypothesis or research design involving a single variable.

Universe See *Population.*

Unobtrusive methods Data collection methods that do not influence the variable under study or the responses of research participants; methods that avoid reactive effects.

Unstructured interviews A series of questions that allow flexibility for both the research participant and the interviewer to make changes during the process.

Validity (1) The extent to which a measuring instrument measures the variable it is supposed to measure and measures it accurately; (2) The degree to which an instrument is able to do what it is intended to do, in terms of both experimental procedures and measuring instruments (internal validity) and generalizability of results (external validity); (3) The degree to which scores on a measuring instrument correlate with measures of performance on some other criterion.

Variable A concept with characteristics that can take on different values.

Verbatim recording Recording interview data word-for-word and including significant gestures, pauses, and expressions of persons in the interview.

Wideband measuring instrument An instrument that measures more than one variable.

Within-methods research approach Triangulation by using different research methods available in *either* the interpretive *or* the positivist research approaches in a single research study.

Words The basic data unit of analysis used in interpretive research studies.

Worker cooperation The actions and attitudes of program personnel when carrying out a research study within an existing social service program; a criterion for selecting a data collection method.

Working hypothesis An assertion about a relationship between two or more variables that may not be true but is plausible and worth examining.

References and Further Reading

Adatto, K. (1990). *Sound byte democracy: Network evening news presidential campaign coverage, 1968 and 1988.* Cambridge, MA: John F. Kennedy School of Government, Harvard University.

Adler, P.A., & Adler, P. (1994). Observational techniques. In N.K. Denzin & Y.S. Lincoln. (Eds.), *Handbook of qualitative research* (pp. 377–392). Thousand Oaks, CA: Sage.

Ainsworth, M.D., Slater, M.D., Blehar, M.C., Waters, E., & Wall, S. (1978). *Patterns of attachment: A psychological study of the strange situation.* Hillsdale, NJ: Erlbaum.

Akbar, N. (1991). Paradigms of African American research. In R.L. Jones. (Ed.), *Black psychology* (3rd ed., pp. 709–725). Berkeley, CA: Cobb and Henry.

Alexander, L.B. (1972). Social work's Freudian deluge: Myth or reality? *Social Service Review, 46,* 517–538.

Allen, M.J. (1995). *Introduction to psychological research.* Itasca, IL: F.E. Peacock.

Allen, M. J., & Yen, W. M. (1979). *Introduction to measurement theory.* Monterey, CA: Brooks/Cole.

Alreck, P.L., & Settle, R.B. (1985). *The survey research handbook.* Homewood, IL: Irwin.

Altheide, D. (1987). Ethnographic content analysis. *Qualitative Sociology, 10,* 62–77.

Altheide, D., & Johnson, J. (1991). Criteria for assessing interpretive validity in qualitative research. In N.K. Denzin & Y. Lincoln (Eds.), *Handbook of qualitative research* (pp. 485–499). Newbury Park, CA: Sage.

American Association on Mental Deficiency (1977). *Consent handbook* (No. 3). Washington, DC: Author.

American Psychological Association. (1971). *Ethical principles in the conduct of research with human participants.* Washington, DC: Author.

American Psychological Association. (1973). *Ethical principles in the conduct of research with human participants.* Washington, DC: Author.

American Psychological Association. (1981a). *Ethical principles in the conduct of research with human participants.* Washington, DC: Author.

American Psychological Association. (1981b). *Specialty guidelines for the delivery of services by counseling psychologists.* Washington, DC: Author.

Anastasi, A. (1988). *Psychological testing* (6th ed.). New York: Macmillan.

Ashcroft, R. (1998). Human research subjects, selection of. In R. Chadwick (Ed.), *Encyclopedia of applied ethics* (Vol. 2, pp. 627–639). San Diego: Academic Press.

Atherton, C., & Klemmack, D. (1982). *Research methods in social work.* Lexington, MA: Heath.

Atkinson, D.R., Morten, G., & Sue, D.W. (1983). *Counseling American minorities: A cross-cultural perspective.* Dubuque, IA: Brown.

Atkinson, J. (1987). Gender roles in marriage and the family: A critique and some proposals. *Journal of Family Issues, 8,* 5–41.

Atkinson, P., & Hammersley, M. (1994). Ethnography and participant observation. In N.K. Denzin & Y.S. Lincoln (Eds.), *Handbook of qualitative research* (pp. 248–261). Thousand Oaks, CA: Sage.

Attneave, C. (1982). American Indians and Alaska Native families: Emigrants in their own homeland. In M. McGoldrick, J.K. Pearce, & J. Giordano (Eds.), *Ethnicity and family therapy* (pp. 55–83). New York: Guilford.

Austin, M.J., & Crowell, J. (1985). Survey research. In R.M. Grinnell, Jr. (Ed.), *Social work research and evaluation* (2nd ed., pp. 275–305). Itasca, IL: F.E. Peacock.

Axelson, J.A. (1985). *Counseling and development in a multicultural society.* Belmont, CA: Wadsworth.

Azibo, D. (1992). Understanding the proper and improper usage of the comparative research framework. In A. Burlew, W. Banks, H. McAdoo, & D. Azibo (Eds.), *African American psychology* (pp. 18–27). Newbury Park, CA: Sage.

Babbie, E.R. (2004). *The practice of social research* (10th ed.). Pacific Grove, CA: Wadsworth.

Badgley, R. (Chairman). (1984). *Sexual offenses against chil-*

dren: Vol. 1. Report of the committee on sexual offenses against children and youths. Ottawa, Ontario: Ministry of Supply and Services.

Bailey, K.D. (1994). *Methods of social research* (4th ed.). New York: Simon and Schuster.

Bainbridge, W. (1989). *Survey research: A computer-assisted introduction.* Belmont, CA: Wadsworth.

Balassone, M.L. (1994). Does emphasizing accountability and evidence dilute service delivery and the helping role? No! In W.W. Hudson & P.S. Nurius (Eds.), *Controversial issues in social work research* (pp. 15–19). Needham Heights, MA: Allyn & Bacon.

Bales, R.F. (1950). *Interaction process analysis.* Reading, MA: Addison-Wesley.

Bane, M.J. (1986). Household composition and poverty. In S.H. Danziger & D.H. Weinberg (Eds.), *Fighting poverty: What works and what doesn't* (pp. 209–231). Cambridge, MA: Harvard University Press.

Barlow, D.H., Hayes, S.C., & Nelson, R.O. (1984). *The scientist-practitioner: Research and accountability in applied settings.* Elmsford, NY: Pergamon.

Barlow, D.H., & Hersen, M. (1984). *Single-case experimental designs: Strategies for studying behavior change* (2nd ed.). Elmsford, NY: Pergamon.

Barton, W.H. (1998). Culturally competent research protocols. In R.R. Greene & M. Watkins (Eds.), *Serving diverse constituencies: Applying the ecological perspective* (pp. 285–303). Hawthorne, NY: Aldine.

Baumeister, R.F. (1988). Should we stop studying sex differences altogether? *American Psychologist, 43,* 1092–1095.

Becerra, R.M. (1997). Can valid research on ethnic populations only be conducted by researchers from the same ethnic group? No. In D. de Anda (Ed.), *Controversial issues in multiculturalism* (pp. 114–117). Needham Heights, MA: Allyn & Bacon.

Becerra, R.M., & Zambrana, R.E. (1985). Methodological approaches to research on Hispanics. *Social Work Research and Abstracts, 21,* 42–49.

Beck, D.F., & Jones, M.A. (1973). Progress on family problems. New York: Family Service Association of America.

Beeman, S.K. (1995). Maximizing credibility and accountability in qualitative data collection and data analysis: A social work research case example. *Journal of Sociology and Social Welfare, 22,* 99–114.

Bellack, A.S., & Hersen, M. (1977). Self-report inventories in behavioral assessment. In J.D. Cone & R. P. Hawkins (Eds.), *Behavioral assessment: New directions in clinical psychology* (pp. 52— 76). New York: Brunner/Mazel.

Bem, D. (1991). Writing the research report. In C. Judd, R. Eliot, & L. Kidder, (Eds.). *Research methods in social relations* (6th ed.). Fort Worth, TX: Harcourt, Brace, Jovanovich.

Benner, P. (Ed.). (1994). *Interpretive phenomenology.* Newbury Park, CA: Sage.

Bennet, M.J. (1986). A developmental approach to training for intercultural sensitivity. *International Journal of Intercultural Relations, 10,* 179–196.

Benney, M., Riesman, D., & Starr, S. (1956). Age and sex with the interview. *American Journal of Sociology, 62,* 143–152.

Berg, B.L. (2004). *Qualitative research methods for the social sciences* (5th ed.). Boston: Allyn & Bacon.

Berkhofer, R.F., Jr. (1969). *A behavioral approach to historical analysis.* New York: Free Press.

Berkowitz, E.D. (1991). *America's welfare state: From Roosevelt to Reagan.* Baltimore, MD: Johns Hopkins University Press.

Berlin, S.B, Mann, K.B., & Grossman, S.F. (1991). Task analysis of cognitive therapy for depression. *Social Work Research and Abstracts, 27,* 3–11.

Bettleheim, B. (1982, March 1). Reflections: Freud and the soul. *New Yorker,* 52–93.

Beveridge, W.I.B. (1957). *The art of scientific investigation* (3rd ed.). London: Heinemann.

Billups, J.O., & Julia, M.C. (1987). Changing profile of social work practice: A content analysis. *Social Work Research and Abstracts, 23,* 17–22.

Bisno, H., & Borowski, A. (1985). The social and psychological contexts of research. In R.M. Grinnell, Jr. (Ed.), *Social work research and evaluation* (2nd ed., pp. 83–100). Itasca, IL: F.E. Peacock.

Blase, K., Fixsen, D., & Phillips, E. (1984). Residential treatment for troubled children: Developing service delivery systems. In S.C. Paine, G.T. Bellamy, & B. Wilcox (Eds.), *Human services that work: From innovation to standard practice.* Baltimore: Paul H. Brookes.

Blaug, M. (1963). The myth of the old poor law and the making of the new. *Journal of Economic History, 23,* 151–184.

Blaug, M. (1964). The Poor Law Report reexamined. *Journal of Economic History, 24,* 229–245.

Bloom, M., Fischer, J., & Orme, J. (2003). *Evaluating practice: Guidelines for the accountable professional* (4th ed.). Englewood Cliffs, NJ: Prentice-Hall.

Blythe, B.J., & Tripodi, T. (1989). *Measurement in direct practice.* Newbury Park, CA: Sage.

Bogdan, R., & Biklen, S.K. (1992). *Qualitative research for education* (2nd ed.). Needham Heights, MA: Allyn & Bacon.

Bogdan, R., Brown, M.A., & Foster, S.B. (1984). Ecology of the family as a context for human development. *Human Organization, 41,* 6–16.

Bogdan, R., & Taylor, R. (1990). Looking at the bright side: A positive approach to qualitative policy and evaluation research. *Qualitative Sociology, 13,* 183–192.

Borden, W. (1992). Narrative perspectives in psychosocial intervention following adverse life events. *Social Work, 37,* 135–141.

Borenzweig, H. (1971). Social work and psychoanalytic theory: A historical analysis. *Social Work, 16,* 7–16.

Borg, W.R., & Gall, M.D. (1989). *Educational research.* White Plains, NY: Longman.

Borowski, A. (1988). Social dimensions of research. In R.M. Grinnell, Jr. (Ed.), *Social work research and evaluation* (3rd ed., pp. 42–64). Itasca, IL: F.E. Peacock.

Bossert, S.T. (1979). *Tasks and social relationships in classrooms.* New York: Cambridge University Press.

Bourgois, P., Lettiere, M., & Quesada, J. (1997). Social misery and the sanctions of substance abuse: Confronting HIV risk among homeless heroin addicts in San Francisco. *Social Problems, 44,* 155–173.

Bowman, P.J. (1993). The impact of economic marginality among African American husbands and fathers. In H.P. McAdoo (Ed.), *Family ethnicity: Strength in diversity* (pp. 120–140). Newbury Park, CA: Sage.

Bretl, D., & Cantor, J. (1988). The portrayal of men and women in U.S. television commercials: A recent content analysis and trends over 15 years. *Sex Roles, 18,* 595–609.

Brieland, D. (1969). Black identity and the helping person. *Children, 16,* 170–176.

Brink, P. (1989). Issues in reliability and validity. In J. Morse (Ed.), *Qualitative nursing research: A contemporary dialogue.* Rockville, MD: Aspen.

Brislin, R.W. (1970). Back-translation for cross-cultural research. *Journal of Cross-Cultural Psychology, 1,* 185–216.

Brody, H. (1992). Philosophic approaches. In B.F. Crabtree & W.L. Miller (Eds.), *Doing qualitative research: Research methods for primary care* (Vol. 3, pp. 174–185). Thousand Oaks, CA: Sage.

Bronson, D.E. (1994). Is a scientist-practitioner model appropriate for direct social work practice? No! In W.W. Hudson & P.S. Nurius (Eds.), *Controversial issues in social work research* (pp. 81–86). Needham Heights, MA: Allyn & Bacon.

Broverman, I.K., Vogel, S.R., Broverman, S.M., Clarkson, F.E., & Rosenkrantz, P.S. (1972). Sex role stereotypes: A current appraisal. *Journal of Social Issues, 28,* 59–78.

Broxmeyer, N. (1979). Practitioner-researcher in treating a borderline child. *Social Work Research and Abstracts, 14,* 5–10.

Burnett, D. (1998). Conceptual and methodological considerations in research with non-white ethnic elders. In M. Potocky & A.Y. Rodgers-Farmer (Eds.), *Social work research with minority and oppressed populations: Methodological issues and innovations* (pp. 71–91). New York: Haworth.

Buros, O.K. (Ed.). (1978). *The eighth mental measurements yearbook* (2 vols.). Highland Park, NJ: Gryphon.

Burt, M. (1996). Homelessness: Definitions and counts. In J. Baumohl (Ed.), *Homelessness in America* (pp. 15–23). Phoenix, AZ: Oryx.

Butterfield, H. (1931). *The Whig interpretation of history.* London: Bell.

Campbell, D. (1956). *Leadership and its effects upon the group.* Columbus: Ohio State University Press.

Campbell, D., & Stanley, J. (1963). *Experimental and quasi-experimental designs for research.* Chicago: Rand McNally.

Campbell, P.B. (1983). The impact of societal biases on research methods. In B.L. Richardson & J. Wirtenberg (Eds.), *Sex role research* (pp. 197–213). New York: Praeger.

Carley, M. (1981). *Social measurement and social indicators.* London: Allen & Unwin.

Carney, T.F. (1990). *Collaborative inquiry methodology.* Windsor, Ontario: University of Windsor, Division for Instructional Development.

Ceci, S.J., Peters, D., & Plotkin, J. (1985). Human subjects review, personal values, and the regulation of social science research. *American Psychologist, 40,* 994–1002.

Chambers, C.A. (1995). *History of social work bibliography: Writings, 1982–1990.* Minneapolis, MN: Social Welfare History Archives, University of Minnesota-Twin Cities.

Chambers, D.E., Wedel, K.R., & Rodwell, M.K. (1992). *Evaluating social programs.* Needham Heights, MA: Allyn & Bacon.

Chandler, S.M. (1994). Is there an ethical responsibility to use practice methods with the best empirical evidence of effectiveness? No! In W.W. Hudson & P.S. Nurius (Eds.), *Controversial issues in social work research* (pp. 106–111). Needham Heights, MA: Allyn & Bacon.

Charges dropped on bogus work. (1989, April 4). *New York Times*, p. 21.

Charmaz, K. (1990). "Discovering" chronic illness: Using grounded theory. *Social Science in Medicine, 30,* 1161–1172.

Cheetham, J. (1992). Evaluating social work effectiveness. *Research on Social Work Practice, 2,* 265–287.

Chwalisz, K., Wiersma, N., & Stark-Wroblewski, K. (1996). A quasi-qualitative investigation of strategies used in qualitative categorization. *Journal of Counseling Psychology, 43,* 502–509.

Cialdini, R.B. (1980). Full-cycle social psychology. In L. Bickman (Ed.), *Applied social psychology annual* (Vol. 1, pp. 21–47). Beverly Hills, CA: Sage.

Coe, D. (1992). *Breaking the Maya code.* New York: Thames and Hudson.

Coleman, H., Collins, D., & Polster, R.A. (1997). Structured observation. In R.M. Grinnell, Jr. (Ed.), *Social work research and evaluation: Quantitative and qualitative approaches* (5th ed., pp. 315–332). Itasca, IL: F.E. Peacock.

Coleman, H., & Unrau, Y. (1996). Phase three: Analyzing your data. In L.M. Tutty, M.A. Rothery, & R.M. Grinnell, Jr. (Eds.), *Qualitative research for social workers: Phases, steps, and tasks* (pp. 88–119). Needham Heights, MA: Allyn & Bacon.

Collins, P.H. (1991). *Black feminist thought: Knowledge, consciousness and the politics of empowerment.* New York: Routledge.

Committee on the Status of Women in Sociology (1985–1986). *The status of women in sociology.* New York: American Sociological Association.

Cook, T.D., & Campbell, D. (1979). *Quasi-experimentation: Design and analysis for field settings.* Boston: Houghton Mifflin.

Cooper, M. (1990). Treatment of a client with obsessive-compulsive disorder. *Social Work Research and Abstracts, 26,* 26–35.

Copeland, A.P., & White, K.M. (1991). *Studying families.* Newbury Park, CA: Sage.

Corcoran, K.J. (1988). Selecting a measuring instrument. In R.M. Grinnell, Jr. (Ed.), *Social work research and evaluation* (3rd ed., pp. 137–155). Itasca, IL: F.E. Peacock.

Coughlin, E.K. (1988). Scholar who submitted bogus article to journals may be disciplined. *Chronicle of Higher Education, 35*(10), A1, A7.

Council for International Organizations of Medical Sciences. (1993). *International ethical guidelines for biomedical research involving research subjects.* Geneva: Author.

Council on Social Work Education. (2003). *Baccalaureate and masters curriculum policy statements.* Alexandria, VA. Author.

Council on Social Work Education (2005). *Baccalaureate and masters curriculum policy statements.* Alexandria, VA. Author.

Cowen, E.L., Hauser, J., Beach, D.R., & Rappaport, J. (1970). Parental perception of young children and their relation to indexes of adjustment. *Journal of Consulting and Clinical Psychology, 34,* 97–103.

Crabtree, B.F., & Miller, W.L. (Eds.). (1992). *Doing qualitative research.* Newbury Park, CA: Sage.

Crawford, K., Thomas, E.D., & Fink, J.J. (1980). Pygmalion at sea: Improving the work effectiveness of low performers. *The Journal of Applied Behavioral Science, 23,* 482–505.

Creswell, J.W. (1994). *Research design: Qualitative & quantitative approaches.* Newbury Park, CA: Sage.

Cresswell, J.W. (1997). Using both research approaches in a single study. In R.M. Grinnell, Jr. (Ed.), *Social work research and evaluation: Quantitative and qualitative approaches* (5th ed., pp. 141–158). Itasca, IL: F.E. Peacock.

Cromwell, R.E., & Ruiz, R.A. (1979). The myth of macho dominance in decision making within Mexican and Chicano families. *Hispanic Journal of Behavioral Sciences, 1,* 355–373.

Cronbach, L.J. (1970). *Essentials of psychological testing* (3rd ed.). New York: Harper & Row.

Cronbach, L.J. (1975). Beyond the two disciplines of scientific psychology. *American Psychologist, 30,* 116–127.

Cronbach, L.J., & Meehl, P.E. (1955). Construct validity in psychological tests. *Psychological Bulletin, 52,* 281–302.

Crowne, D.P., & Marlow, D. (1960). A new scale of social desirability independent of psychopathology. *Journal of Consulting Psychology, 24,* 349–354.

Cumberbatch, G., Jones, I., & Lee, M. (1988). Measuring violence on television. *Current Psychological Research and Review, 7,* 10–25.

Curtis, G.C. (1996). The scientific evaluation of new claims. *Research on Social Work Practice, 6,* 117–121.

Dale, A., Arber, S., & Proctor, M. (1988). *Doing secondary analysis.* Boston: Allen & Unwin.

Dangel, R.F. (1994). Is a scientist-practitioner model appropriate for direct social work practice? Yes! In W.W. Hudson & P.S. Nurius (Eds.), *Controversial issues in social work research* (pp. 75–79). Needham Heights, MA: Allyn & Bacon.

Darley, J.M., & Latane, B. (1968). Bystander intervention in emergencies: Diffusion of responsibility. *Journal of Personality and Social Psychology, 8,* 377–383.

Davis, L.V. (1994). Is feminist research inherently qualitative, and is it a fundamentally different approach to research? Yes. In W.W. Hudson & P.S. Nurius (Eds.), *Controversial issues in social work research* (pp. 63–68). Needham Heights, MA: Allyn & Bacon.

Delumeau, J. (1977). *Catholicism between Luther and Voltaire.* Philadelphia: Westminster Press.

DeMaria, W. (1981). Empiricism: An impoverished philosophy for social work research. *Australian Social Work, 34,* 3–8.

Denmark, R., Russo, N.F., Frieze, I.H., & Sechzer, J.A. (1988). Guidelines for avoiding sexism in research: A report of the Ad Hoc Committee on Nonsexist Research. *American Pyschologist, 43,* 582–585.

Denzin, N.K. (1978). *The research act: A theoretical introduction to sociological methods* (2nd ed.). New York: McGraw-Hill.

Denzin, N.K. (1989). *The research act: A theoretical introduction to sociological methods* (3rd ed.). Englewood Cliffs, NJ: Prentice-Hall.

Denzin, N.K. (1994). The art and politics of interpretation. In N.K. Denzin & Y.S. Lincoln (Eds.), *Handbook of Qualitative Research.* Thousand Oaks, CA: Sage.

Denzin, N.K., & Lincoln, Y.S. (Eds.). (1994). *Handbook of qualitative research.* Newbury Park, CA: Sage.

DePoy, E., & Gitlin, L.N. (1994). *Introduction to research: Multiple strategies for health and human services* (pp. 3–14, 28–39). St. Louis: Mosby.

Derogates, L.R., Rickles, K., & Rock, A.F. (1976). The SCL-90 and the MMPI: A step in the validation of a new self-report scale. *British Journal of Psychiatry, 128,* 280–289.

Diamond, J. (1987, August). Soft sciences are harder than hard sciences. *Discover, 8,* 34–39.

Diaz, J.O.P. (1988). Assessment of Puerto Rican children in bilingual education programs in the United States: A critique of Lloyd M. Dunn's monograph. *Hispanic Journal of Behavioral Sciences, 10,* 237–252.

Dillman, D.A. (1999). *Mail and internet surveys: The tailored design method* (2nd ed.). New York: Wiley.

Dodd, D.K., Foerch, B.J., & Anderson, H.T. (1988). Content analysis of women and racial minorities as newsmagazine cover persons. *Journal of Social Behavior and Personality, 3,* 231–236.

Dohrenwend, B.S., Colombatos, J., & Dohrenwend, B.P. (1968). Social distance and interview effects. *Public Opinion Quarterly, 32,* 410–422.

Dollard, J., & Mowrer, O.II. (1947). A method of measuring tension in written documents. *Journal of Abnormal and Social Psychology, 42,* 3–22.

Dolnick, E. (1984, July 16). Why have the pollsters been missing the mark? *The Boston Globe,* pp. 27–28.

Doyle, C.A. (1901/1955). *A treasury of Sherlock Holmes.* Garden City, NY: Hanover House.

Dozois, D.J., Dobson, K.S., & Ahnberg, J.L. (1998). A psychometric evaluation of the Beck Depression Inventory-II. *Psychological Assessment, 10,* 83–89.

Duehn, W.D. (1985). Practice and research. In R.M. Grinnell, Jr. (Ed.), *Social work research and evaluation* (2nd ed., pp. 19–48). Itasca, IL: F.E. Peacock.

Eagly, A.H. (1987). Reporting sex differences. *American Psychologist, 42,* 756–757.

Eichler, M. (1988). *Nonsexist research methods: A practical guide.* Boston: Allen & Unwin.

Eisner, E.W. (1979). *The educational imagination.* New York: Basic Books.

Eisner, E.W. (1991). *The enlightened eye: Qualitative inquiry and the enhancement of educational practice.* New York: Macmillan.

Emerson, R.M. (1983). Introduction. In R.M. Emerson (Ed.), *Contemporary field research* (pp. 1–16). Boston: Little, Brown.

Engram, E. (1982). Methodological problems in the study of the Black family. In E. Engram (Ed.), *Science, myth, and reality: The Black family in one-half century of research* (pp. 78–87). Westport, CT: Greenwood.

Epstein, I. (1988). Quantitative and qualitative methods. In R.M. Grinnell, Jr. (Ed.), *Social work research and evaluation* (3rd ed., pp. 185–198). Itasca, IL: F.E. Peacock.

Erlandson, D.A., Harris, E.L., Skipper, B.L., & Allen, S.D. (1993). *Doing naturalistic inquiry: A guide to methods.* Newbury Park, CA: Sage.

Esping-Andersen, C. (1990). Three post-industrial employment regimes. In J.E. Kolberg (Ed.), *The welfare state as employer* (pp. 148–188). Armonk, NY: M.E. Sharpe.

Fabricant, M. (1982). *Juveniles in the family courts.* Lexington, MA: Lexington.

Fairweather, G., & Tornatsky, L. (1977). *Experimental methods for social policy research.* Elmsford, NY: Pergamon.

Federal Register. (1978, May 4). Washington, DC: Government Printing Office.

Fetterman, D.M. (1989). *Ethnography: Step by step.* Newbury Park CA: Sage.

Field, M.H. (1980). Social casework practice during the "psychiatric deluge." *Social Service Review, 54,* 482–507.

Fielding, N., & Fielding, J. (1986). *Linking data.* Thousand Oaks, CA: Sage.

Fielding, R., & Lee, R. (Eds.). (1991). *Using computers in qualitative analysis.* Newbury Park, CA: Sage.

Fineman, H. (1995, February 27). The brave new world of cybertribes. *Newsweek, 125,* 30–33.

Finkelhor, D. (1984). *Child sexual abuse: New theory and research.* New York: Free Press.

Firestone, W.A. (1993). Alternative arguments for generalizing from data as applied to qualitative research. *Educational Researcher, 22,* 16–23.

Fischer, C.S. (1992). *America calling: A social history of the telephone to 1940.* Berkeley, CA: University of California Press.

Fischer, D.H. (1970). *Historians' fallacies: Toward a logic of historical thought.* New York: Harper & Row.

Fischer, J. (1993). Evaluating positivistic research reports. In R.M. Grinnell, Jr. (Ed.), *Social work research and evaluation* (4th ed., pp. 347–366). Itasca, IL: F.E. Peacock.

Fischer, J., & Greenberg, J. (1972). *An investigation of different training methods on indigenous nonprofessionals from diverse minority groups.* Paper presented at the National Association of Social Workers Conference on Social Justice, New Orleans.

Fogel, R.W. (1970). Historiography and retrospective economics. *History and Theory, 9,* 245–264.

Fraiberg, S. (1970). The muse in the kitchen: A case study in clinical research. *Smith College Studies in Social Work, 2,* 101–134.

Frankfort-Nachmias, C., & Nachmias, D. (1992). *Research methods in the social sciences* (4th ed.). New York: St. Martin's Press.

Franklin, C. (1996). Learning to teach qualitative research: Reflections from a quantitative researcher. *Marriage and Family Review, 24,* 241–274.

Franklin, C., & Jordan, C. (1995). Qualitative assessment: A methodological review. *Families in Society, 76,* 281–295.

Franklin, C., & Jordan, C. (1997). Qualitative approaches to the generation of knowledge. In R.M. Grinnell, Jr. (Ed.), *Social work research and evaluation: Quantitative and qualitative approaches* (5th ed., pp. 106–140). Itasca, IL: F.E. Peacock.

Freedman, D.A. (1991). Statistical models and shoe leather. In P.V. Marsden (Ed.), *Sociological methodology* (pp. 291–313). Oxford: Basil Blackwell.

Freidel, F. (Ed.). (1974). *Harvard guide to American history* (2 vols., rev. ed.). Cambridge, MA: Harvard University Press.

Gabor, P.A., & Grinnell, R.M., Jr. (1994). *Evaluation and quality improvement in the human services.* Boston: Allyn & Bacon.

Gabor, P.A., Unrau, Y.A., & Grinnell, R.M., Jr. (1998). *Evaluation for social workers: A quality improvement approach for the social services* (2nd ed.). Boston: Allyn & Bacon.

Garmezy, N. (1982). The case for the single case in research. In A.E. Kazdin & A.H. Tuma (Eds.), *New directions for methodology of social and behavioral sciences* (pp. 517–546). San Francisco: Jossey-Bass.

Garrett, G., & Schutt, R. (1990). Homelessness in Massachusetts: Description and analysis. In J.A. Momeni (Ed.), *Homeless in the United States: Vol. 1. State surveys* (pp. 73–90). Westport, CT: Greenwood.

Garvin, C.D. (1981). Research-related roles for social workers. In R.M. Grinnell, Jr. (Ed.), *Social work research and evaluation* (pp. 547–552). Itasca, IL: F.E. Peacock.

Geertz, C. (1973). *The interpretation of culture.* New York: Basic Books.

Geismar, L.L., & Krisberg, J. (1967). *The forgotten neighborhood.* Metuchen, NJ: Scarecrow.

Geismar, L.L., & Wood, K.M. (1982). Evaluating practice: Science as faith. *Social Casework, 63,* 266–272.

Gilbert, K.R., & Schmid, K. (1994). Bringing our emotions out of the closet: Acknowledging the place of emotion in qualitative research. *Qualitative Family Research, 8,* 1–3.

Gilgun, J.F. (1988). Decision-making in interdisciplinary treatment teams. *Child Abuse and Neglect, 12,* 231–239.

Gilgun, J.F. (1992a). Definitions, methodologies, and methods in qualitative family research. In J.F. Gilgun, K. Daly, & G. Handel. (Eds.), *Qualitative methods in family research* (pp. 22–40). Newbury Park, CA: Sage.

Gilgun, J.F. (1992b). Observations in a clinical setting: Team decision-making in family incest treatment. In J.F. Gilgun, K. Daly, & G. Handel (Eds.), *Qualitative methods in family research* (pp. 236–259). Newbury Park, CA: Sage.

Gilgun, J.F. (1994a). A case for case studies in social work research. *Social Work, 39,* 371–380.

Gilgun, J.F. (1994b). Avengers, conquerors, playmates, and lovers: Roles played by child sexual abuse perpetrators. *Families in Society, 75,* 467–480.

Gilgun, J.F. (1994c). Hand into glove: The grounded theory approach and social work practice research. In E.

Sherman & W.J. Reid (Eds.), *Qualitative research in social work* (pp. 115–125). New York: Columbia University Press.

Gilgun, J.F. (1995). The moral discourse of incest perpetrators. *Journal of Marriage and the Family, 57,* 265–282.

Gilgun, J.F. (1997). Case designs. In R.M. Grinnell, Jr. (Ed.), *Social work research and evaluation: Quantitative and qualitative approaches* (5th ed., pp. 298–312). Itasca, IL: F.E. Peacock.

Gilgun, J.F., & Connor, T.M. (1989). How perpetrators view child sexual abuse. *Social Work, 34,* 349–351.

Gilgun, J.F., Daly, K., & Handel, G. (Eds.). (1992). *Qualitative methods in family research.* Newbury Park, CA: Sage.

Gilligan, C. (1982). *In a different voice: Psychological theory and women's development.* Cambridge, MA: Harvard University Press.

Ginsberg, L. (Ed.). (1995). *Social work almanac* (2nd ed.). Silver Spring, MD: NASW Press.

Glaser, B.G., & Strauss, A.L. (1967). *The discovery of grounded theory: Strategies for qualitative research.* Chicago: Aldine.

Gleick, J. (1990, July 15). The census: Why we can't count. *The New York Times Magazine,* pp. 22–26, 54.

Glisson, C.A., & Fischer, J. (1982). Use and non-use of multivariate statistics. *Social Work Research and Abstracts, 18,* 42–44.

Gochros, H.L. (1970). The caseworker-adoptive parent relationships in post-placement services. In A. Kadushin (Ed.), *Child welfare services.* New York: Macmillan.

Gochros, H.L. (1978). Counseling gay husbands. *Journal of Sex Education and Therapy, 4,* 6–10.

Gochros, H.L. (1988). Research interviewing. In R.M. Grinnell, Jr. (Ed.), *Social work research and evaluation* (3rd ed., pp. 267–299). Itasca, IL: F.E. Peacock.

Gogolin, L, & Swartz, F. (1992). A quantitative and qualitative inquiry into the attitudes toward science of nonscience college students. *Journal of Research in Science Teaching, 29,* 487–504.

Golden, M.P. (Ed.). (1970). *The research experience.* Itasca, IL: F.E. Peacock.

Goldfinger, S.M., Schutt, R.K., Tolomicenko, G.S., Turner, W.M., Ware, N., & Penk, W.E., et al. (1997). Housing persons who are homeless and mentally ill: Independent living or evolving consumer households? In W. Breakey, & J.W. Thompson (Eds.), *Mentally ill and homeless: Special programs for special needs* (pp. 29–49). The Netherlands: Harwood Academic.

Goldman, J., Stein, C.L., & Guerry, S. (1983). *Psychological methods of clinical assessment.* New York: Brunner.

Goldstein, H. (1983). Starting where the client is. *Social Casework, 65,* 267–275.

Goleman, D. (1995). *Emotional intelligence.* New York: Bantam.

Gordon, L. (1994). *Pitied but not entitled: Single mothers and the history of welfare, 1890–1935.* New York: Free Press.

Gottman, J.M. (1979). *Marital interaction.* New York: Academic Press.

Gouldner, A.W. (1970). *The coming crisis of western sociology.* New York: Basic Books.

Graham, J.R., & Lilly, R.S. (1984). *Psychological testing.* Englewood Cliffs, NJ: Prentice-Hall.

Green, G.R., & Wright, J.E. (1979). The retrospective approach to collecting baseline data. *Social Work Research and Abstracts, 15,* 25—30.

Greene, J.C., Caracelli, V.J., & Graham, W.E. (1989). Toward a conceptual framework for mixed-method evaluation designs. *Educational Evaluation and Policy Analysis, 11,* 255—274.

Greenstein, F. (1968). New light on changing American values: A forgotten body of survey data. In S. Lipset & R. Hofstadter (Eds.), *Sociology and history: Methods* (pp. 292—310). New York: Basic Books.

Greenwald, R.A., Ryan, M.K., & Mulvihill, J.E. (1982). *Human subjects research.* New York: Plenum.

Grigsby, R.K., Thyer, B.A., Waller, R.J., & Johnston, G.A. (1999). Chalk eating in middle Georgia: A culture-bound syndrome of pica? *Southern Medical Journal, 92,* 190–192.

Grinnell, F. (1987). *The scientific attitude.* Boulder, CO: Westview.

Grinnell, R.M., Jr., Rothery, M., & Thomlison, R.J. (1993). Research in social work. In R.M. Grinnell, Jr. (Ed.), *Social work research and evaluation* (4th ed., pp. 2–16). Itasca, IL: F.E. Peacock.

Grinnell, R.M., Jr., & Siegel, D.H. (1988). The place of research in social work. In R.M. Grinnell, Jr. (Ed.), *Social work research and evaluation* (3rd ed., pp. 9–24). Itasca, IL: F.E. Peacock.

Grinnell, R.M., Jr., & Williams, M. (1990). *Research in social work: A primer.* Itasca, IL: F.E. Peacock.

Grob, G.N. (1973). *Mental institutions in America.* New York: Free Press.

Groves, R.M. (1988). *Telephone survey methodology.* New York: Wiley.

Groves, R.M., & Cialdini, R.B. (1992). Understanding the decision to participate in a survey. *Public Opinion Quarterly, 56,* 475–496.

Guba, E.G. (1981). Criteria for assessing the trustworthiness of naturalistic inquiries. *Educational Communication and Technology Journal, 29,* 75–91.

Guba, E.G. (1990). *The paradigm dialog.* Newbury Park, CA: Sage.

Guba, E.G., & Lincoln, Y.S. (1981). *Effective evaluation.* San Francisco: Jossey-Bass.

Gulliksen, H. (1950). *Theory of mental tests.* New York: Wiley.

Hakim, C. (1982). *Secondary analysis in social research: A guide to data sources and methods with examples.* London: Allen & Unwin.

Hammersly, M. (1992). *What's wrong with ethnography?* New York: Routledge.

Hansen, J.F. (1979). *Sociocultural perspectives on human learning: An introduction to educational anthropology.* Englewood Cliffs, NJ: Prentice-Hall.

Hanson, J. (1989). *The experience of families of people with a severe mental illness: An ethnographic view.* Unpublished doctoral dissertation, University of Kansas.

Harding, S. (1991). *Whose science? Whose knowledge?* Ithaca, NY: Cornell University Press.

Harding, S. (1993). Introduction: Eurocentric scientific illiteracies—A challenge for the world community. In S. Harding. (Ed.), *The "racial" economy of science* (pp. 1–22). Bloomington and Indianapolis: Indiana University Press.

Hartman, A. (1978). Diagrammatic assessment of family relationships. *Social Casework, 59,* 465–476.

Haynes, S.N. (1983). Behavioral assessment. In M. Hersen, A.E. Kazdin, & A.S. Bellack (Eds.), *The clinical psychology handbook* (pp. 397–425). Elmsford, NY: Pergamon.

Heckathorn, D. (1997). Respondent-driven sampling: A new approach to the study of hidden populations. *Social Problems, 44,* 174–199.

Heineman, M.B. (1981). The obsolete scientific imperative in social work research. *Social Service Review, 55,* 371–397.

Hempel, C.G. (1966). *Philosophy of natural science.* Englewood Cliffs, NJ: Prentice-Hall.

Herek, G.M., Kimmel, D.C., Amaro, H., & Melton, G.G. (1991). Avoiding heterosexist bias in psychological research. *American Psychologist, 46,* 957–963.

Herzogg, E. (1959). *Some guidelines for evaluative research.* Washington, DC: U.S. Department of Health, Education, and Welfare.

Hess, D.J. (1995). *Science and technology in a multicultural world.* New York: Columbia University Press.

Hewitt, S.K. (1994). Preverbal sexual abuse: What two children report in later years. *Child Abuse and Neglect, 18,* 821–826.

Hexter, J.H. (1971). *Doing history.* Bloomington: Indiana University Press.

Hill, C.E., Gelso, J., Mohr, J., Rochlen, A., & Zack, J. (1997). *The qualitative study of successful long-term therapy.* Unpublished manuscript.

Hill, C.E., Thompson, B.J., & Williams, E.N. (1997). A guide to conducting consensual qualitative research. *The Counseling Psychologist, 25,* 517–527.

Hochschild, A. (1989). *The second shift: Working parents and the revolution of the home.* New York: Viking.

Hoffart, I., & Krysik, J. (1993). Glossary. In R.M. Grinnell, Jr. (Ed.), *Social work research and evaluation* (4th ed., pp. 439–450). Itasca, IL: F.E. Peacock.

Hofstede, G., Neuijen, B., Ohayv, D.D., & Sanders, G. (1990). Measuring organizational cultures: A qualitative and quantitative study across twenty cases. *Administrative Science Quarterly, 35,* 286–316.

Hogerty, G.F., & Ulrich, R. (1972). The discharge readiness inventory. *Archives of General Psychiatry, 26,* 419–426.

Holmes, S. (1994, May 16). Census officials plan big changes in gathering data. *The New York Times,* pp. A1, A13.

Holmes, S. (1996, February 29). In a first 2000 census is to use sampling. *The New York Times,* p. A18.

Holsti, O. (1969). *Content analysis for the social sciences and humanities.* Reading, MA: Addison-Wesley.

Hooker, E. (1957). The adjustment of the male overt homosexual. *Journal of Projective Techniques, 21,* 18–31.

Hops, H., & Greenwood, C.R. (1981). Social skills deficits. In E.J. Mash & L.G. Terdal (Eds.), *Behavioral assessment of childhood disorders* (pp. 347–394). New York: Guilford.

Howard, A., & Scott, R. (1981). The study of minority groups in complex societies. In R.H. Munroe, R.L. Munroe, & B. Whiting (Eds.), *Handbook of cross-cultural human development* (pp. 113–152). New York: Garland.

Huck, S.W., Cormier, W.H., & Bounds, W.G. (1974). *Reading statistics and research.* New York: Harper & Row.

Huck, S.W., & Sandler, H.M. (1979). *Rival hypotheses: Alternative interpretations of data-based conclusions.* New York: Harper & Row.

Hughes, D., Seidman, E., & Williams, N. (1993). Cultural phenomena and the research enterprise: Toward a culturally anchored methodology. *American Journal of Community Psychology, 21,* 687–703.

Hughes, M. (1998). Turning points in the lives of young inner-city men forgoing destructive criminal behaviors: A qualitative study. *Social Work Research, 22,* 143–151.

Humphrey, N. (1992). *A history of the mind: Evolution and the birth of consciousness.* New York: Simon & Schuster.

Humphreys, L. (1970). *Tearoom trade: Impersonal sex in public places.* Chicago: Aldine.

Hyde, J.S. (1991). *Half the human experience: The psychology of women* (4th ed.). Lexington, MA: Heath.

Hyden, M. (1994). Woman battering as a marital act: Interviewing and analysis in context. In C.K. Reissman (Ed.), *Qualitative studies in social work research* (pp. 95–112). Newbury Park, CA: Sage.

Hyman, H.H. (1954). *Interviewing in social research.* Chicago: University of Chicago Press.

Hyman, H.H. (1987). *Secondary analysis of sample surveys: With a new introduction.* New York: Harper & Row.

Ihilevich, D., & Gleser, G.C. (1982). *Evaluating mental health programs.* Lexington, MA: Lexington.

Jackson, G.B. (1980). Methods for integrative reviews. *Review of Educational Research, 50,* 438–460.

Jacob, E. (1987). Qualitative research traditions: A review. *Review of Educational Research, 57,* 150.

Jacobson, J.L. (1992). Gender bias: Roadblock to sustainable development (Paper No. 110, ISBN 1–87071-10–6). Washington, DC: Worldwatch Institute.

Jarrett, R.L. (1992). A family case study: An examination of the underclass debate. In J.F. Gilgun, Daly, K., & Handel, G. (Eds.), *Qualitative methods in family research* (pp. 172–197). Newbury Park, CA: Sage.

Jenkins, S. (1975). Collecting data by questionnaire and interview. In N.A. Polansky (Ed.), *Social work research: Methods for the helping professions* (Rev. ed., pp. 140–155). Chicago: University of Chicago Press.

Jenkins, S., & Norman, E. (1972). *Filial deprivation and foster care.* New York: Columbia University Press.

Jick, T. (1979). Mixing qualitative and quantitative methods: Triangulation in action. *Administrative Science Quarterly, 24,* 602–611.

Jick, T. (1983). Mixing qualitative and quantitative methods: Triangulation in action. In J. Van Maanen (Ed.), *Qualitative methodology* (pp. 135–148). Thousand Oaks, CA: Sage.

Johnson, J.M. (1975). *Doing field research.* New York: Free Press.

Jordan, C., & Franklin, C. (2003). *Clinical assessment for social workers: Quantitative and qualitative methods* (2nd ed.). Chicago: Lyceum.

Jordan, C., Franklin, C., & Corcoran, K. (1993). Standardized measuring instruments. In R.M. Grinnell, Jr. (Ed.), *Social work research and evaluation* (4th ed., pp. 198–220). Itasca, IL: F.E. Peacock.

Jordan, C., Franklin, C., & Corcoran, K. (1997). Measuring instruments. In R.M. Grinnell, Jr. (Ed.), *Social work research and evaluation: Quantitative and qualitative approaches* (5th ed., pp. 184–211). Itasca, IL: F.E. Peacock.

Jorgensen, D.L. (1989). *Participant observation: A methodology for human studies.* Newbury Park, CA: Sage.

Judd, C.M., Smith, E.R., & Kidder, I.H. (1991). *Research methods in social relations* (6th ed.). Fort Worth, TX: Harcourt Brace.

Junker, B.H. (1960). *Field work.* Chicago: University of Chicago Press.

Kadushin, A., Kadushin, G. (1997). *The social work interview: A guide for human service professionals* (4th ed.). New York: Columbia University Press.

Kahn, R. (1997, January 3). A last drink on New Year's. *The Boston Globe,* pp. B1, B2.

Kalberg, S. (1975). The commitment to career reform: The settlement movement leaders. *Social Service Review, 49,* 608–628.

Kaplan, A. (1964). *The conduct of inquiry: Methodology for behavioral science.* New York: Harper & Row.

Katz, D. (1942). Do interviewers bias polls? *Public Opinion Quarterly, 6,* 248–268.

Kazdin, A.E. (1981). Drawing valid inferences from case studies. *Journal of Consulting and Clinical Psychology, 49,* 183–192.

Keele, H.M., & Kiger, J.C. (Eds.). (1984). *Foundations.* Westport, CT: Greenwood.

Kenney, C. (1987, August 30). They've got your number. *The Boston Globe Magazine,* pp. 12, 46–56, 60.

Kent, R.N., & Foster, S.L. (1977). Direct observational procedures: Methodological issues in naturalistic settings. In A.R. Ciminero, K.S. Calhoun, & H.E. Adams. (Eds.), *Handbook of behavioral assessment* (pp. 217–328). New York: Wiley.

Kerlinger, F. (1986). *Foundations of behavioral research* (3rd ed.). New York: Holt.

Kiecolt, K.J., & Nathan, L.E. (1985). *Secondary analysis of survey data.* Newbury Park, CA: Sage.

Kirk, J., & Miller, M.L. (1986). *Reliability and validity in qualitative research.* Thousand Oaks, CA: Sage.

Klaassen, D.J. (1995). Archives of social welfare. In *Encyclopedia of social work* (19th ed., Vol. 1, pp. 225–231.). Washington, DC: NASW Press.

Kleinman, J.C., & Kessel, S.S. (1987). Racial differences in low birthweight: Trends and risk factors. *New England Journal of Medicine, 317,* 749–753.

Kogel, P., & Burnam, A. (1992). Problems in the assessment of mental illness among the homeless: An empirical approach. In M.J. Robertson, & M. Greenblatt (Eds.), *Homelessness: A national perspective* (pp. 77–99). New York: Plenum.

Kraemer, H., & Thiemann, S. (1987). *How many subjects? Statistical power analysis in research.* Newbury Park, CA: Sage.

Krathwohl, D. (1991). *Methods of educational and social science research: An integrated approach.* New York: Longman.

Krueger, R.A. (1997). *Focus groups: A practical guide for applied research.* Newbury Park, CA: Sage.

Krysik, J., & Grinnell, R.M., Jr. (1997). Quantitative approaches to the generation of knowledge. In R.M. Grinnell, Jr. (Ed.), *Social work research and evaluation: Quantitative and qualitative approaches* (5th ed., pp. 67–105). Itasca, IL: F.E. Peacock.

Krysik, J.L., Hoffart, I., & Grinnell, R.M., Jr. (1993). *Student study guide for the fourth edition of Social Work Research and Evaluation.* Itasca, IL: F.E. Peacock.

Kuhn, T. (1970). *The structure of scientific revolutions* (2nd ed.). Chicago: University of Chicago Press.

Kunzel, R.G. (1993). *Fallen women, problem girls: Unmarried mothers and the professionalization of social work, 1890–1945.* New Haven, CT: Yale University Press.

Kushman, J.W. (1992). The organizational dynamics of teacher workplace commitment: A study of urban elementary and middle schools. *Educational Administration Quarterly, 28,* 5–42.

LaGory, M., Ferris, J., & Mullis, J. (1990). Depression among the homeless. *Journal of Health and Social Behavior, 31,* 87–101.

Lancy, D.F. (1993). *Qualitative research in education: An introduction to the major traditions.* White Plains, NY: Longman.

Landrine, H., Klonoff, E.A., & Brown-Collins, A. (1992). Cultural diversity and methodology in feminist psychology. *Psychology of Women Quarterly, 16,* 145–163.

LaPiere, R.T. (1934). Attitudes and actions. *Social Forces, 13,* 230–237.

Larossa R., & Wolf, J.H. (1985). On qualitative family research. *Journal of Marriage and the Family, 47,* 531–541.

Lasch-Quinn, E. (1993). *Black neighbors: Race and the limits of reform in the American settlement house movement, 1890–1945.* Chapel Hill, NC: University of North Carolina Press.

Lavrakas, P.J. (1987). *Telephone survey methods: Sampling, selection, and supervision.* Newbury Park, CA: Sage.

LeCompte, M.D., & Goetz, J.P. (1982). Problems of reliability and validity in ethnographic research. *Journal of Educational Research, 52,* 31–60.

LeCroy, C.W., & Solomon, G. (1997). Content analysis. In R.M. Grinnell, Jr. (Ed.), *Social work research and evaluation: Quantitative and qualitative approaches* (5th ed., pp. 427–441). Itasca, IL: F.E. Peacock.

Lee, B.A., Jones, S.H., & Lewis, D.W. (1990). Public beliefs about the causes of homelessness. *Social Forces, 69,* 253–265.

Leedy, P.D. (1993). *Practical research: Planning and design* (3rd ed., pp. 128–131). New York: Macmillan.

LeVay, S. (1996). *Queer science: The use and abuse of research into homosexuality.* Cambridge, MA: MIT Press.

Levine, C. (1991). AIDS and the ethics of human subjects research. In F.G. Reamer (Ed.), *AIDS and ethics* (pp. 77–104). New York: Columbia University Press.

Levine, R.J. (1988). *Ethics and regulation of clinical research* (2nd ed.). New Haven, CT: Yale University Press.

Lewis, M.R. (1976). Social policy research: A guide to legal and government documents. *Social Service Review, 50,* 647–654.

Lewis, O. (1966). *La Vida: A Puerto Rican family in the culture of poverty—San Juan and New York.* New York: Random House.

Lincoln, Y., & Guba, E. (1985). *Naturalistic inquiry.* Newbury Park, CA: Sage.

Link, B., Phelan, J., Stueve, A., Moore, R., Brenahan, M., & Struening, E. (1996). Public attitudes and beliefs about homeless people. In J. Baumohl (Ed.), *Homelessness in America* (pp. 143–148). Phoenix, AZ: Oryx.

Loewenberg, F., & Dolgoff, R. (1996). *Ethical decisions for social work practice* (5th ed.). Itasca, IL: F.E. Peacock.

Loth, R. (1992, October 25). Bush may be too far back, history of polls suggests. *The Boston Globe,* p. 19.

Lowenthal, L. (1944). Biographies in popular magazines. In P.F. Lazarsfeld & F.N. Stanton (Eds.), *Radio research in 1942–43* (pp. 505–548). New York: Duell, Sloan, and Pearce.

Mackey, R.A, & Mackey, E.F. (1994). Personal psychotherapy and the development of a professional self. *Families in Society, 75,* 490–498.

Maeser, N., & Thyer, B.A. (1990). Teaching boys with severe retardation to serve themselves during family-style meals. *Behavioral Residential Treatment, 5,* 239–246.

Magill, R.S. (1977). Who decides revenue sharing allocations? *Social Work, 22,* 297–300.

Maloney, D.M. (1984). *Protection of human research subjects: A practical guide to federal laws and regulations.* New York: Plenum.

Maluccio, A.N. (1979). *Learning from clients.* New York: Free Press.

Mandell, N. (1984). Children's negotiation of meaning. *Symbolic Interaction, 7,* 191–211.

Marin, G., & Marin, B. (1991). *Research with Hispanic populations.* Newbury Park, CA: Sage.

Marsh, J.C. (1983). Research and innovation in social work practice: Avoiding the headless machine. *Social Service Review, 57,* 584–598.

Marshall, C., & Rossman, G.B. (1995). *Designing qualitative research* (2nd ed.). Newbury Park, CA: Sage.

Marson, S.M. (1999). Uncovering UnCover. *The New Social Worker, 6,* 23–24, 28.

Mathison, S. (1988). Why triangulate? *Educational Researcher, 17,* 13–17.

Matsumoto, D. (1994). *People: Psychology from a cultural perspective.* Pacific Grove, CA: Brooks/Cole.

McClelland, D.C. (1961). *The achieving society.* New York: Free Press.

McClelland, R.W., & Austin, C.D. (1996). Phase four: Writing your report. In L.M. Tutty, M.A. Rothery, & R.M. Grinnell, Jr. (Eds.), *Qualitative research for social workers: Phases, steps, and tasks* (pp. 120–150). Boston: Allyn & Bacon.

McGrath, J.E., & Brinberg, D. (1983). External validity and the research process: A comment on the Calder-Lynch dialogue. *Journal of Consumer Research, 10,* 115–124.

McMahon, A., & Allen-Meares, P. (1992). Is social work racist? A content analysis of recent literature. *Social Work, 37,* 533–540.

McMurtry, S.L., & McClelland, R.W. (1995, March). *Alarming trends in faculty/student ratios in MSW programs.* Paper presented at the meeting of the Council on Social Work Education, San Diego, CA.

McNicoll, P. (1999). Issues in teaching participatory action research. *Journal of Social Work Education, 35,* 51–62.

Merton, R., Fiske, M., & Kendall, P. (1956). *The focused interview.* Glencoe, IL: Free Press.

Meyer, C. (1983). *Clinical social work in the eco-systems perspective.* New York: Columbia University Press.

Meyer, C. (1993). *Assessment in social work.* New York: Columbia University Press.

Miles, M.B., & Huberman, M. (1994). *An expanded sourcebook: Qualitative data analysis* (2nd ed.). Thousand Oaks, CA: Sage.

Miles, M.B., & Huberman, M. (1995). *Qualitative data analysis: A sourcebook of new methods.* Newbury Park, CA: Sage.

Miles, M.B., & Weitzman, E. (1995). *Computer programs for qualitative data analysis.* Newbury Park, CA: Sage.

Miles, M.B., & Weitzman, E. (1999). *Computer programs for qualitative data analysis* (2nd ed.). Thousand Oaks, CA: Sage.

Milgram, S. (1963). Behavioral study of obedience. *Journal of Abnormal and Applied Social Psychology, 67,* 371–378.

Milgram, S. (1965). Some conditions of obedience and disobedience to authority. *Human Relations, 18,* 57–75.

Milgram, S. (1974). *Obedience to authority: An experimental view.* New York: Harper & Row.

Miller, C., & Swift, K. (1980), *The handbook on nonsexist writing.* New York: Barnes and Noble.

Miller, L.K., & Miller, O.L. (1970). Reinforcing self-help group activities of welfare recipients. *Journal of Applied Behavior Analysis, 3,* 57–64.

Mindel, C.H., & McDonald, L. (1988). Survey research. In R.M. Grinnell, Jr. (Ed.), *Social work research and evaluation* (3rd ed., pp. 300–322). Itasca, IL: F.E. Peacock.

Mischel, W. (1968). *Personality and assessment.* New York: Wiley.

Mook, D.G. (1983). In defense of external invalidity. *American Psychologist, 38,* 379–387.

Moon, S.M., Dillon, D.R., & Sprenkle, D.H. (1990). Family therapy and qualitative research. *Journal of Marital and Family Therapy, 16,* 357–373.

Morgan, D. (1988). *Focus groups as qualitative research.* Newbury Park, CA: Sage.

Morse, J.M. (1991). Approaches to qualitative-quantitative methodological triangulation. *Nursing Research, 40,* 120–123.

Morse, J.M., & Field, P.A. (1995). *Qualitative research methods for health professionals* (2nd ed.). Newbury Park, CA: Sage.

Murguia, E., Padilla, R.V., & Pavel, M. (1991). Ethnicity and the concept of social integration in Tinto's model of institutional departure. *Journal of College Student Development, 32,* 433–439.

Myers, D.G. (1983). *Social psychology.* New York: McGraw-Hill.

Myers, L.M., & Thyer, B.A. (1997). Should social work clients have the right to effective treatment? *Social Work, 42,* 288–298.

Naipaul, V.S. (1979). *A bend in the river.* New York: Knopf.

Navarro, M. (1990, March 25). Census questionnaire: Link to democracy and source of data. *The New York Times,* p. 36.

National Academy of Science. (1993). Methods and values in science. In S. Harding (Ed.), *The "racial" economy of science* (pp. 341–343). Bloomington and Indianapolis: Indiana University Press.

National Association of Social Workers. (1995). *Encyclopedia of social work* (19th ed.). Washington, DC: NASW Press.

National Association of Social Workers. (1996). *Code of Ethics of the National Association of Social Workers.* Washington, DC: Author.

National Commission for the Protection of Human Subjects of Biomedical and Behavioral Research. (1978). *The Belmont Report: Ethical principles and guidelines for the protection of human subjects of research.* Washington, DC: Author.

Neimeyer, R.A. (1993). An appraisal of constructivist psychotherapies. *Journal of Consulting and Clinical Psychology, 61,* 221–234.

Nelson, R., & Barlow, D.H. (1981). Behavioral assessment: Basic strategies and initial procedures. In D. Barlow (Ed.), *Behavior assessment of adult disorders* (pp. 13–43). New York: Guilford.

Neuman, W.L. (2003). *Social research methods: Qualitative and quantitative approaches* (5th ed.). Needham Heights, MA: Allyn & Bacon.

Newfield, N., Sells, S.P., Smith, T.E., Newfield, S., & Newfield, F. (1996). Ethnographic research methods: Creating a clinical science of the humanities. In D.H. Sprenkle & S.M. Moon (Eds.), *Research methods in family therapy* (pp. 25–63). New York: Guilford.

Norris, P. (1987). *Politics and sexual equality: The comparative position of women in western democracies.* Boulder, CO: Lynne Rienner.

Nunnally, J.C. (1975). *Introduction to statistics for psychology and education.* New York: McGraw-Hill.

Nunnally, J.C. (1978). *Psychometric theory* (2nd ed.). New York: McGraw-Hill.

Nurius, P.S., & Hudson, W.W. (1993). *Human services: Practice, evaluation, and computers.* Pacific Grove, CA: Brooks/Cole.

Olesen, V. (1994). Feminisms and models of qualitative research. In N.K. Denzin & Y.S. Lincoln. (Eds.), *Handbook of qualitative research* (pp. 33–44). Thousand Oaks, CA: Sage.

Ortega, D.M., & Richey, C.A. (1998). Methodological issues in social work research with depressed women of color. In M. Potocky & A.Y. Rodgers-Farmer (Eds.), *Social work research with minority and oppressed populations: Methodological issues and innovations* (pp. 47–70). New York: Haworth.

Oyen, E. (1990). *Comparative methodology: Theory and practice in international social research.* Newbury Park, CA: Sage.

Padgett, D.K. (1998). *Qualitative methods in social work research: Challenges and rewards.* Thousand Oaks, CA: Sage.

Palys, T. (1997). *Research decisions: Quantitative and qualitative perspectives.* Toronto: Harcourt Brace.

Papell, C.P., & Skolnik, L. (1992). The reflective practitioner: A contemporary paradigm's relevance for social work education. *Journal of Social Work Education, 28,* 18–26.

Patterson, T.E. (1994). *Out of order.* New York: Vintage.

Patton, M.Q. (1980). *Qualitative evaluation methods.* Thousand Oaks, CA: Sage.

Patton, M.Q. (1990). *Qualitative evaluation and research methods* (2nd ed.). Newbury Park, CA: Sage.

Pedersen, P. (1988). *A handbook for developing multicultural awareness.* Alexandria, VA: American Association for Counseling and Development.

Pedersen, P. (1991). Multiculturalism as a generic approach to counseling. *Journal of Counseling and Development, 19,* 6–12.

Phillips, D.C. (1987). Validity in qualitative research: Why the worry about warrant will not wane. *Education and Urban Society, 20,* 9–24.

Phinney, J.S., & Landin, J. (1998). Research paradigms for studying ethnic minority families within and across groups. In V.C. McLoyd & L. Steinberg (Eds.), *Studying minority adolescents: Conceptual, methodological, and theoretical issues* (pp. 89–109). Mahwah, NJ: Erlbaum.

Pivin, F.F., & Cloward, R.A. (1971). *Regulating the poor: The functions of public welfare.* New York: Vintage.

Polkinghorne, D.E. (1991). Two conflicting calls for methodological reform. *The Counseling Psychologist, 19,* 103–114.

Pollner, M. (1998). The effects of interviewer gender in mental health interviews. *Journal of Nervous and Mental Disease, 18,* 369–373.

Pomeroy, W. (1972). *Dr. Kinsey and the sex institute.* New York: Harper and Row.

Pope, W. (1976). *Durkheim's suicide: A classic analyzed.* Chicago: University of Chicago Press.

Poser, E.G. (1966). The effects of therapists' training on group therapeutic outcome. *Journal of Consulting Psychotherapy, 30,* 283–289.

President's Commission for the Study of Ethical Problems in Medicine and Biomedical and Behavioral Research. (1982). *Making health care decisions: The ethical and legal implications of informed consent in the patient-practitioner relationship* (Vol. 3). Washington, DC: Government Printing Office.

Prucha, F.P. (1994). *Handbook for research in American history: A guide to bibliographies and other reference works* (2nd ed.). Lincoln: University of Nebraska Press.

Pumphrey, R.E., & Pumphrey, M.W. (1961). *The heritage of American social work: Readings in its philosophical and institutional development.* New York: Columbia University Press.

Rafuls, S.E., & Moon, S.M. (1996). Grounded theory methodology in family therapy research. In D.H. Sprenkle & S.M. Moon (Eds.), *Research methods in family therapy* (pp. 64–80). New York: Guilford.

Rauch, J.B. (1975). Women in social work: Friendly visitors in Philadelphia, 1880. *Social Service Review, 49,* 241–259.

Reamer, F.G. (1983). The concept of paternalism in social work. *Social Service Review, 57,* 254–271.

Reamer, F.G. (1987). Informed consent in social work. *Social Work, 32,* 425–429.

Reamer, F.G. (1998). *Ethical standards in social work: A critical review of the NASW Code of Ethics.* Washington, DC: NASW Press.

Reamer, F.G. (1999). *Social work values and ethics* (2nd ed.). New York: Columbia University Press.

Reason, P., & Rowan, J. (1981). Issues of validity in new paradigm research. In P. Reason & J. Rowan (Eds.), *Human inquiry: A sourcebook of new paradigm research* (pp. 239–262). New York: Wiley.

Reid, P.N., & Gundlach, J.H. (1983). A scale for the measurement of consumer satisfaction with social services. *Journal of Social Service Research, 7,* 37–54.

Reid, W.J., & Shyne, A. (1969). *Brief and extended casework.* New York: Columbia University Press.

Reid, W.J., & Smith, A.D. (1989). *Research in social work* (2nd ed.). New York: Columbia University Press.

Reinharz, S. (1992). Feminist survey research and other statistical research formats. In S. Reinharz (Ed.), *Feminist methods in social research* (pp. 76–94). New York: Oxford University Press.

Richards, L., & Richards, T.J. (1992). Analyzing unstructured information: Can computers help? *Library Hi-Tech, 10,* 95–109.

Riesman, D., Glazer, N., & Denny, R. (1950). *The lonely crowd: A study of the changing American character.* New Haven, CT: Yale University Press.

Riessman, C.K. (1994). *Qualitative studies in social work research.* Newbury Park: CA: Sage.

Robinson, D., & Rhodes, S. (1946). Two experiments with an anti-Semitism poll. *Journal of Abnormal and Social Psychology, 41,* 136–144.

Rodwell, M.K. (1998). *Social work constructivist research.* New York: Garland.

Roethlisberger, F.J., & Dickson, W.J. (1939). *Management and the worker: An account of a research program conducted by the Western Electric Co. Hawthorne Works, Chicago.* Cambridge, MA: Harvard University Press.

Rogers, G., & Bouey, E. (1996). Phase two: Collecting your data. In L.M. Tutty, M.A. Rothery, & R.M. Grinnell, Jr. (Eds.), *Qualitative research for social workers: Phases, steps, and tasks* (pp. 50–87). Boston: Allyn & Bacon.

Rogler, L.H. (1999). Methodological sources of cultural insensitivity in mental health research. *American Psychologist, 54,* 424–433.

Rokach, A. (1988). The experience of loneliness: A tri-level model. *Journal of Psychology, 122,* 531–544.

Rollins, J. (1985). *Between women: Domestics and their employers.* Philadelphia: Temple University Press.

Romanofsky, P. (Ed.). (1978). *Social service organizations.* Westport, CT: Greenwood.

Rosenhan, D. (1973). On being sane in insane places. *Science, 179,* 250–258.

Rosenthal, R. (1994). *Homeless in paradise: A map of the terrain.* Philadelphia: Temple University Press.

Rosser, S.V. (1991). AIDS and women. *AIDS, 3,* 230–240.

Rossi, P.H. (1989). *Down and out in America: The origins of homelessness.* Chicago: University of Chicago Press.

Rossi, P.H., & Freeman, H.E. (1993). *Evaluation: A systematic approach* (5th ed.). Newbury Park, CA: Sage.

Roth, D. (1990). Homelessness in Ohio: A statewide epidemiological study. In J.A. Momeni (Ed.), *Homeless in the United States:* Vol. 1. State surveys (pp. 145–163). Westport, CT: Greenwood.

Roth, D., Bean, J., Lust, N., & Saveanu, T. (1985). *Homelessness in Ohio: A study of people in need.* Columbus, OH: Department of Mental Health.

Rothery, M.A., Tutty, L.M., Grinnell, R.M., Jr. (1996). Introduction. In L.M. Tutty, M.A. Rothery, & R.M. Grinnell, Jr. (Eds.), *Qualitative research for social workers: Phases, steps, and tasks* (pp. 2–22). Needham Heights, MA: Allyn & Bacon.

Rothman, D. (1971). *The discovery of the asylum: Social order and disorder in the new republic.* Boston: Little, Brown.

Rubin, A., & Babbie, E. (2005). *Research methods for social work* (5th ed.). Pacific Grove, CA: Wadsworth.

Rubin, H., & Rubin, I. (1995). *Qualitative interviewing: The art of hearing data.* Thousand Oaks, CA: Sage.

Ruckdeschel, R. (1994). Does emphasizing accountability and evidence dilute service delivery and the helping role? Yes! In W.W. Hudson & P.S. Nurius (Eds.), *Controversial issues in social work research* (pp. 9–14). Needham Heights, MA: Allyn & Bacon.

Russell, D. (1984). *Sexual exploitation: Rape, child sexual abuse, and workplace harassment.* Newbury Park, CA: Sage.

Salgo v. Leland Stanford Junior University Board of Trustees, 317 P.2d 170 (Cal. Ct. App. 1957).

Sanders, J.R. (Ed.). (1994). *The program evaluation standards* (2nd ed.). (Joint Committee on Standards for Educational Evaluation.) Newbury Park, CA: Sage.

Sattler, J.M. (Ed.). (1988). *Assessment of children* (3rd ed.). San Diego: Jerome M. Sattler.

Scarr, S. (1988). Race and gender as psychological variables: Social and ethical issues. *American Psychologist, 43,* 56–59.

Schacter, D.L. (1999). The seven sins of memory: Insights from psychology and cognitive neuroscience. *American Psychologist, 54,* 182–203.

Schele, L., & Freidel, D. (1990). *A forest of kings: The untold story of the ancient Maya.* New York: Morrow.

Schinke, S.P., & Gilchrist, L.D. (1993). Ethics in research. In R.M. Grinnell, Jr. (Ed.), *Social work research and evaluation* (4th ed., pp. 79–90). Itasca, IL: F.E. Peacock.

Schloendorff v. Society of New York Hospital, 211 N.Y. 125 (1914).

Schmeckebier, L., & Eastin, R.B. (1969). *Government publications and their use* (2nd ed.). Washington, DC: Brookings Institution.

Schneidman, E. (1985). At the point of no return. *Psychology Today, 19,* 55–58.

Schön, D.A. (1983). *The reflective practitioner: How professionals think in action.* New York: Basic Books.

Schuman, H. (1972). Two sources of antiwar sentiment in America. *American Journal of Sociology, 78,* 513–536.

Schuman, H., & Converse, J.M. (1970). The effects of black and white interviewers on black responses. *Public Opinion Quarterly, 35,* 44–68.

Schutt, R.K., & Garrett, G.R. (1992). *Responding to the homeless: Policy and practice.* New York: Plenum.

Schutt, R.K., & Goldfinger, S.M., & Peck, E. (1997). Satisfaction with residence and with life: When homeless mentally ill persons are housed. *Evaluation and Program Planning, 20,* 185–194.

Schutt, R.K., Meschede, T., & Rierdan, J. (1994). Distress, suicidality, and social support among homeless adults. *Journal of Health and Social Behavior, 35,* 134–142.

Schwitzgebel, R. (1964). *Street-corner research.* Cambridge, MA: Harvard University Press.

Seaberg, J.R. (1988). Utilizing sampling procedures. In R.M. Grinnell, Jr. (Ed.), *Social work research and evaluation* (3rd ed., pp. 240–257). Itasca, IL: F.E. Peacock.

Seidl, F. (Ed.). (1995). Biographies. In *Encyclopedia of Social Work* (19th ed., Vol. 3, pp. 2569–2621). Washington, DC: NASW Press.

Seidman, E. (1978). Justice, values, and social science: Unexamined premises. In R.J. Simon (Ed.), *Research in law and sociology* (pp. 175–200). Greenwich, CT: JAI.

Seidman, E. (1991). *Interviewing as qualitative research.* New York: Teachers College Press.

Seidman, L.J. (1997). Neuropsychological testing. In A. Tasman, J. Kay, & J. Lieberman (Eds.), *Psychiatry* (pp. 498–508). Philadelphia: W.B. Saunders.

Sells, S.P., Smith, T.E., Coe, M.J., Yoshioka, M., & Robbins, J. (1994). An ethnography of couple and therapist experiences in reflecting team practice. *Journal of Marital and Family Therapy, 20,* 247–266.

Selznick, P. (1957). *Leadership in administration.* New York: Harper & Row.

Sherman, E. (1994). Discourse analysis in the framework of change process research. In E. Sherman & W.J. Reid (Eds.), *Qualitative research in social work* (pp. 228–241). New York: Columbia University Press.

Shin, H., & Abell, N. (1999). The Homesickness and Contentment Scale: Developing a culturally sensitive measure of adjustment for Asians. *Research on Social Work Practice, 9,* 45–60.

Shorter, E. (1975). *The making of the modern family.* New York: Basic Books.

Siegel, D.H. (1988). Integrating data-gathering techniques and practice activities. In R.M. Grinnell, Jr. (Ed.), *Social work research and evaluation* (3rd ed., pp. 465–482). Itasca, IL: F.E. Peacock.

Siegel, D.H., & Reamer, F.G. (1988). Integrating research findings, concepts, and logic into practice. In R.M. Grinnell, Jr. (Ed.), *Social work research and evaluation* (3rd ed., pp. 483–502). Itasca, IL: F.E. Peacock.

Simon, J. (1969). *Basic research methods in social science*. New York: Random House.

Singer, E., Frankel, M.R., & Glassman, M.B. (1983). The effect of interviewer characteristics and expectations on response. *Public Opinion Quarterly, 47*, 68–83.

Singleton, R.A., Jr., Straits, B.C., & Miller-Straits, M. (1993). *Approaches to social research* (2nd ed.). New York: Oxford University Press.

Sluckin, A. (1989). Behavioral social work treatment of childhood nocturnal enuresis. *Behavior Modification, 13*, 482–497.

Smith, A.W. (1993). Survey research on African Americans: Methodological innovations. In J.H. Stanfield (Ed.), *Race and ethnicity in research methods* (pp. 217–229). Newbury Park, CA: Sage.

Snow, D.A., & Anderson, L. (1987). Identity work among the homeless: The verbal construction and avowal of personal identities. *American Journal of Sociology, 92*, 1336–1371.

Snow, D.A., & Anderson, L. (1991). Researching the homeless: The characteristic features and virtues of the case study. In J.R. Feagin, A.M. Orum, & G. Sjoberg (Eds.), *A case for the case study* (pp. 148–173). Chapel Hill: University of North Carolina Press.

Specht, H., & Courtney, M.E. (1994). *Unfaithful angels: How social work has abandoned its mission*. New York: Free Press.

Snyder, T.D. (1994). *Digest of education statistics*. (NCES Publication No. 94–115). Washington, DC: US Department of Education, Office of Education Research and Improvement.

Sosin, M., Colson, P., & Grossman, S. (1988). *Homelessness in Chicago: Poverty and pathology, social institutions and social change*. Chicago: Chicago Community Trust.

Sperry, R.W. (1968). Hemisphere deconnection and unity in conscious awareness. *American Psychologist, 23*, 723–733.

Spradley, J.P. (1979). *The ethnographic interview*. New York: Holt, Rinehart, and Winston.

Spradley, J.P. (1980). *Participant observation*. New York: Holt, Rinehart, & Winston.

Staats, A.W., & Butterfield, W. (1965). Treatment of nonreading in a culturally deprived juvenile delinquent: An application of reinforcement principles. *Child Development, 36*, 925–942.

Stake, R.E. (1995). *The art of case study research*. Newbury Park, CA: Sage.

Stanfield, J.H. (1993). *Race and ethnicity in research methods*. Newbury Park, CA: Sage.

Stanfield, J.H. (1994). Ethnic modeling in qualitative research. In N.K. Denzin & Y.S. Lincoln (Eds.), *Handbook of qualitative research* (pp. 175–188). Thousand Oaks, CA: Sage.

Steinberg, L., & Fletcher, A.C. (1998). Data analytic strategies in research on ethnic minority youth. In V.C. McLoyd & L. Steinberg (Eds.), *Studying minority adolescents: Conceptual, methodological, and theoretical issues* (pp. 279–294). Mahwah, NJ: Erlbaum.

Stern, D.N. (1985). *The interpersonal world of the infant*. New York: Basic Books.

Stocks, J.T., Thyer, B.A., & Kearsley, M. (1987). Using a token economy in a community-based residential program for disabled adults: An empirical evaluation leads to program modification. *Behavioral Residential Treatment, 1*, 173–185.

Stout, D. (1997a, March 23). Officials are starting early in their defense of the 2000 census. *The New York Times*, p. 37.

Stout, D. (1997b, May 4). Senate panel opposes use of sampling in next census. *The New York Times*, p. 31.

Straus, M.A. (1987). *Qualitative analysis for social scientists*. New York: Cambridge University Press.

Straus, M.A. (1991). *Beating the devil out of them: Corporal punishment in American families*. New York: Macmillan.

Straus, M.A., & Corbin, J. (1998). *Basics of qualitative research: Grounded theory procedures and techniques* (2nd ed.). Newbury Park, CA: Sage.

Straus, M.A., & Gelles, R. (1986). Societal change and change in family violence from 1975 to 1985 as revealed by two national surveys. *Journal of Marriage and the Family, 48*, 465–479.

Straus, M.A., Gelles, R., & Steinmetz, S. (1980). *Behind closed doors: Violence in the American family*. Garden City, NY: Anchor.

Straus, M.A., & Hafez, H. (1981). Clinical questions and "real research." *American Journal of Psychiatry, 138*, 1592–1597.

Stuart, P. (1979). *The Indian Office: Growth and development of an American institution, 1865–1900*. Ann Arbor, MI: UMI Research Press.

Stuart, P. (1985). Administrative reform in Indian affairs. *Western Historical Quarterly, 16*, 133–146.

Stuart, R. (1967). Behavioral control of overeating. *Behavior Research and Therapy, 5,* 357–365.

Sudman, S. (1976). *Applied sampling.* New York: Academic Press.

Sue, D.W., & Sue, D. (1990). *Counseling the culturally different: Theory and practice* (2nd ed.). New York: Wiley.

Sunberg, N.D. (1977). *Assessment of persons.* Englewood Cliffs, NJ: Prentice-Hall.

Survey Sampling, Inc. (1990). *A survey researcher's view of the U.S.* Fairfield, CT: Author.

Survey Research Center. (1960). *Interviewer's manual.* Ann Arbor: Survey Research Center, Institute of Social Research, University of Michigan.

Survey Research Center. (1976). *Interviewer's manual* (Rev. ed.). Ann Arbor: Survey Research Center, Institute of Social Research, University of Michigan.

Swarns, R. (1996, October 15). Moscow sends homeless to faraway hometowns. *The New York Times,* pp. A1, A12.

Swigonski, M.E. (1994). The logic of feminist standpoint theory for social work research. *Social Work, 39,* 387–393.

Taylor, J. (1977). Toward alternative forms of social work research: The case for naturalistic methods. *Journal of Social Welfare, 4,* 119–126.

Taylor, S., & Bogdan, R. (1984). *Introduction to qualitative research methods: The search for meanings.* New York: Wiley.

Tesch, R. (1990). *Qualitative research: Analysis types and software tools.* New York: Falmer.

Test of journals is criticized as unethical. (1988, September 27). *New York Times,* pp. 21, 25.

Thomas, K.M., Phillips, L.D., & Brown, S. (1998). Redefining race in the workplace: Insights from ethnic identity theory. *Journal of Black Psychology, 24,* 76–92.

Timmer, D., Eitzen, S., & Talley, K. (1993). *Paths to homelessness: Extreme poverty and the urban housing crisis.* Boulder, CO: Westview Press.

Todd, T.A., Joanning, H., Enders, L., Mutchler, L., & Thomas, F.N. (1990). Using ethnographic interviews to create a more cooperative client-therapist relationship. *Journal of Family Psychotherapy, 1,* 51–63.

Trattner, W.I. (Ed.). (1987). *Biographical dictionary of social welfare in America.* Westport, CT: Greenwood.

Trattner, W.I. (1994). *From poor law to welfare state: A history of social welfare in America* (5th ed.). New York: Free Press.

Trattner, W.I, & Achenbaum, W.A. (1983). *Social welfare in America: An annotated bibliography.* Westport, CT: Greenwood.

Tutty, L.M. (1993). After the shelter: Critical issues for women who leave assaultive relationships. *Canadian Social Work Review, 10,* 183–201.

Tutty, L.M., Grinnell, R.M., Jr., & Williams, M. (1997). Research problems and questions. In R.M. Grinnell, Jr. (Ed.), *Social work research and evaluation: Quantitative and qualitative approaches* (5th ed., pp. 49–66). Itasca, IL: F.E. Peacock.

Tutty, L.M., Rothery, M.L., & Grinnell, R.M., Jr. (Eds.). (1996). *Qualitative research for social workers: Phases, steps, and tasks.* Boston: Allyn & Bacon.

Unrau, Y.A. (1993). A program logic model approach to conceptualizing social service programs. *The Canadian Journal of Program Evaluation, 8,* 33–42.

Unrau, Y.A. (1997a). Implementing evaluations. In R.M. Grinnell, Jr. (Ed.), *Social work research and evaluation: Quantitative and qualitative approaches* (5th ed., pp. 588–604). Itasca, IL: F.E. Peacock.

Unrau, Y.A., & Coleman, H. (1997). Qualitative data analysis. In R.M. Grinnell, Jr. (Ed.), *Social work research and evaluation: Quantitative and qualitative approaches* (5th ed., pp. 501–472). Itasca, IL: F.E. Peacock.

Unrau, Y.A., & Gabor, P.A. (1997). Implementing evaluations. In R.M. Grinnell, Jr. (Ed.), *Social work research and evaluation: Quantitative and qualitative approaches* (5th ed., pp. 588–604). Itasca, IL: F.E. Peacock.

Unrau, Y.A., Gabor, P.A., & Grinnell, R.M., Jr. (2001). *Evaluation in the Social Services.* Belmont, CA. Wadsworth.

U.S. Bureau of the Census. (1987). *Statistical abstract of the United States, 1988.* Washington, DC: Author.

U.S. Department of Health, Education, and Welfare. (1971). *Effect of some experimental interviewing techniques on reporting in the health interview survey.* Washington, DC: Author.

U.S. Department of Health, Education, and Welfare. (1978). *Code of federal regulations, Title 45: Public welfare.* Washington, DC: U.S. Government Printing Office.

Valentine, C.A. (1971). The culture of poverty: Its scientific significance and its implications for action. In E.B. Leacock (Ed.). *The culture of poverty: A critique* (pp. 193–225). New York: Simon & Schuster.

van de Vijver, F., & Leung, K. (1997). *Methods and data analysis for cross-cultural research.* Thousand Oaks, CA: Sage.

Van Maanen, J. (1988). *Tales of the field: On writing ethnography.* Chicago: University of Chicago Press.

Van Maanen, J., Dabbs, J.M., Jr., & Faulkner, R.R. (Eds.). (1982). *Varieties of qualitative research.* Newbury Park, CA: Sage.

Vogt, W.P. (1993). *Dictionary of statistics and methodology: A nontechnical guide for the social sciences.* Newbury Park, CA: Sage.

Wagner, D. (1991). Reviving the action research model: Combing case and cause with dislocated workers. *Social Work, 36,* 477–482.

Walker, L. (1979). *The battered woman.* New York: Harper & Row.

Warwick, D., & Lininger, C. (1975). *The sample survey: Theory and practice.* New York: McGraw-Hill.

Watts, T.D. (1985). Ethnomethodology. In R.M. Grinnell, Jr. (Ed.), *Social work research and evaluation* (2nd ed., pp. 357–369). Itasca, IL: F.E. Peacock.

Webb, E., Campbell, D., Schwartz, R., & Sechrest, L. (1981). *Unobtrusive measures: Nonreactive research in the social sciences.* Boston: Houghton Mifflin.

Weber, R.P. (1984). Computer-aided content analysis: A short primer. *Qualitative Sociology, 7,* 126–147.

Weijer, C. (1998). Research methods and policies. In R. Chadwick (Ed.), *Encyclopedia of applied ethics,* (Vol. 3, pp. 853–860). San Diego: Academic Press.

Weinbach, R.W., & Grinnell, R.M., Jr. (2004). *Statistics for social workers* (6th ed.). Boston: Allyn & Bacon.

Weingarten, H.R. (1988). Late life divorce and the life review. *Journal of Gerontological Social Work, 12,* 83–97.

Weiss, C.H. (1968). Validity of welfare mothers' interview responses. *Public Opinion Quarterly, 32,* 622–633.

Weitzman, E.A., & Miles, M.B. (1995). *Computer programs for qualitative data analysis: A software sourcebook.* Newbury Park, CA: Sage.

Welfare study withholds benefits from 800 Texans. (1990, February 11). *Dallas Morning News,* p. 1.

Whitbeck, C. (1998). Research ethics. In R. Chadwick (Ed.), *Encyclopedia of applied ethics* (Vol. 3, pp. 835–843). San Diego: Academic Press.

White, K. (1988). Cost analyses in family support programs. In H.B. Weiss & F.H. Jacobs (Eds.), *Evaluating family programs* (pp. 429–443). New York: Aldine de Gruyter.

Whitnah, D. (Ed.). (1983). *Government agencies.* Westport, CT: Greenwood.

Wicker, A.W. (1981). Nature and assessment of behavior settings: Recent contributions from the ecological perspective. In P. McReynolds (Ed.), *Advances in psychological assessment* (Vol. 5, pp. 22–61). San Francisco: Jossey-Bass.

Wilkinson, W.K., & McNeil, K. (1997). Cultural factors related to research. In R.M. Grinnell, Jr. (Ed.), *Social work research and evaluation: Quantitative and qualitative approaches* (5th ed., pp. 605–630). Itasca, IL: F.E. Peacock.

Williams, J.A., Jr. (1964). Interview-respondent interaction: A study of bias in the information interview. *Sociometry, 27,* 338–352.

Williams, M., Tutty, L.M., & Grinnell, R.M., Jr. (1995). *Research in social work: An introduction* (2nd ed.). Itasca, IL: F.E. Peacock.

Williams, M., Unrau, Y.A., & Grinnell, R.M., Jr. (1998). *Introduction to social work research.* Itasca, IL: F.E. Peacock.

Williams, M., Unrau, Y.A., & Grinnell, R.M., Jr. (2005). *Research methods for social workers* (5th ed.). Peosta, IA: Eddie Bowers.

Williams, T.M. (1989). *Cocaine kids: The inside story of a teenage drug ring.* Reading, MA: Addison-Wesley.

Williams, T.M. (1992). *Crack house: Notes from the end of the line.* Reading, MA: Addison-Wesley.

Williamson, J.B., Karp, D.A., Dalphin, J.R., & Gray, P.S. (1982). *The research craft.* Boston: Little, Brown.

Wong, S.E., Woolsey, J.E., & Gallegos, E. (1987). Behavioral treatment of chronic schizophrenic patients. *Journal of Social Service Research, 4,* 4–35.

Woodroofe, K. (1962). *From charity to social work in England and the United States.* Toronto: University of Toronto Press.

Woodrum, E. (1984). Mainstreaming content analysis in social science: Methodological advantages, obstacles, and solutions. *Social Science Research, 13,* 1–19.

Wright, J., & Weber, E. (1987). *Homelessness and health.* New York: McGraw-Hill.

Yllo, K. (1988). Political and methodological debates in wife abuse research. In K. Yllo & M. Bograd (Eds.), *Feminist perspectives on wife abuse* (pp. 28–49). Newbury Park, CA: Sage.

Zmora, N. (1994). *Orphanages reconsidered: Child care institutions in progressive-era Baltimore.* Philadelphia: Temple University Press.

Zook, A., Jr., & Sipps, G.J. (1985). Cross-validation of a short form of the Marlowe-Crowne social desirability scale. *Journal of Clinical Psychology, 41,* 236–238.

Zuckerman, M. (1990). Some dubious premises in research and theory on racial differences. *American Psychologist, 45,* 1297–1303.

Zyzanski, S.J., McWhinney, I.R., Blake, R., Crabtree, B.F., & Miller, W.L. (1992). Qualitative research: Perspectives on the future. In B.F. Crabtree & W.L. Miller (Eds.), *Doing qualitative research: Research methods for primary care* (pp. 231–248). Thousand Oaks, CA: Sage.

Credits

Box 1.1. Council on Social Work Education (2003). *Curriculum Policy Statement.* Washington, DC: Author.

Box 1.2. National Association of Social Workers (1996). *Code of ethics.* Silver Spring, MD: Author.

Box 5.1. Adapted from: *Research in Social Work: A Primer,* by Richard M. Grinnell, Jr., and Margaret Williams, copyright © 1990 by F.E. Peacock Publishers; *Research in Social Work: An Introduction* (2nd ed.), by Margaret Williams, Leslie M. Tutty, and Richard M. Grinnell, Jr., copyright © 1995 by F.E. Peacock Publishers; and Margaret Williams, Yvonne A. Unrau, and Richard M. Grinnell, Jr., *Introduction to Social Work Research,* copyright © 1998 by F.E. Peacock Publishers.

Box 5.2. by Patricia Fisher, as cited in *Research Methods for Social Work* (2001), by Allen Rubin and Earl Babbie (4th ed., p. 155), Belmont CA: Brooks/Cole.

Box 5.3. Adapted from: *Research in Social Work: A Primer,* by Richard M. Grinnell, Jr., and Margaret Williams, copyright © 1990 by F.E. Peacock Publishers; *Research in Social Work: An Introduction* (2nd ed.), by Margaret Williams, Leslie M. Tutty, and Richard M. Grinnell, Jr., copyright © 1995 by F.E. Peacock Publishers; and Margaret Williams, Yvonne A. Unrau, and Richard M. Grinnell, Jr., *Introduction to Social Work Research,* copyright © 1998 by F.E. Peacock Publishers.

Box 6.1. Adapted from: "Phase One: Introduction," by Michael A. Rothery, Leslie M. Tutty, and Richard M. Grinnell, Jr., in *Qualitative Research for Social Workers: Phases, Steps, and Tasks* (p. 222), edited by Leslie M. Tutty, Michael A. Rothery, and Richard M. Grinnell, Jr., copyright © 1996 by Allyn & Bacon.

Box 9.1. Adapted from: "Survey Research," by Michael J. Austin and Jill Crowell, in *Social Work Research and Evaluation* (2nd ed.), edited by Richard M. Grinnell, Jr., copyright © 1985 by F.E. Peacock Publishers.

Box 13.1. Adapted from: *Research in Social Work: An Introduction* (2nd ed.), by Margaret Williams, Leslie M. Tutty, and Richard M. Grinnell, Jr., copyright © 1995 by F.E. Peacock Publishers.

Box 13.2. Adapted from: *Research in Social Work: An Introduction* (2nd ed.), by Margaret Williams, Leslie M. Tutty, and Richard M. Grinnell, Jr., copyright © 1995 by F.E. Peacock Publishers.

Box 13.3. Adapted from: *Research in Social Work: An Introduction* (2nd ed.), by Margaret Williams, Leslie M. Tutty, and Richard M. Grinnell, Jr., copyright © 1995 by F.E. Peacock Publishers.

Chapter 1. Adapted from: "Chapter 1: Introduction to Social Work Research," by Margaret Williams, Yvonne Unrau, and Richard M. Grinnell, Jr., in *Research Methods for Social Workers* (5th ed., pp. 2–29) by Margaret Williams, Yvonne Unrau, and Richard M. Grinnell, Jr., copyright © 2005 by Eddie Bowers Publishing.

Chapter 3. Adapted from: "Chapter 25: Research Ethics," by Frederic G. Reamer, in *The Handbook of Social Work Research Methods* (pp. 429–444), edited by Bruce A. Thyer, copyright © 2001 by Sage Publications Inc. Reprinted by permission of Sage Publications.

Chapter 4. Adapted from: "Chapter 4: Using Existing Knowledge," in *Research Methods for Social Workers* (4th ed., pp. 63–80), by Bonnie L. Yegidis and Robert W. Weinbach, copyright © 2002 by Allyn & Bacon. Reprinted by permission.

Chapter 5. Adapted from: "Chapter 2: The Quantitative Research Approach," by Margaret Williams, Yvonne Unrau, and Richard M. Grinnell, Jr., in *Research Methods for Social Workers* (5th ed., pp. 30–51), by Margaret Williams, Yvonne Unrau, and Richard M. Grinnell, Jr., copyright © 2005 by Eddie Bowers Publishing.

Chapter 6. Adapted from: "Chapter 3: The Qualitative Research Approach," by Margaret Williams, Yvonne Unrau, and Richard M. Grinnell, Jr., in *Research Methods for Social Workers* (5th ed., pp. 52–71), by Margaret Williams,

Mindel, in *Social Work Research and Evaluation* (4th ed.), edited by Richard M. Grinnell, Jr., copyright © 1993 by F.E. Peacock Publishers.

Figure 12.1. Adapted from: *Research in Social Work: A Primer*, by Richard M. Grinnell, Jr., and Margaret Williams, copyright © 1990 by F.E. Peacock Publishers; *Research in Social Work: An Introduction* (2nd ed.), by Margaret Williams, Leslie M. Tutty, and Richard M. Grinnell, Jr., copyright © 1995 by F.E. Peacock Publishers; and Margaret Williams, Yvonne A. Unrau, and Richard M. Grinnell, Jr. *Introduction to Social Work Research*, copyright © 1998 by F.E. Peacock Publishers.

Figure 12.2. Adapted from: *Research in Social Work: A Primer*, by Richard M. Grinnell, Jr., and Margaret Williams, copyright © 1990 by F.E. Peacock Publishers; *Research in Social Work: An Introduction* (2nd ed.), by Margaret Williams, Leslie M. Tutty, and Richard M. Grinnell, Jr., copyright © 1995 by F.E. Peacock Publishers; and Margaret Williams, Yvonne A. Unrau, and Richard M. Grinnell, Jr. *Introduction to Social Work Research*, copyright © 1998 by F.E. Peacock Publishers.

Figure 12.3. Adapted from: *Research in Social Work: A Primer*, by Richard M. Grinnell, Jr., and Margaret Williams, copyright © 1990 by F.E. Peacock Publishers; *Research in Social Work: An Introduction* (2nd ed.), by Margaret Williams, Leslie M. Tutty, and Richard M. Grinnell, Jr., copyright © 1995 by F.E. Peacock Publishers; and Margaret Williams, Yvonne A. Unrau, and Richard M. Grinnell, Jr. *Introduction to Social Work Research*, copyright © 1998 by F.E. Peacock Publishers.

Figure 12.4. Adapted from: *Research in Social Work: A Primer*, by Richard M. Grinnell, Jr., and Margaret Williams, copyright © 1990 by F.E. Peacock Publishers; *Research in Social Work: An Introduction* (2nd ed.), by Margaret Williams, Leslie M. Tutty, and Richard M. Grinnell, Jr., copyright © 1995 by F.E. Peacock Publishers; and Margaret Williams, Yvonne A. Unrau, and Richard M. Grinnell, Jr. *Introduction to Social Work Research*, copyright © 1998 by F.E. Peacock Publishers.

Figure 12.5. Adapted from: *Research in Social Work: A Primer*, by Richard M. Grinnell, Jr., and Margaret Williams, copyright © 1990 by F.E. Peacock Publishers; *Research in Social Work: An Introduction* (2nd ed.), by Margaret Williams, Leslie M. Tutty, and Richard M. Grinnell, Jr., copyright © 1995 by F.E. Peacock Publishers; and Margaret Williams, Yvonne A. Unrau, and Richard M. Grinnell, Jr. *Introduction to Social Work Research*, copyright © 1998 by F.E. Peacock Publishers.

Figure 12.6. Adapted from: *Research in Social Work: A Primer*, by Richard M. Grinnell, Jr., and Margaret Williams, copyright © 1990 by F.E. Peacock Publishers; *Research in Social Work: An Introduction* (2nd ed.), by Margaret Williams, Leslie M. Tutty, and Richard M. Grinnell, Jr., copyright © 1995 by F.E. Peacock Publishers; and Margaret Williams, Yvonne A. Unrau, and Richard M. Grinnell, Jr. *Introduction to Social Work Research*, copyright © 1998 by F.E. Peacock Publishers.

Figure 12.7. Adapted from: *Research in Social Work: A Primer*, by Richard M. Grinnell, Jr., and Margaret Williams, copyright © 1990 by F.E. Peacock Publishers; *Research in Social Work: An Introduction* (2nd ed.), by Margaret Williams, Leslie M. Tutty, and Richard M. Grinnell, Jr., copyright © 1995 by F.E. Peacock Publishers; and Margaret Williams, Yvonne A. Unrau, and Richard M. Grinnell, Jr. *Introduction to Social Work Research*, copyright © 1998 by F.E. Peacock Publishers.

Figure 12.8. Adapted from: *Research in Social Work: A Primer*, by Richard M. Grinnell, Jr., and Margaret Williams, copyright © 1990 by F.E. Peacock Publishers; *Research in Social Work: An Introduction* (2nd ed.), by Margaret Williams, Leslie M. Tutty, and Richard M. Grinnell, Jr., copyright © 1995 by F.E. Peacock Publishers; and Margaret Williams, Yvonne A. Unrau, and Richard M. Grinnell, Jr. *Introduction to Social Work Research*, copyright © 1998 by F.E. Peacock Publishers.

Figure 12.9. Adapted from: *Research in Social Work: A Primer*, by Richard M. Grinnell, Jr., and Margaret Williams, copyright © 1990 by F.E. Peacock Publishers; *Research in Social Work: An Introduction* (2nd ed.), by Margaret Williams, Leslie M. Tutty, and Richard M. Grinnell, Jr., copyright © 1995 by F.E. Peacock Publishers; and Margaret Williams, Yvonne A. Unrau, and Richard M. Grinnell, Jr. *Introduction to Social Work Research*, copyright © 1998 by F.E. Peacock Publishers.

Figure 12.10. Adapted from: *Research in Social Work: A Primer*, by Richard M. Grinnell, Jr., and Margaret Williams, copyright © 1990 by F.E. Peacock Publishers; *Research in Social Work: An Introduction* (2nd ed.), by Margaret Williams, Leslie M. Tutty, and Richard M. Grinnell, Jr., copyright © 1995 by F.E. Peacock Publishers; and Margaret Williams, Yvonne A. Unrau, and Richard M. Grinnell, Jr. *Introduction to Social Work Research*, copyright © 1998 by F.E. Peacock Publishers.

Figure 15.1. Adapted from: *Research in Social Work: A Primer*, by Richard M. Grinnell, Jr., and Margaret Williams, copyright © 1990 by F.E. Peacock Publishers.

Figure 15.2. Adapted from: *Social Research Methods: Qualitative and Quantitative Approaches* (3rd ed.), by W. Lawrence Neuman, copyright © 1997 by Allyn & Bacon.

Figure 16.1. Adapted from: *Filial Deprivation and Foster Care,* by Shirley Jenkins and Elaine Norman. Copyright © 1972 by Columbia University Press.

Figure 17.1. Adapted from: "Survey Research," by Charles H. Mindel and Lynn McDonald, in *Social Work Research and Evaluation* (3rd ed.), edited by Richard M. Grinnell, Jr., copyright © 1988 by F.E. Peacock Publishers.

Figure 17.2. Adapted from: "Test Administration," by William V. Clemens, in *Educational Measurement* (2nd ed.), edited by Robert L. Thorndkie, copyright © 1971 by the American Council on Education.

Figure 17.3. Adapted from: "Test Administration," by William V. Clemens, in *Educational Measurement* (2nd ed.), edited by Robert L. Thorndkie, copyright © 1971 by the American Council on Education.

Figure 17.4. Adapted from: *Mail and Telephone Surveys: The Total Design Method,* by Don A. Dillman, copyright © 1978 by John Wiley & Sons, Inc.

Figure 17.5. Adapted from: *Mail and Telephone Surveys: The Total Design Method,* by Don A. Dillman, copyright © 1978 by John Wiley & Sons, Inc.

Figure 17.6. Adapted from: *Mail and Telephone Surveys: The Total Design Method,* by Don A. Dillman, copyright © 1978 by John Wiley & Sons, Inc.

Figure 23.3. From: "Univariate Analysis," by Donald W. Beless, in *Social Work Research and Evaluation,* edited by Richard M. Grinnell, Jr., copyright © 1981 by F.E. Peacock Publishers.

Figure 23.5. From: "Univariate Analysis," by Donald W. Beless, in *Social Work Research and Evaluation,* edited by Richard M. Grinnell, Jr., copyright © 1981 by F.E. Peacock Publishers.

Figure 23.7. From: "Univariate Analysis," by Donald W. Beless, in *Social Work Research and Evaluation,* edited by Richard M. Grinnell, Jr., copyright © 1981 by F.E. Peacock Publishers.

Glossary.

Some of the terms in the glossary may have been adapted and modified from: "Glossary," by Yvonne A. Unrau, in *Evaluation and Quality Improvement in the Human Services,* by Peter A. Gabor and Richard M. Grinnell, Jr. Copyright © 1994 by Allyn & Bacon; *Evaluation for Social Workers: A Quality Improvement Approach for the Social Services* (2nd ed.), by Peter A. Gabor, Yvonne A. Unrau, and Richard M. Grinnell, Jr., copyright © 1998 by Allyn & Bacon; *Research in Social Work: A Primer,* by Richard M. Grinnell, Jr., and Margaret Williams, copyright © 1990 by F.E. Peacock Publishers; *Student Study Guide for the Fourth Edition of Social Work Research and Evaluation,* by Judy Krysik, Irene Hoffart, and Richard M. Grinnell, Jr., copyright © 1993 by F.E. Peacock Publishers; *Student Study Guide for the Fifth Edition of Social Work Research and Evaluation: Quantitative and Qualitative Approaches,* by Yvonne A. Unrau, Judy L. Krysik, and Richard M. Grinnell, Jr., copyright © 1997 by F.E. Peacock Publishers; *Student Study Guide for the Sixth Edition of Social Work Research and Evaluation: Quantitative and Qualitative Approaches,* by Yvonne A. Unrau, Judy L. Krysik, and Richard M. Grinnell, Jr., copyright © 2001 by F.E. Peacock Publishers; *Research in Social Work: An Introduction* (2nd ed.), by Margaret Williams, Leslie M. Tutty, and Richard M. Grinnell, Jr., copyright © 1995 by F.E. Peacock Publishers; *Statistics for Social Workers* (1st, 2nd, 3rd, 4th, 5th, 6th eds.), by Robert W. Weinbach and Richard M. Grinnell, Jr., copyright © 1987, 1991, 1995, 1998, 2001, and 2004 by Allyn & Bacon; "Glossary," by Irene Hoffart and Judy L. Krysik, in *Social Work Research and Evaluation* (4th ed.), edited by Richard M. Grinnell, Jr., copyright © 1993 by F.E. Peacock Publishers; and *Evaluation in the Human Services,* by Yvonne A. Unrau, Peter A. Gabor, and Richard M. Grinnell, Jr., copyright © 2001 by F.E. Peacock Publishers.

Index

Page numbers in *italics* indicate graphics.